Balboa Films

Balboa Films

A History and Filmography of the Silent Film Studio

by JEAN-JACQUES JURA *and*
RODNEY NORMAN BARDIN II

with assistance in research for the filmography by
Claudine Burnett

McFarland & Company, Inc., Publishers
Jefferson, North Carolina, and London

The present work is a reprint of the library bound edition of Balboa Films: A History and Filmography of the Silent Film Studio, *first published in 1999 by McFarland.*

LIBRARY OF CONGRESS CATALOGUING-IN-PUBLICATION DATA

Jura, Jean-Jacques, 1950–
  Balboa films : a history and filmography of the silent film studio / by Jean-Jacques Jura and Rodney Norman Bardin II ; with assistance in research for the filmography by Claudine Burnett.
    p. cm.
  "Filmography of Long Beach studios": p.
  Includes bibliographical references and index.

  ISBN-13: 978-0-7864-3098-7
  softcover : 50# alkaline paper ∞

  1. Balboa Amusement Producing Company — History. I. Bardin, Rodney Norman, 1957– . II. Title.
  PN1999.B36J87 2007
  384'.8'06579493 — dc21   98-33441

British Library cataloguing data are available

©1999 Jean-Jacques Jura and Rodney Norman Bardin II. All rights reserved

No part of this book may be reproduced or transmitted in any form or by any means, electronic or mechanical, including photocopying or recording, or by any information storage and retrieval system, without permission in writing from the publisher.

Cover photograph: The Balboa Studios quadrangle

Manufactured in the United States of America

McFarland & Company, Inc., Publishers
  Box 611, Jefferson, North Carolina 28640
    www.mcfarlandpub.com

To the memory of the Horkheimer Brothers,
Herbert Morris Horkheimer and Elwood David Horkheimer,
and all who worked so loyally at Balboa Studios.
These talented pioneers of silent movies gave
Long Beach and the world an unforgettable legacy.

Thanks to my Dad, Rodney, Sr., who got me interested in reading and gave me the fever for history and also taught me how to use my hands and solve problems. My mom, Viola, who has been there when I needed her, the good times and the bad. Longtime friend Jerry, aka "Old Timer." His love for Long Beach history is great. He and I worked on many films together, the best cameraman I ever worked with. I'll never hear the end of that. My brothers, David and Steven, along with my sisters, Cathy, and Devera (Coke). Jeanette, whom I need to get to know better. And when I was feeling low, Soumada Khan, an up-and-coming television personality. All of them were there when I needed them. And to Jacques for putting all of these words together and making sense out of them. Bob and Susan Dodson for their prayers, and Nick Hart for his generosity. —*Rodney Bardin*

Contents

Acknowledgments ix
Prologue: Setting the Stage 1

Reel 1 1893–1913: The Early Years 5
"Lights, Camera, Action — Long Beach" 10
Early Studios in California 12
The Edison Outpost 24

Reel 2 Something Ventured, Something Gained 31
The Inheritance 34
The Sea Wolf's Bite 37
The Fruits of Loyalty and Troubleshooting 41

Reel 3 1913–1918: An Innovative and Productive Studio 61
Timeline of the Balboa Amusement Producing Company 62
Long Beach: Home of the Stars and Headline Stories 79
The Mystery Man, Director Extraordinaire 93

Reel 4 Major Stars and Their Box Office Hits 103
Henry King 105
Jackie Saunders 112

Ruth Roland	119
Daniel Gilfether	124
Mollie McConnell	128
Roscoe "Fatty" Arbuckle	132
Baby Marie Osborne	135

Reel 5   1918–1925: The Beginning of the End — 145
 Acts of God: World War I and the Long Beach Oil Strike — 152
 The Changing of Hands — 159

Reel 6   Epilogue: Back to the Future — 179

Filmography of Long Beach Studios — 193
Bibliography — 271
Index — 275

Acknowledgments

We wish to thank those organizations and persons who assisted in researching and compiling this book. With their aid, it has evolved into a richer and more complete chronicle of Long Beach's golden age as a movie and entertainment center. We are most grateful for the data provided by the American Film Institute; the technical help from El Camino College Innovation Center; the expertise and support of the Historical Society of Long Beach, Long Beach Heritage, and the Long Beach Public Library; and the assistance of Pierce Brothers in Hollywood and the *Press-Telegram*. We are grateful as well for the personal contributions of the following individuals: Julie Bartolotto, Kaye Briegel, Claudine Burnett, Karen Clements, Kelly Quinn, Aimie Gervais, Hilda Lu, Vivian Reed, Dan Ridder, Frani Ridder, Jackie Saunders, Jr., Tony Scott, Ruth Stewart, Sabrina Vincent, Marc Wanamaker, Josephine Woodman, Mark Wu, Marie Osborne-Yeats, and Victor Yushenko.

Prologue: Setting the Stage

> Fame, we may understand, is no sure test
> of merit but only a probability of such;
> it is an accident, not a property of a man.
>
> —*Carlyle*

Moviegoers around the world stir at the mighty roar of the MGM lion. No other logo announces so vociferously the magic appearing on the silver screen. Established in 1924, Metro-Goldwyn-Mayer Studios produced quality films on the cutting edge of technological progress, and produced them in great numbers. Louis B. Mayer liked to boast that his innovative film plant "had more stars than the heavens"—and the number of hits was at least equal to the number of stars.

This book, however, tells the lesser-known story of an earlier film plant, the Balboa Amusement Producing Company. Instead of the roaring lion, Balboa's logo portrayed the mute head of Spanish explorer Vasco Núñez de Balboa, the discoverer of the Pacific Ocean. History has too often overlooked both silent and talking heads, especially those lost to the rapidly changing competition in movieland. The purpose of this book is to afford long-overdue recognition to Balboa Studios, a film plant that eventually lost its lead to equally daring sailors of fortune in neighboring Los Angeles. "The winner take all" outcome typifies how unfairly renown may be bestowed to supposedly accredited contributors. For example, the prototype of modern film plants, Star Film, allowed its creator, Georges Méliès, to raise motion pictures to an art form by way of his technical innovations, production, and distribution planning, along with his marketing and magical skills; yet Méliès died, like too many pioneers, penniless and forgotten in the streets. Pathé Frères replaced Star Film as the premier film business across the globe until the Great War, eventually making Star Film's prototype seem meaningless in comparison.

Balboa Films is not only a story of the pioneering, glamorous, and risk-taking film plant in Long Beach, California. It is mostly about the unsung heroes—founders, artists, technicians, and businessmen who made the plant for five glorious years the most productive independent studio in the world, before there was even an establishment called Hollywood. *Balboa Films* also examines the innovations of the cameramen, directors, and writers at the studio. It provides an overdue explanation of Balboa's significance and the reasons for its untimely demise. Finally, it explores the reasons why Long Beach seemed to take so little pride in the site before the movie studios closed their stages permanently in 1923 and were demolished in 1925 for subdivisions of the parcels.

From the beginning, Long Beach offered an ideal setting for the movie industry. Enjoying a sunny seaside climate, the city was already a theatre town with a steady pool of talented actors, directors, and technicians. Along the Pike, there were eight film houses and two stock company theatres. As early as 1908, Roscoe "Fatty" Arbuckle had been singing in Long Beach, and he even got married on stage that same year at the successful Byde a Whyle Theatre, an adjunct to the elegant and gigantic Hotel Virginia. Moreover, Long Beach enjoyed the busy commerce of its port and railway systems that made the city the fastest growing municipality in the United States of America. In 1910, Long Beach claimed only 17,000 inhabitants, but by 1920 the city had grown to 56,000. Balboa Studios had become Long Beach's biggest employer and biggest tourist attraction by 1917. From 1910 through 1913, at least two other film companies had preceded Balboa Studios in Long Beach, at the very same site. These companies changed hands many times from 1918 to 1925.

Overlooked by historians and ignored in the very town where so many quality movies were made between 1913 and 1918, Balboa Studios shone as a jewel of the silent era.

Today, film buffs the world over recognize the mighty roar of the MGM lion. MGM made history, and its contributions are properly documented and remembered. In contrast, the roar of Balboa was never heard. A studio that should have made history remains silent, like the movies produced there. Of the countless quality films produced at Balboa, the few that remain have been turning to dust as the result of nitrate decomposition and neglect.

Unlike MGM's well-preserved productions, Balboa's films have nearly all been erased from our collective memory. Why? Movies at Balboa were also made big and done well. Like MGM, Balboa was productive and extravagant, boasting luminaries like Jackie Saunders, Ruth Roland, Henry King, Lewis Cody, and William Desmond Taylor, the latter acclaimed as a multitalented director, actor, and writer. Baby Marie Osborne and many other silent stars and directors also began their illustrious and successful careers at Balboa.

Since Balboa has yet to break its silence, many historians are still unaware that it existed. At one time, however, Balboa bore considerable prestige in movieland, even though it was situated in a sometimes hostile climate where certain citizens scorned the very industry that had spurred Long Beach's growth. There were concerns about "those types," some of whom were consuming drugs and alcohol in a dry and righteous town. People were sometimes uncomfortable with the sight of actresses sporting skimpy gowns and bathing suits, lounging around with too much playtime and money to spare. Yes, there were drug and sex scandals in early movieland, before some drugs were even illegal. William Desmond Taylor, who was vehemently opposed to the use of drugs in movieland, may even have been killed by the hitman of a drug ring, several of which infiltrated the early movie industry. Taylor's murder in 1922 remains to this day a mystery; there may have been a cover-up to protect the industry from further scandal during times of bad publicity in the early 1920s.

Like MGM, Balboa made remarkable innovations in studio management and film development, including new methods for shooting night scenes and new techniques for color tinting. The studio often set industry standards regarding quality props and wardrobe, including their maintenance, storage, and care. In fact, Balboa was so highly efficient that its productivity nearly glutted the movie market, with as many as 10 movie companies shooting simultaneously at the studios. Balboa Studios comprised 20 buildings on 8 acres downtown, with 11 additional acres for outdoor shooting in Signal Hill, a separate township enclosed within the city of Long Beach. To accommodate this high productivity, an elaborate and unique film distribution system at Balboa evolved with multiple companies, Fox and Pathé among them; at any one time there were as many as five distributors. Balboa's motto might very well have been that of Louis B. Mayer: "Make it big, make it right."

The story of Balboa chronicles not only part of the untold story of movieland but also that of the city of Long Beach. Above all, if motion pictures represent the greatest chroniclers and storytellers of our century, movies help mark our development as a people on the move. We who love movies are all indebted to our predecessors in cinema. Movies can instruct, amuse, and keep us spellbound. Though they are fragile in their chemical composition, these "living pictures" have the power to transport us across spatio-temporal barriers and beyond the usual dimensions of the performing arts on stage. As an art form, the magic lantern projects a wonderfully mnemonic quality, casting remembrances against the screen for all to explore at the same time, bringing us in the hall to view them together, though we might never agree on what we saw in those same pictures.

Unfortunately, the much celebrated art of cinema has endured severe casualties. Preservation statistics are dismal: 80 percent of all silent movies in the world have disappeared because of nitrate decomposition or neglect, while 40 percent of all movies produced prior to 1952 have also vanished forever, never to be restored. Should we care? What do we owe our predecessors anyway? Why should we remember Balboa? Actually, we owe it to our predecessors and ourselves to recognize the continuity of early filmmakers' influence in our lives today. *Balboa Films* recognizes the historical importance of movie pioneers in Long Beach and their influence in the world, then and now. We need to mark the points in the past that help explain our present and possibly our future. Our knowledge of predecessors helps us understand our own progress and where we stand today.

Balboa Studios produced countless quality pictures for five extraordinarily successful years, for moviegoers around the world. Long before MGM's lion ever stepped onto the stage and became king, Balboa roared—and soared.

To tell this story in the tradition of our predecessors, let's begin by proclaiming loud and clear: *"Lights, camera, action!"*

Reel 1

1893–1913: The Early Years

When someone refers to the movie capital of the world, Hollywood immediately comes to mind, but this unrivaled Mecca did not yet exist when the first studio came to Long Beach in 1910. At that time the idea of producing films in the Far West was still a novelty. In 1910, when the California Motion Picture Manufacturing Company built the first movie studio in Long Beach, it was also the first studio west of Chicago. New York was the film center of the United States. Europe ruled vast empires around the world, and European capitals called the shots with the power and prestige of their currencies, armies, navies, and industries. In particular, Europe's enormous commercial successes represented for many people the very standards of modernity and fashion itself during the heady years of Europe's belle époque, before the calamity of the Great War. Until the First World War erupted in 1914, Europe, and specifically France, reigned as the movie capital of the world, providing state-of-the-art equipment and techniques, along with world-class methods of productivity, distribution, and marketing.

The European empires that were riding so high earlier this century have since dissolved or evolved into new entities, and the center of technological, military, and commercial power has established itself firmly in the North American continent. Admirers of American know-how and efficiency might easily overlook the predecessors abroad who contributed along the way to the achievements made in the United States. Undeniably, the American film industry is the most developed commercially in the world. Hollywood deserves its fame and glory, but predecessors, abroad and at home, did influence Hollywood. Some of these contributors are well documented and remembered, while others have never been sufficiently recorded. While most of Hollywood's superior studios are chronicled and well known, the place of Balboa Studios in movieland's hall of fame lacks documentation and, consequently, recognition. Balboa's contributions need to be examined and explained. On the other hand, French contributions at the beginning of early cinema have been well documented and remain undeniable facts to film historians. Nonetheless, even these French contributions become hidden in the shadows of Hollywood's towering achievements. The French contributions to world-class cinema during the early days of the film industry, when Hollywood was not yet top-dog, might serve as an example of how innovative predecessors are too often overlooked.

Prior to the First World War, the emergence of movie palaces, special effects, feature films, and the development of genres in the United States followed the European prototypes. For instance, the first movie palace in the world, the Omnia, which was built by Pathé, opened in Paris, December 15, 1906. It was followed five years later by the gigantic Gaumont Palace, which opened in Paris, November 30, 1911. This theatre had been a former hippodrome and even a roller-skating center before Gaumont transformed it into the largest movie theatre in the world, with a seating capacity of 3,400. The first animated movie in the world, *Fantasmagorie* by Emile Cohl, was shown at the Théâtre du Gymnase in Paris, August 17, 1908. Moreover, the novelty of the major feature was born in Italy in 1912 with *Quo Vadis* by Enrico Guazzoni. The Europeans were the original pacesetters in developing the Seventh Art into respectable and decidedly artistic entertainment, seriously investing time and effort into all kinds of technical problems, filming, and distribution logistics, and all phases of marketing. Thanks to Ferdinand Zecca, who joined Pathé Frères in 1900, the French film industry launched standards that were to be assimilated around the world, including by the studios of California. Zecca is credited with having perfected the chase scene and influencing Sennett's Keystone Kops, while France's very original Max Linder created a comic character from whom Charlie Chaplin adapted certain body movements and expressions reflected in the creation of his Little Tramp. It was also France's serial *Nick Carter* by Victorin Jasset that introduced the episodic crime stories in the silent era. Afterwards, Gaumont Pictures perfected this serial genre with its big smash hits *Fantômas* (1913–1914) and *Les Vampires* (1915–1916). Moreover, between 1899 and 1913 Georges Méliès had produced more than 400 movies with his company called Star Film. Although Méliès used neither long shots nor close-ups, world cinema will always be indebted to him because he did originate significant camera tricks, including the dissolve, fade-out, superimposition, double exposure, stop motion, and slow motion. His company was also the first to produce a newsreel, a genre further advanced by the year 1908 by both Pathé (*Pathé journal*) and Gaumont (*Actualités Gaumont*).

At the very beginning of France's cinematography preeminence, the new art was inaugurated in March 1895 by Louis Lumière with his *La Sortie des usines Lumière*. On March 19, 1895, the first showing in Lyon, France, failed because of mechanical problems. Three days later in Paris on March 22, 1895, the film was successfully viewed by 200 persons. History marks, however, the date of the Lumière Brothers' inauguration as December 28, 1895, the day when they commercially screened their amazing *cinématographe*, from which were coined the words *cinematography*, *cinematographer*, *cinema*, and other derived terms denoting this new photographic art. Edison soon followed with an improved projection process shown to the public on April 23, 1896. In fact, Edison had earlier commissioned an assistant, William Dickson, to devise a motion picture camera that was patented in 1893, but Edison's camera, the Kinetograph, was immovable, weighing more than 1,000 pounds, and consequently was not so attractive to the earliest cinematographers. Edison's first motion picture camera operated well enough as an inert heavyweight but did not allow for projection of what it photographed. In contrast, the Lumière Brothers' camera weighed less than 20 pounds and was a hand-cranked invention that served both as a camera for filming and as a projector for showing the movies. The versatility and ease of operation of the Lumière invention explains why it became the preferred instrument used to establish many international cinemas, including the Russian, the Australian, and the Japanese movie industries. The Lumière Brothers also introduced with their method of projecting pictures the first big-screen viewing, and the crowd-filled movie theatre as we know it today was born.

By 1897, Georges Méliès in France had an impressive list of original procedures that reflect the seriousness and the dedication with which he engineered his craft: the first world-class film plant, the first use of in-studio photos for publicity, the first movie star (himself), the first chain of permanent viewing halls affiliated with his Star Film productions. Nonetheless, early cinema in France was never all rosy. In March 1902, Georges Méliès presented to exhibitors in Paris his *Le Voyage dans la Lune*, adapted from the literary works of Jules Verne and H. G. Wells. The film became such a coveted success with the public that countless pirated copies were reproduced in the United States and around the world. Not a penny of this global box-office hit went into Méliès' pockets. From this negative experience, Méliès, Pathé, and Gaumont learned to protect themselves in the future by creating American and foreign agencies to take advantage of the copyright protection laws in major countries. For even greater protection against piracy, the French studios even began to employ their company logos in the décor and the scenes of their films; Star Film used the star, Pathé used its rooster, and Gaumont employed its logo, daisies.

Along with Star Film, Gaumont Pictures (founded in 1895) and Pathé Frères (founded in 1896) continued to advance France's lead in production, distribution, and innovations in world cinema until the Great War. France, not Hollywood, was the original movie capital of the world. Gaumont opened foreign offices and acquired theatre chains. With the financial support of some of France's largest corporations, Charles Pathé bought the Lumière patents in 1902, commissioning the creation of an improved camera. Until the end of the First World War in 1918, 60 percent of all film companies in the world used the Pathé camera for their productions. Pathé's world-class operation included the assembly-line manufacturing of Pathé's own film stock, along with its ever-expanding production capacity. Like Gaumont Pictures, Pathé Frères began opening agencies abroad, becoming a formidable, international concern: Spain (1906), Russia (1907), Italy (1908), England (1909), and the United States (1910). Between 1905 and 1914, with Méliès, Gaumont, and Pathé in the lead, French studios were the largest in the world, dominating world movie production, exhibition, and sales.

Most of France's cinematography successes were absolutely reputable and original, while Pathé's predominance might best be described as a curious mix of cunning, guts, corporate spying and downright trickery. Comparable perhaps to a Gallic version of Horatio Alger, Charles Pathé began as a shoeless boy of a butcher family, suffering poor health, but he became one of the twentieth century's greatest capitalists. While France was still building the Panama Canal, young Charles had gone to South America seeking adventure and a fresh start, only to flee suddenly from the jungle because of the yellow fever epidemic. Always the undaunted sailor of fortune, when Charles returned to France, he began selling Edison phonographs. Soon he was engaged in contraband, selling counterfeit Kinetoscopes from England. As Alan Williams explains in *Republic of Images* (p. 42), during his smuggling days Charles worked very hard and did very well. Then he met Henri Joseph Joly, who suggested he quit the black market and that the two of them invest their efforts in the manufacturing and sale of their own "original" film products. It is uncertain whether they obtained the Lumière Brothers' patent, but Charles Pathé's redesigned instrument also had the dual capacity to serve as both a camera and a projector. Joly did not remain in the picture, however, and some claim that Pathé stole the prototype before dumping Joly. After receiving a family inheritance, Charles and three of his brothers formed a new enterprise at the end of 1896, calling it the *Société Pathé Frères*. Eventually the new enterprise would be simply called *Pathé Frères*, but not before two of the four brothers dropped out during a lawsuit against them for nondelivery of goods (Williams, p. 43). Charles and Emile maintained the company and worked harder than ever, with rewarding results. Eventually Pathé Frères revolutionized the marketing of movie production by initiating the idea of renting copies, which were previously and routinely sold to exhibitors. This allowed filmmakers to own their products indefinitely while cashing in on the exhibitors' rental fees. This practice started by Pathé Frères continues today. Thanks to Pathé Frères, the movie industry was set on a profitable and efficient course. Without a doubt, Charles and Emile Pathé were among early cinema's most daring entrepreneurs, but they were clearly not the last.

At the same time, in the United States, similar patterns were developing in the movie business with consolidations of industry-wide monopolies, with ownership and control based on stringent patent rights involving the production, distribution, and exhibition of films. Edison and the East Coast dominated the North American film industry's production and system of film exchange. Film exchanges were the middlemen of the industry, acting as brokers between the producers and the exhibitors, providing films from the producers and leasing them to the exhibitors. According to Griffith and Mayer's *The Movies* (p. 20) by 1907 the film exchanges were amassing more revenue than the legitimate theatre and vaudeville combined. Thomas Alva Edison disdained the movies as a poor man's entertainment, but he could smell the cash. Instead of suing all his competitors for violation of his patents, Edison invited his greatest competitors to form an invincible trust, calling it the Motion Picture Patents Company. In 1909 ten partners emerged to announce that they and they alone had the exclusive right and license to produce motion pictures, a right backed by the patent laws of France, Germany, Italy, the United Kingdom, and the United States (Griffith and Mayers, p. 20). The trust comprised the leading American and French film companies at the time: Biograph, Essanay, Kalem, Kleine, Lubin, Selig, and Vitagraph in the United States and Méliès and Pathé Frères in France.

Along with its exclusive right to produce movies, the trust also went after the independent film exchanges by creating the General Film Company. The trust informed the independent exchanges that they had to let the General Film Company take them over because the patent rights also involved the distribution and exhibition of film products. The trust did not fear the antitrust laws of the Sherman Act because its monopoly was based on patent protection. This takeover plan was not well received by the independents, and two in particular stand out for resisting the pressure to yield to the coercive ultimatum of the trust: Sell your exchange now or be forced to sell it to the trust.

Two independent film exchanges resisted from the start the trust's ultimatum, one headed by William Fox and the other by Carl Laemmle. In the long run, the trust's ultimatum backfired. Following the bold example of Fox and Laemmle, the independents took the industry into their own hands despite the trust and succeeded in flourishing not only as independent exchanges but also as independent producers of films. While William Fox at first simply ignored the trust's ultimatum, Carl Laemmle from the beginning openly criticized in letters and newspaper articles the trust's manipulations of the movie market. When the trust cut off supplies of movies to Laemmle, he became an independent movie producer, forming the Independent Motion-Picture Company (IMP), in defiance of the trust's threats. The move toward more and more independent exchanges and movie producers actually guaranteed better quality films for the public because the independents took more care to provide quality movies for a growing and competitive market. The trust eventually succumbed to the forces of the open market created by the defiant independents, and it was already powerless to impose its special privileges before it was abolished by judicial decision in 1915. Once again the Americans fought for a free market on their own turf, struggling against the imposition of seignorial fees without representation in another war of independence for the sake of free enterprise and the Seventh Art.

At the height of this war, an historical occasion brought film distributors, exhibitors, and producers to the Hotel McAlpin in New York on August 29, 1914, to incorporate a new alliance called the National Independent Motion Picture Board of Trade that legally challenged Edison's Motion Picture Patents Company, popularly called the "trust." It was the intention of these assembled independent producers and exhibitors and producers to become as powerful as Edison's "trust" but with a higher purpose, opposing the trust's special privileges and unfair trade practices. *Motion Picture News* published the intentions of the newly incorporated group, citing the high aims they offered in their "declaration of independence" in an article entitled "Independent Board of Trade Organized":

> To foster trade and commerce and the interests of those engaged either as manufacturers, distributors and exhibitors of motion pictures, to reform abuses relative thereto, to secure freedom from unjust or harmful exactions, to eliminate unfair competition and restraint of trade, and combinations in restraint of trade, to obtain legislation necessary to correct certain present harmful conditions to the motion picture business, and to regulate trade and commerce in that business so that the same shall be free, open, unrestrained and fair to all; to diffuse accurate and reliable information as to the standing of manufacturers, distributors and exhibitors, and other matters to procure uniformity and certainty in the customs and usages of trade and commerce, to obtain a standardization of machines, films, appliances and appurtenances to the said business, to settle and arbitrate differences between and among its members, and to promote a marked enlarged and friendly intercourse between and among the members thereof. (*Press Clippings*, vol. 1, p. 71)

William Fox led the group and called the meeting in which the assembled parties represented almost $75,000 of capital. It was a defiant show of force against Edison's trust. H. M. Horkheimer was among the hundred people attending that day; he was one of the five vice presidents nominated, and he also was chosen to be one of the directors of the National Independent Motion Picture Board of Trade. The president of the new alliance was William Fox, whose legal counsel, Gustavus A. Rogers, directed the legal battle against Edison's trust. The executive committee of the new board consisted of its newly elected officers and directors. The officers were as follows:

William Fox, representing the William Fox Amusement Co., President

H. J. Sawyer, representing Sawyer, Inc., Vice President

J. M. Shear, representing Solax Co., Vice President

H. M. Horkheimer, representing Balboa Feature Films, Vice President

B. K. Bimberg, representing Schuyler Amusement Co., Vice President

S. Schwalbe, representing Electric Theatre Supply Co., Vice President

Winfield R. Sheehan, representing Box Office Amusements Co., Treasurer

Jesse L. Goldberg, representing Life Photo Film Corp., Secretary

Walter Sammis, Executive Secretary

The directors were William Fox, L. J. Selznick, A. H. Sawyer, H. M. Horkheimer, and Louis Rosenbluh; four others were to be named later.

During this period, the Horkheimers and William Fox continued to have close associations regarding film production and distribution, both in New York and in Long Beach. For example, Charles Mortimer Peck, who was connected with William Fox's Box Office Attraction publicity department, took up the duties of assistant general manager of the Balboa Amusement Producing Company at Long Beach, and the Horkheimers intended to maintain an office in New York on a permanent basis, probably because H. M. was an officer and director in the newly formed National Independent Motion Picture Board of Trade. However, in an article dated November 14, 1914, entitled "Peck Assistant Manager for Balboa," *Motion Picture News* implies, that there was a more extensive relationship between the parties. Fox and the Horkheimers shared several levels of production, distribution, and management: "It is understood that H. M. and E. D. Horkheimer, owners of the [Balboa Amusement Producing] company, will in the near future open an office in New York City and one partner will be there all of the time, and both a part of the time; thus the management of their producing company on the West

The Lasky Barn, in Hollywood, was converted, December 1913, into the original studio of "Hollywood." Today the building houses the Hollywood Heritage Museum.

coast will be looked after in their absence by Mr. Peck" (*Press Clippings*, vol. 1, p. 125).

Lights, Camera, Action — Long Beach

Long Beach has the historical distinction of being the home of the very first film plant in the United States to have its headquarters west of Chicago. The first studio in Long Beach, and the first film plant to originate in California, was called the California Motion Picture Manufacturing Company and was founded in 1910. In January 1913, Edison, with his movie headquarters in the Bronx, New York, also targeted Long Beach for one of his western outposts. He leased the studio already in place, renaming it the Edison Motion Picture Company. By coincidence, in December of that same year, Cecil B. DeMille, who was heading west from New York, left Flagstaff, Arizona, since he was unable to film there because of inclement weather, and he took his film crew further west to California. DeMille ended up at an unassuming barn in Hollywood and telegraphed his partners in New York, Jesse Lasky and Samuel Goldwyn, to ask if they would approve his renting the barn for $75 per month. His partners warily replied: "Authorize you to rent barn, but on month-to-month basis. Don't make any long commitment. Regards, Jesse and Sam" (Callard, p. 29). At the time, Hollywood was simply the location of a barn, not the emblem par excellence for the movie industry. In a short time, more and more moviemakers would make the move to California. Not only could the independent producers escape to some degree the stranglehold of the trust back East, but who could deny the good climate and diverse scenery in Southern California?

In January 1913, J. Searle Dawley of the Edison Motion Picture Company had arrived in Long Beach with his stock players and technicians and resided in the elegant Hotel Virginia. A few months later Balboa Amusement Producing Company established itself as the third film plant in Long Beach, again at the very same

Balboa's facility began as the first movie studio to originate in California: the California Motion Picture Manufacturing Company in Long Beach, incorporated October 1910. Also the site of the Edison western outpost, beginning production in January 1913 (courtesy of Marc Wanamaker).

site. It would not be the last film plant in Long Beach, but all of them would close by 1923.

By 1915 the North American film center was rapidly gravitating toward the West; that year 50 percent of all U.S. films were being produced in California. In fact, by 1915 the film industry had become the fifth largest industry in the United States. Within a few years, the studios of Los Angeles County, including those in Long Beach, would transform Southern California into the film capital of the world. During the Great War in Europe, the Far West was recapturing the lead in this expanding industry, not only in the United States, but as the movie production center of the world. During the European calamity, before there was even an establishment called Hollywood, Balboa launched itself for five glorious years, 1913–1918, as the home of the largest glass studio in the industry and one of the most productive plants in the history of world cinema. Balboa Studios in Long Beach, along with its neighboring pioneers in Los Angeles, helped make Southern California the movie capital of the world, with Balboa contributing to California's lead in the industry by producing countless quality films such as *St. Elmo, Little Mary Sunshine, Who Pays?* and *The Awakening.* Hollywood still reigns today as movieland's supreme emblem of movie magic, while Balboa Studios in Long Beach, though having made it big-time and having contributed to Southern California's supremacy in the film industry, vanished almost completely from the moviegoers' collective memory. While movie history was being made in Long Beach, Balboa Studios offered some of the industry's most ambitious triumphs, before the studios fell into near oblivion during the exploding growth and change of the movie industry in Los Angeles County. Today in Long Beach, Balboa's traces and undeniable legacy can still be claimed, making possible eventual recognition of Balboa Studios' significant contributions to California's movie history and Long Beach's rightful place in movieland's hall of fame.

On March 3, 1914, H. M. Horkheimer, head of Balboa Studios, explained in the *Daily Telegram* why Long Beach was the ideal location for making feature films: almost perpetual sunshine, proximity to ships and docks at San Pedro, proximity to mountains and seashores, aid of local people, and ocean breezes that kept the air free of haze (*Press Clippings*, vol. 1). Today many people still recognize Long Beach as an ideal location for films, not knowing that it was once a moviemaking center. Several modern films have used the city either as a major or minor location. The *Press Telegram*, September 19, 1995, announced that the Association of Film Commissioners International Conference was being held in Long Beach. Ironically, overlooking Long Beach's little-known movie history, the association's president, Leigh Von Der Esch, noted, "Your community is getting a reputation for being film friendly." Scott Dewees, a Long Beach alumni and winner of the professional of the year award, also remarked, "It's an area that hasn't been overshot. It's friendly. It is very diverse in its looks." Like Horkheimer, Von Der Esch and Dewees expressed similar compliments about Long Beach as an ideal location for films. The *Press Telegram* article cites some of the recent blockbusters shot in Long Beach: *Spy Hard*, Leslie Nielsen's spoof on action-adventure films; *Nixon*, Oliver Stone's look at the life of President Richard Nixon, with Anthony Hopkins in the title role; *Air Time*, wherein Michael Jordan made his film début; *Batman Forever*; *Speed*; and *Stargate*, just to mention a few. Fortunately, Long Beach still maintains its movie heritage, though most people remain totally in the dark about its glorious moviemaking past.

Early Studios in California

In its December 10, 1910, issue, *Variety* exclaimed: "Chicago is the only city west of the Alleghenies with the exception of one plant at Los Angeles where the motion picture is manufactured." Was there really only one "California" studio in Los Angeles County at the end of 1910? Yes and no. There were at least six studios established by that time in California, but only one, the California Motion Picture Manufacturing Company, was not an outpost of a company located in either New York or Chicago. The following list gives, more or less in chronological order, the first six studios in Southern California, all but one of them with headquarters back East. Some of the following descriptions give specific months and years when the studios were established in California, while the time period when other film companies relocated in California cannot be precisely determined. In any case, the California Motion Picture Manufacturing Company was among the first six film plants operating in California at the end of 1910, and it was the fourth studio erected in Los Angeles County. Nonetheless, the California Motion Picture Manufacturing Company has the marked distinction of being the very first film plant originating in California, with its headquarters in Long Beach, rather than in Chicago or New York.

New York Motion Picture Company

First established in New York and organized by Adam Kessel, Jr., this was one of the first independent motion picture companies in the United States. This company's California outpost was started in the fall of 1909 under the management of producer Fred Balshofer (Slide, p. 244).

Selig Polyscope Company

Selig, one of the earliest film companies in the world, was founded in Chicago by William N. Selig on April 9, 1896. In 1909–1910, Selig built the earliest permanent studio in California, in Edendale, on Allesandro Street; it was managed by James L. McGee (*Encyclopedia of Movie Studios*).

Biograph Company

Biograph was one of the earliest film companies in the world; it was founded in 1895 by

Henry Norton Marvin in New York. Two studios were established in Los Angeles at separate time periods, the first of these operating from January to April 1910 at Grand Avenue and Washington Street, the second operating from 1911 to 1915 at Georgia Street and Girard Street (Slide, p. 40).

Essanay Film Manufacturing Company

This company was incorporated in Chicago, February 5, 1907, by George K. Spoor and G. M. Anderson. On September 8, 1909, G. M. Anderson left Chicago and headed west. He stopped at Denver, El Paso, and Santa Barbara before settling in Niles, California, near Oakland, in 1909. According to Marc Wanamaker, Essanay took over the Majestic Studio in East L.A. in 1915. It was located at 651 Fairview Avenue in Boyle Heights, then called Brooklyn Heights.

California Motion Picture Manufacturing Company

This film studio is the only one on the list that originated in California, and that fact may account for the name of the company, which was incorporated on October 15, 1910, at the corner of Sixth Street and Alamitos Avenue in Long Beach. It was managed by five directors: C. H. Lovell, M. C. Lovell, H. R. Davis, M. F. Brooks, and T. L. Howland.

Kalem Company, Incorporated

This film company was founded in Chicago in early 1907 by George Kleine, Samuel Long, and Frank Marion. A Kalem studio was later established in California at Verdugo Canyon, Glendale, on December 11, 1910, by director Kenean Buell, along with William Wright (Slide, p. 182).

Of all the locations in California for a film plant, one might ask "Why Long Beach?" Actually, this seaside resort was a perfect choice. Long Beach had been known as a theatre town, with many actors and technicians at its doorstep. Legitimate theatre and vaudeville prospered in Long Beach before the studios and silver screens were erected. Theatrical talent was abundant, with companies like the Keith and Orpheum Circuit, and many early film actors started out as comedians or vaudevillians. In 1908, for example, "Fatty" Roscoe Arbuckle, who later returned to live and work in Long Beach, had been doing summer stock in Long Beach, receiving $50 a week as a singer and comedian. That summer Arbuckle performed at the fashionable Pike amusement area of Long Beach at the Byde A Whyle Theatre, one of the most elegant structures owned by the equally majestic Hotel Virginia. During Arbuckle's theatre tour in Long Beach, he met and fell in love with a young dancer, Minta Durfee. In his article, "Long Beach Story: The Balboa Amusements Producing Company" (p. 22), Chris Callard reports that Arbuckle proposed marriage to the dancer while strolling along the Pine Avenue Pier.

Arbuckle must have possessed many fond memories associated with Long Beach. According to Callard, when Arbuckle's marriage proposal to Durfee was made public, the theatre manager made special arrangements to have the wedding performed on stage. On August 5, 1908, after doing two shows before a full house, Roscoe and Minta were married by the Long Beach mayor himself. Callard notes that Roscoe and Minta received many signs of genuine kindness from the people of Long Beach, the newlyweds being flooded with wedding gifts from citizens they didn't even know. The gifts were even displayed in the windows of Long Beach's downtown Buffum department store. It is understandable that Arbuckle loved Long Beach and returned there to make movies and to build himself a home. Before the movies ever came to town, Roscoe Arbuckle's much celebrated wedding reflected Long Beach's heartfelt goodwill toward talented and likable artists.

Not only were the inhabitants of Long Beach most welcoming to theatrical companies, but the climate and terrain of Southern California also drew crowds, along with Long

The elegant Hotel Virginia, at Ocean Boulevard and Magnolia Avenue, on the bluff overlooking the beach. The Pike amusement zone appears to the left.

Hotel Virginia — grand stairway.

Beach's expanding commerce. In fact, Long Beach in 1913 was hailed as the fastest growing municipality in the United States. Everywhere one looks in Long Beach, even today, one can find scenery of all types, with the ocean, port, and beaches just a few steps away, mountains in reach within two hours by car, the city limits being equally close to both rocky deserts and alpine woods, with rivers and marshlands intersecting the city, left and right, with Santa Catalina Island just off the coast of Long Beach. What more could a filmmaker want than a city

Hotel Virginia — main lobby

full of theatrical talent, a welcoming populace, and an ideal location?

In the early days, film studios were already valued as commercial industries and were often called plants or manufacturing companies. Occasionally these film manufacturing sites were even called factories. The first film plant in Long Beach and the first American studio to originate west of Chicago was called the California Motion Picture Manufacturing Company. In October 1910, the Long Beach Chamber of Commerce was informed of the interest of certain businessmen — C. H. Lovell and M. C. Lovell from Los Angeles; and H. R. Davis, M. F. Brooks, and T. L. Howland from Long Beach — to establish a motion picture plant in the city. In their initial proposal, these entrepreneurs intended to spend $1,500 for a developing house and other edifices necessary for the film studio, with a total output between $15,000 and $20,000, a considerable investment at the time. Among this group of investors, Howland, who was motivated by his business ties with the Bijou Theatre in Long Beach, was particularly interested in the film plant's lucrative potential. Howland lamented the insufficient number of films released by both Edison's trust and the independent filmmakers. He complained that there simply weren't enough films available to exhibitors, not only in Long Beach but across the nation. In the *Long Beach Press*, Howland explained that the new film industry in Long Beach would stimulate the local economy and also satisfy the ever-growing national demand for more movies:

> All the films will be branded, "Made in Long Beach." There are now only from twenty-three to twenty-seven independent new pictures released weekly and they are distributed among 5,000 show houses. The trust releases about as many pictures. Long

Beach uses about twenty-seven films a week, which makes it necessary to show some old films at times. The demand is much greater than the supply. (Oct. 20, 1910, 1:4)

The new company was incorporated on October 15, 1910, and the five directors, M. F. Brooks, T. L. Howland, H. R. Davis, C. H. Lovell, and M. C. Lovell, rushed and pushed the establishment of this enterprise together faster than any other company in Long Beach. Everyone involved seemed convinced of the boon these motion picture headquarters would offer the expanding economy of Long Beach. Among the seven elaborate purposes outlined in the Articles of Incorporation of the California Motion Picture Manufacturing Company, the second purpose states:

> The purpose[s] for which said Corporation is formed and framed are as follows: To engage in and carry on the business of manufacturing moving or motion pictures. To engage in the art and manufacture and sale of photographic motion picture films for the purposes of advertising, instruction, amusement, and such other profitable uses and purposes, as the Board of directors may direct.

The directors' bold ambitions seem to have had no limits, matching in power and scope nothing short of a precursor of the amusement parks launched by Walt Disney, a sort of EPCOT Center in Long Beach:

> To conduct amusement enterprises in all the branches pertaining thereto and thereof; consisting of summer gardens, parks, hotels, dance halls, bathing beaches, roof gardens, theaters, nickelodeons, and to run steamboats and other boats for excursion and other purposes; to operate any plays, operas, songs, musical or dramatical performances and other things relating thereto which may be used for amusements of persons in public and private places, and to conduct amusement enterprises of all kinds; to buy, purchase, lease, option, or otherwise acquire, own, exchange, sell or otherwise dispose of, mortgage and deal in real estate, lands, or buildings for the erection and establishment of theaters, halls, offices, stores and ware-houses, with suitable plants, engines and machinery for the furtherance of the businesses named herein; to construct, carry out, maintain, improve, manage, work, control or superintend any private mills, factories, ware-houses and other works and conveniences, which may seem directly or indirectly conducive to the objects of the Company, and to contribute to, subsidize or otherwise aid, or take part in such operations.

The Chamber of Commerce secretary, Mr. Camp, was instructed to meet with the five directors of the California Motion Picture Manufacturing Company to look over available locations for the new studio. Motion picture expert V. L. Duhem from Oakland had already been scouting out the region for the new plant. He had reported to his associates that Long Beach would be an ideal location for manufacturing the newfangled productions, sometimes called "moving pictures." Of the many locations considered, Duhem believed that the land occupied by the Electric Manufacturing Company on the corner of Sixth Street and Alamitos Avenue in Long Beach, as well as several locations around Signal Hill, would be ideal for motion picture productions. One tract of land had already been considered, but that deal fell through. The scouts had been eyeing property near Zaferia Junction that belonged to the Pacific Electric Company, but another buyer, the Southern Pacific Company, beat the movie crowd to the draw, so the search went on. Local men affiliated with the company, M. F. Books, P. L. Howland, and H. R. Davis, were looking for two to three acres to allow ample space for all the necessary paraphernalia used to film action scenes, to construct all types of scenery, and to erect building fronts.

No stone was left unturned during the search, with several locations taken into consideration. Howland would eventually become the president of the California Motion Picture

Manufacturing Company and would work with the Chamber of Commerce, leasing the studios to various production companies, including the Edison Motion Picture Company, Famous Players Company, and Pilot Films Company, until the Horkheimer purchase of the site in 1913. At one point, the newly formed California Motion Picture Manufacturing Company was planning to take over the former Buckle factory building on East Fourth Street, east of Alamitos Avenue. During the company's relentless search, P. L. Howland was quoted in the *Daily Telegram*: "We are going out with Mr. Camp of the Chamber of Commerce tomorrow, and are pretty sure we can find something to suit us. We need at least two or three acres, the more the better, because some of the scenes will require much action and quite a lot of ground. The company will go pretty strong on comedy pictures, which seems to be what the public mind craves more than any other" (Oct. 20, 1910, 8:6).

This historical moment for the early film industry in Southern California looked very promising for the ambitious city of Long Beach. The decision was finally made to build the studio at the intersection of Sixth Street and Alamitos Avenue. The Long Beach *Daily Telegram* dated January 27, 1911, ran this headline: "California Motion Picture Manufacturing Company Begins Active Operations." At an initial expense of $20,000, the new manufacturing company would spare no cost for the different departments or for the equipment needed to produce high-class motion picture films. The film plant was set up to lease its facilities to movie producers, with a projected weekly payroll of at least $300. For the value of the dollar at that time, these sums were considerable outlays. As a point of reference, the average annual income at the time would have been around $1,000. Fortunately, Duhem, the general manager, was a practical man with important experience in this expensive and burgeoning industry that was full of exciting novelties in cinematography. He took it under his own direction to buy the best European lenses, Pathé cameras, and other necessary materials to assure the best quality films.

Actors had been secured and other company workers would be selected as soon as competent people could be found. Only the best people would be employed to promote the highest quality film production capacity. In Long Beach, the stage was being carefully prepared to lure film companies from the East and to promote increased productivity of the motion pictures that were so much in demand in the growing entertainment market.

According to Claudine Burnett, head of literature and history at the Long Beach Public Library, Long Beach's enthusiastic involvement with movies began at the turn of the century. In Burnett's account titled "Long Beach Motion Picture Industry: 1911–1923," she reports that the first motion picture was shown on June 22, 1900, in the old Tabernacle, at the northeast corner of Third Street and Locust Avenue. It was an Edison picture with a combat scene and marine scenes. The Tabernacle was an historical building that had been erected in the 1880s by the Chautauqua Assembly of Long Beach. In 1900 the Tabernacle was the only theatre in Long Beach, a small town then having a population of 2,252 inhabitants. For a small town, the Tabernacle could serve and did serve many functions at the same time — theatre, lecture hall, and church.

In 1907, La Petite Theatre at 236 Pine Avenue became the first establishment especially built as a movie house. Burnett states that patrons could see a movie at La Petite for ten cents and view Edison's latest productions: *The Bell-Ringer's Daughter*, *The Flexible Man,* and *The Fairy of the Spring*. The program was changed Monday, Wednesday, and Friday evenings. Burnett states that the manager of La Petite, Mr. Erwin, attempted to have only the most recent films, but despite his efforts to make La Petite a great success, his enterprise failed to make enough profit, and the theatre closed in 1908.

Claudine Burnett further recounts that in 1902 the arrival of the Pacific Electric Railway and the building of the amusement zone called the Pike not only put Long Beach on the map but made the city's population explode. From 1900 to 1910, the population of Long Beach

The Pike, Long Beach's amusement zone, circa 1910 (courtesy of Long Beach Public Library).

grew a whopping 691 percent as the city became a major entertainment and seaside resort center (Burnett, p. 2).

The Pike was a perfect draw for the motion picture industry and was the location where the first motion picture plant originating in California would be formed. In 1901 a retired railroad magnate from Arizona, Charles R. Drake, conceived the idea of an amusement area in Long Beach. It was Drake who arranged for the Pacific Electric rail line to come into Long Beach to bring in the people to visit his new amusement center. Why was the area called the "Pike"? According to Claudine Burnett, the name was suggested by one of the attractions at the Louisiana Purchase Exposition of 1904, where there was a "Ten Million Dollar Pike." One of the definitions of the term *pike* is a narrow and pointed piece of land. Thus the name was appropriate for the narrow strip of private concessions and amusement rides at the Louisiana Purchase Exposition, as well as the similar arrangement for the entertainment center in Long Beach.

With the new amusement center in place, theatre managers at the Pike in Long Beach took advantage of the opportunities afforded by the new movie industry. After the California Motion Picture Manufacturing Company had established itself in Long Beach, a convention of motion picture producers and distributors convened inside the halls of the Chamber of Commerce of Long Beach. F. Du Ree, the manager of the Bijou Theatre, declared to a reporter from the *Long Beach Press*: "This is the most important gathering of the men engaged in this business that has ever been held in the southwest." Du Ree continued his boast, "It is the first official gathering of those engaged in the moving picture business that has ever been held in this part of the country." This convention provides one more example of the earliest stirrings of the motion picture industry in Southern California, again in the commercially expanding city of Long Beach.

As Burnett also explains, there were many important issues open to discussion at this historic conference, especially the possible enactment of laws to protect the production and distribution of motion pictures. Coming from all parts of Southern California and Arizona, over 200 people attended the conference. The

The Pike looking east toward the Pine Street Pier (courtesy of Long Beach Public Library).

program started with a tour of the Pike, after which everyone sat down to discuss and exchange ideas. At the same time, the gathering served as a trade show, displaying the latest theatre chairs, curtains, machines, and moving picture supplies. Since the people attending the convention were particularly concerned about making the new film industry respectable, they promoted the making of films that would encourage respectability through temperance and the highest moral conduct by avoiding any scenes of murder, saloon brawls, and drunken behavior. This policy reflected, of course, the politically correct temperance movement of the day.

By 1911 the Pike was a thriving, active, and state-of-the art amusement park, the Coney Island of the Pacific. The Pike included a playground, day nursery, a carousel, a roller-skating rink, a miniature railway, and a monstrously large Ferris wheel. Along with all the other sources of entertainment, the Pike also provided year-round vaudeville programs. The stage was set for a bustling theatre and cinema center for Long Beach, not to mention for all of Los Angeles County. Long Beach was clearly a bold contender in Southern California's motion picture industry because the city was already a world-class entertainment center and seaside resort.

Following the historical founding of the California Motion Picture Manufacturing Company in Long Beach in 1910, there would be other film plants settling in the foothills of Los Angeles County, such as Universal Studios and Paramount in 1912. For the U.S. movie industry, the march had begun that would shift the center of the film industry from the East to the West. There was a new kind of rush for the gold in Californy, and the studio trains were packing to make the long haul, their banners flapping "California or bust!" Universal and

Paramount gained lasting fame and glory, but the film industry in Long Beach remains to this date almost forgotten, even though it was one of the very first and most successful prospectors in early movieland.

In April 1911, U.S. marshals seized all the cameras and equipment at the California Motion Picture Manufacturing Company's offices in Los Angeles in accordance with the rights of the Motion Picture Patent Company, Edison's trust, to prevent the illegal use of such equipment by independent producers. This interruption did not prevent the company from going ahead with its ambitious plans; that month it filmed its first comedy in Long Beach. In fact, that same April, seven months before the Gaumont Palace, with its enormous seating capacity of 3,400, opened its doors to the Parisian public, the California Motion Picture Manufacturing Company had begun its own ambitious building on the Pike, laying the foundation of a modern, up-to-date motion picture theatre, to provide the first of a series of public viewing halls connected with the film producers at the Long Beach studio. Excavation and construction began directly north of the Unique Theatre and west of the Bernice Apartments on April 13, 1911. With a staff of eight persons permanently employed and several part-time workers, the California Motion Picture Manufacturing Company was planning on the continued growth of all the town's businesses, with particular attention, of course, directed toward the exciting potential of the new film industry. The company would show all its own movies and import others. On May 13, 1911, the new California Motion Picture Company's theatre at the Pike opened its doors without a roof, showing its first comedy, *On Matrimonial Seas*. The company wanted to meet its own deadline, though there had been construction delays. Therefore the first shows were at night, when no roof would be needed to keep out daylight.

There was no dragging of feet in Long Beach while putting the new movie plant in order. An article dated April 13, 1911, does not reveal the identity of a certain mysterious Easterner, "the best picture-making artist," who would be in charge of movie production in Long Beach. The article does claim that the mystery man would bring with him a large troupe of actors from back East to produce photoplays. Unfortunately, none of these early professional artists coming to Long Beach are identified. If the mystery man worked for Edison films, then it must have been someone other than J. Searle Dawley, who arrived in Long Beach two years later, in January 1913. Nonetheless, with a seating capacity of 800, the new movie theatre would be proudly showing productions filmed in Long Beach, providing the public the first views of Long Beach as the setting and background for the photoplays performed by actors who would soon be making their homes and spending their cash in this developing movie town.

The California Motion Picture Manufacturing Company had pulled out all the stops. The company had already received a large consignment of raw film stock that was being perforated in the company's laboratories, with another large order on the way. To entice movie producers to come to town, the California Motion Picture Manufacturing Company offered to pay the rent for the ground they occupied in the amount of $18,000. These early entrepreneurs spent big money because they had big dreams and wanted to see industries of all sorts expand in Long Beach. Besides housing the movie theatre, the new construction would also provide seven storage rooms facing the fashionable and busy Pike, each one to be leased on an annual basis. The forward-looking manufacturing company hoped to attract a film producer from the East, where the American film capital was located at the time. The Long Beach businessmen tried to make the film plant in California appear as attractive as possible by having a string of theatres extending up and down the California coastline as far north as the Oregon border as part of the package in Long Beach, so that film producers could exhibit their productions with the already established convenience of these affiliated theatres. What more could any film company want — a city bending over backwards to be business-friendly, a complete movie outfit furnished and raring to go, not to mention a seaside resort, beautiful weather, and plenty of sunshine?

Even today many citizens in Long Beach have watched motion pictures being shot around town. The crew sets up lights as makeup artists powder the faces of the stars and the commanding director shouts instructions to the crew. A Panavision platinum sits on a dolly and tracks the shot with the cameraman riding this Rolls-Royce of cameras. Sync cables connect the camera to the sound system, and soundmen adjust booms mounted with microphones attached to the cables. These days hundreds of people comprise motion picture crews, and millions of dollars are spent for a single production.

By contrast, when the California Motion Picture Manufacturing Company first invited movie companies to film at its studios, motion pictures were less technologically complex, and had no sound; cameramen used a 20-pound, hand-cranked camera. Most of the time the filmmakers had to use natural outdoor lighting enhanced with diffusers when photographing a scene. Armies of men and women work in the crews of today, but only a handful of people made these early silent pictures, at a fraction of the millions spent now.

One of the first shoots for the California Motion Picture Manufacturing Company concerned what we might call an infomercial about the city of Long Beach, which was to be shown in the East to help draw reputable movie companies to Long Beach's new movie facilities. Made with the cooperation of the Long Beach Chamber of Commerce, spearheaded by secretary Camp, this promotional film was to be sent all over the country. Its scenario was the work of one Harry Wilhelm, a 19-year-old author from Signal Hill.

This first Long Beach production was accomplished in the blink of an eye at a pace unimaginable today, when a movie on the average takes a year to shoot. In a modern-day film, during a 12-hour shooting, only one minute of those 12 hours can be counted in the finished product. At any rate, the California Motion Picture Manufacturing Company's first movie was nothing more than a calculated advertisement, showing the city's best features, to entice film companies to make the long haul from the East to Long Beach, where they could establish a permanent film base.

It was early morning on January 6, 1911, when the first movie production in Long Beach began to roll. The cast was to consist of the Long Beach Fire Department, though along the way the production attracted a lot of extras (kids on bikes, crowds in the streets, people visible in windows, and a Mr. J. J. Mottell — "among the first to witness the shooting," said the papers).

The fire department went through a series of stunts. The cameras rolled, showing the setting off of an alarm, followed by a scene of the fire department headquarters at Third Street and Pacific Avenue, where the alarm was answered in a hurry. Various autos and other fire equipment came rushing out from the building. Next the cameraman took his place at the southeast corner of Pine Avenue and Ocean Boulevard, where the police tried to hold the excited crowd of onlookers back, out of the camera's view. Tearing down Pine Avenue, the fire engine sounded its mighty whistle and gongs, attracting the typical "fire crowd."

The scenario for this affair might well have read something like this:

Sets — Exterior Only

Fire alarm
Entrance of Fire Department Headquarters
   Corner of Third and Pacific
   Departmental vehicles and equipment
Run down Pine Avenue
Run down First Street
Run down East Ocean Boulevard at the foot of Locust
Run from Pine proceeding east toward American (Long Beach Boulevard today)

FADE IN

1   EXT. VIEW, IDEAL WEATHER   1
      CONDITIONS — EARLY MORNING

    Close-up of clanging fire alarm.

2	EXT. VIEW, IDEAL WEATHER CONDITIONS — EARLY MORNING	2

Fire department's downtown hall in full action. From entrance depart the various apparatus. The cameraman shoots the emerging departmental vehicles and equipment at the corner of Third and Pacific.

3	EXT. VIEW, IDEAL WEATHER CONDITIONS — EARLY MORNING	3

Thundering with terrific speed, the department vehicles go down Pine Avenue.

4	EXT. VIEW, IDEAL WEATHER CONDITIONS — EARLY MORNING	4

The spectacular run continues, seen at First Street, the fire engine tooting its whistle, clanging the gongs, bringing out crowds onto the sidewalks and at the windows of the downtown buildings. Hundreds of curious spectators line the sidewalks and curbs along the route of the run. Several boys on bicycles excitedly stop and watch the engine pass them by.

5	EXT. VIEW, IDEAL WEATHER CONDITIONS — EARLY MORNING	5

East Ocean Boulevard, at the foot of Locust, where the cameraman is stationed, the run proceeds east toward American. The fire department will make a spectacular rush towards the camera. J. J. Mottell watches, believing it's a real chase.

FADE OUT

A 600-foot film was completely used up after four different rolls were taken of the department in action. This promotional film even required a second take because the driver of the truck took off before the cameraman was ready. As is still true today, people tried to get in the picture by following the camera while it was shooting a scene. The boys on their bicycles tried to become the first extras in this film, and by not being careful, they almost caused accidents. The company decided not to use professional actors for this production; instead amateurs were hired and taught how to perform. The company hired eight to ten persons to act for its promotional movies.

The day following this shoot, officials of the California Motion Picture Manufacturing Company announced that this promotional footage would be shown in mid-January at the Bijou Theatre at the Pike. It was to be viewed only by city officials, firemen, and newsmen behind closed doors. This spectacular run would not be shown to the general public. The film had been sent to San Francisco to be developed. When the film was shipped back to Long Beach, it was returned with a complete developing machine to be used in Long Beach for developing future films. Howland stated that the promo film came out perfectly.

Most of the scenarios for the company's promotional films would come from private authors. Several were written by the aforementioned Harry Wilhelm. Displaying much talent, Wilhelm had already written several scenarios for the Independent Moving Picture Company (Imp), the Bison Company, and many others.

With the approval of city officials, the California Motion Picture Manufacturing Company began filming in earnest February 15, 1911. These promotional films would be shown after March 1, 1911, but none of these initial films would be exhibited first by the local Long Beach theatres. Before the local theatres would show them publicly, those films had to be sold directly to the exchanges, which would then rent them to the national theatre chains for general distribution. Long Beach theatres would have to wait their turn.

Consequently, inquiries began pouring in from leading exchanges around the world. An exchange in London wanted to secure rights for distribution of future productions from the California Motion Picture Manufacturing Company in England and throughout Europe. Requests came in daily to Howland, president of the company. Stock footage was already being shot to be spliced into future films.

The second promo film was entitled *Winter Sports in Southern California*. This film was not what the film crew had intended to shoot when they went south on location. While out to get film of the Mexican Revolution, the crew decided to take a detour through a more peaceful San Diego where two thousand feet of film were shot. What was the event that had drawn them away from Mexico? A yacht race in San Diego provided excellent diversion, showing two yachts, the *Azota* and the *Gretchen*, doing stunts and coming close to a collision. The filmmakers in San Diego also displayed their aerial ladder against the side of the new U.S. Grant Hotel to show how quickly they could get set up to take other views of the harbor.

In praise of Long Beach's growing number of high-quality films, Howland boasted, "They are the equal of any ever put out by any company and that already they have several offers for these films" (*Daily Telegram*, Mar. 14, 1911, 5:7). These films would be shown at the Bijou Theatre on the Pike on March 15 and 16, 1911. The first film was described as proudly displaying the U.S. submarine *Pike* maneuvering in the harbor, as she trims the waves, shows her dive, and then comes out of a totally submerged position. Also seen was a torpedo with the warhead on alert for immediate use.

In addition to these promo films, the California Motion Picture Company began filming on April 27, 1911, its first photoplay, *On Matrimonial Seas*, which premiered at the Pike in Long Beach on May 13, 1911. The cast included Hampton Del Ruth, Mrs. Blakeney, Roy Patchin, Miss Elora, Miss Sanchez, and Miss McLean. This was to be the first movie filmed on Ocean Boulevard, the Pike, and the beach to appear in the new theatre built on the Pike for the California Motion Picture Manufacturing Co. On April 27, 1911, in an article titled "Good Films Are Taken," the *Daily Telegram* stated that there had been a big crowd of spectators and "followers" on location and that many Long Beach people would see themselves in the movie. Company president Howland encouraged the public to be at the beach scenes while the principal actors were bathing. Interestingly enough, Hampton Del Ruth, who starred in this early film, would return in the 1920s to start his own film company at the former Balboa site.

These three films are the only examples of the earliest productions at Long Beach for which documentation has been found. These films and any others made at the California Motion Picture Manufacturing Company have probably faced the same fate as most nitrate films made in the silent era, dissolving, alas, into dust. The full story of this company is not known. These unanswered questions just add more mystery to the story of silent film companies located in Long Beach. The local press did note, however, the existence of another motion picture company in Long Beach at the time: the International Moving Picture Company, founded on May 23, 1911. The company was a joint U.S. and Japanese venture, with films made in both countries. Organized with a capital of $15,000, this international company was headed by Ichiro Asai, a Japanese citizen who lived in Long Beach and worked for John Bowers. After Bowers was shot to death in a lover's triangle, the newspapers never made any other mention of Asai's company.

Along with the increased film production in Long Beach, there was also an increase in the number of movie theatres. Comfort and luxury became serious concerns in erecting these movie houses. For example, in June 1912 the *Long Beach Press* reported that workmen were busy remodeling and redecorating the old Arrowhead Theatre, to be renamed "Joyland," the "Homeland of the Silent Actors." At this renovated theatre there would be loges at the rear of the audience that would be equipped with movable and individual chairs, and have a total seating capacity of 100 persons. There would also be a special box for private parties in one corner, and the newspaper emphasized that the moving picture machine would be operated from a fireproof cabinet.

A couple of months later, on August 3, 1912, yet another movie house was erected at the Pike; it was called the American Theatre. In this new theatre, a player piano had been installed, and as advertisement for the theatre, an enormous electric rendering of the American flag was placed on the front of the building. As Claudine Burnett explains, on account of the great success of the American Theatre, the proprietors of the theatre, Helen and A. C. Frist, decided to build the most elaborate theatre at the time ever constructed in Long Beach. On December 25, 1912, the Fairyland Theatre opened its doors. This latest addition to Long Beach's extravagant movie houses prided itself on its rich medieval terra cotta designs. Besides showing movies, the Fairyland Theatre would also serve as a performing arts center for live entertainment.

Claudine Burnett recounts how this growing market for entertainment in Long Beach resulted in some of the businessmen at the Pike trying to control all revenues generated by the movie industry. In fact, the theatre owners at the Pike mustered enough clout in Long Beach to obtain a city ordinance forbidding commercial films to be shown anywhere in the city except in the amusement zone called the Pike. Just as Fox and Laemmle had broken Edison's trust, however, the Los Angeles amusement magnate W. H. Clune broke the Pike's movie privilege in Long Beach when he decided to show his film of the life of Christ at the Municipal Auditorium instead of following the city ordinance that required him to show films at the Pike. Before the businessmen with their ordinance could stop Clune, he had already advertised his film, *From Manger to Cross*, explaining that it would be shown at the auditorium. Of course, the theatre owners at the Pike protested, but Clune outwitted them. To win over city officials, Clune announced that he would build a modern, reinforced, concrete theatre to seat a minimum of 1,800 spectators on a site he owned at the Pike. This announcement very much pleased the city fathers. In planning his counterattack, Clune also knew the Achilles' heel of the theatre owners — fire inspections. In addition to the bribe offered to city officials, Clune also made a threat against the theatre owners once he had gained the favor of the city officials. Clune had convinced the city to prepare fire inspections of all the movie houses in the amusement zone at the Pike.

Although the theatre owners at the Pike had the law on their side, Clune had tricked them. Fearful of the findings of the fire inspections, the theatre owners agreed to relax the city ordinance and let Clune's film run at the municipal auditorium.

The Edison Outpost

In 1913, Long Beach was the "fastest growing city in the United States," according to government statistics. Long Beach also prided itself on having one of the nation's premier amusement zones. When he moved his productions westward in January 1913, Edison logically chose Long Beach as a base for his productions. According to the *Daily Telegram*, by March 1913 the Edison Motion Picture Company had a weekly expenditure of $3,000 to $4,000. Edison Studios in Long Beach employed 40 to 60 actors and mechanics, headed by J. Searle Dawley, one of the most reputed managers in the movie industry. The same article in the *Daily Telegram* calls J. Searle Dawley "one of the most thorough and artistic stage managers in the business" (Mar. 22, 1913, 2:1). His assistant stage director, James Gordon, was an actor of note. The regular members of the company included Laura Sawyer, Jessie McAllister, Betty Harte, Sidney Ayres, Anna Dodge, Ben F. Wilson, Charles Sutton, Richard Allen, Gordon Sackville, Cy Palmer, Dick La Reno, Duane Wager, and James Gordon. One of the earliest of these productions, starring Laura Sawyer and James Gordon, was based on the Ramona story, an historical romance about early California entitled *The Old Monk's Tale*. It is also interesting to note that Harold Lloyd's first movie involved the California Motion Picture Manufacturing Company and was filmed in San Diego. That movie was called *The Jewels of the Madonna*; Harold Lloyd performed as an extra, being paid $3 to dress up as a Yaqui Indian and carrying a tray of food to white men.

In 1910 the California Motion Picture Manufacturing Company was the first movie studio originating west of Chicago, but by 1913

House Peters.

Ben Wilson.

article — as a barn that Cecil B. DeMille began renting 11 months after Edison came to Long Beach. DeMille had arrived in Los Angeles sometime in December 1913, paying $75 a month to "rent" Hollywood (Callard, p. 29). Before DeMille came to rent the barn in Hollywood, Edison's company transformed Long Beach's barnlike structure into "the most complete motion-picture workshop on the coast and the only one of the 27 operating west of Chicago, with one exception, that is equipped with an indoor studio" (Mar. 22, 1913, 2:1).

This increased productivity in Long Beach benefited the city. The same article explains that the films became more elaborate and included a variety of stories. They depicted all sorts of historical eras, necessitating vast arrays of costumes, large numbers of horses and automobiles, and endless lists of props, "like schedule K of the tariff." These items were being fabricated or purchased in Long Beach, thus stimulating the local economy. The actors too resided in Long Beach and spent their money in the rapidly expanding movie town. With the added security of annual contracts, there were already 27 film plants in operation west of Chicago. The studios were beginning to mushroom in Southern California, with Long Beach among the first and the most thriving of the locations. The previously cited article in the *Daily Telegram* recounts how production at the Edison studio in Long Beach was carried on relentlessly, seven days a week, "dealing with society life, scenes from early California days, events supposed to occur on [the] great northwest border, and stories of sea life." Evidently, the Edison company had much expanded the former California Motion Picture Manufacturing Company's facilities, transforming the studio into one of the most complete film plants, one of the rare ones that included an indoor studio. The same article states that prior to Edison's productions in Long Beach, the Long Beach studio was nothing more than a barn. That's also how Hollywood got started nearly a year later, according to Chris Callard's some of the actors enjoyed top billing and international renown. Dawley, who liked to produce films with large casts, would also choose young men and women of Long Beach, however, amateurs doing work for which they could not find better pay in any other line of trade. This hiring practice also benefited the local population. In addition, Edison's films honored the city by premiering the productions in Long Beach before sending them to New York. Not only was Long Beach producing Edison films, but the city was also the fashionable place where movie fans could see some of the newest releases before anyone else in the country. For example, one of the last movies produced by Edison in Long Beach, *The Dances of the Ages*, premiered at the American Theatre. The film was considered quite original for its special effects, "the most spectacular ever turned out at the local studio." The Long Beach newspaper called it "poignant" and "delightfully" executed (*Daily Telegram*, Apr. 12, 1913).

In April 1913, according to the *Daily Telegram*, the Famous Players Film Company also leased the Long Beach studios from Mr. Howland, the president of the California Motion Picture Manufacturing Company. The same year Edison was leaving Long Beach, the Famous Players Film Company would be producing pictures including famous stage actors. In those early days of cinema, most legitimate stage actors considered the movies beneath them. It was a Hungarian emigrant, however, who helped change this attitude in the United States. Adolph Zukor, another Horatio Alger, like Charles Pathé before him, had worked his way up the ranks from floor sweeper to movie tycoon. Along his way to fame and fortune, Zukor had purchased the American rights of a four-reel French movie, *La Reine Elizabeth*, with Sarah Bernhardt in the leading role of the English monarch. Inspired by the movie's success, Zukor established the Famous Players Film Company in partnership with Daniel Frohman. The box-office success of *La Reine Elizabeth* had given Zukor the idea of matching famous plays with famous players, hence the name of the new company.

The Famous Players Film Company may also have used the Long Beach studio for staging the picture plays in which many of its famous actors appeared. The first famous player to appear in Long Beach was supposed to have been John Drew (*Daily Telegram*, Apr. 12, 1913, p. 1). However, according to Daniel Blum's *A Pictorial History of the Silent Screen* (p. 27), John Drew is among the important stage stars of the period who never performed in films, afraid perhaps that such condescension would damage an otherwise respectable career on stage. Blum cites the following actors and actresses as those who refused to do films: Maude Adams, David Warfield, Julia Marlowe, Mary Mannering, Henry Miller, Eleanor Robson, Rose Stahl, and John Drew. On the other hand, Blum explains that several successful stage stars did become hits in the movies, in fact, bigger stars of the screen than of the stage, including Douglas Fairbanks, Marie Dressler, John and Lionel Barrymore, Marguerite Clark, George Arliss, Nazimova, Elsie Ferguson, Pauline Frederick, and Victor Moore.

To add to the jumble and expansion going on at the Long Beach studio, the Balboa Amusement Producing Company purchased the plant in April 1913, about the same date the *Daily Telegram* announced that the Famous Players Film Company was leasing the site to make movies. One can imagine that these production companies sometimes shared the same facilities during this period of multiple leasings and takeovers. According to film historian Marc Wanamaker, Fred Mace, a Keystone comedian and director, had left Keystone in April 1913 to run for mayor of Los Angeles and had also purchased an interest in the Balboa Amusement Producing Company in Long Beach. Fred Mace would make comedies for Balboa, but at the time, the new Balboa company was not filming in Long Beach. According to Marc Wanamaker's timeline for Balboa, the company had leased a tract of land adjoining the Revier studio and laboratory at Vine Street and Selma Avenue in Hollywood. This was a temporary lease, but in April 1913, Balboa was not yet filming in Long Beach. Fred Mace and his comedy company had begun work at the Revier studio. They would make split reel comedies there and at the Thanhouser/Imp lot at 651 Fairview Avenue in East Los Angeles. Hollywood had not yet been defined, and obviously this sharing of facilities seemed to be a rather common occurrence among film companies of Los Angeles County. Therefore, in the spring of 1913, Edison would be preparing to leave the Long Beach studio, Famous Players would be filming there, and by May 1913, Fred Mace's comedy company would be making films for Balboa, probably in Los Angeles, with some shooting in Signal Hill and at the Pike, on location in the Long Beach area. Nonetheless, by the end of 1913, Balboa would have made approximately fifty movies at its new studios in Long Beach, but only a few are identified. The few films listed below by Famous Players Film Company and Pilot Films Corporation were most probably produced in Long Beach, among other productions by various film companies shooting there in 1913:

Chelsea 7750. Four-reel detective drama. Famous Players Film Co. Released Sept. 20, 1913, by State Rights. *Director*: J. Searle Dawley. *Scenario*: J. Searle Dawley. *Cameraman*: H. Lyman Broening. *Cast*: Henry E. Dixey (*Detective Kirby*), Laura Sawyer (*Kirby's daughter, Kate*), House Peters (*Professor Grimble*).

The Daughter of the Hills. Four-reel historical drama. Famous Players Film Co. Released Dec. 20, 1913, by State Rights. *Director*: J. Searle Dawley. *Scenario*: J. Searle Dawley. *Cast*: Laura Sawyer (*Floria*), Wellington A. Playter (*Sergius*), David Davies (*Floria's father*), Frank Van Buren (*the Apostle Paul*), P. W. Nares (*Nero*), Alexander Gaden (*a slave*), Carmen De Gonzales (*leader of the dance*), Ben Breakstone (*opposing gladiator*).

Hoodman Blind. Five-reel drama. Pilot Films Corp. Released Dec. 22, 1913, by State Rights. *Director*: James Gordon. Based on the play *Hoodman Blind* by Henry Arthur Jones and Wilson Barrett (London, Aug. 18, 1885). *Cast*: Wilson Barrett (*Lennon*), Betty Harte (*Jess/Nance*), Herbert Barrington (*Jack Yeulett*), James Gordon (*Tom, the Romany*).

An Hour Before Dawn. Four-reel detective drama. Famous Players Film Co. Released Oct. 20, 1913, by State Rights. *Director*: J. Searle Dawley. *Scenario*: J. Searle Dawley. *Cast*: Laura Sawyer (*Kate Kirby*), House Peters (*Kate's father*).

The Port of Doom. Four-reel detective drama. Famous Players Film Co. Released Oct. 20, 1913, by State Rights. *Director*: J. Searle Dawley. *Scenario*: J. Searle Dawley. *Cast*: Laura Sawyer (*Kate Kirby*), House Peters (*Kate's father*), Dave Wall (*Fuller*), Peter Lang (*Fornton*), Hattie Forsythe (*Vera Fornton*), Hal Clarendon (*Captain Giles*), Henrietta Goodman (*Fuller's wife*).

If Famous Players leased the Long Beach film plant, indicators also point to other companies having possibly leased the California Motion Picture Manufacturing Company between 1911 and 1913. New evidence might prove other companies and stars worked at Long Beach during these early years. For example, Josephine Woodman, born in November 1912, has provided a photo of herself in an early Edison movie filmed in Long Beach when she appeared as a four-month-old in a Western entitled *Bill's Sweetheart*. In the photo, little Josephine, wrapped in a blanket, is being held in the arms of Sydney Ayres, encircled by a crew of cowboys and one lonely cow. There is even some question whether Mary Pickford might have done work at Long Beach during this same time period. At about this time, the famous silent star left Biograph to do stage work for David Belasco once more, while also doing some films for Famous Players. Might she have also worked in Long Beach for Famous Players, then leasing the Long Beach studio? Interestingly enough, Mary Pickford was among those who attended Balboa's Christmas gala on December 24, 1913, but this may be coincidence and may merely reflect the establishment of Long Beach as an entertainment and film production center among the numerous studios burgeoning then in Los Angeles County. Mary Pickford's attendance at the Christmas gala at the Hotel Virginia does,

Bill's Sweetheart (Edison) 1913: Baby, Josephine Woodman, née Munger, in the arms of Sydney Ayres. The other actors are not identified (courtesy of Mrs. Josephine Woodman).

however, raise some speculation about her possible involvement with filmmaking in Long Beach.

By January 1913, Southern California was teeming with film plants; there were already forty companies in operation in Los Angeles County, with more on the way. Among the film companies and troupes in Los Angeles County, there were thirty-one companies that represented the Edison trust—Selig (four troupes), Pathé, Vitagraph, Kalem (two outfits), Essanay (two companies), Edison, Biograph, Mutual Film Company, Kay-Bee, Broncho, Keystone (two troupes), American (two companies), Thanhouser, Majestic, Film Supply Company, and Universal [Nestor (three outfits), Powers (two companies), Rex (two troupes), and Bison (two companies)]. Among the nine independent producers in California by January 1913, one could count Kinemacolor (three outfits), the Eagon (four companies), the Monopol Feature Film Company, and the Amex (American-Mexican) Company. It is not clear which of these forty companies and troupes in Los Angeles County during this period besides Edison, Famous Players, and Biograph might have leased the established and well-equipped studio in Long Beach.

One should not overlook the fact that Los Angeles County constituted the shared turf of these companies, and Long Beach had already established itself as a viable and important movie center in 1910 with the California Motion Picture Manufacturing Company. There was confusion then as there is now about the parameters of Southern California's movieland, later to be called Hollywood. Within these mobile boundaries, on February 23, 1914, the *Daily Telegram* of Long Beach announced that Carl Laemmle's Universal Film Manufacturing Company, described in the article as the largest motion picture producing organization in the world, was preparing to move from its ranch site at Universal City near Los Angeles. With studios located in New York, New Jersey, and California, the Universal Company would make its new home a permanent center for the movie industry. Carl Laemmle, whose

Imp Company was doing well, had founded the Universal Film Manufacturing Company on June 8, 1912. Capitalized at $2,000,000, Laemmle's company had become the chief competitor of the Edison trust, though the Universal conglomerate was not quite two years old in February 1914 and had been started on little real cash. The removal of the studio from Los Angeles to Long Beach never occurred, but according to the *Daily Telegram* (Feb. 23, 1914, 1:4), eager city fathers of Long Beach attempted every possible enticement to encourage Universal to make Long Beach its home and Long Beach waited impatiently for the bigwigs from the studio to visit Long Beach's facilities and environs: "Local boosters for the project point out that Long Beach could offer more than is asked in this line having hills, valleys, the mountains, the ocean, the harbor, industrial enterprises for the staging of factory scenes and many other natural resources necessary for the staging of the movies."

Secretary R. L. Bisby was expecting Universal to make the move, the visit having been delayed, most unfortunately, because of severe rain and flooding that made travel difficult between Los Angeles and Long Beach. Universal's removal from Los Angeles to Long Beach was thought to be inevitable because of the expiring lease on the huge plant near Hollywood, a lease unlikely to be renewed because of the astronomical hike in fees. The new plant in Long Beach would have required a property from 600 to 1,200 acres, along with ample areas to build stages and studios. I. Bernstein, general manager of the California studios for Universal, was handling the negotiations for Carl Laemmle, president of Universal. At the time of these negotiations, the Universal organization included the following members: Imp, Rex, Bison, Nestor, Gold Seal, Victor, Eclair, Crystal, Frontier, Powers, Joker, Animated, and Universal Ike. If this historical negotiation had succeeded, then the movie world of Southern California would have shifted from Los Angeles to Long Beach. In early 1913, Universal spent approximately $20,000 a week in Los Angeles, an annual business expenditure of $1,000,000. Universal employed 500 people, not including scores of extras for the larger productions. If Universal had made the move, Long Beach would have become Hollywood by the Sea. Other auxiliary companies that normally furnish the various supplies for the movie industry would have sprung up in Long Beach with the number of jobs and tradesmen skyrocketing and payrolls soaring.

The studio did not make the move, however, and it is possible that the proposed removal of the studio to Long Beach was merely a ploy to lower the lease at Universal City. Moreover, it has not yet been determined whether Universal ever made an inspection trip to Long Beach. Could it be that Long Beach failed to become the movie capital of the world only because of one bad season of winter rains? Fate is a fickle schemer. In the land of perpetual sunshine, during the winter of 1913–1914 too much rain fell on the seaside resort, which was the fastest-growing municipality in the United States and a growing entertainment and cinema center. That fateful winter season, torrential rivers overflowed, dashing the hopes of the ambitious city fathers, and the movie industry over the next decade would firmly anchor itself in the neighboring city of the angels.

Nonetheless, in 1913, Long Beach remained a healthy contender among the movie plants of Los Angeles County. That year two daring and venturesome brothers would bolster the movie preeminence of Long Beach, creating for five glorious years, 1913–1918, the world's most productive film plant, the Balboa Amusement Producing Company. In 1913, California was emerging as the film production center of the world, thanks in great part to the Balboa Studios in Long Beach. Herbert Morris Horkheimer and Elwood David Horkheimer, two brothers in Long Beach, helped make Los Angeles County the movie capital of the world. Before there was an establishment called Hollywood, Balboa was to become king of the silver screen, producing as much as 20,000 feet of negative film a week, with as many as 10 film companies working simultaneously, three shifts a day. At a breathtaking pace, the Horkheimer Brothers made it big-time, but they have yet to be honored for their many contributions to the cinematography arts and sciences. Fortunately, at the time of writing this book, this neglect is about to end because the Horkheimers' accomplishments are in the process of being commemorated with the support and the involvement of various Long Beach citizens, historical and heritage societies, and fans of the arts. In due time, Balboa and the Horkheimers will find once again their proper place in movieland's hall of fame.

Claudine Burnett has written most eloquently about the "meteoric" sensation of the early movie industry in Long Beach in one of her yet unpublished manuscripts entitled "Long Beach Motion Picture Industry: 1911–1923":

> A rare celestial spectacle occurred over the skies of Long Beach on May 23, 1910 — the appearance of Halley's Comet and a total eclipse of the moon. Portents could be read into such an occurrence, if one was superstitious. Ancients viewed the erratic behavior of comets against the harmonious order of the heavens with awe. Combining a total eclipse of the moon with the appearance of a comet could signify that something significant was about to occur.
>
> Coincidentally, perhaps, the same year did bring something significant to Long Beach. It brought the birth of a new industry — that of motion pictures. It was an industry that was to have a prolonged effect on the city, as well as the world. (p. 1)

A few lines later Claudine Burnett points to one of the reasons the movie industry was displaced from Long Beach: "For many years the fledgling Long Beach industry flamed like a comet in the movie world, but in 1921 the local movie business was eclipsed by a new industry — oil."

From 1910 to 1923, over forty film companies used the Long Beach studios for their productions to take advantage of the most complete and compact film plant in Southern California, which at its height covered eight acres in downtown Long Beach and eleven acres in Signal Hill. Some of the silent era's greatest actors, directors, and technicians lived and worked in Long Beach, including Henry King, Jackie Saunders, Baby Marie Osborne, William Desmond Taylor, "Fatty" Arbuckle, Buster Keaton, Ruth Roland, Pearl White, and Theda Bara, just to name a few. Long Beach was a thriving movie town of the silent era. In fact, in 1917 the film industry in Long Beach was the biggest tourist attraction and the biggest employer in town. Most importantly, after inheriting an established movie plant, the Horkheimer brothers expanded it to make movie history on the grandest scale.

The Horkheimers' meteoric rise provides a fascinating and entertaining account of men and women who forged ahead in this new industry, refusing to give up, no matter what the odds, no matter what the obstacle. Only acts of God would finally derail their course toward undying fame and glory. In the long run, as the French say, "l'homme propose, mais Dieu dispose," and the Horkheimers' film legacy would temporarily disappear from view after the debilitating blows of the Great War and the unexpected arrival of the town's newest darling, the most spectacular industry to hit Long Beach — oil. Subterranean floods of petroleum would displace the former walk of the stars. These debilitating blows could not have been foreseen by the dedicated and loyal cofounders of Balboa, and these later upheavals would eventually obscure Long Beach's reign in movieland, until searching eyes would look up and spy once more, among the shining stars in the heavens, the glorious traces of Balboa's ascent as one of the greatest luminaries of the silent era.

Reel 2

Something Ventured, Something Gained

Herbert Morris Horkheimer, a great but overlooked American, was born in Wheeling, West Virginia, on July 9, 1882, five days too late to be called a Yankee Doodle Dandy. Herbert's father was a German immigrant named Morris Horkheimer, and Herbert's mother, Cecelia Hirsch, was born and raised in Pennsylvania. H. M. and Elwood's achievements in the early cinema mark another example of an immigrant's children who seized opportunities and tasted sweet success in America. Despite the Horkheimer brothers' deserved claim to fame during the silent era, however, H. M. and Elwood both sank into obscurity after they left Balboa. This negligence on the part of film historians has been the result, understandably enough, of missing evidence of the Horkheimers' involvement, if any, as producers and filmmakers after leaving Balboa. Nonetheless, during the silent era, both men were heralded for their prominence and high profiles in the American movie industry. *Press Clippings*, vol. 1, p. 245, contains an article dating from 1914 entitled, "H. M. Horkheimer a Magnate of the Amusement Producing Art." This article lauds the ambitious and youthful film magnate, who, as general manager at the age of 30, was the youngest of all the chiefs of the motion picture plants in the United States. On the other hand, the writer of the article politely glosses over Herbert Morris Horkheimer's education, explaining that H. M. had simply received a rudimentary one in his home district of Wheeling in Virginia, before leaving that state as a youth to work in a New York mercantile firm. H. M. soon discovered, however, his passion and knack for theatrical productions.

H. M. serves as another example of a Horatio Alger rise to success during that fecund period of self-taught and capable entrepreneurs. Sadly enough, however, when H. M. died of an acute pulmonary edema on April 25, 1962, at Cedars of Lebanon Hospital in Los Angeles, his death went unnoticed. There were no visitors at the Pierce Brothers Mortuary in Hollywood, and not a single memorial folder was printed. No one deserves that much obscurity. The body was cremated, and his ashes were returned to his wife in a cardboard box. Until his death, H. M. had been living very close to the stars whom he loved, frequently

The Horkheimers, a family portrait. Mother, Cecelia, seated at left; H. M., seated on ground in middle with hat at knee; father, Morris, seated at right; Elwood at right, next to father (courtesy of Jackie Saunders, Jr.).

recalling no doubt his meteoric rise to fame during the silent era, as he resided at 1720 North Whitley Avenue, less than a block from the Walk of the Stars on Hollywood Boulevard. On H. M.'s death certificate, his second wife, Agnes, had listed his latest occupation as that of a producer in the theatrical industry — but where and when, after Balboa? It is a pity that both brothers were denied, while they were living, the recognition that they so much deserved.

Although H. M. was educated by the school of hard knocks, he knew, nevertheless, what Shakespeare meant when the bard described the world as a stage. The same *Press Clippings* article enumerates several instances when H. M. Horkheimer sent theatrical troupes and companies on the road: the actress Violet Dale starred in *A Message from Reno*, and one of his companies enacted *Paid in Full*, a celebrated drama by Eugene Walter. During the same time, H. M. also put on stage Clyde Fitch's play *Girls*, while successfully managing an unidentified but supposedly large company from Rochester, New York, with Julia Booth and William Ingersoll in the starring roles of the following productions: *The Girl of the Golden West*, *The College Widow*, *Great Divide*, and *Soldiers of Fortune*. In addition, the article reports that H. M. had also collaborated in the writing and staging of the following productions: *Caught by Wireless*, *The Child*, and *The Strugglers*.

Later, when H. M. converted to filmmaking, he exhibited the same bold versatility and multiple talents as he had for theatrical productions. For example, in 1915, while busy with his new film studio, H. M. collaborated with H. O. Stechhan at the Balboa Amusement Producing Company in writing an historical pageant called *Balboa* that was one of the featured productions at the Panama-Pacific International Exposition in San Francisco. H. M. directed this pageant, which included a cast of several hundred players. Coincidentally, this production is often cited as the source of the name given to the Horkheimer studio. Vasco Núñez de Balboa had been the discoverer of the Pacific Ocean, and the exposition commemorated that discovery, and promoted California's world trade, celebrating also the Panama Canal, which had opened to traffic on August 15, 1914. It is also interesting to remark that the pageant did not draw the attendance expected because the advent of World War I kept away the anticipated crowds. Reflecting the great expectations and hoopla, the U.S. Postal Service issued a 1¢ postage stamp with Balboa's bust on it.

With their typical versatility, both H. M. and Elwood did not hesitate to work in every facet of filmmaking at Balboa Studios. They served as directors, laboratory chemists, scenario writers, camera operators and worked in any and all other areas of what people in 1915 sometimes used to call cinematography — *motography*. H. M.'s considerable energies also involved him in more than his movie business; he was an active Mason and Elk, and was a member of the National Association of Theatrical Producing Managers, the Friars Club of New York, the Gamut Club of Los Angeles, and the Automobile Club of Southern California.

Elwood David Horkheimer, who was born February 8, 1881, and died August 14, 1966, would soon join his younger brother, H. M., in California to become secretary and treasurer of the Balboa Amusement Producing Company, and both brothers would reside in California the remainder of their lives. Nonetheless, there were marked differences between the two brothers that actually helped complement each other's talents. For example, while the two

E. D. Horkheimer (courtesy of Jackie Saunders, Jr.).

brothers shared the same family zeal for success and salesmanship, Elwood was the more formally educated of the two brothers; he had graduated from Cornell University with degrees in both electrical and mechanical engineering. The more cultivated of the two brothers, Elwood was the one who closed the Balboa business deals in Europe — in London in 1914, with Balboa's exclusive European distributor, Bishop, Pessers, and Co., Ltd., as well as in Paris, where he used his knowledge of French to finalize a contract in December 1914 with Pathé Frères. As another telling point of contrast, H. M. was proud to be a member of the Automobile Club of Southern California, but Elwood put off learning to drive in the state famous for its car culture until he was 45 years old.

On July 9, 1914, a British magazine, *The Cinema* (p. 52), issued an interview with Elwood conducted by Alured, that appears in *Press Clippings*, vol. 1, and is entitled, "A Powerful Combination, A Chat with Mr. Elwood D. Horkheimer." During the interview, Elwood demonstrates decidedly Yankee salesmanship equal in boldness of delivery to that of his brother, as he confidently foretells the bright future of Balboa Studios. When Elwood was asked whether he was expecting Balboa to do well in Great Britain, he responded, "Most certainly I am, but I should like to make it quite plain that we're not out for money, but for glory and undying fame!" At this point the interviewer explains to his readers that he could not help but gasp at Elwood's remark. Elwood obviously made his point without considering a moment the British penchant for understatement. One can only imagine that this first gasp was not the last from the Englishman interviewing Elwood Horkheimer. The older brother continued: "Yes, sir, glory and undying fame is our mark with the Balboa films. And we shall earn both without any doubt. I tell you that when people see our pictures they will proclaim them artistic triumphs — everyone of them. Each picture will have something original in it. When I tell you they positively took the United States by storm you will understand they are *just* out of the ordinary."

The same article also includes more boasting by Elwood about the studio's logo, the bust of the Spanish explorer Balboa, explaining how the trademark had been used by the U.S. Postal Service on their 1¢ postage stamp to commemorate the Panama-American Exposition. Elwood finishes the interview by praising the most celebrated star at Balboa at the time, the actress who would later become his wife and the love of his life, Jackie Saunders, the "Maid of Long Beach": "Some people call her 'the second Mary Pickford,' but I call that talented young lady 'the second Jackie Saunders!'" Elwood's know-how and Yankee-styled salesmanship could make any Englishman gasp; he never minced words to clear his way to fame and glory during Balboa's meteoric rise.

In 1912–13 and on February 14, 1915, 334,796,626 Balboa 1¢ green stamps were issued; the value of the stamp varies from $.75 to $4.50. According to Elwood Horkheimer, the bust was based on the Balboa Amusement Producing Company's logo, but the original issue date preceded the founding of the movie studio. Californians awaited the opening of the Panama Canal with impatience because the great canal would be linking the far western states to many of the commercial centers back East and around the globe. The Panama Canal would shorten voyages for national and international cargo from coast to coast (collection of Rodney Bardin).

The Inheritance

Throughout his years as a theatrical producer, H. M. had known many ups and downs, and he had learned to roll with the punches prior to taking over the former Edison studio on Sixth Street and Alamitos Avenue in Long Beach in 1913. Before he had ever seen a motion picture camera, Herbert Morris Horkheimer decided to produce movies in California, where he arrived in 1912. Like his brother Elwood, H. M. Horkheimer remained a persistent and persuasive salesman; he had connections and experience with the legitimate theatre, beginning as a hawker of circus tickets before rising to become a manager of stage productions. What prompted H. M. Horkheimer's move to California and his bold venture in the new medium? With an inheritance from father Horkheimer's woolen mills in the amount of $7,000, a considerable sum at the time, H. M. Horkheimer had entered the movie business and had deftly smooth-talked himself into a contract with the renowned novelist Jack London to do a film based on his best-seller, *The Sea Wolf*.

Not only had H. M. Horkheimer inherited a pile of money, but he also had the good fortune to choose one of the important and early centers of filmmaking in California when he decided to purchase the Long Beach studio. When H. M. purchased the studio, which was being leased by the Edison Motion Picture Company, J. Searle Dawley was still producing movies there. In 1913, at the time of the purchase, the Edison Company in Long Beach comprised one small building and a platform serving as a stage (25' × 75'), along with some diffusers. Later, H. M. Horkheimer and his brother E. D. Horkheimer would convert the original Edison building into a laboratory and a wardrobe department for their expanding Balboa Amusement Producing Company. In April 1913, however, Elwood David Horkheimer had not yet joined his brother in California. While Edison was still using the studio in Long Beach, H. M. Horkheimer was obliged to film elsewhere, going to Los Angeles, where he leased some land next to the Revier Studio and laboratory at Vine and Selma Avenue in Hollywood, where he had a stage and temporary buildings erected until he could return to Long Beach to produce movies there. Fred Mace, who owned an interest in Balboa Studio, was waiting for the Edison filmmakers to leave Long Beach because he had asked the Horkheimers to erect a revolving stage for his comedies. He did all the lab work with the Harry Revier laboratory, cranking out his comedies at the Thanhouser/Imp lot at 651 Fairview Avenue in East Los Angeles. Exactly how long H. M. and Fred Mace worked together in Hollywood has not yet been determined. When H. M.'s brother Elwood arrived in California from the

Jackie Saunders (courtesy of Jackie Saunders, Jr.).

East, the brothers began as a loyal duo to operate in Long Beach the Balboa Amusement Producing Company, with H. M. as president–general manager and Elwood as secretary-treasurer, along with Charles M. Peck as vice-president and assistant manager.

With the building of the stage in Long Beach and production under way for Mace at

Elwood, Florence, and H. M. Horkheimer, sole proproprietors of the Balboa Amusement Producing Company (courtesy of Jackie Saunders, Jr.).

ning as their business and studio manager. When they moved permanently into the Long Beach facilities, they determined that the recently vacated studio was lacking sufficient materials and equipment for them to operate on the scale they intended to produce films in this newly acquired Long Beach venue.

At the southeast corner of Alamitos Avenue and Sixth Street stood the original barnlike studio that was built by the California Motion Picture Manufacturing Company and later improved and enlarged by the Edison company. All under one roof at the same corner were the business offices, carpentry department, property department, and film laboratory, as well as the dressing rooms for the players. To put the studio into good working order, the Horkheimers ended up investing $9,000, which was $2,000 more than they had expected and $2,000 more than the temporary installations in Los Angeles, it is difficult to fix the exact date when Balboa films actually began to be entirely shot in Long Beach for the Balboa Amusement Producing Company. It is equally difficult to fix the date when Dawley's crew left Long Beach. Who actually vacated the studio in Long Beach just before the Horkheimers' arrival? Were there any other companies leasing the site in Long Beach? Edison or Famous Players? It is not clear when Fred Mace sold his holdings in the Balboa Amusement Producing Company. Nor is it clear whether the Horkheimers' sister Florence was a silent partner from the start. She did, however, play an important part in determining the fate of the studio in its last phase of operation, when she did not always agree with her brothers and was unwilling to sell her shares. In any case, when the Horkheimers did eventually move their film productions to Long Beach, they installed Arthur A. Lotto as assistant general manager and Norman Man-

Florence Horkheimer. Note the Balboa logo (courtesy of Jackie Saunders, Jr.).

their inheritance. Despite the tight squeeze on funds, the brothers and their assistant managers mustered a decent crew, attracting some actors from the Lubin studio in San Diego, along with a few carpenters and stagehands, a cameraman, and some lab assistants. The first week's payroll included 12 employees, with an operating expense of $500. These were promising beginnings for big dreamers, and the returns would be worth it, as the ambitious and hard-working Horkheimers began their ascent to fame and glory. Balboa Studio would make over fifty films in 1913, mostly one- and two-reelers, including an uncopyrighted racing film, *In the Stretch*, as well as some juvenile movies starring the child actor Fred J. Whitman.

Unfortunately, trouble was already brewing before the studio's first year ended. The special deal struck between H. M. Horkheimer and the very popular novelist Jack London would turn sour and plague the studio for years with enormous court costs and lawyers' fees. In an issue of *Motion Picture News,* November 29, 1913, George D. Proctor explained that H. M. Horkheimer was the major catalyst in a quarrel between movie producers and authors over interpretations of what constituted public domain, "involving the validity of book copyrights [which] may yet reach the U.S. Supreme Court, according to the threat of the Authors' League of America, 30 Broad St., N.Y.C." Dame Fortune would smile on the Horkheimers, who were counting on their spunk and resolve to pull them through, but the monies and energy spent would take their toll on the struggling studio.

Elwood D. Horkheimer (courtesy of Jackie Saunders, Jr.).

The Sea Wolf's Bite

The Horkheimers signed a five-year contract with the Jack London Motion Picture Company. It should have been the dream team to give the studio global recognition because Jack London was enormously popular and world-renowned. Above all, the Horkheimers wanted fame and glory. Instead, the movie deal with Jack London became a nightmare that tested their mettle.

Better known by his nom de plume, Jack London, this great American writer was born on January 12, 1876, in San Francisco as John Griffith Chaney. Young Jack did not enjoy a happy childhood. First, his parents were terribly poor. To add to the problem of poverty, Jack's father abandoned the young boy and his mother when Jack was still very young. Second, though Jack's parents had interesting occupations, they were plagued by financial worries that they were never able to resolve. Jack's father was an astrologer without any regular employment, and Jack's mother was a spiritualist who was struggling to make ends meet. Their talented son John wanted to grow up to be wealthy, and Jack London did grow up to be an adventurer both rich and famous, but he died young, before attaining his fortieth year, on November 22, 1916, from a drug overdose. His death was suspected to be suicide. Despite his sad beginnings and mournful end, Jack London knew fame and glory in his brief lifetime.

Jack took his surname, London, from his stepfather. At 14 years of age, he set out on his own looking for adventure and riches. In San Francisco, Jack became a part-time thief, while also landing a job with an interesting twist. One of his first occupations was that of an oyster pirate, stealing oysters. As he stole oysters, young Jack concurrently was employed as a member of the fish patrol, working for the government. This ideal double life suited Jack's rebellious character and daring fancy, enabling him to be a "guardian-thief." He was able to rob the very goods he was hired to protect.

Later London began roving the high seas as a sailor of fortune, journeying to the exciting and exotic shores of Japan. Afterwards, he worked in the North Pacific as a seal hunter before returning to the United States. There the latest means of transportation would transform him into an untamed land-rover riding the iron horses, living the hobo life aboard the long and lonely hauls on the mighty freight trains of North America. All these adventures and experiences transpired before Jack was twenty years old. Among his most memorable adventures were escapades during the Klondike Gold Rush. Many of his books use the Klondike Gold Rush as a setting, a veritable microcosm where strong-willed individuals are pitted against nature's unfriendly forces and the violent threats of human opponents. London thus showcases the exceptional determination of his supermen, so much a hallmark in his literary works. Understandably enough, as an autodidactic man of letters, London's thinking reflected what he learned at the public libraries, centering on philosophy, as well as the latest theories concerning the social and natural sciences. Charles Darwin, Karl Marx, and Friedrich Nietzsche were the sources of London's ideas about the survival of the fittest.

When London returned to California from the Klondike, he wrote at least 1,000 words every day until he died. In seventeen years, he wrote fifty books. Despite London's early years of poverty, he would become one of the most-loved and best-paid writers of the modern age. One of his best novels, *Martin Eden* (1909), was based on his own life. London's first novel was called *The Son of the Wolf*. His Klondike experiences were often used in stories about Alaska such as *Call of the Wild* (1903), *White Fang* (1906), and *Burning Daylight* (1910). Even though London was paid well for his novels, he spent his money quickly, frequently giving it to the poor or to a socialist cause. The quality of his writing is often considered uneven, but his popularity continues even today, its uninterrupted longevity being a remarkable accomplishment in itself. Being impulsive, making money and spending it quickly, London was sometimes obliged to write very quickly to maintain a certain revenue. Despite the time constraints imposed on some of his work, London's books are still among the most popular in the world and the most widely read. London believed in making his heroes superhuman, able to overcome impossible odds; consequently, an anxious generation facing an unknown and awesome new century found solace in the bold determination and willpower of London's characters, who could survive anything, even the harsh wilderness of Alaska.

When the Horkheimers signed their contract with Jack London, they bagged, it seemed, a golden egg with this legendary writer at the very peak of his success. London's persona seemed grander than any movie hero, and he appeared larger than life at the dawn of a brave new millennium. How could a movie deal with such a writer ever go wrong? The new age, however, brought new questions, among them the issue of the bounds of copyright laws for movies based on Jack London's literary works.

Copyright disputes arose early in the silent movie era, and one of the earliest and most far-reaching to determine the future of motion picture rights occurred during the legal proceedings between Balboa Studio and Jack London. Movies were still a new medium, and Jack London and the Horkheimers tested the limits of copyright and helped rewrite some of the copyright laws. The results favored authors who wanted to control their writings that were being transformed into the new motion picture medium. For example, in December of 1907, Kalem produced *Ben Hur*, almost twenty years before MGM's famous silent version. Kalem had done the movie without even considering the necessity of acquiring the rights to Lew Wallace's drama, and the studio was promptly sued for $25,000. Until the suit involving Kalem, however, motion picture rights were unknown and frankly still undefined.

Before the clash between Balboa Studios and the Jack London Motion Picture Company, the contract seemed like the perfect win-win agreement between the equally ambitious Horkheimers and Jack London. On April 28, 1913, Jack London was in Long Beach announcing in the *Daily Telegram*:

> I have just completed a deal by which I shall appear as the leading actor in all my own short stories and novels dramatized into motion pictures. I am going into the pictures to give them "the punch" that is almost impossible to communicate to another. What is my definition of the "punch"? Well, it would take many volumes to communicate it properly but, briefly, it is making the impossible possible.

In late July 1913, storm clouds were definitely gathering into ominous darkness, just before London would deliver the lightning punch the Horkheimers were not expecting. Sydney Ayres, who had been working on films at Long Beach since the Edison days, was also working on Balboa's *The Sea Wolf* and claimed breech of contract against the Horkheimers. Ayres declared the studio chiefs' signed contract to be invalid because the July 1, 1913, shooting deadline had not been met for the first picture. According to the *Daily Telegram*, the plaintiffs claiming violation of copyright law were Jack London and Frank A. Garbutt. Alleging misappropriation of two of London's stories, *A Piece of Steak* and *The Sea Wolf,* which were under production at Balboa in Long Beach, these two plaintiffs, London and Garbutt, were heard by Federal Judge Willborn: "The prayer is for an injunction enjoining the defendant corporation from appropriating the stories for moving picture purposes, and assessing damages in $20,000 for the alleged unlawful and illegal use of the publication. It is claimed that the rights of dramatization are more than $10,000" (Oct. 1, 1913, p. 4:3).

The defendants, the Horkheimers, counterclaimed that the publication of these stories in magazines made them public domain. The stories originally appeared in the *Saturday Evening Post* and in the *Century Magazine*, and had also been published in book form by MacMillan Company. Despite the Horkheimers' claim to a five-year contract with London, the famous author vowed he had assigned all movie rights to Frank A. Garbutt. The Horkheimers must have felt betrayed, dealing with a renowned author and "superman" who turned against them in favor of his filmmaking buddies who wanted to use his stories. Nonetheless, the Horkheimers put up a fight, but it cost them dearly. The defendants were represented by Ligon Johnson of New York, one of the great copyright authorities in the world and the author of the copyright laws as they exist in the federal statutes today, so the Horkheimers thought they had a fighting chance against the rich and powerful Jack London.

Jack London had decided to grant exclusive movie rights to Frank Garbutt and Hobart Bosworth, who was an actor and close friend of London's, at a time when Bosworth was just beginning his own film production in Los Angeles. London dropped his agreement with the Horkheimers to help his friends, and the conflict between London and the Horkheimers had as its result the strong protection through legislation of American authors' copyrights. This legislation covered not only movies based on literary pieces, but also adaptations of literary works that were being transformed into any number of newfangled technologies yet on their way during the scientifically advanced twentieth century. Concurrently attacking Balboa Amusement Producing Company and renouncing his contract with the Long Beach studio, Jack London turned his back on the Horkheimers to grant all copyright and renewal options to his buddies Frank Garbutt and Hobart Bosworth. At the time of the suit, H. M. Horkheimer had already spent between $7,000 and $8,000 for production of his motion picture version of *The Sea Wolf*. He had also spent $14,000 on improvements at the studio to enhance the quality of his production of London's work. The Horkheimers had counted on the written contract with Jack London. H. M. and E. D. Horkheimer had already prepared a three-reel production of the story, to be released in December 1913, but Hobart Bosworth, a close personal friend and professional associate of Jack London, had himself prepared his own movie of the same story, a seven-reel version of *The Sea Wolf*, to be released the same month. To protect the interests of Bosworth and his own authorship, London sought an injunction against the commercialization and exhibition of Balboa's version of the story. At first, the federal court in Los Angeles refused to grant London's injunction against the Balboa Amusement Producing Company, but it granted, nonetheless, the right to reopen the case.

H. M. Horkheimer based his totally justifiable defense on two grounds: the preexisting contract with London and the existing copyright laws of the day. First, H. M. had a signed contract with London to make movies based on some of London's literary works. *Moving Picture World*, December 20, 1913, announced that several Jack London stories were being prepared at Balboa, including *A Piece of Steak*, based on London's *When God Laughs*, and *The Sea Wolf* and *To Kill a Man* based on London's *The Night Born*. The announcement also stated that the following other works by London were being prepared as movies at Balboa: *Martin Eden*, *John Barleycorn*, *The Call of the Wild*, *Smoke Bellew Series*, and *The Valley of the Moon* (*Press Clippings*, vol. 1, p. 31). Second, in addition to citing the signed contract with London, H. M. claimed there had been no violation of copyright laws because the stories he was filming had already appeared in magazine publications, and according to the interpretation of the copyright laws current at that time, this placed them in the public domain. Fortunately for writers who wanted to protect their copyright privileges after stories had appeared in magazines, London counterattacked and won. Despite the preexisting laws of the day, the Horkheimers lost. In effect, this historic court case between London and the Horkheimers redefined the copyright laws in the United States. Ironically, London, the former "oyster pirate," called the Balboa's producers "pirate producers" for claiming film rights of magazine stories. Spurred on by his victory against Balboa, London helped found the Authors' League of America with Rex Beach, Booth Tarkington, Ellen Glasgow, and other writers to extend the protection of copyright into novel types of media because twentieth-century technology was ever evolving. Their united force helped influence Congress to change laws to favor writers so that "piracy" would be redefined, especially concerning film productions based on literary works. This victory for writers was achieved at the expense of the Balboa Studios' contract with Jack London, with the Horkheimers losing a pearl of a deal.

Instead of being discouraged by this powerful punch delivered by Jack London, the Horkheimers continued to use literary sources as the basis of many of their features. They succeeded wonderfully in the years to come as innovative adapters of literary works, always respecting copyright laws and by their example paving the way for all future screen versions based on popular works of literature.

The Fruits of Loyalty and Troubleshooting

As a result of their stormy association with Jack London, the Horkheimers would thereafter insist on loyalty at the Balboa Amusement Producing Company. "Loyalty" became the password and proved to be the saving grace at the studio as it proceeded along its bumpy road. H. M. and Elwood had been punched in the wallet by the London suit, and they would be put through the wringer several more times. They had learned, however, from the London suit to demand and promise loyalty between themselves and their employees. At the studio's first gala Christmas dinner on December 24, 1913, the program lists 43 members of the studio staff, including all aspects of production — actors and actresses, cameramen, directors, producers, scenarists, etc. The gala's program championed loyalty, with the following names presented in the following order, as members of the "Roll of Loyalty": Mary Brotherton, Dora Stollar, Edward M. Langley, Lewis O. Morris, Louis P. Hansen, Leroy Frechette, William Whittlesey, Miles Burnett, Joseph Brotherton, Robert Brotherton, William Beckway, John Wyse, George Crane, Bert Stevens, Percy Dewey, Ralph Sutton, Bruce Randall, Robert G. Thurman, Arthur A. Lotto, Clifford Howard, James W. Brewester, Carrie Browning Nash, Bertram Bracken, David Porter, Belle Bennett, Jackie Saunders, Augusta Bolle, Madeline Lenard, Mollie McConnell, Gypsy Abbott, Harriet Jansen, Nina Deal, Marguerite Bowles, Billie Bennett, Henry King, Raymond Gallagher, Robert H. Grey, Charles Dudley, Henry Stanley, Fred Whitman, Frank Erlanger, Richard Johnson, and Clara Beyers. Not surprisingly, Jack London's name does not appear on the list, but neither does H. M's, who was the host at the Hotel Virginia that Christmas Eve. In addition to the 43 names just given, the newspapers announced a grand total of 60 persons in attendance, including the guests not directly involved at the time with Balboa: Mary Pickford and Mrs. Pickford, Warren Kerrigan, Laura Oakley, Ruth Roland, Paul Grant, Mr. and Mrs. Nash, Mr. and Mrs. Isidore Bernstein, Francis Grandin, Mr. and Mrs. William Clifford, Miss Bertha Rush, Miss Gladys Rutledge, Lawrence Flatau, and Velma Whitman.

If anyone doubts the strong bonds created by the Horkheimers' policy on loyalty, there are several examples in Balboa's history when loyalty among the staff helped pull the plant out of troubled waters. Despite a very high level of productivity during 1914, the following year looked bleak, primarily because of the loss of outlets in Europe with the Great War in full swing. At one point, Balboa's payroll was 11 weeks in arrears, in the amount of $25,000. A small number of employees quit the studio, but 40 "loyals" remained and bore the burden together. In this instance, everyone's loyalty and perseverance paid off. They pulled together to purchase raw film stock, essential to continue production, during the studio's cash-flow problems at the start of World War I. About 6 of the 40 loyals voluntarily withdrew $500 each from their savings and placed the money into the empty coffers of the film company so that Balboa would not fail. When one unidentified loyal offered her entire savings. H. M. tried to refuse her generous offer, but she insisted, having full faith in his know-how to overcome the temporary setback. They all had faith that H. M. could manage to turn the studio around, if only given the chance. The investment did pay off, as the American film market recovered, creating new outlets, and depending less on the European ones that were in turmoil during the war. Balboa soon sold all its collectively backed films in New York, paid all salaries, even those in arrears, and redeemed everyone's savings, with money to spare. This episode was indelibly etched in the memory of Henry King, who endured these hard times at Balboa and called the unpleasant episode "the struggle."

For the sake of loyalty, the Horkheimers were always finding ways to create a community spirit at the studio, organizing softball games with a picnic atmosphere in public parks of Long Beach, along with company dances and dinners, not to mention the Horkheimers' patriotic service to country and fighting men during the Great War. For the Horkheimers, loyalty was not just a business tactic, it was a way of life. One can only admire the drive the Horkheimers demonstrated towards the war effort. For example, H. M. organized actors throughout the country to work for the Red Cross. Since many of the players had spare time in their motion picture career, especially between pictures, H. M. conceived the idea of having a Red Cross auxiliary in every studio across the nation, with the actors often preparing garments and surgical dressings for the servicemen overseas. H. M. also organized a special committee, along with the Laskys, D. W. Griffith, and Mrs. Cecil B. DeMille, to collaborate with the Red Cross; at one point he wired President Wilson to ask for his endorsement of their collective war efforts. The Horkheimers represented a humane and socially active film community, with a keenly moral conscience.

Besides organizing the Red Cross volunteer work to assist the war effort, during the local sardine run off the coast of Long Beach, H. M. also engineered fishing expeditions every Sunday for the local fisheries, supplying 5,000 cases a day to the Allies from local canneries. These canneries represented one of the biggest industries of Long Beach, and by October 1916, local papers announced that the season's packing was well ahead of the previous year, with a total output of 90,000 cans packed in Long Beach. It was a smelly job, but somebody had to do it. Four years later, however, on December 30, 1920, the residents of Long Beach living at the west end of town near the fisheries requested the dismantling and removal of these prosperous canneries, declaring them a public nuisance on account of their odor. Nevertheless, during the war years, despite the disagreeable side to working with fish, H. M. and his staff donated their time and energies, and any money made went back to the fishermen to improve their fishing gear and equipment. As a movie town, Long Beach represented most admirably a stellar community that knew how to roll up its sleeves and help at home and abroad, acting with plenty of heart and soul.

After the Christmas gala at the Hotel Virginia, the Horkheimers forged ahead with an ambitious program of expansion for 1914 in all areas of production, marketing, and public relations. They knew how to roll with the punches and how to seize opportunities. After opening their first business office in Los Angeles in January 1914 at the Security Building, Suite 806, the Horkheimers began to increase the production capacity of their facilities in Long Beach, constructing a new stage (50' x 120') for a third acting company that would be installed by April 1914. Then the William Fox Box Office Attractions Company in New York revolutionized the distributing business, and Balboa was the first film producer to supply movies for this company. A studio press release dated February 10, 1914, announced that it would be the first time that a firm of motion picture exhibitors had arranged to purchase films, which spoke "volumes for the high-class merit and quality of the Balboa brand of features." The brothers delivered their first coup that year by allying themselves with Fox. In the same press release, Balboa also announced arrangements for opening a distributing office in London for output of Balboa feature films in Europe, these negotiations having begun before the outbreak of war. To meet the demand for their movies, the Horkheimers lost no time in stepping up production and hiring at their studio in Long Beach.

During its first year, Balboa quadrupled, buying another acre at the studio site for $30,000, despite the difficulties with the Jack London lawsuit. In contrast, when initial production began in Los Angeles, April 1913, the Balboa Amusement Producing Company had but one director, six players, and an additional working staff of six. A year later, by April 2, 1914, there were over 200 employees at the fully operational studio in Long Beach. Moreover, the studio possessed ten automobiles for driving to mountain and seaside locations. Also in April 1914, H. M. Horkheimer presented his wife a birthday present, a luxurious European car, a 90-horsepower Belgian Métalurgique limousine. The future looked a lot rosier after Balboa's first year.

There were several impressive indicators of Balboa's expansion that first year. Over 200 films were produced at Balboa in 1914.

Running full blast, the studio had three shifts, with an output of 6,000 feet of negative film per week and 150,000 feet of positive film per week. The Horkheimers invested $50,000 to install a complete and up-to-date film printing department that was the largest of its kind west of Chicago. At the time, most films made in California were shipped to Chicago or New York for the printing of positive copies. With its new printing department, Balboa was able to make its own releases and deliver them to the exchanges ready for immediate projection onto the screens. At Balboa, it was even possible in theory to complete filming before noon and then release the finished product to the exchanges and movie theatres in the evening. To maintain this high productivity, the studio had the most modern equipment. In another press release from *Press Clipping*, vol. 1, dated February 24, 1914, the studio boasted of having a mammoth automatic film-washing tank, with a capacity of washing 2,000 feet of film every ten minutes, feeding the film directly into the drying room. Electrically driven, revolving drivers would receive the washed film in the completely modern drying room with a capacity of drying 40,000 feet of film a day. Each drum could be operated independently of the other drums, which allowed quick action on any special piece of work.

It would be wrong to assume that the Horkheimers aimed only for quantity. On the contrary, their expert technicians and state-of-the-art equipment guaranteed top quality in photographing, printing, and processing films, much superior to the quality of the average production during the silent era. The Brothertons were among the best technicians at the studio. Mary Brotherton was in charge of assembly of the films, while Robert Brotherton was chief chemist. John Wyse worked as stage manager, and William Beckway was a premier cameraman. To guarantee successful processing, all the air in the drying room and in the other laboratory apartments was filtered and made thoroughly free from dust. At the same time, Balboa had added a commodious and fully equipped projecting theatre where company officials and critics would inspect the newly made films to determine whether there were any defects in the scenes, subtitles, and other parts of production. Always keenly aware how efficiency worked hand in hand with quality, the Horkheimers kept in mind the "big picture." To be more efficient as a quality studio, the Horkheimers added another feature to their expanding film plant. They strategically located the scenario department inside the studio building, an innovation at the time, so that the screenwriting could be brought into closer conjunction with the actual production of special features, a novelty in studio planning that the Horkheimers conceived as a pacesetting departure among the filmmaking centers on the Pacific coast. More and more settled in their studio at Long Beach, the Horkheimers finally moved their business offices from Los Angeles to Long Beach in the spring of 1914.

Along with all the expansion going on at the studio, the Horkheimers launched a publicity campaign without precedent, advertising a contest in more than 400 daily newspapers in the United States and Canada through which they invited the public to submit scenarios at market price. In its advertising campaigns, Balboa Studios was one of the first film plants to recognize the value of trade journals. In the December 25, 1914, issue of *Variety*, there appeared an article by Charles M. Peck, assistant general manager of Balboa Amusement Producing Company, entitled "How Advertising Sells Pictures." In Balboa's campaigns, efficient and well-chosen advertisements would help both the public and exhibitors identify "quality" pictures. Imitating Balboa's novel advertising pitches, some local newspapers launched their own ads. The newspapers also wanted to draw writers and movie fans directly into the movie business; they advertised that anyone could learn to write photoplays by buying their pamphlets giving advice to scenarists. In one advertisement, a man claimed to have made $3,500 in six months. Of course, not all submissions could be used, and F. M. Wiltermood, scenario editor at Balboa, had to prepare the following rejection notice for those who might have missed the mark:

Thank you for submitting the enclosed scenario, regretting that it is unsuited to the company's needs. On one or more of the following reasons a check mark is placed to show unavailability: Does not contain a good romance; the plot is not important enough; would cost very large amount of money to produce; similar story already filmed; plot is not novel, interesting or practical; would be rejected by censorship boards; calls for locations not readily obtainable; narrative is too gloomy and morbid. The company's policy is to avoid themes that censorship boards reject, as: degradation of women, crime, the exploitation of crime and the making of a hero out of a criminal; defamation of public officials; drunkenness; kidnapping; lost money; sacrilegious acts; gambling; disrobing views; sad death episodes and other depressing subjects.

Alas, today moviegoers are more than willing to pay good money to see most of these "unsuitable" subjects that would have been rejected by the self-imposed codes at the Balboa Amusement Producing Company.

In February 1914, along with the material resources in full expansion, Balboa managed to attract important human resources to its Long Beach studio, signing contracts with some major stars, including leading ladies Ruth Roland, Belle Bennett, Nan Christie, Neva Gerber, and Jackie Saunders; important leading men Lew Cody and Charles Dudley; an important character actor, Archibald Warren; and the comic duo Ben Deely and Marie Wayne. In fact, Marie Wayne and Ben Deely would star later that year with Charles Dudley, Archibald Warren, and Nan Christie in a early detective series called *Ima Simp*, directed by William Wolbert, with camera work by Percy De Gaston.

The expansion continued at a breathtaking pace till the end of 1914. In April 1914, Balboa announced its recent signing of new "loyals": Pop Leonard, a comic actor, and Lucille Younge, formerly with Majestic and Usonia. In April 1914, an additional director, Harry Wulze, also joined Balboa. In May 1914, Balboa extended its operations across the street to an outdoor stage where most of the interiors would be shot. They also built a new vault, 16 feet high, to store the finished film stock and added a garage to house seven cars and a truck. At the new operations across the street, 12 new dressing rooms were completed and a water cooling system was installed through all the enclosed buildings. On May 27, 1914, Balboa sent to 35 newspapers a press release confirming one of the biggest producer-distributor alliances ever negotiated in the history of the silent era — an alliance between the Balboa Amusement Producing Company and William Fox. Fox would handle exclusively the entire output of Balboa for the film markets of the United States and Canada, Balboa putting out more than 300,000 feet of positive print per week for Fox. In the same press release, the Horkheimers announced that they had also signed with Bishop, Pessers, and Co., Ltd., their exclusive European distributor, to provide the same amount of print for distribution in Europe as that promised for Fox. To accommodate these enormous orders, the working staff and laboratory doubled at Balboa so that the studio could make prompt deliveries of "Balboa Feature Films." In the same press release, the Horkheimers also mentioned the latest addition and innovation to their studio grounds, the wild animal farm in Long Beach for exotic animals needed for some of their productions.

The Horkheimers consistently sought both comfort and style during the constant changes that took place at their studios. The Balboa Company had originally purchased in 1913 the former studio of the Edison Motion Picture Manufacturing Company, which consisted at that time of one small building and one platform stage, with diffusers. By 1915 the Horkheimers had added eight stages and at one corner of Sixth Street and Alamitos Avenue, there were two bungalows, one for general offices and the other for the press and scenario departments. The one original Edison building had been converted into a laboratory and a wardrobe department. The vacant lot on the fourth corner was leased for large sets. Besides the eight acres in town, Balboa studios covered eleven acres in Signal Hill, most probably situated at the junction of Alamitos and Orange avenues. In Signal Hill, Westerns and outdoor scenes were filmed. At the expanding studio downtown, the buildings were well maintained; palm trees were planted and white sculptures erected. All studio buildings were meticulously painted green with white trim. During the studio's meteoric rise, the city of Long Beach much appreciated Balboa's business and fame. City officials were friendly from the start toward the movie plant and were even willing to have the dirt streets at the intersection of Sixth Street and Alamitos Avenue routinely oiled to keep dust down to a minimum. In this way, the city officials helped contribute to quality photography and film processing at the Long Beach plant.

By June 1914, the Horkheimers had added to their outstanding luminaries William Desmond Taylor, who would excel as a Balboa feature-film director. That summer William Wolbert also joined the Balboa ranks as a comedy director. Around the same time, actors Henry King and Edwin August joined Balboa, the latter having had three years experience with the Biograph Company and two years at the Universal Company; Bertram Bracken was hired for general production. Among the numerous three- and four-reel dramas released that summer by the William Fox Box Office Attraction Company, at least three movies featured Jackie Saunders: *Little Jack, Little Sunbeam,* and *The Will O' the Wisp,* photographed by Joseph Brotherton. Two Balboa productions were directed by Bertram Bracken: *Sacrificial Fires* and *The Square Triangle*:

Little Jack. Three reels. Balboa Amusement Producing Co. Made for William Fox. Released Nov. 3, 1914, by Box Office Attraction Co.

Little Sunbeam. Three reels. Balboa Amusement Producing Co. Made for William Fox. Released Oct. 19, 1914, by Box Office Attraction Co.

Sacrificial Fires. Three-reel drama. Balboa Amusement Producing Co. Made for William Fox. Released Feb. 28, 1914, by Box Office Attraction Co.

The Square Triangle. Three reel drama. Balboa Amusement Producing Co. Made for William Fox. Released Sept. 28, 1914, by Box Office Attraction Co.

The Will O' the Wisp. Four-reel drama. Balboa Amusement Producing Co. Made for William Fox. Released July 1914 by Box Office Attraction Co.

That autumn Balboa put out another press release, dated October 29, 1914, keeping the public informed of the prompt deliveries promised in Balboa's deal with Fox. H. M. Horkheimer was in New York for two months, where he had sold the entire output of the plant from June 1 to August 1, comprising 104,000 feet of negative film. During H. M.'s visit to New York, Elwood produced in Long Beach an additional 75,000 feet of negative film, producing two-, three-, and four-reel dramatic features. To meet Balboa's obligations with Fox by December 1, with five casts working simultaneously, the film vaults at Balboa would stock an additional 100,000 feet of brand new negatives—20 two-reelers, 12 three-reelers, and 6 four-reelers. In the same press release, Balboa claimed that its films, despite accelerated production, reflected unequaled quality of photography and film-processing:

> There is no company in this country that achieves such perfect photographic results—none that devotes more care to essential details—none that is more capable or has a more versatile group of all-star casts—none that insists more strenuously upon attaining, in every effort, the highest possible degree of motion picture perfection. This is why Balboa Feature Films are known as the "The Pictures Beautiful"—why exhibitors demand them—why the public calls for more and more of them. When a picture doesn't meet this standard of quality, it is never released under the Balboa name—to maintain uniform excellence.

While still producing for various other film companies, Balboa remained obliged to supply great quantities of films to Fox. During this busy season, Balboa released *St. Elmo*, a six-reel drama that broke all box-office records when it showed for a week in New York at the grandest motion picture house of the day, the Strand Theatre. *St. Elmo* repeated this box-office success at nine other movie theatres:

St. Elmo. Six-reel drama. Balboa Amusement Producing Co. Made for William Fox. Released Aug. 1914 by Box Office Attraction Co.

Before the Pathé contract went into effect and while still filling the tall order for Fox, Balboa produced many other releases between 1913 and 1914 for other film companies, including *The Counterfeit*, produced for University Film Company, *The Intrigue*, produced for Kalem, *The Path of Sorrow*, produced for Warner Features, and *Tricks of Fate* with Neva Gerber, directed by William Desmond Tayor with William Beckway as cameraman.

The Counterfeit. Two-reel drama. University Film Co.
The Intrigue. Two-reel drama. Kalem. Released Mar. 4, 1914, by General Film Co., made for Kalem Co.
Path of Sorrow. Three-reel drama. Warner's Features, Inc.
Tricks of Fate. (no further information available)

William Fox's contract with Balboa was truly a special mark of distinction for the Long Beach studio. In the summer of 1914, after war had been declared in Europe, William Fox explained to the American public that he was no longer going to distribute European movies, though he still considered them to be among the best ever put out. Fox had noticed a grave mistake by the European producers, who would "dump" their flops on the enormous American market, trying to obtain some return on their investments for their poorer products. Fox could see that this decision by the European producers had gravely hurt the European movies in the United States, seemingly beyond repair. Although Europe continued to produce excellent films up to the Great War and afterwards as well, American distributors had already taken note of the American public's mounting dislike of the European flops that began flooding the market, insulting the American audiences who were looking for quality productions. Fox blamed the Europeans for making a bad name for themselves by not considering the greater expectations and higher tastes of the American public, and because of the soured opinion in the United States about European films at the time, Fox himself did not want to risk exhibiting European movies to an already wary American public. In prescreening foreign films, William Fox determined that out of a group of 20 perhaps only two or three would cut the mustard. Fox simply wouldn't take any chances with the American public. The Box Office Attraction Company decided that its exhibitors should be furnished with a feature films service the public wanted, without insulting their intelligence. Fox turned to Balboa to supply these quality films because Balboa films were considered among the best in the world market and were proudly made in the USA.

That same summer, around the time that William Fox made his pledge to exhibit only American films, Elwood Horkheimer was predicting in the *Long Beach Telegram* the best was yet to come for the American film business. In an article in *Press Clippings*, vol. 1 (Aug. 21, 1914, p. 107) entitled "Horkheimer Is Back Home — Says War Will Benefit American Movie Industry," Elwood Horkheimer announced that until the beginning of the Great War, 25 percent of the world's supply of movies came from Europe. That supply was cut off with the war. Although the U.S. market also suffered during the war, the United States remained the only viable producer of movies during the war years because the Great War had paralyzed the film industry in Europe. Before the Great War, however, European films were shown widely in the United States, Canada, and Australia. During the war, however, the United States found itself virtually without any competition in the global film industry.

Elwood also pointed out in the article that Southern California was becoming the

American film capital, replacing both New York and Chicago; he claimed that 85 percent of U.S. films were being produced in the Golden State. Elwood could only imagine increased cinematographic activity and demand, greater than ever before. Today, in Southern California's diverse economy, it is easy to overlook the enormous importance of moviemaking in California's prosperity. In fact, moviemaking was for decades Southern California's major industry, particularly between 1916 and 1946. Elwood was correct in his prediction about the rosy future of the film industry in Southern California, foreseeing greater prosperity among the film producers of Los Angeles County, where Balboa was located.

Elwood continued to cite figures, saying that there were more than 30,000 people in the film industry by the summer of 1914; the Horkheimers expected that figure to double in a few years. Moreover, after the Great War, only U.S. films were available even in Europe because no production occurred during the war in France, Germany, Austria, and England. By the end of the war, Australia and Canada had already replaced their dependency on European films with those from the United States. The irreversible displacement of European movies by American ones was decisive and complete in the global market. As Elwood had predicted, the United States came out the winner in the global market for the production, commercialization, and distribution of quality motion pictures.

When Pathé Frères first entered the American market, it arrived with a world-renowned reputation for quality, often being called the supreme "House of Serials," with its crowing rooster as its trademark. Like William Fox, Charles and Emile Pathé understood that greater profits in the film industry would be realized in film distribution, not production, though Pathé Frères continued to produce movies after becoming a releasing house. Pathé Frères had arranged to release its Balboa productions in the United States simultaneously with the Eclectic Film Company, the latter having a national distribution system, being part of the Motion Picture Patents Company that managed Eclectic's distribution through the General Films Company. In a bold move similar to Laemmle and Fox's defiance toward the trust, on May 9, 1914, Pathé Frères announced it would release its movies without the trust's approval in 16 leading cities across the United States (Lahue, p. 58). Later, in January 1915, Eclectic and Pathé Frères combined under a joint name, calling the combination Pathé Exchange, Inc. However, it was Balboa's association with Pathé Frères that would promote internationally the first-class image of its feature films, launching a slogan that would greatly appeal both to the trade journals and to the high expectations of American movie fans: "Balboa/Pathé—The Pictures Beautiful."

Not using its own production units in most cases, Pathé Frères in the United States became a releasing house of the first category. Pathé Frères imposed stringent quality controls for two major reasons. First, the Great War had made film materials rare, so that each reel counted. Second, Pathé Frères established its Pathé Film Committee for quality control as a watchdog to review the productions of its independent filmmakers. Since Pathé Frères was so exacting, it quickly developed a deserved reputation as the most prestigious releasing house for the commercialization of American films.

By October 1914, Balboa made public its future dealings with Pathé Frères, as one of the first independent producers in the United States working for the French company, supplying four of the early serials with the famous crowing rooster. Balboa announced its newly formed association with Pathé Frères, signing definitively that December a contract in Paris. Balboa would be doing four of its earliest serials with the crowing rooster of Pathé: *Who Pays?*, *Neal of the Navy*, *The Red Circle*, and *The Neglected Wife*. The popular *Who Pays?* series consisted of 12 individual stories by Will M. Ritchey, head of the Balboa scenario department. This popular series starred Ruth Roland and actor/director Henry King, with supporting actors Daniel Gilfether, Edwin J. Brady, and Mollie McConnell and direction by Harry Harvey. The first episode was copyrighted March 21, 1915, and the twelfth was copyrighted October 13, 1915. *Neal of the Navy* (December 30, 1915), also directed by Harry Harvey, was a serial written by William Hamilton Osborne, but this series was made too hastily to pass the stringent controls of the Pathé Film Committee. Harvey was offered a bonus of $500 if he could make the serial in 12 weeks. Finishing eight episodes in six weeks, Harvey completed the task well ahead of schedule, but to the detriment of this serial's quality. Moreover, *The Red Circle*, starring Ruth Roland, along with Philo McCullough and Frank Mayo, contained 14 episodes, and again, Pathé ordered retakes of some of the episodes because the quality was not up to its standards. Finally a new Balboa/Pathé serial was contracted, with episodes copyrighted between December 1916 and April 1917. This latest serial was called *The Neglected Wife* and also starred Ruth Roland. The production of this serial was enhanced by the erection of a new $50,000 stage by the Horkheimers' studio.

The first photoplays at Balboa released under the new slogan with Pathé, "Balboa/Pathé: The Pictures Beautiful," would include *An Eye for an Eye, Coveted Heritage, Saved From Himself, The Tip-Off*, and the serial *When Fate Was Kind*.

- ***An Eye for an Eye.*** Four-reel drama. Balboa Amusement Producing Co. Copyright Dec. 28, 1914, Pathé Frères, LU4037. Released by Pathé Frères.
- ***Coveted Heritage.*** Copyright Dec. 28, 1914. Released by Pathé Frères (*Encyclopedia of the Movie Studios*, p. 232).
- ***Saved From Himself.*** Copyright Dec. 30, 1914. Released by Pathé Frères (*Encyclopedia of the Movie Studios*, p. 232).
- ***The Tip Off.*** Copyright, Dec. 16, 1914. Released by Pathé Frères (*Encyclopedia of the Movie Studios*, p. 232).
- ***When Fate Was Kind.*** Three-reel drama. Copyright Eclectic Film Co., Oct. 23, 1914. Pathé Frères. Released by Eclectic Film Co. (*Encyclopedia of the Movie Studios*, p. 232).

In order to speed up production of films to meet the growing public demand for more movies, Pathé began to subsidize independent filmmakers, advancing funds prior to actual production, with each contractual arrangement particular to each case and some producers receiving regular payments as episodes were released. Of course, such a financial arrangement suited the Horkheimers, who expanded their facilities and feverishly pumped out features without stopping.

With the signing of their contract with Pathé in December 1914, the Horkheimers received advanced monies for a series of episodes to be produced at the Balboa Amusement Producing Company for Pathé's network of exchanges throughout the United States. Whenever Pathé made special financial arrangements with its producers, the terms often changed, but Pathé did always insist on controlling the quality of the work with the Pathé Film Committee. The Horkheimers were riding a crest at the end of 1914, with the good fortune of having both Fox and Pathé as their distributors. The following excerpt from an advertisement in the *Moving Picture World* reflects the Horkheimers' heady self-confidence:

> More than two hundred dramatic features and a score of comedies made by the Balboa Amusement Production Company of Long Beach, California, have been sold to leading exchange organizations in the U.S. during the past year. The two, three and four-reel Balboa dramas are proportionally magnetic, the photography is above criticism, the scenes brilliant and beautiful and the acting superb. The plays and the stories back of them are absorbingly interesting—thrilling—gripping and never fail to hold the spellbound attention of the audience. In all of those essentials that entitle motion pictures to a high place among the various forms of public amusement, Balboa Feature Films are supreme.

At the end of 1914, the Horkheimers had lured into their honorable troupe of photoplayers the famous Henry Walthall, celebrated for his performance in D. W. Griffith's *The Birth of a Nation*. As a Balboa star, Walthall

Complete cast of "The Red Circle," Balboa-Pathe release. Left to right, first row: Gordon Sackville, Philo McCullough, Corenne Grant, Ruth Roland, Frank Mayo, Mollie McConnell, Andrew Arbuckle. Second row: Bruce Smith, Bert Francis, Ruth Lackaye, Myrtle Reeves, Daniel Gilfether, Makato Inokuchi, Fred Whitman, Frank Erlanger.

An unidentified press clipping (courtesy of Marie Osborne-Yeats).

would earn an astronomical $1,000 per week. Walthall would, by the following spring, pull out of his contract with the Horkheimers without much explanation, but Balboa did have the power to draw some of the greatest and most celebrated players, artists, and technicians of the silver screen. By May 1915, directors Charles E. Hayden and Sherwood MacDonald also signed contracts with Balboa. All of Elwood's earliest and boldest predictions of undying fame and glory seemed destined to bear fruit.

A full-page advertisement in the *Moving Picture World* at the end of 1915 listed Balboa's impressive roll of players: Lillian Lorraine, Ruth Roland, William Courtleigh, Jr., Mollie McConnell, Daniel Gilfether, Madeleine Pardee, Frank Mayo, Andrew Arbuckle, Joyce Moore, Victory Bateman, Lucy Blake, Ethel Fleming, Paul Gilmore, Charles Dudley, Corinne Grant, Henry Stanley, Fred Whitman, Lillian West, Edwin J. Brady, Jack Livingstone, Ruth Lackaye, Philo McCullough, Marguerite Nichols, Richard Johnson, R. Henry Grey, Frank Erlanger, William Conklin, Bert Francis, Robert Gray, Gordon Sackville, Jackie

This flyer for exhibitors shows Ruth Roland on her way out the window (courtesy of Marie Osborne-Yeats).

Saunders, Mae Sterling, Lewis Cody, William Lampe, Dixie Jarrel, Florence Hansen, Edith Reeves, Gladys Webber, William Reed, Phyllis Gray, and Bruce Smith.

With William B. Ritchey as head of the scenario department, the reference library there had been fully expanded and stocked. The Horkheimers had decided to cease one- and two-reel productions and to manufacture instead three- and five-reel features. Eventually, the Horkheimers would decide on making their features four-reelers, setting the standard for feature lengths for years to come. Four-reelers were considered neither too short nor too long and also allowed for the time required to change the reels during a showing. In 1915 the Horkheimers planned another stage to double the space for production of their features, all original stories.

In 1915, visitors and observers were often struck by the tidiness and efficiency at the Horkheimers' film plant: 8,000 square feet of stage space, sufficient for five directors to work simultaneously at ease; diffusers with brand-new canvases that were controlled by ropes to drop shade in a jiffy to any part of the stage; a mirror (6' x 5') at the side for actors to see their own reflections; a 1½-inch fire main extending throughout the plant with fire plugs at five different points; all trucks rolling across the stages on rubber wheels to provide smooth motion and little noise.

With the Horkheimers holding all the stock of the Balboa Amusement Producing Company, their film plant represented an investment of $300,000 after two years of operation. Apart from the stages and film processing buildings, their investment included also the property rooms, paint and carpenter shops, scene docks, laboratory, dressing rooms, wardrobe quarters, general offices, and miscellaneous departments in over a dozen buildings. By this time, there were 250 people on the payroll all the time, though the number might double during productions. Balboa continued to expand, as it always had done. By 1916 there were as many as 18 buildings, with improvements in several departments. In many ways, Balboa was a pacesetter in the maintenance and recycling of properties and wardrobe. Contrary to many early studios that rented props and never recycled wardrobes, Balboa kept its wardrobe well protected during storage, simply modifying clothes slightly to suit different movies. At its height, Balboa would boast having over 100,000 props in storage. There was even a blacksmith's forge to provide metal works for the sets, along with a gown-making department, a zoo to house exotic and ordinary animals for films, and a camera department in which each cinematographer had his own compartment with a lock. Balboa Amusement Producing Company was a highly organized and admirably spotless working environment, breaking ground in every direction.

Long Beach's reputation as a movie town grew by leaps and bounds, thanks to the Horkheimers' success. A few additional film companies expressed plans to move to Long Beach, and these reports give testimony to the interest generated about Long Beach as a film center during the silent era. For example, in July 1915, the Geographical Feature Film Corporation announced plans to locate in Long Beach. G. H. Howling, an Eastern filmmaker, also visited Long Beach on December 6, 1915, for the Metropolitan Motion Picture and Producing Company, seriously considering relocating somewhere towards the eastern section of the city, several blocks from the beach.

In spite of the ups and downs, the Horkheimers maintained their sang-froid and urbane cordiality until the end, even when their creditors came knocking at the door. While H. M. and Elwood enjoyed the undying devotion of certain loyals, there were disgruntled employees like Henry King who complained bitterly of delayed salaries. The most celebrated example of the brothers' agility with indebtedness occurred when a sheriff came with a writ of attachment on behalf of a creditor's judgment. It appeared that H. M and Elwood would be required to close the doors to their bustling studios. Instead of acquiescing to the intent of the papers being served, the brothers invited the sheriff and his deputy to

Fred Whitman.

tour the studio grounds. The lawmen were dazzled by what they saw throughout the plant, evidently enjoying fully the sights, quite forgetting to serve the writ at the end, especially after the sheriff and his deputy completed their "visit" by posing in flatteringly heroic parts before the camera. Once more, Balboa was saved during financial straits, papers once more being delayed, and the temporary crisis was eventually smoothed over by the Horkheimers' next surge of production investments. "Something ventured, something gained" might well have been the motto to describe the Horkheimers' meteoric but bumpy ride to fame and glory.

In 1916 few companies of the original old guard American film plants would survive the proliferation of independent producers and escalating costs. Only Vitagraph, Essanay, and Pathé withstood the onslaught of competition from the vastly expanding companies exemplified by the exciting developments at the Balboa Amusement Producing Company. Balboa's productions that year started with the spectacularly colored feature, *The Shrine of Happiness*. It was followed by Marie Osborne's smash hit, *Little Mary Sunshine*, which launched several sequels directed by Henry King, bringing to the world Shirley Temple's precursor of the silent screen, Baby Marie, and raising Marie Osborne to worldwide stardom as one of the greatest child talents and box-office successes. Additional Baby Marie films that year would be *Shadows and Sunshine* and *Joy and the Dragon*. Other Balboa hits in 1916 included *Matrimonial Martyr*; *The Sultana*; the serial *The Grip of Evil*, starring Jackie Saunders and Roland Bottomley; and *The Twin Triangle*. The list for all the years of production at Balboa goes on and on. The filmography in this book offers the reader interesting comments and reviews, as well as several summaries of these and many other films produced at the ambitious Long Beach studios.

Jackie Saunders (courtesy of Jackie Saunders, Jr.).

Lewis J. Cody.

Corinne Grant.

Ever expanding, Balboa Studios announced on September 16, 1916, that it would produce under other trademarks, including Knickerbocker Star Features. Balboa contracted with the General Film Company to make these Knickerbocker Star Features. Knickerbocker had been located in New York beginning in 1915, but in February 1917, the film company, distributed by General Films, was purchased by the growing Long Beach plant. When Balboa took the reins of Knickerbocker, Henry King and Reeves Eason were to become Knickerbocker's directors, and the players included Jackie Saunders, Frank Mayo, Mollie McConnell, Marguerite Nichols, Gordon Sackville, Daniel Gilfether, Margaret Landis, Lillian West, Fred Whitman, and Virginia Norden. A million-dollar contract was awarded to Balboa by the General Film Company for 52 Knickerbocker feature photoplays of four reels each. This was said to be the largest order ever placed in the film world for picture-plays. One production was to be released each week on the general film program as a "Knickerbocker Star Feature," featuring Vola Vale, Winnifred Greenwood, Louis Sothern, Kathleen Kirkman, Mignon LeBrun, Arthur Shirley, Clifford Gray, Melvin Mayo, Cullen Landis, Lewis King, and James Warner (*Encyclopedia of the Movie Studios*, p. 238). Many of the stories were written by prominent authors, and countless readers were interested in seeing them on the screen. There would be no copyright problems this time around. The Horkheimers would not receive another London punch. To fulfill this mind-boggling contract, four companies

Leon Perdue and Daniel Gilfether costarred with Baby Marie in *Sunshine and Shadows* (courtesy of Marie Osborne-Yeats).

would work simultaneously (*Daily Telegram*, Jan. 29, 1917, 10: 6).

With the arrival of 1917, Balboa would continue to see impressive growth until the spring of 1918. This was a big year for the Horkheimers who expected only the best for their company for many years to come. In 1917, Balboa was the largest employer in Long Beach and the greatest tourist attraction in a town well known as an entertainment center, with its thriving amusement zone called the Pike, along with seven miles of sparkling beaches studded with world-class hotels. In addition to the new trademark, Knickerbocker Star Features, the Horkheimers also splashed across the screen another new brand with a group of films called "Falcon Features," employing a hooded falcon as the trademark. These features were also to be produced and released by General Films. However, these ambitious plans fizzled prematurely. Falcon Features began in August 1917 and ceased production in February 1918.

Nonetheless, there were significant successes with these new trademarks. Among the successful Falcon Features were *The Mainspring*, based on the story "The Mainspring" by Louis Joseph Vance in *Popular Magazine*; *The Martinache Marriage*, directed by Bert Bracken, based on the story "The Martinache Marriage" by Beatrix Demarest; *The Phantom*

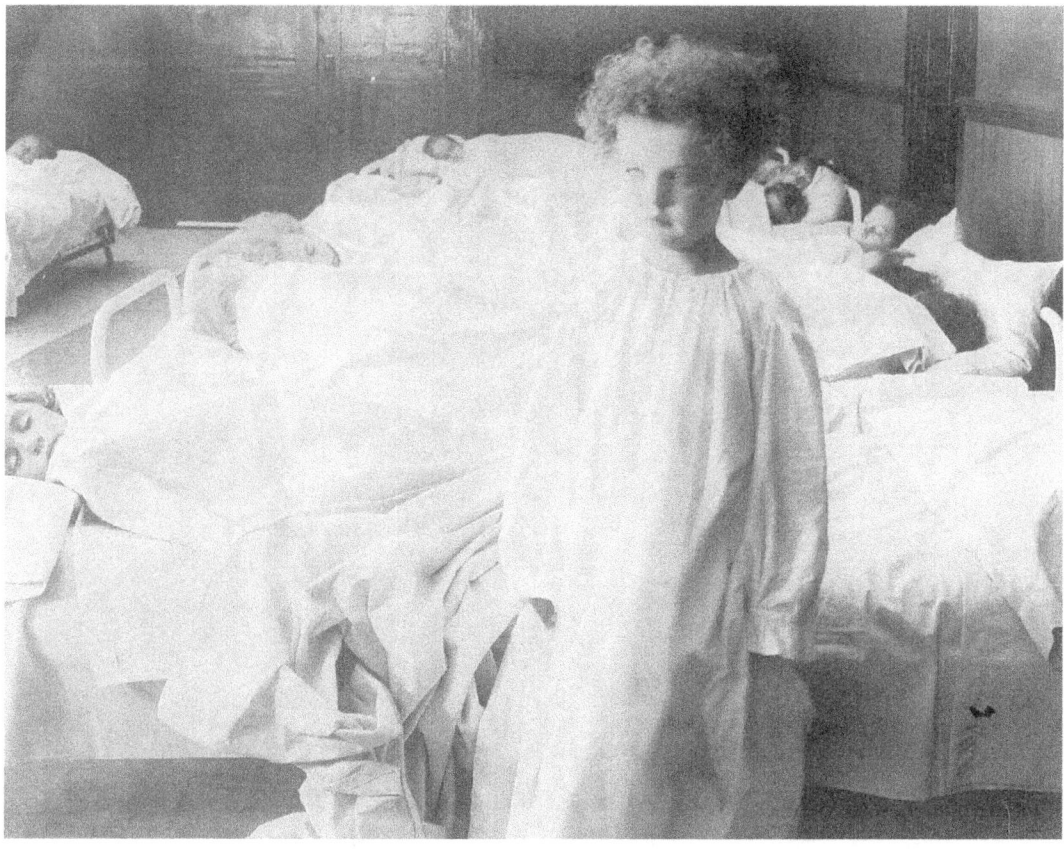

Joy and the Dragon (courtesy of Marie Osborne-Yeats).

Shotgun, directed by Harry Harvey; *The Secret of Black Mountain*, a four-reel Western directed by Otto Hoffman, featuring Vola Vale, Philo McCullough, Charles Dudley, George Austin, Henry Crawford, Mignon LeBrun, James Warner, Lewis King, Jack McLaughlin, T. H. Gibson Gowland, and H. C. Russell. Other Falcon Features that year included *The Stolen Play*, written by H. O. Strechhan, featuring Ruth Roland, Edwin J. Brady, William Conklin, Lucy Blake, Harry Southard, Ruth Lackaye, and Makoto Inokuchi, as well as the two films *The Understudy* and *Zollenstein*.

It is also interesting to note that Baby Marie continued to make films at Balboa that year, including *Sunshine and Gold*, *Told at Midnight*, *Twin Kiddies*, and *Twin Rays of Sunshine*. Moreover, Paramount Pictures in 1917 would make its first serial at Balboa, called *Who is "Number One"?* This serial was shown in 19 episodes, produced by H. M. Horkheimer, with the story by Anna Katherine Green, starring Kathleen Clifford and Cullen Landis. Moreover, Pathé was still represented in a release entitled *Sold at Auction*, directed by Sherwood MacDonald.

Trade journals in March 1917 stated that the facilities in Long Beach proved to be too cramped, so the Horkheimers had bungalow offices built on the southwest corner of Sixth Street and Alamitos Avenue across from the original Edison studio. Attached to these new buildings, the Horkheimers added a garage for 20 cars, along with a papier-mâché department, in addition to several large warehouses, allowing more space for Balboa's magnificent stock of props and furnishings. With the first expansion across the street from the original Edison studio, on the northeast corner of the Balboa lots, large sets had been erected for the

Twin Kiddies: Henry King and Baby Marie in foreground; Lon Chaney, an extra wearing cap, at center in background.

indoor stages. At the cost of $20,000, the finest stage in Southern California was started. It would have hardwood floors and an overhead system for controlling the diffusers from a central station. This stage measured 200 feet square and would extend another 100 feet in the near future. The new stage would be flanked on one side by a battery of 13 private offices for directors. On the other side, 20 of the most modern dressing rooms were built. By the following spring, ground was broken for a glass studio (150' x 200') with further enlargement projected. At this point in its growth and development, Balboa Amusement Producing Company represented an investment of $400,000, a whopping sum in 1917.

Regarding the ever-expanding and promising studio, H. M. remarked optimistically in 1917 about the future of Balboa Amusement Producing Company to a reporter of the Long Beach *Daily Telegram*: "While I do not pose as a prophet, yet I have every reason for believing that the biggest improvements in pictures is still ahead. We of Balboa would not be spreading out so if we did not have faith in the industry. The films are here to stay and so are the Balboa Studio and Horkheimer Brothers as producers thereof, as well" (*Press-Telegram Southland Magazine*, Aug. 1, 1948).

In December 1917, yet another leasing company would use the Balboa site. One of Long Beach's favorite celebrities, "Fatty" Arbuckle, would return with his Comique Film Corporation to the town in which he had married. The Comique Film Corporation had been started by Joseph M. Schenck in the spring of 1917 for the comedy films of "Fatty" Arbuckle, along with Buster Keaton, which

In 1917–1918, Balboa's glassed-in studio was the biggest in the industry. This view also shows the outdoor stage in front of the glass structure (courtesy of Marc Wanamaker).

were to be released by Paramount. The first movie, released April 23, 1917, *The Butcher Boy*, was made at the studios of the Norma Talmadge Film Corporation in New York. Comique would move to Long Beach and do six movies there before finally moving to the Diando studios in Glendale in 1918, though Arbuckle's original intention had been to produce films indefinitely at Long Beach.

In December 1917, Balboa Studios built a separate glass studio, the world's biggest, for the Comique Film Corporation. The new structure measured 100' x 200' and was used for producing Arbuckle's *The Country Hero*. In February 1918, the Arbuckle company was still filming a series of movies at Balboa, and Charlie Chaplin came to visit the Balboa Studios and was photographed on Arbuckle's set. In February 1918, the road to fame and glory seemed well-trodden by the Horkheimers and was still very promising to them. In a few months, however, the bottom would fall out, as the Horkheimers and their famous studios would fade in and out, positioning themselves for a comeback in the 1920s. Alas, despite several bold attempts made by many film plants between 1918 and 1923, as well as by H. M.

Horkheimer in 1923, to make Long Beach once more a thriving movie center, the city would never again take the lead it so enjoyed that all the loyals had worked so hard to achieve.

The new year, 1918, was expected to be very promising, but Lady Luck would make it a disaster for the Horkheimers. That year would prove to be a difficult one for many of the old guard among the most renowned American film companies. The film industry was in the doldrums, and several major companies would go under, overcome by the most competitive of the newest independent movie companies. First, World Film Company had lost its prestige with the departure of Selznick from its ranks. Second, Mutual's days were limited, while Essanay and Selig too were beginning to topple. By 1918 the Edison Company had quit the filmmaking scene entirely, while Vitagraph and Pathé were fighting to keep up with the competition. Who would have thought it possible that such a rapid changing of the guard would occur? By 1919, the Triangle Film Company and Mutual Film Corporation actually ceased to operate. As H. M. and Elwood had rightly predicted, the best was yet to come for the burgeoning movie

Left to right: Charlie Chaplin at camera; Lou Anger, manager for Arbuckle; H. M. Horkheimer; and Buster Keaton. Charlie Chaplin visited the Balboa Studios on three separate occasions. Apparently he was genuinely interested in working at the studio (courtesy of Marc Wanamaker).

industry in Southern California, but Balboa, among others, would not, as the Horkheimer brothers had expected, be part of the Hollywood crowd to enjoy the global recognition granted those fortunate competitors who survived intact to transform California into the undisputed film capital of the world. From 1916 until 1946, moviemaking would remain Southern California's biggest industry. It would take another world war to displace moviemaking in California and replace its preeminence with those myriad industries directly aligned with the war effort, including aviation.

In the spring of 1918, fate finally caught up with the Horkheimers. All the Horkheimers' savvy and all their loyals could not keep the creditors away from the movie plant. Balboa had glutted the sagging market with its prolific productivity. The studio stacked up seventeen pictures during an economic slump, and its distributor, Pathé, could not and would not release the films to exhibitors, after having repeatedly told Balboa to slow down production during the Great War. In the past, the Horkheimers' productivity had always somehow paid off, but not this time. Without being able to market the films, the studio saw its income cease, and the Horkheimers, the sole owners of all the company stock, went broke. Three Long Beach banks emerged as their most prominent creditors. On March 25, 1918, the Horkheimers declared voluntary bankruptcy. By April 1918, with very heavy hearts, H. M. and Elwood assigned their studio to the Los Angeles Wholesalers Board of Trade for liquidation, while they secretly prayed for the Wheel

Opposite: Some of those who attended the dance given by the Horkheimer Brothers in honor of Roscoe Arbuckle on the occasion of the dedication of Balboa's new glassed-in studio in which this picture was taken. *In foreground:* Fatty Arbuckle between the army and navy (courtesy of Marc Wanamaker).

of Fortune to bring them another chance in the volatile market. Surely the brothers would make a comeback. They had known reverses before. By agreement, the Balboa Studios would stay in operation by the new trustees. This arrangement left the Horkheimers a window of opportunity in the future. The window of opportunity was left ajar another seven years at the Long Beach plant for the Horkheimers and other filmmakers in Long Beach until the studios were finally demolished in 1925. The doors had shut on H. M. and Elwood's beautiful dreams of undying fame and glory. After making countless quality films between 1913 and 1918, never again would the Horkheimers produce another movie, either in Long Beach or in Los Angeles, although in 1923, H. M. would make an ill-fated attempt at a comeback in Long Beach.

Reel 3

1913–1918: An Innovative and Productive Studio

The important contributions of Balboa Amusement Producing Company to California's early movie history are still being rediscovered today. Unfortunately, like the countless nitrate films once carefully guarded in Balboa's vault, the studio's impressive history has mostly dissolved into dust, but not entirely. A few rare and fascinating traces give testimony to Balboa's significance. In time, more research will lead to general recognition of Balboa's innovations and quality productions. In the following timeline, readers will note the many ways in which Balboa was a pacesetter in organizing its film plant and in marketing, distributing, and adding technical innovations to its productions. For example, cameraman Robert Brotherton, an ex-Selig cameraman who was also a chemist, worked on toning and tinting film. By 1914 he was able to give films various colors without distorting the balance of the hues of actors' faces. Robert Brotherton also developed a process to wash out the highlights of the tints on the positive prints to leave flesh tones a natural color. At a time when colored film was either too strong or faded, Brotherton was able to give an amber glow on one side of a strip of film, as when lighting a room, with pale blue moonlight streaming into an adjoining room.

Balboa's significant chapter among the pioneer studios of the silent era reads at times like its movies — full of adventure, risks, secret love affairs, the whole place buzzing with life and exuberance, involving also mystery and intrigue. For instance, one of Long Beach's major directors, William Desmond Taylor, was murdered in 1922, a case that remains to this day a movieland mystery. The demise of the studio was mysterious; when it was seemingly riding a crest, the cofounder and president of Balboa Amusement Producing Company, H. M. Horkheimer (1882–1962), stunned the movie industry in 1918 by declaring voluntary bankruptcy. H. M.'s character and track record should have allowed him to weather the worst of times and come out a winner in the end, but H. M. and Elwood simply seemed to fade away from the Hollywood scene. Without the whole story, the eventual and complete disappearance of the Horkheimers baffles researchers to this day. What happened? Why would such enterprising men like H. M. and Elwood abandon the movie industry? These men knew how to roll with the punches, and in their meteoric rise to fame, they had proved themselves multitalented in all aspects of producing and marketing movies. Moreover, after their departure from Long Beach, both brothers would live another 50 years, without ever leaving another mark on California's film heritage.

In 1918 the Balboa plant was valued at a whopping $450,000 when the Horkheimers walked away. After the bankruptcy, however, despite a good number of attempts to revitalize the movie industry in Long Beach, the studio never picked up steam again. At first, Balboa was leased to the Art Film Company, and then 14 other companies leased space over the next four years. The property changed hands three or four times between 1919 and 1923 before the studio was demolished in 1925. Today very few people remember Balboa's name and fame. Nonetheless, Balboa's legacy has the power to make moviegoers marvel at all that excitement stirring in Long Beach 80 years ago, all of which ended so mysteriously and much too soon.

Timeline of the Balboa Amusement Producing Company

Most of the timeline information that follows was gleaned from four reliable sources: (1) the Balboa press releases from February 10, 1914, through October 29, 1914, in the archives of the Historical Society of Long Beach, entitled *Press Clippings,* vol. 1, property of the Balboa Amusement Producing Company, 1913–1914; (2) two Long Beach daily newspapers, the *Daily Telegram* and the *Long Beach Press,* from 1910 to 1923, which were thoroughly searched by Claudine Burnett, as well as *Variety,* from June 11, 1910, to February 28, 1919, with all information regarding film studios in Long Beach noted and indexed in the *Long Beach Collection Newspaper Index*; (3) the unpublished timeline on the Balboa Amusement Producing Company in the *Encyclopedia of the Movie Studios* by Marc Wanamaker; (4) Marie Osborne Yeats' two scrapbooks filled with clippings and memorabilia.

1913

April 1913: Using his $7,000 inheritance, H. M. Horkheimer purchased from the California Motion Picture Manufacturing Company the studio site in Long Beach. Fred Mace, comedian and director, also purchased an interest in the Balboa company. Fred Mace made comedies for Balboa at the temporarily leased Revier studio in Hollywood until the Long Beach site was vacated. Harry Revier did all the laboratory work for Mace. In the beginning, the Balboa Amusement Producing Company had but one director, six players, and an additional working staff of six.

April 28, 1913: Jack London was in Long Beach announcing that some of his stories would be produced by the Balboa Amusement Producing Company. This association between Jack London and the Horkheimers would test the limits of copyright and help rewrite some of the U.S. copyright laws, favoring authors who wanted to control their writings as they were being transformed into the new motion picture medium.

September 8, 1913: The Balboa Amusement Producing Company was reported to be in a very precarious state. The Jack London suit plagued the new studio.

October 1, 1913: The *Daily Telegram* announced that Jack London and Frank Garbutt were proceeding with their attempt to enjoin the Balboa Amusement Producing Company for alleged unlawful use of London's publications. After winning this case, London helped found the Authors' League of America with Rex Beach, Booth Tarkington, Ellen Glasgow, and other writers to extend protection of copyright into novel types of media. During this case, their united force helped influence Congress to change laws to favor writers.

December 24, 1913: The Balboa Amusement Producing Company threw its first Christmas gala at the elegant Hotel Virginia. During the dinner, Bertram Bracken, managing director, presented H. M. with a silver loving cup on behalf of the entire studio staff. In a short speech, H. M. Horkheimer thanked the loyal company for the beautiful gift. Then after the dinner more guests began to arrive for the ball, including Mary Pickford. By 10:30 P.M. the ballroom was full. Popular ragtime and tango music filled the air, with the orchestra under the baton of William Perlus. According to *Press Clippings*, vol. 1, encores followed each regular dance. During the dance that evening, a buffet lunch was served.

1914

January 1914: The Horkheimers opened their first business office in Los Angeles, at the Security Building, Suite 806. At the same time they were expanding their facilities in Long Beach, having just built a new stage, 50' x 120'.

January 16, 1914: In an article entitled "Children's Troupe for Film Work Is Formed," the *Los Angeles Tribune* announced that Frank D. Williams would launch at Balboa a series of juvenile films called the Kid Komedy Kompany, a precursor of Hal Roach's Our Gang. The Kid Komedy Kompany was directed by Frank D. Williams and featured child players such as Georgie Stone, Dorothy Moulton, Olive Johnson, and Violet Radcliffe. The article explained that Frank D. Williams already had considerable experience as a director of juvenile actors, having done juvenile comedies for Keystone, Sterling, Alco, Essanay, and Pathé Frères. Williams was to begin filming a farce on January 17 to be entirely enacted by tots. His leading lady was Olive Johnson, three and a half years old, who had recently been a star in "kid" comedies produced by the Sterling Company. Williams directed the films, did the camera work, wrote the scenarios, set the scenes, and produced the kid comedies. In fact, he was the only grown-up in the troupe (*Press Clippings*, vol. 1, p. 52).

February 1914: The Balboa Amusement Producing Company attracted important actors and actresses to its Long Beach studio: Ruth Roland, Belle Bennett, Nan Christie, Neva Gerber, Jackie Saunders, Lewis Cody, Charles Dudley, Archibald Warren, Ben Deely, and Marie Wayne.

February 24, 1914: The Balboa Amusement Producing Company boasted having a mammoth automatic film-washing tank, with a capacity of washing 2,000 feet of film every ten minutes, feeding the film directly into the drying room. Electrically driven, revolving drivers received the washed film in the completely modern drying room with a capacity of drying 40,000 feet of film a day.

February 27, 1914: The Balboa Amusement Producing Company installed its complete printing department at an investment of $50,000; it was to be the largest of its kind west of Chicago. With its new printing department, Balboa was able to make its own releases and deliver them to the exchanges directly.

March 1914: Balboa's general offices were removed from downtown Los Angeles to the Long Beach studio site. Along with its expert technicians and state-of-the-art equipment, Balboa maintained top quality in photography, printing, and film processing, turning out productions that were superior to most others of the silent era. Mary Brotherton was in charge of the assembly of the films; Robert Brotherton was chief chemist. John Wyse worked as stage manager, and William Beckway was one of Balboa's premier cameramen. Another novelty at Balboa included the placing of the scenario department inside the studio building, so that screenwriting could be close to the actual production of features, a novelty in studio planning that the Horkheimers conceived as a pacesetting standard for all future movie plants. While some of the early studio sites resembled shanty towns, Balboa's buildings and ground were beautifully maintained.

March 26, 1914: The *Long Beach Telegram* gave details about the luxurious dressing rooms to be furnished at Balboa. In an article entitled "Balboa Studio Dressing Rooms: Theatrical Men Overlook Nothing for Benefit of Their Employees," it was noted that H. M. and E. D. Horkheimer had learned from experience that comfort for actors would "preserve their good humor and thus bring out to the utmost their dramatic talents." Balboa's dressing rooms were reportedly the most up-to-date in the world, with many amenities: running water

British publicity (courtesy of Marie Osborne-Yeats).

hydrants, enameled washing stands, electrical fans, carpet on the floors, extension telephones, padlocked closets for costumes and street wearing apparel, swinging mirrors and other "aristocratic" devices (*Press Clippings,* vol. 1, p. 62).

April 1914: Balboa announced its recent signing of new "loyals": actors Pop Leonard and Lucille Younge and director Harry Wulze. A press release dated April 2, 1914, stated that a third company had been added to Balboa's troupes of actors, and that the city had installed hydrants to provide greater protection against fires. Eventually, to prevent fires, there would be two watchmen, one with a time clock, 16 stations, hourly rounds, a total of 22 hydrants, with an average of 50 feet of hose each, one hang hose cart with 250 feet of 2½ inch hose, 3 thirty-gallon "deluge" chemical engines, 43 three-gallon chemical extinguishers, 4 one-gallon chemical extinguishers, 51 pyrene extinguishers, 16 dry powder extinguishers, 42 sand pails, 42 water pails, 6 fire hooks, 9 fire axes, 6 alarm bells, with ladders to all roofs, metal waste cans, 5 city double hydrants, and a city fire alarm box near the plant (*Insurance Map of Long Beach, California*, p. 48). During this month, the studio boasted having ten automobiles at its disposal and one limousine.

May 1914: *Motion Picture News* reported that Balboa was expanding, with the studio superintendent, Edward Langley, officiating at the groundbreaking ceremony. Balboa extended its operations across the street to include a new outdoor stage, 50' x 100', where most of the interiors would be shot, a scene dock, 50' x 75', and a property room, 50' x 75'. The Long Beach studio also built a new vault that was 8' x 14' and was 16' high to store the finished film stock and added a garage to house seven cars and a truck.

May 9, 1914: *Moving Picture World* announced that at the new operations across the street, 12 new dressing rooms were completed and freshly painted. Balboa was also installing a water air-cooling system which would deliver clean and cool air to each dressing room. In the winter the system would be changed so that hot air would be sent into the same rooms. A concrete floor was laid in the drying room, which had 36 drums with a capacity of 400 feet of film on each cylinder. Two big water-air coolers and cleaners had also been placed in the dust-proof room. Not only had the city oiled the streets near the studio, but the railway company that ran through the studio grounds along Alamitos Avenue promised to do the same in the path of its right of way (*Press Clippings*, vol. 1, p. 66).

May 27, 1914: Balboa sent to 35 newspapers a press release confirming one of the biggest producer-distributor alliances ever negotiated in the history of the silent era, involving the Balboa Amusement Producing Company and William Fox. Fox would handle exclusively the entire output of Balboa for the film markets of the United States and Canada, Balboa putting out more than 300,000 feet of positive print per week for Fox. In the same press release, the Horkheimers announced that they had also signed with Bishop, Pessers, and Co., Ltd., their exclusive European distributor, to provide the same amount of print for distribution in Europe as that promised for Fox in North America. This deal with the British agency was the first time American films were marketed in Europe before being released in the United States. British addresses included S. W. Bishop, managing director, Bishop, Pessers, and Co., Ltd., 29a Charing Cross Road, W., London, W.C.; C. Foster Wicks Film Agency, 72 E. Street, Sittingbourne, Glasgow; Balborama, 132 West Nile Street, Glasgow; Balboa Film Agency (Bishop, Pessers, and Co., Ltd.) 18 Castle Arcade, Cardiff, South Wales.

May 30, 1914: *Motion Picture News* announced in an article entitled "Lorimore with Fox" that Alec Lorimore had resigned as sales manager for Gaumont and as publicity manager of Méliès to take over at Box Office Attraction Company. Lorimore would travel around the United States making arrangements with state rights buyers for the handling of the new Balboa features which the Box Office Attraction Company had recently bought (*Press Clippings*, vol. 1, p. 83).

N.B.—*State Rights distributor:* Before there was a national system of film distribution, independent producers would lease their films to an exchange or distributor in each state or territory, hence the term "state rights." The exchanges then would lease the film to a theatre that would promote the film. Each exchange would have an exclusive to the titles it would lease out. This system was dominant throughout the teens of the early twentieth century. From the producers' point of view, State Rights was not the most efficient system for three reasons: 1) most exchanges were owned by exhibitors, so they were not too eager to let other exchanges have films to be used against them in the competitive market; 2) most exchanges were handling many films from many producers and could not give very much attention to promoting any one title at any given time; 3) certain exchanges were less than honest in reporting their rentals when they received them on a percentage basis or they would "bicycle" the print to an unlicensed exhibitor and keep the rental fees without reporting them (Slide, p. 326).

June 1914: The Horkheimers had added to their luminaries William Desmond Taylor, who would excel as a Balboa feature film director. That summer other cameramen, directors, and actors would join the prestigious ranks at Balboa: Percy DeGaston, William Wolbert, directing Balboa comedies, Bertram Bracken, Henry King, and Edwin August. William Fox also announced that he would no longer distribute European movies. Fox turned to Balboa to supply quality films. This was the first time an American independent distributor turned to an independent producer for such a massive market. During the summer, Wiltermood, chief of the Balboa scenario department, wrote a note to Elwood D. Horkheimer to express his pleasure that the censors had for the most part approved *The Cruise of the Hell Ship*: "This looks good, eleven reels and only a few insignificant cutouts" (*Press Clippings*, vol. 1, p. 188). The censors had made the following recommendations for deletions and changes in the film: "Entire sea burial scene; throwing man over board; all scenes showing rifling of pockets; shorten both man choking scenes to flash; shorten forcible kissing of girl scene to flash."

June 16, 1914: Running full blast, Balboa had three shifts, with an output of 6,000 negative feet of film per week and 150,000 feet of positive film per week. Long Beach had the distinction of being the only city on the Pacific coast to have a complete printing plant for the developing of positive prints.

June 27, 1914: *Motion Picture News* announced that Alec Lorimore would be selling 11 Balboa features, disposing of state rights for *St. Elmo, Will o' the Wisp, The Cruise of the Hell Ship, Sacrificial Fires, The Unexpected, The Hunchback of Cedar Lodge, Gypsy Love, Sands of Life, The Human Soul, The Call of the Heart,* and *The Rat* (*Press Clippings*, vol. 1, p. 99).

August 8, 1914: *Motion Picture News* announced (*Press Clippings*, vol. 1, p. 120):

> When Box Office Attractions took over the productions of the Balboa amusement Company some time ago, they endeavored to find state right buyers who would interest themselves primarily in Balboa productions.
>
> This line of output was found almost impossible as nearly every state right approached was tied up by prior contracts with other manufacturers; therefore, they have been forced to open their own exchanges in cities already announced in *The Motion Picture News* and also additional exchanges in Denver, Los Angeles, San Francisco, Portland, Seattle, Salt Lake City and Vancouver, B.C. By this means they will obtain maximum selling power on all productions handled by them.

August 15, 1914: *Motion Picture News* announced that William Desmond Taylor, a director at the Balboa Amusement Producing Company, was elected as the first vice president of the Photoplayers Club (*Press Clippings*, vol. 1, p. 30).

August 21, 1914: Elwood Horkheimer announced in the *Long Beach Telegram* that Southern California was becoming the American film capital, replacing both New York and Chicago. Elwood expected bigger and better things for Balboa, with over 30,000 persons employed in the U.S. film industry by the summer of 1914 and the Horkheimers anticipating the figure would double within a few years. By 1914 the motion picture industry had become the fifth largest industry in the United States, with only steel, agriculture, railroads, and mining ahead of filmmaking.

August 29, 1914: Independent American distributors and producers of films met for an historic occasion at the Hotel McAlpin in New York on this date to incorporate a new alliance called the National Independent Motion Picture Board of Trade, declaring war against

Edison's Motion Picture Patents Company, popularly called the "trust." It was the alliance's intention to become as powerful as Edison's "trust" but with a higher purpose. H. M. Horkheimer was one of the five vice presidents and one of the directors of the National Independent Motion Picture Board of Trade.

September 1, 1914: The *Daily Telegram* reported that Robert Brotherton, chief chemist at Balboa, had discovered new tinting and toning techniques for three-exposure scenes.

September 5, 1914: The *Daily Telegram* announced that cameraman Percy DeGaston at Balboa had devised a new chemical compound providing enough actinic light to film night scenes, the newspaper explaining that the movies "appear wondrously realistic and signify a new era in lighting effects in cinematography." An ad for the film *An Eye for an Eye*, copyrighted January 1915 claimed this movie produced at Balboa was the first to use successful night photography.

September 6, 1914: The *New York Telegraph* reported a new breakthrough at the Balboa Studios in an article entitled "Balboa Expert Makes Tinting Discoveries." The new process was reported to be permanent, and films treated would show the initial brilliance of the tinting as long as the film texture lasted. Previously, specially colored prints soon lost their original bright hues. Robert Brotherton at Balboa, however, overcame that difficulty after many years of almost constant research. In the same article, Brotherton was reported to be working on a special attachment to be placed on the lenses of cameras and theatre projectors whereby color photography would become an inexpensive and direct process, with the negative film capable of receiving every hue shown in the scenes. This novel system of color photography would be available and user-friendly for everyone. At this point in his career, Brotherton had 15 years of laboratory experience behind him, having first worked as an apprentice in England for several years before moving to Chicago to work for nine years at the Selig company, among other laboratories, before finally settling at Balboa in 1913 (*Press Clippings*, vol. 1, p. 172).

September 12, 1914: The *Daily Telegram* published a copy of Balboa's suggestions to amateur scenarists. This public relations project was an enormous success, and the studio was inundated with scripts from all over the United States and Canada. Balboa received 701 scenarios as a result, but only 11 of those were considered for use in Balboa's production lineup (*Press Clippings*, vol. 1, p. 140).

September 26, 1914: *Motion Picture News* printed an article entitled "Alex Lorimore Promoted:" "Alex Lorimore, who among his other duties at the Box Office Attractions Company has been handling the booking of state rights subjects, has been made business manager of his concern's recently formed producing companies."

October 1914: Before signing the contract in Paris, December 1914, the Horkheimers made public their association with Pathé Frères, Balboa being one of the first independent producers in the United States working for Pathé Frères, supplying four of the early serials with Pathé's famous trademark: *Neal of the Navy*, *The Red Circle*, *The Neglected Wife*, and *Who Pays?* Another breakthrough was also accredited to Balboa Studios. An article appeared this same month in the *Long Beach Telegram* entitled "Camp Fire Scene Is Now Filmed." Percy DeGaston had experimented for years with a chemical composition that would allow filming at night, something that was impossible to do until his discovery. When a scene was being photographed at night, DeGaston's discovery allowed the area to be illuminated for several hundred feet distant, the great violet-white flame burning steadily for two minutes (*Press Clippings*, vol. 1, p. 175).

October 12, 1914: On this date appeared an amusing article, "Brewery Sends Actor Bill; Repudiates Debt," in the *Los Angeles Tribune*. Henry King had received a bill for $16 accrued by an impostor using the star's name in Olathe, Kansas, Prohibition country. The impostor had the bill sent to the Long Beach star; as the article noted, "some Kansan admirer jokingly slipped one over on him" (*Press Clippings*, vol. 1, p. 183).

October 24, 1914: Fox took over the

from **PATHE EXCHANGE, Inc.**
25 West 45th St., New York City

1c PAID
New York, N. Y.
Permit No. 373

MISS RUTH ROLAND,
℅ BALBOA FILM CO.,
LONG BEACH, CAL.

POSTMASTER—If this be undeliverable kindly notify us in accordance with section 637, P. L. and R. and we will remit postage for its return.

Pathé Exchanges

Albany	398 Broadway
Atlanta	111 Walton Street
Boston	7 Isabella Street
Buffalo	47 W. Swann Street
Butte	124 W. Granite Street
Charlotte	6-8-10 S. Graham Street
Chicago	5 South Wabash Avenue
Cincinnati	217 E. Fifth Street
Cleveland	750 Prospect Avenue, S. E.
Dallas	2012½ Commerce Street
Denver	16th & Larimer Streets
Des Moines	316 Locust Street
Detroit	40 E. Larned Street
Indianapolis	27 Willoughby Bldg.
Kansas City	928 Main Street
Los Angeles	732 South Olive Street
Milwaukee	133 Second Street
Minneapolis	712 Produce Exchange Bldg.
Newark	6-8 Mechanic Street
New Orleans	836 Common Street
New York	115 East 23rd Street
Omaha	1312 Farnam Street
Philadelphia	1235 Vine Street
Pittsburg	938 Penn Avenue
Portland	392 Burnside Street
Salt Lake City	68 So. Main Street
San Francisco	67 Turk Street
Seattle	246 Central Bldg.
St. Louis	3210 Locust Street
Washington	Seventh & E Streets, N. W.

Main Office
25 WEST 45TH STREET, NEW YORK CITY

AGENCIES IN CANADA

SPECIALTY FILM IMPORT, Ltd.:

Calgary, Alberta	Leeson & Lineham Block
St. John, N. B.	167 Prince William
Toronto, Ontario	56 King Street West
Winnipeg, Man.	382 Donald Street
Montreal	313 Bleury Street
Vancouver	553 Granville Street

Pathé Exchanges/R. Roland flyer.

former Pathé studio in New York and opened another studio at Linoleumville with J. Gordon Edwards. It was announced that four companies had been engaged for the anbitious productions scheduled for the Box Office Attraction Company's weekly and monthly program of film production and distribution. *Motion Picture News* explained in an article entitled "Box Office Opens 13 Branch Exchanges" that these productions were adaptations from well-known novels and plays. The thirteen branches involved the following cities, to which would be added 11 more, and later still more: Cleveland, Boston, Syracuse, Philadelphia, Pittsburgh, St. Louis, Kansas City, Dallas, San Francisco, Denver, Minneapolis, Chicago, and Seattle. It was the intention of Fox's organization to release three features a week and three elaborate features a month throughout the United States and Canada, with single-reel comedies to fill in between the features (*Press Clippings*, vol. 1, p. 179). Balboa was one of these four production companies, along with Nemo, White Star, and Fox's own emerging production company, Fox Features, and perhaps even Joy. Interestingly enough, all of these production brands worked at some time during this period at Long Beach's Balboa studios.

On the same date, October 24, 1914, in an unidentified periodical an article appeared entitled "Creator of Great Number of Paintings Now Scenic Artist of Balboa Studios" (*Press Clippings*, vol. 1, page 231). The article summarizes in a laudatory manner LeRoy J. Frechette's contribution to Balboa's quality films. Frechette is described as a scenic artist at Balboa who has won distinction as the creator of paintings, indoor embellishments, stained glass windows, curving stairways, fountains, fireplaces, art stands, and other interior settings that have brought much admiration from directors, players, and diverse studio owners. Frechette at the time had been at Balboa for over a year. The article explains how some of his copies of paintings by the old masters were nearly exact duplicates of the originals. In fact, one of his stained glass windows in beautiful colors showed two strutting peacocks, and "when this pictorial garniture was set in place in the drawing room, a flood of sunlight was reflected through the window with large mirrors, thus affording an illumination that made the hand-painted glass glow sublimely." The film made of the scene was tinted to correspond to the window hues, and when the pictures were shown in the Balboa projection theatre, the gorgeous colorings brought praise from all the cinema experts present. The article also states: "Another handsome studio set made by Mr. Frechette, an old Dutch fireplace mantel, twelve feet high, shows bricks and tiling of the most artistic design, with secret tilting niches in which the scenario characters can hide precious documents, wills, mortgages, bonds and money. Many of these creations were made from prints found in antique volumes on European art, Mr. Frechette studying the ancient books to learn the best patterns for the elegant interiors desired."

October 31, 1914: *Moving Picture World* issued an article, "Box Office to Release Seventeen Reels," which was subtitled "Will Institute Program in Which a Feature Each Week Will Be a Broadway Star in Broadway Play." According to the article:

The Box Office Attractions Company is about to institute a program of seventeen reels a week. The brands and the number of reels to be released under each every seven days are the Balboa, of two or three reels; White Star, three reels; Nemo, three reels; Fox Features, four reels; Wonderful Plays and Players, four or five reels. This latter brand will represent the work of Mr. Fox's own organization. The first release of this company, which is designed to produce Broadway stars in Broadway plays, will be *The Walls of Jericho*, Alfred Sutro's play of modern society. In this production there will be featured Edmund Breese, the creator of John Burkett Ryder, in *The Lion and the Mouse*.

Mr. Fox has opened fourteen exchanges in different parts of the country. He owns and controls twenty-two theaters in New York State and New England. Many of these are noted for their size and elaborateness. It is his intention to put out such pictures as will please the clientele of his own houses, which he considers the best. At work on these subjects are such directors as Frank Powell, lately with Pathé; J. Gordon Edwards, formerly managing producer at the Academy of Music; Edgar Lewis, who directed *The Littlest Rebel*; Lloyd B. Carlton, long time with Lubin, and the director of many of the larger productions of that studio, and George De Carlton.

Mr. Fox has the control of the rights of *A Fool There Was*, Porter Emerson Browne's story; *The Idler*, by C. Haddon Chambers, the adaptation for which has been made by Roy McCardell; and Israel Zangwill's *Children of the Ghetto*; in which Wilton Lackaye will play Reb Schmudl, which character he played in the original production. (*Press Clippings*, vol. 1, p. 131)

In light of the shared interests between Fox and the Horkheimers, who combined their efforts in the production and distribution of quality films, more research might explain whether some of Fox's earliest films used the production facilities at Balboa. *Life's Shop Window* is interconnected with three Fox productions, none of which is usually associated with Balboa. The three other movies include *The Children of the Ghetto* (1915), with the same cast as that found in *Life's Shop Window* (1914); *The Thief* (1914), also with the same cast; and *The Walls of Jericho* (1914). An unidentified article in *Press Clippings*, vol. 1, page 25, lends credence to this idea of a Balboa connection because the unidentified article claims that Claire Whitney and Stuart Holmes, who had already performed in Balboa's *St. Elmo*, would be in another release for the Balboa company—*Life's Shop Window*.

November 1914: Director William Desmond Taylor produced *Tricks of Fate*, starring Neva Gerber, with cameraman Billy Beckway. Billy Beckway used innovative double exposure for this film, devising a novel attachment for his camera. At the end of 1914, the Horkheimers also lured to their studio the famous player Henry Walthall, celebrated for his performance in D. W. Griffith's *The Birth of a Nation*. As a Balboa star, Walthall would earn the astronomical salary of $1,000 per week.

December 1914: In Long Beach, the movie theatres were mostly located at the amusement zone along the beach called the Pike. Motion pictures were very big business there and nationally. Businessmen at the Pike estimated that local people spent nearly $200,000 on movies during 1914. The theatre owners at the Pike estimated they showed nearly 500,000 feet of film per month, totaling about 150 miles of motion pictures per annum in Long Beach alone. Long Beach supported ten theatres, with an average capacity per theatre of 400 persons. The movie industry was a lucrative and expanding business for the city.

December 25, 1914: Balboa was one of the first film companies to recognize the value of advertising in the trade journals. *Variety* released an issue on this date in which appeared an article by Charles Peck, assistant general manager of Balboa Amusement Producing Company, which was entitled "How Advertising Sells Pictures." Balboa would use the trade journals to run efficient and well-chosen advertisements to help both the public and exhibitors identify quality pictures. One of Balboa's most successful publicity campaigns, which was without precedent, was a contest advertised in more than 400 daily newspapers in the United States and Canada in which Balboa invited the public to submit scenarios at market price, effectively drawing writers and movie fans into the movie business, suggesting that anyone could be a part of the exciting new movie industry.

1915

January 1915: Balboa by this date had been enjoying the award-winning contributions of the scenic artist Leroy J. Frechette, who had worked before for Pathé Frères in Versailles, as well as for Keystone, Alco, and Essanay. In 1915, H. M. Horkheimer would also be planning an enormous pageant in San Francisco for the Panama-Pacific International Exposition. To commemorate this exhibition, the U.S. Postal Service had issued (1912–13) a 1¢ postage stamp using the bust of Vasco Núñez de Balboa. This is also the year when the Balboa Amusement Producing Company would be known as a serial house, producing, among other films, *Neal of the Navy, Who Pays?* and *Who Is Guilty?* Serials constituted a new genre, and Balboa was in the vanguard of this new type of entertainment. During this period, the Horkheimers decided to cease production of one- and two-reel productions. Eventually, they established a precedent by making their features four-reelers, equivalent to approximately eighty minutes, thus setting the standard for feature lengths for decades to come.

March 1915: Balboa released through Alliance its smash hit *Beulah*, which was produced by H. M. Horkheimer. Bertram Bracken directed, with assistant director Alden Willey. The scenario was written by Will M. Ritchey. The cast included Henry B. Walthall (*Dr. Guy Hartwell*), Joyce Moore (*Beulah Benton*), Mae Prestell, Clifford Gray, Marguerite Nichols, Elsie Allen, Gypsy Abbott, Corinne Grant, Leopold Medan, Mollie McConnell, Henry Stanley, Gordon Sackville, Hazel Henderson, Sylvia Ashton, Charles Dudley, and Margaret Mulvane. "The Price of Fame," the first episode of the successful serial *Who Pays?* was copyrighted this month.

April 1915: After two years in operation, the Balboa Amusement Producing Company represented an investment of $300,000. Apart from the stages and film-processing buildings, their investment included also the property rooms, paint and carpenter shops, scene docks, laboratory, dressing rooms, wardrobe quarters, general offices, and miscellaneous departments in over a dozen buildings. By this time, there were 250 persons on the payroll all the time, though the number might double during productions. Balboa continued to expand, as it always had done.

May 1915: The important directors at Balboa included Harry Harvey, Charles E. Hayden, and Sherwood MacDonald. Charles M. Peck was assistant general manager of the studio, and Norman Manning was business manager.

June 17, 1915: Balboa announced it would make extensive additions to the studio, buying more ground, increasing the stage space, and erecting new buildings. The Horkheimers would add eight stages. At one corner of Sixth Street and Alamitos Avenue, there would be two bungalows to serve as general offices and the press and scenario departments. The one original Edison building had been converted into a laboratory and a wardrobe department. The vacant lot on the fourth corner was leased for large sets. Besides the eight acres in town, Balboa Studios would cover eleven acres in Signal Hill.

December 1915: At the end of 1915, *Moving Picture World* listed Balboa's impressive roll of players: Lillian Lorraine, Ruth Roland, William Courtleigh, Jr., Mollie McConnell, Daniel Gilfether, Madeleine Pardee, Frank Mayo, Andrew Arbuckle, Joyce Moore, Victory Bateman, Lucy Blake, Ethel Fleming, Paul Gilmore, Charles Dudley, Corinne Grant, Henry Stanley, Fred Whitman, Lillian West, Edwin J. Brady, Jack Livingstone, Ruth Lackaye, Philo McCullough, Marguerite Nichols, Richard Johnson, R. Henry Grey, Frank Erlanger, William Conklin, Bert Francis, Robert Gray, Gordon Sackville, Jackie Saunders, Mae Sterling, Lewis Cody, William Lampe, Dixie Jarrel, Florence Hansen, Edith Reeves, Gladys Webber, William Reed, Phyllis Gray, and Bruce Smith. In 1915, visitors were often struck by the tidiness and efficiency at Balboa: 8,000 feet of stage space, sufficient for five directors to work simultaneously at ease; diffusers with brand-new canvases that were controlled by ropes to drop shade quickly to any part of the stage; a mirror (6' x 5') at the side for actors to see their own reflections; a 1½-inch fire main extending throughout the plant with fire plugs at five different points; trucks that rolled across the stages on rubber wheels to provide smooth motion and little noise.

1916

January 1916: By 1916, the Balboa studio contained as many as 18 buildings, with improvements in several departments. In many ways, Balboa was a pacesetter in the maintenance and recycling of properties and wardrobe. Contrary to many early studios that rented props and never recycled wardrobes,

Balboa kept its wardrobe well protected during storage, simply modifying clothes slightly to suit different movies. At its height, Balboa would boast of having over 100,000 props in storage. There was even a blacksmith's forge to provide metal works for the sets, along with a gown-making department, a zoo to house exotic and ordinary animals for films, and by September a camera department in which each cinematographer had his own compartment with a lock. Balboa Amusement Producing Company was a highly organized and admirably spotless working environment, breaking ground in every direction.

March 3, 1916: This is the month that Balboa released *Little Mary Sunshine*, with Baby Marie. This movie started the worldwide trend of promoting better films for children. This photoplay was used as an example and promoted by many groups, including the women's clubs of America. This movie launched Baby Marie into global stardom and broke all records for five-reel photoplays. Pathé immediately contracted with Balboa to do six more movies with Baby Marie in the leading role, with Henry King directing: *Shadows and Sunshine, Joy and the Dragon, Twin Kiddies, Told at Midnight, A Little Ray of Sunshine*, and *Sunshine and Gold*. It was the first time that a juvenile actor held the leading part in a feature film, and the Little Mary Sunshine features made Henry King world-famous as a director.

May 23, 1916: Balboa Amusement Producing Company celebrated its third anniversary in Long Beach. With the growing fame and popularity of Balboa Amusement Producing Company, the name "Balboa" became fashionable as a mark of distinction and quality. It was used for a beach resort in Southern California, a shirt manufacturer of the day, several hotels, a number of stores, a bank, and a movie theatre in Los Angeles at the corner of Vermont and Manchester.

June 19, 1916: *The Matrimonial Martyr*, a five-reel comedy, was released by Pathé Exchange. Sherwood MacDonald was the director, and William Beckway was the cameraman. The film featured Ruth Roland (*Erma Desmond/Bertie Stanley*), Andrew Arbuckle (*Professor Stanley*), Marguerite Nichols (*Phyllis Burnham*), R. Henry Gray (*Elbert Chetwynde*), Madeleine Pardee (*Mrs. Baddly Bytton*), Lulu Bowers (*Gilberta Stanley*), Fred Whitman (*Chester Clynch*), and Daniel Gilfether. According to *The American Film Institute Catalog* (p. 600), this film was hand-colored in the Pathé color process.

July 17, 1916: The first episode of *The Grip of Evil* was copyrighted. The serial was made for Pathé and featured Philo McCullough, Jackie Saunders, and Roland Bottomley. The first chapter was copyrighted on July 17, 1916, and the last chapter was copyrighted on September 28, 1916. The 14 chapters, each containing two reels, were *Fate; The Underworld; The Upper Ten; The Looters; The Way of a Woman; The Hypocrites; The Butterflies; In Bohemia; The Dollar Kings; Down to the Sea; Mammon and Moloch; Into the Pits; Circumstantial Evidence;* and *Humanity Triumphant*. This was a grandiose production. According to the *Daily Telegram*, the Balboa Company went into the Long Beach market and hired the services of about 7,000 extras for this production. Much raw material in the way of film, new props, lumber, and art was used in the production, which was shown weekly for 14 weeks. Each installment consisted of two reels of film, so there were twenty-eight reels in all. This was not a series as most serials were; rather it was a big picture book, with moving pictures, each story complete in itself, although each installment dealt with the same general theme, the object of all of them being to answer the question "Is the world in the grip of evil?" Long Beach's own star, Jackie Saunders (now billed as Jacquelin), was the featured player, and she was seen in 14 separate and distinct characterizations. The *Daily Telegram* noted, "This girl has won millions of friends in all parts of the world and Long Beach is proud to label her 'Maid of Long Beach.'" Roland Bottomley, the distinguished English actor, played opposite Saunders, and his character of John Burton, according to the *Daily Telegram* (Oct. 13, 1916, 5:4), "will long live as the most unique in filmdom." Almost the entire personnel of the Balboa stock company was to be seen in this serial.

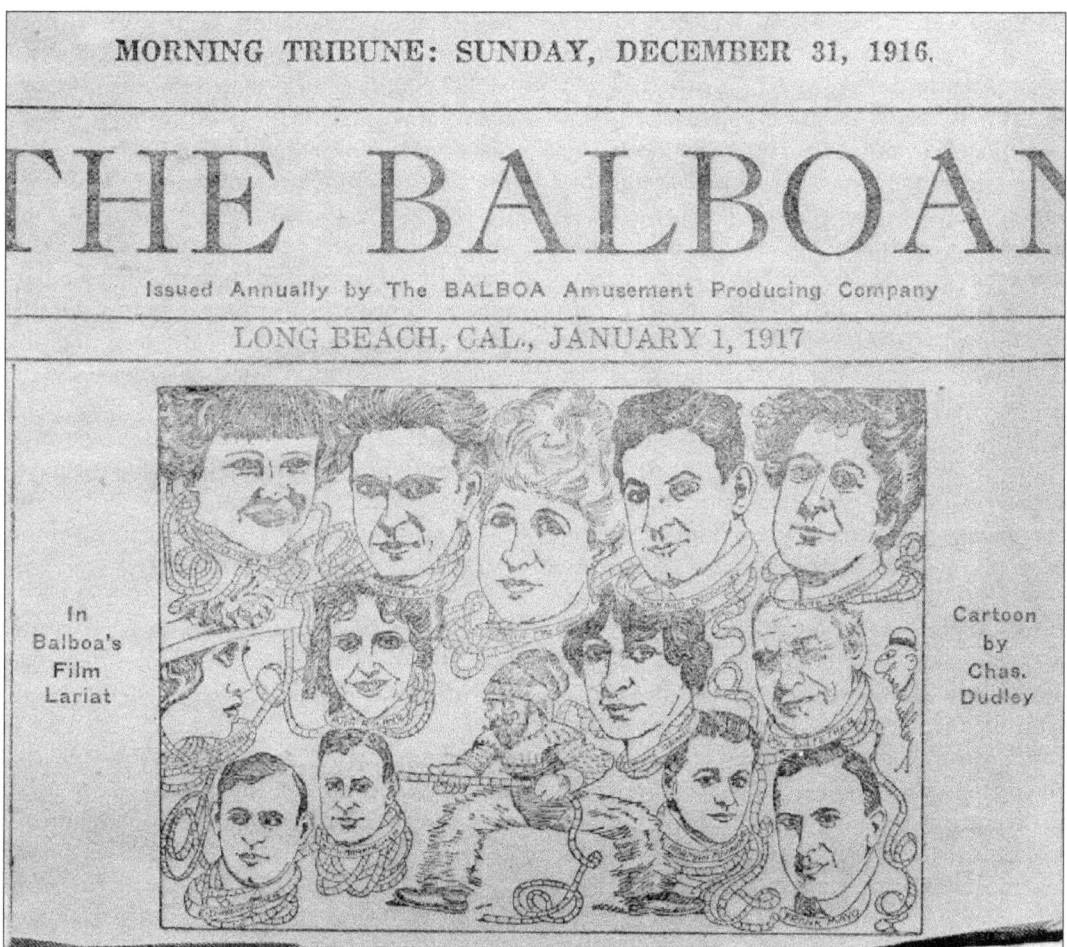

Front page of *The Balboan*, as reprinted in the *Morning Tribune*.

September 16, 1916: Balboa announced that it would produce some films under other trademarks, including Knickerbocker Star Features. Balboa would contract with the General Film Company to make Knickerbocker Star Features. Knickerbocker had been located in New York beginning in 1915, but in February 1917, the film company, distributed by General Films, was taken over by the growing Long Beach plant.

December 1916: Of the six American films sent to France in 1916 to be hand-colored by Pathé, five were Balboa productions: *The Adventures of a Madcap, The Shrine of Happiness, Rose Among the Briers, The Matrimonial Martyr,* and *The Sultana*. This special honor indicated the exceptional quality of the Horkheimer films because they must have possessed unusual merit to be selected for such expensive treatment as Pathé's esteemed hand-coloring process. Balboa motion pictures were widely famed for their photographic excellence.

December 16, 1916: The *Morning Tribune*, Sunday, December 16, 1916, showed the first page of *The Balboan*, a studio newsletter to be issued annually by the Balboa Amusement Producing Company from Long Beach, California; the copy in the *Morning Tribune* showed *The Balboan* for January 1, 1917.

1917

February 1917: This would be another big year for the Horkheimers, who expected only the best for their company and a rosier future. In 1917, Balboa was the largest employer in Long Beach and the greatest tourist attraction in a town already famous as an entertainment center. Balboa announced another new brand among its productions, "Little Mary Sunshine Plays," starring Baby Marie Osborne. Baby Marie had become a world-class star. Other films that year made at Balboa featuring Baby Marie would include *Sunshine and Gold*, *Told at Midnight*, *Twin Kiddies*, and *Twin Rays of Sunshine*. Moreover, the studio announced that a new glass stage would be built. When Balboa took over the reins of Knickerbocker Star Features in February, Henry King and Reaves Eason became Knickerbocker's directors, and the players included Jackie Saunders, Frank Mayo, Mollie McConnell, Marguerite Nichols, Gordon Sackville, Daniel Gilfether, Margaret Landis, Lillian West, Fred Whitman, and Virginia Norden. A million-dollar contract was awarded to Balboa by the General Film Company for fifty-two Knickerbocker feature photoplays of four reels each. This was said to be the largest order ever placed in the film world for picture-plays. Many of the stories were by prominent writers and were known to countless readers who were interested in seeing them on screen. One production for Knickerbocker was to be released each week, and to fulfill this demanding contract, four companies would work simultaneously (*Daily Telegram*, Jan. 29, 1917, 10: 6).

February 7, 1917: The Balboa studio was threatened by a fire, but the damages were negligible. The studio was well prepared and protected in case of fires.

March 1917: The Horkheimers built the largest glass studio in the industry. The trade journals stated that the facilities in Long Beach needed to expand. The Horkheimers had the bungalow offices moved to the third corner of Sixth Street and Alamitos Avenue. They added a garage for 20 cars, along with a papier-mâché department and several large warehouses that would provide more space for Balboa's magnificent stock of props and furnishings. With the first expansion across the street from the original Edison studio, on the northeastern corner of the Balboa lots, large sets had been erected there for the indoor stages. At the cost of $20,000, the finest stage in Southern California was started. It would have hardwood floors and an overhead system for controlling the diffusers from a central station. This stage measured 200 feet square and would extend another 100 feet in the near future. The new stage would be flanked on one side by a battery of 13 private offices for directors. On the other side, 20 of the most modern dressing rooms were built. That spring, ground was broken for a glass studio (150' x 200'), with further enlargement projected. At this point in its growth and development, Balboa Amusement Producing Company represented an investment of $400,000, an enormous sum in 1917.

March 3, 1917: The *Moving Picture World* (p. 1363–64) described in glowing terms a visit to the Balboa Studios in an article entitled "Visiting the Balboa Studios: Norman Manning Has Introduced Efficiency System at Horkheimer Brothers' Plant." G. P. Von Harleman, the author of the article, was much impressed with the Long Beach film plant:

> We paid a visit this week to the studios of the Balboa Amusement and Producing Company, at Long Beach, California. Balboa has now one of the most attractive and elaborate studios on the Pacific Coast. We had the pleasure of a chat with H. M. Horkheimer, the general president, and were conducted through the plant by Norman Manning, business manager and efficiency expert. Mr. Manning has so arranged everything around the plant that there is not a prop nor an article, however unimportant, that he cannot lay his hands on within a fraction of a second. It isn't a matter of card indexing and filing systems, but the man actually has all these things at his finger tips, and can tell any employee of the big plant where to find anything from a spool of thread to a grand piano. Almost everything in the studios is on rollers and Mr. Manning has devised a thousand and one time-saving schemes for handling scenery and props and taking care of same. Everything is kept in tip-top condition. In

the glassware department there is enough glass to fit out a five-and-ten-cent store. Not a speck of dust anywhere, and a man was polishing glasses like a first-class bartender. Mr. Manning's pet department evidently is the automobile garage. The company owns twenty cars and sometimes hires as many more.

August 1917: In addition to their new trademark, Knickerbocker Star Features, the Horkheimers splashed across the screen another new brand with a group of films called "Falcon Features," employing a hooded falcon as their trademark. These features were also to be produced and released by General Films. Falcon Features began in August 1917 and ceased production in February 1918, at the start of the worst crisis ever for the filmmaking careers of the gifted Horkheimers.

August 11, 1917: Again the *Moving Picture World* (p. 948) discussed enthusiastically the elaborate production of a Balboa serial, *The Twisted Thread*:

> Balboa studio is rapidly becoming a serial factory. The Horkheimers announce that they propose to build bigger and better serials. "The Twisted Thread" will mark the beginning of this new policy, and productions to follow will be constructed along lines more elaborate than before attempted.
>
> A large and well equipped single outdoor stage has just been completed and will be devoted exclusively to the building of serials. The newest ideas in filmcraft have been incorporated in the new plant.

October 26, 1917: *Variety* thought that Balboa's *Who Is "Number One"?* was a magnificent film, sumptuous in the extreme. The magazine noted that the Horkheimers had spared no expense in building sets. *Variety* (October 26, 1917, p. 33) also wrote that the detail in the serial was wonderfully worked out and stated its hopes that the remaining 15 episodes would do equally well. There would be 19 episodes.

According to the *Daily Telegram* (November 1917), this was the first serial ever handled by Paramount Pictures. H. M. Horkheimer produced the movie, Anna Katherine Green wrote the story, and the film starred Kathleen Clifford and Cullen Landis.

November 15, 1917: The Horkheimers promoted and initiated Red Cross auxiliaries in U.S. film studios. Besides the Red Cross volunteer work, during the local sardine run off the coast of Long Beach, H. M. engineered fishing expeditions every Sunday for the local fisheries to help supply the U.S. allies from local canneries.

December 1917: Yet another leasing company used the Balboa site. One of Long Beach's favorite celebrities, "Fatty" Arbuckle, returned to Long Beach, the town where he had been married and where he had always been well received.

The Comique Film Corporation had been started by Joseph M. Schenck in the spring of 1917 for the comedy films of Fatty Arbuckle and Buster Keaton, which were to be released by Paramount. The first movie, *The Butcher Boy*, which was released April 23, 1917, was filmed at the studios of the Norma Talmadge Film Corporation in New York. Comique would move to Long Beach and do six movies there before finally moving to the Diando studios in Glendale in 1918.

The Horkheimers and Arbuckle had expected a longer association, but Dame Fortune intervened. To better accommodate Arbuckle's ambitious production plans in Long Beach, the Horkheimers had a separate glass studio built, the world's biggest, for the impressive lineup of films to be made in Long Beach by the Comique Film Corporation. The new structure measured 100' x 200' and was used for Arbuckle's *The Country Hero*.

1918

February 1918: The future still looked bright for the Horkheimers. Arbuckle's company was filming a series of movies at Balboa and had plenty of big plans ahead in Long Beach. Charlie Chaplin was photographed clowning around on Arbuckle's set during one of his three visits to Balboa. Marc Wanamaker reported that Chaplin was interested in doing his own productions, and was carefully eyeing the Balboa facilities.

March 25, 1918: The Horkheimers declared voluntary bankruptcy.

March 27, 1918: H. M. Horkheimer reported to the local papers that all the studio's financial difficulties would be overcome.

April 1918: H. M. and Elwood assigned their studio to the Los Angeles Wholesalers Board of Trade for liquidation. By agreement, the Balboa Amusement Producing Company would stay in operation under the new trustees.

Although H. M. Horkheimer always hoped to make a comeback, publicly announcing his intentions in 1923, neither he nor his brother produced another movie after 1918. Defending his honor at an embarrassing and painful moment, H. M. was quoted in *Moving Picture World*:

> The attachment of the studios on Monday, by the Los Angeles Wholesalers Board of Trade, was made at my suggestion and by which agreement was made with all of the studio's creditors. It is a well known fact that the sales market from a sales standpoint has been upset for sometime, as a direct result of which larger producers and Balboa have been pinched and had to retrench. I have been looking for a favorable turn in the market any day, but none have showed. When this happened, I took the matter up with our three most important creditors, and after going over the situation, we decided to have an attachment proceed to save the assets from complete liquidation. E. D. Horkheimer, my brother, has made the financial arrangements with the new trustees. Under the circumstances, there were only two courses open for us. One would have been the easiest, but we chose assignment.

Four companies were working at the time at the Balboa site: The Kathleen Clifford Company, the Anita King Company, the Mona Lisa Company, and the Comique Film Company. It is interesting to note that the first three companies were headed by women. H. O. Stechhan remained as the assistant to the general manager of the Balboa studio.

July 8, 1918: Buster Keaton left Long Beach and Arbuckle's film company to serve as an American soldier in Europe.

July 17, 1918: To disassociate himself from the bad rumors circulating about the Balboa studio, Roscoe "Fatty" Arbuckle sought another location, leaving Long Beach and continuing his productions in Glendale.

September 23, 1918: It was reported that Balboa studios might be dismantled and sold unless one of two deals materialized. One of the deals involved the Goldwyn Pictures Corporation.

October 3, 1918: Newspapers announced that Goldwyn Pictures Corporation was planning to lease the Balboa film plant. Samuel Goldwyn in New York reportedly wanted to lease the Balboa plant for $36,000 until January 1, 1920. He was supposedly willing to lease the compact and complete studio in Long Beach, with the option to buy it for $125,000. F. A. Knight, the attorney representing Balboa's creditors, did not believe Goldwyn Pictures would actually buy the site in the end, even if Goldwyn were to lease it.

The reasons for this hesitation on the part of the creditors and Knight are not clear. Goldwyn had been experiencing financial problems in 1917, but by the end of the war, two great financial contributions bolstered the Goldwyn company, the first being the $7,000,000 invested by the du Ponts, and the second being the $50,000 in Liberty Bonds donated by Mabel Normand, a close and generous friend of Samuel Goldwyn. Nonetheless, Balboa's creditors were impatient for more return on their investment because they had been feeling jittery since the bankruptcy, and the deal with Goldwyn eventually fell through. Knight and the creditors considered Balboa a real gem of a prize and expected another rich buyer to snatch it up, especially since the war had caused a shortage of much that was available at Balboa. A new owner would be able to start production immediately in Long Beach, with all kinds of materials and supplies already on site. Once again, just as had happened earlier in Long Beach's history, when Universal once considered locating its film plant by the city's beach, Goldwyn Pictures too would consider the same option, nearly changing the course of future Hollywood.

The creditors would, however, have to wait a few more months. On February 13, 1919, the *Daily Telegram* of Long Beach announced that the New Art Film Corporation, organized in Des Moines, Iowa, would be the new owner. It was the first in a file of new owners over the next five or six years.

H. M. and Elwood, along with their sister, Florence, had been the sole owners of Balboa Amusement Producing Company once Fred Mace quit the partnership early in Balboa's history. The Horkheimers were unwilling to sell their shares, and Florence was more reluctant than her brothers. Even after H. M. and Elwood eventually agreed to sell, Florence adamantly held out. What had gone wrong on the Horkheimers' spectacular path to fame and glory?

Ever vigilant about cost and quality control, Pathé had asked, as early as 1916, that the Horkheimers slow down production. While the strength of Horkheimers may have been their zeal for success, along with their diversified and innovative marketing and distribution approaches, in the end, the brothers made a fatal error in turning a deaf ear to Pathé.

The Great War had made film stock rare and expensive because the same chemicals were also used to fabricate explosives. The whole movie industry had entered a slump, with many prestigious companies folding, though studios in California would emerge victorious and supreme. Good relations between producers and distributors became essential by 1917, during this turning point in the film industry. Unfortunately, several studios, including Balboa, would fail to fathom fully the ramifications of the necessary marriage between producers and distributors to assure their mutual success and longevity.

When Pathé finally refused to release films in the same volume as in previous years, the Horkheimers and their creditors squirmed as they never had before, incredulous towards the suddenly bleak market ahead of them, having believed that their studio and its quality films were a permanent fixture in the movie capital of the world. In 1917, H. M. Horkheimer had firmly expressed his confidence in the future of the film plant in Long Beach, and as late as February 1918, Balboa was heralded as a world-class studio with a most promising and bright future.

Tragically, H. M. never fully grasped the consequences of his grave mistake with Pathé, expecting a turn in the market any day after Balboa was assigned to the Los Angeles Wholesale Board of Trade for liquidation. Embarrassed but still determined, H. M. discussed matters of honor in a fickle market. On March 27, 1918, in the *Daily Telegram*, he explained that the assignment had been done voluntarily to hold all the assets together for the benefit of all the creditors. Simple bankruptcy would have been easier but less honorable because then the Horkheimers would have rid themselves of all their financial obligations, but H. M., a man of his word from West Virginia, was promising to pay off the debts amounting to $200,000. H. M., after all, was always resourceful and never a quitter. In fact, by 1923, H. M. would announce in Long Beach his comeback, but predictions of his return to the Long Beach film plant would not be realized, in spite of all his efforts, hopes, and dreams.

Description of the Long Beach Studio Grounds and Facilities

The following four aerial sections were drawn according to information and details in the Sanborn maps at the Long Beach Public Library, which show the studio quadrangle at the four corners of Sixth Street and Alamitos Avenue in Long Beach. The Sanborn maps present each successive addition at the studio site, as new buildings were being constructed

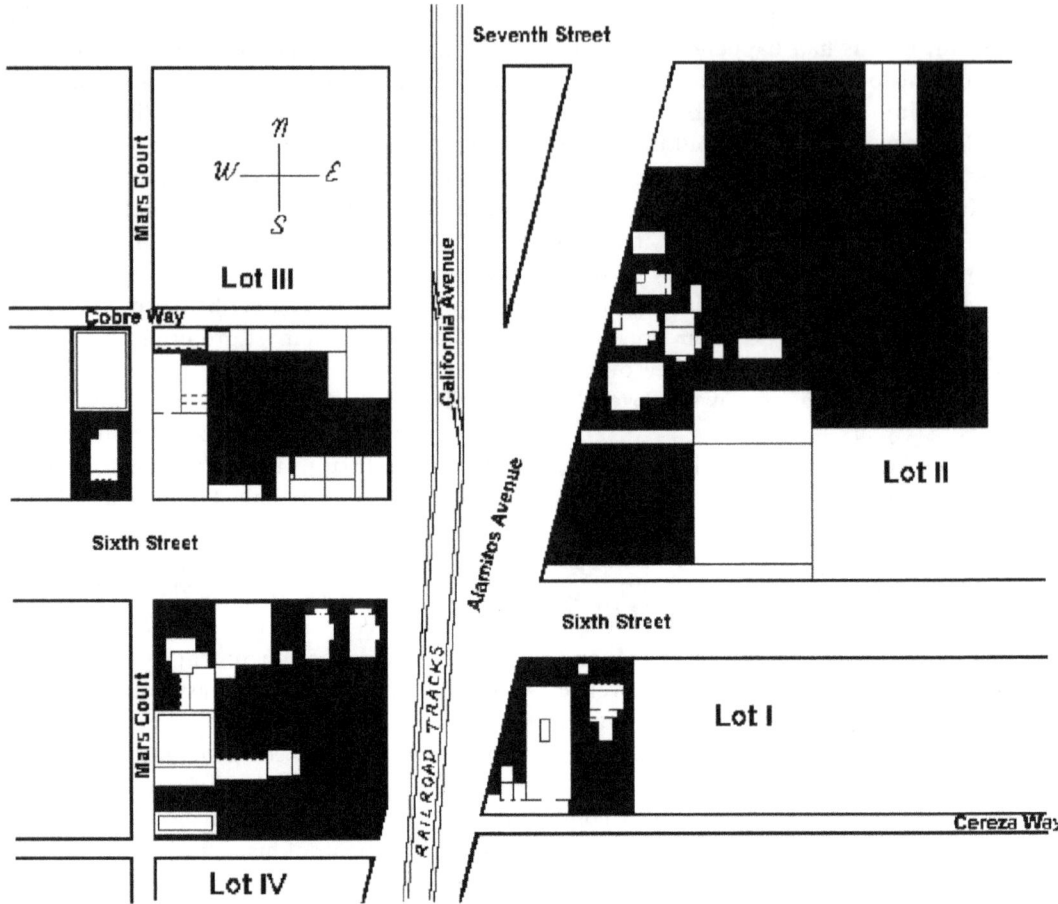

Aerial view of the Balboa Amusement Producing Company, circa 1917–1918 (graphics by J. J. Jura).

at the Balboa Studios. Despite the archeological rigor with which each peeling was carefully performed to unveil the underlying layers, our research never did identify the location of the Balboa zoo, nor did the peelings uncover the exact location of the eleven acres of studio grounds in Signal Hill. Unfortunately, some underlying layers were permanently removed and discarded during the building up of layers, one on top of the other, between 1914 and 1942.

Apart from the Sanborn maps, we consulted escrow and trust papers that had been donated by Aimie Gervais to the Historical Society of Long Beach around 1985, among tons of papers being dumped from a title company's archives in Pasadena. Fortunately, Gervais appreciated the historical value of these dusty papers concerning the purchase of the studio site in September 1919 by Master Pictures. Instead of driving directly to the disposal site, he took the time and effort to contact many different societies about the papers he had retrieved. Fortunately for the sake of preserving records of the Balboa Amusement Producing Company, the Historical Society of Long Beach most enthusiastically accepted these "lost" treasures. These title papers proved to be extremely valuable in cross-referencing details with the Sanborn maps and furnished measurements and appraisals about both the real estate and the improvements of the film plant at Long Beach. Lots I–IV of the following maps are arranged in a counterclockwise sequence, starting from the original site of the Edison studio at the southeast corner of Sixth

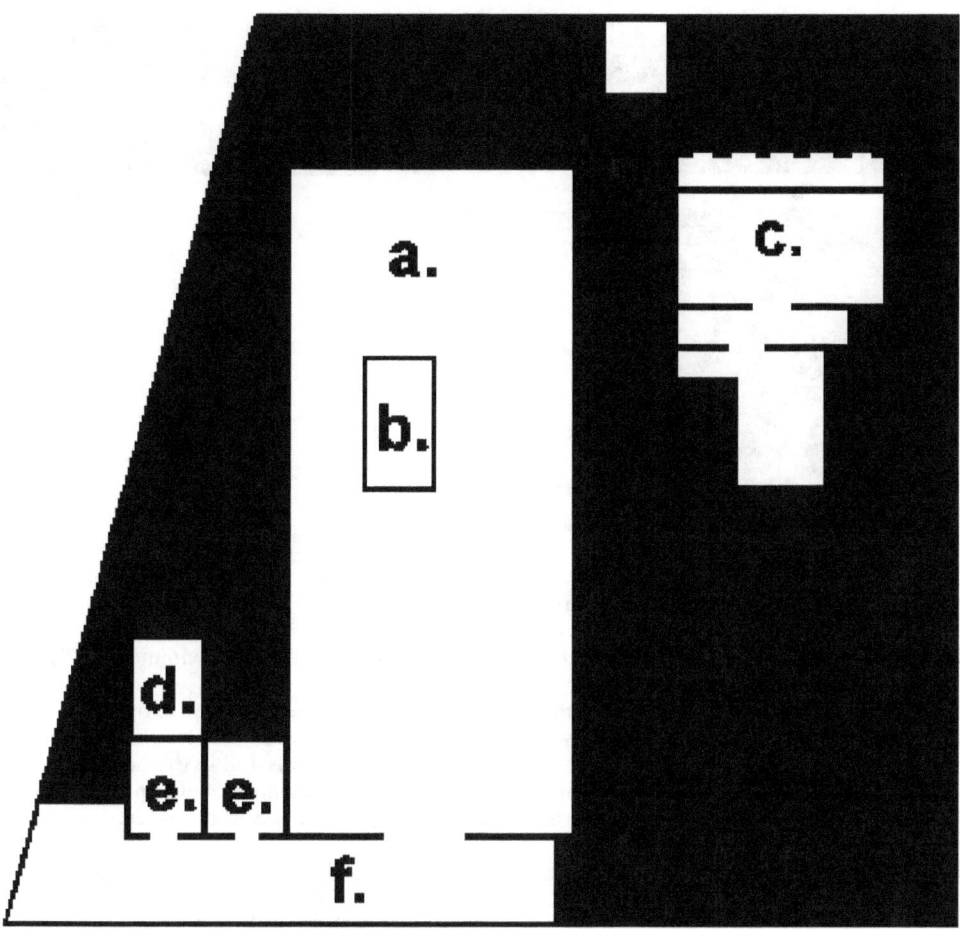

Lot I, southeast corner of the Balboa Studios quadrangle, the original site of the California Motion Picture Manufacturing Company (1910) and of the Edison studio (1913). The addresses of this lot include either 901 and 935 Sixth Street or 610, 622, 630, 636, and 638 Alamitos Avenue (graphics by J. J. Jura).
- a. Development & Wardrobe Storage. Floor area approximately 12' × 32'.
- b. Fireproof Film Vault
- c. Office. Area of approximately 16' × 10'.
- d. Tank House. Area of approximately 4' × 5'.
- e. Printing Rooms. Area of approximately 4' × 5'.
- f. Dry Lab Rooms/Heating — Gas. Area of approximately 5' × 24'.

Street and Alamitos Avenue, Lot I, and ending with the southwest corner of the studio quadrangle, Lot IV.

The photographs of the studio that appear following the maps were selected from the collection at the Long Beach Public Library. With a little effort, readers can match the photographs with the following aerial views, the photographs transforming the flat surfaces into three-dimensional views of the stunning Balboa Studios. Of particular interest are the details in the photographs, including the white sculptures, the magnificent glass studio, and the outdoor stages with towering scaffolding used to control and harness the overhead diffusers and canvases. This pictorial evidence showcases some of Balboa's beauty during its reign as a pacesetting film plant.

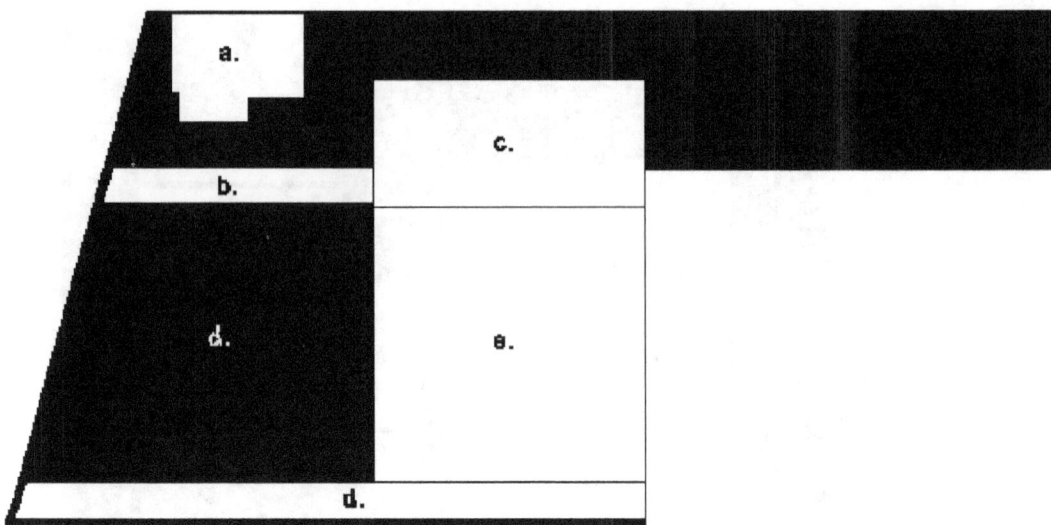

Lower half of Lot II, northeast corner of the Balboa Studios quadrangle (graphics by J. J. Jura).
   a. Scenario Offices, 630 Alamitos Avenue
   b. Scenery Storage, 622 Alamitos Avenue
   c. Double-Deck Scenery Storage, 626 Alamitos Avenue. Floor area of approximately 107' × 40'; one water pressure elevator; property room and office.
   d. No. 2 Stage, 610 Alamitos Avenue. One open air stage with an area of approximately 128' × 108', with all overhead timbering for wires, defusers, and lighting; on Sixth Street side, offices, dark rooms, directors' rooms, two three-way toilet rooms, along with furniture rooms and switchboard room.
   e. One Glass Studio, 612 Alamitos Avenue. Steel construction, with an area of approximately 107' × 135', with comfortable dressing rooms and washrooms, flooring, and tanks under stage.

Long Beach: Home of the Stars and Headline Stories

Studio policy required Balboa's stars to reside in Long Beach, and the city glittered with celebrities of the silent screen. In fact, Theda Bara and "Fatty" Arbuckle were neighbors on Ocean Boulevard. Long Beach streets became the daily walkways for these early stars: Pearl White, Ruth Roland, Henry King, Jackie Saunders, William Desmond Taylor, Baby Marie Osborne, "Fatty" Arbuckle, Buster Keaton, Al St. John, and many others. Even a local version of the Brown Derby, Joe's Restaurant, stood in the triangle formed where Martin Luther King, Jr., Avenue (then California Avenue) and Alamitos Avenue meet, on the northern edge of the four corners of the Balboa Amusement Producing Company. There a customer could order a "Jackie Saunders Special" and an "Arbuckle Appetizer," among other dishes that thrilled the palates and imaginations of the stargazers in Long Beach.

On August 1, 1948, Garald Lagard wrote in the *Press-Telegram Southland Magazine* an article entitled "Long Beach Film Quadrangle," which reflected on the movie colony that encircled the studio site during the silent era. Many contract players lived near or directly next to the studio. Hazel Tranchell, who did more than 150 films at Balboa, lived with her husband, Hugh E. Tranchell, and their daughter, Katherine, on the northeast corner, next to that part of the studio facing Alamitos. Not only were the contract players often seen on location at favorite sites, such as the seven-mile stretch of beaches and the Pike, but many extras were drawn from Long Beach residents, who were paid five dollars a day for participating in Balboa's serials and other production shoots. Those residents who were lucky enough to be selected could even watch themselves on their hometown screens. During Long Beach's

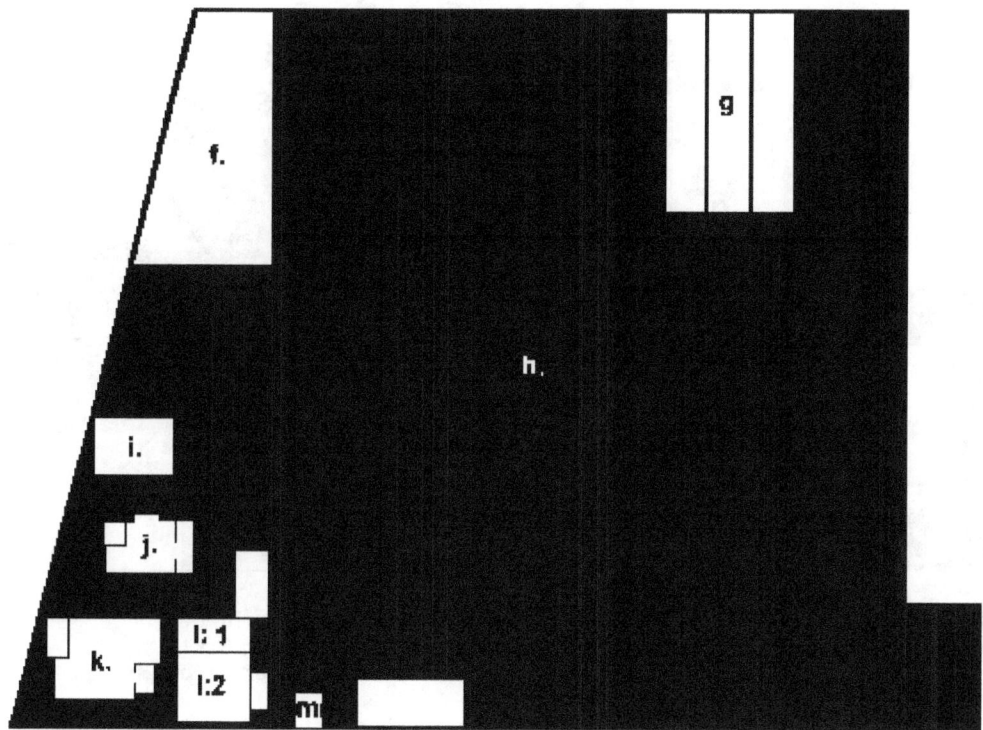

Upper half of Lot II, northeast corner of the Balboa Studios quadrangle (graphics by J. J. Jura).

    f. Plumbing

    g. Scenery Storage, 1030 Seventh Street. Partitioned in three sections, total area approximately 48' × 74', or 3,552 square feet.

    h. Lot. Area of lot, 175' x 198.3', or 34,702.5 square feet, filled with cheap, movable buildings for motion picture productions.

    i. Restaurant, 648 Alamitos Avenue

    j. Dwelling. Now the Barcelona Brasserie, 640 Alamitos Avenue

    k. Ladies' Dressing Room and Hospital. Now property management offices for Gumbiner real estate investments, 638 Alamitos Avenue. Dressing rooms all equipped with toilet and washrooms of latest construction.

    l. Blacksmith Shop (l:1)/Storage (l:2), 636 Alamitos Avenue

    m. Transformer Room

heyday *Neal of the Navy* played an installment every Saturday at the old Bijou Theatre at the West Pike. One of Hazel Tranchell's movies, *Uneven Match*, with "Slim" Pickett, was showing at the old Liberty Theatre on Ocean Boulevard, opposite the Pacific Electric Station. For a while, Long Beach could have been called "Hollywood by the Sea."

Moreover, as early as 1914, Norman Manning, the youngest studio manager in the film industry and one of the wisest and most efficient in the business, arranged a display for the Balboa Amusement Producing Company at the Long Beach Drug Company, at the corner of Pine Avenue and Ocean Boulevard in downtown Long Beach. The publicity in the display effectively piqued the insatiable appetite of the stargazing tourists, showcasing some of Balboa's hit films, with a pictorial spread of Balboa's actors and actresses, along with studio accessories of moviemaking magic. Among the articles on display, one could see an oil painting of Jackie Saunders, the "Maid of Long Beach," and photos of Henry King, Richard Johnson, and Mollie McConnell. The Horkheimers never overlooked the chance to

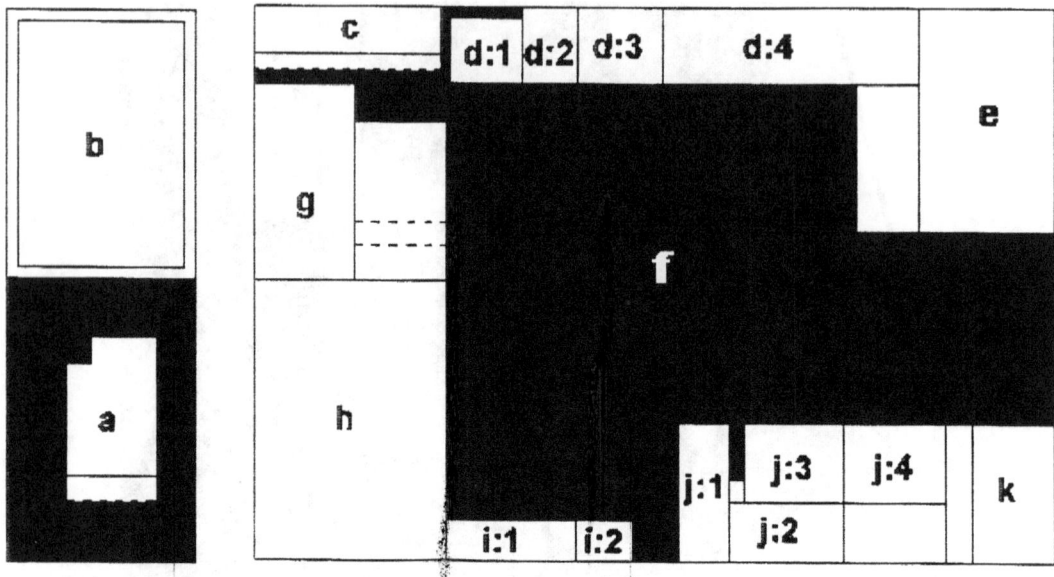

Lot III, northwest corner of the Balboa Studios quadrangle (graphics by J. J. Jura).
   a. Mens' Dressing Rooms, 827 Sixth Street. Floor area of approximately 8' × 14'.
   b. Furniture Storage/Some Cabinet Work, No. 2, 829 Sixth Street. Floor area of approximately 16' × 23'.
   c. Dressing Rooms, 611 Cobre Way. Floor area of approximately 16' × 6'.
   d. Storage and Rooms. Floor areas of approximately 6' × 5' (d:1) and 7' × 39' (d:2, d:3, d:4 [613, 615, and 619 Cobre Way] collectively).
   e. Scenery Storage and Wood Working, 621 California Avenue. Floor area of approximately 16' × 12'.
   f. No. 1 Stage, between 621 and 601 California Avenue. Area of approximately 35' × 50'.
   g. Print and Paper Room, 839 Sixth Street. Floor area of approximately 16' × 16'.
   h. Carpentry and Scenery Manufacturing, 837 Sixth Street. Floor area of approximately 16' × 24'.
   i. Storage (i:1) and Fire-Proof Camera Vault (i:2), 843 and 845 Sixth Street. Floor area of approximately (4' × 16').
   j. Storage (j:1), Electrical Fixture Room (j:2), Electrical Shop (j:3), and Drapery Department (j:4), 855 and 861 Sixth Street. Total floor area of approximately 12' × 20'.
   k. Property Room, 869 Sixth Street. Floor area of approximately 6' × 12'.

generate more attention and interest in their growing studio and in Long Beach as a movie town.

Along with the glitter and excitement of being a movie town, Long Beach also had to endure the scandalous living of the rich and famous. The list of scandals would, of course, be much longer and detailed if all the traces were still clear, but they are not. Only bits and pieces have been culled from the remaining fragments, most of them contained in *Press Clippings*, vol. 1 (1913–1914), Balboa's publicity scrapbook preserved at the Historical Society of Long Beach. Other fragments were gleaned from Marie Osborne-Yeats' personal scrapbooks, which were generously lent to the authors of this book during our research.

January 16, 1914: The *Los Angeles Tribune* announced in an article entitled "Film Performers Have Thrilling Auto Ride" that William D. Taylor and players near Chatsworth Park were filming scenes in a melodrama on some wild and rocky terrain. In one scene Jackie Saunders and Norman Manning made a wild auto ride through a pass, going 50 miles per hour. They hit a bump that made the vehicle leap 30 feet, but it fell safely to earth, the riders holding their seats without any injury (*Press Clippings*, vol. 1, p. 52).

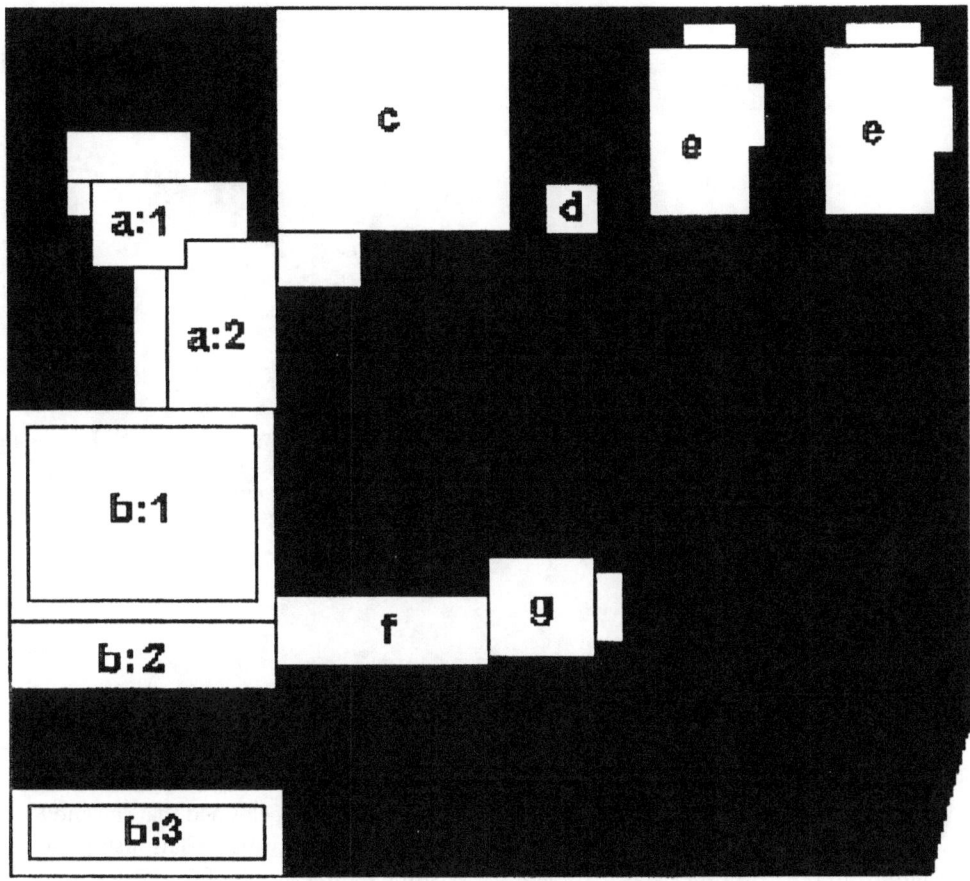

Lot IV, southwest corner of the Balboa Studios quadrangle (graphics by J. J. Jura).
  a. Plaster of Paris Room (a:1) and Lumber Shed (a:2), 832 Sixth Street. Floor area of approximately 20' × 10'.
  b. Property and Scenery Storage (b:1), Auto House, No. 1 (b:2), and Auto House, No. 2 (b:3), 832 Sixth Street. Total floor area of approximately 21' × 18'.
  c. Auto Repair Shop, 850 Sixth Street. Made of concrete, floor area of approximately 16' × 16'.
  d. One Small Building. Floor area of approximately 4' × 4'.
  e. Two Office Buildings, 866 Sixth Street or 557 Alamitos Avenue. Each building includes five offices elaborately finished.
  f. Auto House, No. 3. Floor area of approximately 14' × 5'.
  g. Storage. Floor area of approximately 7' × 7'.

March 3, 1914: The *Long Beach Telegram* reported in an article entitled "Comedian Badly Hurt" that "Pop" Leonard fell through a window during a movie scene at the Balboa Studios in which he was leaning and gesturing at a window. His fall resulted in one broken rib and a severely sprained back. Dr. R. A. Terry stated, "Mr. Leonard will be confined to his bed for a number of days." It was said that Pop joked with his physician all the way to his home at 644 Lime Avenue (*Press Clippings*, vol. 1, p. 64).

March 4, 1914: The *Los Angeles Examiner* reported a juicy story about a handsome Italian attorney and confidence man who embezzled $4,311, by kissing all the girls and "investing" their money, before skipping out of town —*O, la dolce vita*. The article was entitled "Riccardi Elusive As His Amours Are Bared." Constantine V. Riccardi was a dapper and

Southeast corner of the Balboa Studio quadrangle, the original site of the California Motion Picture Manufacturing Company (1910) and the Edison studio (1913).

likeable young attorney with a wide circle of friends whom one could call "fans." After Riccardi's flight from L.A., his office was searched, and there were found photographs and burning love letters from his many admirers. In Riccardi's desk at the International Bank Building, his office associates discovered pictures of Belle Bennett, a star at Balboa. Not only did Riccardi possess photos of Belle Bennett, but some of them were autographed and even personalized, rather tamely from our modern point of view—"To Mr. Riccardi." Nonetheless, these "hot" items were considered rather scandalous. Bennett, who stayed at the Hotel Virginia, defended herself: "I have known Mr. Riccardi for about a year, and was in his company frequently but always as a member of a party. I did not know that he had left the city. I had not seen him nor heard of him for probably 2 months" (*Press Clippings*, vol. 1, p. 55).

March 7, 1914: The *Los Angeles Examiner* released an update on Riccardi's escape entitled, "Wireless Is Used to Hunt Riccardi." Riccardi had successfully fled the country via Mexico. This time Bennett claimed that she and Riccardi had only had a platonic relationship, but in her ensuing enumeration of Riccardi's charms, one detects more than mere friendship. For Belle Bennett, this con man possessed four outstanding qualities: (1) a fascinating personality, (2) a handsome face, (3) unfailing good nature, (4) attention to the most trivial wants of those about him (*Press Clippings*, vol. 1, p. 56).

March 8, 1914: This news item created a stir by eliciting the sympathies of the film world. The *Los Angeles Herald* released an article entitled, "Seen and Heard in Filmland" announcing that Joseph E. Singleton, working with director Bertram Bracken at the Balboa Amusement Producing Company, was badly injured in the face. While working at the Long Beach studio on March 7, 1914, Singleton was wounded by a blank cartridge that exploded in his face. When the members of the Photoplayers' Club learned the news through a telegram sent by Francis McDonald, there was much expression of concern and regret. Later the film world was relieved to hear that the injuries

Northeast corner of the Balboa Studios quadrangle.

were not so serious as to cause disfigurement (*Press Clippings*, vol. 1, p. 68).

April 4, 1914: The *Los Angeles Tribune* announced that William Jossey, author and actor at Balboa, had recently been stricken with apoplexy but was expected to return to work after a period of convalescence (*Press Clippings*, vol. 1, p. 64).

April 14, 1914: On this date, the *Long Beach Telegram* reported that a pedestrian was knocked down by the Horkheimer touring car and the pedestrian's left ankle was run over. The pedestrian's name was William L. Weller of Long Beach. The article was entitled "Run Down and Hurt by Auto." Mrs. H. M. Horkheimer was riding alone in the car driven by her chauffeur. The accident occurred the very day of the article, April 14, 1914. Weller was struck at 1:30 P.M. and knocked down as one of the wheels of the car passed over his left ankle. He was carried to Pacific Park, where Dr. L. A. Perce dressed the injuries. In Weller's statement he puts the blame on his own carelessness and bad timing. Weller explained the mishap by saying that he was walking west on Ocean Boulevard and attempted to get around an ice wagon and team of horses directly in his path by stepping out onto the Pacific Electric right of way, directly in front of a car. Stepping still further out into the street to avoid the first car, Weller got in front of the Horkheimer's car going east on Ocean. The Horkheimer chauffeur had no time to prevent the accident. Later, Horkheimer arrived to drive the car back, and he took the injured man to his home. Although everyone may have been unnerved, there were apparently no hard feelings and no lawsuits (*Press Clippings*, vol. 1, p. 64).

April 24, 1914: This event concerns a fund-raiser for the Hollywood baseball league. The Hollywood studios were blending filmdom with America's favorite sport. It was a

Northwest corner of the quadrangle.

wonderful public relations concept to be able to watch the favorite stars playing the country's favorite sport. The *Long Beach Press* discussed a big dance to promote the league. The article was entitled "Moving Pictures Ball May First." It was Balboa's first "movie" ball at the Majestic Pavilion, under the management of Norman Manning. It was announced as a terpsichorean fête, a benefit ball as never before seen in Long Beach. The dance would provide funds to back Balboa's moving picture baseball team just then entering the Southern California Motion Picture Baseball League, with games to be staged regularly on a local diamond in Long Beach. At the benefit ball, there would be actors and actresses from various film companies in and around Los Angeles.

The Balboa Amusement Producing Company was to be the host of the ball. After the gala event, it was reported that in the first ball game including Balboa, Universal City had swamped Balboa 14 to 1 in Long Beach. Horace Huff, the Universal pitcher, was given credit for the victory, holding the Long Beach players at his mercy (*Press Clippings*, vol. 1, p. 65).

June 25, 1914: The *Los Angeles Tribune* reported in an article entitled "Motion Picture Man, Fleeing Speed 'Cop,' Pays $115 for Dash," that G. P. Thurman, who worked at Balboa, fled from a county motorcycle officer, Fred Nelson, along Long Beach Boulevard in Long Beach. The police officer had chased the speedster for 13 miles, the officer sometimes traveling at 75 miles per hour. Justice Forbes gave Thurman a choice of paying the maximum fine of $50 or spending 30 days in jail. Thurman quickly opted for the fine. In addition to the county fees, a Long Beach magistrate imposed an additional $65 fine for excessive speed.

July 1914: *The Will O' the Wisp* was released. In *Press Clippings*, vol. 1, p. 118, there is an article from an unidentified publication entitled "Jackie Saunders Back at Work" that recounts a poisoning (probably from poison ivy in the rugged country):

> Miss Jackie Saunders, whose current release, *The Will O' the Wisp*, has received such favorable comment, is now able to return to the studio of the Balboa Amusement Company, after an absence of two weeks made necessary because of poisoning.

Southwest corner of the quadrangle.

"It was that horrible trip up Fish Canyon; where we climbed up straight rocks that almost caused me the loss of my beauty," the popular actress said with a sly wink, "for it was then that I was poisoned. You should have seen me last week when my face was puffed out of shape — it was a cartoon. I thought I would have to go in for comedy."

July 18, 1914: Both the *Los Angeles Herald* and the *Long Beach Telegram* reported legal suits against Balboa. Edwin August, a famous actor and producer, and Henry Otto, also a producer at Balboa, filed suit against their former employer. August claimed he was owed his $217 weekly salary according to contract, along with remuneration for scenarios he had written and produced under contract with Otto for Balboa. Balboa alleged that August and Otto were discharged because August submitted and produced for the Balboa Amusement Producing Company a scenario, *The Actor*, which August had already used for the Universal company. This practice of using the same work twice, pretending that it was original, was called "repeating." The article in the *Los Angeles Herald*, "Film Actors Sue Balboa Company" and the one in the *Long Beach Telegram*, "Trouble in 'Movie' World: Balboa Dismisses Two of Its Stars," try to be objective, but the papers sympathize with the Horkheimers. To give the reader a perspective on salaries, here are a few examples. At Balboa, Edwin August enjoyed one of the highest salaries among all the screen actors of Hollywood, with a salary per annum of $10,400, roughly $217 per week. For comparison, according to Robert Giroux, in his book *A Deed of Death* (pp. 188–89), Mabel Normand in 1914 was receiving $250 per week, Mary Pickford in 1914 was earning $385, being the highest paid actress in Hollywood at the time, and although his salary skyrocketed in 1916, Charlie Chaplin was making $150 per week in 1915. The average annual income for Americans was only around $1,000 per annum. These were big bucks for the stars of filmdom. Nonetheless, before being fired, August also claimed that there was owing to him in his suit against Balboa, besides his lost salary, $25 for each reel for all the scenarios he had submitted and produced, as well as a royalty in sum of 6¢ a foot for all negatives produced from the original film. In response to these accusations, the Horkheimers insisted that there were no such clauses in the contract. H. M. Horkheimer was so outraged by August's assertions that he promised to fight to the bitter end the suit initiated by August and Otto, who had been

View from roof at northwest corner, across southwest corner, to southeast corner of the quadrangle.

working for several months at the studio. Balboa's chiefs sent letters to the leading producing companies of the world outlining the trouble between themselves and August and Otto. Unfortunately, sources fail to disclose the details of the proceedings and the outcome (*Press Clippings*, vol. 1, p. 106).

July 25, 1914: *Motion Picture News* reported "Balboa's Fox Steals Chickens." There had been several calls for the police after both a fox and a coyote escaped from Balboa's zoo. The coyote eventually returned to the studio on his own, stepping right back into his cage after two days on the prowl, but the fox, true to his crafty and independent nature, was still at large, the supposed culprit who had been stealing and eating chickens in Long Beach, along his merry way to freedom (*Press Clippings*, vol. 1, p. 95).

September 26, 1914: *Moving Picture World* announced a birthday dinner for the dean of Balboa Studios, Daniel Gilfether: "Major Daniel Gilfether, approaching his sixtieth year, of which forty years has been spent on the stage, is to be tendered a dinner, by his friends among the Balboa players at Long Beach, California. The Major appeared first with Frank Mayo in 'Davy Crockett,' and he has been all along the line. He is a member of Elk's Lodge No. 1 of New York" (*Press Clippings*, vol. 1, p. 119).

October 17, 1914: In an article entitled "Husband Goes on Rampage," the *Long Beach Telegram* covered a story about domestic violence. Ben Deely, the assailant, had been leasing the Balboa Studios to produce films for his own company. His wife and he had previously separated and then attempted reconciliation. It was during their reconciliation that this scandal occurred, an episode that some sources blame on excessive drinking. The couple had residences at both Long Beach and Los Angeles. In Long Beach, the Deelys stayed at the fashionable Schuyler apartments. There were two victims in the assault. The first victim was the Deelys' friend, E. W. Maxwell. On the evening of October 16, 1914, after an argument with Maxwell, Ben Deely punched him in the face at the Deely's apartment, breaking his nose. Maxwell was taken to the Seaside Hospi-

Filming *Neal of the Navy* (1915) (courtesy of Marc Wanamaker).

tal in a private car. About 30 minutes later, Mrs. Deely, 24 years old, quarreled with her husband and was then beaten by him. She had already notified the police in the past about fearing the violent streak in her husband. The police were called, but Mr. Deely had fled. Mrs. Deely suffered a cut face, and her right eye was swollen shut. Neither Maxwell nor Mrs. Deely was expected to remain long in the hospital (*Press Clippings*, vol. 1, p. 224).

These preceding headline stories were gleaned from *Press Clippings*, vol. 1 (1913–1914), and are thus limited to 1914. More research in the future will undoubtedly reveal other tasty items for the gossip-seekers in all of us, but we will have to wait for those. Before delving more into the unsolved murder of William Desmond Taylor, we will close this segment with two headline stories concerning both William Desmond Taylor and Baby Marie Osborne, two celebrities at Balboa. Most of the information regarding William Desmond Taylor was obtained from Robert Giroux's fascinating account of Taylor's mysterious life and death entitled *A Deed of Death*, and the unhappy "kidnapping" of Baby Marie was a news item taken from the star's scrapbook full of movie memorabilia carefully and lovingly collected by the juvenile star's foster parents.

At Balboa, William Desmond Taylor, already an experienced actor approaching 40 years of age, turned to directing. His directorial début occurred in the film *The Awakening*, during which he fell in love with the starring actress Neva Gerber, a well-to-do actress who was also from a prominent family. *The Awakening* was a three-reel drama that was made for William Fox by White Star and was released October 5, 1914, by Box Office Attraction Co.

Neva Gerber would appear in the next four Taylor productions at Balboa, and their love affair would last five years, beyond Taylor's stay at Balboa. Taylor and Gerber hoped to marry each other after Gerber divorced her husband. Unfortunately for the two lovers, Gerber was never able to divorce her husband, who categorically refused to give her a divorce, though he was aware of the affair. Eventually, Gerber and Taylor went their separate ways, remaining friends. They had always been honest with each other, each being aware of the other's marriage. Gerber was married but separated from her husband when the extramarital liaison began. Taylor too had been married, but he had abandoned his wife and daughter in New York in 1908. As a result of the abandonment, Taylor's wife divorced him in 1912 on grounds of adultery. After their separation as lovers, Gerber acknowledged Taylor's lapses into amnesia and his spells of depression, these being the principal causes, according to Taylor, for his leaving his wife and daughter. He claimed to be quite unaware at the time of his ties to them. Even after they went their separate ways, Gerber could only praise this "great" man of enormous generosity and romantic sensibilities, who suffered terrible bouts of depression, headaches and occasional amnesia: "He would walk the floor and wring his hands, asking, 'Why do I have to keep up this battle? Is it worthwhile to continue this struggle of existence?'" (Giroux, p. 82).

Even juvenile players failed to escape the occasional pangs of sorrow at Balboa during the silent era. Baby Marie Osborne was also the target of headlines and sometimes too much attention in the press. Not only had she broken all records for five-reel movies, but her example became a cause célèbre for critics of juvenile actors exploited by the movie industry or their own movie moms. It was once falsely reported that Baby Marie had been kidnapped. A nude picture of her as a ward of the court was displayed for shock effect on some front pages, in a sensational and potentially harmful custody battle between her foster parents and the court. In fact, the young actress had been placed in a foster home as an infant but had never really been adopted. At four years old, Baby Marie was already world-famous and adored by her fans by many names—"Little Majesty Marie," "Baby Grand," "Little Mary Sunshine" and "Merry Sunshine," a weighty sobriquet created by *Motion Picture Magazine*, which called her "Baby Bernhardt," comparing her stardom to that of the famous French actress, Sarah Bernhardt. In the Spanish-speaking world, Baby Marie was called "El Rayito de Sol." Newspapers often tried to hook readers, as they do today, by targeting the corrupting influences of money among the rich and famous, and the papers had a bone to pick about the "exceedingly" high salary for Baby Marie, $90 per week, equivalent in those days to the salary of a bank president.

An article appeared on August 20, 1916 in the *Seattle Sunday Times* entitled, "Real Romance of the Movies—$," in which it was lamented that while Baby Marie enjoyed financial security, her guardianship required a judge, depriving her of a stable home base for a toddler of only four years of age. As it turned out, the reported kidnapping was a misunderstanding between her foster parents, who had been quarreling and not communicating to each other. The three of them had gone on location in Orange County, when the foster father decided it was inappropriate for his daughter to attend another studio's party after the shooting because she was on contract with Balboa. When he left the gathering with Marie, not telling his wife, she and Henry King thought Marie had been kidnapped and reported her missing to the police. The bold kidnapping headline appeared, September 27, 1916, in the *Morning Tribune* of Los Angeles: *LITTLE MARY SUNSHINE STOLEN!*

Before the California legislature enacted the Child Actors Bill in the 1930s, popularly called the Coogan Law, to protect the personal and financial concerns of juvenile actors, H. M. Horkheimer devoted much effort to bringing harmony into Baby Marie's life. H. M. specifically underlined the importance of Marie's continuing her education and having sufficient playtime at the studio. H. M. also posted at the studio the following mandate in order to protect Baby Marie's interests and safety at the studio:

TO ALL CONCERNED
Effective Upon Publication.

Rules to be observed
in regard to Little Mary Sunshine.

While on the stage the child is not to be touched by anyone excepting her director, her attendant or those assisting the director or participating in the scenes in which she appears.

She is not to be teased at any time.

She is not to be shouted at nor addressed in slang.

She is not to be given sweet meats nor presents of any description while at work on the stage or on location. All presents must be sent to her dressing room or left at the general offices of the studio.

She is not to be coddled nor handled unnecessarily. The idea of the management being hands off. You must adore her from afar.

Threatening or addressing the baby star in loud or unseemingly language or using objectionable language in her presence shall be cause for instant dismissal.

Every person connected with this studio should feel moral obligation looking after the moral and physical welfare of Little Mary Sunshine and the Balboa management insists upon surrounding her with unexceptionable conditions.

By order of the President.
H. M. Horkheimer

When Baby Marie appeared on the cover of *Moving Picture Stories* (November 24, 1916), a weekly magazine devoted to photoplays and players, all the negative press seemed to have evaporated, leaving the distilled essence of what made her such a grand success around the world. The magazine had this to say about the famous star on the cover:

Helen Marie Osborne
(Our Wonderful Baby Star on the Cover)

LITTLE MARY SUNSHINE, the celebrated play by Dan F. Whitcomb, which is partly responsible for the world-wide movement to produce better pictures for children, was filmed by Balboa for the House of Pathé in 1915. Its success has been so unparalleled that Pathé has contracted with Balboa for six additional plays all to star the same baby artiste who gave the play "Little Mary Sunshine" such a tremendous vogue. This wonderful child is Helen Marie Osborne, and she lives at Long Beach, California, in the shadow of Balboa's studio, but throughout the Americas and even in England and war-torn Europe she is known as Little Mary Sunshine, and doubtless this charming sobriquet will stick to her through life. At Balboa studio she is known also as the "Baby Grand," and she is in truth a baby grand. The difference between Little Mary Sunshine and most other children in motion pictures is this: Other children come and go, appearing in a few scenes, being entirely incidental to the story, but the Balboa wonder-child actually takes the leading lady's part, carrying the story through five reels of film, with the action written around her and she being the star in fact and name. This baby star is only four and a half years old, and she is as much a baby now as the first day she stepped before a camera. There isn't anything stagey about her at all. Her director, Henry King, himself a moving picture headliner, sees to that. Mr. King is only in his twenties and yet he knows more about children than men with large families. Anyhow he knows more about Little Mary Sunshine. To see Mr. King at work with his protégée before the camera is a joy. What he seems to do is to get right into the scene with her and prevent her from acting. The minute a child begins to act she gets self-conscious and it's all off. Balboa's proudest laurel is the place unanimously awarded it as pioneer of the movement for better films for children, and that its standard is to be maintained is evidenced by the reports that the Little Mary Sunshine pictures soon to be released are equal to the ones that captured the hearts of the whole world.

TO ALL CONCERNED

Effective Upon Publication.

Rules to be observed in regard to Little Mary Sunshine.

While on the stage the child is not to be touched by anyone excepting her director, her attendant or those assisting the director or participating in the scenes in which she appears.

She is not to be teased at any time.

She is not to be shouted at nor addressed in slang.

She is not to be given sweet meats nor presents of any description while at work on the stage or on location. All presents must be sent to her dressing room or left at the general offices of the studio.

She is not to be coddled nor handled unnecessarily. The idea of the management being hands off. You must adore her from afar.

Threatening or addressing the baby star in loud or unseemingly language or using objectionable language in her presence shall be cause for instant dismissal.

Every person connected with this studio should feel a moral obligation in looking after the moral and physical welfare of Little Mary Sunshine and the Balboa management insists upon surrounding her with unexceptional conditions.

---

of the President.

Mandate to protect Baby Marie Osborne (courtesy of Marie Osborne-Yeats).

The Mystery Man, Director Extraordinaire

In Robert Giroux's story of William Desmond Taylor's yet unsolved murder, *A Deed of Death* (p. 78), there are ironically embedded some delightfully blissful impressions of the period. James Shelley Hamilton, an early film critic, may never have realized all the worries and details involved in the production and marketing of silent films. Giroux quotes him as saying: "…You can't imagine how different it was in those days. We all felt that a new era, and a marvelous art, had begun. No cost accounting, no efficiency experts, no ironclad schedules — all that came later." In another quotation, Charlie Chaplin expresses with equal innocence the joy of finding himself so young in the face of such unbelievably sweet success. "Each studio was like a family. It was 1914 and I was 25 years old, in the flush of youth and enamored of my work — not alone for the success of it, but for its enchantment." We must avoid, however, their mistake of idealizing any epoch that precedes the one in which we live, somehow imagining that all the people of that bygone era were more blessedly content and satisfied than we are1. Moviemaking appeals to us still today in part because of the illusions created on the screen; the magic lantern still has the power to transport us into fantastic kingdoms of the imagination, more beautiful than what many viewers must face in their daily lives outside the theatre. All movies have the power to render a more idealized world than the reality found at the very stages and backdrops where these beautiful films were produced. In the modern era, moving pictures remain the most innovative narrative form of all the performing arts and one of the greatest sources of affordable entertainment for people around the globe. We all rally around the screen, spellbound by the seductive and glorious illusions of master filmmakers.

In 1914, however, many people were disillusioned, as they are today and will be tomorrow, by the horrendous events in a turbulent world with an uncertain future. In 1914, drug addiction was at an all-time high, and Western society seemed to be tottering precariously toward an abyss. World War I does mark an extremely anxious period of transition for the West, with many lost souls unable to find peace and happiness because of the turmoil. In contrast, during the proud and positivist parade that preceded the Great War, Western faith in technological miracles marched headily towards a magnificent future, hand in hand with the shining beauties of progress and prosperity, the three invincible graces of the Belle Époque. Despite the high hopes of this technically advanced age, World War I produced a rude awakening, as even dream-makers in Hollywood understood the vulnerability of their own illusions on screen in the aftermath of the state-of-the-art warfare that had exploded to bits some of the oldest empires in the world, revealing the destructive and disturbing potential of mankind to commit ruthless acts of aggression.

The mystery man, William Desmond Taylor, wrote with romantic verve the following poem about the inescapable sorrow of his era, a poem about mankind's Sisyphus-like progress in which modern sailors of fortune found themselves paradoxically both degraded and ennobled by the apparent absurdity of human perseverance:

The Knowledge

Man — do you know, have you felt, and seen,
In the wastes of the earth have your footsteps been?
Have you tasted the salt, the deserts trod,

Forsaken all else, forgotten your God?
At the beck and call of a woman's nod,
Have you walked the paths that are mean?

Have you eaten the sweets and spat the gall,
Has your heart beat high at the wanderlust call,
Had rope in hand, or gun in fist,
Been cursed and loved and beaten and missed,
And slept where the wind your brow has kissed?
Have you fought with your back to the wall?

Even so, and from fate you never ran
Though held 'neath narrow society's ban,
Ne'er taken an innocent girl in tow,
Nor lied, nor struck a fallen foe —
Then you have felt and seen and know
And you'll die as you've lived, a man.

(Giroux, pp. 71–72)

William Desmond Taylor was the stage name of William Cunningham Deane-Tanner. The actor-director was born into an upper-middle-class Anglo-Irish family, for whom Taylor's choice of a career in the theatre was nothing less than a scandal. In part, Taylor's stage name was created to protect his family back in Great Britain, though Taylor himself had already been rejected by his father after a terrible quarrel when he was still a lad, before he began acting on the stage. The dispute between father and son was so serious that William's father at first kept him isolated on the family estate in a small shed and then sent his 19-year-old son to an American reform colony located in southwest Kansas for 18 months. The ranch in Kansas, which was especially established for the black sheep of well-to-do British families, was called Runnymede; it was founded by an Anglo-Irishman, Ned Turnley.

Once in the United States, Taylor decided to remain there and make a fresh start. He changed jobs frequently, working as a common laborer, a waiter, a restaurateur, a railroad hand, a gambler, an adventurer, a canvasser for magazine subscriptions, and finally as an actor on the stage and on the screen. William D. Taylor was universally appreciated wherever he worked for his qualities as a gentleman of breeding. He was manly, good-natured, well-mannered, and generous to a fault and was also learned, well-read in several languages, and able to speak fluently both French and German. Nonetheless, he also had a checkered and dark side that made him something of a puzzle to those closest to him. Once Taylor confided in H. M. Horkheimer about a tragically romantic episode in his past, disclosing that he had spent three years in prison over a matter of honor regarding a woman. This confession was later converted into a movie entitled *The Judge's Wife* that was produced by the Horkheimers and directed by William Desmond Taylor himself. *The Judge's Wife* was a three-reel drama by White Star, that was made for William Fox and was released October 12, 1914, by Box Office Attraction Co.

Robert Giroux explains in his book *A Deed of Death* that Taylor left Balboa, where he had begun his career as a film director, to work in Santa Barbara at the American Film Company, popularly called "The Flying 'A.'" There he took over as director for the ambitious serial entitled *The Diamond from the Sky*, a 60-reel, 30-episode extravaganza. Jacques Jaccard had been the intended director of this production until he received a better offer at Universal. This last-minute switch in directors gave Taylor the break that would launch his fame beyond the scope he had enjoyed at Balboa. In *The Diamond from the Sky*, one episode dealing with morphine addiction reflected Taylor's newly born crusade against the proliferation of drug rings in the movie industry. His crusade against drugs, beginning in 1915, would escalate once he decided to help Mabel Normand. He spent as much as $50,000 of his own personal wealth trying to rehabilitate Normand, one of the women he truly loved, who was also one of the sweetest and kindest stars of the silent era, but unfortunately an inveterate drug addict. During the Great War, drugs abounded among the wealthy elite of Hollywood, especially opium, morphine, cocaine, and heroin. Drug addiction was greater in the period 1914–1918 in the United States than in the 1950s. To King Vidor, Allan Dwan testified regarding Taylor's personal crusade against drugs:

> I do know that Taylor had a thing about the use of dope, and was very much against its use on the set. He actively tried to stop the drifters who used to come up from Los Angeles with cocaine and opium. There were as many dope dealers as there were prostitutes and, believe me, there was never a shortage of prostitutes. Taylor was known to throw a mean lecture on the evils of drugs to his company of actors. (Giroux, p. 90)

As Giroux explained in his book (p. 32–33), drug addiction in 1914 involved one out of every 400 citizens, while in 1957, only one out of every 3,500 was an addict. Some of the most famous addicts in Hollywood in the 1920s were Juanita Hansen, Barbara La Marr, Mabel Normand, Jack Pickford — brother of Mary Pickford, Wallace Reid, Alma Rubens, and Olive Thomas.

After decades of personal struggle to find his niche and a "family," the next seven years, 1915–1922, would be the most satisfying for Taylor because during this time he would shine as a noted director at Paramount. At the same time he was nobly trying to rescue the woman he loved, Mabel Normand. Jesse Lasky at Paramount, where Taylor would direct more than 40 movies, described Taylor as one of the few gentlemanly celebrities in movieland, the best example of "cultivated Hollywood." Taylor's popularity among his colleagues was reflected in his tenure as head of the Motion Picture Directors Association for five of the first seven years of the society. Taylor's domestic staff and some of his closest friends make one question, however; why would he surround himself with so many marginal types in movieland? For example, his former cook and secretary, Edward F. Sands, who had been recommended by Paramount studios, would one day forge Taylor's checks in excess of $5,000, and he stole Taylor's car, jewelry, and finest clothes while Taylor was on a trip to England in 1921. In addition, while trying to save Mabel Normand from her own drug dealers, Taylor was reported to have taken the law into his own hands by beating up traffickers more than once at Mabel's residence, confiscating their goods and their loot to save his beloved Mabel. Even at the time of Taylor's murder in 1922, his black valet and cook, Henry Peavey, was an exhibitionist homosexual, who was arrested for exposing himself at a local park. Of course, Taylor paid Peavey's $200 bail, and true to Taylor's loyal character, he had agreed to come to Peavey's defense in court on February 2, 1922, the very day Taylor's corpse was discovered. Although he was a learned gentleman with polished manners, Taylor had himself been a rebel and the black sheep of his proud, Anglo-Irish family. Many might even have called Taylor a drifter because he had run away from home, had been sent to a reform colony, had deserted his wife and daughter in New York, had prospected in Alaska and Canada, had held various odd jobs, including menial labor, and had changed names and identities more than once, before giving his all to the directing career and those whom he considered part of his extended family in Hollywood. Rather than chastise Taylor for being morally deficient, it seems more appropriate to describe him as those who loved him did, as a prodigal son who was unusually understanding, patient, and generous at the apex of his success. Most appropriately, Taylor's favorite motto suited his noble character: "The only things we really keep are the things we give away" (Giroux, p. 101).

Taylor's friend William Russell had worked with Taylor in several episodes of *The Diamond in the Sky*. After the murder, Russell defended Taylor's character, though many newspapers claimed the murdered director was an evil Don Juan who might even have deserved the bullet in the back that ended his life:

> If women were infatuated with him, it was only natural. His manner, his very aloofness, attracted them, and if they wrote him wild love notes [a reference to Mary Miles Minter], was he to blame? If he gave women money, it was because in the generosity of his big heart he wanted to help them, wanted to keep them from the necessity of asking other men for it. If Taylor sometimes associated with people who were not altogether what they should be morally, it was because he had faith that in every human being there is a spark of divinity. He not only tried but often succeeded in assisting many to rise above the lesser things of earth. (Giroux, p. 92)

What makes Taylor so remarkable may have more to do with his complex and tragic persona. Robert Giroux finds Taylor's greatness more in the duplicity of his rebellious and gentlemanly persona than in the creativity of his directorial achievements:

> Taylor, as a movie director, was a professional, a workmanlike and reliable craftsman who got the job done while keeping disruptive problems to a minimum — the

kind of director most producers would prefer. Assuming he had the capacity to break out of the conventional mold, he either never had the opportunity to do so or chose not to. In the history of films, as in other arts, there have been only a few persons one would call great — from pioneers like Méliès, Griffith, and Chaplin to Kurosawa, Bergman, Orson Welles, and John Huston in more recent times. They usually, though not always, succeeded in doing what they (rather than some backer) wanted. William Desmond Taylor is an interesting figure for many reasons, but not for unusual creative qualities as a director. (Giroux, p. 111)

William Desmond Taylor was born in Cork, Ireland, April 26, 1872, the second of four children, in a family of distinguished achievers — architects, doctors, government officials, military officers. William's father was an officer in the British army and was reportedly very tough on William, though the exact reason for the rupture between the two remains uncertain. Giroux suspects that William may have had a row with his father over William's involvement with women, while William himself covers this matter up by explaining that by failing an eye test, he was prevented from pursuing an honorable career in the British army, implying that his lack of a military career might have upset his family. Problems with his lady friends seem the more likely point of dispute between young William and his father, however, because William later confessed to H. M. at Balboa that he had spent three years in prison for the honor of a woman. According to Giroux, William D. Taylor drew an enhanced picture for the press about his education to fit his background, claiming to have had a formal British education at Clifton College in England, where he supposedly succeeded as a scholar and an athlete, but evidence shows it was his younger brother Denis who attended Clifton College, not William. For all of William's polish and knowledge, he was, like H. M. Horkheimer and Jack London, a self-taught graduate from the school of hard knocks. Taylor probably also profited from private tutors as a child, while his linguistic skills may have been developed not only from voracious readings in foreign languages, but also from his sojourns in both Germany and France.

While Taylor's comportment and learning reflected his gentlemanly, Anglo-Irish background, his eventual Americanization was evidenced at its best by his democratic and friendly demeanor, even toward strangers. These American qualities were saluted ten days after Taylor's murder in a February 12, 1922, *Daily Telegram* (B4:2) article entitled "Taylor Was Director at Old Balboa Studio, Photographer Tells." The photographer, William Wilson, who had taken a number of stills for Taylor's films produced at Balboa, recalled: "He was a fellow one would remember because he was democratic and friendly. He asked me at length about my experience, and manifested an active interest in my work. Taylor was very much a gentleman, and his unselfish interest in others gave me a favorable opinion of him."

When this article appeared, Taylor's name was still inscribed over the door to one of the rooms at Balboa, seven years after his departure from Long Beach, and another room at the old Balboa Studios bore above its portico the name "Fatty Arbuckle," despite the scandal that ensued. This practice of inscribing celebrity names over the entrance of different studio rooms was another example of the Horkheimers' manner of recording the studio's history in its architecture, paying tribute to their stars, a sign of the brothers' appreciation for those who helped build Balboa into such a prosperous enterprise during its meteoric rise to fame.

Nonetheless, there is the disturbing side to William Desmond Taylor, for example, the abandonment of his wife and daughter. Does amnesia justify this criminal lack of commitment on Taylor's part to his wife and child, and can one approve of Taylor's unwillingness to seek reconciliation with the family he abandoned? Taylor's wife was the one who chose closure after years of neglect, deciding to divorce Taylor. Was Taylor's reported generosity then merely a selfish and irresponsible impulse to mask his darker nature, contrary to what his friends claimed? For artists, amnesia would be debilitating to their creativity. We will never know if Taylor really suffered amnesia or whether he chose to forget what he could not face. Was he a master director or a master actor, or both, on and off the stage? To call a film director, or any artist, amnesiac seems a contradiction in terms. Who will say the lines if they are forgotten? According to the ancient Greeks, the nine Muses of the liberal arts, sister goddesses who guided artists during their artistic masterpieces, all had the same mother, Mnemosyne, the personification of memory. In identifying memory as the mother of the fine arts, the Greeks implied that artists necessarily rely on their memory to create, that is to say, artists use their memory to restage, reinterpret, and represent life's raw experiences, transforming them through the clearinghouse of reflection, a retrieval process whereby remembrances become essential to the development of artistic expressions. In twentieth-century literature, this retrieval and representation of remembrances reflects the major impetus of writers like Marcel Proust and James Joyce. Then again, in the literary works of Samuel Beckett, confused remembrances offer an ironic twist to the narrative voice, where lack of clear recollection baffles both the narrator and the reader because the narrator has no steady recall, with no clear focus to the telling of the tale.

Robert Giroux seems to invite a modern dramaturge to pick up the pieces of evidence recorded about Taylor's murder, to write a scenario that makes sense of Taylor's mysterious death. The authors of the present work have answered the invitation with the scenario that follows. In modern Greece, the artist might simply call Lieutenant Columbo to the rescue, but literary tradition would invoke to help the detective the sister goddesses, those cunning daughters of Mnemosyne. The Muses will help unravel the secrets of Taylor's murder. Which of the nine sisters will best resolve the baffling murder case — Clio, Euterpe, Thalia, Melpomene, Terpsichore, Erato, Plymnia, Urania, or Calliope? Three will do — Calliope, the chief Muse who knows how to use her beautiful voice to keep the audience spellbound; Clio, who proclaims in historical terms Taylor's demise; finally, Erato, whose love poetry suits the romantic nature of Taylor's tragic life and death.

Rouge on the Pane:
The Last Good-bye

Supervisors

CALLIOPE   The Chief Muse
CLIO   The Proclaiming Muse Who Renders Historical the *Deed of Death*
ERATO   The Muse Whose Poetry Pays Homage to the Director's Love Life

Scenario

Based on Mabel Normand's statement in the *Deed of Death* (pp. 25–30) by Robert Giroux

Cast

William Desmond Taylor (*Director Extraordinaire*), Mabel Normand (*Taylor's loved one*), Henry Peavey (*Taylor's black valet and cook*), Grant Floyd Hartley (*service station owner*), L. A. Grant (*service station helper*), Christine Jewett (*a neighbor's maid*), Faith MacLean (*Taylor's neighbor*), Howard Fellows (*Taylor's chauffeur*), Edna Purviance (*actress, Taylor's neighbor*), Mr. X (*Taylor's murderer*).

Sets—Exterior

Alvarado Court bungalow, residence of William Desmond Taylor, corner of Maryland Street and Alvarado Street
Mabel Normand's car on Alvarado
The bungalow courtyard

Sets—Interior

Taylor's rooms, upstairs and downstairs

FADE IN *(February 1, 1922)* Exterior: Alvarado Court bungalow, residence of William Desmond Taylor, corner of Maryland Street and Alvarado Street

1   EXT. VIEW, COLD CONDITIONS —   1
    EARLY EVENING

6:00 P.M.—At the Hartley Service Station, on the corner of Sixth and South Alvarado, Mr. X talks to Grant Floyd Hartley and his helper, L. A. Grant. The stranger asks them where Taylor lives, and they point the way. Later, they will describe the stranger to reporters as a man around 26 or 27 years, about 165 lbs., with dark hair, wearing a dark suit. No policeman will ever question Hartley and Grant about what they saw that night.

2   EXT. VIEW, COLD CONDITIONS—   2
         EARLY EVENING

7:00 P.M.—On Alvarado Street, Mabel's chauffeur parks her car. Mabel walks toward Taylor's bungalow. Taylor rarely ever locked his front door, even at night. Mabel rings the bell, and Henry Peavey comes to the door. Taylor is inside talking on the telephone. Taylor speaks to two different people that evening around the same time, first, to a friend, Antonio Moreno, an actor asking advice; and the second call is to Taylor's financial adviser. Mabel insists on waiting outdoors until Taylor finishes his second call. Peavey tells Taylor that Mabel is waiting, so Taylor concludes his call to his financial adviser, Marjorie Berger, going to the door with a smile, holding out both hands.

TAYLOR

Hello, Mabel darling; I know what you've come for—the two books.

MABEL

Righto, my bright duck, and I've brought you a present. Guess what it is.

Mabel holds a bag of peanuts behind her back, keeping it out of view.

TAYLOR

No man could possibly guess what you'd buy, but I'll bet it's something nice. Come on in and have some dinner. I'm finishing, but Peavey can fix you something.

MABEL

No, Mamie's going to feed me in bed tonight. I'm working on location tomorrow and have to retire early.

FADE OUT

FADE IN *(February 1, 1922)* Interior: Alvarado Court bungalow, residence of William Desmond Taylor, corner of Maryland Street and Alvarado Street

1   INT. VIEW, TWO-ROOMS   1
       DOWNSTAIRS—EARLY EVENING

7:05 P.M.—Mabel has entered Taylor's bungalow and can see through the arch separating the two rooms downstairs, the table covered with dishes.

MABEL

Why don't you finish your dinner?

TAYLOR

I don't want dessert, but you'll have a cocktail with me, won't you?

MABEL

Sure, and I've got just the thing for your dessert, Bill, a bag of peanuts.

Taylor laughs, placing the bag on top of the piano. The bag, still full, will be found by the police at the same spot the next morning. Taylor calls out to Peavey asking him to prepare two cocktails, sits in front of his desk, covered with cancelled checks in preparation for his income tax report, due in that era on March 15. Taylor points to some checks forged by Edward Sands. Taylor picks one up and compares it to one he signed himself.

TAYLOR

Who could tell the difference?

MABEL

It's a perfect match. What do you plan to do about Sands?

TAYLOR

What on earth can I do? He's been missing since my return. I'm afraid I'll never get it straightened out.

7:15 P.M.—Christine Jewett, a neighbor's maid, hears Mr. X in alleyway. Henry Peavey, in a white coat, sporting his spotless butler attire, brings the cocktails, despite the U.S. Prohibition then in full force. Mabel and William are served the latest alcoholic postwar rage, Orange Blossoms (gin and orange juice). Peavey places the tray, tall cocktail shaker, and glasses on the table where they will be found the next morning by the police after the murder. Taylor encourages Peavey to head home.

TAYLOR

You may go after you clear the dinner dishes.

Peavey hastens to complete his work in the kitchen, climbs the stairs hurriedly to change clothes upstairs, coming down dressed like a neon dandy: green golf stockings, yellow plus fours, and a purple tie. 7:20 P.M.—Peavey leaves. After Peavey shuts the door, Mabel smiles and comments to Taylor about Peavey's attire, referring to his recent arrest for indecent exposure at West Lake Park.

MABEL

If you'd let him play golf more often, he wouldn't get in any more trouble at the park.

Taylor returns the smile, stands up, and moves toward the shelves to remove some books. Recently purchased for Mabel, the books are still covered in paper. Unwrapping them, Taylor sits next to Mabel, placing the books on the table in front of them:

TAYLOR

Rosa Mundi by Ethel M. Dell. This novel could be nicely adapted for one of your movies. And here's a mind-tingler about Nietzsche. Mabel, darling, I hope you're making progress with your French. Don't forget your French-Canadian heritage, and remember French writers offer a treasure trove worth exploring, better yet in the original.

The two friends sit close to each other turning the pages, chatting distractedly and lovingly about publications. Mabel blurts out, during their chatting, to show off her knowledge about *Three Soldiers*:

MABEL

It's by that Chicago newspaperman, John Dos Passos.

TAYLOR

Right you are. Say, your new film, *Susanna*, you're pleased with production?

MABEL

So far so good. Going on location early tomorrow. Bill, what about your *Green Temptation*?

TAYLOR

Do I look green? Really... directing has given me a wonderful life. But let's not talk shop. Let's go see the Harold Lloyd film this week and have dinner together. Lloyd makes us laugh so, and these tax papers are driving me mad.

MABEL

Yes, Lloyd makes great company, but I have to get going now. My car is waiting. On location early tomorrow. Don't get angry, Bill, but Nietzsche never makes me even smile. But since you insist...

TAYLOR

Let me call you later.

MABEL

Please don't make it a late call. Mamie will not disturb me after I've gone to bed.

TAYLOR

I'll call you at 9:00.

FADE OUT

FADE IN *(February 1, 1922)* Exterior: Alvarado Court bungalow, residence of William Desmond Taylor, moving toward Alvarado Street.

1   EXT. VIEW, COLD CONDITIONS—   1
    EARLY EVENING

Mabel Normand

7:45 P.M.—Taylor helps Mabel into her car before it drives away. Mabel peers back longingly as the two blow kisses to each other, until it's impossible to see each other. Mabel even presses her lips against the window pane to deliver the final kiss, leaving lip rouge that will be found on the glass by detectives after the murder. It is their last good-bye. Bill and Mabel will never again be able to exchange gestures of affection.

7:58 P.M.—Taylor's neighbors, the MacLeans et al., hear a gunshot.

8:02 P.M.—Faith MacLean sees Mr. X leaving Taylor's home. With the smoking gun in his pocket, he exits Taylor's apartment to face Faith MacLean at her door, straight in front of him. With aplomb, Mr. X casually returns to Taylor's door, making it seem he had forgotten something there. Mrs. MacLean assumed she had only heard a car backfiring.

7:40 P.M.—Taylor escorts Mabel to her car. Taylor laughs upon seeing the peanut shells Mabel's chauffeur had swept out of the car. Taylor also spies a copy of *Police Gazette* inside the car where Mabel had juxtaposed Freud's *Interpretation of Dreams*.

TAYLOR

Who else in this world could straddle two such extremes? Mabel, my darling, I'm afraid you're hopeless! Sometimes I wonder what's to become of you, my dear. Oh Mabel, what a lovely thing it would be if perfect love and trust could come into your strange life.

Taylor looks at Mabel and shakes his head, for he loves Mabel. Mabel tugs Bill's ear lobe, saying:

MABEL

Don't be silly, Bill. You don't believe it, but I bought that *Police Gazette* for the cover girl's pose.

William Desmond Taylor

8:04 P.M.—Mr. X goes through the alley before boarding the trolley.

8:15 P.M.—Taylor's chauffeur, Howard Fellows, rings the bell at Taylor's home—no response.

(February 2, 1922) Midnight—Taylor's neighbor, Edna Purviance, notices lights still on in Taylor's apartment.

7:30 A.M.—Peavey discovers Taylor's corpse.

FADE OUT

Robert Giroux presents ten names of people who were considered in 1922 as possible suspects in the murder, eliminating all but one, Mr. X, as he goes over their possible motives: Mrs. Charlotte Shelby, Julia Crawford Ivers, Mary Miles Minter, Mabel Normand, Ms. X, Edward Sands, Denis Deane-Tanner, Henry Peavey, Mack Sennett, and finally, Mr. X. According to Giroux's careful weighing of evidence, none of these suspects pans out, save Mr. X, a hired gunman. Hollywood in 1922 was trying to clean up its image and to avoid scandal at all costs. Although there were sex and dope scandals, the public had no idea of the extent of drug trafficking in movieland. Journalists also jumped at the opportunity to make a wicked Don Juan out of Taylor, highlighting his popularity with women, especially younger women half his age. Diverting attention away from the drug scandals in Hollywood pleased the studios that wanted to keep their public image in good standing, while newspapers sold bundles of sordid articles defiling Taylor's image. It was better for everyone in power to cover up any and all indications of drug rings and assassins in Hollywood. Such a revelation clearly wouldn't have helped the movie business.

Strongly suggesting a cover-up, Giroux describes the odd omission of key witnesses at the inquest and its brevity:

> The coroner's inquest was convened at the Ivy Overholtzer mortuary at 10:00 a.m. on a rainy Saturday morning, February 4, 1922, three days after the murder. It was unusual in at least two respects: for brevity—it lasted less than an hour, as compared with the inquest for the Fatty Arbuckle case, which took seven hours—and for the fact that Coroner Frank A. Nance asked only five people to testify, when thirteen people had been served with subpoenas. Oddest of all was the fact that Faith MacLean, sitting in the room, was not put on the stand. (Giroux, p. 162)

By 1930, William C. Doran, the deputy in 1922 to the district attorney during the murder case, considered three probable motives: "(1) a crime committed by a dope ring; (2) love and jealousy; and (3) revenge" (Giroux, p. 232). Of these three motives, Giroux notes that a dope ring was never mentioned during the inquest. Giroux also argues that the nonchalance of Mr. X, witnessed by four men and two women, denotes the uninvolved professional style of a paid assassin. Seventy-five years later, it is unlikely that the murderer still lives, nor is it likely that his identity will ever be known. Hollywood survived the scandal by hiding the truth, while national newspapers had a field day destroying Taylor's reputation. Taylor was maligned by most reporters covering the murder, but he was missed by his loyal friends and devoted lovers. Taylor's death was an extraordinary exit for an extraordinary master of theatrical illusions.

Reel 4

Major Stars and Their Box Office Hits

In the movie journal *Classic Images*, Billy H. Doyle remarks in his article "Lost Players" that among the illustrious actors in 1914 listed in the "Who's Who in the Film World," many were key Balboans, including Bertram Bracken, Charles Dudley, Henry King, Mollie McConnell, Jackie Saunders, Henry Stanley, Gypsy Abbott, and Fred J. Whitman. Doyle laments that only Henry King is remembered among moviegoers today, primarily because of King's long and stellar preeminence in Hollywood, though all the others in the above list were also prominent stars in 1914, known nationally and internationally, along with the Balboa Feature Film brand. Moreover, some Balboans even married each other, while on contract at the Long Beach studios or sometime before or after joining Balboa. Roscoe Arbuckle married Minta Durfee on stage in Long Beach; Henry King married his fellow Balboan, Gypsy Abbott; the Balboan Dorothy Davenport became the wife of screen idol Wallace Reid; and after leaving Balboa, Lewis Cody would hitch up on a whim in a platonic and unusual marital alliance with one of the silent era's most famous comediennes, Mabel Normand. Of course, finally, there was the stellar attraction at Balboa that led to matrimony between one of the studio's chiefs, Elwood D. Horkheimer, and Jackie Saunders, the studio's major star.

Of the myriad Balboans who made a splash on the silent screen, we have chosen but a select few to cover in this reel, including the following celebrities: Henry King, Jackie Saunders, Ruth Roland, Daniel Gilfether, Mollie McConnell, Roscoe "Fatty" Arbuckle, and Baby Marie Osborne. They represent a slice of the varied personalities and talents that contributed to the success story that became the legacy of Balboa during its meteoric rise to fame.

Several Balboans enjoyed successful careers for years before joining Balboa, while many others learned the ropes of filmdom in Long Beach. For instance, among the most illustrious Balboans, Bertram Bracken started humbly enough as a bank clerk in Texas and a member of the 15th U.S. Cavalry prior to beginning his theatrical career in 1898 at the Hay Market Theatre in Chicago doing juvenile roles. Doyle explains that Bracken wrote and produced *College Life* and toured the United States with his own company before he entered films in

1910, joining the French interest, Star Film in the United States, doing heavy roles under the direction of Gaston Méliès. Bracken then toured the world as managing producer for Star Film, traveling to the South Seas, Australia, and Asia. When he returned from the Orient, he joined the Western Lubin Company as director before joining Balboa as a seasoned actor and director. Charles Dudley had 12 years of stage experience in musical comedy, comic opera, and grand opera before making his film début with the Universal Film Company; he also appeared for Monopol and Keystone before joining Balboa in 1913. On the other hand, Henry Stanley's career at Balboa, 1914–1916, is less clearly traceable. Educated in both England and France, Henry Stanley first appeared on stage at the early age of 14 years, in comic opera, stock, and vaudeville, before joining Méliès' Star Film in New York. Henry King's first wife, Gypsy Abbott, made her film start for the St. Elmo company after an extensive career in vaudeville touring the United States; she joined Balboa in 1914, where she married Henry King. The last actor listed for 1914 in "Who's Who in the Film World," Fred J. Whitman, began his stage career in 1904 doing stock productions in both the South and the Midwest, prior to joining Balboa in November 1913.

The list of celebrated Balboans could be an endless one of impressive curricula vitæ on stage and on screen. As early as 1915, *Moving Picture World* listed Balboa's stunning roll of players: Lillian Lorraine, Ruth Roland, William Courtleigh, Jr., Mollie McConnell, Daniel Gilfether, Madeleine Pardee, Frank Mayo, Andrew Arbuckle, Joyce Moore, Victory Bateman, Lucy Blake, Ethel Fleming, Paul Gilmore, Charles Dudley, Corinne Grant, Henry Stanley, Fred Whitman, Lillian West, Edwin J. Brady, Jack Livingstone, Ruth Lackaye, Philo McCullough, Marguerite Nichols, Richard Johnson, R. Henry Grey, Frank Erlanger, William Conklin, Bert Francis, Robert Gray, Gordon Sackville, Jackie Saunders, Mae Sterling, Lewis Cody, William Lampe, Dixie Jarrel, Florence Hansen, Edith Reeves, Gladys Webber, William Reed, Phyllis Gray, and Bruce Smith.

Before centering special attention in this reel on the seven major Balboans — Henry King, Jackie Saunders, Ruth Roland, Daniel Gilfether, Mollie McConnell, Roscoe "Fatty" Arbuckle, and Baby Marie Osborne — let's first take a glimpse at what the *San Francisco Rounder* (*Press Clippings*, vol. 1, p. 34) printed about both the established and the emerging figures at Balboa as early as 1914:

Clara Beyers, well known on the legitimate stage, has joined the Balboa company and will be seen in all future releases. Miss Beyers is making her debut in the silent drama after nine years' successful work in well known stock companies in Philadelphia, Omaha, San Francisco and Vancouver. Miss Beyers is a striking brunette of a type that assures her success in the photoplay world. In addition to being a clever actress Miss Beyers is an all around athletic girl, which will be valuable in pictures where accomplished swimming and riding is required.

Henry W. Otto, for a number of years feature player and producer for the Selig company, has joined the Balboa company and will start shortly with an all star company to produce two and three reel feature films. The addition of Mr. Otto to the Balboa company is another step forward in making the Balboa company one of the best known in this country.

Miss Belle Bennett, leading woman of the Balboa company, recently proved her ability to master any role assigned to her. The picture she was playing in required the difficult role of a Japanese maiden. Miss Bennett informed Director Bracken she would be able to play the part. A few minutes later Miss Bennett appeared from her dressing room, looking all the world like a Japanese lady, with proper obi, kimono and shoes. The makeup was so natural that a number of her fellow workers could hardly believe it was the clever star. Miss Bennett will play all the leads in the coming Balboa feature films under the direction of Mr. Bracken.

Miss Nina Deal, who was associated with the Pathé Western company for some time, is now with the Balboa company. Miss Deal has a great future in pictures if her past work can be taken as a criterion. Miss

Deal is a petite blonde, well suited for ingenue parts.

Miss Harriet Jansen has returned to the Balboa company and is at present playing minor parts. Miss Jansen has had some experience on the legitimate stage, but is almost a newcomer in pictures. In a recent Balboa picture, "The Rise of the Sunset," Miss Jansen played the ingenue part in a finished manner, which brought forth much deserved praise from the reviewers.

Raymond Gallagher, juvenile of the Balboa company, is about to become a motorist. Ray has to be in Los Angeles every evening and does not like the long trip in the Pacific Electric automobiles; therefore the determination to own his own. When the happy event is over Ray will probably reside in Long Beach, as the rest of the Balboa players are doing. Ray is doing clever work with the company under Director Bracken.

R. Henry Grey, Balboa company, candidate for honors as the "handsomest man in motion pictures," has already started an active campaign among his friends in the various studios. Bob's long list of admirers in all parts of the world are also going to be asked to vote.

Miss Madeline Lenard is busy on a new book, "Friends I Have Known and Liked." Miss Lenard, in addition to being one of the Balboa stars, is also a clever writer. Her ability to write has probably been inherited from her illustrious ancestor, Noah Webster. Miss Lenard's new book is being anxiously watched for by her friends, who are legion.

Clifford Howard, the well known author and magazine writer, who is scenario editor of the Balboa company, is one of the busiest men in Filmdom today. Mr. Howard reads on an average fifty scenarios a day from photoplaywrights all over the world. To impartially decide on the merits of a screen story takes a great deal of work and time. Mr. Howard, in his spare moments, outlines his own stories for the future Balboa features.

A few of the élite group of seven stars featured in the following pages were mentioned in the article just quoted, but we didn't include them in the above entries because we shall describe them at greater length in this next section. While the careers of some of these famous stars extended years beyond their important contributions to the Long Beach studios, we have chosen to discuss principally their fame and tenure at Balboa. Most appropriately, we shall begin with the most prominent Balboan, the great actor-director who would become the most celebrated and the long-lived Hollywood celebrity connected with the Balboa Amusement Producing Company — Henry King.

Henry King

Henry King, one of the best assets at Balboa, became one of the biggest success stories in Hollywood. From humble beginnings, he reached the top of the ladder. Born on a farm near Christianburg, Virginia, on January 24, 1888, Henry King lived a long life of 94 years, dying a world-class celebrity on June 29, 1982. As a young boy, Henry King attended public schools, dreaming of the stage. Against his family's wishes, his earliest ambition was to become an actor, but the handsome, fair-haired, six-foot thespian would eventually find his niche in directing, a little disappointed at first to step permanently to the opposite side of the lens.

At the age of 15, King quit school to work in the machine shops of the Norfolk and Western Railroad, through an offer made by an older brother. He was soon bored with the railroad, however, and joined a road show for $15 a week, doing juvenile parts for one year. According to an interview in the *Movie Pictorial*, June 27, 1914, Henry King received good training touring the South with the Arnold Stock Company during which time he learned to sing and dance, performing in both musical comedies and plays (*Press Clippings*, vol. 1, p. 103). He devoted himself to the theatrical profession against the wishes of his family, who wanted him to become a Methodist minister. Only Henry's mother supported his idea of a career in the theatre. During the season following his tour with the Arnold Stock Company, Henry did not have a promising theatrical tour; he worked for as many as 11 companies during a nine-month period. In the same press clipping, it is noted that Henry King was only 19 years old when he commenced a Shakespearean repertoire with Anna Boyle Moore, followed by a trip to New York, where he secured the part of Jefferson Ryder in *The Lion and the Mouse*, under the management of Henry B. Harris. Other performances for King included *The Devil*, *Graustark*, *The Common Law*, and *The House of a Thousand Candles*.

Despite these successes on stage, a friend, Wilbur Melville, persuaded Henry King to switch to movies. They both went to Los Angeles. King first acted in movies for the Lubin Company in 1913, before both he and Bertram Bracken left Lubin to work at the Balboa Amusement Producing Company in Long Beach. At Lubin, King was receiving $35 per week, while Balboa won him over with $75 per week. With his acting talent and manly good looks, King had begun acquiring roles as a romantic lead. It was at Balboa, however, that he started to show promise as a director, and he eventually began to write and direct films for Balboa.

At Balboa, King established a reputation for being totally dedicated to his work. In later years, King would tend to belittle the Balboa studio, perhaps because he believed he had not been appreciated there or he was confused about the facts during his tenure at Balboa from 1913 to 1918. In the following quotation, however, which was taken from the *Movie Pictorial* interview, King's tone is one of genuine gratitude and praise for the opportunities given to him by the Horkheimers:

> Perhaps I shouldn't be quite so devoted to the work, if I hadn't been with the Horkheimers almost from the start. But after being here with them through the struggle, I feel so much a part of it all that I'd hate to give it up.
>
> Then too, if you're on the road for ten months with a show, or in New York, why when the season's over, it's over. That's all. No one feels any sentimental regret over it. But, after ten months in California, working all day in the same studio with the same people, going home to dinner every night down the same street, to your own bungalow ... well, if you ask me whether I'll stay

Henry King.

in the movies, my answer now and always, will be the same: You bet I will!

In 1915, King married Gypsy Abbott, who also performed in a few pictures at Balboa until she quit acting to become a full-time mother and wife in 1917. Also in 1915, Henry King directed and wrote an episode of *Who Pays?* starring Ruth Roland. In the book *Henry King, Director* (Frank Thompson, ed., pp. 17–18), the former Balboa star spoke during an interview about his start as a director in Long Beach: "Although I was hired at Balboa as an actor, I wanted to branch out to other things. I wrote one original story, *The Brand of Man* (1915) and got $75.00 for it. It was one of the first five-reel pictures. I also wrote a chapter of the serial *Who Pays?* (1915) from something I saw when I was fifteen years old in Abingdon, Virginia."

After his earliest directing experience, King's career really took off when he began directing and starring with Baby Marie Osborne in the "Little Mary Sunshine" series for Pathé, beginning in March 1916. A reviewer for the *New York Dramatic Mirror* said, "Handling of the 'little things,' the 'tremendous trifles' in direction of this feature shows him to

Joy and the Dragon (1916). Henry King, Baby Marie Osborne, and cameraman Georges Rizard (courtesy of Marie Osborne-Yeats).

be an artist of depth and certainty." The series was a box-office hit and a critical one as well, enabling King to direct at least five more movies in the series for Balboa, such as *Joy and the Dragon, Shadows and Sunshine,* and *Sunshine and Gold.*

In *Henry King, Director,* the famous Balboan recalls asking Dan Whitcomb, a writer on the old *Los Angeles Herald Express* and a scenarist for Balboa, to do a story for Baby Marie Osborne and King together. When Whitcomb asked King what kind of story he had in mind, King replied: "I have no idea. But I'm just getting tired of changing leading ladies on every story." When King took the idea to the Horkheimers, Elwood did not yet have a child of his own and didn't think the public would accept a juvenile leading lady in a full-length feature movie, while H. M., who had a child already, thought Henry King should give the idea a go. *Little Mary Sunshine* became a smash hit, and as King noted in an interview, "It also was the first full-length picture that I ever directed" (*Henry King, Director,* p. 23).

In an article entitled "Youngest Leading Lady" appearing in the *London Film Censor* on November 10, 1915, Henry King offered many kind remarks about the young starlet, Marie Osborn(e): "Miss Osborn doesn't require as much rehearsing as the average adult. I tell her once what I want and she does it. The child is a marvel. Many children have played prominent parts in silent dramas. But Helen Marie Osborn has the distinction of doing the first real lead" (Mary Osborne-Yeats' scrapbook). King had one last remark in the same article that still captures Marie Osborne's spunky vigor today. When King was asked if the child star had a hobby, he replied: "Oh, yes! Automobiles. Anything on wheels that goes will win her. The faster, the better!"

With the worldwide hit of the "Little Mary Sunshine" series, Henry King reiterated his gratitude toward the Horkheimers. In an article entitled "The Actor-Director's Viewpoint" that appeared in *Motography*, December 4, 1915, Henry King presented a very different image of Balboa than he did in his interviews given in his senior years, when he had apparently forgotten the advantages of having worked for the once-prestigious Long Beach film plant, where he enjoyed the special camaraderie that allowed for artistic freedom and professional cooperation:

> The standing I have achieved in pictures as an actor and a director I owe almost entirely to the Horkheimer brothers and the opportunities they have given. Before coming to Balboa, I had one other studio engagement. I stuck to my present employers through the dark days, when I had various offers to go elsewhere. At the time,

Henry King with Baby Marie in his arms, in front of a crowd of children at Balboa Studios.

H. M. Horkheimer said that I would never be sorry and I am not. He has made good every promise and done even more. Today Balboa is among the largest independent producing concerns in the world and I am proud to be identified with it and to have played a modest part in its growth.

For a man to get results, he must be satisfied, happy in his affiliations. The conditions existing at the Long Beach studio I believe to be unique in the film world. It is more like one big family than anything else. Directors, actors and all other employees work harmoniously to the common end of producing good pictures for their employers. Unprejudiced observers tell us there is a steady improvement in our output. The increasing demand is further evidence.

In conclusion, as an actor-director I might say I am primarily interested in achieving as nearly a perfect picture as possible. Whenever I feel that I can interpret the part best, I play it; otherwise, someone else is cast for it. At times, I write my own stories and do them. I know what I want to get over and I am glad to say that I have the hearty co-operation of my assistants. They help me as much as I help them. The mind in front, so to speak, simply pulls the strings. The others respond according to their individuality and understanding [from Marie Osborne-Yeats' scrapbook].

King had an extraordinary eye for choosing telling details and for setting the scene with the viewer in mind. In *Henry King, Director*, King notes that he tried to shoot his silent films with as few titles as possible, believing that it was more important to show the story development than to have the audience read about it.

Sometime in 1918, Henry King left Balboa to work for the American Film Company, popularly known as the "Flying A"; he later worked as a director for United Artists, 20th–Century

"Peek-a-boo!" calls Mary Sunshine to Bob Daley, and has as much fun in rehearsals as if it wasn't work.

Fox, Metro-Goldwyn-Mayer, and Paramount. Some of King's most lavish productions were filmed during the Cinemascope era, in the 1950s. Back in 1919, before he had achieved true glory and job security, King had gone to the Thomas Ince Company, where he made a major hit with an army comedy called *23½ Hours Leave*. This production made a star out of Douglas MacLean, but the movie cost King his job because he went over budget. Ince was gone when King lost his job, but when he returned, he viewed the movie, finding it superb. Ince then fired the studio manager for having given King the boot.

A similar experience had happened earlier to King at Balboa. When offered a position at another studio, he went to Elwood Horkheimer and told him that he had been offered $500 a week to direct elsewhere. H. M. Horkheimer was out of town that fateful day, so Elwood, treasurer and secretary of Balboa, bluntly told King that the studio could not match such an offer. Thereafter King would recall Balboa with mixed feelings. Although he had launched his directing career there, he felt unappreciated when he did not receive a serious counteroffer, not even a hint from Elwood, to try to keep him at Balboa. King left Balboa to accept a higher salary, but he felt rejected by the Horkheimers and had a bitter taste in his mouth the rest of his life about the Long Beach studio. In fact, King later erroneously stated that Elwood had died during the 1920s, even though he actually lived until 1966. Obviously, the breach between the two men was a permanent one. Furthermore, though King found H. M. more "reasonable" and friendly than Elwood, most of King's recollections about H. M. portray the former Balboa mogul as being a penniless and pathetic loser after the closing of the Long Beach studios. It is unfortunate that the relationship between King and the Horkheimers was not better and did not last longer. When H. M. returned that fateful day from his business trip in New York, after Henry King had left Balboa, H. M. told Elwood that they had made a big mistake in letting King go, but it was too late to change the course of King's illustrious career.

In later years, King's success grew, as he scored high marks introducing innovative techniques to his movies. For example, to enliven fighting scenes on the screen, King used his own personal recollections as a boy in combat, incorporating these personal remembrances and angles in his movies. On the other hand, when soundtracks became part of movie

Who Pays? (1914–1915) Chapter 12, *Toil and Tyranny* (1915), starring Henry King, Daniel Gilfether, Edwin J. Brady, and Ruth Roland.

production in the late 1920s, King, along with other directors, felt frustrated during this transitional period with sound equipment. The directors dared not budge the microphones for fear of making horrendous interference; consequently they had to freeze much movement and action that had known no such technical barriers during the silent era. Soon enough, however, improved technology came to the rescue and freed the action once again.

King also discovered several prominent stars, including Ronald Coleman and Dean Stockwell. Among his other achievements in the business, Henry King was one of the founders of the Academy of Motion Pictures Arts and Sciences and the Directors Guild of America. Active all his life, Henry King was still logging around 12,000 miles a year in his airplane as late as 1978, at the age of 90, and he was at that time the oldest licensed pilot in the history of American aviation. In fact, King was the first to use airplanes to scout for film locations. It was the blend of his personal touch along with professional standards that generated Henry King's long-standing success. In an unidentified article in Marie Osborne's scrapbook there is a "Recipe for Movies" that expresses Henry King's flair for cooking up a movie and whetting the appetite of the public:

Director Henry King, who is producing the Little Mary Sunshine plays for Balboa, declares that when he first went into the game, moving pictures were made after the following formula:

Take one husky hero and one perfectly good villain or "heavy," mix them up thoroughly, hero on top. Add hatred and introduce gently one heroine with curls. Stir them all together, add the villain's gang and let it soak the hero and put him in a cool or hot place to simmer. Take one "longarm of co-incidence," one dispensation of Providence, and two parts of luck, scramble them and let the whole batch ferment. Presently the hero will "raise," surround the heroine and the villain will "fall" and boil over into the fire. Add one stage robbery, one sheriff, one bar-room ruction, three lies, a little horseback riding, two teaspoonfuls of tears, kisses to taste and a hungry looking Indian.

A Partial List of King's Films at Balboa

Abide With Me. One-reel drama. Pathé Frères. Released Mar. 11, 1914, by General Film Co.

The Brand of Man. Balboa Amusement Producing Co. Released in 1915 by Pathé Frères.

By Impulse. One-reel drama. Pathé Frères. Released Nov. 19, 1913, by General Film Co.

Called Back. Balboa Amusement Producing Co. Released May 1914.

The Climber. Four-reel drama. Falcon Features. Released Sept. 1917 by General Film Co.

The Crooked Road. Balboa Amusement Producing Co., a Fortune Photoplay. Released in 1917.

Faith's Reward. Balboa Amusement Producing Co. Released 1916 by Pathé Exchange, Inc.

The Imprint. One-reel drama. White Star. Released Nov. 13, 1913, by Box Office Attraction Co., made for William Fox.

Joy and the Dragon. Five-reel drama. Balboa Amusement Producing Co. Released Dec. 31, 1916, by Pathé Exchange, Inc.

Letters Entangled. Balboa Amusement Producing Co. Released in 1915 by Pathé Frères.

Little Mary Sunshine. Five-reel drama. Balboa Feature Film Co. Released Mar. 3, 1916, by Pathé Exchange, Inc., Gold Rooster Plays.

A Little Ray of Sunshine. Pathé Exchange, Inc. Balboa Feature Film Co. Released by Pathé Exchange, Inc.; Gold Rooster Plays.

The Locked Heart. Probably Balboa Amusement Producing Co. Released July 20, 1918, by American Film Co., Oakdale Productions/General Film Co.

The Mainspring. Four-reel Western. Falcon Features. Released Aug. 17, 1917, by General Film Co.

The Mask. Two-reel drama. White Star. Released Nov. 3, 1914, by Box Office Attraction Co., made for William Fox.

The Moth and the Flame. Two-reel drama. Pathé Frères. Released Dec. 27, 1913, by General Film Co.

Nerve. One reel. Balboa Amusement Producing Co. Released by Box Office Attraction Co., made for William Fox.

No Children Wanted. Probably Balboa Amusement Producing Co. Released in 1918 by Oakdale Productions/General Film Co.

Oath of Hate. Knickerbocker Star Features. Released in 1916.

Pay Dirt. Five-reel drama. Knickerbocker Star Features. Released June 18, 1916, by General Film Co.

The Power of Evil. Five-reel drama. Balboa Amusement Producing Co. Released Oct. 1, 1916, by B. S. Moss Motion Picture Corp., made for B. S. Moss Motion Picture Corp.

The Power of Print. Two-reel drama. Pathé Frères. Released Jan. 29, 1914, by General Film Co.

The Rat. Two-reel drama. Balboa Amusement Producing Co. Released by Box Office Attraction Co., made for William Fox.

Sacrificial Fires. Three-reel drama. Balboa Amusement Producing Co. Released Feb. 28, 1914, by Box Office Attraction Co.

The Sand Lark. Balboa Amusement Producing Co. Released in 1916 by Pathé Frères.

Sands of Life. Two-reel drama. Balboa Amusement Producing Co. Released by Box Office Attraction Co., made for William Fox.

Saved from Himself. Balboa Amusement Producing Co. Copyright Dec. 30, 1914. Released by Pathé Frères.

The Sea Wolf. Three-reel drama. Balboa Amusement Producing Co.

Seeds of Jealousy. Three-reel drama. Nemo. Released Oct. 26, 1914, by Box Office Attraction Co., made for William Fox.

Shadows and Sunshine. Five-reel comedy-drama. Pathé-Balboa. Released Nov. 12, 1916, by Pathé Exchange, Inc., Gold Rooster Plays.

Should a Wife Forgive? Five-reel drama. Released Nov. 8, 1915, by World Film Corp.

Silver Lining. Three-reel drama. Balboa Amusement Producing Co. Released by Box Office Attraction Co., made for William Fox.

The Stranger. Two-reels. White Star.

Sunshine and Gold. Five-reel comedy-drama. Balboa Amusement Co. Released Apr. 29, 1917, by Pathé Exchange, Inc., Gold Rooster Plays.

The Test of Manhood. Three-reel drama. Balboa Amusement Producing Co. Released Oct. 12, 1914, by Box Office Attraction Co., made for William Fox.

Through Night to Light. Three-reel drama. Nemo. Released Oct. 5, 1914, by Box Office Attraction Co., made for William Fox.

Told at Twilight. Five-reel drama. Balboa Amusement Producing Co. Released Mar. 25, 1917, by Pathé Exchange, Inc., Gold Rooster Plays.

Tomboy. Balboa Amusement Producing Co. Released in 1915 by Pathé Frères.

Twin Kiddies. Five-reel drama. Balboa Amusement Producing Co. Released Jan. 28, 1917, by Pathé Exchange, Inc.; Gold Rooster Plays.

The Unexpected. Three-reel drama. Balboa Amusement Producing Co. Released Feb. 28, 1914, by Box Office Attraction Co., made for William Fox.

Vengeance of the Dead. Four-reel (drama?). Balboa Amusement Producing Co., a Fortune Photoplay. Released Mar. 1917? by General Film Co.

When Might Is Right. Knickerbocker Star Features. Released in 1916.

Who Pays? Serial. Released by Pathé Frères.

The 12 chapters: *The Price of Fame, The Pursuit of Pleasure, Where Justice Sleeps, The Love Liar, Unto Herself Alone, House of Glass, Blue Blood and Yellow, Today and Tomorrow, For the Commonwealth, The Pomp of the Earth, The Fruit of Folly,* and *Toil and Tyranny.* The first chapter was copyrighted Mar. 21, 1914, and the last chapter was copyrighted Oct. 13, 1915.

The Will O' the Wisp. Four-reel drama. Balboa Amusement Producing Co. Released July 1914 by Box Office Attraction Co., made for William Fox.

You've Got to Pay. Pathé Frères. Released Dec. 10, 1913, by General Film Co.

Jackie Saunders

Jackie Saunders was surely the most well-known actress during the heyday of Balboa and was called the "Maid of Long Beach." H. M. Horkheimer also nicknamed her "Little Sunbeam," after her role in *Little Jack*, and the popular actress was also known as the Mary Pickford of the West.

After starting her career in New York, both on stage and as an artist's model, posing for noted masters such as Howard C. Christy, Harrison Fisher, and Clarence Underwood, Saunders did her first stage work in Atlantic City with a troupe of dancers. Eventually she acted on stage and in films, under contract in New York with D. W. Griffith, who discovered her. Moving west, she joined Balboa in December 1913, and under contract at Balboa, Jackie became a national and then an international sensation almost overnight.

A native of Germantown, Philadelphia, of Franco-German lineage, Jackie Saunders was born Anna Jackal, on October 6, 1892. She was educated at St. Joseph's Convent in Chestnut Hill, Philadelphia. Baptized in the Catholic church, Jackie later joined the Church of Religious Science and Unity. Her parents moved to Quaker City, and Jackie gravitated towards the theatre. She seemed to bloom beautifully in the spotlight, against the wishes of her parents, who were "staid" Pennsylvanians according to the *Moving Picture World.*

Before entering the movie business, Jackie had joined the Orpheum Stock Company, and she later accepted a position as a star with Dawson's Dancing Dolls, making three road tours with that company doing child roles and ingenue parts. Jackie loved to dance and was considered an expert in the tango, the Maxie, the hesitation, the waltz, and other dances. Her talents also included athletic abilities, especially horseback riding and swimming; both sports came in handy for several of her movie stunts.

When Jackie joined Balboa, she was 21 years old and capable of lighting up the screen with her glowing personality. On September 5, 1914, the *Photoplayers' Weekly*, in an article written by Balboa's Frank M. Wiltermood, described the special appeal of the rising star, calling her "an unassuming, thoroughly charming actress of the most democratic demeanor and tastes." Wiltermood continued, "Her fame is growing so rapidly that within the near future she will be acclaimed throughout the world as a leading woman of the first rank in genius and talents" (*Press Clippings*, vol. 1, p. 185). Another article, entitled "Miss Jackie Saunders," that appeared in the *Moving Picture World* (p. 1793) on September 26, 1914, also praised the Balboa star:

Jackie Saunders in *The Will O' the Wisp* (1914) (courtesy of Jackie Saunders, Jr.).

In as much as Miss Saunders has won thousands of enthusiastic followers throughout the country, it has been decided to arrange for her a tour of the principal cities.

Picture fans everywhere will be given an opportunity to see this winsome little lady vivacious and sparkling with good humor, her personality is one that attracts the admiration of women as well as men.

By October 1914, *Motion Picture News* was eagerly announcing that Balboa's star would be featured in six productions by Fox's Box Office Attraction Company: *Little Sunbeam*, *The Square Triangle*, *Rose of the Alley*, *The Hunchback of Cedar Lodge*, and *Little Jack* (*Press Clippings*, vol. 1, p. 28). At the time, Jackie was 22 years old, measured 5'2" tall, weighed 125 lbs., and was known for her grey-blue eyes, beautiful dark-blond hair, and sunshiny smile. In fact, Jackie first appeared in films at Biograph and then worked at Universal's West Coast studios, before joining Balboa in December 1913; she was a sensation on the screen from the very start.

Jackie had to adjust, however, to being a stage actress playing before an impersonal and clicking camera, without the supportive spectators to encourage her. Jackie Saunders explained succinctly the awkwardness she felt trying to connect with her part in front of the lens without a live audience:

When I first joined the Universal, it was impossible for me to put forth my best efforts. The stimulus of an applauding audience was lacking, and my sensibilities seemed to be dormant. I am sure that I was painfully mechanical, but gradually this feeling wore away. The pictures require more self-control, more self-reliance, and one's imagination must be on the alert. I always have a great curiosity to see myself on the film, but this privilege is seldom offered. The fact that I am in continuous demand therefore, must furnish consolation enough. (*Moving Picture World*, p. 1793)

Thanks to the Horkheimers, many of the loyal artists at Balboa branched out and participated in several diverse facets of filmmaking. Not only was Jackie Saunders a successful photoplayer of renown, but she was credited with being the author of at least two scenarios that became Balboa feature films: *The Rose of the Alley* and *A Mix-Up in Clothes*. In Wiltermood's article in the *Photoplayers' Weekly* cited above, Jackie expressed her concern as a screenwriter. Still pertinent nowadays are her comments about the need for quality scenarios if filmmakers hope to please the viewers. Jackie's comments reflect both her personal views and those of the Horkheimers, who were making serious efforts to provide the best scenario department in the business.

The Horkheimers' efforts allowed Balboa films to gain critical acclaim on many counts, and this enabled the Horkheimers to attract talented or experienced writers to Balboa. For example, one of Balboa's directors, Harry Harvey, had a seasoned and diversified background, as Tony Scott explains in "Southern Exposure" (p. 116). He had written 37 photoplays and produced 29 films before joining Balboa. Prior to signing with one of Balboa's production companies, Harvey had had 12 years experience, having spent time at Mutoscope, Edison, Cameraphone, Pathé Frères, Gaumont (in France), Yankee, Solax, Kay Bee, Frontier, Universal, and Reliance. Harvey had also been Pathé's first American leading man. In Wiltermood's article (*Press Clippings*, vol. 1, p. 185),

Jackie Saunders conveys Balboa's view on the importance of quality screenplays:

Moving picture producers apparently have got to come to the belief that to obtain a great feature photo-drama they must first secure a first class story for the groundwork of the picture. Theatergoers want to see an interesting, original and otherwise meritorious story told in a drama. They evidently do not care to enter a theater merely to see a pageantry, a lot of people marching past the camera, but they desire to see the recital of a heart-gripping narrative, the chief elements of which move them to sympathy and admiration and fondness for the heroic roles in the play.

I have written several good movie dramas myself and will strive in the future to create some scenarios that would win praise. I know that excellent stories are next to good acting, the greatest requirements at present in the cinema field. The director who is fortunate enough to obtain a meritorious narrative and a group of good actors and actresses has little need to worry much about backgrounds and locations, for the story and the players will lift the picture into stellar rank.

In 1914, among other Balboa releases for Fox appeared *The Will O' the Wisp*, a thrilling story filled with danger that captured the breath-taking sight of flood waters filmed between Long Beach and Compton. The *Moving Picture World* (p. 1793) said of Jackie Saunders' work in this film, "no stunt or task is too difficult for her to attempt." These releases for Fox occurred when Fox handled on an exclusive basis the entire output of Balboa Feature Films. Balboa's exclusive network of distribution, first with the Box Office Attraction Company in Canada and in the United States, and then with Bishop, Pessers, and Co., Ltd., in the United Kingdom, guaranteed Jackie Saunders fame, international attention, and critical acclaim.

With Jackie Saunders very much in demand, Elwood D. Horkheimer negotiated with Mutual Film Corporation in 1916 to distribute a blockbuster deal involving six five-part

Jackie Saunders (courtesy of Jackie Saunders, Jr.).

productions with Jackie Saunders in the starring role, the first to be released on March 26, 1916. The six negotiated films included *Sunny Jane, The Checkmate, The Wild Cat, A Bit of Kindling, Betty Be Good,* and *Bab the Fixer.* In addition, *The Grip of Evil* (1916) was the start of Jackie Saunders' success in serials at Balboa, and as a serial queen she would rival Pearl White and another Balboa star, Ruth Roland. *The Grip of Evil* was a grandiose production which was shown weekly for 14 weeks. Each installment consisted of two reels of film, so there were twenty-eight reels in all. Jackie Saunders was on top of the world, and so was Balboa. According to Jackie Saunders, Jr., daughter of Jackie and Elwood Horkheimer, the star and Balboa chief were married that same year, 1916.

In Long Beach, Jackie had been billed with many of the top stars of the time, such as Henry King, Daniel Gilfether, Lewis Cody, Philo McCullough, and the English actor Roland Bottomley, just to name a few. Later Jackie Saunders also appeared in a Western that is still available today for viewing; it was mostly shot on Santa Catalina Island. In this movie, *Drag Harlan* (1920), Jackie rode her horse like Bronco Bill through the hilly terrain, starring with William Farnum; Fox rereleased the film in 1925.

After the closing of Balboa Studios, Jackie worked in films with other companies, especially Fox, and was a stock player at Warner Bros. during the 1930s. According to Jackie Saunders, Jr., her famous Balboan mother returned to do stage work in New York, after leaving Long Beach. Many attributed her continuing success partly to her glowing screen and stage presence and her stunning features; she had abundant, gorgeous, dark-blond hair, a perfect nose, and limpid, grey-blue eyes. Her good looks and athletic yet feminine motions could capture an audience and hold the viewers spellbound. In the 1920s, Jackie

Drag Harlan (1920). William Farnum and Jackie Saunders.

enjoyed mostly supporting roles with other screen celebrities, such as Alice Lake in *The Infamous Miss Ravell* (1921), Irene Rich in *Defying Destiny*, and Dorothy Davenport, wife of Wallace Reid, in *Broken Laws* (1924).

While at Balboa, Jackie Saunders married Elwood D. Horkheimer, whom she divorced in 1920 or 1921. Their daughter, born September 1, 1917, was also named Jacquelin, and was often called Jackie Saunders, Jr. In anticipation of her birth, Balboa set up a delivery room at the studio, though the girl was actually born not on a movie stage, but at the Horkheimers' home in Long Beach. Jackie Saunders, Jr., also appeared in the movies after graduating from the Pasadena Playhouse School of the Theatre, as well as from Stanford University. In films, she became a contract player with Warner Bros., while doing leads in regional theatres, and playing in *The Man Who Came to Dinner* and *The Philadelphia Story*. Jackie Saunders, Jr., also appeared in *The Gold Diggers of 1937* (1936). Like her community-spirited father and uncle, she remembered the servicemen at the U.S.O., performing as an actress on stage, as well as a prestidigitator in New York, the Aleutians, and the Philippines.

The talented daughter still remembers vividly the day in 1925 when she witnessed her father, after four or five years spent apart from his ex-wife, begging her mother not to remarry. Outside the Gables Beach Club, seven-year-old

Jackie was alone in her mother's car while her parents, just a few steps away, discussed their future. During their entire separation, Elwood never went out with other women, not until they were divorced and his ex-wife finally remarried. Jackie Saunders had been the love of Elwood's life. He had hoped until the end that if he walked the line, he and Jackie would find the means to reconcile their differences. For Jackie Saunders, however, her first marriage terminated irrevocably in divorce, and her conjugal bliss would be found in her second marriage with Joseph Ward Cohen.

Jackie Saunders and J. Ward Cohen were married at the El Mirasol Hotel in Santa Barbara in 1925. On June 29, 1927, their daughter was born. She too would grow up to be a very successful stage and screen actress, using the stage name Mary Ann Gibson.

Jackie Saunders also promoted fund-raising programs and discovered talent for Hollywood's growing film industry. In 1927, she founded the Film Welfare League and became its first president. The organization still raises funds for people in the industry who need assistance, those who may not qualify for aid from the Motion Picture Guild. According to Jackie Saunders, Jr., the first person to benefit from the Film Welfare League's fund-raising efforts through fashion shows, luncheons, and dinner/ball affairs was Ella Wickersham. Ella Wickersham wrote a motion picture column for the *Los Angeles Examiner*. Ella's brother, Billie Wickersham, cared for his sister, and they shared the same residence. They had been dancers together, when one day her brother accidentally dropped her, resulting in her being paralyzed for life. The League gave Ella a beautiful new wheelchair to replace her dilapidated wicker one. Ella's brother remained truly and completely devoted to his sister, tending her lovingly. Ella, who was stunningly beautiful, and her brother were a very popular pair in Hollywood society from the mid-twenties throughout the thirties, until her death, according to Jackie Saunders, Jr.

Mother and daughter, Jackie, Sr. and Jackie, Jr. (courtesy of Jackie Saunders, Jr.).

In the late 1930s, Jackie Saunders' first husband, Elwood D. Horkheimer, remarried. Elwood's second wife, Vivian, had persuaded him to invest his second fortune, the inheritance he received after his mother's death, in a silver mine in which Vivian's father already held an interest. Unfortunately, the silver mine was a dud, and the investment was a total loss. Vivian too worked in the movie industry, behind the scenes, as a draper and assistant for Adrian at MGM.

Jackie Saunders also discovered the famous designer, Irene, who replaced Adrian. Jackie Saunders had found Irene operating a small shop near the University of Southern California and took the very talented young woman under her wing, becoming her sponsor and promoter. Jackie Saunders introduced Irene to her friends in the industry and enabled her to give fashion shows at the Gables Beach Club. Jackie Saunders' second husband, J. Ward Cohen, was an energetic entrepreneur-builder, being the owner and president of the Gables Beach Club (1925), proprietor of the Edgewater Beach Club (1927-1928), and owner of the Sonoma Mission Inn (1930) and the Boyes Hot Springs Resort (1931). He was also a wine merchant for several wineries in Napa Valley and developed a hotel–golf club at the end of his life. With her own connections in the film industry and the business contacts of her second husband, Jackie Saunders was able to promote Irene's career and persuaded her to move to a studio in Hollywood, where she was much in demand. After Irene left MGM, she engaged in custom designing for Bullocks Wilshire until the time of her death by suicide. During Irene's illustrious career, her costumes were extremely expensive and exquisitely fashioned.

In the end, Jackie Saunders would pass away before Elwood D. Horkheimer who died in 1966 in the Beverly Hills Hospital, after having lived at a board and care facility in West Los Angeles, still married to Vivian. After his death Elwood D. Horkheimer donated his remains to the University of California Los Angeles Medical Center. Jackie Saunders, Jr., remembers her father as a great scholar who sold his complete library to Warner Bros. in the 1930s for thousands of dollars. All of the Warner Bros. archives were transferred decades later to the Burbank Public Library.

Jackie Saunders' second husband, J. Ward Cohen, died of cancer at Cedars of Lebanon Hospital in Los Angeles in 1950. On Bastille Day, July 14, 1954, Jackie Saunders died of pneumonia at 62 years of age in Palm Springs, California, where she had retired to relieve somewhat the excruciating pain of severe arthritis that plagued her in her final years. After leading an exciting and rich life, Jackie was buried in a small cemetery called Wellwood at the top of Alejo Street, next to the mountains in Palm Springs, California. It is only appropriate that the "Maid of Long Beach" should remain on top of the world to the end, close to the desert's inimitable splash of sparkling and expansive evening sky.

A Partial List of Saunders' Films at Balboa

The Adventures of a Madcap. Four-reel comedy-drama. Balboa Amusement Producing Co. Released by Pathé Exchange, Inc., Nov. 3, 1915.

Bab the Fixer. Five-reel comedy-drama. E. D. Horkheimer. Released Aug. 13, 1917, by Mutual Film Corp.

Betty Be Good. Five-reel comedy-drama. Balboa Amusement Producing Co. Released July 16, 1917, by Mutual Film Corp., made for Mutual Star Productions.

A Bit of Kindling. Five-reel drama. Mutual Film Corp., Horkheimer. Released June 18, 1917, by Mutual Film Corp., made for Mutual Star Productions.

Broken Laws. (no further information available)

The Checkmate. Five-reel drama. Mutual Film Corp., Horkheimer. Released May 21, 1917, by Mutual Film Corp., made for Mutual Star Productions.

Defying Destiny. (no further information available)

Drag Harlan. Six-reel Western. Fox Film Corp. Released Oct. 24, 1920, by Fox Film Corp.

The Grip of Evil. Serial. Made for Pathé of New York.

The 14 chapters (two reels each): *Fate, The*

Underworld, The Upper Ten, The Looters, The Way of a Woman, The Hypocrites, The Butterflies, In Bohemia, The Dollar Kings, Down to the Sea, Mammon and Moloch, Into the Pits, Circumstantial Evidence, and *Humanity Triumphant*. The first chapter was copyrighted July 17, 1916, and the last chapter was copyrighted Sept. 28, 1916 (*Filmarama*, vol. 1).

Gypsy Love. Three-reel drama. Balboa Amusement Producing Co. Released July 20, 1914, by Box Office Attraction Co., made for William Fox.

The Hunchback of Cedar Lodge. Three-reel drama. Balboa Amusement Producing Co. Released by Box Office Attraction Co., made for William Fox.

Ill Starred Babbie. Five-reel drama. Balboa Amusement Producing Co. Released Dec. 7, 1914, by the Alliance Films Corp.

The Infamous Miss Ravell. (no further information available)

The Intrigue. Two-reel drama. Kalem. Released Mar. 4, 1914, by General Film Co., made for Kalem Co.

Little Jack. Three reels. Balboa Amusement Producing Co. Released Nov. 3, 1914, by Box Office Attraction Co., made for William Fox.

Little Sunbeam. Three reels. Balboa Amusement Producing Co. Released Oct. 19, 1914, by Box Office Attraction Co., made for William Fox.

The Man with Green Eyes. (no further information available)

A Mixup in Clothes. Three-reel drama. Balboa Amusement Producing Co., made for William Fox, released in 1914.

A Romance in the Hills. Balboa Amusement Producing Co.

The Rose of the Alley. Three-reel drama. Balboa Amusement Producing Co. Released Oct. 5, 1914, by Box Office Attraction Co., made for William Fox.

The Shrine of Happiness. Five-reel drama. Balboa Feature Film Co. Released Feb. 18, 1916, by Pathé Exchange, Inc., Gold Rooster Plays.

The Square Triangle. Three-reel drama. Balboa Amusement Producing Co. Released Sept. 28, 1914, by Box Office Attraction Co., made for William Fox.

Sunny Jane. Five-reel comedy-drama. Jackie Saunders Series. Balboa Amusement Producing Co. Released Mar. 26, 1917, by Mutual Film Corp.

Through Night to Light. Three-reel drama. Nemo. Released Oct. 5, 1914, by Box Office Attraction Co., made for William Fox.

The Wildcat. Five reels.

Will o' the Wisp. Four-reel drama. Balboa Amusement Producing Co. Released July 1914 by Box Office Attraction Co.

Ruth Roland

This popular star of the early movies was born August 26, 1892, in San Francisco, California, and began a theatrical career as a youngster known as "Baby Ruth," appearing in Ed Holden's stage company as a little girl. According to Tony Scott's article "Southern Exposure" in *Variety* (p. 118), David Belasco spotted Baby Ruth in San Francisco when she was playing Little Lord Fauntleroy at age four. Belasco considered the moppet a crowd-pleaser. Baby Ruth had also performed in vaudeville, even going on tour to Honolulu, where she appeared for the royal Hawaiian family. Baby Ruth continued on the stage until she was 11 years old and then busied herself with private schooling. This schooling, however, was not all academic. The vivacious and indomitable Ruth managed to learn all types of extraordinary skills: driving cars, horseback riding, boxing, fencing, playing tennis, football, baseball, jumping, swimming, swinging Indian clubs, bowling and running. Not only was Ruth an all-round athlete, she was a modern version of Annie Oakley and Robin Hood, expertly wielding rifles, pistols, and bows and arrows. In short, Ruth could not have been better prepared to enter the serial movie business.

As a Balboan, Ruth Roland was the Horkheimers' action-adventure serial queen and a major box-office smash. During her tenure at Balboa, she enjoyed enormous popularity, second in the world only to Pearl White in action-adventure movies, and like Balboa Studios itself, where she was under contract, Roland

Ruth Roland

helped inaugurate the novel genre of serial films. Having first signed in 1911 with the Kalem Company in Santa Monica when she was 19 years old, Ruth Roland was once billed as the "Kalem Girl," a budding bathing beauty, bold and athletic. Other notable photoplayers also worked at the Kalem studios: Marin Sais, Ed Coxen, and Marshall Neilan. As Tony Scott notes, Roland started appearing in Westerns before branching out to do detective and comedy dramas such as *Ruth Roland, Detective, The Pasadena Peach,* and *Wanted, An Heir.*

In early 1914, The "Kalem Girl" signed with Balboa, and her popularity soared to new heights. Ruth Roland started at Balboa a few months after Jackie Saunders' arrival at the studios in Long Beach. Coincidentally, both Ruth Roland and Jackie Saunders were the same age, and both stars were outstanding leading ladies and sportswomen, doing their own stunts and offering audiences thrilling screen entertainment with much derring-do. Before there were professional stuntmen, serial kings and queens prided themselves on never using doubles for their stunts, though some producers thought the stars were taking too many risks because those same producers were placing their bets on the continuing returns that would be halted if a serious accident were to occur. Originally, Ruth Roland had signed for only one year with Balboa, but she stayed until 1917. During her first year, Roland starred with Henry King in the serial *Who Pays?* which was presented in 12 episodes, each three reels long; she also starred in another serial entitled *The Red Circle*, which was H. M.'s own brainchild.

Ruth Roland's numerous hair-raising adventure serials produced at Balboa, including *The Adventures of Ruth* and *Ruth of the Rockies,* were well received, but she also garnered accolades for performances in more dramatic features produced in Long Beach, such as, *Should a Wife Forgive?* with Baby Marie Osborne. In this movie, Baby Marie made her official début playing the part of a small boy. Moreover, as Roland's popularity continued to grow, so did her successes at Balboa. Her serials followed each other at a quick pace. Another of her hits was *Neal of the Navy*, a patriotic wartime saga. Her reputation soaring, Roland also starred in Pathé's hand-tinted *A Matrimonial Martyr*, followed by *The Tiger's Trail*, with live tigers carted in from Colonel Selig's Zoo located up at Eastlake Park in Los Angeles. Roland also starred in *Comrade John* and another successful Balboa serial, *The Neglected Wife*; the exotic Astra adventure series *Hands Up* was one of her last films produced at Balboa.

According to Pathé's announcements for *Hands Up*, the world-famous "House of Serials" offered the viewer Pathé's first Western serial with this production, which it called "the most ambitious Western production ever filmed." George Fitzmaurice, a noted director of big extravaganzas, was supervisor of this Astra production. Louis J. Gasnier also worked on this Western serial, following his successful host of serials: *The House of Hate, Pearl of the Army, The Shielding Shadow,* and *The Fatal Ring,* all distributed by Pathé.

Balboa Amusement Producing Company

Scene from *Should a Wife Forgive?* (Equitable) (from Marie Osborne-Yeats' scrapbook).

announced publicly that the studio had originally hired the vivacious Roland "because she represents the higher and more finished type of motion picture actress — because she is an exponent of the more refined school of dramatic expression as it relates to the science of cinematography. ... [Balboa] is determined to furnish her with vehicles that will enable her to harmoniously blend her inherent powers over the risibilities of amusement loving humanity" (Scott, pp. 118-20). Superbly capable of dramatic acting, Ruth Roland performed at times in defiance of stereotypes. For example, many of her Western serials depicted a tomboyish heroine who was a capable match, in both characterization and in physical skill, to most male leads. These heroic leading parts for women have generally been rare throughout the history of film, and for that reason alone, Ruth Roland, Jackie Saunders, and Pearl White deserve much credit for being the early vanguards who opened new avenues for actresses in the movies.

H. M.'s brainchild, *The Red Circle*, did, however, challenge the dramatic talents of Ruth Roland. The plot hinted of Shakespeare's psychologically disturbed Lady MacBeth, though Horkheimer's heroine only suffered from a benignly induced red stain. In contrast to Lady MacBeth, Ruth's character was not a murderess with a guilty conscience. According to the *Daily Telegram* (December 2, 1915, 3:6), the title is based on the birthmark that appears on the hand of the heroine, June Travers, who is played by Ruth Roland. The birthmark was noticeable only in times of stress and excitement, and a number of complications arose through this fact because there was a curse attached to this red circle. Those who had it were made to steal. June was a good girl who

H. M. Horkheimer and Ruth Roland (courtesy of Marc Wanamaker).

suffered from this hereditary taint, but she used it for good. Her first crime was stealing a moneylender's notes, returning them to his victims. Such an idea must have greatly appealed to the indebted H. M. In fact, though the story was written by the scenario editor of the Balboa Company, Will M. Ritchie (sometimes spelled Ritchey), the fundamental plot was based upon an idea furnished by the studio's chief, H. M. Horkheimer. As Tony Scott ("Southern Exposure," p. 120), explains, "the character was in emotional distress, and only the detective on the scene, played by Frank Mayo, could manage to clean the mental block away through his love; the public adored it, as did Balboa; Ruth Roland would appear in 11 more chapter plays."

Ruth Roland's career would outlive the Balboa Studios, and she saved enough money to finance her own pictures, but her most popular films were the serials she made at Balboa. *Variety*'s 1937 obituary lauded the serial queen for the diversity of her performances at Kalem and Balboa, where the actress was forever "undergoing many dangers and often escaping death or serious injury by the proverbial hair's breadth." Her departure from Long Beach seemed to erase some of the stargazing frenzy that had permeated the city during Balboa's heyday. Tony Scott (Southern Exposure," p. 114) quotes a local columnist, Lou Jobst, who himself cited a retired banker in Long Beach who reminisced about the excitement of having big stars roaming the city: "I can remember Ruth Roland, dressed in form-fitting riding habit, walking into the bank on pay day and all the vice presidents scrambling toward her."

The legendary Ruth Roland died of cancer in Hollywood, California, before attaining 40 years of age; she was one of the greatest serial queens of the silent era. By investing her money wisely and carefully, like Mary Pickford, Ruth Roland had become one of the most prominent businesswomen of movieland and owned some of the most valuable residential real estate in Los Angeles. The *Press Telegram* (Sept. 22, 1937, A1–6) announced Ruth Roland's death the very day of her passing, September 22, 1937, boasting about the star's wise and lucrative real estate investments:

Realty circles have told a story of the film star's operations which illustrated the fast movement of the business in the days when she began to buy land. She had purchased a corner, now an exceedingly valuable one, on Wilshire Boulevard, but then only a potential money-maker. After the deal was consummated she was said to have regretted the investment and asked the agent who handled it to take the property back. He argued with her and finally persuaded her that she had made a wise purchase.

Time proved he was right and the Wilshire Boulevard corner, which she retained and finally subdivided and sold, today was one of the highest priced properties on the street which runs from the heart of the Los Angeles business district to the sea at Santa Monica.

At 39, Ruth Roland died at her home, where she had been confined by her grave illness. Understandably enough, her death in 1937 came as a shock to the entire film industry. Despite all the fury and passion that Ruth Roland had put into her film career and real estate investments, she passed away quietly before her time, after having worked with most of the major stars at Balboa, as well as with other great performers of the silent era, including Charlie Chaplin, Mabel Normand, Marguerite Clark, William S. Hart, and many others. Her husband, Ben Bard, producer and theater operator, and her aunt, Edith Thompson, were at her bedside when Roland breathed her last sigh. A few days later her funeral services took place at the Forest Lawn Mortuary in Glendale.

Ruth Roland may have also planned her own monument, and one can be grateful that she did. Mimicking the adventures about hidden treasures that were so much a part of her

Ruth Roland as a cowgirl.

films, she stored in her backyard a cement vault containing many of her treasured Balboa films. When it was uncovered after her death, the nitrate film was still in good condition. This thrilling find helped preserve a monument to this stellar and original Balboan, who, like the Long Beach studio itself, rose and fell before her time. Without such a monument, with so few vestiges remaining these days of the once celebrated and numerous Balboan productions, Ruth Roland's legacy would be a faded memory.

A Partial List of Roland's Films at Balboa

Comrade John. Five reels. Balboa Amusement Producing Co. Released Oct. 27, 1915, by Pathé Frères.

The Devil's Bait. Four-reel drama. Balboa Amusement Producing Co., a Fortune Photoplay. Released Mar. 1917 by General Film Co.

Hands Up! A Cyclonic Western Serial. Astra Film Corp. Released by Pathé Exchange, Inc.

The Matrimonial Martyr. Five-reel comedy. Balboa Feature Film Co. Released June 19, 1916, by Pathé Exchange, Inc., Gold Rooster Plays.

The Neglected Wife. Serial. Copyright Dec. 18, 1916. Released by Pathé Frères.

The 15 chapters: *The Woman Alone, The Weakening, In the Crucible, Beyond Recall, Under Suspicion, On the Precipice, The Message on the Mirror, A Relentless Fate, Deepening Degradation, A Veiled Intrigue, A Reckless Indiscretion, Embittered Love, Revolting Pride, Desperation,* and *A Sacrifice Supreme.* Chapter 1 was copyrighted Dec. 18, 1916, and Chapter 15 was copyrighted Apr. 25, 1917 (*Filmarama*, vol. 1).

The Red Circle. Serial. Balboa Amusement Producing Co. Released by Pathé Frères.

The 14 chapters (two reels each): *Nevermore, Pity the Poor, Twenty Years Ago, In Strange Attire, Weapons of War, False Colors, Third Degree* or *Two Captives, Peace at Any Price, Dodgin' the Law, Excess Baggage, Seeds of Suspicion, Like a Rat in a Trap, Branded as a Thief,* and *Judgment Day.* Chapter 1 was copyrighted Feb. 30, 1915, and Chapter 14 was copyrighted Sept. 3, 1916 (Filmarama, vol. 1).

Ruth of the Rockies. Serial.

The Stolen Play. Four-reel drama. Falcon Features. Released Sept. 1917 by General Film Co.

The Sultana. Five-reel crime/drama. Balboa Amusement Co. Released Feb. 18, 1916, by Pathé Exchange, Inc., Gold Rooster Plays.

The Tiger's Trail. (no further information available)

Who Pays? Serial. Released by Pathé Frères.

The 12 chapters: *The Price of Fame, The Pursuit of Pleasure, Where Justice Sleeps, The Love Liar, Unto Herself Alone, House of Glass, Blue Blood and Yellow, Today and Tomorrow, For the Commonwealth, The Pomp of the Earth, The Fruit of Folly,* and *Toil and Tyranny.* Chapter 1 was copyrighted Mar. 21, 1914, and Chapter 12 was copyrighted Oct. 13, 1915 (*Encyclopedia of the Movie Studios*, p. 234, and Scott, "Southern Exposure," p. 118).

Daniel Gilfether

Born in 1849, Daniel Gilfether had the dubious distinction of being the dean of the Balboa Amusement Producing Company. The eldest Balboan was a native of Boston who had had an acting career that spanned 40 years before he joined three of Balboa's troupes of players at the quickly expanding studios in 1914. At Balboa, Daniel Gilfether's senior status gained him the nickname "Major." Despite his advanced age, he was one of the most active players at Balboa, and his recurring name among the thespians listed in prominent features produced at Long Beach attests to Gilfether's steady stream of work during his tenure at the prestigious Long Beach film plant. Unfortunately, there is little information available concerning his private life. For example, we have found no data to determine whether he ever married and whether he had any favorite pastimes or hobbies.

Some details are available, however, about Gilfether's professional career. In 1869, as a young man of 20, Daniel Gilfether decided to devote his services to the stage as a member of Frank Mayo's company during a presentation of *Davy Crockett*. Gilfether's devotion to the theatre is described in *Press Clippings*, vol. 1, in an article that appeared on September 13, 1914, "Major Gilfether Honored," from the *Press Telegram*. The article reports that after several seasons with Frank Mayo's company, Gilfether traveled to Sacramento, California, where he joined Joseph Proctor's stock company at the historical Metropolitan Theatre. During the

Told at Twilight (1917). Baby Marie and Daniel Gilfether (courtesy of Marie Osborne-Yeats).

1870s, a few years after the close of the Civil War, Proctor's troupe of players enjoyed particular success with a drama with a theme about pioneers and Indians entitled *Jibenosay*. Afterwards, Major Gilfether performed for two seasons with Annie Pixley, a celebrated actress from the West Coast. Gilfether was associated with other well-known stars and organizations, including the Sol Smith Russell companies, with whom he toured the United States doing *Edgewood Folks*, *A Poor Relation*, and *Peaceful Valley*. Afterwards, Gilfether spent three years with Daniel Frohman's Prince and Pauper organization and eight seasons with Augustus Pitou's company, which was headed by Chauncey Olcott. Gilfether also spent a year and a half with the elder Salvini and later starred in *Darkest Russia*, *Othello*, *Richelieu*, *Virginius*, and other famous plays of the day. Finally, Gilfether spent five years with William A. Brady's companies doing character and heavy roles, supporting Robert Mantell in Shakespearean dramas, and for three years he toured the United States with Wright Lorimer in *The Shepherd King*. Daniel Gilfether also starred in Barley Campbell's *My Partner*, and he starred in *A Messenger from Jarvis Section* in his popular role as "Uncle Dan'l." Gilfether's experience on stage was complete and seemingly exhaustive, yet the actor would find more untapped reserves of energy to burn on the screen.

How and when Gilfether left the stage to become a "photoplayer" has escaped our detection. There are some indications that he made a smooth transition to the screen, being especially well liked by his colleagues at Balboa. The article "Major Gilfether Honored" records that members of three of Balboa's troupes gave an elaborate reception involving a dinner and

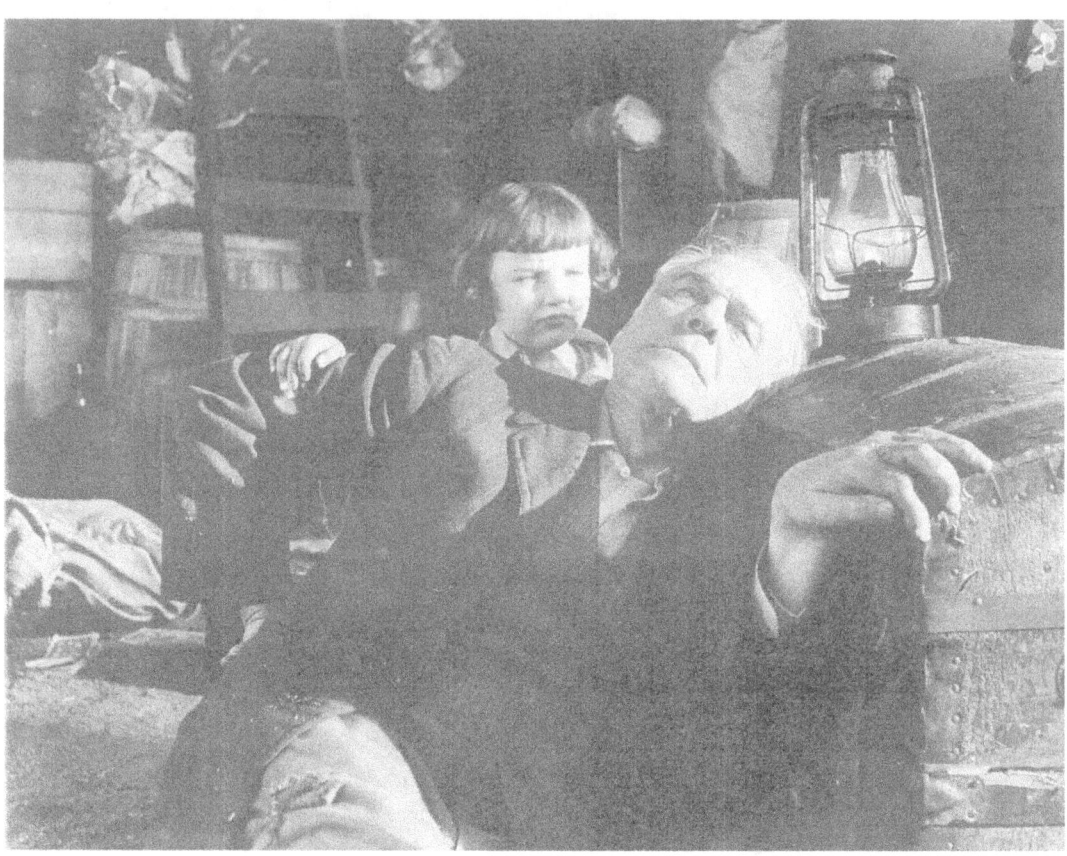

Sunshine and Gold (1917). Baby Marie and Daniel Gilfether (courtesy of Marie Osborne-Yeats).

dance in September 1914 to celebrate the Major's sixty-fifth birthday. After all the theatrical touring and traveling across the United States for 40 years, Daniel Gilfether seemed ready and happy to settle down to the life of a film actor. It was an especial advantage to be able to work close to home, doing more regular hours with a familiar group of stock players. Another article announcing the same birthday party appeared in the *Long Beach Telegram* on August 22, 1914. Entitled "To Honor an Old Veteran," the article noted the pleasure Gilfether experienced residing in Long Beach, close to the Balboa film plant: "[The] patriarchal thespian has located himself here permanently, a result brought about by a casual visit he made to Long Beach several months ago, at which time he became greatly enamored with the city's manifold attractions" (*Press Clippings*, vol. 1, p. 149).

Besides his acting career, Gilfether was an active member of Elk Lodge, No. 1, of New York and was a member of a Balboa organization, presumably a studio club to promote goodwill, which was called the "Mother Assembly," in reference to Mollie McConnell's nickname at Balboa — "Mother." True to the jolly actor's friendly nature, he was also a charter member of the Actor's Order of Friendship instituted by Edwin Forrest. From these memberships alone, one can imagine that Major Gilfether was a congenial and likeable colleague, esteemed for both his professionalism and for his affable nature.

Five years after his sixty-fifth birthday party, Gilfether had hit the big time on the silver screen with his successful film career at Balboa, despite his golden years. On May 3, 1919, the respected actor died of kidney disease in his adopted town of Long Beach, perhaps pained to see his fellow Balboans, even the Horkheimers, pack up and leave town. The talented dean of the Balboa Amusement Producing Company passed away in the beautiful seaside resort of Long Beach, bowing out quietly from the entertainment community he loved after contributing at the end of an exciting theatrical career to the newfangled and expanding movie business of Southern California.

A Partial List of Gilfether's Films at Balboa

Brand's Daughter. Four-reel drama. Falcon Features. Released Nov. 1917? by General Film Co.

The Checkmate. Five-reel drama. Mutual Film Corp., Horkheimer. Released May 21, 1917, by Mutual Film Corp., made for Mutual Star Productions.

The Criminal Code. Four-reel drama. Balboa Amusement Producing Co. Released Sept. 28, 1914, by Box Office Attraction Co., made for William Fox.

The Girl Angle. Five-reel Western. Horkheimer Studios. Released Oct. 5, 1917, by World Film Corp.

His Old-Fashioned Dad. Four-reel drama. Falcon Features. Released by General Film Company.

The Judge's Wife. Three-reel drama. White Star. Released Oct. 12, 1914, by Box Office Attraction Co., made for William Fox.

The Locked Heart. American Film Co., Oakdale Productions (probably Balboa Amusement Producing Co.). Released July 20, 1918, by General Film Co.

The Matrimonial Martyr. Five-reel comedy. Balboa Feature Film Co. Released June 19, 1916, by Pathé Exchange, Inc., Gold Rooster Plays.

No Children Wanted. Probably Balboa Amusement Producing Co. Released in 1918 by Oakdale/General.

Pay Dirt. Five-reel drama. Knickerbocker Star Features. Released June 18, 1916, by General Film Co.

The Red Circle. Serial. Balboa Amusement Producing Co. Released by Pathé Frères.

The 14 chapters (two reels each): *Nevermore, Pity the Poor, Twenty Years Ago, In Strange Attire, Weapons of War, False Colors, Third Degree* or *Two Captives, Peace at Any Price, Dodgin' the Law, Excess Baggage, Seeds of Suspicion, Like a Rat in a Trap, Branded as a Thief*, and *Judgment Day*. Chapter 1 was copyrighted Feb. 30, 1915, and Chapter 14 was copyrighted Sept. 3, 1916 (*Filmarama*, vol. 1).

Shadows and Sunshine. Five-reel comedy-drama. Pathé-Balboa. Released Nov. 12, 1916, by Pathé Exchange, Inc., Gold Rooster Plays.

Should a Wife Forgive? Five-reel drama. Equitable Motion Pictures Corp. Released Nov. 8, 1915, by World Film Corp.

The Sultana. Five-reel crime/drama. Balboa Amusement Co. Released Feb. 18, 1916, by Pathé Exchange, Inc.; Gold Rooster Plays.

Sunshine and Gold. Five-reel comedy-drama. Balboa Amusement Co. Released Apr. 29, 1917, by Pathé Exchange, Inc.; Gold Rooster Plays.

The Test of Manhood. Three-reel drama. Balboa Amusement Producing Co. Released Oct. 12, 1914, by Box Office Attraction Co., made for William Fox.

Told at Twilight. Five-reel drama. Balboa Amusement Producing Co. Released Mar. 25, 1917, by Pathé Exchange, Inc., Gold Rooster Plays.

Twin Kiddies. Five-reel drama. Balboa Amusement Producing Co. Released Jan. 28, 1917, by Pathé Exchange, Inc., Gold Rooster Plays.

Who Pays? Serial. Released by Pathé Frères.

The 12 chapters: *The Price of Fame, The Pursuit of Pleasure, Where Justice Sleeps, The Love Liar, Unto Herself Alone, House of Glass, Blue Blood and Yellow, Today and Tomorrow, For the Commonwealth, The Pomp of the Earth, The Fruit of Folly*, and *Toil and Tyranny*. Chapter 1 was copyrighted Mar. 21, 1914, and Chapter 12 was copyrighted Oct. 13, 1915 (*Encyclopedia of the Movie Studios*, p. 234, and Scott, "Southern Exposure," p. 118).

Zollenstein. Four-reel drama. Falcon Features. Released Dec. 4, 1917, by General Film Co.

Mollie McConnell

In May 1913, Mollie McConnell made her film début; she was directed by Edwin August at Universal Film Company before joining Balboa the same year (Scott, p. 114). Prior to McConnell's tenure at Balboa and prior even to her début at Universal, she had enjoyed an esteemed reputation as one of the most talented and artistic "grandes dames" of the English and United States stages, and like Gilfether, Mollie McConnell performed many years in the legitimate theatre before doing movies. She also shared Gilfether's attachment to Long Beach, enjoying the city's fresh sea breezes and its prosperous commerce and amusement zones. Mollie was especially drawn to the camaraderie for which the Balboa Amusement Producing Company was known. The *Photoplayers' Weekly* published an article entitled "Mollie McConnell, Leading Character Woman of the Balboa Co." on September 26, 1914, explaining the happy coincidence between Mollie's temperament and the atmosphere at the studio: "In her charming personality is shown the dominant spirit of the Horkheimer Brothers' big plant, the ever-present purpose to be guided always by the Golden Rule" (*Press Clippings*, vol. 1, p. 189).

Mollie McConnell eventually attained international fame, making theatrical tours on two continents, but in the beginning her education did not direct her toward the theatre. Born on September 24, 1865, in Chicago, Illinois, she was educated at Mills Seminary in Oakland, near San Francisco, California. Before returning to her native town of Chicago, Mollie McConnell was reportedly also a graduate of an unnamed but exclusive and classical college in the West. After graduation from this private school, she attended Miss Grant's college in Chicago, but just before finishing her term there, Mollie decided to quit her academic studies to become an actress.

The *Photoplayers' Weekly* article summarized McConnell's impressive theatrical career, beginning with her comic roles that preceded her serious and dramatic work. Apparently, the great actress met success from the start, first as a comedienne; her initial role in a farce production *The Kitty* won her praise, with fellow cast members W. A. Mestayer, Theresa Vaughn, and Thomas Wise. The title of her next comedy might make the reader guffaw. Some months after doing *The Kitty*, Mollie McConnell joined the Donnelly and Girard Company in *Natural Gas*, in which she toured the United States for several years with great success. How could such a title fail? Then in 1890, John Russell, manager of the same company, organized the City Directory Company, taking with him Mollie McConnell and a number of other troupe members of *Natural Gas*. Among the other members of the new company were William Collier, May Yohe, Charlie Reed, and May Irwin.

That very same year, 1890, Mollie's career took a very dramatic and successful turn. She did more than charm the spectators; she became part of an important alliance in the theatrical industry. In the autumn of 1890, Mollie married Will A. McConnell, a leading writer and theatrical magnate of New York City. About the time of their marriage, Mr. McConnell had formed the American Theatrical Exchange, and his first customer was Charles Frohman, who immediately handed him a check for $500 and assured him he would aid in every way the success of the new venture. The McConnells could not have had a better helping hand. Charles Frohman was the leading theatrical manager of the day, the one who laid the foundation for the Theatrical Syndicate, the body that once controlled U.S. theatres. He also founded the Empire Stock Company, promoted important playwrights of the day such as Clyde Fitch, David Belasco, and Augustus Thomas, and launched stars like John Drew, Ethel Barrymore, William Gillette, and Otis Skinner. Frohman had an extraordinary talent for picking winners and dominated the U.S. theatrical business during an explosive growth period of some 25 years. His domination ended, sadly enough, when his life and his reign were cut short by the sinking of the British ocean liner

Mollie McConnell and Baby Marie in arms of unidentified actress (courtesy of Marie Osborne-Yeats).

Lusitania, which was torpedoed by a German submarine on May 7, 1915.

In 1890, Mollie McConnell and her husband enjoyed the complete support of Frohman's business savvy. With Frohman interested in Mollie's stage work, the actress became a star and a member of Frohman's leading New York company, where she worked with Mrs. Leslie Carter, William Gillette, Maude Adams, and other celebrities promoted by Frohman. After a long engagement with Frohman's companies, Mollie joined Aubrey Boucicault in his premiere production of *Old Heidelberg,* which was staged with an all-star cast: Boucicault as Prince Karl, Robert Loraine as the student, and Theodore Roberts as the valet, with Minnie

Dupree, Max Freeman, and Morton Selten in other roles. In fact, the ever-familiar and well-liked melody, "Love's Old Sweet Song" was written and dedicated to Mollie McConnell, who sang it for the first time in public in the *Old Heidelberg* production, with 17 recalls, while the author, composer, and Mollie's husband, Will McConnell, then editor of the *New York Morning Telegraph*, sat in a box. It was in this production that Mollie McConnell created and played the part of Frau Ruder. What a glorious memory that song must have evoked for Mollie; it was a crowning moment and remains a melodic monument to her fame.

Some months later Richard Mansfield bought the play *Old Heidelberg*, from the Shuberts, starring himself in the drama as Prince Karl, with Mollie again appearing in her celebrated role as Frau Ruder. She was flying high with this production and did two seasons as Frau Ruder, along with other leading characters in Mansfield's repertoire.

After Mollie's husband died in 1905, she became a member of Frohman's London company for several seasons in the Duke of York's Theatre and other playhouses under Frohman's management.

Later Mollie went to Los Angeles to visit her father, W. F. Sherwood. In fact, her stage name had been Mollie Sherwood, while in movies she was known as Mollie McConnell. During her visit to her father, Mollie received an offer to work in movies and joined Balboa in 1913, the same year the studio was bought by the Horkheimers. The partial list of films Mollie produced at Balboa indicates how very busy she was at Long Beach, with many hits to her credit there, including *Will O' the Wisp*, *St. Elmo*, *The Red Circle*, and *Who Pays?*

The *Daily Telegram* (Dec. 14, 1920, 2:5) announced Mollie McConnell's death in Los Angeles in December 1920 in an article entitled "Body of Grande Dame of Picture World Is Cremated at L.A." and subtitled "Mollie McConnell Starred in Pictures Made Here:"

> The body of the late Mollie McConnell, who died last Thursday in Los Angeles, was cremated yesterday at the Los Angeles crematory. A large number of friends, both professional and personal, were present and flowers from many celebrated film stars marked the high regard in which Mollie McConnell, grande dame of the pictures, was held. Mrs. McConnell lived in Long Beach for six years, during the regime of the Balboa studio, and appeared in all of the best productions of that company, notably "The Red Circle," "Neglected Wife" and others.

The same article mentions that her last picture, unnamed in the article, was a Metro production. Always imposing and brilliant on the screen, Mollie McConnell was one of the grandes dames of silent pictures. It is worthy to note, however, that with her good-hearted modesty, Mollie let her fellow Balboans affectionately call her "Mother" on the set and backstage.

A Partial List of McConnell's Films at Balboa

Bab the Fixer. Five-reel comedy-drama. E. D. Horkheimer. Released Aug. 13, 1917, by Mutual Film Corp.

The Best Man. Four-reel social drama. Falcon Features. Released Oct. 21, 1917, by General Film Co.

The Checkmate. Five-reel drama. Mutual Film Corp., Horkheimer. Released May 21, 1917, by Mutual Star Corp., Mutual Star Productions.

The Criminal Code. Four-reel drama. Balboa Amusement Producing Co. Released Sept. 28, 1914, by Box Office Attraction Co., made for William Fox.

The Crooked Road. Balboa Amusement Producing Co., a Fortune Photoplay. Released in 1917.

The End of the Bridge. Three-reel drama. Balboa Amusement Producing Co. Released Oct. 26, 1914, by Box Office Attraction Co., made for William Fox.

The Girl Angle. Five-reel Western. Horkheimer Studios. Released Oct. 5, 1917, by World Film Corp.

His Old-Fashioned Dad. Four-reel drama. Falcon Features. Released by General Film Co.

Baby Marie and Mollie McConnell in unidentified still (courtesy of Marie Osborne-Yeats).

The Hunchback of Cedar Lodge. Three-reel drama. Balboa Amusement Producing Co. Released by Box Office Attraction Co., made for William Fox.

The Intrigue. Two-reel drama. Kalem. Released Mar. 4, 1914, by General Film Co.

Joy and the Dragon. Five-reel drama. Balboa Amusement Producing Co. Released Dec. 31, 1916, by Pathé Exchange, Inc.

Little Mary Sunshine. Five-reel drama. Balboa Feature Film Co. Released Mar. 3, 1916, by Pathé Exchange, Inc., Gold Rooster Plays.

The Martinache Marriage. Four-reel drama. Falcon Features. Released Sept. 1917 by General Film Co.

Pay Dirt. Five-reel drama. Knickerbocker Star Features. Released June 18, 1916, by General Film Co.

The Red Circle. Serial. Balboa Amusement Producing Co. Released by Pathé Frères.

The 14 chapters (two reels each): *Nevermore, Pity the Poor, Twenty Years Ago, In Strange Attire, Weapons of War, False Colors, Third Degree* or *Two Captives, Peace at Any Price, Dodgin' the Law, Excess Baggage, Seeds of Suspicion, Like a Rat in a Trap, Branded as a Thief,* and *Judgment Day.* Chapter 1 was copyrighted Feb. 30, 1915, and Chapter 14 was copyrighted Sept. 3, 1916 (*Filmarama*, vol. 1).

A Romance in the Hills. Balboa Amusement Producing Co.

St. Elmo. Six-reel drama. Balboa Amusement Producing Co. Released Aug. 1914 by Box Office Attraction Co., made for William Fox.

Shadows and Sunshine. Five-reel comedy-drama. Pathé-Balboa. Released Nov. 12, 1916, by Pathé Exchange, Inc., Gold Rooster Plays.

Should a Wife Forgive? Five-reel drama. Equitable Motion Pictures Corp. Released Nov. 8, 1915, by World Film Corp.

The Square Triangle. Three-reel drama. Balboa Amusement Producing Co. Released Sept. 28, 1914, by Box Office Attraction Co., made for William Fox.

Tricks of Fate. (no further information available)

The Twin Triangle. Five-reel drama. Balboa Amusement Co. Released May 1, 1916, by Equitable Motion Pictures Corp., World Film Corp.

The Understudy. Four-reel drama. Falcon Features. Released Oct. 5, 1917, by General Film Co.

The Unexpected. Three-reel drama. Balboa Amusement Producing Co. Released Feb. 28, 1914, by Box Office Attraction Co. Made for William Fox.

Who Pays? Serial. Released by Pathé Frères.

The 12 chapters: *The Price of Fame, The Pursuit of Pleasure, Where Justice Sleeps, The Love Liar, Unto Herself Alone, House of Glass, Blue Blood and Yellow, Today and Tomorrow, For the Commonwealth, The Pomp of the Earth, The Fruit of Folly,* and *Toil and Tyranny*. Chapter 1 was copyrighted Mar. 21, 1914, and Chapter 12 was copyrighted Oct. 13, 1915 (*Encyclopedia of the Movie Studios*, p. 234 and Scott, "Southern Exposure," p. 118).

The Will O' the Wisp. Four-reel drama. Balboa Amusement Producing Co. Released July 1914 by Box Office Attraction Co., made for William Fox.

Roscoe "Fatty" Arbuckle

Roscoe Arbuckle's family moved to Santa Ana, California, when he was only a boy. Although he was at first a plumber's assistant, Fatty Arbuckle's involvement with Long Beach's entertainment industry goes back to the beginning of the century when he did vaudeville and sang at the Byde A Whyle Theatre at the Pike during summer stock in 1908, the same summer he married Minta Durfee on stage. The citizens of Long Beach loved the entertainer, and he would always feel at home at the seaside resort. Arbuckle's attachment to Long Beach was profound and genuine, and these feelings help explain why he jumped at the opportunity to lease the Balboa Studios shortly after he headed his own film company, the Comique Film Corporation, beginning in 1917. While leasing the Balboa Studios, Arbuckle resided in a sumptuous beachfront house at 1817 Ocean Boulevard, which was demolished for redevelopment in 1971. Arbuckle's house even had a specially constructed tunnel that connected his property to the shore, where he would take daily swims, sometimes reportedly frolicking with the passing dolphins.

Some of the films Arbuckle produced at

Fatty Arbuckle.

Balboa were quite extravagant; one example is *A Country Hero*. According to *Frame-up* (p. 296), this movie was filmed at Jazzville, a rural village set built for Arbuckle at the Balboa Amusement Producing Company. Jim Kline's *The Complete Films of Buster Keaton* (p. 39) notes that the film contained an elaborate nightclub free-for-all in which Roscoe heaved a piano at a rival, along with a spectacular two-car auto wreck with a passing locomotive. Arbuckle spent over $20,000 staging the wreck scene alone, an incredible amount of money to splurge on just one scene for a two-reel comedy. Unfortunately, no known copy of this film exists today.

Expecting Arbuckle to produce an endless chain of successful films at Balboa, the Horkheimers had invested in the building of the industry's largest glassed-in studio for the very popular Arbuckle. While at Balboa, Arbuckle's troupe of players included Buster Keaton and Al St. John, the latter having been a former lifeguard at Long Beach before launching his film career with Arbuckle as a Keystone Kop.

Buster Keaton, Roscoe Arbuckle, and Al St. John.

Of course, Buster Keaton would become a legend, after first experiencing a meteoric rise to fame with his popular, hilarious, and agile character on the screen.

Arbuckle remains to this day, in the memories of filmgoers around the world, one of the earliest and greatest film stars, even though he was associated sadly and wrongly with the first giant scandal in the film industry. In his book about William Desmond Taylor, *A Deed of Death*, Robert Giroux also discusses the Arbuckle case and laments the way he was framed. Arbuckle was accused of sexually assailing and mortally wounding a starlet, Virginia Rappe, and was the defendant in three infamous trials beginning September 21, 1921, and ending, January 22, 1922. During the first two trials, the jury was unable to arrive at a verdict. The third trial exonerated him, and the foreman of the jury apologized for "the great injustice that has been done him" (Giroux, p. 40). Rumors circulated describing how Arbuckle had forced his 266 pounds of weight on Miss Rappe, thrusting a Coca-Cola bottle into her private parts, crushing her under his "tonnage," leaving her bleeding to death. Despite Arbuckle's acquittal and the shame of the trumped-up charges, the negative publicity forced him into early retirement as a comedian, though he did continue as a film director for a short period, changing his name to the pseudonym Will B. Good.

Because of Hollywood's string of scandals in the early 20s—beginning with Wallace Reid's death from drug addiction, William Desmond Taylor's unsolved murder, and especially with the publicity of the gruesome case involving Fatty Arbuckle, the U.S. film industry instituted the Hays Office to police and censor the activities of the "decadent" tendencies in the film industry. Hollywood's moguls united—Adolph Zukor, Marcus Loew, Winfield Sheehan, William Fox, Courtland Smith, Samuel Goldwyn, Carl Laemmle, R. H. Cochrane, Lewis J. Selznick, et al. They hired Will Hays, a member of President Warren Harding's cabinet and chairman of the Republican National Committee, to be in charge of the newly formed Motion Picture Producers and Distributors Association, making Hays the new "moral czar" for the film industry, with a whopping salary of $100,000 per annum, a greater salary at the time than that of the president of the United States of America (Giroux, p. 36). Even the irreverent humor of Arbuckle's pseudonym was suspect and was quickly "corrected" by the Hays Office; Arbuckle obediently changed Will B. Good to William B. Goodrich.

Giroux notes that the real truth about Arbuckle's "murder" case was only publicly disclosed in 1976. He states that Virginia Rappe was not the victim of Arbuckle at all, nor of any other party-goer in Arbuckle's crowded San Francisco hotel suite. Although the information was not publicized before 1976, Virginia Rappe showed up at the party already pregnant and very infected with gonorrhea as the sad result of her bed-hopping lifestyle; the disease had greatly damaged her bladder. Doctors who treated Rappe falsified the postmortem report to protect themselves, concealing the fact that she had died in a maternity

The beautiful and tragic Virginia Rappe.

ward after an illegal abortion procedure. At the party, Rappe had asked Fatty Arbuckle for money for the abortion. Known for his big-heartedness and liberal donations while he was a star on Easy Street, Arbuckle promised to help her. Giroux points out that the false accusations of sexual assault against Arbuckle were actually launched by a greedy third party who could smell the potential of netting a lot of cash. According to Giroux, Mandy Delmont, an older woman, framed Arbuckle, wreaking havoc to milk him for more money. During the preliminary inquest, Mandy Delmont telegraphed her lawyer to announce: "We have Roscoe Arbuckle in a hole here. Chance to make some money out of him" (Giroux, p. 39).

Two years after he was acquitted, still haunted by the damaging publicity, Roscoe Arbuckle returned to Long Beach on June 30, 1924, to attend a city council meeting in order to request the right to appear on stage at the Hoyt Theatre in Long Beach. Long Beach had many admirers of the film star, but his enemies were multiplying. The Long Beach Ministerial Union protested the idea of having Arbuckle perform on any stages in Long Beach because of the murder case, considering Arbuckle guilty of "moral delinquency," if not of murder. In fact, Councilman Fillmore Condit denounced Fatty at the council meeting, and Long Beach Councilman Arnold seconded the condemnation. The City Council members did not know that Arbuckle was in the audience, and Fatty surprised the crowd when he stood up during the motion to speak, directing his first question to Condit. According to the *Long Beach Press*, July 1, 1924, council members were dumbfounded when Arbuckle asked Condit: "Upon what facts do you base your motion? Be specific. What is the objection based on now, since I was cleared of the murder charge by a jury of twelve Americans?" The councilman replied: "Drunkenness. That in itself was a violation of the laws of this state." To Condit's response, Arbuckle made this plea, as he reportedly stiffened:

> I had no liquor in my apartments. There is no evidence of drunkenness in the record. I was the victim of circumstances and bad company that time. But, gentlemen of the Council, I found my God in that prison cell in San Francisco. I decided to change. I am a decent man now. My heart is clear. I went through the fire and it purged me. I am in debt $134,000 and I ask the chance to earn and pay it in the only way I know how.

Interrupted by thunderous applause, Arbuckle had once again won over his Long Beach supporters. Even in the Long Beach Council, the councilmen overwhelmingly favored Arbuckle's request, approving the motion to table Condit's resolution to prevent Arbuckle from appearing at the Hoyt Theatre. Only Condit and Arnold voted "nay" to tabling their previous motion.

In Long Beach that summer of 1924, Roscoe Arbuckle played to a full house at the Hoyt Theatre, with standing room only. The majority of citizens in Long Beach still loved the much-maligned comedian, watching enthusiastically the program that began with a short film, followed by Arbuckle emerging from behind the curtain, pleading for a second chance to perform for the American public. As

Arbuckle pondered his future in the entertainment industry, he was greeted on stage with deafening applause and a standing ovation. It was a heart-warming homecoming at the Hoyt Theatre, but the Long Beach welcome could not break Roscoe's eventual banishment from show business, and his future on the screen could not really be salvaged by a few loyal fans. Despite the goodwill on display that evening at Long Beach, public support would wane for Fatty Arbuckle. The self-righteous and self-serving forces in movieland would sacrifice Fatty Arbuckle as a scapegoat, pushing the famous actor away from the spotlight into one of the darkest corners of the wings in one of the most unfair character assassinations in movieland history.

A Complete List of Arbuckle's Films at Balboa

- ***The Bell Boy.*** Two-reel comedy. Comique Film Corp. Released Mar. 18, 1918, by Paramount Pictures.
- ***The Cook.*** Two-reel comedy. Comique Film Corp. Released Sept. 15, 1918, by Paramount Pictures.
- ***A Country Hero.*** Two-reel comedy. Comique Film Corp. Released Dec. 10, 1917, by Paramount Pictures.
- ***Good Night, Nurse.*** Two-reel comedy. Comique Film Corp. Released July 8, 1918, by Paramount Pictures.
- ***Moonshine.*** Two-reel comedy. Comique Film Corp. Released May 13, 1918, by Paramount Pictures.
- ***Out West.*** Two-reel comedy. Comique Film Corp. Released Jan. 20, 1918, by Paramount Pictures.

Baby Marie Osborne

Of all the celebrities at the Balboa Amusement Producing Company, only one Balboan has been able to share her memories in person with the authors of this book—Baby Marie Osborne. In working with Marie Osborne-Yeats since 1995, we have come to know a star of the first category who is as agile, vivacious, and enchanting in her mature years as she was as the three-year-old "Mary Sunshine" some 80 years ago on the silver screen. Many youngsters appeared as juvenile actors in early films, but Baby Marie was one of the first to make such a tremendous and lasting impression on the viewers. Before there were Baby Peggy, Jackie Coogan, and Shirley Temple, Baby Marie reigned as an international star loved the world over. The *Bristol Courier* in Pennsylvania printed on May 1, 1916, an article entitled "Baby Marie Osborne, the Youngest Leading Woman in the World," which defined the essence of the popular appeal of the young actress. While reviewing Marie's smash hit, *Little Mary Sunshine*, the writer of the article might very well have captured the little lady behind her screen persona:

> Baby Marie Osborne loves her amateur standing as a guileless kid and assumes the professional dignity of an honest-to-goodness leading lady in "Little Mary Sunshine" a Pathé Gold Rooster play that propels us with an urgent, though delicate, touch, back to the free spaces of the "never-never land."
>
> "Little Mary Sunshine" is one of those "once upon a time" butterflies, through whose gauzy wing we see life in rare and delightful tints. Five reels isn't a scene too long for "Little Mary," who, thank heaven, doesn't realize the charm of her fat little self and never overdoes the "saccharine stuff." Her utter unconsciousness of herself is a revelation in art, particularly in one so young, and points encouragingly to a brilliant stage career. Director Henry King, who also plays the male lead in the picture, deserves more than passing notice for his masterly handling of the child, and his delicate, knowing touch on a play that was woven of Fancy's wool. He is an actor of intelligence and subtlety, and a personality that is impressive. His handling of the "little things," the "tremendous trifles" in the direction of this feature, shows him an artist of depth and certainty.
>
> Baby Osborne can honestly and truly lay claim to be the youngest leading woman in the land, for she has just turned three years of age. Far from being "camera shy," she

Baby Marie (courtesy of Marie Osborne Yeats).

gurgles and laughs as though she were having the time of her life and goes through her scenes as though to the manner born. Almost invariably the child player of the stage is oppressed with a feeling of self-importance. Little Marie is not — she is just a wholesome, mighty clever, unspoiled baby, of whom any mother would be proud. Her debut in pictures makes us hope we will see others in which she is featured.

It has been a pleasure and an honor to know the former Balboan, not only for her impressive achievements in early cinema, but also for her delightful combination of spirited enthusiasm, attentive tact, and unaffected generosity. Marie Osborne-Yeats remains to this day an unspoiled, beguiling, and independent grande dame of the entertainment industry, of the same extraordinary ilk as the other six notable Balboans whom we have just presented in this reel. In fact, Marie Osborne-Yeats represents the special family atmosphere at Bal-

The youngest of Balboa's biggest stars (courtesy of Marie Osborne-Yeats).

boa, where the most popular players were given special nicknames as members of one big studio family: "Mother" Mollie McConnell, "Major" Daniel Gilfether, and "Pop" Lenard, to mention but a few. Despite the fierce competition and hard knocks that tend to wear people down in the movie industry, Marie Osborne-Yeats remains a very private, respectable, and genteel lady who knows, nonetheless, how to speak her mind and to raise bemused eyebrows. In sum, she represents the Balboa hallmarks of team loyalty and goodwill. We can only suggest to our readers the surprising blend of qualities possessed by this attractive movie star, who is still called Baby Marie by her close friends. Her many charms warm the heart and haunt the memory. To her own self, Baby Marie has stayed true-blue. Despite some sad circumstances in her life, Marie Osborne-Yeats lives very much in the present, while also being energetically forward-looking.

Scene from *Little Mary Sunshine* (Pathé, 1916).

Born Helen Alice Myres, November 5, 1911, Baby Marie Osborne was a native of Denver, Colorado. Unfortunately, 11 days after her birth, Baby Marie was placed in the Colorado State Home for Dependent and Neglected Children. In February 1912, Leon and Edyth Osborn[e] took the infant home, never formally adopting her; they renamed her Marie. From her foster parents, Marie received much loving and devoted care. As Michael G. Ankerich explains in his interview with Marie Osborne-Yeats in *Broken Silence*, it was not until Marie was 22 years old that she learned her foster parents were not her natural parents, despite earlier newspaper reports when she was a tot that called her a "ward of the court." Although she was surprised to learn the news and curious to know her real parents, even making an unsuccessful attempt to track down her natural parents, in the end Marie Osborne-Yeats appreciated even more the only parents she had known and loved, deciding to turn the page to the next chapter in her life without ever discovering more about her natural parents.

Not only did her foster parents love and care for Baby Marie, they also inadvertently introduced their daughter to a successful movie career. Around 1914, the Osbornes left Colorado, heading directly for California to try their luck in the growing movie business. They traveled to Long Beach where they became stock players under contract at the Balboa Amusement Producing Company. Mr. and Mrs. Osborne enjoyed bit parts over the years there, working with some of the celebrated photoplayers at Balboa: Ruth Roland, Cullen Landis, Lewis J. Cody, and Daniel Gilfether, among others.

It was never the intention of Marie's parents to have their daughter perform in movies; nor did they ever play in any of Marie's films once she became a movie star. They never wanted to infringe on their daughter's stardom. In fact, Baby Marie stumbled accidentally into the movie business. She appeared for the first time in *Maid of the Wild* (1915), playing in a pinch the part of a small boy, at the last moment replacing the lad who failed to show up for the scheduled shooting. Even though her name did not appear in the credits, Pathé and

"Newsie" Baby Marie (courtesy of Marie Osborne-Yeats).

the public noticed the Wunderkind. Henry King also fell in love with the charmer, asking Daniel Whitcomb to create a script at Balboa that would team Baby Marie and him as the film's leading man and leading lady. Pairing a toddler and a grownup as the leading couple in a feature film represented a novel idea, but the new formula became a roaring success. After all the noise about *Little Mary Sunshine* spread around the world, Pathé would back at least six more "Mary Sunshine" productions at Balboa, insisting on using in each the same leading couple, that sensational little lady and that talented actor-director — Baby Marie and Henry King.

Most of Baby Marie's films at Balboa included Henry King, but after they left Balboa and went their separate ways, the duo did not work together again till the 1930s. According to Tony Scott, from three to eight years of age, Baby Marie made 28 five-reel films and 2 two-reel films, and some claim that she performed at Balboa as late as 1919. Some newspaper articles imply that Marie did return to Balboa, her film company leasing the Long Beach studio after 1917, but it is clear that most of her movies after April 1917 were being made in Los Angeles, or more usually in Glendale at the Diando Studios. Of the 30 movies produced with Baby Marie, only 10 to date have been absolutely identified as having been filmed at Balboa, though others may well have been made there too. The following Baby Marie movies are known to have been produced at Balboa: in 1915, *Maid of the Wild, Should a Wife Forgive?*; in 1916, *Joy and the Dragon, Little Mary Sunshine, A Little Ray of Sunshine, Shadows and Sunshine*; in 1917, *Sunshine and Gold, Told at Twilight, Twin Kiddies, Twin Rays of Sunshine*.

So spectacular was Baby Marie's success that her salary became a heated issue, and her parents considered forming their own film company to feature their daughter exclusively, Baby Marie having become a veritable box-office hit before she was four years old. According to the *Los Angeles Record*, in an undated newspaper clipping entitled "Baby Marie Osborne Is Offered $300 a Week," the Horkheimers were even willing to pay a superstar's salary to keep the leading lady at the Balboa

Studios. The same article reveals, however, that Mr. and Mrs. Osborne knew they had a gold mine and decided to form their own film company:

> Not all of the salary holdouts are in the big league of baseball. Some are in the motion picture game. Take, for instance, the case of Baby Marie Osborn, the "Merry Sunshine" of picture-land. Baby Marie until recently was with the Balboa Amusement Co. of Long Beach.
>
> Upon the expiration of her contract with that firm, however, the parents of the child, Mrs. Edith Osborn and her husband, Leon Osborn, also film players, refused to sign up a new contract for the tiny star, declaring that the salary offered was insufficient.
>
> The little girl is not yet 5 years old. H. M. Horkheimer, president of the Balboa Co., offered to draw a contract with the child for $300 a week. BUT THE PARENTS TURNED DOWN THE OFFER, STATING THAT IT WAS NOT ENOUGH.
>
> The Balboa studio is now in the market for a new child star and Baby Marie Osborn is looking for a job. The parents contemplate organizing a company especially to produce "Merry Sunshine" films. They claim that local capital is ready to back them.
>
> Pres. Horkheimer was offered 20 per cent of the stock in the new company providing he would manage it, but he refused. And he has not withdrawn his offer of $300 a week to the baby star [from Baby Marie Osborne-Yeats' scrapbook].

In 1917, Leon Osborne and W. A. S. Douglas took over the old Kalem studio in Glendale, christening the studio the Diando Film Company, the name based on the "D" of Douglas and the "O" of Osborne, that is to say — the D and O Film Company, with Baby Marie being the major attraction. As Marie's fame and films spread like wildfire throughout the world, the young actress reportedly earned as much as $1,000 per week, living on Easy Street under the careful surveillance of her parents. In fact, after Marie became a star, her mother ceased acting in films altogether, becoming her daughter's escort and accompanying her famous child,

Baby Marie and a Balboa camera.

and she was always driven to and fro in high style by their chauffeur.

Before Baby Marie was an adolescent, she quit performing in the movies and stopped doing her national tours on stage, during which she had been accompanied by both her parents. Unfortunately, shortly thereafter Marie's foster parents divorced, and their daughter's trust fund evaporated. The glorious days of being an international star seemed like a dream as the family returned to more ordinary daily concerns. In fact, Marie enjoyed an adolescence away from the spotlight, going to school and growing up sharing time separately with her divorced mother and father, along with friends who had nothing to do with Hollywood. It seemed as if her Hollywood days were history.

Quite detached from the Hollywood glamour she had known as a tot, by 22 years of age, Marie was working as a saleswoman for $16 a week in a yardage department. Unexpectedly that same year, Marie's name hit the papers once more, with sensational stories that

British "Baby Marie" poster (courtesy of Marie Osborne-Yeats).

Baby Marie's natural father had been looking for her for the past five years. Marie's natural father was supposedly a man by the name of H. L. Shriver, who in 1927 sought his daughter through the Colorado State Home for Dependent and Neglected Children, explaining to the authorities that he, the natural father, and the natural mother of Marie intended to marry. The superintendent of the home tried to find Marie, but the former actress had left the limelight and was difficult to trace. Ironically, once Marie discovered the surprising news, her natural father could not be located. Was the story of her natural parents a mean hoax? Marie attempted to contact her natural parents through the home without success. In her usual fashion, after fate threw Marie this curved ball, she simply closed the chapter and moved on, perhaps reminded by the unplanned publicity that the movies might still be a viable option for the former film star.

It was about this time that Marie decided to return to films, including a little radio in Los Angeles — KFI's "Hollywood Extra Program." Never again, however, would Marie play the leading lady, except as a stand-in. According to a 1934 article entitled "Former Noted Child Star Stages Comeback as Extra Girl in Films" that was one of the unidentified newspaper clippings found in Marie's scrapbook, she was not really interested in turning back the clock. She was just taking advantage of the only business she had known, other than her low-paying work as a salesclerk. Returning to the movie industry definitely offered her greater opportunities for a brighter future.

The world-famous Hollywood director Henry King would enter once again Marie's life, lending a hand by opening doors. Marie would appear in his film *Caroline* (1934), as well as in films at other movie studios. At Fox she did stand-in work for Ginger Rogers in *Change of Heart* (1934), and also appeared in *The Gay Divorcee* (1934); she later did stand-in work for Deanna Durbin. In films for Paramount, she did stand-in work for Betty Hutton. Eventually, however, Marie would quit working before the camera altogether, as she sought more regular hours, acquired a new interest, and developed a new talent. In time she would become an outstanding costumer. Her apprenticeship began with the Western Costume Company, where she worked for two years before moving on to the movie studios, beginning with Republic. Marie quickly learned the ropes of the trade, how to handle the orders that would come in from high schools with plays in production, as well as costume requests from TV shows, learning also how to take care of the billing and shipping paperwork. She scurried from the fitting rooms

Unidentified newspaper clipping from 1934 (courtesy of Marie Osborne-Yeats).

to making costume selections, carefully reading the scripts ahead of time to envision all the costume changes during a theatrical or screen production. In *Broken Silence* (p. 232), Michael G. Ankerich explains Marie's impressive career as costumer:

> Marie worked on such films as *Guys and Dolls* (1955) with Marlon Brando and Jean Simmons, *This Earth is Mine* (1959) with Rock Hudson and Jean Simmons, *Spartacus* (1960) with Kirk Douglas, Laurence Olivier, and Jean Simmons, *Circus World* (1964) with John Wayne and Rita Hayworth, *The Chase* (1966) with Jane Fonda and Robert Redford, *The Legend of Lylah Clare* (1968) with Kim Novak and Peter Finch, *The Way We Were* (1973) with Barbra Streisand and Robert Redford, *Mame* (1974) with Lucille Ball and Bea Arthur, and many others.

Marie Osborne-Yeats emphasizes that what she most enjoyed as a costumer was being part of the team that put the movies together.

Among the many directors with whom she worked as a costumer, she most vividly recalls Fritz Lang for his professionalism and expertise. She harbors very fond memories of being part of these many movie crews, back on the sets where every day was different, where every film offered surprises, challenges, and rewards. For example, in a pinch Marie once had to take charge unexpectedly of the men's wardrobe because of a union walkout while she was working on *The Godfather, Part II*. As a costumer, Marie also enjoyed the traveling. For *The Godfather, Part II*, she journeyed from the Dominican Republic to Lake Tahoe to New York. The hours were long and hard but most satisfying. During her illustrious career as a costumer, Marie was the special costumer for Elizabeth Taylor in *Cleopatra* (1963), for whom there were as many as 40 costumes, not to mention all the accessories. Marie's rich experiences as a costumer explain her sharp eye today for detail and her appreciation for finishing touches in apparel. Close friends and neighbors say even today that Marie is always well coiffed and impeccably groomed, even in the most modest daily attire. In contrast to the rare instances of privacy accorded the most famous actors, costumers enjoy a higher measure of anonymity, an advantage that Marie much prefers. Order and maintenance, self-reliance, tact, the Golden Rule, and her eye for fine details constitute the humming gears that drive Marie's engine.

Despite Marie's self-reliant spirit and love of privacy, she has been married twice and has raised a family. Her first marriage did not last, but her second marriage was a loving match. Married a little more than five years to Frank J. Dempsey, a draftsman whom she had met at a church function, Marie divorced him in 1936. They had a daughter, Joan, and Marie took custody of their daughter after the divorce. In the 1940s, Marie married her second husband, Murray F. Yeats, a fellow actor with whom she enjoyed a conjugal life for nearly thirty years before she became a widow in 1975.

Baby Marie has always looked forward to the future and is totally aware of current events with her daily doses of voracious reading. She manages to face and accept change very well, inspired too on a daily basis by her perception of the beauty all around her. Whatever the challenge, Baby Marie has always made the best out of any circumstance. Her spirit is strong, untiring, and passionate, though prudent and tactful, never obliging others. Marie does follow the Golden Rule, and since she herself cherishes her own privacy and independence, she would be horrified to deprive others of the same. With her undaunted courage and optimism, Baby Marie has always savored the moment, exhibiting a kind and responsible tenderness toward those around her: family, friends, and all living things, including, of course, her special appreciation of the animal world. In order of importance, Marie is most grateful for her Roman Catholicism, for her most excellent health that she has enjoyed throughout her full and interesting life, for her cherished daughter, Joan, and for the beauty of nature.

One of Marie's favorite pastimes as a child — besides eating ice-cream cones — involved the care and company of animals. She still adores having pets at home, such as her rescued raccoon, one of the charges in her current life, and her many cats. As a child star, Marie was often featured in newspapers accompanied by her furry and feathered friends at home, including does, monkeys, ospreys, a donkey, a lion, an ocelot, even her beloved Pete the bear, who played a part in *Little Mary Sunshine*, and plenty of dogs of course — especially her boon companions, Rowdy and Toodles, her pet collie, Sandy, a poodle named Tiny, a pony named Dobbins, kittens, canaries, rats, and chipmunks.

It is only fitting that Baby Marie should still like being on the move and still adore ice-cream cones, although she consumes them in moderation these days to maintain a healthy cholesterol count. She to this day, at the age of 87, prefers to drive than to be driven. Wearing her leather gloves, she handles the turns, cautiously but masterfully, enjoying every moment behind the wheel, shifting gears like a venturesome yet careful spirit, totally in control of her Saab 9000S. As Henry King pointed out in the early days at Balboa, Marie enjoys fully the speed and power of a car. This forward-looking star moves steadily to the next bend in the road, and that perspective has dominated her point of view throughout life. She is prepared for tomorrow, yet is always caring and generous with her time at any given moment, be it for her friends, her neighbors, her Bible study group, or her fans in Long Beach or around the world who still send her fan letters.

We witnessed one example of Marie's generosity with her time when she arranged to drive up from San Clemente to Long Beach with her neighbor to deliver copies of *Broken Silence* and *Henry King, Director* to us, as well as to the Historical Society of Long Beach, and to the Long Beach Public Library. Not only did she deliver the books in person because "that's the way these things are done, my dear," but she insisted on driving us through the maze of one-way streets in downtown Long Beach. While we were at the civic center, it began to rain, and Baby Marie, always vigilant and prepared for rain or shine, insisted on trekking back alone inside the parking structure to her car to fetch an assortment of her own umbrellas, each one a different color and pattern. She passed them out, while eyeing and matching each umbrella to what each passenger was wearing. Never did our costumer ask for a hand, nor did she take the elevator up and down, and up and down again in the parking garage, nor would she allow someone else to do "her" job. These actions speak louder than any words about Baby Marie's conscientious and self-reliant nature.

Everyone in Long Beach who has been touched by Baby Marie's special aura has fallen in love with her. This love affair is part of the town's living heritage, that special link between the stars of Balboa and the townspeople who are awed by the Balboans' magnetic personalities and honored by their contributions to the exciting history of movie magic. Balboans will reign forever in Long Beach, and we can say with confidence that Baby Marie's continuing presence in our town makes the future look much brighter.

A Partial List of Osborne's Films at Balboa

Joy and the Dragon. Five-reel drama. Balboa Amusement Producing Co. Released Dec. 31, 1916, by Pathé Exchange, Inc.

Little Mary Sunshine. Five-reel drama. Balboa Feature Film Co. Released Mar. 3, 1916, by Pathé Exchange, Inc., Gold Rooster Plays.

A Little Ray of Sunshine. Balboa Feature Film Co. Released by Pathé Exchange, Inc., Gold Rooster Plays.

Maid of the Wild. Three reels. Balboa Amusement Producing Co. Released Oct. 9, 1915, by Pathé Frères.

Shadows and Sunshine. Five-reel comedy-drama. Pathé-Balboa. Released Nov. 12, 1916, by Pathé Exchange, Inc., Gold Rooster Plays.

Should a Wife Forgive? Five-reel drama. Equitable Motion Pictures Corp. Released Nov. 8, 1915, by World Film Corp.

Sunshine and Gold. Five-reel comedy-drama. Balboa Amusement Co. Released Apr. 29, 1917, by Pathé Exchange, Inc., Gold Rooster Plays.

Told at Twilight. Five-reel drama. Balboa Amusement Producing Co. Released Mar. 25, 1917, by Pathé Exchange, Inc., Gold Rooster Plays.

Twin Kiddies. Five-reel drama. Balboa Amusement Producing Co. Released Jan. 28, 1917, by Pathé Exchange, Inc., Gold Rooster Plays.

Twin Rays of Sunshine. Four-reel drama. Balboa Feature Film Co. Released Mar. 8, 1917, by Pathé Exchange, Inc., Gold Rooster Plays.

Reel 5

1918–1925:
The Beginning of the End

As early as March 10, 1916, *Variety* published an article entitled "Survival of the Fittest" that decried the fierce competition mounting in the film industry. The writer of the article specifically claimed that many companies were going under in the newfangled industry because they had grown too fast, producing more films than the market could handle. As explained in Reel 2 of this book, during the Great War, the film industry was in the doldrums, and several major companies went under, overcome by the most competitive independent movie producers and movie distributors. World Film Company had lost its prestige with the departure of Selznick from its ranks, and Mutual's days were limited, while Essanay and Selig too were beginning to topple. By 1918 the Edison Company had quit the filmmaking scene entirely, while Vitagraph and Pathé were fighting to keep up with the competition.

Most film historians accuse the Horkheimers of ineptly overproducing their films and glutting the market, but such excess of supply seems inevitable with any emerging and popular product, war or no war, until the balance between supply and demand is normalized. Problems of overproduction can still plague the most experienced film companies today; Disney Productions will be cutting back on its movies after recently saturating the market. Overproduction alone explains little about Balboa's collapse. On the contrary, H. M.'s optimism, even at the time of the bankruptcy, reflected his acceptance of both the ups and downs of market forces and the problems involved in taking calculated risks. By 1916, most of the older film plants were unable to keep up with the younger set of independent producers and distributors, and that younger breed of producers was represented by Balboa's pacesetting methods of production, innovative publicity, and an intercontinental system of distribution. In fact, the Horkheimers invested wisely in all three of these domains to keep their successful plant on the cutting edge, adaptable to the latest tastes, trends, and equipment in the movie business. Balboa had neither an obsolescent product nor a narrow system of commercialization.

There were, assuredly, other adversities that would intervene to make the Balboa Amusement Producing Company lose the

January 5, 1918: One of Charlie Chaplin's three visits to Balboa. President H. M. Horkheimer and Charlie Chaplin sit on the fence together and talk about the high cost of moving pictures. The cherubic expressions must be caused by a little bird who whispered something in their ears (courtesy of Marc Wanamaker).

At Balboa Studios (1918): *left to right*—(1) Buster Keaton, (2) Alf Reeves, Chaplin studio manager, (3) Charlie Chaplin, (4) unidentified, (5) H. M. Horkheimer, (6) unidentified, (7) Lou Anger, manager for Arbuckle.

support of its financial backers. These adversities were for the most part what one might call "acts of God"—principally the Great War and the discovery of petroleum in Long Beach. Over the next seven years, after the Horkheimers declared bankruptcy, adverse conditions displaced the movie industry in Long Beach, and these conditions were totally beyond the Horkheimers' control. Despite the bankruptcy, the Horkheimers were among those film pioneers who adapted well to change, being cognizant of the global and expanding market for movies. The brothers ran calculated risks to maintain their competitive edge in the swiftly changing entertainment industry.

Lacking the business acumen manifested by the Horkheimers, some filmmakers were unable to adapt to change, just as many carriage makers could not adapt to automobile manufacturing in the twentieth century. Hundreds of carriage factories vanished in the United States practically over night, except for Studebaker, one of the few carriage makers that was able to switch to producing automobiles. Once automobiles became affordable to the general public, there was no turning back, and the more advanced technology of automobiles would replace the horse-drawn carriages forever. Movies too replaced the preeminence of earlier theatrical performances, including the legitimate theatre, opera, and vaudeville. Without a crystal ball in hand, who would have thought possible a complete and irreversible conversion from carriage to automobile, or who would have imagined the performing artist at the theatre being upstaged by his flickering counterpart on the silver screen? The carriage makers could not see into the future, nor could they make a comeback once the new technology took over, so they simply sank in the unrelenting tide and drowned. The same

Here at least, all is not vanity. Anita King, the Balboa star, entertains a party of "just kids," suspending work on location to be photographed with them (courtesy of Marc Wanamaker).

fate faced the earliest filmmakers who could not adapt to the rapidly changing movie industry. Despite the Horkheimers' good track record as part of the younger set of independent producers and their excellent backers and distributors, once Balboa lost Pathé's financial support and distribution services, its competitive edge evaporated into thin air. The famous studio was damaged beyond repair, and the death blow was delivered by the adverse market conditions during the Great War.

It is difficult in today's global market to keep up with rapid changes. Enormous investments are necessary to adapt to the expensive and incessant advances in technology and remain competitive in the fashion-conscious and volatile high-tech consumerism that predominates around the world. What suffices in terms of manufacturing equipment during one season may become obsolete the next. In the same vein, certain products, while enjoying popularity one season, unexpectedly lose their appeal, only to collect dust in the overstocked warehouses. These volatile forces in the global market have always been in play for the ever-changing film industry.

By specializing in film production and leaving distribution, national and international, to specialists, the Horkheimers had established at Balboa the appropriate prototype for the entire industry. Felix Malitz of Piedmont Corporation, formerly the vice president and general manager of Pathé Frères and Pathé Exchange, tried to warn the film industry against the idea of having producers both manufacture and distribute their own films. Less than four months after the Horkheimers declared voluntary bankruptcy, on July 6, 1917, Felix Malitz hit the nail on the head in an article in *Moving Picture World* entitled "Producing and Distributing Should Be Strictly Separated." He claimed that production costs, which were passed on to the consumers at the movie theatres, could be reduced and efficiency heightened if producers did not distribute their own films. The Horkheimers seemed to understand this principle because they associated themselves back in 1914 with two major distributors, Fox and Pathé. The marriage between Pathé and Balboa failed by 1918, however, during a slump in the market, forcing the Horkheimers to lose the very strong partnership that Malitz advocated so vociferously between producers and distributors in order to avoid

"Reading the Script": standing, left to right, Janet M. Sully, Mr. Kirk, Mr. Smith, assistant cameraman; seated, left to right, Mr. Clark Bard, cameraman; Charlie Spear, leading man; Jack, assistant director; Eddie Saunders (Jackie Saunders' brother); Dorothy Wood, leading lady (courtesy of Marc Wanamaker).

unnecessary costs and delays in both production and distribution. Malitz noted, "Very often pictures cost by far too much money because they have not been produced with efficiency and alacrity, just because the boss [producer] may be or has been away for several weeks to attend to the placing of his previous picture." Malitz also warned producers in 1917 about an enduring truism — not to expect an excellent production to sell itself on its own merits or to expect a movie to succeed simply because a lot of money was spent on advertising. Instead, a reputable and expert distributor would be the only key to box-office success at home and abroad. Comparable marketing savvy would be impossible for a serious producer to master if he or she wanted to concentrate his or her talents on the manufacturing of quality movies, first and foremost. Malitz continued to insist on recognizing production and distribution as two distinct specialties that required separate attention and focus for a movie's success at the box office:

> An efficient and reliable selling organization costs money. It requires familiarity with the domestic and all foreign markets, many personal business relations and heavy expenses, and it is impossible for every producer to have such an organization of his own at his disposal. When he wants to avail himself of a selling organization built up by others, he must of course first of all be sure that he deals with people of high standing, clean reputation and high efficiency; to such an organization he will be able to concede advantageous terms for the selling of his state and foreign rights, because this organization means a real — an inestimable — help in the disposing of his pictures.

Circa 1916: Henry King always claimed in interviews that Balboa only depended on natural light for filming, but this view of the outdoor stage shows high-power electric lamps on the right, brought out and turned on to produce photographic possibilities on cloudy days. The lights were also used to help out the sunlight, which could not always penetrate darkened corners in stage sets (courtesy of Marc Wanamaker).

Malitz insisted that both producer and distributor remain absolutely independent in their specialties. Without that independence, neither one would do his best work:

> One important point which the producer must not overlook is to see that he deals with a selling representative not only of high standing, but who can give him a fair and square deal, which can be accomplished only when the selling agent feels himself absolutely independent in every way, and not, directly or indirectly, financially interested in any picture he handles; for then alone he will be in a position to give fair attention to every picture handled by him, because there is none to be given preference to for financial reasons.

Although the Horkheimers set masterfully their course for success, the economic trends during the Great War dashed their plans. After the Horkheimers submitted on March 26, 1918, a statement of their assets and liabilities to a meeting of their creditors, *Variety* printed it a few days later on April 5, 1918. The statement showed a robust enterprise:

Real estate and buildings	$105,292.54
Investment	2,610.64
	$107,903.18
Less mortgage	-14,900.00
	$93,003.18
Equipment	112,551.63
Supplies	10,771.60
Contract rights, scenarios, etc.	55,318.35
Pictures	174,032.02
Accounts receivable	3,269.92
Petty cash	100.14
Total assets	$449,046.84
Bank loans, etc.	$48,729.44
Bank overdraft	5,811.88
Salaries payable	57,959.79
Trust funds	44,032.90
Trade and miscellaneous accounts	63,433.09
Liabilities	$219,967.70
Capital	83,350.00
	$ 303,317.70
Surplus	145,729.14
	$449,046.84

The *Variety* article, which was entitled "Balboa Plant to Be Operated By a Committee of Creditors," reported the total assets at $449,046.84 and the liabilities at $219,967.70, including $48,729.44 in bank loans, with $100.14 in petty cash. The same article claimed that the company would not be placed in bankruptcy. Most of the nearly 200 creditors in attendance at the meeting rejected the idea of bankruptcy, deciding that the movie plant should be handled by a committee of creditors consisting of three representatives of the banks at Long Beach, three representatives of general creditors, and three labor claimants, or employees of the company. The article concluded:

> The Balboa studio was attached last week by the Wholesalers' Board of Trade, to satisfy debts and the Labor Commission present[s] claims for salaries which have been incurred since the Horkheimers began operations.
> According to a statement made by the company, the liabilities are around $20[0],000, with assets consisting of studio property, completed films, etc., $40[0],000.
> The plant will continue to run in order to complete unfinished pictures, but outside executives will be brought in. (*Variety*, Apr. 5, 1918, p. 49)

As late as May 29, 1918, trade journals expected Balboa would rebound, and they reported that the Balboa Amusement Corporation would begin production of a series to be released in five-reel parts for ten weeks, a new venture about which film circles were buzzing. The serial was supposed to total 50 reels, to be the longest of its kind ever offered. The new serial involved the latest discovery by the Horkheimers, their nascent star Mona Lisa, who bore a striking resemblance to Leonardo da Vinci's original. The Horkheimers, however, could not bridge the widening gap developing during the slump in the market in the aftermath of the war which greatly reduced trade with Europe. The Great War had made Pathé more cautious in a war-torn economy, and when Pathé withdrew financial backing, the punch forced the Horkheimers to bow out in the months to come, abandoning their successful movie business, the preeminent industry of Southern California that the Horkheimers had helped forge during their meteoric rise to fame and glory.

Acts of God: World War I and the Long Beach Oil Strike

The havoc generated by the Great War resulted in immeasurable material damage, economic paralysis, and an enormous loss of human life. Like a monstrous tornado, the war spread haunting winds of despair to millions of disillusioned and wailing souls. All the countries, winners and losers alike, suffered terribly. In its scope and totality, the Great War ushered in a violent age of international warfare, ironically, at the inception of an emerging millennium of global expansion and interdependence. Never before had a war exhausted so many human and material resources among the richest nations of the world. Europe bled itself dry, and its wounds scarred both the psyche and the face of Europe. The number of casualties in previous wars had no equal to the almost 9,000,000 servicemen who perished in the combined armed forces of the Allied and Associated powers as well as the Central Powers. Besides the terrible loss of soldiers, the direct war expenditure of the Allied and Associated powers totaled approximately $145,400,000,000, including as well British, French, and U.S. loans of around $20,000,000,000 to other fighting countries. For the Central Powers, the cost totaled around $63,000,000,000, with German loans of $2,400,000,000. Farms, villages, factories, and homes turned to dust in the most industrialized departments of France, effacing the signs of the region's former prosperity.

At war's end, many Europeans could not return to the lives they had led before. Some countries ceased to exist, including many of the grandest empires that had reigned for centuries on European soil — the Austro-Hungarian Empire, the Russian Empire, the Prussian Empire (the second German Reich), and the Ottoman Empire. The conflagration of war ushered in much turmoil and confusion with unstable governments, changing boundaries, and exhausted national economies. Starting anew seemed impossible even for the winners who remained intact and enhanced, so to speak, such as the British and French empires. Before the war, France boasted of having the enviable position of being the number one producer in the world of some of the industrial age's most prestigious items — automobiles, airplanes, and motion pictures. As a consequence of the war, technological preeminence in these key industries would shift eventually from war-weary Europe, mostly to the stabler shores of the United States. The transfer of the movie capital from France to the United States was definitely accomplished by war's end, and that period of transfer coincides, not accidentally, with the Horkheimers' meteoric rise to fame and glory between 1913 and 1918.

Unfortunately, between 1914 and 1918, France's northeastern departments served as the primary military front, being the battleground for entrenched enemy and allied forces. So much of France's prime property was under fire that industrial production dropped 40% in France during the war, while the nation's currency in international exchanges was gravely weakened. The French government only finally stabilized the franc ten years later in 1928, by which time the French monetary unit had lost 80% of its prewar value. The Great War had set back economic growth in France a whole decade, dismantling, of course, the French movie industry in the bargain. Given these economic conditions, one can better understand why Pathé was concerned about cutting costs and refused to distribute more of Balboa's productions.

Pathé's woes shook the French-based company's worldwide operations. Pathé was well established not only throughout the United States, but also throughout the world: in Europe, including Kiev and Budapest, and Asia, including Calcutta and Singapore. Before the Great War, Pathé was expanding rapidly, seemingly both unbeatable and ubiquitous. That permanence was only illusory. The Great

War shut down many of Pathé's operations in Europe and throughout the world, causing absolute chaos in many of its subsidiaries. When the First World War began in 1914, Pathé, in his usually cautious manner, made efforts to protect his important American market, which was managed through the Pathé Exchange, but he could not have imagined the extent to which his European enterprise would be in tatters by the end of the war. The weakened French franc and destroyed industries in France caused production costs to soar astronomically, and the deluge of American films irrevocably replaced French films in Europe and across the globe. To make matters even worse for Pathé, the American market had been steadily rejecting European films since Fox made the decision to distribute only American movies, a decision that favored Balboa productions. Seeing the American market as essential to the success of his international operations, Pathé even specified to his European producers to tailor their film productions to American tastes in a last ditch effort to keep the French film industry competitive at the end of the war, but his efforts could not save his company.

By 1918, Pathé, like France itself, had to admit the profound and painful consequences of the Great War. After so much success and hard work, Pathé was forced to dismantle his film empire over the next few years, including his association with Balboa, as he removed certain affiliates from his worldwide operations. In fact, as explained by Ephraim Katz in his work *The Film Encyclopedia*, Merrill, Lynch & Company acquired the controlling interest in Pathé's company in the United States in 1923, and this interest would then be sold to Blair and Company in 1926. By 1929, Pathé had sold the rest of his holdings, and he withdrew permanently from all his business ventures. His name did linger, however, once the Pathé company was sold to RKO in 1931, because the firm continued to provide film financing and laboratory services in the United States. Ephraim Katz remarks that the name "Pathé" even experienced a certain resurrection in the 1990s when Pathé Communications Corporation owned MGM/UA, renaming it MGM-Pathé.

Despite American preeminence in world cinema by the end of the Great War, there were difficulties to overcome and a slump in the American market. A series of articles in *Variety* beginning August 30, 1918, and running through November 15, 1918, discussed new problems plaguing the American movie industry. First, as the industry grew, the U.S. government determined it an essential business for winning the war. Consequently, the film industry encountered more and more governmental intrusion at all levels of production, distribution, and exhibition. Second, with the manpower required to fight the war, many male employees were no longer available. At the same time, labor unions began to make demands that created other restrictions and difficulties for studios. When the Horkheimers bowed out, they were by no means the only moguls facing mounting complications in the entertainment industry, both during and after the catastrophes of the Great War.

The ruling by the U.S. government that films were essential to the nation was a mixed blessing for the industry because it meant all branches of the industry, from production and distribution to exhibition, would be subject to governmental intervention. For purposes of public morale and military propaganda, the film industry acquired a unique status protected by the federal government. As a result, the U.S. government regulated whom to hire and how to budget the films, protecting "essential" workers in the film industry, except for young male employees needed for the armed services, who were replaced with women. Productions were to be on tighter budgets, eliminating surplus shooting to avoid waste. The government also asked that old films be returned to be recycled into explosives for the war effort because the chemicals used in producing nitrate film resemble those of guncotton, the chemicals needed for manufacturing explosives. In an August 30, 1918 article (p. 42), *Variety* stated that the film industry was becoming the ward of the federal government, which was beginning to take charge of the industry for the public good:

The Priorities Committee of the War Industries Board in Washington last Friday declared the motion picture industry essential in all its branches.

This is a very important ruling in that it is the only industry in the United States so passed upon. This action by the Board was announced officially by Chairman Bernard M. Baruch.

The declaration is the result of a conference between the Priorities Committee of the Board, headed by Judge Edwin B. Parker and a committee of the National Association of the Motion Picture industry, headed by Pres. William A. Brady.

Plans were agreed upon for the conservation of film in every way deemed feasible, and hereafter the general custom of "shooting" five times as much negative as is finally used will be eliminated. The necessity for this conservation is due to the fact that the chemicals utilized in the manufacture of the base celluloid are required in many forms of explosives. All waste film must be returned to the manufacturer together with all old film when it has outlived its usefulness for exhibition.

The major concern of those involved in the motion picture industry was determining who would be deemed essential. The armistice that put an end to the war was not signed until November 11, 1918. Until then, recruiting and patriotic propaganda for the war effort affected the filmmaking community. In the same article, which was entitled, "'Essential Ruling' for Films Takes in Experienced People," *Variety* explained who would be considered essential in the ruling from the government's point of view: "It can be stated with authority that the ruling includes producers, directors, actors and actresses, managers of theatres and exchanges, assistant managers, and does not embrace any male employees who can be replaced by women. For instance, if a woman can be secured to run a machine or do clerical work in an office, sell or take tickets, etc., the men they may replace can be called by the Government."

Before the signing of the Armistice, *Variety* followed closely the continuing woes in the industry arising from stricter governmental controls and the all-consuming war effort throughout the Western world. In an October 18, 1918, article entitled, "Decision to Close Studios Follows New Release Ban," *Variety* reported that as a matter of voluntary compliance, the federal government had asked the industry to shut down its studios and refrain from releasing any new pictures for four weeks. The United States government had the cooperation of almost all the movie studios. In fact, Vitagraph was the only film plant that refused to shut down. This period of strict governmental intervention occurred at the same time that the Horkheimers were hoping and waiting for an upturn in the market. Unfortunately, the timing could not have been worse for optimism in the industry. Besides cutting off production, the government promoted a rigorous program of downsizing throughout the industry's network of production, distribution, and exhibition, according to *Variety* (Oct. 18, 1918, p. 92): "With but one exception all the releasing concerns are laying off a number of their executives, and the exception has adopted a plan of withholding 50 per cent of all executives receiving salaries of over $25 a week for the four weeks of inaction, paying the money so withheld at a later date." Although it was not officially ordered, the closing of the studios was considered a patriotic duty and a health precaution because of the influenza epidemic sweeping the nation. Actors under contract could still insist on payment for their layoffs, and *Variety* was unable or unwilling to disclose to the public any dissenting voices from the actors but explained that most of the exchanges in New York also laid off a portion of their sales personnel and office forces at the same time. The shutdown was far-reaching in the industry: "The General, Mutual, Universal, Sherry and the First National all gave enforced vacations to various members of their staffs" (*Variety*, Oct. 18, 1918, p. 42).

Pathé, the Horkheimers' major distributor, was ahead of the game, perhaps because it was based in war-torn France, where so much of the commercial paralysis began during the Great War. The October 18, 1918, *Variety* article described Pathé, the "House of Serials," as being the film-producing interest in the United States that was the least affected by the new ruling. Not only did Pathé have a reputation for efficiency and quality control, it had tightened its belt early, as is evidenced by its refusal to distribute that same year any more of Balboa's productions. Moreover, the French-based company pleased the U.S. government by shifting its productions from general features to educational films and propagandistic war pictures, and it was also releasing the Official War Review for the U.S. government. In part, Pathé had new priorities for the war effort, and Balboa no longer seemed to fit into the picture. The same *Variety* article (Oct. 18, 1918, p. 42) declared: "While all Pathé feature films are equally affected by the new ruling, they will suffer the least, since most of their feature films have already been released. Their serial pictures, educationals and war films are in no way affected."

Shortly after publishing the article just cited, *Variety* wrote about the pros and cons of the war years, summarizing the activities affecting the movie industry during the four years of hostilities, and mentioning another thorn in the side of the aching industry — labor troubles. This article, which appeared on October 25, 1918, was entitled "Bankruptcy in Pictures Laid to War Conditions." Once again the industry was described according to terms borrowed from the theory of Darwinism. Evolution in the industry had been ruthless, permitting only the strongest and the fittest to survive. The Horkheimers had survived the competition, but that survival preceded the intrusion of the U.S. government in the film industry. Owners of small studios were being devoured by their more able competitors because of the war and the way it had changed the public's demand "for greater and better pictures." Exhibitors with small businesses faced the same fate as the small film companies; they were unable to compete with the million-dollar motion picture palaces springing up across the nation, subsidized in part by the 20 billion dollars to be released by the U.S. government for war purposes.

Consequently, the war and the subsequent subsidization by the U.S. government actually helped determine the rise and fall of large and small film producers, distributors, and exhibitors. One of the consequences of the Great War throughout the West would be bigger government and its growing involvement in the private sector. Ironically, "survival of the fittest" often meant the survival of the most subsidized or those most favored by governmental intervention. Free market forces did not come into play much during this slump in the film market. New forces were changing the film industry — intervention by the federal government and labor unions efforts to organize inside the studios:

> As a medium or propaganda, the motion picture theatre has many points of advantage over the press, and as a source of revenue to Uncle Sam it is a mint. But the serious question which is now puzzling the gentlemen who control the industry is the extent to which the Government, on the one hand, and the labor unions, on the other, are likely to confiscate the bullion without disrupting the business [*Variety*, Oct. 25, 1918, p. 37].

The movie industry was besieged by those who wanted a piece of the scrumptious pie. On the one hand, the U.S. government was playing Robin Hood by redistributing the wealth to its chosen favorites, while emerging labor unions fought hard to profit also from the riches generated at the studios. At the same time, the federal government had to protect public health during the devastating influenza epidemic, choking in its grasp the very goose that was laying the golden eggs. Local boards of health shut down every place of amusement in Greater New York. Despite the governmental shut-down of studios and the influenza scare, however, new taxes imposed on the movie industry assured a steady flow of money into governmental coffers, making Uncle Sam a meddler with sticky fingers. The movie industry had been doing too well for the federal government not to try to poke its hand in the cookie jar. The October 25, 1918, article in

Variety stated: "With a tax of one-quarter per cent on raw film and one-half per cent on finished film; a ten (or twenty) per cent tax on admissions to theatres; and advance in the salaries of players, operators, photographers, carpenters, property men, clay-modelers, electricians, musicians and even ushers, averaging about 25 per cent, and higher pay among the mechanics at the studios, the film industry is beset on every hand by an army of Olivers asking for money."

The International Alliance of Theatrical Stage Employees, which included the moving picture machine operators in the United States and Canada, had been formed as early as July 17, 1893, becoming international on October 1, 1902. During the same period of governmental intervention during the Great War, the studios of Los Angeles experienced the first real labor trouble in the history of movieland. The I.A.T.S.E., with 1,100 members, went on strike, demanding a raise in wages "from $5 to $6 per diem, with a working day of eight hours, with time and one-half for overtime and Sundays." According to the October 25, 1918, *Variety* article: "Griffith, Astra Films, Chaplin, Fox, Hart, Ince, Kerigan, L-KO, Metro, Sennet, Universal, Weber, Yorke studios acceded to the demands of the union, but nine of the producers determined to fight. Extra men were called upon to do the work of the mechanics; but being gentlemen of leisure, they refused duty. An order restraining operators, or grips, from working in the theatres is a retaliatory measure threatened by the Federal Labor Council."

As if governmental intervention and labor troubles were not enough to plague the studios, there was also a killer that attacked the entertainment industry and the whole world with a vengeance. The influenza epidemic of 1918 deserves special attention. In 1918, influenza killed as many as 40 million people around the world. As if the Great War had not done enough to depress the war-weary populations, an unusually potent virus killed more American soldiers than had died in combat during the war. Recent studies by Dr. Jeffrey K. Taubenberger and his research team have furnished the first direct evidence on the genetic makeup of the 1918 virus, determining that the killer virus developed along normal channels, with nothing aberrant about its origin. Such an epidemic, though unusual, could happen again. Until the research by Dr. Taubenberger and his team, there had only been indirect clues about the nature of the virulent outbreak. First, viruses were unknown in 1918, so scientists had to depend on antibody patterns among survivors of the epidemic, but antibodies give incomplete data about any virus. Lung tissue preserved in formaldehyde from U.S. soldiers who fell victim to the disease was studied at the Armed Forces Institute. This recent research by Dr. Taubenberger was able to piece together parts of five different genes from the killer strain, less than ten percent of the entire genome.

The influenza epidemic climaxed in September 1918, and in October 1918, it reached Long Beach. In September 1918, the influenza struck a military camp outside of Boston. Many of the soldiers fell instantly and gravely ill, turning blue, bleeding from the nose, dying within 48 hours. In one day 90 soldiers died. The epidemic entered Southern California via an infected ship in the harbor of San Pedro, next to the port of Long Beach. On October 11 1918, all schools, theatres, and public meeting places were closed throughout the county of Los Angeles. In Long Beach, January 8, 1919, a new flu ban was imposed against public assemblies at high school football games and sporting events. On January 21, 1919, Long Beach proclaimed a discontinuance of all public gatherings. By January 23, theatres in Long Beach were closed on account of the influenza, but all the restrictions were lifted by January 31, 1919. Despite all the precautions, the influenza spread like wildfire, as Claudine Burnett describes:

> In the first 2 weeks of October between 400 and 500 cases had been reported in Long Beach and 5 deaths had occurred. Before it was over in February of 1919, there were 148 deaths of the flu in Long Beach (compared to 60 Long Beach lads who lost their lives in World War I). In the United States

alone more people died of the flu (550,000) in 1918 than the U.S. military lost to combat in both World Wars, Korea and Vietnam. ("Influenza Ghosts")

Years later it was decided that the influenza had probably started on a pig farm in Iowa. According to Claudine Burnett, after the annual Iowa Cedar Rapids Swine Show in September 1917, millions of pigs fell ill and thousands died. The virus first spread among animals — moose, elk, bison, and sheep — before reaching the human population in North America. Doctors failed to acknowledge the epidemic until American troops had transported the dreaded disease to an already devastated Europe.

The movie industry also experienced a shutdown because of the flu. On November 15, 1918, four days after the armistice was signed that ended the war, *Variety* (p. 50) printed an article, entitled, "Industry Resumes Releasing After Five Weeks' Shutdown." Once again, however, the Horkheimers would not experience an upswing in the market because of yet another catastrophe. It would take at least a year for the industry to recover from the paralysis caused by the influenza epidemic: "The exchanges throughout the country where the epidemic closed down the theatres were also shut down and the incomes of the producing and distributing companies was cut to almost nothing because of the countrywide closing of the houses. It was a tremendous blow to the industry and those that are at its head say that it will be at least a year before the companies can recover from the body blow that it has received."

As if world war, governmental intrusion, a global epidemic, and heated labor disputes were not enough to discourage the Horkheimers' return to filmmaking, another unexpected discovery altered physically and economically the city of Long Beach, transforming it from an entertainment and resort town to a world-class port and industrial center for Southern California. In 1921 the world's richest oil deposit in terms of barrels of crude oil per acre gushed out of Signal Hill. Within the first 50 years of drilling 2,400 wells, over 859,000,000 barrels of petroleum were extracted in Signal Hill and the Long Beach area. The new darling of Long Beach was dinosaur juice, not celluloid, with the city going wild over the revenues generated by the plentiful natural resource oozing below the former stages of the city's movie community. The following timeline, recorded by Claudine Burnett at the Long Beach Public Library, touches briefly upon the spectacular highlights of the oil strike in Long Beach and its economic consequences.

April 5, 1921: Inventor Jonathan Beggs, at 96 years of age, predicted an oil strike in the Signal Hill area, saying that millions of dollars would be made.

May 2, 1921: Signs of oil in Signal Hill caused excitement throughout the city of Long Beach.

May 24, 1921: Crude oil flowed from a well at Signal Hill.

May 25, 1921: Fifty Signal Hill lots were sold in one day.

May 27, 1921: The city of Long Beach became the proprietor of 36 acres in the "oil belt" of Signal Hill, with the municipality standing a chance of having an extraordinary means of producing revenues for the city, perhaps ending all city taxation.

June 24, 1921: A Shell gusher set Long Beach wild: black fluid shot high in the air at different times during the night.

October 26, 1921: A new well on Signal Hill caved in with the mighty rush of oil.

November 17, 1921: A second "gasser" gushed out of control, the well roaring loudly throughout Signal Hill area.

November 28, 1921: Oil spouted from the municipal oil hole, with 200 barrels shooting above the top of the derrick.

November 29, 1921: The city's income increased $360 per day thanks to the oil well.

December 1, 1921: Visions of riches dazzled Long Beach officials. They scrapped plans to build a city park to focus on oil production, expecting millions in income from the municipal well.

Oil gusher.

December 10, 1921: Long Beach imposed a "hands off" policy in the city's eagerness to claim oil rights, claiming exclusive rights to profits, saying those profits belonged to Long Beach's water department.

December 13, 1921: A third "gasser" erupted on the hill, Wilbur No. 1, a roaring geyser of pure gas flame; a workman was badly burned.

March 2, 1922: The biggest Signal Hill gusher yet erupted with a resounding roar.

June 2, 1922: Oil revenues to fill city cash basis fund: black gold receipts to July 1 would total $19,675.40.

July 29, 1922: Income for the year was $511,000, from the city's new well.

August 24, 1922: The first step was taken to establish a taxless city for Long Beach, with all oil monies to go into the general fund.

December 31, 1922: Long Beach oil revenues for the year 1922 exceeded $200,000.

April 29, 1923: It was decided that oil revenues would not lower the city's tax rate, but a new fund would be created.

May 12, 1923: City coffers were enriched by the oil money — revenues for the fiscal year totaling $400,000.

During this exciting period of oil drilling and gushing derricks, Long Beach was becoming richer than it had ever dreamed, transforming itself into a new industrial center and international port. On the other hand, the physical transformation — oil derricks here, there, and everywhere in town — hurt the appearance of the seaside resort. Although the movie industry would continue to produce a good number of films in Long Beach until the mid-twenties, gone were the days when Balboa would compete for the crown of movie capital, and no longer would the film plant of "Hollywood by the Sea" represent the biggest employer in town and the greatest tourist attraction for Long Beach. Oil money would drench the city and steal the show. In a few more years, the studio site would shrink in size as real estate development closed in, and the final coup de grâce would be delivered in

Oil wells on Signal Hill.

January 1925, with the demolition of the famous glassed-in stage and its surrounding buildings. At that time, the Balboa Amusement Producing Company became history.

The Changing of Hands

As mentioned in Reel 2 of this book, the Balboa plant was turned over to creditors, on March 25, 1918. During its management by the creditors, Balboa was leased or sold to a number of companies. Although the studio continued to be managed by the Balboa trustees for most of the seven years, the trust being a corporation of the studio's major creditors, there were a few failed attempts to sell the site and a few successful ones. Potential sales were hindered in part by the slump in the market and by buyers with bad credit; they were even blocked purposefully at times by the shareholding interests of the Horkheimers, who were reluctant to give up entirely the reins of the studio. Despite the changing of hands from 1918 to 1925, people continued to call the plant the Balboa Studios, and its walls were faithfully repainted with the Balboa name until the plant's demolition in 1925, despite all the new "owners" who tried to reclaim the site. For the last seven years of operation, the Balboa plant never regained the glory of its past, and the creditors failed to find the right buyer. Although the new operators raved about the facilities and made ambitious plans, mismanagement and misfortune blocked Balboa's road to recovery. Throughout those painful seven years of unrelenting decline for the movie industry in Long Beach, H. M. Horkheimer was still waiting eagerly in the wings for one last fling at eternal fame and glory. Unfortunately, with all the failed attempts to recapture its past as a buzzing film center, Balboa Studios never succeeded in netting the right buyer, and all the prospective deals fizzled out, one after the other, during the sour market and the difficult times that followed the First World War.

By the beginning of 1919, enthusiastic producing companies and interested buyers emerged on scene to try their luck at the Balboa Studios. In February 1919, only three months after the signing of the armistice, the Balboa plant was leased by the New Art Film Company, which was headed by George D. Watters, vice president and general manager of the concern. Watters had been a prominent figure in show business in the Midwest. The owners of New Art, based in Des Moines, Iowa, considered purchasing the studio, but the negotiations were never finalized. Among others on the staff was Fred Sullivan, former general director with Thanhouser Film Company. The first picture was announced in the *Daily Telegram*, February 13, 1919; it was entitled *The Warning*, directed by Fred Sullivan. The New Art Company had been hiring for its Long Beach productions a number of actors and actresses, including Edward Cecil and Kate Lester, the two leading actors in *The Warning*. Jack Mulhall of Famous Players had also been lent to New Art for a lead in *The Warning*, which was a production backed by the U.S. government. Other players associated with New Art who were announced in the *Daily Telegram* were Ann Schaefer; Edward Jobson; Irene Aldwyn; Pauline Curley; Helene Chadwick, a Pathé star; Leo Pearson; Charles Spere, who had starred with Mary Miles Minter; and Gordon Griffith, who had played young Tarzan in *Tarzan of the Apes*. Despite this announcement of great things to come at Long Beach, no more information has been gleaned about *The Warning* or the other New Art Company productions at Long Beach.

Three months after the New Art Film Company first stepped in, its lease was overridden by interested buyers who borrowed money for the purchase but ultimately had trouble meeting their obligations. On April 14, 1919, F. C. Delano, representing the corporation organized for the purpose, among other things, of holding and administering the Balboa property in trust, proceeded to sell the Long Beach studio to William S. Forsyth and Charles M. Furey, whose company name was Master Pictures Corporation. Forsyth and Furey had agreed to borrow from W. J. Conner the sum of $350,000. An appraisal of the real estate and the studio properties was made May 2, 1919. The total real estate value was determined at $37,563 and the total improvements (buildings and amenities) were appraised at $326,850, the grand total being $364,413. Most of the former Balboa Amusement Producing Company was intact for this purchase. As an omen of things to come, however, it appears from cross-referencing and studying the Sanborn maps that some of the real estate, especially on the northeast corner, had already been sold since 1918 in small parcels to some of the expanding retail businesses in the neighborhood, reducing the studio's former northeastern border that had skirted most of the block along Seventh Street.

Furey and Forsyth began to have difficulties making payments by the autumn of 1919, as is attested by a writ of assignment that was delivered to them by the Superior Court of California via the sheriff's office on September 20, 1919, by a plaintiff named Thomas R. Mills. The Retail Merchants Credit Association of Los Angeles, which was associated with the Balboa trustees, another plaintiff against Master Pictures, claimed on October 14, 1919, that the judgment was still in full force and unsatisfied against the debtor. An attachment was served to Master Pictures against money or papers belonging to W. J. Conner, W. S. Forsyth, and B. M. Furey, co-partners of Master Pictures. Interestingly enough, the plaintiffs in the latter case included the Title Insurance and Trust Company, the Bank of Italy, the National Bank of Pasadena, the Crown City Trust and Savings Bank, R. De MoLouis, the City Center Company, and the Baby Marie Osborne Film Company.

While these financial problems were plaguing the prospective buyer, Master Pictures was leasing the facilities to various production companies with significant rosters of players and technicians. For example, at the end of 1919, the Mercury Comedy Company started work at Balboa, producing Morante comedies. Milburn Morante's troupe also included Joe Bonner, juvenile player; H. Hewston, character actor; Ray Hampton, character actress; Grace Gordon and Florence Gilbert,

Texas Guinan.

ingénues; Grover Jones, writer and director; Al Morante, assistant director; M. J. Burns, cameraman; T. Caswell, assistant cameraman; R. C. Currier, editor; J. Morante, technical director; and Charles Everett, master of properties (*Daily Telegram*, Dec. 3, 1919, 3:5). The Morante company was so pleased with the studio and its equipment that it encouraged other leasing companies to join it at Long Beach — the Holly Comedy Company, making two-reel comedies featuring Syd Smith; the Spinx Serial Company, producing at Balboa a 30-reel serial entitled *The Fatal Thirty*, written by Grover Jones; and the Texas Guinan Company, making two-reel Westerns featuring the woman lead Texas Guinan.

In January 1920, financially troubled Master Pictures was in the process of arranging to sell the film plant to the firm of McCauley and Hunt of the International Film Company. The

International Film Company was also formed to rent space to independent producers, with W. Welch as the manager of the studio, which had three companies making Bull's Eye films. Once again, however, obstacles interrupted ambitious attempts to resuscitate the studio. In February 1920, the *Daily Telegram* announced that both partners of the International Film Company had died. On February 17, 1920, the newspaper explained that John William McCauley, a retired broker, had passed away from pneumonia at his apartments at 63 years of age, about two weeks after his partner, George J. Hunt, had died of heart trouble. Sadly enough, Hunt's son, who came from Bridgeport, Nebraska, to Long Beach to attend the funeral also died of pneumonia during his train ride home after the funeral.

Nonetheless, by April 1920, movie production involved a total of ten companies leasing the facilities at Balboa: (1) the Morante Motion Picture Company, directed by Al Morante, (2) the Paragon Pictures Corporation of America, headed by Fred Jefferson, (3) Acme, (4) the Columbia Film Company, with Jack Kiefer as production manager, (5) Special Pictures Corporation, headed by Ward Lascelle, (6) the David Trattner Production Company, (7) the Kelsey Company, producing a five-reel feature starring Helen Hunt, (8) the Atlas Film Corporation, (9) the Long Beach Motion Picture Company (a.k.a. Long Beach Studios, Inc.), and (10) the Marie Osborne Film Company. According to Marc Wanamaker, the Edith Sterling Productions, with William J. Beckway as cameraman, was also using the Balboa Studios that same year. Many of these companies considered purchasing the studios, but none did.

In March 1920, the *Daily Telegram* described some of the productions underway at Balboa by the companies leasing the studio. The David Trattner Production Company was operating at Balboa, presenting Irene Hunt, a well-known former Griffith star, in an interesting series of two-reel comedy dramas from the pen of Miriam Michelson, author of *In the Bishop's Carriage*. David Trattner was president of the company, and E. M. Rosenthal was vice president, with Erwin Trattner serving as secretary and treasurer, and Shields Lawson as business manager. In the series there would be 26 stories concerning the adventures of a local newspaper woman that were formerly published in the *Saturday Evening Post*. Along with Irene Hunt, the leading parts would include Clyde McCoy, who had worked as director and actor with Oakley and Selig productions. The first episode, called *Back on the Job*, was directed by Fred A. Kelsey, who was associated with the Majestic and Reliance production companies, with Ed Gheller as cameraman.

At this time, the Paragon Film Company was the oldest established production company using the Balboa Studios. According to the *Daily Telegram* (April 7, 1920, p. 20), the company was expected to purchase the entire plant. The company's general manager and supervisor, G. Le Roi Clarke, stated that Paragon produced two-reel situational comedies and that the staff had found the Balboa equipment, particularly the interior sets, very "desirable." The article presented more of Clarke's favorable impression of the site: "And also it is advantageous for a comedy concern to be located here where those ever popular beach and bathing girl scenes can be 'shot' and many comic 'stunts' worked out on the Pike amusements." The same article names the latest comedy filmed by Paragon, *Bill and Coo and Ouija Board*, which was Paragon's first release produced at the Long Beach studios.

Unfortunately, once again, on April 13, 1920, the *Daily Telegram* reported that managers and directors of the diverse companies at the Balboa plant were despairing, like H. M. Horkheimer in the wings, hoping for a turn in the market. To encourage all the "boosters" trying to promote the floundering movie industry in Long Beach, the *Daily Telegram* on May 12, 1920 (3:5) announced enthusiastically a promising recent production: "a comedy picture made in Long Beach by a local company from the Balboa Studios. The title of this picture is 'A Barnyard Romance,' and because of the exclusive Long Beach scenes portrayed in the picture and the local people who are seen as spectators wherever the many different scenes were being enacted, it is believed that the picture will attract large audiences at every performance it is shown at the Strand."

Having more trouble than anticipated finding a reliable buyer, the creditors of the old Balboa Amusement Producing Company by August 1920 organized themselves and proposed forming a new film corporation themselves. Their film company would be worth $500,000, and its creation would be settled through Los Angeles and Long Beach brokerage offices. The new company would be called the Long Beach Studios, Inc. The brokers were estimating more than an 8% return on the proposed investment. The plan was to issue $250,000 worth of preferred stock, paying $150,000 for the plant and using $100,000 as working capital. A bonus of one share of common stock with every share of preferred stock was also proposed. The Los Angeles Wholesalers' Board of Trade, the assignee, was in charge of the big plant while it was being leased to the various producing companies described above.

Even if business was slow in 1920 for the film producers in Long Beach, Marc Wanamaker of Bison Archives affirms that the Atlas Film Corporation was renting space at Balboa, making a comedy series with the famous silent screen star, Chester Conklin. The city also still managed to draw other companies to town, even to other parts of town. According to the *Daily Telegram* (Dec. 18, 1920, 11:1) R. D. Films, Inc., was leasing, building, and equipping a studio site for the production of one-reel comedies at the rate of one a week on the west side of Coronado Avenue between Anaheim and Fourteenth Streets. Articles of incorporation for the R. D. Film company were reportedly filed that week, with a capitalization of $100,000. The manager of R. D. Films was to be Denver Dixon, formerly a star of Vitagraph Westerns. The assistant manager was to be Clyde McClary, and the directors were to be A. F. Devereaux and S. B. Drum of Long Beach and W. C. Rae of Pasadena.

In February 1921, Harry Corson Clarke at the Hotel Virginia did an interview for the *Daily Telegram* (Feb. 2, 1921, 17:3) extolling Long Beach as the best spot in the Southland for film work. Clarke was a promoter and a booster for the film industry in Long Beach. He was especially impressed with the Balboa Studios, where the Milburn Morante Comedy Company was still busy making one-reelers. Clarke commented about the large capacity for filmmaking at the studio and the actual shortage of producers utilizing the space and the accommodations. This movie promoter was much impressed and noted that the large plant was "a credit to Long Beach." Clarke added, "There should have been 10 companies at least working there."

Clarke was a world traveler and a showman, well acquainted with the Morante "family" and its international team:

> It's a small world. I've encircled it four times and each time it seems to grow smaller. I hadn't met "Mil" Morante since the old days when his father, Joseph (Dad) had his two boys, Mil and Al, out with the first Edison moving picture machine, giving shows thru the Middle West. And now they have as smooth a working company as I have seen in many a day.
>
> Milburn is the star, Tom Gibson writes and directs, and is a wizard at the megaphone, Al Morante [is] Gibson's right hand assistant director. Miles Burns, a cameraman deluxe whom I had the pleasure of meeting in the Hawaiian Islands, is ably assisted by "Spike" Vanderpool; while sets that are sets are built by our old friend "Dad" Morante and furnished by one of the best property men in the business, Chas. (Shorty) Everett, I know as he was with me in Australia. Alfred (Tex) Hueston is a wonder with makeup and rated as an A1 character actor while Ray Hampton as a character actress has few equals. I tried to corral this lady for my last world's tour but she had gone to Alaska. Then there is Harry Belmore, a good all round man, George Gyton, a young actor I met in New Zealand, and Joe Cush at the switchboard, "Joe" was one of my staff in Denver. (*Daily Telegram*, Feb. 2, 1921, 17:3)

In the same article, Clarke reminded the Long Beach business community of the advantages of the film industry's growth in the city:

At Balboa Studios: William Bertram with Baby Gloria Osborne, sister of Baby Marie Osborne (courtesy of Marie Osborne-Yeats).

"Taken as a whole, this outfit is a credit in Long Beach. They work in Long Beach, they spend their money in Long Beach. It's a Long Beach institution, and, Oh, you Long Beach boosters! With this little band as a start, get busy, do some shouting and let's place Long Beach on the map as a moving picture producing center. It can be done."

The Morante company made a departure from comedies to begin filming a series of Western dramas. Milburn Morante starred in the series, supported by Evelyn Nelson, with Morante's four-year-old daughter as "the baby." After the first Morante Western, *Hearts of the Range*, was released in early 1921, seven Westerns were scheduled for production beginning March 1921 by the film company based in Long Beach. Later articles in the *Daily Telegram* would cover the company's travels to Madera County to shoot on location for scenes photographed in the rugged and sylvan terrain. All the interior shots, of course, were filmed at Balboa. In the town of Raymond, in Madera County, the film crew set up headquarters.

On June 22, 1921, the *Daily Telegram* (4:3) reported that the Long Beach Motion Picture Company had also gone to Hornitos on location. William Bertram was directing the picture, a mining story. The cast included Leo Maloney, Dixie Lamont, Gus Scoville, and 35 other actors. The company was to spend a total of about two weeks there and then move on to Wawona. While at Hornitos, the Long Beach Motion Picture Company brought the old ghost town to life, reenacting in the mining story the Gold Rush days, inviting all the inhabitants of the surrounding country for one frolicking evening, with a huge display of entertainment. It was estimated that around 2,000 persons attended the dance. An old gold miner living in the Hornitos area who joined the festivities, Emilio Campodonico, had not seen so many people in the town at one time since the good old days: "The dance was scheduled for 8 o'clock, but early in the afternoon machines began rolling in from Livingston, Bear Valley, Atwater, La Grand, Merced, Madera, Merced Falls, Mt. Ballion, Snelling, Fresno, Bagby and Mariposa. By 7:30 the usually deserted streets were jammed with machines and people thronged the thorofares."

That splendid evening, before there was a Knott's Berry Farm, the atmosphere of Hornitos revived the ambiance of the Gold Rush days. The same article described the excitement: "Across the street from the dance hall, in the aged Pat Garate saloon, where much of California's early history transpired, near beer and soda water crossed the bar while the drinkers swapped yarns of the days of gold. On the street back of the hall stands the famous Hornitos hotel, which has been taken over by the film company as headquarters, and in the barroom 30 gallons of ice cream, 40 cakes and 1800 sandwiches were served to the visitors by the film folk."

That same month, June 1921, negotiations began between the industrial bureau of the Long Beach Chamber of Commerce and the Balboa Amusement Producing Company, which was seeking a long-term lease of the film studios. With local capital, the trustees would organize a local film company called the Long Beach Comedy Company, to be directed by Fred A. Jefferson and to star Le Roi Clarke. If the negotiations succeeded, the company

Daily Telegram, August 20, 1921: Fred A. Jefferson, handing over check for new 1922 Columbia, while his wife looks on.

would hire about 50 persons to begin productions within six weeks. Obviously, businessmen would support the film industry, even at the end of June 1921, after the first gushers already began to change the course of history for Long Beach.

The *Daily Telegram* on July 26, 1921, indicated that the new company did not immediately materialize. A new company, Meteor Pictures Corporation, was using some of the same actors who had been slated to appear with the Long Beach Comedy Company. George Le Roi Clarke had finished his contract with Paragon Pictures, having done 52 one-reel slapstick comedies for the Reelcraft series, and he was now starring in a Meteor film. His leading lady was to be Celeste Zimlick, and they were to be supported by fellow actors George Austin, Harry Belmore, Hazel Tranchell, Tiny Harding, and Amelia Gilson. A. B. Montgomery was general manager, and Eddie Welch was business manager. Fred Jefferson would be directing, with George Clarke co-directing, and Eddie (Dutch) Blake serving as cameraman. The company, which had a board of directors that included A. B. Montgomery, Charles E. Philippi, E. W. Welsh, Amelia P. Gillson, and J. L. Darnall, had rented space at Balboa. In fact, the Meteor Pictures Corporation was capitalized at $50,000, being the first enterprise to file articles of incorporation under the new state law requiring the original copies of the articles be sent to the secretary of state. Under the old law, the secretary of state received the first copy, while the county clerk received the original copy.

On August 12, 1921, the *Daily Telegram* (17:1) announced a private showing of the first film completed by the Long Beach Motion

Picture Company. William Bertram was the author and the director of this film, *The Dashing Ranger*, and it helped launch a whole series of films that romanticized and glamorized the Canadian Mounted Police. Leo Maloney had the leading part, performing sensational stunts on horseback, including crossing a two-board trestle 60 feet high. He also leaped off a building through a wooden awning. Dixie la Monte was the leading lady, Harry Bellmour was the heavy, and Gus Scoville played another leading character. This is the film and the series that began filming at Hornitos, in Mariposa County, which was full of the Gold Rush ambiance of 1849. In fact, the production company had leased the hotel at Hornitos for one year to be able to continue filming future productions there. At the time of this announcement in the *Daily Telegram*, the Long Beach Motion Picture Company was working on a cooperative basis, not having incorporated as yet. There were no paid officers; partners simply shared in the financial returns.

That summer Long Beach boosters imagined "a second Hollywood" with Long Beach growing to be a formidable center of the motion picture industry, but it was also the same summer of gushing oil madness and mushrooming oil derricks all over the city. Before petroleum displaced the capital invested in the movie industry at Long Beach, the city fathers were still actively inviting studios to the city. The manager of the industrial bureau of the Long Beach Chamber of Commerce, George Alisey Brown, announced that seven motion picture companies were planning to locate in Long Beach that year, including the Long Beach Community Producers, the Olympian Production Company of New York, and the Meteor Pictures Corporation. (The latter was already established in Long Beach by July 1921.) Brown claimed that better rental and living conditions in Long Beach, along with the amenities of the sea air and the Pike amusement zone were attracting the movie folk to the city. It was also claimed that Hollywood studios were facing difficulties in expanding their lots because of prohibitive real estate costs in Los Angeles, already the biggest metropolis in the state of California. The movie boosters and business-friendly chamber of commerce in Long Beach were trying to draw the movie communities to the seaside resort, where there were still plenty of building sites at reasonable prices.

As a point of reference, that same year when the Morante company was busy producing comedies and dramas at the Balboa Studios, Fatty Arbuckle was arrested for murder on September 12, 1921. Although he was no longer working in Long Beach, the popular comedian had a long association with the city's entertainment business. But by April 18, 1922, the Ebell Club in Long Beach endorsed a move against all of Arbuckle's films. Even in Long Beach, Roscoe could not escape persecution.

The general manager of the Morante Producing Company, F. D. Fowler, left for the nation's financial capital, New York, on February 1922 to sign a contract for a series of five-reel comedy dramas, a contract worth a stunning $126,000. At the time, the Morante company was producing five-reel dramas in Long Beach under contract with George Chesbro, who distributed the pictures through the Clark-Cornelia agency. The Chesbro contract called for eight five-reel pictures, and by February 6, 1922, just four days after William Desmond Taylor's murder, the fourth picture in the series had already been completed. The Chesbro contract concerned the northwestern mounted police, with the scenarios written by J. Inman Kane, a former Long Beach High School student. The continuities were handled by Richard Gilson and the productions were directed by Tom Gibson, who formerly worked at Universal and other Hollywood studios. Other members of the cast in the mounted police series included Alfred Hewston, formerly with Fairbanks and Universal, Vivian Rich, a former Fox star, Mr. and Mrs. M. L. Barber, Frank Coffray, Henry Arris, and E. L. MacManigal. The local Long Beach papers explained that the Morante company was a closed corporation, having sold no stock; it was owned by a group personally interested in the future of movies at Long Beach. The exteriors were filmed in the Lake Tahoe area and in the mountains near California Hot Springs. Interior scenes, of course, were produced at the Balboa Studios. The fifth picture of the Chesbro contract, to be released in March 1922, was entitled *Menacing Past* and was directed by Gibson.

By February 1922, the holding company that managed the Balboa Studios had big plans, starting with repairs to entice film activity at the site. The city was bidding once more to become a center of the motion picture industry of Southern California. Along with other Long Beach capitalists, J. E. Logan and E. F. Thorine purchased the studio and its surrounding grounds, putting into escrow $115,000 in fulfillment of the terms of an option taken earlier on December 15, 1921. This move did not please Florence Horkheimer and her brothers. In response to this action, Florence tried to impose an injunction to restrain the receiver from passing title to the new owners, claiming her interests as part owner had not been protected. A hearing was scheduled in Los Angeles to determine whether the Horkheimer injunction would prevent the transfer of property to the collective group of Long Beach businessmen. The money for the purchase was already in escrow, and all indicators favored the new buyers. The Morante company was leasing the studio, as well as a second company, and a third producing company was expected to commence the filming of five-reel comedies at the Balboa Studios. All these steps forward to accelerate film production at Balboa motivated the eager potential purchasers. At the same time, expanding businesses were snatching up studio property whenever they could, diminishing with time the original dimensions of the studio grounds. The Drummer Manufacturing Company on the eastern section of Sixth Street at the Balboa quadrangle was awaiting action of the court before moving its offices and work rooms into larger quarters inside some of the Balboa buildings.

Following the injunction suit by his sister and the murder of William Desmond Taylor in February 1922, H. M. Horkheimer was back in Long Beach for the first time in many years. H. M. had just returned from a trip to New York, traveling to Los Angeles County via New Orleans. The local papers revealed on March 4, 1922, their conjectures about H.M.'s visit to Long Beach, during which he stopped at the Hotel Virginia to meet with local businessmen and old associates. Reporters wished to interview H.M. about the scandals so much in the news involving the former stars of Balboa's glory days, Taylor and Arbuckle. The *Daily Telegram* also hoped to question the pioneer producer H.M. about his dealings back East, where he had been given a contract to produce five pictures at a cost not to exceed $300,000. It was understood that Florence wanted very much to retain the ownership of the studio, and perhaps all three of the Horkheimers would return to work at the studio they had once made world-famous.

The injunction suit filed in the Los Angeles court may have precipitated H.M.'s visit to Long Beach because the Horkheimers perhaps hoped to prevent the transfer of the Balboa property from the receivers, in whom the control had been vested. Exact reasons for H.M. Horkheimer's return to Balboa could not be ascertained because he left before the reporters could question him on the matter. Unfortunately, despite the injunction the sale of the Balboa Studios went through. Even four years after the Horkheimers had departed, the Balboa Studios were considered to be in fairly good shape, and the property was deemed to still have a very high value. Only H. M. seemed to be much changed physically; he had put on weight and resembled his rotund father, Morris.

All the negative publicity in filmdom around 1922 — Wallace Reid's overdose, William Desmond Taylor's murder, and Fatty Arbuckle's scandal — would provoke a movement to return in the entertainment business to moral programming and fundamental Christian values. This movement was especially noticeable among moviemakers in Long Beach, who were trying to clean up Hollywood's image. Several producers came to town to film religious movies under the auspices of Long Beach and Los Angeles ministers and members of the chamber of commerce. One such company, the Scripture Film Company,

Hampton Del Ruth, from an unidentified newspaper clipping. Del Ruth is shown assembling his cast for the first picture to be taken at the Long Beach Studios, Inc., of which he was production manager.

was mentioned in the *Daily Telegram*, April 1, 1922, which claimed that Long Beach had become one of the main centers for this movement specializing in Christian filmmaking. It was not specified whether the organization would use the Balboa Studios because they had recently changed hands. The article in the paper was enthusiastic, however, about the possibility of having a zoo established in Long Beach, if the Scripture Film Company left the animals they used for their productions for eventual public viewing.

In 1922, Tod Sloan, hailed as the greatest jockey America had ever known, was also considering Long Beach as a base for moviemaking. While staying at the Hotel Virginia, Sloan mentioned the possibility of producing films at Balboa: "Just what my future plans are I cannot say at this time. But this I will say, that Long Beach is a real city, and I should think, ideally located for the filming of high class pictures. As soon as I have more time I will look into the situation and come to a definite conclusion" (*Daily Telegram*, Apr. 20, 1922, 21:4). Tod Sloan would not, however, be the one to try to revitalize the film plant in Long Beach. By May 1922, another hat was tossed into the ring.

On May 24, 1922, the *Daily Telegram* announced that Hampton Del Ruth, the famous director for Sennett and Fox, would be in charge of new film productions and that the sizable Balboa plant would be remodeled. Del Ruth had a formidable reputation, and many hoped he would have what it took to bring the stagnant film industry at Long Beach to its former days of glory. As one of the best-known directors in the industry, Del Ruth would be making five-reel features and a number of shorter length comedies with all-star casts.

Hampton Del Ruth had been in Long Beach at the beginning of the movie industry, even starring in one of Long Beach's earliest films, *On Matrimonial Seas* (1911), which was produced by the original movie company of California, the California Motion Picture Manufacturing Company, the first such company both originating in California and having its headquarters in the Sunshine State. In 1922, Hampton Del Ruth returned to Long Beach as a seasoned filmmaker with many credits to his name.

With his reputation for making "clean" films, Del Ruth was much praised in the local press. He had started his movie career at the Selig-Polyscope Company and had directed the first filming of Alexandre Dumas' *The Count of Monte Cristo*. For six years, Del Ruth had been in charge of productions at the Mack Sennett Studios, making some of the first feature-length comedies. As production manager there, he made over 700 of the popular Keystone farce comedies. Most remarkable among these early comedies was the movie entitled *Tillie's Punctured Romance*, starring Charles Chaplin, Marie Dressler, and Mabel Normand. Del Ruth was also responsible for the production of one of the most popular films of the silent era, *Mickey*, as well as *Skirts*. After his work with Sennett, Del Ruth became managing director for two years for the William Fox Sunshine Comedies.

J. E. Logan and his associates had purchased the studios in Long Beach from the receivers who had taken over the Horkheimer enterprise. In May 1922, Logan and Thorine sold the Balboa Studios to a group of businessmen, with production headed by Hampton Del Ruth. This new corporation dropped the Balboa name, christening itself the Long Beach Studios Corporation, and their films boasted the trademark "Made in Long Beach." The incorporation papers were filed on June 19, 1922. These new incorporators included A. H. Brewster and B. P. Glenn of the Brewster-Glenn Insurance and Bond Company of Los Angeles, Glenn being the more prominent member of the group. Having helped organize the Long Beach Chamber of Commerce, Glenn was a well-known entrepreneur in the city, as well as a director of the California Bank in Los Angeles. Earlier, Glenn had also been a representative of a railway company, the Salt Lake Railroad, the track of which ran straight through the Balboa property to the end of the line, where Long Beach had an open market with livestock, which provided a rodeo and carnival atmosphere very close to the studio site. The other incorporators were various Long Beach and Los Angeles businessmen, who would invest heavily to improve the film plant to the sum of about $50,000, adding roofing over the open stage adjoining the glassed-in studio, entirely remodeling and reequipping the laboratories, and rewiring the studio to provide direct current for more artificial lighting.

The new corporation announced many ambitions plans and featured many exciting programs to make the movie industry in Long Beach once more both prolific and "clean." Not only was the studio buzzing with remodeling and rewiring, but the incorporators intended to acquire about 20 acres of property in or near Long Beach to be used for large exterior sets, street scenes, and spectacular effects. Furthermore, on May 25, 1922, the *Daily Telegram* announced the arrival of other producing companies that would lease the Long Beach plant, including, as a sign of the conservative times in movieland, religious filmmakers who were determined to keep the business respectable, such as the Historical Films Company, in which Mr. Brewster and Mrs. Glenn were said to be interested. In fact, Logan insisted on producing educational and biblical pictures; the slogan characterizing the plant was to be "A Clean Studio for Clean Films." The Historical Films Company would provide film programs for churches and schools, to include an educational feature, a biblical film, a short comedy, and a travelogue. No records have been found, however, of the Historical Films Company productions in Long Beach. Two other religious producers of films are mentioned in the same article, the Commonwealth Company, specializing in biblical photoplays, supplemented with other educational features, and the William Thompson Company that had reportedly just completed a Bible subject production at Long Beach. Again, no records of these companies have been found.

Besides the Morante company, which had been on site for a number of years, continuing to specialize in five-reel Westerns with Vivian Rich, there was also the Bob Horner organization, which was starting film productions in Long Beach with the new incorporators. On June 11, 1922, the *Daily Telegram* announced that Horner would begin a series of five feature Western photoplays and an Arabian spectacle movie. Contracts had been finalized with "Ranger" Bill Miller and Patricia Palmer to do the leading parts in the series. The first picture was named *Twin Six O'Brien*. Miller was reportedly among the first cowboys to play leading parts in motion pictures. He had begun as an extra in the Lubin company, after arriving from Texas. Palmer had been with the Famous Players–Lasky corporation before joining the Horner company. Horner himself happened to be without legs because of a train accident when he was a youth, but this handicap never prevented him from becoming a successful film producer specializing in Western movies.

In a move to mix movie stars with the Long Beach crowd, the local post of the American Legion presented "A Night in Movieland" at the Long Beach studio on June 26, 1922. Long Beach business associations were eager to support the movie industry in town, looking forward to a highly entertaining and enthusiastic evening of spreading the movie fever in town.

In fact, on June 19, 1922, the *Daily Telegram* was predicting that the Long Beach Studio Corporation was planning to produce films more extensively than had the Horkheimers at the height of their prolific output of films. The Long Beach paper reported that incorporation papers had been filed and the Balboa Studios would thereafter be renamed the Long Beach Studios. The organizers — A. B. Brewster, B. P. Glenn, Hampton Del Ruth, L. Davis, and L. C. Thorne, all of Los Angeles — would be the directors of the corporation, with the controlling interest, while associates from Long Beach would be financial backers. At the time of this announcement other companies were already at work, including the Milburn Morante group, the Starke-Statter Corporation, the Commonwealth Pictures Company, and the "Bill" Thompson organization, while several other producing companies were also still negotiating for use of the Long Beach Studios. The Starke-Staller organization, with Pauline Starke as their star, also planned to produce a series of 8 seven-reel pictures, one of which was entitled *Pawnee Bill*.

Hampton Del Ruth was hoping for a revival of the movie industry in Long Beach and planned to begin shooting his first picture around July 20, 1922. On June 26 he and his wife, a movie star by the name of Alta Allen, registered at the Hotel Virginia, where H. M. Horkheimer had also resided during his tenure as chief at Balboa Studios. For his first Long Beach production, Del Ruth had decided on a cast that included many notable film celebrities: Henry Walthall, James Kirkwood, Lon Chaney, and Anna Q. Nielsson; Alta Allen was also in the Del Ruth productions. Del Ruth was the principal stockholder in the Long Beach Studios, Inc. In an article entitled "Picture Making Will Start Soon; All-Star Casts," he predicted there would be many productions, beginning the first year with 4 special five-reel pictures with an all-star cast and 12 two-reel comedies. "During our second year we will double our production," he added (*Daily Telegram*, June 27, 1922, 4:5).

In late July 1922, the *Daily Telegram* announced that Hampton Del Ruth would direct an impromptu picture, inviting every person in Long Beach to participate who was interested in entering the motion picture field. The stars participating in the impromptu film were to include Lon Chaney, one of the greatest character actors; Milton Mills, a popular leading man; Henry Walthall; Tully Marshall, a popular character man; Alta Allen; and Irene Rich. The production chief would be Del Ruth; the director, Tom Gibson; and the cameraman, Elmer G. Dyer. In short, Del Ruth was inviting the public to an open and gigantic screen test, again mixing the stars with the general public. The event was considered a novelty. It drew a crowd of 1,000 persons, who were organized by a team of movie boosters: Mrs. Wallace Reid; Mr. Gibson; Eugene Wither, dramatic editor of the *Daily Telegram*; C. E. Freshwater, assistant manager of the Empire Theatre in Long Beach; Edward Marshall, the nationally known artist and correspondent of *Variety*, the vaudeville and movie trade journal; and H. R. Connor and Henry Rhea, publicity directors of the Empire Theatre. In scope and ambition, it was the kind of publicity stunt that the Horkheimers might have devised. Gibson told the *Daily Telegram* on July 30, 1922:

> Instead of employing some actress who has already achieved stardom and bringing her to Long Beach to appear in our productions, we are going to find some Long Beach girl who shows possibilities and give her every opportunity to go far along the road to screen fame. I believe these screen tests will be invaluable in starting our search for worthy local talent, and they may result in the discovery of a real star. Some of the best known screen stars today have been developed after such tests, and this particular one seems especially promising. The large participation in the event indicates that all Long Beach is interested in Southern California's greatest industry and in giving this city a prominent place in it.

Of course, camera tests had been done before, but seldom with such a great mixture of celebrities and open to such a large public. Consequently, the experiment was watched closely by the film industry in Southern California. Mrs. Wallace Reid, whose late husband had been a screen idol, gave the women a discussion on screen technique and helped them with their appearance before the camera. She herself had played at the Balboa Studios during the Horkheimer years under the name of Dorothy Davenport. She answered questions put to her about the business in general and about her famous and deceased husband. She also worked with the small children before the camera. The impromptu film was then filed in the studio library to be available for casting directors of the dozen companies located at the Long Beach plant. The *Daily Telegram* (9:4) outlined the conditions of the invitation: "Everybody has the cordial invitation of all concerned in making the event's success to participate in the tests and informal reception. There are no requirements and no entrance formality, other than to be at the Empire theatre at 11 o'clock." The article finished with a flourish: "Come to Mrs. 'Wallie' Reid's 'Movie Party.' Empire Theatre lobby at 11:00 A.M. tomorrow. 10 people will be chosen for an actual appearance in a forthcoming production."

The newspaper articles described the open screen test as a raving success. As a result, the *Daily Telegram* announced the choice of 20 women who showed the most promise. It was decided, however, to ask the public to help in the "star search." On August 3, 1922, in an article entitled "Leading Screen Candidates Will Be Given Roles," the newspaper announced that Gibson and Dyer were searching for a new star, if possible from local talent, if someone could be found who had the right qualities and the proper screen presence. The winners would play bit parts or leading roles. The studio was waiting for the return of Patricia Palmer from Wyoming, where she was on location with the Lasky company, working with Mary Miles Minter, Tom Moore, and Eugene O'Brien. Upon Palmer's return, Tom Gibson at the Long Beach Studios would direct, with Elmer Dyer as cameraman, the next "Ranger Bill" photoplay using the ten lucky women selected from the star search.

Since the studio authorities found it impossible to pick from the large number of candidates, audiences at the Empire Theatre were asked to watch the screen test and to vote by secret ballot, using code numbers pinned to the candidates to identify the women on the screen. The top ten would be given parts immediately, while the other ten winners would stand an excellent chance of receiving parts later. Everybody participating—women, men, boys, and girls—would be considered for future movies, the screen test being kept in the studio library. On August 9, 1922, the *Daily Telegram* (p. 11, col. 1) announced the names of the top ten women: (1) Caroline Geiger, (2) Alice Jean Wood, (3) Irene Cadmus, (4) Audrey Homer, (5) Helen Kelly, (6) Linnette Brown, (7) Irene Shupe, (8) Alta Lenore, (9) Winifred Nimmo, (10) Betty Gayton.

Not only was the new studio attempting a comeback for Long Beach's movie industry, but Hampton Del Ruth made every effort to prepare a smash hit to get the ball rolling. Hampton Del Ruth himself had penned an original scenario for his star-studded production, *The Marriage Chance*, including such famous players of the silver screen as Alta Allen, Milton Sills, Irene Rich, Henry Walthall, Lon Chaney, Tully Marshall, Nick Cogley, and Laura La Varnie.

Hampton Del Ruth's wife, Alta Allen, took the lead in the film. She was a resident of Long Beach, a city that pleased her, as she revealed in an interview: "I'm very much in love with Long Beach. You see my home is here, and I really think it's grand to be able to live by the ocean. What is my hobby? Well, I like to study vocal music and classic dancing. I play tennis, too" (*Daily Telegram*, August 20, 1922, B5).

While playing the lead in a musical revue in San Francisco, Allen had been discovered by William Fox. Alta Allen had played the leading part in *Skirts* in a Sunshine Comedy film for Fox. Afterwards, she had starred opposite Gareth Hughes in *The Lure of Youth* and with the French comic movie star Max Linder in his American productions, *Seven Years Bad Luck* and *Be My Wife*.

On the other hand, Milton Sills, who played opposite Allen in *The Marriage Chance*, was preparing to teach as a college professor before he decided to become an actor for the silver screen. Sills had originally planned a career in academia and studied philosophy at Chicago University. He had been a teaching fellow there before mounting the stage to become a thespian. The scholarly Sills imagined movies becoming more evolved and cultured, presenting in time more Shakespearean works and other classic productions. Besides performing on stage and screen, he enjoyed hunting, fishing, and all sorts of sports.

Also among the stars of *The Marriage Chance* figured Henry B. Walthall, who had become famous for his part as the Little Colonel in Griffith's classic masterpiece, *The Birth of a Nation*. After a successful career on stage, Walthall broke into the movies in 1909. In fact, Walthall had worked a short spell with Balboa under contract with the Horkheimers. Other films with Henry Walthall include *The Raven* and *The Avenging Conscience*. While working at Long Beach in 1922, Walthall was known to rise early and to be splashing in the surf by 6 A.M. He worked long and hard hours for Del Ruth, but he, like Sills, also enjoyed the sports of hunting and fishing, especially in the high Sierras or some nearby mountain stream.

Among other leading actors in *The Marriage Chance*, Tully Marshall had worked on the stage for 30 years, starting his theatrical career as a call boy in San Francisco. He had played with many great stars in stage productions such as *Paid in Full*, *The City*, and *The Talker*, and he had been a director and producer for a while. Eventually, he went back to acting, working in pictures with Norma Talmadge, Jane Grey, and Seena Owen. Marshall worked for Griffith in *Sable Torch*, *The Devil's Needle*, *The Streets of Paris*, and *Intolerance*.

For all the major roles in *The Marriage Chance*, Hampton Del Ruth had selected seasoned and well-known actors skilled in doing character parts and slapstick comedy. Del Ruth intended to use most of the same star-studded cast in future pictures, his intention being to keep all the Long Beach productions of the highest quality. The stakes were high, but the prospects looked very good. The Long Beach boosters and much of the established Hollywood crowd were rooting for a return to the former prosperity that the Horkheimers had attracted to Long Beach the previous decade. Consequently, the stage was being set when four promising contracts were signed for feature pictures to be made in Long Beach. At the Long Beach Studios on August 22, 1922, A. H. Jage, assistant manager of the United States branch of the American Releasing Corporation, and J. E. Logan, general manager of the Long Beach Studios, Inc., signed the contracts to assure the success of the films being produced by Hampton Del Ruth. *The Marriage Chance* had already been sold to William H. Jenner, the West Coast manager of the American Releasing Corporation.

The efforts of the Long Beach Studios, Inc., seemed relentless and untiring. At the Lions' Club in Long Beach, September 8, 1922, Hampton Del Ruth, supervising managing director; Byron P. Glenn, president; E. C. Bennett; and J. E. Logan, general manager of the Long Beach Studios, comprised the guests of honor at the weekly meeting of the club, held at the Hotel Virginia. Each presented a speech on the movie industry, promoting the ambitious plans of the new concern at the former Balboa Studios. In an article appearing in the *Daily Telegram* (Sept. 8, 1922, 27:6), Glenn described the studio as the best equipped on the Pacific coast, potentially the best in the world: "The motion picture industry is the most abused, the most criticised business in the world. It is because of the mystery and the lure which surrounds movieism. People are anxious to know what is going on behind the high board fences of the studios and are allowing their imaginations to run wild." Glenn emphasized to the members of the Lions' Club the continuing growth of the film industry and its world capital located in Southern California: "About Los Angeles there are approximately 200 producing companies and 65 studios. The value of the yearly output is $200,000,000. About 50,000 people are constantly employed. The motion picture houses in the United States number about 25,000."

In the hurry and flurry of all the promises and contracts made by the Long Beach Studios, the *Daily Telegram* announced on October 18, 1922, in an article entitled "Eastern Capitalist and Local Director Associated in Plans" that the day before, October 17, 1922, all existing contracts and future contracts of the Long Beach Studios were sold to R. S. Baddeley, an Eastern capitalist. A special Pullman car bearing in gold letters the names of the Long Beach Studio and the name of the director, Del Ruth, would be touring the country by train. advertising Long Beach, its film studio, the studio's first movie, *The Marriage Chance*, and the stars. It would take along a motion picture projector to show moving pictures of Long Beach. On the national railroad tour, Hampton Del Ruth was accompanied by Mr. Baddeley, the new owner, several personal friends of Mr. Baddeley, and Thurlow W. Brewer, a former Essanay manager and director. The same promises outlined earlier by Del Ruth were announced by the new owner: (1) production of four feature films with all-star casts, (2) the contracts for the release of these productions were already signed, (3) 12 two-reel comedies to be filmed each year, and (4) all movies to be personally directed by Hampton Del Ruth. Baddeley also stated that very morning that leasing contracts would be negotiated with prominent producing companies, resulting in the studio at Long Beach being actively engaged throughout the year, year after year. Baddeley was totally convinced of the profitability of investing in Long Beach's dormant but potentially successful movie studio:

> I have become a California enthusiast and have decided to make a business connection which will enable me to spend a large part of my time here. It is a surprise to me that a plant of this magnitude has been allowed to stand idle so many months and I have become interested to the extent that I can assure production from this time on. I have contracted with Hampton Del Ruth and have tentative contracts for future productions with some of the leading artists. I can assure the public of Long Beach that the best of pictures will be produced here and that the features which will follow "The Marriage Chance"— a success already — will be a credit to this city and this community. (Daily Telegram, Oct. 18, 1922, 14:1)

Unfortunately for Hampton Del Ruth and the Long Beach film industry, *The Marriage Chance* was an enormous box-office flop. In November 1922, Hampton Del Ruth and backers purchased the Balboa/International Film Company, and the name was changed to the Hampton Del Ruth Studios. O. A. Greybeal owned the greatest share of the studio. Despite all of Del Ruth's efforts to revive the former glory days of the Balboa Studios, there appear no other newspaper articles about Hampton Del Ruth continuing to do other productions in Long Beach. He, like his ill-fated predecessors, eventually threw in the towel.

Hampton Del Ruth's removal from the scene did not, however, spell the end of attempts to kick-start the movie industry in Long Beach. The *Long Beach Press* (Jan. 25, 1923, 7:6) reported in an article entitled "Shoot First Scenes in New Universal Peace Story Soon" that the Super-Feature Film Corporation would be leasing the site and starting to film its educational films at the Balboa Studios. Super-Feature's first movie in Long Beach would be an eight-reel antiwar movie, conceived in response to the mounting tension after the economic slump in Europe and the implementation of the unsuccessful Treaty of Versailles. The corporation doing the picture included a board of directors, unnamed in the article but all Long Beach businessmen, and all of the scenes were scheduled to be shot in and about Long Beach, "and some of the strongest scenes will be 'shot' among the Signal Hill oil derricks." This was the first time Long Beach's new face as a petroleum town was scheduled to be a setting for a movie. Supposedly, the corporation had already acquired international rights to the story, and one of the features already done by the Super-Feature Corporation outside of Long Beach had been shown in most Long Beach churches before it toured the country. This completed film by Super Feature, *Palestine*, was a six-reel educational film also spurred by the war, but Super-Feature planned to cut *Palestine* to four reels, adding two new reels to be filmed in and about Long Beach. No other information has been retrieved regarding Super-Feature's film productions in Long Beach.

Then the long-awaited return of the Horkheimers was finally realized. The changing of hands had come full circle. On March 30, 1923, the *Long Beach Press* announced the former owner would resume production in Balboa's remodeled buildings: "Balboa Studios Sold to H. M. Horkheimer; Will Make Pictures." This announcement breathed new hope into the financially troubled and disappointing decline of the once-famous studio. The article claimed that H. M. purchased the studio from O. A. Greybeal for $300,000. When the committee of creditors was formed in 1918 to take over the Horkheimers' holdings, Greybeal was a member of the committee. He later became the sole owner, after the parade of potential buyers and renters, by purchasing the holdings of all the other associates in the committee. At the time of this announcement, H. M. was living in Los Angeles, with his office in the Loew State Building. Of course, H. M. was expected to move his offices as a producer back to the Balboa Studios. He announced eloquently his pleasure in working with the citizens of Long Beach, along with the prospect of returning to do films in Long Beach:

> I came to this city because I like it and want to help it. I don't ask anything of the municipality but its moral support. I expect to employ from 300 to 500 people, and from time to time thousands of extras. I presume that my payroll will run close to $30,000 per week.
>
> On every picture I put out there will be a trailer attached which shall read, "Made in Long Beach." (*Long Beach Press*, March 30, 1923, 8:3)

The article concluded by stating that H. M. would be the sole supervisor of the studio, though he would not be directing productions as he had in the past. H. M. would spend all his time overseeing the work of the plant, diligently bringing it back into the superior working conditions that had brought fame and fortune to Long Beach's movie industry in the past. The article claimed that observers considered the buildings at Balboa Studios to be adequate for the largest productions and to contain sets of considerable value. H. M., nonetheless, planned to remodel the site to restore parts of the studios that had been converted to other commercial uses, as the studio grounds had begun to shrink with the encroaching spread of other businesses all around. The same article mentioned that two serials would be among the first in line under H. M.'s supervision, with production to start within 30 days.

On May 13, 1923, however, the newest director at the Balboa Studios was named in the *Long Beach Press* without any mention of H. M.'s connection to that director. A. S. McCarthy, who had experience as a director in Hollywood, was to open a company of his own in Long Beach. Was he cooperating with H. M., or was H. M. only leasing the site to him? McCarthy was busy gathering his crew and preparing for the leasing of several stars from the Hollywood studios, but he intended to use local talent for the supporting roles in his films. Like H. M. and Del Ruth, McCarthy announced a slogan for his films: "Long Beach Made and Played." His first feature was to be a Midwest story, the scenario having been written by C. P. Huntsman of Long Beach.

H. M. Horkheimer's name does reappear a few days later on May 17, 1923, again in the *Long Beach Press*, in an article entitled "Studio Closed to Wrestling Match." H. M. Horkheimer had offered to allow his studio to hold a wrestling match. Afterwards, H. M. changed his mind, abiding by the judgment of the city council. H. M. also issued a statement explaining that he would have to respect the city's wishes by not holding the match, though he regretted, no doubt, the lost revenues. The promoter of the match, Mr. Daro, had earlier obtained a license from the city clerk to put on the bout, having made arrangements with H. M. Horkheimer, manager of the studios, to hold the match on the studio grounds. The reasons for the objections on the part of the city council are not explained, other than that some parents denounced the violent sport that was to be performed at the site. Horkheimer had written the city council asking for its approval, however, even though he had already obtained a license. Apparently this was a move to remain in good standing with the council. Horkheimer's diplomacy did not seem to impress anybody, however, and Daro was the greatest loser because he had invested money to arrange and advertise the match, and the last minute cancellation, the day before the scheduled event, must have caused him much chagrin.

Horkheimer issued a statement to the sports reporter of *Long Beach Press* (May 17, 1923, 14:8) explaining his position on the whole affair:

> I am most willing to do anything to help Long Beach, for charity or anything else that comes under my observation, and which tends to benefit the city. I think I have stated most clearly in my letter that I would take no chance of violating any of the views of the council — and I have therefore refused to allow the match to be staged, since the city council failed to approve the request of Mr. Daro.
>
> I am sure that citizens of Long Beach have every faith and confidence in their mayor, their manager and their chief — the very fact that these citizens have elected them, is proof sufficient of the confidence they repose in them — and it would therefore be most unfitting in me to suggest to them what they should allow and what not to allow. If their opinion is good enough for the citizens, it is good enough for me — and I am therefore abiding by their unanimous vote in disapproving the match.
>
> I sincerely hope you will give me space enough in your paper to bring my viewpoint on this matter before the notice of the public.

After the canceled wrestling match, there appeared no news about the studio until November 1923, and H. M. Horkheimer's name never again figured in any other reports about the studio after May 1923, nor was there any more mention of making movies at Balboa, despite the renovations during 1923.

No news in this case was not good news. Instead of being used for movie productions, on November 23, 1923, the Balboa Studios were the scene of a Christmas charity circus given by the local lodge of Elks. An army of decorators constructed booths along the sides of the "big top," a real circus tent placed at the front of the main stage of the studio, which was decorated in red, white, and blue. The receipts went to the Christmas charity fund and also to defray the expense of the big convention to be held the following year by the Elks. All the automobile agencies in Long Beach also displayed their models at the week-long circus spectacular, where there were booths and 15 acts, including trapeze artists, trained dogs, acrobatic skaters, contortionists, prize fighters, musicians, and of course clowns. How and when H. M.'s goal to revive the studio evaporated, we cannot say, but quite literally the Long Beach studios had degenerated into a charity case, full of buffoons swaggering on location, a veritable *danse macabre* before the final blow. The circus lasted seven days, and was attended by more than 65,000 persons. It was a symbolic farewell to the Balboa Amusement Producing Company. Soon the final curtain would close. For the loyals of Balboa, the circus may very well have served as a disguised wake.

The interment was delayed another year. In the meantime, the laying of the shroud could not drown out completely the noise and rumble of demolition. On December 8, 1923, Charles W. Harlow purchased the plot from O. A. Greybeal. Horkheimer was never mentioned during this period of mourning. Sadly enough, H. M. never succeeded in reviving the studios and was never able to claim them once again as his own; he probably only acted as manager of the studios owned by Greybeal. Not only had H. M. hoped for a revival, but so did the Long Beach press in March and May of 1923. How does one explain H. M.'s involvement at the studio throughout the spring of

March 22, 1925: "Long Beach–Balboa Studios Fall in Path of Progress." From the *Los Angeles Times*: "Remains of Famous Film Factory."

that year except as a temporary manager for Greybeal? Nonetheless, the last remaining parcel of Balboa Studios, by then reduced to a mere two and a quarter acres at the northeast corner of Sixth and Alamitos Avenues, was sold to Mr. Harlow, a local oil man and financier, for $260,000.

As a result, the big stage and other film property was removed, the ground cleared, and the property subdivided into business lots. The interment was performed as simply as that. There were no tears and no eulogies at this burial, nothing to commemorate the passing of this golden age in early cinema. The flattened remains of the once-proud Balboa Studios would be further subdivided into twenty-one lots, with a frontage of 243 feet on Alamitos and another 231 feet on Sixth, with a depth of 418 feet. Harlow reportedly had already purchased all the previous parcels of the studio grounds a few months before the circus came to town for approximately $100,000, the total of all the tracts being worth an impressive $360,000, a figure indicating that the value of the studio property had never really fallen since the Horkheimers relinquished their control, even though the grounds had been diminished in size over the years.

When the buildings on the last tract were razed to the ground, all the earlier parcels had already been resold to various neighboring businesses. At the time of the last demolition involving the glassed-in studio and surrounding buildings, the other corners of the former Balboa quadrangle had already been replaced by a two-story building containing nine stores and by 11 apartments occupying the site where once stood the Balboa offices. The big stage had been replaced by a bungalow court, and on another slice of the grounds there already loomed the Palmdale Apartments. The last section of the former studio to be redeveloped would be the 2½ acre tract purchased by Harlow, who planned to subdivide it for more apartment buildings and store fronts.

Balboa's obituary was published in the *Los Angeles Times* on March 22, 1925. There was even a photograph showing the flattened remains of the "Famous Film Factory," where the glassed-in studio once reigned. The article headed "Long Beach–Balboa Studios Fall in Path of Progress" stated:

> Unimaginative workmen at Long Beach have written "finis" to an early phase of the motion-picture industry. With the final demolition of the old Balboa Studios there has passed out of existence the cradle in which many cinema stars, past and present, first pantomimed their way into the hearts of a not too exacting public. Gone are many of the stars — gone are the Horkheimer Brothers and gone is the Balboa Studio. ...
>
> But the fall of the studios was as meteoric as the rise. Reaching its heyday in 1916, when as many as ten companies were working on its stages, there was every promise that the fortunes of the Horkheimers and

Balboa's studio sign illuminated at night, shining like stars in the heavens (courtesy of Marc Wanamaker).

those who worked for the enterprising brothers were made. Production became too rapid, however, and finally Pathé Frères, through which Balboa films were being distributed and marketed, issued a warning to the Horkheimers to slow down, but it was too late.

Then came the big slump and in the vaults of the studios there were no less than seventeen completed pictures which the Pathé interests were unable to dispose of. Work on the big stages stopped with a bang, and actors, actresses, camera men, property men and the host of others who had cast their fortunes with the Horkheimers were out of work. (Sect. II, p. 10)

The obituary attempted to describe the last days of Balboa Studios, when the enterprise was frozen in suspended animation, unwilling to pass on to the afterlife until Harlow abandoned altogether the idea of making movies.

After the circus had paraded for one week like a cortege in one of Federico Fellini's magical spells, the studio was emptied of its moviemaking wares and nailed shut. An eerie silence took over the site until total demolition irrevocably transfigured Balboa's towering frame forever:

[Then] followed a period of inactivity. Stage props and furniture, rugs and furnishings to the value of many thousands of dollars, were stored in the property rooms and the latter were nailed shut. There was silence on the big 100-foot square stage, broken only by the footfall of the night watchman or the sudden noises of the studio cats in hot pursuit of a rat. In the vaults there lay fourteen of the seventeen unsold pictures costing thousands of dollars to make.

Then came Charles W. Harlow, wealthy oil producer who, realizing the rapid development and growth of Long Beach, purchased outright three acres of the studio grounds, together with the buildings and their contents. The fourteen pictures were sent to New York by representatives of the oil producer and there sold.

About a year ago [circa March 1924] the contents of the studios were [sold] at public auction and hundreds of men and women gathered to bid for the elaborate sets of furniture, the framed pictures, hundreds of statues, swords, spears, rugs, bedding and the thousands of other things that stage directors and property men find use for in the making of cinema thrillers. (Sect. II, p. 10)

This poignant closing chronicled the passing of an age in Long Beach. The Balboa Amusement Producing Company, once so prominent in early cinema, was fast becoming a faded memory. Nonetheless, from 1910 to 1923, the Long Beach film plant offered the venturesome pioneers a ticket to fame and glory. By a strange set of circumstances, some still unexplained, suddenly the Horkheimers took a sharp and undeserved turn toward obscurity and defamation. The majestically glassed-in studio, the jewel of the plant, was the last to vanish, its 100-square-foot structure having weathered the tide for eight years, from 1917 to 1925, without a single supporting column to impede interior photography. During the plant's glorious but brief career, more than $2,000,000 was invested in the studio. Unfortunately, the prolonged economic slump destroyed the Horkheimers' reign in movieland as it would also destroy a few years later Charles Pathé's film empire throughout the world. A new guard would reign in Hollywood. In fact, the changing of hands at Balboa attests to the numerous and vigorous attempts made to revive Long Beach's once major film plant.

While we have tried to present the major factors that contributed to the meteoric rise and fall of Balboa, the final years of inactivity still remain essentially an enigma. What really prevented the studio's revival after the Horkheimers left in 1918, or after H. M. returned in 1923, despite the many other businessmen, producers, and directors who tried vigorously to make the film plant hum, all marveling until the very end at the film plant's enormous potential? Although the Horkheimer Brothers have journeyed by now to the Elysian Fields beyond the Golden Gates, may their memory live forever in movieland, and may these pioneer moviemakers, H. M. and Elwood, know at last the undying fame and glory they themselves bestowed to Hollywood when she was still only a babe in the cradle.

FADE OUT

Reel 6

Epilogue: Back to the Future

Long Beach today is a major international port in Los Angeles County, situated on San Pedro Bay. Commerce has always figured prominently in the history of the location because the community first began as an Indian trading camp. It later became part of both Spanish and Mexican commercial enterprises, first with Rancho Nieto in 1784, then as part of the enormous Ranchos Los Alamitos and Cerritos. In 1881 the American businessman W. E. Willmore planned Willmore City, a seaside resort incorporated in 1888. It was later renamed Long Beach because of the popularity of the town's then 8½-mile-long strand. Long Beach is a relatively young city, but it has a rich and fascinating history as a movie town and an entertainment center. Although Long Beach is one of the biggest cities in the state of California, with a population of about 450,000 inhabitants, the city has a small-town ambiance, reflecting many different faces in each of its diverse districts. Moreover, Long Beach enjoys an excellent climate throughout the year, along with one of the best public transportation systems around, with electric trains, buses, and tour boats connecting visitors to the city's many points of interest.

Even though the Balboa Studios were demolished in 1925, Long Beach has continued over the years to attract busy film crews from Hollywood. The complete list of movies using Long Beach as a location would be encyclopedic in scope and volume, and the prospects today in Long Beach for moviemaking look brighter than ever. The *Press-Telegram* opened the new year, January 1, 1997, with this title on its front page, "Movie, TV deal signed for dome."

The dome refers to the former Spruce Goose hangar in Long Beach, which is now being leased to Warner Bros. as a movie and TV production facility. In effect, Warner Bros. is paying $1,000,000 per annum for the converted soundstage. The *Press-Telegram* (A1ff.) announced the deal with much enthusiasm:

LONG BEACH — Look out, Hollywood. Long Beach is getting a movie studio.

The old Spruce Goose dome will be turned into a film and television production stage next year under a deal with Warner Bros.

The deal will allow Warner Bros. to use the dome for filming for the next three years, with an option for a fourth year. The studio will pay $1 million a year in rent to the RMS Foundation, which leases the dome and the nearby Queen Mary from the city. Meanwhile, revenues generated from film production will go to the city.

Five days later, January 6, 1997, the *Press-Telegram* (B1ff.) continued the story by the same staff writer, Luis Monteagudo, Jr., entitled "Lights, Action...Long Beach," explaining that the booming movie industry in Southern California was too big for Hollywood to handle alone:

> A box-office boom is resulting in a bonanza in Long Beach. When it was announced last week that Warner Bros. had agreed to operate a full-time production stage at the old Spruce Goose dome, it was a sign that the boom in California's movie business is paying off for cities outside Hollywood.
>
> Entertainment production activity in Los Angeles County jumped more than 30 percent during the first 11 months of 1996, according to the Entertainment Industry Development Corp., which was formed last year after the merger of the county and city film offices.

After signing the lease for the dome in Long Beach, Warner Bros. transformed it into a full-time soundstage in a lease that will surely keep the studio busy into the new millennium. At 130 feet high, the dome easily accommodates large sets. In fact, over the past three years, other Hollywood studios besides Warner Bros. have signed short-term leases so that several blockbuster action-adventure films could be produced there. In MGM/UA's movie *Stargate*, starring Kurt Russell, the dome served as the stage for the laboratory in the film where the Stargate device was used to enter another world. The same dome also housed the 60 foot tall, two-leveled Batcave for *Batman Forever*, becoming again the set for the laboratory of the Riddler, who was played by Jim Carrey. The dome also served in the same film as the lair for Two-Face, played by Tommy Lee Jones.

Moviemaking still fills the city's coffers. Monteagudo explained in his article that *Batman Forever* cost Warner Bros. over $100,000,000 to make, while the studio spent around $750,000 in Long Beach for food, materials, and various supplies. Long Beach's local economy was also replenished another $1,000,000 during the filming of *Batman and Robin* at the dome, while city film permits collected $12,000 for the same movie. In total, Long Beach received $160,000 from all film permit fees during the period July 1, 1995, through September 30, 1996. As Monteagudo noted, the city requires daily fees for filming, in the amount of $650 for the first day, then $400 per diem thereafter.

Here are a few of the movies and TV shows partially produced on location in Long Beach over the past few years: *Batman Forever*, *The Cable Guy*, *Stargate*, *Heat*, *Congo*, *Space Jam*, *Matilda*, *Multiplicity*, *Tin Cup*, *Escape from L.A.*, *Executive Decision*, *Nixon*, *How to Make an American Quilt*, *Baywatch*, *Dark Skies*, and *JAG*.

As a sequel to Monteagudo's article in the *Press-Telegram*, Tim Grobaty began on January 18, 1997, a special weekly column, "On Location," about moviemaking in Long Beach. The first column was entitled, "Long Beach: One Giant Film Set for Hollywood." Why Long Beach? The reasons presented in the column by JoAnn Burns, director of special events in Long Beach, are the same as the reasons given over 80 years ago by H. M. Horkheimer: "There are so many different looks around the city." John Robinson is also quoted in the same article (A4) as saying, "Long Beach can look like Anytown, USA."

For example, in *Tin Cup*, starring Kevin Costner and Rene Russo, Long Beach's magnificent El Dorado Park became North Carolina. In *Nixon*, El Dorado Park transformed itself into Washington, D.C., and then El Dorado changed into tropical Panama in the Harrison Ford thriller *Clear and Present Danger*. The vast and verdant park is a striking beauty, and El Dorado has many different facades with ample vegetation, ponds, and streams. Furthermore, the same park was used in Albert Brooks' *Defending Your Life*. With the seashore looming brightly at the city's doorstep, Long Beach has even posed as the French Riviera for the TV miniseries "Rich Man, Poor Man."

Long Beach is also a motor town, and one of the favorite locations for Hollywood, used repeatedly in freeway scenes, has been Shoreline Drive, near to Long Beach's *Queen Mary* and the Shoreline Village. This happens only when the Grand Prix is not in town because at that time each spring the race roars and steals the show. Since Shoreline Drive is easily closed to traffic, filmmakers have chosen it for scenes in *Speed*, *Demolition Man*, and *To Live and Die in L.A.* In fact, in the charming comedy *Forget Paris*, Billy Crystal was filmed there stuck in rush-hour traffic, patiently clutching his sperm sample. As an interesting coincidence, *Speed*, filmed in 1994, was also shot at the same location, with the crazed runaway bus careering down Ocean Boulevard, the very same thoroughfare where the first silent movie in Long Beach was filmed back in 1911.

Even a certain hospital in Long Beach has attracted the Hollywood crews recently. St. Mary Medical Center, in the heart of town at Linden Avenue and Tenth Street, was chosen for scenes in the feature movie *Blade* about a vampire killer played by Wesley Snipes. *Blade* was coproduced by Stan Lee and was based on one of Lee's comic book characters. St. Mary's entry into Hollywood's circle began, according to Tim Grobaty, when the Robert De Niro–Al Pacino thriller *Heat* used the Long Beach hospital for the opening scene of the film, in which De Niro swipes an ambulance. The hospital was also featured in the same movie again when Pacino takes his daughter to the emergency room after she has attempted suicide. The 74-year-old hospital draws more cameramen each month; scenes were recently filmed there for *Gunshy*.

Yet another "Mary" in town has been the cameramen's favorite — the *Queen Mary*, the ocean liner permanently docked at Long Beach. She made her film debut back in 1972, posing as the ill-fated vessel in the blockbuster hit *The Poseidon Adventure*, starring Red Buttons, Ernest Borgnine, and Shirley Winters. Since 1972, the *Queen Mary* has maintained an impressive portfolio as a Hollywood extra in *The Godfather II*, *The Execution of Private Slovick*, *W. C. and Me*, *The Lonely Guy*, *The Natural*, *Tucker*, and *Barton Fink*. Most recently the ship has appeared in John Carpenter's *Escape from L.A.* and *Multiplicity*. To be able to film the *Queen Mary*'s handsome hull, Hollywood crews must pay dearly. The royal extra charges a regal fee of $4,000 per diem, while the city imposes an additional $600 a day in permit fees. When cameras put the queen on the screen, she knows how to deal as a shrewd businesswoman.

Steven Spielberg's film *Amistad* used a smaller Long Beach vessel, the *Californian*, which is docked at Shoreline Village. *Amistad* is based on a true story about a slave uprising against a Spanish crew in 1839. After having committed mutiny on board, the men were sailing back to Sierra Leone in Africa, when they were captured off the coast of Long Island. During their trial, former president John Quincy Adams, who was 73 at the time, pleaded their case before the U.S. Supreme Court.

The waters off Long Beach also include the Naples district of town, where canals, bridges, and gondolas grace the Mediterranean setting and Hollywood crews sometimes perch atop the Vincent Thomas Bridge, fooling TV viewers into believing that Long Beach can be Italy or the home of the Golden Gate Bridge. The Vincent Thomas Bridge was in fact used on the old *Ironsides* series. There are even spooky locations in Long Beach, as Claudine Burnett explains in her book, *Haunted Long Beach*, published by the Historical Society of Long Beach. Those who enjoy the spine-tingling magic of horror films might recall the low-budget, box-office success entitled *Phantasm*, which was filmed in the oldest graveyard in Long Beach, the Municipal Cemetery, located at the junction of Orange and Willow near Signal Hill, where Hollywood's werewolves, goblins, and vampires like to gather for the cameras. Even intergalactic life forms have visited Long Beach. At Lincoln Park, near the Civil War Memorial, the main public library was used for the massacre of the peace delegation in the pilot episode of *Battlestar Galactica*.

By an eerie coincidence, Hollywood has even returned to the very site of the old Balboa quadrangle, where now stands the gymnasium of St. Anthony High School, to film a basketball game for the movie *Pleasantville*. The film features Jeff Daniels, as well as nominees for best supporting actress and actor for the Academy Awards of 1997 — Joan Allen and William H. Macy. Other institutions of higher education in Long Beach have attracted Hollywood cameramen. The giant Pyramid at the campus of California State University, Long Beach, which was built for basketball games and special events, was also used for the science-fiction terror *Starship Troopers*, directed by Paul Verhoeven. For this film, a futuristic indoor football game was shot in the Pyramid. Recreation Park, the rolling and wooded terrain that was once part of the magnificent Rancho Los Alamitos, houses Blair Field, the baseball stadium in Long Beach used for the movie productions *Space Jam*, *The Scout*, and *Angels in the Outfield*. Joe Jost's, the historical tavern on Anaheim Street that is one of Long Beach's most popular "watering holes" and surely the one with the most character, was used in *The Vanishing*, as well as in *The Bodyguard*, starring Kevin Costner and Whitney Houston. The present owner of the tavern, Ken Buck, who is Joe Jost's grandson, tried to explain the appeal of the establishment to the Hollywood crowd: "Art directors love the look of the place, and agents call me all the time, but our main business is being Joe Jost's. I'll maybe close it down four or five times a year, but that's about it. I have to keep our loyal customers happy" (*Press-Telegram*, Mar. 8, 1997, A9).

Besides the big Hollywood studios using Long Beach, there are some independent filmmakers coming to town. For instance, *Phoenix* is a star-studded movie produced by Prickly Pear Productions that stars Anjelica Huston, Ray Liotta, and Daniel Baldwin. In order to transform Long Beach into Phoenix, Arizona, a little "makeup" was required, as explained by Tim Grobaty of the *Press-Telegram* (April 28, 1997, D1):

> For the scene — which will be held in an area sealed off from the public — rain machines will be brought in to change the climate for a brawl, including actor Liotta, in the alleyway, at the foot of a stairwell that once led to the darkroom above Terry's Camera on Broadway.
>
> "It's a very cool-looking area," said Blue Cafe co-owner Vince Jordan. "It's all brick back there, and it really looks great in a vintage sort of way. I've always pictured it as having some purpose. Whoever picked it out for filming did a great job, because it's a really cool location." ...
>
> Following the rough-housing behind the Blue, the crew and cast move across town on Saturday and next Monday to an apartment complex on Carson Street in Bixby Knolls for some drive-up and drive-away shots, as well as some interiors.

The residents of Long Beach were upset, however, when the *Phoenix* crew replaced the Typewriter City front on Broadway at the Promenade with the sign LIVE NUDE GIRLS, in enormous letters. Citizens bombarded the police and city hall with calls of complaint, outraged at the prospect of such decadence in town, but the only stripping was that of the sign after the shot was completed. Obviously, Long Beach's moviemaking days are still in full swing.

In fact, on May 10, 1997, the *Press-Telegram* published an article, "And the Oscar Goes to...Long Beach?" Will the Academy Awards ceremony move to Long Beach? Such a proposition would be valid for historical reasons and because of the continuing filmmaking in Long Beach. City representatives and Long Beach Convention and Entertainment Center officials played host to members of the Academy of Motion Picture Arts and Sciences who visited the Terrace Theatre in Long Beach to investigate the site as the possible venue for the 1999 telecast, and the members were impressed with the theatre and the support space and parking area. Lack of suitable accommodations for the media at the Shrine Auditorium and scheduling conflicts at the Dorothy Chandler Pavilion in downtown Los Angeles prompted this visit to Long Beach. Wouldn't the Horkheimers have liked the awards ceremony to take place near their old studios?

Movie glamour might never have come to

The original Long Beach roller coaster at the Pike, 1907–1914.

Long Beach, however, if the Pike amusement zone had not already been established in 1902. With the advent of the new millennium just around the corner, not only has Warner Bros., a thriving film studio, returned to Long Beach, but a new amusement zone may also take us "back to the future." Ken Jillison of Laguna Beach is proposing the return of the famous roller coaster called the Cyclone Racer as part of the redevelopment plan for Long Beach along the Shoreline Drive area of the city. This roller coaster was the third one built in the Long Beach amusement zone and received its first riders on Memorial Day, 1930. The first roller coaster in Long Beach was built in 1907, and Long Beach crowds enjoyed the second roller coaster, called the Jackrabbit Racer, from 1915 to 1929 until the Cyclone Racer replaced it. Thrill-seekers took 25 million rides on the Cyclone from 1930 to 1968, making Long Beach a tourist mecca known for its beaches and for having the most celebrated amusement zone in Southern California.

At the Long Beach Pike, the Cyclone was heralded as the main attraction. Located on the Silver Spray Pier, jutting out against the Pacific Ocean, it was described as the biggest wooden roller coaster in the world. It was a beauty to behold and a sensation to ride, a claim supported by the authors of this book, who had the pleasure of taking several spins on the Cyclone. Darren James, exhibit coordinator and volunteer at the Historical Society of Long Beach, promises by August 1997 to present a scale model of the Cyclone, along with a Pike amusement zone exhibit with photos and artifacts to be housed at the Historical Society of Long Beach on Pine Avenue.

The amusement zone outlived the Balboa Studios by about 50 years. Unfortunately for Long Beach, newer parks eventually eclipsed the former glory of the Pike as an amusement center, with the arrival of Disneyland in 1955 in Anaheim, the development of Knott's Berry Farm in Buena Park, in competition with Disneyland, and finally with the opening in Valencia of Magic Mountain in 1971. To the great disappointment of Pike aficionados, the Cyclone was demolished in 1968 to make way for Shoreline Drive, while the Pike's other rides and attractions closed ten years later in 1978, except for the Life-a-Line game, which still

The Jackrabbit Racer, the second roller coaster at the Pike, 1915–1929.

operates in the historic Looff Hippodrome in Long Beach. By 1981, however, most of the Pike rides and buildings had been razed.

Bill Hillburg wrote a special front-page report for the *Press-Telegram* (May 16, 1997, A11), "Back to the Future," in which he ardently described the glorious past of Long Beach's amusement zone as a battle begun by Long Beach against competing and neighboring townships trying to draw tourists and prospective home buyers to the growing beach communities of Long Beach, Seal Beach, Venice, and Santa Monica:

> Long Beach opened the battle in 1902, when Col. Charles Rivers Drake opened a bathhouse and a small amusement area near the Pine Avenue Pier. Drake's son, Gene, named the area The Pike.
>
> Drake teamed with Charles I. D. Looff, a park developer and ride designer who had built his first carousel at New York's Coney Island in 1876. Looff and his son, Arthur, would go on to create more such parks.
>
> The Looffs, who built carousels and other rides at their Hippodrome Factory in Long Beach, also created Shady Acres, a miniature golf complex that once drew crowds to North Long Beach.

Like the Drakes and the Looffs before them, Ken Jillison and Joseph Prevratil, the latter being the operator of the *Queen Mary*, are busy promoting a revival of Long Beach's glory days as an amusement center. In addition to the replica of the Cyclone, Jillison and Prevratil would like to see a mixture of the old and the new. They are trying to bring back the nostalgia but only the best elements that drew people to town to spend an enjoyable day at the beach; they want to make sure that the public feels safe with plenty of reasons to make return visits. The *Press-Telegram*, May 16, 1997, describes the numerous potential amusements:

The Cyclone Racer, 1930–1968 (courtesy of the *Press-Telegram*).

Cyclone Racer: Reproduction of the wooden roller coaster that was a Long Beach landmark from 1930 to 1968. Two separate tracks would each have a pair of coaster cars, racing in tandem. Riders would whip to and fro at up to 55 mph on a one-mile course with numerous curves and 100-foot drops.

Junior Cyclone Racer: A pint-sized, less terrifying replica of the Cyclone Racer for kids who are under the big coaster's 48-inch height safety limit. Young riders would get a coupon good for a free spin on the Cyclone Racer once they're 48 inches tall.

Waltzing Waters: The amusement zone's centerpiece would be a fountain show with syncopated music and lights, like the old Dancing Waters attraction at the Disneyland Hotel in Anaheim.

Tilt-a-Whirl: A classic midway ride featuring spinning and dipping cars and plenty of chances to experience vertigo. It would be updated with new safety features.

Rotor: Another classic thriller. Centrifugal force pins riders against the wall of the cylinder as the floor drops away.

Carousel: A new or vintage merry-go-round. It would be housed in a structure modeled after the Looff Building that still stands as the last vestige of the Long Beach Pike.

Theater arcade: A vintage theater building, possibly modeled after the Pike's old Strand movie house, that would be filled with both antique and high-tech arcade machines.

Birthday Pavilion: Shaped like a candle-topped birthday cake, it would be the venue for catered kiddie parties.

Filling Station: An old-time gas station that would house a bump'em cars ride.

Red Baron: A kiddie ride featuring

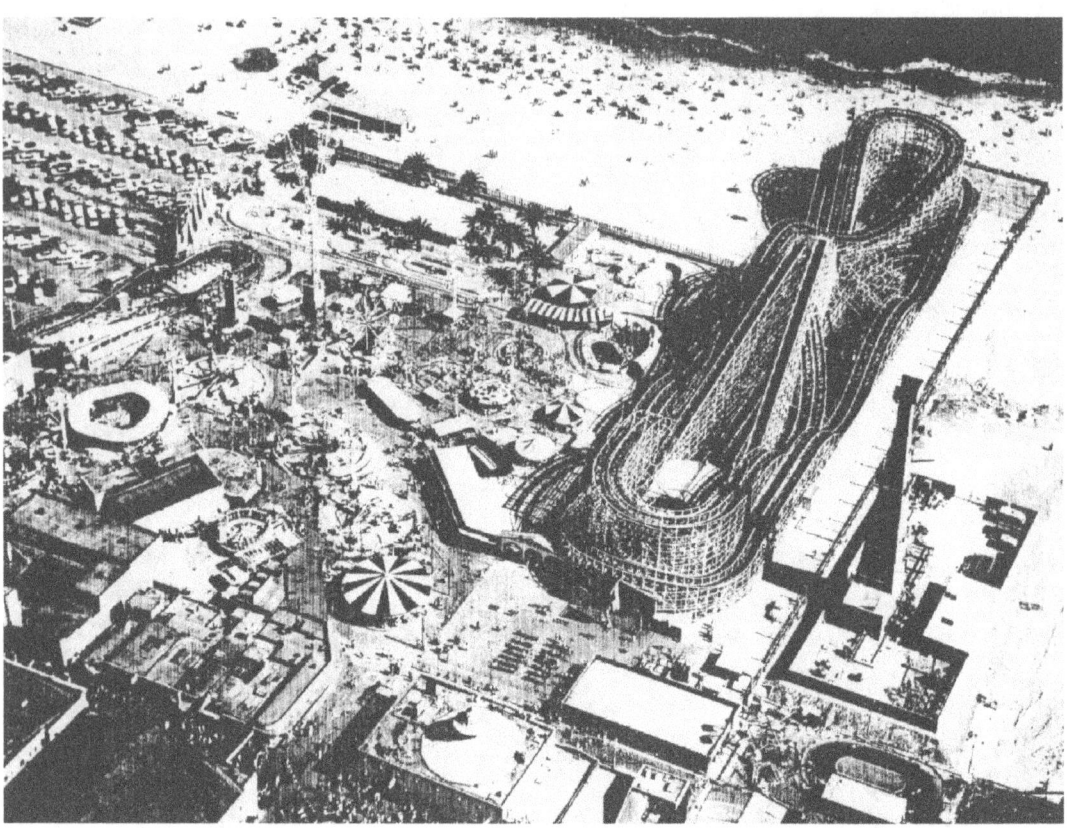

Aerial view of the Pike, circa 1960 (courtesy of Pierre and Carolyn Jura).

miniature biplanes that would spin around a control tower modeled after Long Beach airport's art deco terminal.

Fire Station No. 8: A full size replica of the old fire and police station on Second Street in Belmont Shore, with a fire engine kiddie ride. Security personnel would be headquartered at the police station.

Pony photos: A photo stand where kiddies could be captured for posterity on horseback.

Miscellany: Theme restaurants, a toy store and souvenir shop, and a beachstyle dining area featuring sand and sun umbrellas.

With so many revivals going on in Long Beach, the authors of this book hope too that Balboa's history and memorabilia may find a home where tourists can examine and enjoy the vestiges of Long Beach's film heritage. The Balboa revival has in fact already started. On November 9, 1996, the Balboa Amusement Producing Company was honored at the first Balboa Film Festival and Studio Tour. Over 450 persons participated at each event in a day-long celebration of Balboa's contributions to early Hollywood. Over 1,000 films were made at Long Beach's Balboa Studios, one of the most prolific film plants in the world during the silent era. Around 35 Balboa films, maybe more, are still available throughout archives in the United States and Canada. Many Long Beach organizations came together in this festival spearheaded by Claudine Burnett of the Long Beach Public Library. After months of planning to put on a really great show, the festival presented three rare episodes from the hit serial *Who Pays?*—Chapter 1: *The Price of Fame*, Chapter 7: *Blue Blood and Yellow*, Chapter 12: *Toil and Tyranny*.

Thanks to Harold Linn, proprietor, the films were shown at the Art Theatre, with

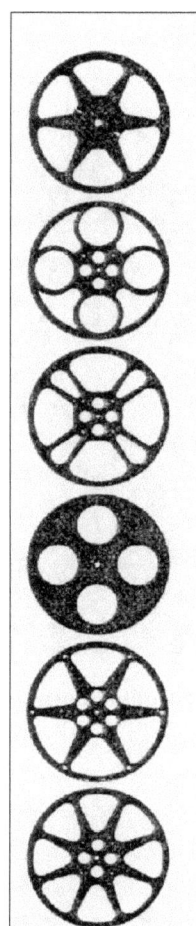

REDISCOVERING LONG BEACH'S FILM HERITAGE

Guided Historical Tour of Balboa Film Studio Site
Hosted by Long Beach Heritage
6th & Alamitos
Saturday, November 9 • 10:00 AM, 10:45 AM, 11:30 AM

Film Program ("The Price of Fame," "Blue Blood & Yellow," "Toil & Tyranny")
Art Theatre, 2025 East 4th Street
Saturday, November 9 • 1:00 PM

On the program are three recently discovered silent movies from the "Who Pays?" series, featuring Ruth Roland and Henry King and filmed at the Balboa Studios between 1914-15. Doors open at 12:30 PM and the program begins at 1:00 PM. Jean-Jacques Jura and Rodney Bardin, authors of a forthcoming book on the Balboa Studios, will be guest speakers. There will also be guest appearances by some of the early stars and other people associated with the studio.

Advance ticket sales for both the guided tours and the film program are $12.50. Please send a check, payable to the Historical Society of Long Beach, along with a **self-addressed stamped envelope** to the Historical Society, PO Box 1869, Long Beach, CA 90801. Advance ticket sales end November 1, 1996. Tickets and other information to early subscribers will be sent out by November 1.

Some tickets will still be available the day of the event. However, on November 9, the cost will be $5 for the tour and $10 for the film program. If you have questions, please contact the Historical Society at (310) 495-1210.

Proceeds will go to the Long Beach Public Library Centennial Book Fund.

Flyer announcing the first Balboa Film Festival and Studio Tour, November 9, 1996, spearheaded by Claudine Burnett of the Long Beach Public Library.

musical accompaniment at the keyboard by David Koehring to help add pathos to the flickering scenes. The Art Theatre, built in 1925, is the last remaining neighborhood movie theatre in Long Beach. All other cinemas in town are now multiple-screen facilities. The former movie palaces of Long Beach have all been permanently removed. On the day of the festival, a studio tour took place at the old Balboa quadrangle, guided by a team of expert docents from Long Beach Heritage who volunteered their time, even wearing costumes to set the mood; their script and maps were coordinated by Karen Clements. The tour would have been impossible without the support of the Museum of Latin American Art, which stands on the quadrangle, with special help from Adam Feldman, property manager, Susan Golden, head of public relations, and Pat House, director of the museum. Benefits from the two events supported the Long Beach Public Library Centennial Book Fund.

The day-long sentimental journey ended with a VIP dinner at the Barcelona Brasserie, situated on the former studio grounds, where some of the studio's few remaining buildings are also clustered. Especially notable among the stars of the day were Marie Osborne-Yeats,

VIP Tour of Balboa Studio quadrangle. J. J. Jura at left, Baby Marie at center, with Claudine Burnett behind Baby Marie.

Interior of the Museum of Latin American Art: from left to right, Marie Osborne-Yeats, Claudine Burnett, Jackie Saunders, Jr.

Available Films Produced at the Balboa Studios

Grapevine Video (http://grapevinevideo.com):
  Drag Harlan (1920/1925) #DHWF, $16.95
  Good Night, Nurse (1918) with four other films, "Buster and Fatty," $19.95
  Out West (1918) together with four other films, "Buster and Fatty," $19.95

Library of Congress: (same episodes* at National Archives of Canada)
  I. Eight Episodes of the 15-Episode Serial, With Their Call Numbers:
    The Neglected Wife, Ep. 2: "Weakening" (1917) Feb 8797-8798 (*1980-0195); Ep. 4: "Beyond Recall" (1917) Feb 8799; Ep. 6: "On the Precipice" (1917) Feb 8800; Ep. 8: "A Relentless Fate" (1917) Feb 8801 (*1980-0195); Ep. 9: "Deepening Degradation" (1917) Feb 8802-8803 (*1980-0195); Ep. 10: "A Veiled Intrigue" (1917) Feb 8804-8805 (*1980-0195); Ep. 11: "A Reckless Indiscretion" (1917) Feb 8806 (*1980-0195); Ep. 14: "Desperation" (1917) Feb 8807 (*1979-0191)
  II. Miscellaneous Films (**Library of Congress**)
    Alien Blood (1917) master material only
    Captain Kiddo (1917) reel 1 only, FEA 8983
    Cleo and Simp (1914-1917?) copy is incomplete, FEA 8996
    The Devil's Bait aka *Devil's Pet* (1917) FEA 6996-6999
    Maid of the Wild (1915) FGE 3486
    Mentioned in Confidence (1917) master material only
    Spellbound aka *The One-Eyed God* (1916) master material only
    Vengeance of the Dead aka *Vengeance of Death* aka *Dungeons of the Dead* (1917)
  III. Miscellaneous Film (**National Archives of Canada**)
    Sunshine and Gold (1917)

Museum of Modern Art:
  Told at Twilight (1917)

Nostalgia Family Video:
  Too Wise Wives (1921) #1995, $19.95

UCLA Film and Television Archive:
  I. All 12 Episodes of the 12-Episode Serial, With Their Call Numbers:
    Who Pays?, Ep. 1: "The Price of Fame" (1915) M18373 (*ready for viewing*); Ep. 2: "The Pursuit of Pleasure" (1915) master material only; Ep. 3: "Where Justice Sleeps" (1915) master material only; Ep. 4: "The Love Liar" (1915) master material only; Ep. 5: "Unto Herself Alone" (1915) master material only; Ep. 6: "House of Glass" (1915) master material only; Ep. 7: "Blue Blood and Yellow" (1915) M55039 (*ready for viewing*); Ep. 8: "Today and Tomorrow" (1915) master material only; Ep. 9: "For the Commonwealth" (1915) master material only; Ep. 10: "The Pomp of the Earth" (1915) M4367, master material only; Ep. 11: "The Fruit of Folly" (1915) master material only; Ep. 12: "Toil and Tyranny" (1915) (*ready for viewing*)
  II. Miscellaneous Films (**UCLA Film and Television Archive**)
    The Checkmate (1917) one of five reels ready for viewing
    Hands Up (1918) promotional film, M20972
    Ruth of the Rockies (1915-1916?) serial, master material only

Unknown Video (unkvid@earthlink.net):
  Little Mary Sunshine (1916)

Listen to *At a Glance* talk radio with Rodney Bardin: VIP dinner, November 9, 1996, at the Barcelona Brasserie, the very site of Balboa Studios. Rodney Bardin and Jean-Jacques Jura, standing behind Marie Osborne-Yeats, with Jackie Saunders, Jr., seated in front (courtesy of Rodney Bardin).

Jackie Saunders, Jr., and Ronnie Lasky, the latter being an actor in his own right and the grandson of the famous Jesse Lasky. All three of these special guests are members of the original Hollywood family of Southern California. Once again, in 1996, Balboa stars and stargazers were able to mingle at the studio quadrangle.

For stargazers interested in history, this closing millennium began in Long Beach with an important and promising marriage between the city's film industry and the amusement zone called the Pike; the latter was established in 1902 and the California Motion Picture Manufacturing Company was incorporated in 1910. Together the Pike and Long Beach's film plant created a viable and healthy team for the city's economy and were part of a rich commercial and artistic heritage. In fact, the film plant and the Pike prospered together as helpmates, and they drew eager crowds to Long Beach seeking entertainment that might confuse, in the most delightful way, "reel" fantasy with "real" pleasure.

In 1910, when the California Motion Picture Manufacturing Company was founded, a comet was sighted over Long Beach. Eighty-seven years later, in the spring of 1997, the comet Hale-Bopp shone across the sparkling skies, portending again perhaps some clues to the mysteries of Long Beach's beginnings, serving as well as a premonition of the city's destiny. Throughout history, stargazers have expressed superstitions about comets as omens. Two amateur astronomers, Alan Hale and Thomas Bopp, discovered the comet Hale-Bopp separately on the same date, July 23, 1995, Hale using a telescope in his driveway in New Mexico, while Bopp in Arizona borrowed a friend's telescope to spy his discovery. Now these two men are immortalized, and the comet that bears their names heads toward deep space, not to return within view from Earth for another 2,500 years.

Stargazers across the globe might also hope for the return of fame to Long Beach, given the city's rich contributions to world cinema. Pieces of comets, meteoroids, enter the Earth's atmosphere and are called "falling stars"

Jean-Jacques Jura and Rodney Bardin (courtesy of the *Press-Telegram*).

Jean-Jacques Jura
P.O. Box 7802
Long Beach, California 90807-7802

Rodney Bardin
P.O. Box 831
Long Beach, California 90801-0831

or meteors. The authors of this book invite all stargazers, amateurs and professionals alike, to share any and all fragments gathered about Balboa by corresponding with us. Please let us know what you have spotted during the meteoric rise and fall of the Balboa Amusement Producing Company. We invite all who enjoy the movements of heavenly bodies to participate in this revival of Long Beach's glorious movie history. May this book be but a springboard "back to the future" for two great pioneers and movieland heroes, H. M. Horkheimer and Elwood D. Horkheimer.

Correspondence regarding Balboa Studios may be addressed to the authors in care of the publisher.

Filmography of Long Beach Studios

Of the countless movies produced in Long Beach, only a few appear on this list. How many Balboa films have survived the ravages of time? Perhaps reader response will bring some of the remaining reels out of dusty storage. Statistics, however, present a dismal picture — 80 percent of all silent movies in the world have disappeared because of nitrate decomposition or neglect, while 40 percent of all movies produced prior to 1952 have also vanished forever, never to be restored. Early motion picture film was often used over and over to keep down production cost. This practice also accounts for the demise of many silent movies. If certain movies won public acclaim, they might sometimes be saved and reissued at a later date as part of a double billing with new releases, but many films were recycled again and again. In addition, though safety film had been developed back in 1908 by Eastman Kodak, this more stable film stock used acetate, which was not flammable like nitrate but was prone to shrinkage and breakage, requiring that the film industry wait decades before flammable nitrate film stock could be replaced by a reliable safety film in 1949.

Anthony Slide explains the dangers of nitrate in *The American Film Industry*. Nitrate will self-ignite at 300 degrees or less. Nitrate film burns 20 times as fast as wood and holds enough oxygen to keep burning even under water. Extremely flammable, burning nitrate emits nitric acid, which is harmful to the lungs and potentially deadly if inhaled. In fact, the chemicals used in producing nitrate film resemble those of guncotton, the chemicals needed for manufacturing explosives. Even if nitrate does not ignite, its decomposition process can occur without fire if it is not stored properly. Keeping nitrate film stock in a humid and cold environment will protect it, as has been proved with some films made in the 1890s that are still in prime condition. If improperly stored, however, nitrate can decompose at any time, beginning with the pictures fading, followed by the film turning sticky and bubbly, and ending with a pile of brown powder. During decomposition, nitrate film often starts a chemical chain reaction of decay among surrounding reels of film (Slide, p. 247). To make matters worse for the fate of silent movies, besides this perpetual threat of nitrate decay, during World War I the U.S. government requested that film manufacturers turn in old reels of film as their patriotic duty to support the war effort in making explosive weapons. When one considers all these factors together, it's a wonder that there are any silent movies still available.

The following filmography is based on information compiled by Claudine Burnett, head of literature and history at the Long Beach Public Library. To this basic information we have added a wealth of details gleaned from Balboa's *Press Clippings*, volume 1, and from entries in *The American Film Institute Catalog*, *Henry King, Director*, and other sources. We are most grateful to Claudine Burnett for her contributions (which reflect five years of research) and her expertise, as well as for her support and encouragement during our research.

Following the chart of studios and distributors, the reader will find the films listed in alphabetical order.

Long Beach Studios/Film Companies	*Distributors*	*Years(s)*
California Motion Picture Manufacturing Company		1910–13
Film Companies	*Distributors*	
Edison Manufacturing Company	unknown	
Famous Players Company	State Rights	
Pilot Films Corporation	State Rights	
Balboa Amusement Producing Company		1913–18
Film Companies	*Distributors*	
Anita King Company	Mutual Film Corporation	
American Film Company	General Film Company	
Astra Film Corporation	Pathé Exchange, Inc.	
*Balboa Amusement Producing Co.	Alliance Films Corporation	
	Bishop, Pessers, and Company, Ltd. (U.K.)	
	Box Office Attraction Company	
	B. S. Moss Motion Pictures Corp.	
	Mutual Film Corporation	
	Pathé Frères/Pathé Exchange, Inc.	
Celebrated Players Film Company	State Rights	
Comique Film Corporation (Arbuckle)	Paramount Pictures	
Eclectic Film Company	Eclectic Film Company	
Equitable Motion Pictures Corporation	Equitable; World Film Corporation	
*Falcon Features	General Film Company	
*A Fortune Photoplay	General Film Company	
*Horkheimer Studios	World Film Corporation	
Joy	Box Office Attraction Company	
Kalem	General Film Company	
Kathleen Clifford Company	Paramount Pictures	
*Knickerbocker Star Features	General Film Company	
Mona Lisa Company	unknown	
Mutual Film Corporation	Mutual Film Corporation	

*These particular film companies at Long Beach were owned by the Horkheimer brothers.

Long Beach Studios/Film Companies	Distributors	Years(s)
Nemo	Box Office Attraction Company	
North Woods Producing Company	State Rights; Atlantic Distributing Corp.	
Pathé Frères	Pathé Frères/General Film Company	
Select Pictures Corporation	Select Pictures Corporation	
University Film Company	University Film Company	
Warner's Features, Inc.	unknown	
White Star	Box Office Attraction Company	
The Art Film Company	unknown	1919
The New Art Company	State Rights; Solitary Sin.	1919

Master Pictures Corporation — 1919–20

Film Companies	Distributors
Fox Film Corporation	Fox Film Corporation
Master Pictures	State Rights
Holly Comedy Company	unknown
Mercury Comedy Company	Bull's Eye
Morante Motion Picture Company	Reelcraft Corporation
Spinx Serial Company	unknown
Texas Guinan Company	unknown

International Film Company — 1920–22

Film Companies	Distributors
Acme	unknown
Atlas Film Corporation	Mt. Olympus Distribution
Bull's Eye Film Corporation	Bull's Eye
Columbia Film Company	unknown
David Trattner Production Company	unknown
Edith Sterling Productions	unknown
Famous Players–Lasky	Paramount Pictures
Kelsey Company	unknown
Long Beach Motion Picture Company	American Distributing Corporation
Marie Osborne Film Company	unknown
Meteor Pictures Corporation	unknown
Morante Motion Picture Company	Reelcraft Corporation
Paragon Pictures Corporation of America	Reelcraft Corporation
Special Pictures Corporation	unknown

**Long Beach Studios, Inc./
Hampton Del Ruth Studios** — 1922

Film Companies	Distributors
Bob Horner Company	unknown
Commonwealth Company	unknown
Historical Films Company	unknown
Long Beach Studios, Inc.	American Releasing Corp.
Morante Motion Picture Company	Reelcraft Corporation
William Thompson Company	unknown
Starke-Staller Corporation	unknown

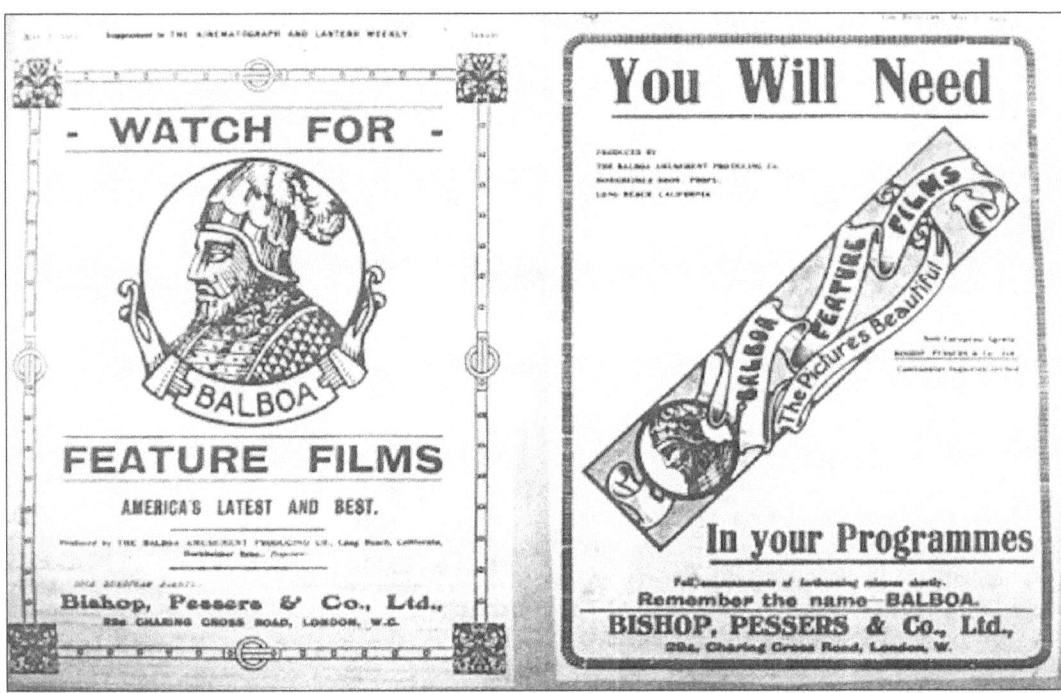

British publicity about Balboa movies taken from *Press Clippings*, vol. 1 (courtesy of Marc Wanamaker).

Abide With Me. One-reel drama. Pathé Frères. Released Mar. 11, 1914, by General Film Co. *Cast*: Henry King (*Ralph Chalmers*), William Wolbert (*his father, a banker*), Augusta Bolle (*Jean Gooding*), Charles Dudley (*the doctor*), Madeline Pardee (*the other girl*) (*Press Clippings*, vol. 1, p. 52).

Commentary: This drama was based on the old hymn of the same name. From beginning to end, it preaches the moral that the way of the sinner is hard and that the only hope for the wayward is complete and absolute repentance.

Summary: Ralph Chalmers is the typical prodigal son to whom the father's wealth is but a demoralizing influence. Meeting by chance an attractive girl coming out of church one morning, Ralph sees in her face the antithesis of what he is and feels the pangs of conscience. Mentally he resolves to turn over a new leaf and be worthy of her, but he soon relapses into his old habits. Enraged by his son's dissipations, Mr. Chalmers disowns him and turns him from the house. The young man goes from bad to worse. One day, crazed by drugs, he wanders into a little mission hall and is astounded to see Jean there singing before the congregation. Her old father having died, Jean has devoted her talents to making the world better. Recognizing her old admirer she sets out to redeem him from his evil ways and, by patience and by the example of her own blameless life, finally drags him from the depths.

Review: According to the *Daily Telegram* (Mar. 1914), "This one reel feature has been hailed by the critics as the best work of the Balboa people who have already built up an enviable reputation for production."

The Acid Test. Copyright Feb. 3, 1915 (*Encyclopedia of the Movie Studios*, p. 234).

The Adventures of a Madcap. Four-reel comedy-drama. Balboa Amusement Producing Co. Released by Pathé Exchange, Inc., Nov. 3, 1915. *Cast*: Jackie Saunders (*Jean*), Frank Mayo (*Jack Aubrey*), Corinne Grant (*Carmio*), Philo McCullough (*Carlos*).

Commentary: According to the *American Film Institute Catalog* (p. 5), this movie was

Fatty Arbuckle at the Balboa Studios (courtesy of Marc Wanamaker).

hand-colored by the Pathé process in Vincennes, France.

Summary: Jean, as a little girl, is adopted by an old flower grower. Having grown up in the country, Jean helps out by selling flowers by the side of the road. A shy neighbor, Jack, loves Jean from afar, not daring to make a move. One day Jean's adoptive father passes away, and the wealthy Gordons, who live in the city, adopt Jean. The confines and manners of city life don't appeal to Jean. Wanderlust pulls at Jean's heart strings, and she runs away seeking adventure and freedom with a band of gypsies. Jean finds too much adventure, however, as Carlos, the son of the Gypsy King, takes a fancy to her. Carlos comes on too strong one day, so Jean escapes and hides in an abandoned hut. Carlos soon locates Jean, but his jealous lover, Carmio, brings a search party to the rescue, including Jack, Jean's secret admirer, and the Gordons. The searchers arrive in the nick of time to save Jean from the clutches of the hot-blooded Carlos. (Drawn from *American Film Institute Catalog*, p 5.)

The Adventures of Ruth. Serial. *Cast:* Ruth Roland ("Southern Exposure," p. 120).

The Alien Blood. Four-reel (drama?). Balboa Amusement Producing Co., a Fortune Photoplay. Released Mar.-Apr. 1917 by General Film Co. *Director:* Burton George. *Scenario:* Captain Leslie Peacocke. *Cameraman:* Garnett (full name unknown). Based on the short story "The Alien Blood" by Louise Rice in *Ainslee's Magazine* (publication date undetermined). *Cast:* Clifford Gray, Winnifred Greenwood.

Commentary: According to *American Film Institute Catalog* (p. 13), this movie was among the last of the Fortune Photoplays filmed at Balboa Studios. One contemporary describes this movie as a Méliès production. There is no plot information since this movie might have had limited release for which reviews cannot be found.

All on Account of Polly. One-reel comedy. Pathé Frères. Released Feb. 13, 1914, by General Film Co. *Cast:* Charles Dudley (*Sailor*

Baby Marie stealing hearts (courtesy of Marie Osborne-Yeats).

Slim), Delia Connor (*Dorothy*), William Wolbert (*the favored suitor, Monk Thorpe*), Carl Erlanger (*Van Tuyl, the troublemaker*).

Commentary: This photoplay was locally made, with actors and actresses familiar to Long Beach citizens; however, it was "Pretty Polly," the parrot, who was the real star of the film.

Summary: The *Daily Telegram* (Feb. 25, 1914, 4:7) recounts the plot as a story about a talkative parrot whose language, which is more forceful than polite, creates complications in the lives of humans around her. Sailor Slim, the owner, sells Polly to a man who has just been rejected by his girlfriend. This man hopes to

```
BALBOA FEATURE FILMS
MANUFACTURED BY
THE BALBOA AMUSEMENT PRODUCING CO.
INCORPORATED

EXECUTIVE OFFICES AND STUDIOS
LONG BEACH, CALIFORNIA
```

OFFICE OF THE PRESIDENT

May
Third
Nineteen Sixteen.

Miss Myrtle Reeves,
% The Studio,
Long Beach, California.

Dear Madam:

    This is to advise that beginning Monday, May eighth, your salary will be increased Five Dollars ($5.00) per week.

    This is given in accordance with our policy, for faithful and loyal services rendered The Balboa Amusement Producing Company.

    We sincerely hope that we will have the pleasure of giving you many more increases in the near future.

    With very best personal regards, beg to remain

    Yours very truly,

President and General Manager,
THE BALBOA AMUSEMENT PRODUCING COMPANY.

HMH-RRR

Copy of a letter from H. M. Horkheimer to Myrtle Reeves (courtesy of Randy Skretvedt).

use the parrot to make trouble between the new pair of lovers and win her back. The new owner places the parrot in the room in which the girl is entertaining her beau. Soon the young woman hears language that should not be used around a lady, and she suspects her new boyfriend. Vainly he protests his innocence before he regains the good graces of his sweetheart.

Almost Crazy. One-reel drama. Joy. Made for William Fox, released by the Box Office Attraction Co. (*Moving Picture World*).

Angel Child. Five-reel comedy-drama. Plaza Pictures (probably started for Balboa Amusement Producing Co.) Released Sep. 9, 1919, by W. W. Hodkinson Corp. *Director:* Henry

HORKHEIMER BROTHERS

Producers of Photoplay Successes for

Paramount	Mutual	General Film	Pathe
"WHO IS 'NUMBER ONE'?" the Mystery Serial Starring **Kathleen Clifford** Story by Anna Katherine Green Picture Synopsis by H. M. Horkheimer This is the first Serial ever released by PARAMOUNT.	Those Rollicking **Jackie Saunders** Comedy-drama hits on the program of "Big Stars Only" Like "Sunny Jane," "The Wildcat," "A Bit of Kindling," etc. All came direct from the HORKHEIMER Studio. There will soon be another series of them.	For this pioneer program **Horkheimer Brothers** Have long been making such brands as Knickerbocker Star Features Fortune Photoplays Falcon Features All of which are evidence of their superiority as motion picture producers par-excellence.	Which right now is releasing one of the biggest serial hits of the year— **"The Neglected Wife"** A BALBOA Production Following such Screen landmarks as "Who Pays," "Neal of the Navy," "The Red Circle," "The Grip of Evil." All BALBOA Serials

BALBOA

Originated the World-famous Photoplays with a "Baby Grand" Star

A new series just completed featuring

Gloria Joy
the Child Wonder

BALBOA

BALBOA

now producing six smashing features starring

Anita King
the Joyous Outdoor Girl

Horkheimer-Mutual Release

BALBOA
BALBOA
BALBOA

The Largest **Actually** Independent Motion Picture Producing Studio in the Industry.
The Studio built on Merit. No stock for Sale.
Now Four Years Old and still Growing.
The Studio where "Fatty" Arbuckle Comedies are Produced for the Paramount Program.

H. M. HORKHEIMER
President and General Manager

The
BALBOA Amusement
Producing Company
(INCORPORATED)

Studio and General Offices:
Long Beach, Cal.

New York Headquarters: 1600 Broadway
H. N. HOLDE, Eastern Representative

E. D. HORKHEIMER
Secretary and Treasurer

Balboa publicity, 1918 (courtesy of Marc Wanamaker).

Otto. *Scenario:* Harl McInroy (sometimes Carl McInroy or Hal McInroy). *Cameraman:* Joseph Brotherton. *Cast:* Kathleen Clifford (*Glory Moore*), Leslie T. Peacock (*Glory's father*), Rita Harlan (*Glory's Mother*), Fred Church (*Richard Grant*), Daniel Gilfether, Neil Hardin, Gordon Sackville (*American Film Institute Catalog*, p. 25).

Commentary: According to the *American Film Institute Catalog*, this production is not credited to Balboa Studios; however, the release date would explain why the producer would be other than Balboa, since Balboa had gone into receivership while the production was still under way. In addition, the director, the cameraman, and the majority of the actors were Balboans. See also *The Law That Divides*, *Petticoats and Politics*, and *Whatever the Cost*, all of which seem to fall into the same category.

Summary: Glory Moore has been driving her mother mad with her pranks, though her father adores his "angel child." The mother gets her way by sending Glory off to finishing school. However, the move does not change the young woman's ways, for Glory continues her prankishness at school. Shortly after his daughter's departure, Glory's father is looking for an important document that will send a business rival to prison. Unknowingly, Glory had rolled up some candy in the letter and tossed it on the ground, where it was picked up by the rival's daughter, who retrieved the letter to protect her own father. Learning her mistake, Glory gets the letter back, with the help of a young lawyer she had met at school, Richard Grant. Glory's day of victory is made complete when she abandons the rigors of finishing school to accept Richard Grant's proposal for marriage.

The Awakening. Three-reel drama. White Star. Made for William Fox. Released Oct. 5, 1914, by Box Office Attraction Co. *Director:* William Desmond Taylor. *Cast:* Neva Gerber (*Jane Conway*), Edwin August (*Herbert Randolph*) (*Press Clippings*, vol. 1, p. 101).

Commentary: Taylor made his directorial début with this film and fell in love with Miss Gerber. Gerber, unable to get a divorce, and Taylor, already divorced, later ended their affair but remained loyal friends until his murder in 1922. According to Robert Giroux, in *A Deed of Death* (p. 80), Neva Gerber appeared in the next four of Taylor's movies at Balboa.

Summary: Herbert Randolph, son of a well-to-do country clergyman, is engaged to Matilda Rankin, a homely and prudish young woman. He has proposed to her to gratify his parents. His ambition is to be an author. He finishes his first novel and takes the manuscript to a publisher. The editor rejects it, calling special attention to the portrayal of the lover experiencing his first thrill of love by kissing the heroine on the forehead, which is the limit of Herbert's own experience. But Jane Conway, the daughter of the editor, becomes interested in him, believing that he has talent. She takes it upon herself to call upon him and offers to assist him in revising his novel, and he very gratefully accepts her assistance. She learns of his engagement to Matilda, sees her picture, and realizes not only that Herbert does not love her, but that with such a woman for a wife he can never hope to succeed in a literary career. Jane determines for Herbert's sake to break the engagement.

While Herbert is out one evening with Matilda and her mother, Jane gets into his room and places cards, poker chips, wine bottles and a pair of her gloves and slippers about the room. Herbert brings Matilda and her mother back to his apartment for some refreshments, and the two women discover the suspicious evidences of a wild bachelor's life. Matilda, ignoring Herbert's protestations of innocence, gives him back his ring, and she and her mother depart in great indignation. Jane, who has been watching the scene outside the French window, falls into the room. Herbert accuses her of the plot, and she admits it, much to Herbert's amazement. Later she comes back for her things, finds him asleep on the couch, kisses him, and runs out. Herbert has been insensibly falling in love with Jane, and this kiss in his sleep awakens him to the full realization of his feelings. Under this inspiration he revises his story, and does it so well that it is promptly accepted. Jane, in the meantime fearing that she has gone too far and that she has offended Herbert, makes it a point to avoid meeting him, not realizing that he has fallen in love with her as she has with him. When he receives the letter from the publisher telling him of his acceptance of his manuscript, he takes it to Jane to thank her for her share in the good luck. He finds her asleep in a chair and kisses her, thus revealing his love for her. (Drawn from *Press Clippings*, vol. 1, p. 101.)

Bab the Fixer. Five-reel comedy-drama. E. D. Horkheimer. *Distributor*: Mutual Film Corp., released Aug. 13, 1917. *Director*: Sherwood MacDonald. *Scenario*: Lee Arthur and Jackie Saunders. *Story*: Lee Arthur. *Cameraman*: William Beckway. *Cast*: Jackie Saunders (*Bab*), Leslie T. Peacocke (*John Porter*), Mollie McConnell (*Adelaide Porter*), Ruth Lackaye (*Mrs. Drexel*), R. Henry Grey (*Leroy Scott*), Arthur Shirley (*Richard Sterling*), Clara Kahler.

Commentary: Jackie Saunders had worked for Biograph in the East and one year for Universal before signing a contract with Balboa. E. D. Horkheimer met with Mutual Film Corp. to arrange the distribution of 6 five-part productions with Jackie Saunders. The first release was *Sunny Jane*, followed soon afterwards by *The Checkmate* and *The Wildcat*, then *A Bit of Kindling*, *Betty Be Good*, and *Bab the Fixer*.

Summary: Leaving behind the fast-track of city life, a financially ruined stockbroker tries to start over by moving west with his wife and daughter. The young girl, Bab, grows up happily as a cowgirl on their ranch. As a young woman, Bab falls in love with a rich neighbor, Richard Sterling, but her mother wants her daughter to go back to the sophisticated life in the East, where her daughter might become part of high society. After oil is discovered in their ranch, Bab's parents can finally send her to finishing school in the East, where Bab can meet the right people. On one of Bab's return trips to her parents, she becomes "the fixer." Nothing seems quite right at home. Her parents are separated, but Bab persuades her folks to get back together, and by the end of the story, Bab "the fixer" has negotiated her own matrimonial arrangements with her beloved Sterling. (Drawn from the *American Film Institute Catalog*, pp. 40–41.)

A Barnyard Romance. Released in 1920.
Commentary: This comedy was produced and filmed in Long Beach (*Daily Telegram*, May 12, 1920, p. 3).

A Bear Escape. One-reel comedy. Joy. Made for William Fox, released by Box Office Attraction Co. (*Press Clippings*, vol. 1, p. 179).

Summary: A burlesque farce in costumes of the romantic drama. Nero is the king, and two of his courtiers have a fight over Ligea, a pretty slave girl, whose nose is twisted and turned sidewise. It depends on one's digestion whether a picture of this kind appeals strongly to one's sense of what is funny or not.

The Bell Boy. Two-reel comedy. Copyright Mar. 7, 1918. Famous Players–Lasky Corp. copyright claimant. Comique Film Corp. Paramount–Arbuckle Comedy No. A–3109. Released Mar. 18, 1918, by Paramount Pictures. *Director/Writer*: Roscoe Arbuckle. *Scene Editor*: Herbert Warren. *Cameraman*: George Peters. *Cast*: Roscoe Arbuckle, Buster Keaton, Al St. John, Alice Lake, Joseph Keaton, Charles Dudley.

Commentary: According to *Frame-up* (p. 296), this production was filmed at Ouchgosh, a rural village set built for Arbuckle at Balboa Amusement Co.

Summary: Jim Kline's *The Complete Films of Buster Keaton* (p. 41), explains that the action takes place in the Elk's Head Hotel, a rural establishment operated by Roscoe and Buster, who appear as bellboys, and Al, the desk clerk. The first Keaton gag is the one of cleaning a pane of nonexistent glass. Roscoe then mops the lobby by sitting on the floor and cleaning one small area before scooting on to another. He next shaves a heavily bearded guest, transforming the man into various historical personages as he removes layers of whiskers and hair. Buster then recreates one of his vaudeville routines when his father, Joe Keaton, shows up as an elegantly dressed guest. While Buster mops the floor, Joe's top hat is knocked off by an overhead conveyor belt carrying hot towels from the kitchen to the barber shop. Suspecting Buster has insulted him, Joe kicks him in the rear, then upends his pail of water onto his head. Other gags follow — an elevator gets stuck between floors, and there is a mock bank robbery to impress a girl when real robbers appear.

Review: *Variety* (Mar. 22, 1918, p. 52) reported that "the rapid, acrobatic comedy of these three slapstick comedians had the audience in hysterics at the Rialto Sunday afternoon." The story was excruciatingly funny.

The Best Man. Four-reel social drama. Copyright Oct. 12, 1917, General Film Co., Inc., LP11539. Falcon Features. Released, Oct. 21, 1917, by General Film Co. *Supervisors:* H. M. Horkheimer and E. D. Horkheimer. *Director:* Bertram Bracken. *Scenario:* Douglas Bronston. *Story:* George Cain. *Cast:* William Ehfe (*Arnold Hammond*), Gordon Sackville (*Pierre Lemoyne*), Capt. Nicholson (*Dr. Storm*), Margaret Landis (*Ruth Storm*), Mollie McConnell (*Mrs. Storm*), Clifford B. Gray (*Blake*), Frank Brownlee (*Capt. Hale*).

Commentary: According to the *American Film-Index 1916–1920* (p. xvi), Falcon Features began production Aug. 1917 and ended Feb. 1918 and were distributed through General Films.

According to the *American Film Institute Catalog* (p. 61), sources vary in crediting a production company. Some credit Balboa, while others credit Falcon. Both companies were owned by H. M. and E. D. Horkheimer.

Summary: Trying to recover from alcoholism, Arnold Hammond, under a doctor's care, moves to a scenic fishing village in Nova Scotia. During his complete rehabilitation, Arnold falls in love with the doctor's daughter, Ruth. On the other hand, Ruth is in love with two men at the same time and must choose the best one. Is it Arnold Hammond or Pierre Lemoyne? The latter is a dashing young man, but he turns out to be dangerous when he drinks. One day Arnold invites Ruth to take a boat ride with him, hiring Pierre, the dashing fisherman, to sail the boat. Before long, Pierre has been drinking on board and suddenly attacks Arnold. During the skirmish, the boat turns over. The three fall into the brine but are saved by passing boaters. This close call gives Ruth the chance to choose the best man. (Drawn from the *American Film Institute Catalog*, p. 61.)

Betty Be Good. Five-reel comedy-drama. Balboa Amusement Producing Co. Made for Mutual Star Productions. Released July 16, 1917, by Mutual Film Corp. *Producer:* E. D. Horkheimer. *Director* Sherwood MacDonald. *Story:* Will M. Ritchey. *Cameraman:* William Beckway. *Cast:* Jackie Saunders (*Betty Brownlee*), Arthur Shirley (*Jimmy Madison*), Leslie T. Peacocke (*Jonathan Brownlee*), Mollie McConnell (*Mrs. Sarah Lenox*), Mrs. Marsh (*Lyda*), Ben Rossier (*Griggs*), Dad Voute (*Police sergeant*), William Reed (*Jeams*), Mignon LeBrun (*Jenny*), Albert B. Ellis (*Mayor Madison*).

Commentary: Jackie Saunders had worked for Biograph in the East and one year for Universal before signing a contract with Balboa. E. D. Horkheimer met with Mutual Film Corp. to arrange the distribution of 6 five-part productions with Jackie Saunders. The first release was *Sunny Jane*, followed soon afterwards by *The Checkmate* and *The Wildcat*, then *A Bit of Kindling*, *Betty Be Good*, and *Bab the Fixer*.

Summary: Two men, Jonathan Brownlee, a millionaire, and Mayor Peter Madison, suspect each other of political wrongdoing. Jimmy Madison, the mayor's son, is posing as a policeman on assignment to be able to infiltrate and uncover corruption on the force. Brownlee believes the mayor is the source of the corruption, based on some documents he has found. One day Betty Brownlee innocently takes her father's car for a spin, unaware of the important documents stashed in the car. During his investigation, Jimmy Madison tails the young woman behind the wheel, stopping her as a suspected thief, but it's love at first sight, and love manages to conquer all the misunderstandings in this political yarn. All the suspicions prove false and are eventually dropped on both sides, as their true identities are made known, with a happy ending for both families. (Drawn from the *American Film Institute Catalog*, p. 64.)

Beulah. Six-reel drama. Balboa Amusement Producing Co. Released by Alliance Films Corp., May 1915. *Producer*: H M. Horkheimer. *Director:* Bertram Bracken. *Assistant Director*: Alden Willey. *Scenario*: Will M. Ritchey. *Cast*: Henry B. Walthall (*Dr. Guy Hartwell*), Joyce Moore (*Beulah Benton*), Mae Prestell, Clifford Gray, Marguerite Nichols, Elsie Allen, Gypsy Abbott, Corinne Grant, Leopold Medan, Mollie McConnell, Henry Stanley, Gordon Sackville, Hazel Henderson, Sylvia Ashton, Charles Dudley, Margaret Mulvane. (Drawn from the *American Film Institute Catalog*, p. 65.)

Commentary: Based on Augusta Evans' Southern novel, adapted for the screen by Will M. Ritchey. It was an expensive film, costing $85,000 with a large cast of 40 players, and was considered a sequel to the successful *St. Elmo* (*Variety*, May 14, 1915, p. 20).

Summary: The story is about an orphan girl named Beulah who is adopted by Dr. Guy Hartwell, a wealthy Southern physician. The doctor is somewhat sour on all women, having been betrayed by the woman he married. In time, the wounds heal with the love of the little orphan. He falls in love with Beulah and proposes to her when she returns from school. She has fallen in love with a younger man, and Dr. Hartwell wishes her happiness. The doctor leaves Beulah behind and travels north, returning to the Southern town when he reads of an epidemic killing many. Beulah is one of the few who survives, and together they try to save as many townsfolk as they can. Beulah discovers that she does love the doctor, and a happy ending results from the tragedy (*Variety*, p. 20).

Review: According to *Variety*, the only two actors who gave a good performance were the two main characters, Walthall and Moore. In fact, the audience laughed at what should have been the most dramatic scenes.

Bill and Coo and Ouija Board. Two reels. Paragon Pictures Corporation of America (*Daily Telegram*, Apr. 7, 1920, p. 20).

Bill and the Baby. Western. Released in 1921. Morante Motion Picture Company. *Cast*: Milburn Morante, Evelyn Nelson, and Morante's four-year-old daughter.

Commentary: According to the *Daily Telegram* (Mar. 19, 1921, p. 9), this movie was filmed in Raymond, in Madera County, with the interiors shot in Balboa Studios.

Birds of Prey. Cast: William Conklin (*Daily Telegram*, Oct. 6, 1916, 4:6).

The Birth of a Man. Five-reel drama. Balboa Amusement Producing Co., Celebrated Players Film Co. Made for B. S. Moss Motion Picture Corp. Released Apr. 1916 by State Rights. *Cast*: Henry Walthall, Joyce Moore, Henry Stanley, Jay Herman, Dick Johnson, William Reed, William Sheer.

Commentary: According to the *American Film Institute Catalog* (p. 70), this movie was made earlier at Balboa Studios. Henry Walthall walked out Mar. 13, 1915, from his Balboa contract, heading first for Majestic, then later to Essanay. One reviewer noted that the movie seemed padded, as if the Balboa film had been lengthened to five reels by the Celebrated Players Film Co. It is also possible that the film was released earlier under another title. The title given here may have been used because Walthall was made famous with the Griffith film entitled *The Birth of a Nation*.

Summary: A formerly arrogant millionaire is robbed and left to die in a burning barn. The millionaire manages to save himself, but, days later, after his ordeal, he returns to the city, worn out and transformed in appearance and in attitude. No one recognizes him. Friends ignore him, and even his own servants shut him out of his own home. He does manage to befriend a poor man who feeds the "homeless" millionaire and helps him break into his own house. Inside his mansion, the millionaire grooms himself and puts on a change of clothes. Back to his old look, the millionaire, however, is not back to the old self. Inspired by the example of the poor man who helped him when he was homeless, hungry, and friendless, the millionaire decides to dedicate himself to the needy. (Drawn from the *American Film Institute Catalog*, p. 70.)

A Bit of Kindling. Five-reel drama. Mutual Film Corp., Horkheimer. Made for Mutual Star Productions, released by Mutual Film Corp., June 18, 1917. *Director*: Sherwood MacDonald. *Story*: Douglas Bronston. *Cameraman*: William Beckway. *Cast*: Jackie Saunders (*Sticks/Alice*), Arthur Shirley (*James Morgan*), J. P. Wade (*chief engineer*), Charles Dudley (*Jim Clauncy*), Ethel Ritchey (*Ruth Borden*), Edward Jobson (*Cyrus Van Hook*), H. C. Russell (*constable*), Daniel Gilfether (*Alice's benefactor*).

Commentary: According to the *American Film Institute Catalog* (p. 73), this movie was also entitled *Sticks*. Although Wid's called this a Balboa production, it is uncertain whether the Horkheimer brothers were producing under the name of Balboa at this time.

Jackie Saunders had worked for Biograph in the East and one year for Universal before signing a contract with Balboa. E. D. Horkheimer met with Mutual Film Corp. to arrange the distribution of 6 five-part productions with Jackie Saunders. The first release was *Sunny Jane*, followed soon afterwards by *The Checkmate* and *The Wildcat*, then *A Bit of Kindling*, *Betty Be Good*, and *Bab the Fixer*.

Summary: A young newsgirl called "Sticks" must fight for her turf in a tough neighborhood. One day Sticks tries to defind one of her favorite clients, who is being attacked by hooligans. The rich client, James Morgan, and Sticks are both beaten unconscious and end up in a baggage car. By the time they awake, they're miles away from home. The two end up starting over where they get off the train, with Morgan working for the railroad and Sticks doing house cleaning. Morgan's father and girlfriend, Ruth Borden, come looking for Morgan. Sticks is still a young girl and misunderstands a discussion she overhears among the reunited adults, thinking that Morgan has given up his good life only to protect his little ward. Unselfishly, Sticks walks away and is adopted by another guardian, a wealthy benefactor. Years pass, and one day by chance Morgan runs into Sticks at her benefactor's home. The special bond and love between Sticks and Morgan had endured all those years, and the two agree to marry each other. (Drawn from the *American Film Institute Catalog*, p. 73.)

Bitter Sweets. Three-reel drama. Nemo. Made for William Fox. Released Nov. 3, 1914, by Box Office Attraction Co. (*Moving Picture World*).

Summary: Clare Mason, a rancher's daughter who is working in the city, becomes infatuated with Bob Storm, an attractive rascal, and agrees to marry him. Bob uses his charm to get money from his fiancée to entertain other women. Clare finds Bob out and attempts revenge, but Carl Knight, a college student, helps to change her mind. Clare becomes ill because of Bob's deceit and is cared for by Carl, who has paid all her bills. Humiliated at receiving charity, Clare returns to the ranch, leaving a photograph and letter of thanks for Carl. With Clare gone, Carl realizes how much he misses her. Could it be love? Carl travels to the ranch, buying an adjoining ranch and raising a banner crop. He impresses her with his honest devotion, and she agrees to marry him. Bob reappears on the scene, fleeing from the police who accuse him of robbery. He tries to get Clare back by threatening to implicate her father in the crime unless she agrees to marry him. All works out in the end, with Bob getting his just reward and Carl and Clare living happily ever after. (Drawn from *Press Clippings*, vol. 1, p. 102.)

Bliss of Ignorance. Copyright Oct. 13, 1915 (*Encyclopedia of the Movie Studios*, p. 234).

Bolt from the Sky. Copyright Oct. 25, 1915 (*Encyclopedia of the Movie Studios*, p. 234).

The Boob and the Bandit. One-reel comedy. Joy. Made for William Fox, released by Box Office Attraction Co. (*Moving Picture World*).

Boots and Saddles. Five-reel drama. Balboa Amusement Producing Co. Made for B. S. Moss Motion Picture Corp. Released Nov. 1916 by Moss Films. *Scenario*: Eugene Walters. *Cast*: R. Henry Grey (*John James English*), Lillian West (*Lucy Ward*), Robyn Adair (*George Ferris), Norman W. Luke (*William Briscoe*), Charles Dudley (*Walter Harris*), George Pheilen (*Charles Tallyen*), Claire Glenn (*Beth Ward*), Gordon Sackville.

Commentary: This was a picture version of the Eugene Walter play with the same name. According to the *American Film Institute Catalog* (p. 89), this movie had its première in New York on Oct. 26, 1916. Some sources state that the film was produced by the B. S. Moss Motion Picture Corp., but Moss did not begin production until later.

Summary: John James English adores Lucy Ward, but she marries the dishonest George Ferris, a gambler, who steals her heart, believing her to be wealthy. Her childhood sweetheart is desolate when she returns his engagement ring, so he joins the army. All three meet again in Las Vegas, where George and Lucy had gone to run a mine. George speculates with company funds and steals the payroll. Troops are called in, and the former fiancé, one of the soldiers, saves the wife from disgrace by refusing to reveal that she mistakenly killed her gambler husband thinking him a burglar. Finally, after other villainy, the former lovers are reunited. (Drawn from *Variety*, Nov. 2, 1916, p. 24, and the *American Film Institute Catalog*, p. 89.)

Review: *Variety* (Nov. 2, 1916, p. 24) thought *Boots and Saddles* was just "so so."

The Bracelet. Three-reel drama. White Star. Made for William Fox. Released Oct. 26, 1914, by Box Office Attraction Co. (*Moving Picture World*).

The Brand of Man. Balboa Amusement Producing Co. Released in 1915 by Pathé Frères. *Scenario*: Henry King (*Henry King, Director*, p. 195).

Brand's Daughter. Four-reel drama. Copyright Nov. 9, 1917, General Film Co., Inc., LP11691. Falcon Features. Released Nov. 1917? by General Film Co. *Supervisors*: H. M. Horkheimer and E. D. Horkheimer. *Director*: Harry Harvey. *Scenario*: Captain Leslie T. Peacocke. *Story*: Harry S. Stabler. *Cast*: Daniel Gilfether (*Roger Brand*), Julien Beaubien (*Alethea Brand*), Gloria Payton (*Annette*), R. Henry Grey (*Spencer Rutherford*), Kathleen Kirkham (*Paula Lavergne*), Melvin Mayo (*Baron Norvinsk*), Robert Weycross (*Anton Hierdoff*).

Summary: Robert Brand is a rich banker who imposes a very special condition before he will allow his daughter to marry one of the bank's lowly cashiers. Alethea, Brand's daughter, will only be able to marry the cashier, Spencer Rutherford, when Rutherford himself has finally amassed a fortune equivalent to that of the daughter. Eager to impress his future father-in-law, Rutherford initiates at the bank an investment with Baron Norvinsk, supposedly a member of the Russian government, when the baron and his "sister," Paula Lavergne, open an account at the bank. Brand is impressed with the new clients and lends them half a million dollars without doing a thorough background check on the crooks. Alethea discovers before the others that the new clients are imposters. To trap the imposters, Alethea risks her own safety. Alethea agrees to run away with the baron, tricking him first to go to the bank's vault, where Alethea and Baron Norvinsk are trapped together inside by a private detective hired to protect the bank. With Alethea's virtue at peril inside the vault with the lusty baron, Spencer Rutherford comes to her rescue just in time by burning through the vault door to save his beloved. In revealing the imposters, Rutherford helps the bank reclaim its half a million dollar loan, and the cashier convinces Brand that this recovery of the loan fulfills the special condition imposed by the rich banker. Brand agrees to the marriage, but the villain comes to a sad end, a victim of a mercy killing. Lavergne murders him to keep the impostor from being sent to prison in Siberia. (Drawn from the *American Film Institute Catalog*, p. 95.)

The Break-Up. Two-reel drama. Nemo. Made for William Fox, released by Box Office Attraction Co. (*Moving Picture World*).

Broken Laws. *Cast*: Dorothy Davenport, Jackie Saunders ("Southern Exposure," p. 114).

Bumping the Bumps. One-reel comedy. Joy. Made for William Fox. Released by Box Office Attraction Co. (*Moving Picture World*).

By Impulse. One-reel drama. Pathé Frères. Released Nov. 19, 1913, by General Film Company. *Director*: Bertram Bracken. *Cast*: William Wolbert, Henry King, Madeline Pardee (*Press Clippings*, vol. 1, p. 21).

Review: *Moving Picture World* (Dec. 6, 1913) appraised the film, briefly recounting the plot:

> The personality of the leading woman is the chief asset of this very acceptable offering. The impulsive heroine takes a position as housemaid in the home of one of her father's best friends, but that is not known to her. A burglar breaks in the first night and she proves quite a heroine, then there's a good laughable ending. It makes a very pleasing picture [*Press Clippings*, vol. 1, p. 21].

Review: The *New York Dramatic Mirror* evaluated the film on Dec. 10, 1913:

> This is a comedy-drama of rather an interesting type, in which William Wolbert, Henry King, and Miss Pardee play the principal roles, and play them well. The story is aided largely by excellent photography. The plot may have a somewhat hurried development, which leaves a taint of inconsistency on the rushing of the lovers to each other's arms without some of the usual preliminaries. On the other hand, what seems a defect may be a point of favor in that it is at least an original touch [*Press Clippings*, vol. 1, p. 22].

The Call of the Heart. Two-reel drama. Balboa Amusement Producing Co. Made for William Fox. Released Nov. 1914 by Box Office Attraction Co. (*Moving Picture World*).

Called Back. Balboa Amusement Producing Co. Released May, 1914. *Director*: Henry Otto. *Cast*: Henry King, Lucille Younge (*Press Clippings*, vol. 1, p. 74).

The Checkmate. Five-reel drama. Mutual Film Corp., Horkheimer. Released May 21, 1917, by Mutual Star Corp., Mutual Star Productions. *Director*: Sherwood MacDonald. *Story*: Capt. Leslie T. Peacocke. *Cameraman*: William Beckway. *Cast*: Jackie Saunders (*Ida Marley/Claire Marley*), Frank Mayo (*Roy Vangrift*), Daniel Gilfether (*Pa Marley*), Mollie McConnell (*Ma Marley*), R. Henry Grey (*Dick Cooper*), Margaret Landis (*Addie Smith*), Cullen Landis (*Bill Meyer*), Edward Jobson (*country minister*).

Commentary: According to the *American Film Institute Catalog* (p. 136), though Wid's referred to this production as a Balboa movie, the Horkheimer brothers may not have been using the name of Balboa for their productions at the time. Moreover, Jackie Saunders had worked for Biograph in the East and one year for Universal before signing a contract with Balboa. E. D. Horkheimer met with Mutual Film Corp. to arrange the distribution of 6 five-part productions with Jackie Saunders. The first release was *Sunny Jane*, followed soon afterwards by *The Checkmate* and *The Wildcat*, then *A Bit of Kindling*, *Betty Be Good*, and *Bab the Fixer*.

Summary: Twin sisters go their separate ways but end up winning the same reluctant suitor. Claire Marley heads for the fast lane of city life, while Ida, the devoted daughter, stays faithfully at home to watch over their aging mother and father. Claire believes that the rich man in the city, whom she loves and who takes care of her, will one day marry her. Roy Vangrift, however, gets cold feet and dumps her. Devastated, Claire takes courage and decides to earn her own living but can't manage well, so she decides to go back to her family. By coincidence, Roy goes on a fishing trip near the home of Claire's family. He falls in love with Ida, Claire's look-alike sister, and confesses that he's madly in love with her. In an interesting twist of repressed passion, Claire gets her man in the end, with the assistance of a minister, standing in for her sister at the wedding ceremony. In learning the true identity of his wife, Roy realizes he has always loved Claire. (Drawn from the *American Film Institute Catalog*, p. 136.)

Chelsea 7750. Four-reel detective drama. Famous Players Film Co. Released Sept. 20,

1913, by State Rights. *Director*: J. Searle Dawley. *Scenario*: J. Searle Dawley. *Cameraman*: H. Lyman Broening. *Cast*: Henry E. Dixey (*Detective Kirby*), Laura Sawyer (*Kirby's daughter, Kate*), House Peters (*Professor Grimble*).

Commentary: According to the *American Film Institute Catalog* (p. 136), this movie was also said to be three reels long. There was a sequel called *An Hour Before Dawn*.

Summary: A paraplegic detective is hard pressed to save his own daughter, who has been kidnapped by a gang of counterfeiters. The leader of the gang, Professor Grimble, also has a bone to pick with Detective Kirby. Evidence provided by Kirby in a previous court case sent Grimble's son to prison on a twenty-year term. Many adventures ensue, made more original by the physical challenges imposed on the paraplegic detective. In one case, firefighters come to the rescue, after Kirby has set his own apartment on fire to attract outside help. Kirby's daughter is equally capable in beating the odds. For example, she uses the telephone to communicate without using her voice by sending a tapped message to her father in Morse code through the receiver. The story ends in a glorious crescendo of spectacular action whereby the daughter saves herself, while an explosion puts an end to Grimble's exploits. (Drawn from the *American Film Institute Catalog*, p. 136.)

The Chief's Day Off. One-reel comedy. Joy. Made for William Fox, released by Box Office Attraction Co. (*Moving Picture World*).

The City of San Francisco. Copyright Jan. 24, 1913. Edison Manufacturing Co. Filmed in San Francisco (*Encyclopedia of the Movie Studios*).

The Clean Gun. Four-reel drama. Copyright Oct. 26, 1917, General Film Co., Inc., LP11626. Falcon Features. Released Oct. 1917, by General Film Co. *Supervisors*: H. M. Horkheimer and E. D. Horkheimer. *Director*: Harry Harvey. *Scenario*: Captain Leslie T. Peacocke. *Cameraman*: Eddie Saunders. Based on the short story "The Clean Gun" by Barr Moses in *People's Magazine* (publication date undetermined). *Cast*: Stanley J. Preston (*Jack Algers*), Edward Jobson (*Dean Grayson*), Kathleen Kirkham (*Matie Norton*), Robert Weycross (*Senator Norton*), William Marshall (*Edward Brantonx*), Harl McInroy (*Doctor Bristow*), Charles Edler (*Stephen Crawfield*), Louise Sothern (*Della Markham*).

Commentary: The cameraman in this movie, Eddie Saunders, was the brother of the great Balboa star, Jackie Saunders.

Summary: This is an original whodunit with a surprising ending. Stephen Crawfield, seeking money in a hurry, proposes marriage to the daughter of his old friend Senator Norton. The senator's daughter, Matie, already has a young beau, Jack Algers, so she rejects on the spot Crawfield's proposal. Matie's beau comes from a well-to-do family, but his millionaire uncle, Dean Grayson, will not give money to his nephew for the wedding. Then Dean Grayson is murdered at Senator Norton's hunting party, where an unidentified stalker was spotted by witnesses. Who is this killer? The gun found at the murder sight looks just like Jack's. Jack entrusts the two guns to Crawfield, and Crawfield betrays Jack by framing him while producing Jack's gun as evidence. With Jack temporarily out of the picture and Jack's reputation in tatters, Crawfield starts courting Matie once more. But Crawfield has a jealous lover, Della Markham, who still loves Crawfield and claims she saw him shoot Grayson. Senator Norton and Matie both overhear this testimony, which leads to replacing Jack with Crawfield behind bars. But who really did shoot Grayson? At the end of the movie, we see the unidentified killer still lurking about. A la Hitchcock, in the final scene the killer buys a ticket and smiles at the audience, explaining that he merely stumbled into the picture. (Drawn from the *American Film Institute Catalog*, p. 148.)

The Climber. Four-reel drama. Copyright, Sept. 28, 1917, General Film Co., Inc., LP11463. Falcon Features. Released Sept. 1917, by General Film Co. *Supervisors*: H. M. Horkheimer and E. D. Horkheimer. *Director*: Henry King. *Story*: George Foxhall and Lela Leibrand. *Cast*:

Henry King (*William Beerdheim Van Broon*), Jack McLaughlin (*Bruce Crosby*), T. H. Gibson Gowland (*Buck Stringer*), Bert Ensminger (*Grafton*), Charles Blaisdell (*Tom Tarney*), James Kerr (*Sweeney*), Bruce Smith (*Slats O'Keefe*), Frank Erlanger ("*Happy*"), Lucille Pietz (*Eva Crosby*), Leah Gibbs (*Ethel Crosby*), Arma Carlton (*Madelyn Rosseau*), Mollie McConnell (*Mrs. Crosby*), Ruth Lackaye (*Mrs. Tarney*).

Commentary: According to the *American Film Institute Catalog* (p. 149), George Foxhall is credited with the story in the copyright entry and the synopsis included in the copyright descriptions, while Lela Leibrand is listed as the "author" in the copyright entry. She may have written the scenario. No reviews were located for this film.

Summary: A poor man who is a descendant of a respectable family works hard against enormous odds in a rough part of town where fighting and double-crossing run rampant. His name is William Beerheim Van Broon, and he has landed a job at a bowling alley. The owner of the bowling alley, Tom Tarney, sees potential in William's punch when William knocks a man out one day. Tarney decides to train William to become a boxer to fight a professional fighter, Buck Stringer. Buck's siblings, Madelyn and Grafton, plan to blackmail their own boss, Bruce Crosby. Crosby and his sister Eva meet trouble with Buck's family near the bowling alley, and William unexpectedly becomes a good Samaritan when he protects Crosby and Eva. William and Eva take an instant liking to each other before double-crossing makes an already difficult situation worse. First, William wins a lighting bout against the local champion, Buck Stringer. Buck's brother and sister are angry about their brother losing the fight; after all, Buck was a champion and William was an upstart in the ring, but Eva stands by her new love, William. Second, matters get worse when the very man William had defended, Crosby, accuses William of being an accomplice in the plot where William had only acted as a good Samaritan. When Eva makes a trip to William's home, she discovers a lawyer there who had identified William's picture in the papers. Suddenly, by good fortune, the lawyer informs William that he is now the heir of a family fortune worth millions of dollars. (Drawn from the *American Film Institute Catalog*, p. 149.)

Comrade John. Five reels. Balboa Amusement Producing Co. Released Oct. 27, 1915, by Pathé Frères. *Cast*: William Elliott, Lewis Cody, Ruth Roland, Burr McIntosh (*Daily Telegram*, Jan. 25, 1916, 2:3).

Summary: In this film, Elliott is given a check for $100,000 to build a dream city for a religious fakir, with the understanding that he is to say that he too is a "comrade" of the group and that the structure was built by a community of believers. The prophet converts a young girl with whom Elliott is in love. He is afraid that she is being taken in by this fakir "faker" and spills the beans about the religious commune to the press.

Review: *Variety* (Nov. 12, 1915, p. 23) thought that Lewis Cody's portrayal of the prophet was exceedingly good and that the film was a fairly good popularly priced feature.

The Cook. Two-reel comedy. Copyright Aug. 20, 1918, Famous Players-Lasky Corp. copyright claimant. Comique Film Corp. Paramount-Arbuckle Comedy No. A-3112. Released Sept. 15, 1918, by Paramount Pictures. *Director/Writer*: Roscoe Arbuckle. *Cast*: Roscoe Arbuckle, Buster Keaton, Al St. John, Alice Lake, Glen Cavender.

Commentary: According to *Frame-up* (p. 297), this production was filmed at the old Balboa Studios by the Comique Film Corporation studios. Arbuckle's company moved to Glendale to complete this movie, the location where "Our Gang" also got started.

According to *The Complete Films of Buster Keaton* (p. 47), *The Cook* is one of the most obscure of all the lost Arbuckle-Keaton films and is often confused with an earlier film called *The Rough House* because of similar plots.

Summary: According to Jim Kline's *The Complete Films of Buster Keaton* (p. 47), in *The Cook*, Roscoe is billed as the chef of a respectable oceanfront restaurant with Buster as his assistant and Alice as a waitress/cashier. Complications result when the cooks, in the name of efficiency, destroy the tranquillity of the restaurant. The finale takes place at a seaside park (probably Seal Beach), where Roscoe battles Al St. John, who plays a restaurant holdup man. Arbuckle's dog, Luke, joins in at the end, chasing Al off into the sunset.

Counsel for the Defense. Copyright Oct. 6, 1915 (*Encyclopedia of the Movie Studios*, p. 234).

The Counterfeit. Two-reel drama. University Film Co. *Characters*: Robert Morton; Wilson; Miss Grace Cameron, the Colonel's niece; Colonel Morton.
   Commentary: The story dealt with the sudden "demonic" change in a man for money, according to *Motion Picture News* (June 20, 1914). It is worth noting that Famous Players also made a film by the same name in 1919.
   Summary: Robert Morton, while on a prospecting trip in the West with his partner, Wilson, receives a letter from his uncle, whom he barely knows, telling him that he would like to make him his heir. Wilson tries to kill Morton and heads east with the letter to claim his inheritance. He manages to ingratiate himself with the millionaire's niece, but just as he is about to marry her, Morton, who had not been killed, arrives on the scene.
   Review: *Motion Picture News* (June 20, 1914) said that there was good camera work and that clever double exposures made the film notable.

A Country Hero. Two-reel comedy. Copyright Dec. 13, 1917, Famous Players-Lasky Corp. copyright claimant. Comique Film Corp. Paramount-Arbuckle Comedy No. A-3107. Released Dec. 10, 1917, by Paramount Pictures. *Director/Writer*: Roscoe Arbuckle. *Scene Editor*: Herbert Warren. *Cameraman*: George Peters. *Cast*: Roscoe Arbuckle, Buster Keaton, Al St. John, Alice Lake, Joseph Keaton.
   Commentary: According to *Frame-up* (p. 296), this movie was filmed at Jazzville, a rural village set built for Arbuckle at the Horkheimer Brothers' Balboa Amusement Producing Co.
   Jim Kline's *The Complete Films of Buster Keaton* (p. 39), explains that the film contained an elaborate nightclub free-for-all in which Roscoe heaves a piano at a rival and a spectacular two-car auto wreck with a passing locomotive. Arbuckle spent over $20,000 staging the wreck scene alone, an incredible amount of money to splurge on just one scene for a two-reel comedy. The film is unfortunately lost.
   Summary: Roscoe is the owner of a blacksmith shop in Jazzville, and Joe, known as Cy Kone, is a rival owner of a garage. The two men, already enemies, come to blows when they vie for the affections of a pretty schoolteacher played by Alice Lake. However, with the arrival of city slicker Al. St. John, Roscoe and Joe join forces to vanquish this new Romeo. The finale takes place during amateur night at the local village ball. (Drawn from *The Complete Films of Buster Keaton*, p. 39.)

Coveted Heritage. Copyright Dec. 28, 1914. Released by Pathé Frères (*Encyclopedia of the Movie Studios*, p. 232).

The Criminal Code. Four-reel drama. Balboa Amusement Producing Co. Made for William Fox. Released Sept. 28, 1914, by Box Office Attraction Co. *Director*: William Desmond Taylor. *Cast*: Neva Gerber (*Betty*), Jack Bryce (*Francis W. Seeman*), William Desmond Taylor (*Roger Neville*), Daniel Gilfether (*Thomas Mills*), Gypsy Abbott (*Gladys Mills*), Joan Pardee (*Joan*), Mollie McConnell (*Mrs. Mills*) (*Press Clippings*, vol. 1, p. 135).
   Summary: Betty, who is sixteen, leaves an orphanage because of harsh treatment. She is adopted and educated by Francis Seeman, a man who makes a business of stealing valuable jewelry, all the while pretending to be a respectable businessman. He wants his new daughter to help him in his endeavors. She is so frightened at the thought of being turned out into the streets that she helps him in his robberies. When it comes to stealing a necklace from one of her old school friends, however,

she rebels. For a time, it looks bad for her, but eventually she finds love and happiness with a young lawyer, Roger Neville. (Drawn from *Motion Picture News*, Oct. 31, 1914.)

Review: *Motion Picture News* (Oct. 31, 1914) called this a melodrama of "unusual excellence" and stated: "The exteriors are well handled. Full advantage has been taken of the California sunlight and scenery."

The *New York Telegraph* (Oct. 25, 1914) complimented the movie:

> Photographically the film is very good. The players are all well cast and give good accounts of themselves. Many of the settings, particularly those at the reception and the picnic, are beautiful.

The Crooked Road. Balboa Amusement Producing Co., A Fortune Photoplay. Released in 1917. *Director:* Bert Bracken. *Cast:* Henry King, Charles Dudley, Mollie McConnell (*Henry King, Director*, p. 197).

The Cruise of the Hell Ship. Three-reel drama. Balboa Amusement Producing Co. Made for William Fox, released by Box Office Attraction Co.

Summary: The story involves a ferryboat which has been wrecked. One man, Walter Van Brunt, is rescued by the Hell Ship. The captain forces him to work as a slave in the kitchen. A few days later a small boat is sighted and a young girl is rescued. Van Brunt protects her from the captain, and the two fall in love. They escape from the Hell Ship and take refuge on a desert island. The captain is subject to violent headaches which leave him totally blind. While in this condition he is left on board by his crew who mutiny by leaving the ship. The ship drifts on and is wrecked on the same island as Van Brunt and the girl. A fight breaks out between the two men, and the captain manages to set fire to the ship. The fire is extinguished, but the captain, Parsons, is so badly burned that he dies. The couple set out for home. But, as the reviewer asks, Who is sailing the boat?

Review: This film was shown at the Second International Exposition of Motion Pictures Art at Grand Central Palace, New York City. The *New York Telegraph* (June 14, 1914) said that the film was exciting in a way but was characterized by some rather amazing inconsistencies of plot. The Hell Ship was shown in one scene high and dry on a sandy shore; a few moments later, it could be seen to rise and fall on a series of ocean waves.

The Dances of the Ages. Two reels. Edison Manufacturing Co. *Cast:* Norma Gould, Ted Shawn (*Encyclopedia of the Movie Studios*).

Commentary: According to Claudine Burnett, Edison's stay in Long Beach only lasted five months, though the Edison Manufacturing Company had planned to rent the California Motion Picture Manufacturing Company's studio for one year. During those five months, the Edison Company made productions of historical interest, including *The Dancer*, a one-reeler, and *The Dances of the Ages*. Choreographer Shawn, a pioneer of modern dance, would later form the Denishawn Dancers with his wife Ruth St. Denis. Their New York school of dance produced Martha Graham, Charles Weidman, and Doris Humphrey.

Summary: This was a tale of an old-fashioned dancing master in his little garret who still clings to the old-fashioned dances of grace and movement. At a banquet table, he meets his old cronies; together they discuss the progress of their art. As these gray-haired men speak, viewers are shown the Dances of the Ages.

On the table before them appear dainty, tiny figures who dance before their gaze. The audience is shown the slow, crawling, weird, snakelike movements of the Dance of the Priest of Ra, before an Egyptian temple in 1200 B.C. This fades away and time creeps to 400 B.C. to the Grecian Bacchanalia, where garlanded maidens give forth their joy in the abandonment of youth and gladness. Then the ancient Orient of 200 A.D. comes before us with all the voluptuousness of that period of veiled maidens and Oriental splendor. Then the stately minuet of 1760 is shown, quickly followed by the wild frolic of the carnival period of France. Afterwards, it's the cakewalk in America and back again to France, where we see the Apache dance, the dreamy waltz, and finally the audience is shown the present era with the modern rag.

Review: The *Daily Telegram* (June 14, 1913, 10:5) remarks, "The picture closes showing the old broken down dancing master trying to keep pace with the times and squirming into the inartistic movements and hops of modern ragtime dances."

The Dancer. One reel, credited to James Oppenheim. Edison Manufacturing Co. Copyright Jan. 10, 1913. *Director*: Ashley Miller. *Cast*: Bessie Learn, William West.

The Dashing Ranger. Western. Released in 1921. Long Beach Motion Picture Company. *Director*: William Bertram. *Scenario*: William Bertram. *Cast*: Leo Maloney, Dixie Lamont, Harry Bellmour, Gus Scoville, and 35 other actors (*Daily Telegram*, June 22, 1921, p. 4, and Aug. 12, 1921, p. 17).

Commentary: In August 1921, the *Daily Telegram* announced a private showing of the first film completed by the Long Beach Motion Picture Company. William Bertram was the author and the director of this film, *The Dashing Ranger*, which helped launch a whole series of films that romanticized and glamorized the Canadian Mounted Police. Leo Maloney had the leading part and performed sensational stunts on horseback, including crossing a two-board trestle 60 feet high and also leaping off a building through a wooden awning.

Dixie la Monte was the leading lady, Harry Bellmour would be the heavy, and Gus Scoville would play another leading character. This is the film and the series that began its filming at Hornitos, in Mariposa County, which was full of the Gold Rush ambiance of 1849. In fact, the production company had leased the hotel at Hornitos for one year to be able to continue filming future productions there. At the time of this announcement in the *Daily Telegram* (Aug. 12, 1921, 17:1), the Long Beach Motion Picture Company was working on a cooperative basis, not having incorporated as yet. There were no paid officers, and the partners simply shared in the financial returns.

The Daughter of the Hills. Four-reel historical drama. Famous Players Film Co. Released Dec. 20, 1913, by State Rights. *Director*: J. Searle Dawley. *Scenario*: J. Searle Dawley. *Cast*: Laura Sawyer (*Floria*), Wellington A. Playter (*Sergius*), David Davies (*Floria's father*), Frank Van Buren (*the Apostle Paul*), P. W. Nares (*Nero*), Alexander Gaden (*a slave*), Carmen De Gonzales (*leader of the dance*), Ben Breakstone (*opposing gladiator*).

Commentary: The *American Film Institute Catalog* (p. 194) explains that there are reviews that describe this movie in three reels and that House Peters might have been cast in this film as well. Exterior scenes were filmed in Virginia.

Summary: During the reign of Nero, Sergius, the prosperous gladiator, encounters a shepherdess and falls deeply in love with her. They marry, but the shepherdess, Floria, has trouble adjusting to the life of luxury she finds in her husband's palace in Rome. One day Floria goes to the arena to watch her husband fight. Horrified at the brutality of the events, she leaves her husband and his sumptuous palace, finding refuge with the apostle Paul. Sergius follows, looking for his wife. When Sergius finds her, Paul urges Floria to rejoin her husband. Miraculously, a conversion takes place, and the rage subsides inside the heart of the fierce gladiator after he hears Paul preach. Sergius refuses to return to fight in the arena, abandoning his many riches and comforts in Rome and returning with his wife, Floria, to the hills where they had met and fallen in love. (Drawn from the *American Film Institute Catalog*, p. 194.)

Defying Destiny. *Cast*: Irene Rich, Jackie Saunders ("Southern Exposure," p. 114).

Detective Dale and Mudflats Gang see **End of the Bridge**

The Devil's Bait. Four-reel drama. Balboa Amusement Producing Co., a Fortune Photoplay. Released Mar. 1917 by General Film Co. *Director*: Harry Harvey. *Story*: Will M. Ritchey. *Cast*: Ruth Roland (*Doris Sheldon*), William

Conklin (*Dr. Royal Sheldon*), Edward J. Brady (*Jason Davies*), Henry King (*Eric Reese*), Lucy Blake (*Madame Delong*), Myrtle Reeves (*Anita*), Gordon Sackville, Lucille Serwill, Zada Marlo, Charles Dudley.

Commentary: This film is also known as *Devil's Pet*.

Summary: A precious ruby is uncovered during a landslide, and the ownership of the prized gem is disputed between two friends at the mine. Dr. Sheldon wins the stone, but Davies plans his retaliation. Ultimately the two former friends end up fighting over the same woman. Although Sheldon weds Anita, Davies underhandedly wins her away from Sheldon with expensive presents. Davies repeats the same efforts with Sheldon's daughter when she grows up, but Sheldon successfully blocks his attempts, thus preventing his daughter from being duped by the scheming Davies. Still Davies doesn't give up his acts of retaliation for losing the precious ruby to his former friend. Finally, Davies uses Madame DeLong to seduce Sheldon. Madame DeLong, however, falls in love with Sheldon and turns informer. Sheldon wants to face Davies and pursues him, for Davies has the prized ruby in his hands, but as Davies attempts to escape, he plunges off a cliff and dies. Sheldon reaches Davies' body, removes the cursed ruby from the dead man's fist, and then tosses the stone into the ocean. (Drawn from the *American Film Institute Catalog*, p. 210.)

Dividing Walls. Two-reel drama? *Director:* William Desmond Taylor. *Cast:* William Desmond Taylor, Jack Byrne, Neva Gerber (*Press Clippings*, vol. 1, p. 2).

Commentary: According to an unidentified clipping in the *Press Clippings*, vol. 1, there were also four children in the cast. This was Taylor's first experience directing children, and the director admitted that the children tested his patience.

Drag Harlan. Six-reel western, 5,038 ft. Copyright Oct. 24, 1920, William Fox, LP15737. Fox Film Corp. Released Oct. 24, 1920, by Fox Film Corp. *Director:* J. Gordon Edwards *Scenario:* H. P. Keeler. *Story:* Charles Alden Seltzer. *Cameraman:* John Boyle. *Cast:* William Farnum (*Drag Harlan*), Jackie Saunders (*Barbara Morgan*), Arthur Millett (*John Haydon*), G. Raymond Nye (*Luke Deveny*), Herschel Mayall (*Lane Morgan*), Frank Thurwald (*Meeker Lawson*), "Kewpie" Morgan (*Red Linton*), Al Fremont (*Laskar*), Erle Crane (*Storm Rogers*).

Commentary: According to the *American Film Institute Catalog* (p. 227), Sidney Franklyn is credited with the role of John Haydon. This movie was reissued in Feb. 1925.

Summary: In pursuit of the murderer of his partner, Drag Harlan stumbles into an ambush on the plains. During the shooting, Drag tries to defend the intended victim, Lane Morgan, and kills one of the ambushers, the very man who had killed Drag Harlan's partner. With his last breath, Lane Morgan beseeches Drag to care for his daughter, Barbara, handing over to Drag at the same time a map to a gold mine. With the map, Drag rides to the town of Lamo, where Barbara is in danger. Luke Deveny and his band of thieves are taking over the place. Even Lane Morgan's ranch foreman, John Haydon, is in cahoots with the thieving band. Drag frees Barbara from the clutches of the band and has a shoot-out with the gang, killing both Haydon and Deveny. With all the villains dead, Drag takes over as ranch foreman, marrying Barbara in the bargain, and the gold mine then becomes theirs to share. (Drawn from the *American Film Institute Catalog*, p. 227.)

Dream of Loco Juan. Two-reel drama. Balboa Amusement Producing Co. Made for William Fox, released Nov. 17, 1914, by Box Office Attraction Co. *Cast:* Dorothy Davenport (*Carmencita Nina*), Archie Warren (*Poncho*), Madeline Pardee (*Santa Guadalupe*), Henry King (*Loco Juan*), Henry Stanley (*Dominguez*), Fred Whitman (*Antonio Sanchez*).

Summary: Loco Juan, a poor woodchopper befriended by Carmencita, a flower girl, incurs the wrath of Señor Dominguez at the cantina. Juan falls asleep in the forest and dreams that a kind fairy transforms him into a dashing hero. In his dream he saves

Carmencita from the advances of Señor Dominguez and wins her love for himself. When the fairy takes the magic bracelet from Juan's arm, the spell is broken, and Juan awakes from his dream, still the half-witted woodchopper, lying under a sunflower in the woods. (Drawn from *Press Clippings*, vol. 1, p. 251.)

Eggs and Water. One-reel comedy. Joy. Made for William Fox, released by Box Office Attraction Co. (*Moving Picture World*).

The End of the Bridge. Three-reel drama. Balboa Amusement Producing Co. Made for William Fox, released Oct. 26, 1914, by Box Office Attraction Co. *Cast*: J. Francis McDonald (*David Dale, the detective*), Madeline Pardee (*Stella Bracket, the heroine*), Frank Cleaver (*"Shark" Manning, chief of the Mudflats Gang*), Fred Whitman (*Dick Brackett, Stella's brother*), Mollie McConnell (*Mrs. Luck Brackett, Stella's mother*), "Pop" Leonard (*Silas Brackett, Stella's father*), Frank A. Erlanger (*Jake, member of the robber gang*), Bruce Randall (*Haley, another member of the band*), Henry Stanley (*Boland, a crook*).

Commentary: The mudflats between Long Beach and Wilmington, an extensive area filled in with silt pumped out of the harbor channels by gigantic dredgers, were immortalized in this film. Also shown in this film are the Salt Lake Railroad Company's massive bascule-lifting bridge, some of the ships and docks at San Pedro, the wharves near the Craig Shipyards, cafés, houses, and lodging establishments along the harbor front in Long Beach, the vast Southern California Edison power plant and many other of the big establishments in and about Long Beach.

Summary: "Shark" Manning is the brutal chief of the Mudflats Gang of robbers. His right-hand man is Dick Brackett, who lives at home with his family. The gang robs some railway freight cars and detective David Dale is sent to get evidence against the robber band. Dale, disguised as a stevedore, visits the Brackett café and falls in love with Stella.

Stella's brother, Dick Brackett, has been converted by a street preacher and persuaded to give up his "evil ways." Shark Manning is angered when Dick refuses to help him and has him shanghaied. Feature scenes show how the hero, detective Dale, and his sweetheart, the heroine, receive word that her brother has been shanghaied onto a ship at San Pedro. The hero and heroine have one hour to get to the harbor before the vessel is scheduled to depart for South Africa. They try to catch a train from Long Beach to go rescue the girl's captive brother but just miss the train. They manage to get the use of a handcar, however, which they pump with all their might, racing toward San Pedro. The villain, Shark Manning, determined to foil the plans of the hero and the girl, steals a horse and rides swiftly after the couple. He speeds along the railroad track and arrives at the bascule bridge just as the couple is crossing the gigantic lifting device. When the "heavy" overpowers the bridge tender and manipulates the bridge machinery, the handcar is caught on the lifting end of the bridge, carrying the detective and the heroine up to a height of 125 feet.

The bridgetender's wife arrives on scene, finds her husband unconscious from Shark's blows, and fights Shark herself. This gives the hero-detective enough time to climb down from his lofty, perilous position, rout the evil plotter, and get the bridge machinery operating to rescue the girl and the handcar. The lovers then speed on to San Pedro and arrive just in time to save the heroine's brother, Dick Brackett, from being forced to take a sea voyage to the land of Boers, diamonds, and lions.

During the action sequence of the film, one of the robber gang drops a stolen $10,000 necklace into the harbor channel to foil the detective. These gems later are pumped up by one of the big dredgers. Shark meanwhile gets near the suction part of the dredger and is drawn to an awful death. Dick recovers the gems, and Dale returns them to their owner. Dick becomes an honest mechanic, and Dale and Stella agree to marry. (Drawn from *Press Clippings*, vol. 1, and *Daily Telegram*, Mar. 10, 1914, 3:4.)

The Explorer. Six-reel adventure. *Scenario*: Frank M. Wiltermood. **Cast:** Frederick A. Cook (*playing himself*) (*Dramatic News*, Oct. 17, 1914, p. 179, in *Press Clippings*, vol. 1).

Commentary: Frederick A. Cook, explorer and chief of the expedition which scaled the summit of Mt. McKinley, was the star of this six-reel film based on his expedition. The scenario contained many interesting scenes to substantiate Dr. Cook's claims that he reached the largest mountain top in North America on Apr. 21, 1908, before Robert E. Peary.

This film should not be confused with a production starring Lou-Tellegen that was released Sept. 27, 1915, by Jesse L. Lasky Feature Play Co., Inc. The Lasky production was based on the novel *The Explorer* by William Somerset Maugham and was a five-reel adventure about explorer Alec McKenzie's mission in Africa. The *American Film Institute Catalog* (p. 157) describes the Lasky production and claims that it marked the film début of Lou-Tellegen.

The Daily Telegram (Oct. 6, 1914, 10:5) claims that many of the most important scenes in the Balboa production were enacted on the snow-clad peaks of the San Bernardino Mountains. Genuine Eskimo dogs, igloo houses, sledges, and other Arctic property were used to make the film realistic. A charming romance, in which Dr. Cook's prowess as an explorer wins him a wealthy bride, forms the basis of the script.

An Eye for an Eye. Four-reel drama. Balboa Amusement Producing Co. Copyright Dec. 28, 1914, Pathé Frères, LU4037, released by Pathé Frères. *Director*: William Desmond Taylor *Cast*: Neva Gerber (*Elsie*), William Desmond Taylor (*Dave Harmon*), Harriet Janson (*Sister*), William Wolbert (*Robert Duncan*), Nan Christie (*Mrs. Duncan*) (*American Film Institute Catalog*, p. 354, and *Press Clippings*, vol. 1).

Commentary: According to the *American Film Institute Catalog* (p. 254), publicity for the movie claimed that this film presented "for the first time successful night photography."

Summary: While hunting in the country, Robert Duncan seduces the youngest daughter at the ranch where he has taken up room and board. The girl's father dies of a broken heart when he discovers that his youngest daughter has run off with this married man. After the duped girl vanishes, no one hears from her anymore. Her older sister, Elsie searches for her younger sister in the city and does find her, just before the heartbroken girl dies. As the title of the movie implies, Elsie plans to get even with Robert Duncan. In the city, Elsie pretends to be a singer in the café that Robert Duncan frequents. He takes the bait, intrigued by the new singer who wears a mask. The villain follows the masked singer to her flat, where the authorities have been waiting to trap the scoundrel. After her sweet revenge, Elsie returns to the family ranch and to the loving arms of the man with whom she will rebuild her life, the foreman of the ranch. (Drawn from the *American Film Institute*, p. 254.)

Faith's Reward. Balboa Amusement Producing Co. Released in 1916 by Pathé Frères. Cast: Henry King (*Henry King, Director*, p. 195).

The Fatal Thirty. Serial. Thirty reels. Spinx Serial Co. *Scenario*: Grover Jones. *Cast*: Johnny Hayes (*Daily Telegram*, Dec. 3, 1919, p. 3).

Feet of Clay. Four-reel mystery. Copyright Nov. 2, 1917, General Film Co., Inc., LP11668. Falcon Features. Released Nov. 2, 1917, by General Film Co. *Supervisors*: H. M. Horkheimer and E. D. Horkheimer. *Director*: Harry Harvey. *Scenario*: Luther Morton. Based on the story "Feet of Clay" by William Morton. *Cast*: Barney Fury (*Brandsby Mordant*), Tom Morgan (*Jeremiah Pew*), Harry F. McPerson (*Herbert Grodney*), William Marshall (*James Crowley*), Frank Erlanger (*Adolph Gassner*), Charles Elder (*Phineas Glenister*), Harl McInroy (*Jefferson Armstrong*), Leota Lorraine (*Marie Marat*), Margaret Landis (*Dorothy Glenister*), R. Henry Grey (*Richard Armstrong*), J. P. Wade (*Bedford*), Bruce Smith (*English detective*), Edward Jobson (*Alexander Greggson*).

Commentary: According to the *American*

Film Institute Catalog (p. 269), there is a news item that states that William Morton's story was originally published in a magazine.

Summary: A complex web of circumstantial evidence implicates a Scotland Yard detective, Brandsby Mordant, who was attempting to get his nephew out of a gang of thieves called "The Four." Framed, Detective Mordant ends up in prison. In fact, the double-crossers were three of Mordant's former associates — Phineas Glenister, Jefferson Armstrong, and Adolph Gassner. But the prison walls cannot keep the clever Mordant from breaking out. Mordant and his wife, Marie Marat, seek revenge, leaving the country together. On the trail of the double-crossers, Mordant and his wife travel to San Francisco. In the meantime, one of the associates is slain, and a daughter of another former associate is kidnapped. These horrendous crimes make Mordant reexamine his plans of vengeance. Eventually, Mordant discovers that the kidnapped daughter is really his own nephew's daughter, Dorothy. Mordant abandons his plans of revenge in this tangled web. At the time that Mordant is planning to start his life over in America, a detective from Scotland Yard finds Mordant, but instead of returning Mordant to the United Kingdom, the British detective is persuaded by Dorothy to go back empty-handed. Mordant stays in America to begin over again. (Drawn from the *American Film Institute Catalog*, p. 269.)

Gentlemen's Agreement. Copyright Oct. 6, 1915 (*Encyclopedia of the Movie Studios*, p. 234).

The Girl Angle. Five-reel Western. Horkheimer Studios. Released Oct. 5, 1917, by World Film Corp. *Producer*: E. D. Horkheimer. *Director*: Edgar Jones. *Scenario*: Julian Lamothe. *Story*: L. V. Jefferson. *Cast*: Anita King (*Maud Wainwright*), Robert Ensminger (*Steve Kennedy*), Ruth Lackaye (*Mrs. Millikin*), Joseph Ryan ("*Three Gun*" *Smith*), Frank Erlanger (*village storekeeper*), Daniel Gilfether (*proprietor of gambling house*), William Reed (*degenerate*), Gordon Sackville (*proprietor of dance hall*), Mollie McConnell (*Maud's aunt*).

Summary: Maud Wainwright is stood up on her wedding day and decides to give up on men. Resettling in the Southwest, she pays no attention at first to two men who want to court her, one a bandit and one a man of the law — "Three Gun" Smith and Sheriff Steve Kennedy. By accident, Smith's gang damages Maud's cabin, so they invite her to Smith's cabin during repairs. While Maud is staying at Smith's home, she uncovers stolen mail and reports the finding to the sheriff. Sheriff Kennedy convinces Maud to help him trap the outlaws, but Maud had the bandits all wrong. While Smith is in jail, Maud discovers that Sheriff Kennedy is the real villain, while Smith is an undercover agent. Maud no longer wants to give up on men because Smith has stolen her heart. She rides to save Smith before he is lynched by vigilantes. The story ends with Maud at last truly in love with the undercover agent she helped save. (Drawn from the *American Film Institute Catalog*, 322–23.)

The Girl That Didn't Matter. Copyright Apr. 5, 1916 (*Encyclopedia of the Movie Studios*, p. 238).

The Girl Who Doesn't Know. Five-reel drama. B. S. Moss Motion Picture Corp. Released Dec. 1916 by State Rights. *Director*: Charles E. Barlett. *Scenario*: John E. Lopez. *Cast*: Marie Empress (*Zelma*), R. Henry Grey (*Reverend Martin*), Zada Barlow (*his sister Ruth*), Henry Stanley (*Deacon Brown*), Ruth White (*his daughter Amy*), George Theilan (*Jack Rance*), Robyn Adair (*Paul Jerome*).

Commentary: This film was probably a Balboa production and was probably distributed by B. S. Moss Motion Picture Corp.

Summary: Zelma moves out of the slums, but instead of finding a better life, she runs into a series of predicaments. Finding work at a casino, she is used by her boss to cheat customers. Depressed by the life she is leading, Zelma attempts suicide, but she is saved in the nick of time by a young preacher. The young minister, Martin, invites Zelma to stay at his family's home. The two quickly fall in love, but Paul, the casino owner, looks for Zelma and begins dating Martin's sister. Paul takes the opportunity to discredit Zelma by telling Martin about her past. Before Martin gives up on Zelma, she persuades him of her good character by warning Ruth, Martin's sister, about her new boyfriend. Paul and Zelma are immediately reconciled and go on with their plans to marry. (Drawn from the *American Film Institute Catalog*, pp. 330-31.)

The Girl Who Won. Copyright Apr. 29, 1916 (*Encyclopedia of the Movie Studios*, p. 238).

Good Night, Nurse. Two-reel comedy. Copyright June 22, 1918, Famous Players-Lasky Corp. copyright claimant. Comique Film Corp. Paramount-Arbuckle Comedy No. A-3111. Released July 8, 1918, by Paramount Pictures. *Director/Writer*: Roscoe Arbuckle. *Scene Editor*: Herbert Warren. *Cameraman*: George Peters. *Cast*: Roscoe Arbuckle, Buster Keaton, Al St. John, Alice Lake, Kate Price, Joseph Keaton.

Commentary: According to *The Complete Films of Buster Keaton* (p. 45), some believe this to be the best film Arbuckle ever made. According to *Frame-up* (p. 297), this movie was filmed at Arrowhead Hot Springs on location and at the Balboa Studios.

Summary: According to Jim Kline's *The Complete Films of Buster Keaton* (p. 45), the plot begins with the obviously drunk Arbuckle standing on a street corner in the pouring rain, trying to light a cigarette. Suddenly a woman (actually Buster in drag) passes by carrying an umbrella. Moments later she literally is blown back into the scene as a gust of wind catches her umbrella; Arbuckle is then joined by an organ-grinder and his monkey, a gypsy dancer, and finally a cop who accompanies Roscoe home. Arbuckle's wife wants her husband out of the home, insisting that her chronically inebriated husband take a drinking cure at the No Hope Sanitarium. After he eats a thermometer, Arbuckle is operated on and when he awakens he plans an escape with fellow patient Alice Lake. Later, after an elaborate getaway, he awakens on the operating table, realizing his antics were only a dream.

A Great Secret. Three-reel drama. White Star. Made for William Fox, released Oct. 19, 1914, by Box Office Attraction Co. *Director*: William Desmond Taylor. *Cast*: Edwin August (*Edwin Tremayne*), Neva Gerber (*Mrs. Edwin Tremayne*), Marion Roth (*Mrs. Hal Tremayne*) (*Press Clippings*, vol. 1, p. 105).

Commentary: This film is apparently based on Guy de Maupassant's short story entitled "La Parure" (The Necklace).

Summary: An unidentified article in *Press Clippings*, vol. 1, p. 105, presents the plot:

Edwin Tremayne and his brother Hal live with their widowed mother in a pretty home beside the seashore. The young men are in love with Neva, the daughter of a widow residing near the Tremayne home. Neva finally decides to become the betrothed of Edwin, and when she announces her decision, Hal becomes embittered and forsakes the village, going to a city where he obtains work in a fashionable hotel as a bellboy. His youth and good looks win the admiration of one of the hotel guests, Miss Ruth Grant, a handsome young woman of wealth. Ruth professes love for Hal, and they marry. In the meantime, Edwin and Neva have been joined in marriage. Hal and Ruth send an invitation to Edwin and Neva to come to the city and visit them. When Edwin and Neva arrive at Hal's home they admire a $10,000 necklace worn by Ruth. Edwin and Neva then decide to make their home in the city and rent a house, which they occupy. Hal and Ruth give a masque ball, and Neva obtains from Ruth the loan of her necklace to wear at the ball. A gang of robbers reads of the forthcoming ball and decides to attend in masquerade costumes. The gang leader manages to steal the necklace from Neva during the dancing. Edwin and Neva fear to tell Hal and Ruth of the theft. They buy a similarly-appearing necklace worth $10,000 from a jeweler, on credit, signing a contract to pay $1,000 a year. This substitute necklace is given to Hal and Ruth. For ten years Edwin and Neva toil from early until late to earn the money to pay the jeweler, undergoing great privations. When they make the final payment the truth of the substitution is revealed to Hal and Ruth, and the latter then tell Edwin and Neva that the original, stolen necklace was only a string of paste, imitation gems.

The Grip of Evil. Serial. Made for Pathé of New York, released 1916. *Cast*: Philo McCullough, Jackie Saunders, Roland Bottomley.

The 14 Chapters (two reels each): *Fate, The Underworld, The Upper Ten, The Looters, The Way of a Woman, The Hypocrites, The Butterflies, In Bohemia, The Dollar Kings, Down to the Sea, Mammon and Moloch, Into the Pits, Circumstantial Evidence, Humanity Triumphant.* Chapter 1 was copyrighted July 17, 1916, and Chapter 14 was copyrighted Sept. 28, 1916 (*Filmarama*, vol. 1).

Commentary: According to the *Daily Telegram* (Oct. 13, 1916, 5:4), the Balboa Company went into the Long Beach market and purchased the services of about 7,000 extras for this production. Much raw material in the way of film, new props, lumber, and art was used in the production. It was shown weekly for 14 weeks. Each installment consisted of two reels of film, so there were twenty-eight reels in all. This film was not a series as most serials were, rather a big picture book with moving pictures, with the stories complete in each installment, although they all dealt with the same general theme, the object of all of them being to answer the question, "Is the world in the grip of evil?"

Long Beach's own star, Jackie Saunders (now billed as Jacquelin), was the featured player, and she was seen in 14 separate and distinct characterizations. The *Daily Telegram* noted, "This girl has won millions of friends in all parts of the world and Long Beach is proud to label her 'Maid of Long Beach.'"

Roland Bottomley, the distinguished English actor, played opposite Saunders, and the *Daily Telegram* stated that his character of John Burton "will long live as the most unique in filmdom." Almost the entire personnel of the Balboa stock company was to be seen in this serial.

Guns and Garlic. One-reel comedy. Joy. Made for William Fox, released by Box Office Attraction Co. (*Moving Picture World*).

Gypsy Love. Three-reel drama. Balboa Amusement Producing Co. Made for William Fox, released July 20, 1914, by Box Office Attraction Co. *Scenario*: Henry W. Otto. *Cast*: Ray Gallagher (*Paul Brooks*), Jackie Saunders (*Daisy Clark*), Robert Grey (*Lorenz, a gypsy poet*), Henry Stanley (*gypsy king*), Charles Dudley (*John Brooks*), Harriet Jensen (*Anita, daughter of the gypsy king*).

Summary: John Moore, a miser, and his little nephew, Paul, nine years old, lose their way in their wanderings. Hungry and ill, the uncle falls by the roadside. Nearby gypsies find the pair and help them the best they can. Moore, after getting the gypsy king's promise to adopt little Paul, turns two treasure bags over to him. He then dies. Paul is adopted by the tribe and becomes the playmate of the gypsy king's little daughter, Anita. One of the stipulations in the uncle's will demands that Paul be sent to college and educated when he becomes a young man. Ten years after Paul's adoption by the tribe, the King tells Paul that the time has come for him to go to college but that he must return to the tribe. At college Paul soon forgets his promise and falls in love with Daisy Martin, daughter of a wealthy merchant. Pretty Anita, waiting in the gypsy camp, can't forget Paul and is blind to the pure, worthy love of Lorenz, a handsome young dreamer in the gypsy camp. Paul realizes that he loves Daisy, but also remembers his pledge to the tribe, and after graduation he sends Daisy a note asking that she forget him. He then goes back to the gypsies and finds that Anita is now a full grown woman. To his amazement, he discovers that she loves him. Daisy still pines for Paul, and her father decides to take him on a hunting trip. Daisy rescues Anita, who is attacked by a tramp.

The two girls become friends. Anita discovers the romance between Paul and Daisy and helps bring them together. Lorenz sees and understands Anita's sacrifice and opens his arms to her; she recognizes his virtues, and accepts his proposal of marriage. (Drawn from *Press Clippings*, vol. 1, p. 156.)

Hands Up! A Cyclonic Western Serial. Astra Film Corp. Released by Pathé Exchange, Inc. *Director*: James W. Horne. *Supervisor*: George Fitzmaurice. *Scenario*: Jack Cunningham. *Screenplay*: Gilson Willets. *Cast*: Ruth Roland (*heroine*), George Chesebro (*Hero, Hands Up*), Easter Alters (*Villain "The Phantom Rider"*).

The 15 episodes: Chapter 1 is *The Bride of the Sun*. The other episodes are not yet determined.

Commentary: According to Pathé's announcements for this serial, the world-famous "House of Serials" offered the viewer Pathé's first Western serial with this production — "the most ambitious Western production ever filmed."

George Fitzmaurice, noted director of big productions, was supervisor of this production. Louis J. Gasnier also worked on this production, following his successful group of serials: *The House of Hate*, *Pearl of the Army*, *The Shielding Shadow*, and *The Fatal Ring*, all distributed by Pathé.

"The Phantom Rider," resembling very much the masked and caped Zorro, who showed up in later films, is a polished villain who poses as a gentleman rancher while secretly being an outlaw leader. Ruth Roland, the heroine, vies for the affection of "Hands Ups," the hero, against her rival adventuress. The dashing hero, Hands Up, is a daring and courageous cowboy who fights the Inca Indian leaders, custodians of the secret treasure. The Indians constantly put the heroine, Ruth Roland, in peril. The adventures abound with love interest, stunts, and thrills galore. The photography captures rugged country and elaborate sets, including the Throne Room of the Incas and the Sacrificial Chamber.

Heart of the Brute. Two-reel drama. Balboa Amusement Producing Co. Made for William Fox, released Sept., 1914, by Box Office Attraction Co. *Director*: Bertram Bracken (*Daily Telegram*, Nov. 16, 1914, 10:7).

Review: *Moving Picture World* (Oct. 3, 1914) finds this Balboa film a success with popular appeal:

> A two-reeler telling the hopeless romance of a man who often acted like a wild brute toward most whom he met; but who had a very kind heart none-the-less. He is contrasted with another kind of villain much to his advantage. It is fresh though there have been pictures something like it; it is pleasingly acted and, like most of these Balboa offerings, it has a decidedly popular flavor — it will go well with the majority. Its scenes are in the west and in a mining region. There are only four chief characters and the tale is simple, clear and entertaining [*Press Clippings*, vol. 1, p. 41].

Hearts of the Range. Western. Released in 1921. Morante Motion Picture Company. *Cast*: Milburn Morante, Evelyn Nelson (*Daily Telegram*, Mar. 19, 1921, p. 9).

Commentary: After the first Morante Western, *Hearts of the Range*, was released in early 1921, seven Westerns were scheduled for production beginning, March 1921 by the film company based in Long Beach. The Morante company made a departure from comedies to begin filming a series of Western dramas. Milburn Morante would star in the series, supported by Evelyn Nelson, with Morante's four-year-old daughter as "the baby." Later, articles in the *Daily Telegram* would cover the travels of the film company to Madera County to shoot on location for scenes photographed in the rugged and sylvan terrain. All the interior shots, of course, were filmed at Balboa. The film crew set up headquarters in the town of Raymond, in Madera County.

His Conquered Self. Copyright Nov. 10, 1915 (*Encyclopedia of the Movie Studios*, p. 234).

His Old-Fashioned Dad. Four-reel drama. Falcon Features. Copyright Nov. 16, 1917, General Film Company, LP11714. *Distributor*: General Film Co. *Supervisors*: H. M. Horkheimer and E. D. Horkheimer. *Cast*: Daniel Gilfether (*Dr. Silas Morton*), Mollie McConnell (*Mandy Morton*), Richard Johnson (*Emory Morton*), Lucy Payton (*Nettie Wright*),

Dan Bailey (*Mr. Wright*), Alice Smith (*Mrs. Wright*), Emil Roe (*surgeon*).

Commentary: In the *American Film Institute Catalog* (p. 412), H. O. Stechhan is credited as author in the copyright entry. Stechhan was the publicity and advertising director at the Balboa studio, where this film was made, and although he wrote scenarios and playlets, the author credit in this case may have been assigned only for copyright claimant reasons.

Summary: The son of a country doctor is sent to medical school thanks to many privations suffered by his parents. Their unappreciative son, Emory Morton, gambles and demands more and more money. The country doctor runs out of money and is forced to sell his livestock. Finally, the father decides to look into Emory's lifestyle. When the country doctor complains because his son is gambling away the last bit of family funds, Emory insults his father, telling him that he is old-fashioned. Heartbroken on his return home, the father crashes his car. In the hospital, the country doctor dreams up a plan to collect on his life insurance by exchanging identities with the dying patient next to him. In the aftermath of this fraud, the widow becomes obsessed in her solitude with chasing tramps off the premises. When the doctor returns home, looking like a tramp, he terrifies his wife and she kills him in self-defense. By this sad point in the story, Emory finally begins to take life seriously, using the insurance money to make a medical breakthrough. In the tradition of the prodigal son, Emory's turnaround also brings him financial success and the respect of the medical community. (Drawn from *American Film Institute Catalog*, p. 412.)

Hoodman Blind. Five-reel drama. Pilot Films Corp. Released Dec. 22, 1913, by State Rights. *Director*: James Gordon. Based on the play *Hoodman Blind* by Henry Arthur Jones and Wilson Barrett (London, Aug. 18, 1885). *Cast*: Wilson Barrett (*Lennon*), Betty Harte (*Jess/Nance*), Herbert Barrington (*Jack Yeulett*), James Gordon (*Tom, the Romany*).

Commentary: According to the *American Film Institute Catalog* (p. 423), a modern source includes Violet Stewart and Mrs. Guy Standing in the cast. The story was also filmed by Fox in 1916, when it was entitled *A Man of Sorrow* and starred William Farnum.

Summary: An auto accident causes Lennon to suffer amnesia. His identity and residence become a mystery, and he forgets that his family even exists. Consequently, his wife and their twin daughters, Jess and Nance, lose the breadwinner and the head of the household. Before she dies, leaving behind two young daughters, Mrs. Lennon asks her close friend, Lezzard, to take care of Nance, but the other daughter, Jess, is brought up by gypsies. Growing up apart, neither twin knows the other exists. Nance becomes a young woman and marries a farmer, Jack Yeulett, though her guardian, Lezzard, had wanted her to marry Lezzard's son, Mark, who loves Nance very selfishly. After Nance's marriage to Jack, Mark is still jealous and finds an opportunity for revenge. The other twin, Jess, is in love with a gypsy by the name of Tom. Mark runs into Jess and plans to get even with Nance by using the twins' resemblance to wreak havoc. Mark arranges to have Jack, Nance's husband, witness the two gypsies, Jess and Tom, in a love scene. This scene ruins Nance's marriage because her husband thinks his wife is cheating on him. Thrown out of their home, Nance and her daughter Kit go to the city. Eventually, the other twin, Jess, is also dumped by her gypsy beau, Tom, and understanding the games that have been played, Jess tries to patch things up between her sister and her sister's husband. One day Lennon, the twins' father, regains his memory, and he goes back to deliver an inheritance for Nance, who had been left in Lezzard's care. The father leaves the inheritance for Nance with Lezzard's son Mark, not knowing of Mark's underhandedness. Of course, Mark keeps the money, but he is nabbed in the end by the authorities. Finally Nance receives her inheritance, and she is reconciled with her husband, while also being reunited with her long-lost sister. (Drawn from the *American Film Institute Catalog*, p. 423.)

An Hour Before Dawn. Four-reel detective drama. Famous Players Film Co. Released Oct. 20, 1913, by State Rights. *Director*: J. Searle Dawley. *Scenario*: J. Searle Dawley. *Cast*: Laura Sawyer (*Kate Kirby*), House Peters (*Kate's father*).

Commentary: According to the *American Film Institute Catalog* (p. 425), this movie was three reels long and was a sequel to *Chelsea 7750*.

Summary: An inventor, Professor Wallace, disapproves of his son's romance with a chorus girl. Shortly thereafter, the corpse of the professor is discovered in his laboratory, and his son Richard is arrested as the prime suspect. Detective Kate Kirby, however, has her own suspicions and takes on the case. Suspecting the chorus girl, Violet, Kate goes undercover as one of the dancers on stage with Violet. In getting to know Violet, Kate learns to admire Violet's character and drops her suspicions about Violet at the same time that Violet turns herself in. Surprised by Violet's confession of guilt, Kate asks for help. Kate asks her father, a retired detective, to assist her in the case. The father, a paraplegic who knows how to get around, examines the professor's work journals and determines in the end that the professor had accidentally killed himself with an explosion of his own creation — death by "infra red ray." (Drawn from the *American Film Institute Catalog*, p. 425.)

The House Divided (*Press Clippings*, vol. 1).

The Human Soul. Three-reel drama. Balboa Amusement Producing Co. Made for William Fox, released by Box Office Attraction Co. *Scenario*: Frank M. Wiltermood. *Cast*: Henry Stanley, Madeline Pardee, Bruce Smith, Jane Dey, Francis McDonald, Robert Grey (*Press Clippings*, vol. 1).

Commentary: F. M. Wiltermood, a scriptwriter at Balboa, supposedly made an extensive study of the principles of psychic, metaphysical and spiritual phenomena before writing this story.

Summary: The story is about a Spanish inventor who comes to settle in California with his wife and daughter. He constructs a wondrously powerful camera, sensitive enough to photograph even the smallest molecules that float in the air. His wife becomes ill, and he dreams that he can take a picture of her soul as she dies. At the moment of her death, to advance the world's belief in the immortality of the human soul, he is able to photograph the flight of his wife's soul from her body.

The Spaniard hides the photo of the soul of his wife behind a regular photograph. He unexpectedly dies, leaving behind his young daughter. Years later the girl has grown into an attractive señorita and is wooed by a young cattleman. A villainous Spaniard appears on the scene, however, and takes her love by storm. As she prepares to leave with the cad, she reaches for her mother's picture and discovers the picture plate behind it. Is it the soul of her mother that sets her straight or the arrival of the handsome cattleman? In any case, the true lover forgives the foolish girl, and they live happily ever after.

Review: Here's what the *Daily Telegram* (Mar. 4, 1914, 4:3), had to say about the film:

> The experts who attended the presentation of the scenes last evening were unanimous in declaring the pictures to be the "creepiest," most uncanny and wonderful photographic views ever made, their praise especially centering on the scene showing the vaporous, spiritual and divinely beautiful soul of the dying woman slowly rising out of her pain-racked, withered form. The photographic achievement was obtained after several weeks of experimenting at the Balboa studios, the results being gotten by a process invented by the camera experts employed by the company. Within a short time the photoplay will be exhibited at hundreds of moving-picture theaters throughout the English-speaking world and is expected to create a wave of discussion among psychological savants everywhere. A special set of the films is being prepared to be sent to Sir Oliver Lodge, who is England's leading student of the occult. For thirty years an official of the English Society for Psychical Research, his

fame has become worldwide, and that he will be greatly interested in the remarkable motion photographs made in Long Beach is beyond question.

The Hunchback of Cedar Lodge. Three-reel drama. Balboa Amusement Producing Co. Made for William Fox, released by Box Office Attraction Co. *Cast*: Jackie Saunders (*Ellen Page, ward*), Ray Gallagher (*Martin Meredith, the Hunchback of Cedar Lodge*), Fred Whitman (*Beverly Meredith, his brother*), Henry Stanley (*John Meredith, the father*), Mollie McConnell (*Aunt Nancy*), George Liepold (*Uncle Ben*) (*Press Clippings*, vol. 1, pp. 127, 134).

Summary: The story is woven around the treachery of a deformed brother who falsely accuses his normal brother of killing their father. *Variety* explained the plot by stating that the hunchback, his brother, and father live together with a young girl who was adopted by the father. The two sons are infatuated with her, and a rivalry exists. The hunchback discovers that his father has a secret hoard of gold. He follows him to the treasure and kills him, but he sets up the crime to look as if his brother had committed the evil deed. The brother sees no way of proving his innocence and leaves for the West, where he becomes wealthy from prospecting. The girl leaves the cripple and becomes a governess. The hunchback gets trapped in the treasure vault and dies there. The rich brother returns home, clears his name, marries the girl, and finds the treasure. (Drawn from *Variety*, Aug. 29, 1914.)

Review: The *Daily Telegram* (Nov. 7, 1914, 15:8) reported: "Jackie Saunders and Ray Gallagher are featured in this production, which is a rare excursion into the field of photographic fiction, with romance, adventure and peril enacted in the forceful and intelligent manner for which the Balboa Stock company of Long Beach is noted."

The *Variety* (Aug. 29, 1914) review had a diametrically opposed critique and listed the title as *The Humpback of Cedar Lodge*. The magazine stated that Balboa, the explorer, would turn in his grave if he could see this picture made by the firm with his name. The reviewer thought that it was terrible to make a poor, defenseless cripple the bad guy in the film. He did, however, think that the photography was excellent, despite the poor attempt to represent a thunder and lightning storm.

Ill Starred Babbie. Five-reel drama. Balboa Amusement Producing Co. Released Dec. 7, 1914, by the Alliance Films Corp. Based on the novel *Ill-Starred Babbie* by William Wilfrid Whalen (Boston, 1912). *Director*: Sherwood MacDonald. *Scenario*: Will M. Ritchey. *Cast*: Jackie Saunders.

Summary: This movie gives the viewer a glimpse of the hard life in the Allegheny Mountains, beginning with the death at childbirth of the wife of a coal miner, Peter Conway. The viewer watches the child, Babbie, grow up and marry an abusive husband. During one of his drunken attacks on Babbie, he smashes a window while striking his young wife, cuts his arm, gets blood poisoning, and dies. Babbie then returns home, where there's more strife awaiting her. Her older sister, Hannah, is in love with Ned Higgins, but he is smitten by Babbie. Babbie, out of respect towards her sister, shuns Ned's advances. Outside the home, strikers are organizing against the company guards. Trying again to reconcile differences, Babbie has a priest intervene to calm down the uprising. A drunken miner, Dominick Kenelly, who has organized the strike, lashes out at Babbie for bringing in the priest, while Ned comes to her defense. At one point, Ned risks his own life while rescuing Babbie from a passing train that narrowly misses her. Ned proposes marriage to Babbie, but she refuses on account of her sister. Then another crisis interrupts Babbie's calamitous life. Babbie's father is unfairly accused and scheduled for execution. While saving her father, Babbie is mortally wounded by a bullet. Dying with Ned at her side, Babbie avows her love to him, beseeching him to give his loving care and devotion to Hannah. (Drawn from the *American Film Institute Catalog*, p. 442.)

Ima Simp, Detective. Serial. Each one-reel comedy-drama. Uncopyrighted. *Director*:

William Wolbert. *Cameramen*: Percy De Gaston and Joseph Z. Brotherton. *Cast*: William Wolbert (*villain*), Marie Wayne, Ben Deely, Charles Dudley, Henry Stanley, Archibald Warren, Brent Carruthers, Suzanne Rogers, Robert Barrow, Alice Brookton, Nan Christie, Nell Frantzen, Myrtle Carruthers, Bruce Randall.

Commentary: The *Daily Telegram* (Aug. 26, 1914, 7:5) remarked that the famed vaudeville team of Ben Deely and Marie Wayne joined the Balboa Studios to film this comedy/ adventure series. While in vaudeville, Deely came up with a variety of ideas surrounding the adventures of Ima Simp, Detective. Deely and Wayne were known for their sketch *The New Bellboy*, which they had performed for more than ten years on the Orpheum and Keith circuits. During their careers they also played Keith's Theatre in Washington and had the honor of playing to President Wilson and Secretary Bryan.

According to *Motion Picture News* (Oct. 24, 1914), in this serial Deely almost invariably posed as a millionaire in evening dress, "while Miss Wayne's beauty was made even more attractive by Parisian gowns, gorgeous millinery creations and palatial indoor sets" (*Press Clippings*, vol. 1, p. 73).

The Imprint. One-reel drama. White Star. Made for William Fox, released Nov. 13, 1913, by Box Office Attraction Co. *Director*: David Porter. *Cast*: Henry King, Robert Grey, Augusta Bolle (*Press Clippings*, vol. 1).

In the Bishop's Carriage. Serial. Released in 1920. David Trattner Production Company. Based on the book by the same title by Miriam Michelson.

Twenty-Six Stories: Story 1—*Back on the Job.* *Director*: Fred A. Kelsey. *Cameraman*: Ed Gheller.

Commentary: According to the *Daily Telegram*, the 26 stories had appeared in the *Saturday Evening Post* (Mar. 25, 1920, p. 5).

In the Hands of the Law. Five-reel drama. Balboa Amusement Producing Co. Made for B. S. Moss Motion Pictures Corp. Released Feb. 1917 by Moss Films but shown in New York in July 1916 to an invited audience which included the police commissioner, the secretary to the mayor, and various legislators. *Producers*: H. M. Horkheimer and E. D. Horkheimer. Based on a novel by William O. H. Hurst. *Cast*: Lois Meredith.

Commentary: According to the *American Film Institute Catalog* (p. 449), certain scenes of this movie were done in St. Augustine, Florida, where the novel took place, including scenes at the home of retired cotton king, D. Ramsey Moore, and at the federal prison in Atlanta, Georgia

Summary: In this story, circumstantial evidence most likely points to the wrong man. In fact, the suspect's own fiancée has been the very person to provide the circumstantial evidence, and the man's conviction, of course, strains to the breaking point the romance between them until an old man tells his own story of a similar tragic case. In the old man's "story within a story," he himself had once suspected his own son of robbing a bank, also on account of circumstantial evidence. There was never any hard evidence, but the son's life was ruined by the suspicion against him, and he spent many years in prison, dying in shame and misery. (Drawn from the *American Film Institute Catalog*, p. 449.)

The Infamous Miss Ravell. *Cast*: Alice Lake, Jackie Saunders ("Southern Exposure," p. 114).

The Inspirations of Harry Larrabee. Four-reel mystery. Balboa Amusement Producing Co., a Fortune Photoplay. Released March 1917 by General Film Co. *Producers*: H. M. Horkheimer and E. D. Horkheimer. *Director*: Bertram Bracken. *Scenario*: Douglas Bronston. Based on the short story "The Inspirations of Harry Larrabee" by Howard Fielding, pseud. of Charles Witherle Hooke (publication undetermined). *Cameraman*: Victor Miller. *Cast*: Clifford Gray (*Harry Larrabee*), Margaret Landis (*Carolyn Vaughn*), Winifred Greenwood (*Madame Batonyl*), Frank Brownlee (*Batonyl, also known as "The Wolf"*), William

Ehfe (*Dr. Stettina*), Charles Blaisdell (*Dr. Seard Wendell*), Tom Morgan (*hallboy*).

Commentary: According to the *American Film Institute Catalog* (pp. 457–58), news items of the era claim that this production was the first release in the Fortune Photoplay series, which was comprised of adaptations of stories that appeared in various Street and Smith publications, including *Popular, People's, Smith's* and *Ainslee's* magazines

Summary: A playwright, Harry Larrabee, is in love with a female tenant in the same apartment building. The young woman's name is Carolyn Vaughn. Carolyn knows a certain Madame Batonyl, who is sent to see Carolyn to look over her jewelry collection. The man who sends Madame Batonyl is a thief known as "The Wolf." During Madame Batonyl's visit, the Wolf sneaks into Carolyn's apartment via the dumbwaiter, surprising her and drugging her with chloroform. The heist begins to unravel, however, when Harry, the playwright, detects the crime going on and rescues Carolyn, taking her to Dr. Wendell to be resuscitated. The jewels are returned to the rightful owner, after the Wolf and his partner in crime, Dr. Stettina, shoot each other in a duel. The criminal plot is finally revealed by a repentant Madame Batonyl, who turns out to have been the wife of the Wolf. She laments in the end having been brutally forced into criminal activities by her dead husband. (Drawn from the *American Film Institute Catalog*, pp. 457-58.)

The Intrigue. Two-reel drama. Kalem. Released Mar. 4, 1914, by General Film Co. *Cast*: Robert Grey (*Ralph Brant, lawyer*), Jackie Saunders (*Jeannette Morton*), Henry Stanley (*George Austin*), Mollie McConnell (*his wife*), Raymond Gallagher (*Press Clippings*, vol. 1, p. 55).

Summary: The Austins mourn the loss of their only child. At the same time, Brant, a young widower, has a four-year-old son, Bob. The child wanders away from his father and later climbs into Mrs. Austin's automobile. He is discovered by the grief-stricken woman. In an insane moment, she decides to keep Bob. Brant searches for his boy, but in vain. Years later Bob, grown to manhood, learns that the Austins are not his parents. Brant, meanwhile has attained prominence as a lawyer. He falls in love with Jeannette, a society girl, and marries her.

As time passes, Brant neglects his young wife for his business. Fate throws Jeannette and Bob together. The boy falls in love with Jeannette and urges her to elope with him. Lonely and believing that her husband no longer loves her, Jeannette consents. On the night of the elopement, an impulse causes her to take an old tintype from the drawer. Bob sees it. It is identical to the one in his possession. After ordering Jeannette to remove her wraps, the boy hastens to his adopted parents and tells them he has found his father. Brant returns and finds the note. His joy in finding his long-lost son is so great, however, that he forgives the culprits and takes them in his arms. (Drawn from the *Daily Telegram*, Mar. 18, 1914, 4:7.)

It Happened One Night. One-reel comedy. Joy. Made for William Fox, released by Box Office Attraction Co. (*Moving Picture World*).

It Will All Come Out in the Wash. One-reel comedy. Joy. Made for William Fox, released by Box Office Attraction Co. (*Moving Picture World*).

The Jewels of the Madonna. Edison Manufacturing Company. Filmed in San Diego.

Commentary: According to Claudine Burnett's "Long Beach Motion Picture Industry: 1911-1923" (p. 9), Harold Lloyd was attending a drama school in San Diego in 1913 when he decided to work as an extra on location for the Edison Company, which was filming this movie. It was Lloyd's first job in films. He was hired as an extra for $3 and was made up as a Yaqui Indian carrying a tray of food to white men. The next week Lloyd worked a whole day in a Dutch costume in another Edison production.

Joy and the Dragon. Five-reel drama. Balboa Amusement Producing Co. Copyright Dec. 18, 1916, Pathé Exchange, Inc., LU9747.

Distributor: Pathé Exchange, Inc., Gold Rooster Plays, released Dec. 31, 1916, by Pathé Exchange, Inc. *Director*: Henry King. *Scenario*: Will M. Ritchey. *Cameramen*: William Beckway, Georges Rizard. *Cast*: Baby Marie Osborne (*Joy*), Henry King (*Hal Lewis*), Mollie McConnell (*the matron*), Cullen Landis (*Slinky Joe*).

Summary: Saved by fishermen, Joy is the only survivor of a shipwreck that has made her an orphan. The little girl is placed in an orphanage that serves as a secret operation for a band of thieves. Joy also has possession of her deceased mother's jewels. The thieves are more interested in the jewels than in the welfare of the little girl. Eventually, Joy runs away from the orphanage, leaving the jewels behind, just to save herself. In her escape, she hides on a train going west. Out West, Joy meets Hal Lewis, the black sheep of a well-to-do Eastern family. The two runaways bond, and in forming a supportive "family" together, Hal becomes more responsible and caring while parenting little Joy. In seeing his own family back East differently, Hal goes back home with Joy, and reconciles himself with his father. To add to the family's good fortune, Hal bravely returns to the orphanage to confront the gang of thieves, and while destroying their ring, he also manages to retrieve Joy's jewels. (Drawn from the *American Film Institute Catalog*, p. 478.)

The Judge's Wife. Three-reel drama. White Star. Made for William Fox, released Oct. 12, 1914, by Box Office Attraction Co. *Director*: William Desmond Taylor. *Cast*: Neva Gerber (*Mrs. Livingston*), Daniel Gilfether (*Judge Livingston*), Harriet Jansen (*Eleanor*), John Revett (*Dick Winthrop*), Tom Moore (*Mr. Johnson*).

Commentary: In *A Deed of Death* (p. 53), Robert Giroux states that the plot of this movie, in which the main character spends time in prison to protect the honor of a woman he loves, was based on a true incident in Taylor's life.

Summary: An untitled press clipping in the Horkheimer scrapbook describes the action of the film:

Judge Livingston, a wealthy jurist, lives happily in a mansion with his young wife Josephine, and his daughter, Eleanor, child of the judge's first wife. Dick Winthrop, the judge's private secretary, is in love with Eleanor, and she returns his affection. They become betrothed, and the judge approves their engagement.

Mrs. Livingston, Eleanor's stepmother, buys goods extravagantly at fashionable shopping places, and has the goods charged to her account. Dick receives a letter from the bank, saying that Mrs. Livingston has overdrawn her account $1,100, and requesting settlement without disturbing Judge Livingston. Dick tries to persuade Mrs. Livingston to attend to the overdrawn account, but she becomes angry and resolves to break Dick's engagement to Eleanor. Mrs. Livingston then tells the judge that Dick is not a proper fiancé for Eleanor.

Eleanor finds recreation in doing settlement work, attracting the attention of several men engaged in white slavery acts. These evil doers forge a note purporting to be from a poor woman, asking Eleanor to come to her aid, and when she arrives at the address given the white slavers seize her and make her a prisoner. Dick accidentally finds the note and rushes to rescue Eleanor, as he feels that the note was forged. Dick arrives at the house where Eleanor is held captive, and after a desperate fight with the plotters, the men are taken prisoners, Eleanor and Dick manage to return home.

The debts Mrs. Livingston owes become pressing; she tries at night to steal funds from her husband's safe, and Dick finds her near the safe. To escape accusation, Mrs. Livingston charges Dick with the theft, and he, to shield her, shoulders the blame in the presence of the judge and Eleanor. The judge believes his wife, and tells Dick he must leave the house forever. Mrs. Livingston then repents, tells her husband she alone is to blame, begs his forgiveness [*Press Clippings*, vol. 1, p. 115].

The Lady in the Library. Four-reel drama. Copyright Oct. 19, 1917, General Film Co., Inc., LP11580. Falcon Features. Released Oct. 1917 by General Film Co. *Supervisors*: H. M.

Horkheimer and E. D. Horkheimer. *Director*: Edgar Jones. *Scenario*: Lela Leibrand. Based on the story "The Lady in the Library" by Frederick Orin Bartlett (publication undetermined). *Cast*: Jack Vosburgh (*T. Huntington Forbes*), Vola Vale (*Mildred Vandeburg*), Robert Weycross (*Augustus Vandeburg*), Ella Pitts (*Mrs. Vandeburg*), William Reed (*Simonds*), Ruth Lackaye (*Mrs. Merriweather*), Harl McInroy (*Rev. Alred Clemons*), Jessylee Roberson (*the mother*), Jane Pepprell (*Meeda Jones*), Barney Fury (*"Spike" Jones*), James Warner (*Gerald Courtney*), Moru Kuan (*"Jap"*), W. N. Carter (*Dan*).

Commentary: According to the *American Film Institute Catalog* (p. 496), Vitagraph produced in 1916 a one-reel film that was based on the same source and was directed by Sidney Drew.

Summary: Mildred Vandeburg, a philanthropist heiress, breaks off her engagement to a selfish gentleman. She prefers to spend her time doing charity work at a hospital she helped build in a poor part of town, while her former fiancé, T. Huntington Forbes, spends all his time with sports and horse racing. At the hospital, there are some unsavory characters among the workers, including a nurse, Meeda Jones, who is the wife of a criminal, Spike. After stealing some jewelry, Spike tries to have his brother sell the stolen property for him. Spike's brother Dan dies at the hands of police during an attempt to arrest him, and Dan's wife, stunned at the news of his death, expires on the spot, leaving a baby girl without parents. Good-hearted Mildred takes charge of the baby girl, and in telling her former beau that someone is expecting him, she announces that there is a "lady in the library." Forbes is transformed by this new responsibility of caring for the infant girl. He devotes so much time and effort to parenting that he forgets his former selfish pastimes. The criminal Spike Jones takes the opportunity to kidnap the little girl, however, demanding a handsome ransom, but Mildred and Forbes beat him to the punch. The story ends happily, with Mildred and Forbes reconciled, planning to marry and to raise the child together. (Drawn from the *American Film Institute Catalog*, p. 496.)

The Law That Divides. Five-reel drama. Plaza Pictures (probably started for Balboa Amusement Producing Co.). Released Oct. 28, 1918, by W. W. Hodkinson Corp. *Director*: Howard M. Mitchell. *Cameraman*: Joseph Brotherton. *Cast*: Kathleen Clifford (*Kathleen Preston*), Kenneth Harlan (*Howard Murray*), Gordon Sackville (*John Douglas*), Corinne Grant (*Mrs. Douglas*), Patrick Calhoun (*Kenneth Douglas*), Stanley Pembroke (*Jack Baggot*), Ruth Lackaye (*Mrs. Baggot*), Mabel Hyde (*Mrs. Preston*) (*American Film Institute Catalog*, p. 507).

Commentary: According to the *American Film Institute Catalog*, this production is not credited to Balboa Studios; however, the release date would explain why the producer would be other than Balboa, since Balboa had gone into receivership while the production was still under way. In addition, the cameraman and the major actors were Balboans. See also *Angel Child*, *Petticoats and Politics*, and *Whatever the Cost*, all of which seem to fall into the same category.

Summary: In their divorce, John Douglas and his wife split the custody of their children. John Douglas takes charge of their son, Kenneth, and Mrs. Douglas takes charge of Kathleen. Later, Mrs. Douglas dies poor, while Kathleen is taken in by Jack Baggot, a thief, and his wife. From the thieving couple, Kathleen learns the tricks of the trade. Later, after Jack is imprisoned, Kathleen is adopted by Mrs. Preston, a rich woman who offers Kathleen a refined and elegant lifestyle. When Jack is released from jail, he forces Kathleen back into a life of crime. She steels for him a valuable diamond necklace belonging to Mrs. Preston. Kenneth, Kathleen's brother, arrives the day of the theft as a guest at the Preston home and falls in love with Kathleen, not knowing she is his sister. To win over the beautiful girl, Kenneth takes the diamond necklace from Jack and entices Kathleen into his room at night. As Kenneth tries to force himself on Kathleen, she kills her assailant. Kathleen's boyfriend, Howard Murray, takes the blame for Kathleen, but Kathleen tells the truth to Kenneth's father, who is her father as well. Realizing the double tragedy of the murder, Kathleen's father sadly clears Howard of all blame. The surviving lovers, Howard and Kathleen, try to begin anew.

The Lesson. Five-reel comedy-drama. Copyright May 3, 1918, Select Pictures Corp., LP12385. Select Pictures Corp. Released May 1918 by Select Pictures Corp. *Director*: Charles Giblyn. *Scenario*: Charles Giblyn. *Adaptor*: Charles Giblyn. *Story*: Virginia Terhune Van De Water. *Cast*: Constance Talmadge (*Helen Drayton*), Tom Moore (*Chet Vernon*), Walter Hiers ("*Tub*" *Martin*), Herbert Heyes (*John Galvin*), Joseph Smiley (*Henry Hammond*), Lillian Rambeau (*Mrs. Hammond*), Dorothy Green (*Ada Thompson*), Christy Walker (*Harriet Reeves*).

Commentary: In the *American Film Institute Catalog* (p. 511), there is only an indirect reference to this movie being connected with the Balboa Studios that states that the first public showing of this film was given at Long Beach, July 29, 1917, to raise funds for a hospital for convalescent servicemen of the U.S. Army. There are no reviews available about this movie.

Summary: Bored with the too familiar routines and people of her quiet little town, Helen Drayton surprises her family and friends when she decides not to wed her number-one beau, Chet Vernon. In her desire to know big-city life, Helen finds her ticket out of the village in the person of a visiting traveler, John Galvin, an architect from New York. Within just a few weeks, without really getting to know each other, the two marry and head for the bright lights of New York. Once in the city, Helen finally opens her eyes to the kind of man she has married and realizes her mistake. She endures painful lessons while living with her selfish husband, until she rejects him. Eventually she decides to go back to her little hometown, where she remarries, this time contently, with her lifetime friend and companion, Chet Vernon. (Drawn from the *American Film Institute Catalog*, p. 511.)

Letters Entangled. Balboa Amusement Producing Co. Released in 1915 by Pathé Frères. *Cast*: Henry King (*Henry King, Director*, p. 195).

The Light in a Woman's Eye. Three reels. *Director*: Harry Harvey. *Scenarist*: F. M. Wiltermood. *Cast*: Caroline Frances Cooke, Constance Johnson, Douglas Gerrard, Howard Davies, William Carroll, Ben F. Clinton.

Commentary: Tony Scott notes the seasoned background of director Harry Harvey who had written 37 photoplays and produced 29 films before joining Balboa. Prior to signing with one of Balboa's companies, Harvey had 12 years experience, having spent time at Mutoscope, Edison, Cameraphone, Pathé Frères, Gaumont, Yankee, Solax, Kay Bee, Frontier, Universal, and Reliance. Harvey had also been Pathé's first American leading man ("Southern Exposure," p. 116).

F. M. Wiltermood wrote this photoplay about an eye specialist ordered at gunpoint to operate on a blind woman he jilted in his youth.

Although it was filmed at Long Beach, according to the *Motion Picture News* (New York, Nov. 21, 1914), the Balboa Amusement Producing Co. contracted with Lorimer Johnston to produce this film (*Press Clippings*, vol. 1, p. 26).

Little Jack. Three reels. Balboa Amusement Producing Co. Made for William Fox, released Nov. 3, 1914, by Box Office Attraction Co. *Cast*: Dan Moran, Jackie Saunders (*Press Clippings*, vol. 1, p. 110).

Summary: *Moving Picture World* (Nov. 14, 1914) recounts the plot:

> A three-reel Balboa offering with Jackie Saunders in the title role, a girl who has been brought up by a rough bandit uncle and is dressed as a boy. She saves a rich lumberman who puts up at their lonely house overnight and then runs away for fear of punishment. She falls in with another gang of thieves and is wounded while helping them rob the city office of the lumberman. Later, on being recognized, she is given a home and in the end is the means of saving her benefactor from the thieving of his dishonest partner. (*Press Clippings*, vol. 1, p. 110)

Review: *Moving Picture World* also presented a critique in the same article:

There is action all through the piece and it is likely to prove a very acceptable entertainer in spite of the fact that it does not tell a strongly convincing story.

Little Mary Sunshine. Five-reel drama. Copyright Mar. 30, 1916, Pathé Exchange, Inc., LU7954. Balboa Feature Film Co., Released Mar. 3, 1916, by Pathé Exchange, Inc., Gold Rooster Plays. *Director*: Henry King. *Assistant Director*: Alden Willey. *Scenario*: Dan F. Whitcomb. *Cameraman*: Harry W. Gerstad. *Cast*: Baby Marie Osborne (*Mary*), Henry King (*Bob Daley*), Marguerite Nichols (*Sylvia Sanford*), Andrew Arbuckle (*Bob's father*), Mollie McConnell (*Bob's mother*), Pete (*the trained bear*).

Commentary: This film is among the ten produced at Balboa Studios with Baby Marie. *Little Mary Sunshine* introduced into cinema the idea of using a tiny tot as the lead in a feature film. In fact, this movie started a world-wide campaign promoting better films for children, and this photoplay was used as an example by many groups, including the women's clubs of America. Most importantly, the "Mary Sunshine" series at Balboa became the forerunner of the wholesome "family" films that would follow, with tiny tots like Jackie Coogan, Baby Peggy, and Shirley Temple — all of whom would also share their leading roles with adult actors. This movie not only launched Baby Marie into global stardom, it also broke all records for five-reel photoplays. Pathé immediately contracted with Balboa to do six more movies with Baby Marie in the leading role, with Henry King directing: *Shadows and Sunshine*, *Joy and the Dragon*, *Twin Kiddies*, *Told at Twilight*, *A Little Ray of Sunshine*, and *Sunshine and Gold*. In addition, the Little Mary Sunshine series would make Henry King world-famous as a director.

Summary: Three-year old Mary is left motherless after her drunk and penniless father beats his wife to death and walks out on his little girl. In a parallel story of another drinking problem from the other side of the tracks, the viewer witnesses how the handsome and elegant Bob Daley lets alcohol come between him and his fiancée. Sylvia, in disgust at Bob's drinking, returns her engagement ring before she begins to experience tremendous feelings of loss. Returning to little Mary, the viewer sees her climb into Bob's hired car just before Bob is seated in back behind the chauffeur. Bob discovers the little girl under a blanket on the floor of the car and decides to take her home with him. Bob and Mary need each other, and Bob's parents are delighted to see the therapeutic effects of the growing bond between Mary and Bob. Despite his depression and sorrow over Sylvia, Bob manages to laugh, enjoying fully the sunshine of the little girl's indomitable courage and bubbly personality. In addition, Bob's parental responsibilities leave him no time for drinking, though he, like Sylvia, is pining over the loss of his wedding pledge. Eventually, as Mary and Bob become more attached to each other and as Bob's rehabilitation proves complete, Bob's father invites Sylvia over to meet the "new woman" in Bob's life. Little does Sylvia know that the new woman is only three years old. During her clandestine visit, Sylvia watches Bob through the curtains as he refuses a drink and tosses the glass into the fireplace, disgusted at his father's offer of a cocktail. When Sylvia also observes how tenderly Bob cares for Mary, she is convinced that it is time for a reconciliation. The three come together, ready and eager to form a loving family. (Drawn from the *American Film Institute Catalog*, pp. 528–28.)

Little Miss Grown-Up. Five-reel comedy. Oakdale Productions (probably Balboa Amusement Producing Co.). Released Oct. 1918 by General Film Co. *Director*: Sherwood MacDonald. *Cast*: Gloria Joy (*Nan Griffing*), Ethel Pepperell (*Grace Griffing*), Mary Northmore (*Ethel Griffing*), Neil Hardin (*Robert Griffing*), Mollie McConnell (*Anna Griffing*), Daniel Gilfether (*James Griffing*), Edward Saunders (*Morgan Thornton*), Charles Dudley (*Simple Simon Magee*) (*American Film Institute Catalog*, p. 528).

Commentary: The majority of the personnel involved were associated with the Balboa Amusement Producing Co., but the film is not usually credited as being produced at Long Beach, since its production would have occurred about the very time that the Horkheimers were facing bankruptcy. However, the Horkheimers had boldly announced that Gloria Joy, the "Child Wonder," would appear in a new series, to follow the example of the "Baby Grand," Marie Osborne, who had left Balboa the previous year to make movies at her own studio in Glendale, the Diando Studios. Other features in this Balboa series with Gloria Joy include *The Locked Heart, The Midnight Burglar, Miss Mischief Maker, No Children Wanted,* and *Wanted—A Brother,* all of which feature Gloria Joy in the leading role.

Summary: Nan Griffing spends her time on her parents' farm playing with Simple Simon Magee. Though an adult, Simple Simon Magee has the mental capacity of a young child. While playing in the attic one day, Nan discovers an old costume her mother used to wear when she performed on stage. Putting on the costume, Nan begs her mom to show her how to dance. Nan's mother, Ethel, agrees, but as the mother shows her daughter how to perform, members of a local church society are horrified to see such sinful behavior. Shortly afterwards, Nan and Simple Simon leave to go to the city on a visit to Nan's grandmother Anna and Aunt Grace. Hiding in the orchard, Simon frightens the servants, who mistake him for a ghost. Aunt Grace has a fiancé, Morgan Thornton, and little Nan takes a strong liking to the young man, innocently proposing marriage to him. Little Nan even sneaks to his house to elope with Morgan. In the meantime, Morgan asks the aunt and grandmother to come to his house, while Nan asks Morgan to choose between his fiancée Grace and herself. In front of the witnesses, Morgan chooses Grace. Little Nan takes it on the chin, turns her back on the city, and heads home to her parents.

A Little Ray of Sunshine. Pathé Exchange, Inc. Balboa Feature Film Co. Released by Pathé Exchange, Inc.; Gold Rooster Plays. *Director:* Henry King. *Cast:* Baby Marie Osborne, Henry King (Marie Osborne-Yeats' scrapbook).

Little Sunbeam. Three reels. Balboa Amusement Producing Co. Made for William Fox, released Oct. 19, 1914, by Box Office Attraction Co. *Cast:* Jackie Saunders in title role.

Summary: Two sisters, Sunbeam and Daisy, are orphaned and go to live with the village blacksmith. Daisy falls for a city slicker and leaves for the big city with him. Sunbeam goes to the city to find her sister and convince her of her mistake. On the train, Sunbeam meets a young artist who wants her to model for him. She agrees, poses for his work and becomes famous. Daisy, in the meantime, is deserted by her lover and left alone in the big city, but Sunbeam comes to her rescue (*Daily Telegram,* Jan. 2, 1915, 4:6).

Review: The story was set in Southern California, and *Variety* (Nov. 7, 1914, p. 23) called it a good picture that "excels the majority of three-reelers turned out by this concern." The reviewer noted that Jackie Saunders was a truly lovely girl and her animation and charm left the audience with a fine impression. All in all, it was a good picture with few faults.

The Locked Heart. American Film Co., Oakdale Productions. (Probably Balboa Amusement Producing Co.) Released July 20, 1918, by General Film Co. *Director:* Henry King. *Scenario:* Daniel F. Whitcomb. *Cameraman:* George Rizard. *Cast:* Gloria Joy (*Martha Mason*), Henry King (*Harry Mason*), Vola Vale (*Ruth Mason*), Daniel Gilfether (*Col. Mason*), Leon Perdue (*The villain*) (*Henry King, Director,* p. 200, and *American Film Institute Catalog,* p. 536).

Commentary: The majority of the personnel involved were associated with the Balboa Amusement Producing Co., but the film is not usually credited as being produced at Long Beach, since its production would have occurred about the very time that the Horkheimers were facing bankruptcy. However, the Horkheimers had boldly announced that Gloria Joy, the "Child Wonder," would appear in a new series, to follow the example of the "Baby Grand," Marie Osborne, who left Balboa the previous year to make movies at her own studio in Glendale, the Diando Studios. Other features in this Balboa series with Gloria Joy include *Little Miss Grown-Up*, *The Midnight Burglar*, *Miss Mischief Maker*, *No Children Wanted*, and *Wanted — A Brother*, all of which feature Gloria Joy in the leading role.

Summary: Called home for an emergency, Harry Mason arrives to find his wife has just died in childbirth. In his despondency, he will not even look at the infant. He leaves the girl in the care of her grandfather, Colonel Mason, and then departs for Europe to grieve in solitude over his enormous loss. Harry continues to travel around the world, but he cannot escape the haunting memory of his deceased wife. Drawn back to his home by an inexplicable pull, he returns years later. In the meantime, his little girl, Martha, has grown to be a charming and vivacious lass. Not recognizing the visitor and not knowing that he is her father, Martha persuades him to open the nursery. The letter left by Harry's wife is still on the dresser. He reads the letter and knows why he has been called back home. In the letter, his beloved wife had requested that Harry devote himself to their child, should anything happen to the mother. Harry unlocks his heart, commits himself to his child, and realizes what a treasure he had abandoned in leaving his daughter. (Drawn from the *American Film Institute*, p. 536.)

Maid of the Wild.

Three reels. Balboa Amusement Producing Co. Released Oct. 9, 1915, by Pathé Frères. *Cast*: Baby Marie Osborne, Marguerite Nichols (*Lucy Bingham*), Gordon Sackville (*James Sterling*).

Commentary: Baby Marie Osborne appeared for the first time in this movie, though her name did not show in the credits. According to Tony Scott, Baby Marie made 28 five-reel films and 2 two-reel films, and some claim that she performed at Balboa till 1919, though most probably she was already making movies in Glendale at the Diando Studios by that time ("Southern Exposure," p. 132). Of the 30 movies with Baby Marie, only 10 have been conservatively listed in this filmography as ones made at Balboa Studios: 1915, *Maid of the Wild*, *Should a Wife Forgive?*; 1916, *Joy and the Dragon*, *Little Mary Sunshine*, *A Little Ray of Sunshine*, *Shadows and Sunshine*; 1917, *Sunshine and Gold*, *Told at Twilight*, *Twin Kiddies*, *Twin Rays of Sunshine*.

Ankerich explains in *Broken Silence* (p. 225) that prior to her first film Baby Marie always accompanied her parents, who played bit parts at Balboa Studio. Unexpectedly, Marie was asked one day to play a little boy because no boy was available the moment production was scheduled to begin. Marie told Ankerich, "I had a Dutch bob, and when they put little boy's clothes on me, I was the little boy they needed." Baby Marie's career was launched with this film. According to Ankerich, both the public and Pathé liked her performance. At the height of her acting career during the silent era, Baby Marie was reportedly making as much as $1,000 per week.

Summary: The maid of the wild is the wife of a trapper in the mountains. There she lives happily with her husband and two children until her husband is killed by a bandit. A neighboring trapper falls in love with her and begins to court the widow, but a "city feller" arrives on the scene — James Sterling, a wealthy bachelor. In leaving the city, Sterling left behind Clarice Driscoll, a society girl who loves him. The city slicker had come to the mountains under doctor's orders to recuperate from the wild life he has been leading in the city. He too falls for the pretty widow, and he marries her.

After the marriage, Sterling takes Lucy and the children back home to the city and introduces her to his friends. Unfortunately, her country ways make her the laughing stock of her new husband's friends. At a dance she drinks too much spiked lemonade, and it goes to her head. Her husband yells at her in a burst of rage because she has humiliated him. She decides she would be better off back in the hills, so she takes her children and runs off. Her husband chases after her and arrives on the scene just as the neighbor has managed to save her from committing suicide. Together in the mountains they rekindle their love for each other and become reunited. The couple make up as a beautifully colored sun sets behind them (*Variety*, Oct. 8, 1915, p. 23, and Marie Osborne's scrapbook.)

Review: *Variety* (p. 23) wrote that this was a drama without much punch and that the story had been told too many times.

The Mainspring. Four-reel Western. Copyright Aug. 17, 1917, General Film Co., Inc., LP11261. Falcon Features. Released Aug. 17, 1917, by General Film Co. *Supervisors*: H. M. Horkheimer and E. D. Horkheimer. *Director*: Henry King. *Scenario*: Frances E. Guihan. Based on the story "The Mainspring" by Louis Joseph Vance in *Popular Magazine* (publication date unknown). *Cast*: Henry King (*Ned Gillett*), Ethel Pepperell (*Frances Hardor*), Bert Ensminger (*"Bellows" Jones*), Charles Blaisdell (*J. J. O'Rourke*), Cullen Landis (*Bellamy Hardor*), Arma Jacobsen (*Peggy Mason*).

Commentary: According to the *American Film Institute Catalog* (p. 567), this was the first of the Falcon Features, a series of four-reel films based on stories appearing in Street & Smith publications. According to an early preproduction news item, *The Mainspring* was to be part of the Horkheimer's Fortune Photoplay series, which ended in June 1917. Tiffany Productions released *Lost at Sea*, which was suggested by the same source, in 1926. It was directed by Louis J. Gasnier and starred Huntley Gordon, Lowell Sherman, and Jane Novak.

Summary: Ned Gillett calls off his engagement to Frances Hardor when he discovers that his father, a banker, has killed himself after speculating with trust funds. Gillett heads West to start a new life. J. J. O'Rourke, an old miner, spots Ned wandering through the countryside, and they both become friends. Bellows Jones, the town bully, attempts to kill Ned and J. J. while trying to take over Mainspring, J. J. O'Rourke's mine. Both of the intended victims barely escape death. At one point, Bellows topples over the shack with two men inside, dragging it down the side of the mountain. Afterwards, Ned hurries to Traver City in order to file a claim before Bellows Jones does. While filing his claim, Ned discovers that Jones fraudulently sold the mine to Bellamy, Frances' brother. After Ned forces Bellamy to pay restitution, Frances refuses to talk to him. Bellamy supports Ned in operating the mine, which becomes very lucrative. Refusing to accept defeat, Bellows sets fire to Mainspring and incites a miners' strike. Ned saves Frances and Bellamy, defeats Bellows Jones, wins the heart of Frances, and gets the mine. (Drawn from the *American Film Institute Catalog*, p. 567.)

The Man with Green Eyes. *Director*: William Desmond Taylor. *Cast*: Henry King, Jackie Saunders (*Press Clippings*, vol. 1).

The Marriage Chance. Six-reel comedy melodrama, 5,840 ft. Uncopyrighted. Hampton Del Ruth Productions. Released Dec. 10, 1922, by American Releasing Corp. *Director/Writer*: Hampton Del Ruth. *Photography*: Dal Clawson. *Cast*: Alta Allen (*Eleanor Douglas*), Milton Sills (*William Bradley*), Henry B. Walthall (*Dr. Paul Graydon*), Tully Marshall (*Timothy Lamb*), Irene Rich (*Mary Douglas*), Mitchell Lewis (*the Mute*), Laura La Varnie (*Martha Douglas*), Nick Cogley (*Uncle Remus*), and Lon Chaney (?).

Commentary: During the production of this movie, the Long Beach press always insisted that Lon Chaney was also among the cast of players and that he was involved also in the publicity during the giant screen test the studio conducted in August 1922 that was open to the public.

Summary: This film begins comically and turns farcical. In the beginning, Eleanor Douglas is about to wed the district attorney, William Bradley. Dr. Paul Graydon gives Eleanor a drink of water and she passes out right away. Dr. Graydon then pronounces her dead, and she is buried. Then a cat drinks from the same glass and seems to die too, but suddenly the cat comes back to life. Bradley removes Eleanor's body from the grave only to find her casket empty. He discovers that Eleanor is lying on Dr. Graydon's operating table, still wearing her wedding gown. Suddenly it is the doctor who is lying dead on the ground. It appears that Eleanor has somehow shot Dr. Graydon. Finally the scene fades out and fades in again to the original wedding. The anxious bride had only fainted, and Eleanor realizes it was all but a dream. (Drawn from the *American Film Institute Catalog*, p. 493.)

Martin Eden. *Scenario*: Jack London. *Director*: Sidney Ayers.

Commentary: The Jack London Motion Picture Company was associated with Balboa Studios, on contract to film *Martin Eden*, *Call of the Wild*, and *The Sea Wolf*. The relationship ended with an infamous court case in 1913 between the two parties. That year, before completing the filming at Balboa Studios, London moved to Bosworth's studio in Los Angeles. Balboa alleged that the scripts, based on London's novels, had been written for Balboa before Jack London and the other plaintiffs obtained their copyright which prevented others from using the stories to make movies. Despite its contract with Jack London, Balboa lost the case. According to the *American Film Institute Catalog*, Bosworth's production was filmed in the fall of 1913, but Bosworth waited until London's contractual agreement expired with Balboa before releasing the film. According to documents in the London collection, some of the scenes were shot in San Francisco, Oakland, and other areas of the San Francisco Bay area.

Moving Picture World (Dec. 20, 1913) announced that several Jack London stories were being prepared at Balboa, including *A Piece of Steak*, based on London's *When God Laughs*, and *The Sea Wolf* and *To Kill a Man*, based on London's *The Night Born*. The announcement further stated that the following works by London were also being prepared as movies at Balboa: *Martin Eden*, *John Barleycorn*, *The Call of the Wild*, *Smoke Bellew Series*, and *The Valley of the Moon* (*Press Clippings*, vol. 1, p. 31).

The *American Film Institute Catalog* (p. 253), explains that the novel *Martin Eden* on which the film was based was first serialized in *Pacific Monthly* from Sept. 1908 to Sept. 1909. This same story was filmed twice more: first, in Russia in 1918 as *Creation Can't Be Bought*, with Vladmir Mayakovsky in the leading role and Nikandr Turkin as director; second, by Columbia in 1942 as *The Adventures of Martin Eden*, starring Glenn Ford, with Sidney Salkow as director.

According to the *American Film Institute Catalog*, these are the details about Bosworth's completed production: Six-reel drama. Based on London's novel *Martin Eden*, published in New York in 1909. Copyright June 22, 1914, Bosworth, Inc., LU3029. Bosworth Inc. Released Aug. 16, 1914, by State Rights; W. W. Hodkinson. Cast: Lawrence Peyton (Martin Eden), Viola Barry (Ruth Morse), Herbert Rawlinson (Arthur Morse), Rhea Haines (Lizzie Connolly), Ann Ivers (Maria Silva), Ray Myers (Russ Brissenden), Elmer Clifton (Cub reporter), Hobart Bosworth, Myrtle Stedman.

Summary: This depressing tale of hard knocks and disappointments begins with a scene of Jack London reading at home. Then the story introduces the main character, Martin Eden, who, weary of the South Seas, returns to Oakland, California. Back in Oakland, Martin saves Arthur Morse from hooligans and the two men become friends. Eventually Martin falls in love with Arthur's sister, Ruth. In an attempt to improve his lot, Martin tries to educate himself but doesn't have enough money, so he goes back to life at sea. While on board ship, Martin begins to write stories, all of which are rejected by publishers. In the meantime, Martin befriends an anarchist, Russ Brissenden, who is also a poet. The two men begin attending socialist meetings and supporting each other in their writings. Martin becomes a socialist, and when Arthur finds out, he is outraged and persuades his sister, Ruth, to forget the radical suitor. Just prior to having his first publication acceptance, Russ kills himself, never knowing of his success as a poet. Martin too publishes work and becomes very successful;, but he turns his back on all his fairweather friends, only caring in the end for Maria, his widowed landlady and her children. Martin ends up despondent about life. Before returning to the sea one last time, he buys a farm for Maria. He later commits suicide out at sea. (Drawn from the *American Film Institute Catalog*, p. 253.)

The Martinache Marriage. Four-reel drama. Copyright Aug. 24, 1917, General Film Co., Inc., LP11279. Falcon Features. Released Sept. 1917, by General Film Co. *Supervisors*: H. M. Horkheimer and E. D. Horkheimer. *Director*: Bert Bracken. Based on the story "The Martinache Marriage" by Beatrix Demarest Lloyd. *Cast*: Margaret Landis (*Sara St. Ypriex*), Philo McCullough (*Col. Horace Martinache*), Mollie McConnell (*Mrs. Martinache*), Leota Lorraine (*Hermia Martinache*), Julien Beaubien (*Irene Lawson*), Vincent Beresford (*Eric Martinache*), Harl McInroy (*Lord Sayle*), Frank Brownlee (*Roscoe Vandercourt*).

Summary: Horace Martinache, a wealthy young American living in Paris, takes a young flower girl to the hospital after hitting her with his car. Before returning to the United States, Martinache leaves money with friends to provide an education for the girl. Years later Horace's nephew Eric brings home from Europe a young actress whom he wants to marry. The family does not approve of the marriage and asks Horace to do something to prevent it. An unmarried colonel, Horace agrees and schemes to break up the match by courting the girl himself. The girl, Sara St. Ypriex, turns out to be the flower girl that Horace had helped educate in France, and she does not seem to mind the new beau. Sara becomes certain of her choice, however, when another suitor, Roscoe Vandercourt, attacks her, and Eric fails to respond to her distress. Horace, however, comes gallantly to her rescue. Vandercourt escapes for the moment, but Sara's father catches him. The capture gives the father much satisfaction because he had once been framed and served a prison term on account of Vandercourt. In the end, Sara gets the right man, as Horace proposes marriage to her. (Drawn from the *American Film Institute Catalog*, p. 593.)

The Mask. Two-reel drama. White Star. Made for William Fox, released Nov. 3, 1914, by Box Office Attraction Co. *Director*: Bertram Bracken (*Daily Telegram*, Nov. 16, 1914, 10:7). *Cast*: Henry King, Dorothy Davenport (*Dorothy Stevens*) (*Press Clippings*, vol. 1, p. 138).

Summary: An unidentified article in the *Press Clippings*, vol. 1, gives the plot:

> Henry King, star man of an Australian detective agency arrives in California to help the police round up a gang of criminals. When Dorothy Stevens is kidnapped in broad daylight, King follows the kidnappers to their hiding place and is there surprised and overpowered by them. Learning that the gang are about to escape next morning on the schooner "Blanche," King manages to get a note to the police and the next morning traps the whole party as they are leaving and rescues Miss Stevens. (*Press Clippings*, vol. 1, p. 138)

The Matrimonial Martyr. Five-reel comedy. Copyright Apr. 29, 1916. Balboa Feature Film Co., LU8186. Balboa Feature Film Co. Released June 19, 1916, by Pathé Exchange, Inc., Gold Rooster Plays. Based on the play *A Message from Reno* (production undetermined). *Director*: Sherwood MacDonald. *Cameraman*: William Beckway. *Cast*: Ruth Roland (*Erma Desmond/Bertie Stanley*), Andrew Arbuckle (*Professor Stanley*), Marguerite Nichols (*Phyllis Burnham*), R. Henry Gray (*Elbert Chetwynde*), Madeleine Pardee (*Mrs. Baddly Bytton*), Lulu Bowers (*Gilberta Stanley*), Fred Whitman (*Chester Clynch*), Daniel Gilfether.

Commentary: According to the *American Film Institute Catalog* (p. 600), this film was copyrighted as *The Matrimonial Martyr*, but most sources called it *A Matrimonial Martyr*. The movie was hand-colored in the Pathécolor process.

According to *Variety* (July 7, 1916), this was a very silly and inconsequential tale whose only redeeming feature was the magnificent hand-coloring.

Summary: In the story, a young girl decides to elope, but upon meeting her sweetheart, she changes her mind and decides to get a job as a companion to a society woman. Remarkably, the two women (both played by Ruth Roland) could be twins. The society woman leaves the young girl in her home to impersonate her while she heads west to get a divorce. All kinds of slapstick situations result, culminating with the wife getting her divorce and the girl marrying the husband. (Drawn from *Variety*, July 7, 1916.)

Menacing Past. Five-reel Western. Serial. Released in March 1922. Morante Motion Picture Co. *Director:* Tom Gibson. *Scenarios*: J. Inman Kane. *Cast*: Alfred Hewston, Vivian Rich, Frank Coffray, Henry Arris, E. L. MacManigal, Mr. and Mrs. M. L. Barber (*Press*, Feb. 6, 1922).

Commentary: According to the *Press* (Feb. 6, 1922, p. 10), exteriors were taken in the Lake Tahoe districts and in the mountains near California Hot Springs, while the interiors and town scenes were taken in Long Beach. This was the fifth of five films in an eight-part series dealing with the Northwestern mounted police; other titles are not known. The scenarist, J. Inman Kane, was a former Long Beach High School student.

Mentioned in Confidence. Four-reel drama. Balboa Amusement Producing Co., A Fortune Photoplay. Released Mar. 1917 by General Film Co. *Director*: Edgar Jones. *Scenario*: Captain Leslie Peacock. *Source*: Based on the short story "Mentioned in Confidence" by Howard Fielding (pseud. of Charles Whitherle Hooke) in *Popular Magazine* (publication date unknown). *Cast*: Vola Vale (*Marjorie Manning*), R. Henry Grey (*Gordon Leigh*), Frank Brownlee (*Mr. Leigh*), Melvin Mayo (*Robert Manning*), Leah Gibbs (*Perda Brentane*), Bruce Smith (*Father Daly*), Gordon Sackville (*Capitalist*).

Commentary: According to The American Film Institute Catalog, this production was the second release in the Fortune Photoplay series at Balboa (p. 604).

Summary: To still the raging feud between two men, one rich and the other of modest means, a priest recounts in confidence a similar story of two other young people in love, though born from the opposite sides of the tracks — Gordon Leigh, a wealthy son, and Marjorie Manning, the daughter of a poor florist. The children in the priest's story had been boon companions as children until the wealthy father objected to their growing friendship. The two families went their separate ways, and the florist eventually became rich, too. Marjorie, the florist's daughter, was living with her well-to-do father when he decided to marry Perda Brentane. Unfortunately for Marjorie, her step-mother was cruel, so Marjorie left her father's house to work as a nurse at a hospital. By coincidence, Gordon Leigh, her childhood playmate, was working as a doctor at the same hospital. Their rekindled friendship blossomed into passionate love. The mean stepmother, who had once loved Gordon, learned of the future marriage of Gordon and Marjorie. In a jealous rage, Perda shot Gordon and killed herself at the same time. Gordon fell into a coma, while Manning was accused of the assault. Coming out of his coma, Gordon explained that Perda attacked him, not Manning. After hearing the end of the priest's story, the two feuding fathers, moved by the example, allow their children to play together.

Mesh of the Net. Copyright Nov. 10, 1915 (*Encyclopedia of the Movie Studios*, p. 234).

Message of the Mind. Three-reel drama. Balboa Amusement Producing Co. Made for William Fox, released Nov. 10, 1914, by Box Office Attraction Co. (*Moving Picture World*). *Cast*: Lucille Younge (*Rosa Rice*), Jack Bryce (*Dr. Rolla*) (*Press Clippings*, vol. 1, p. 105).

Summary: An unidentified article in the *Press Clippings*, vol. 1, gives the plot:

> Dr. Rolla, an Italian revolutionist misappropriates legacy funds belonging to his wards, Arthur Rice and his sister Rosa. Fearing exposure, Rolla instructs two of his associates to place Arthur in an asylum. When the men attempt to take Arthur away, a struggle takes place, in which Rolla's ward is killed. Rosa is singing in another part of the house, and the shock of the murder causes her to lose her mind. Harry French, a blind young man wanders into the hallway, just as the murderers drag their victim away. Two years later, Harry regains his sight, and falls in love with Rosa when they meet on the street, though neither knows they have met before. Rolla's

companions induce Harry to marry Rosa, and not until after the ceremony does he learn that his wife's mind is weak. One evening Harry plays the tune Rosa sang the night her brother was slain, and it restores her memory. The conspirators are captured as revolutionists in Milan, Italy, and shot by the soldiers. (*Press Clippings*, vol. 1, p. 137)

The Midnight Burglar. Five-reel comedy-drama. Oakdale Productions (probably Balboa Amusement Producing Co.). Released Aug. 26, 1918, by General Film Co. *Director*: Bert Ensminger. *Cast*: Gloria Joy (*Marylee Depue*), Neil Hardin (*John Cromwell Depue*), Ethel Ritchie (*Emily Depue*), Charles Dudley (*Jones*), Mrs. Pepperell (*Mrs. Jones*), Daniel Gilfether (*Dr. Baxter*), Ruth Lackaye, Frank Erlanger (*American Film Institute Catalog*, p. 608).

Commentary: The majority of the personnel involved were associated with the Balboa Amusement Producing Co., but the film is not usually credited as being produced at Long Beach, since its production would have occurred about the very time that the Horkheimers were facing bankruptcy. However, the Horkheimers had boldly announced that Gloria Joy, the "Child Wonder," would appear in a new series, to follow the example of the "Baby Grand," Marie Osborne, who had left Balboa the previous year to make movies at her own studio in Glendale, the Diando Studios. Other features in this Balboa series with Gloria Joy include *Little Miss Grown-Up*, *The Locked Heart*, *Miss Mischief Maker*, *No Children Wanted*, and *Wanted—A Brother*, all of which feature Gloria Joy in the leading role.

Summary: John Cromwell Depue, Marylee's father, is unwilling to spend the money to upgrade the tenements he owns, even though many of his tenants are falling ill from the unsanitary conditions. John's wife, Emily, does charity work for show only, to impress her friends, rather than to assist the poor. On a trip to the tenements with her mother, Marylee witnesses misery for the first time. After the trip to the tenements, Marylee dresses as a beggar and asks money from the guests at her mother's ball. That very night, Marylee goes off to the tenements and visits Jones, whose wife is gravely ill with typhoid. Eager to help the ailing wife, Marylee returns home, where she swipes food to give it to Jones' wife. Marylee returns to the tenements, but Jones takes Marylee back to her home when Marylee falls ill. In the end, Marylee's illness is nothing more than indigestion, and her parents, John and Emily, learn an important lesson from their daughter's example. The Depues decide to lower the rent and to upgrade the tenements.

A Midnight Call. One-reel drama. Pathé Frères. Released Dec. 8, 1913, by General Film Co. (*Press Clippings*, vol. 1, p. 21).

Summary: *Moving Picture World* (Dec. 6, 1913) explains the plot:

Will Harvey and Jack Fielding are roommates at college and in love with the same girl, Katherine. She is in doubt as to which one she prefers. Spending a day at the beach Jack refuses to go in bathing with the others, as he was nearly drowned when a boy and has dreaded the ocean ever since. Katherine while rowing in a boat alone is upset and nearly drowned. Harvey is the man who rushes to her assistance and because he came to the front when Jack held back, Katherine gives her love to him. Jack is considered a coward not only by his roommate and Katherine, but by the college boys as well.

Ten years later Katherine and Harvey are married and have a little daughter. One night when the parents are spending the evening at the theatre, the little girl, who is not feeling well, is left in charge of the maid. The maid deserts the child in order to flirt with a policeman. Later in the night Fielding, who has become a physician and a specialist of note, while going by the house, hears the wailing of a child in apparent agony. He enters the house, finds no one at home, and tracing the source of the cries sees that the child is sick with smallpox. The health officers are telephoned for and the house put under quarantine. Only the frantic mother is permitted to enter the house. Dr. Fielding has had a struggle with himself when he has learned whose child it is, but he buries his personal feelings under the influence of duty. He brings the little girl through her illness, but falls a victim to the disease himself, and pays for his self-sacrifice with his life [*Press Clippings*, vol. 1, p. 21].

Miss Mischief Maker. Five-reel comedy. Oakdale Productions (probably Balboa Amusement Producing Co.). Released Aug. 17, 1918, by General Film Co. Director: Sherwood MacDonald. *Cast*: Gloria Joy (*Sallie O'Brien*), Nell Saalman (*Mrs. O'Brien*), Ruth Lackaye (*Bridget Cassidy*), Edward Jobson (*James Wilson*), Edward Saunders (*Richard Wilson*), Ethel Pepperell (*Marjorie Wilson*), Albert Rockett (*Frederick Mason*), Charles Dudley (*Patrick Cassidy*) (*American Film Institute Catalog*, p. 619).

Commentary: The majority of the personnel involved were associated with the Balboa Amusement Producing Co., but the film is not usually credited as being produced at Long Beach, since its production would have occurred about the very time that the Horkheimers were facing bankruptcy. However, the Horkheimers had boldly announced that Gloria Joy, the "Child Wonder," would appear in a new series, to follow the example of the "Baby Grand," Marie Osborne, who had left Balboa the previous year to make movies at her own studio in Glendale, the Diando Studios. Other features in this Balboa series with Gloria Joy include *Little Miss Grown-Up*, *The Locked Heart*, *The Midnight Burglar*, *No Children Wanted*, and *Wanted — A Brother*, all of which feature Gloria Joy in the leading role.

Summary: Little Sallie O'Brien sells newspapers on the city streets. The landlady, Bridget Cassidy, adopts little Sallie when the girl's mother dies. The landlady does not properly care for the child, treating her cruelly. James Wilson realizes the situation and takes the waif to his big and comfortable home. James Wilson's own children treat Sallie in two different ways. His son, Richard, befriends Sallie, but his daughter, Marjorie, dislikes Sallie. Marjorie is a young woman with a boyfriend. Marjorie proves herself difficult with her boyfriend too. Marjorie has a romantic nature, and she finds her boyfriend lacking in bravery and chivalry. Sallie realizes that Marjorie's beau, Frederick Mason, is in love with Marjorie, when she overhears his proposal to Marjorie. Impish in nature, Sallie plays a prank on Marjorie, by convincing the landlady's son, Patrick, to seduce Marjorie by posing as "the Duke of Galway." Mrs. Cassidy's arrival reveals the ruse. Marjorie ends up accepting Frederick as he is, and Richard intervenes in time to save Sallie from a whipping.

A Mixup in Clothes. Three-reel drama. Balboa Amusement Producing Co. Made for William Fox, released in 1914. *Scenario*: Jackie Saunders. *Cast*: Jackie Saunders in leading role.

Commentary: Not only was Jackie Saunders a successful photoplayer of renown, but she was the author of at least two scenarios that became Balboa feature films *The Rose of the Alley* and *A Mix-Up in Clothes*. In Wiltermood's article in the *Photoplayers' Weekly* (Sept. 5, 1914), Jackie expressed her concern as a screenwriter about the need for quality scenarios if filmmakers expect a successful future. Her comments still apply today.

The Moods of Medora. Copyright Sept. 14, 1916 (*Encyclopedia of the Movie Studios*, p. 238).

Moonshine. Two-reel comedy. Copyright May 6, 1918, Famous Players-Lasky Corp., copyright claimant. Comique Film Corp. Paramount-Arbuckle Comedy No. A–3110. Released May 13, 1918, by Paramount Pictures. *Director/Writer*: Roscoe Arbuckle. *Scene Editor*: Herbert Warren. *Cameraman*: George Peters. *Cast*: Roscoe Arbuckle, Buster Keaton, Al St. John, Charles Dudley, Alice Lake, Joe Bordeau.

Commentary: According to *Frame-up* (p. 296), this production was filmed in the San Gabriel Canyon near Los Angeles and at Balboa Studios. The Balboa Amusement Producing Company ceased operations April 1918, while *Moonshine* was in production, but Roscoe Arbuckle continued to use the studio in Long Beach for his own productions under the name of Comique Film Corporation Studios, Roscoe Arbuckle Comedy Company .

Summary: Jim Kline's *The Complete Films of Buster Keaton* (p. 43) explains that in this movie Buster and Roscoe play revenue agents responsible for tracking down moonshiners in the backwoods of Virginia. Buster and Roscoe arrive in a chauffeur-driven limousine from which a ridiculous number of people exit. Roscoe is captured by the moonshiners and thrown into the cellar of their hideout shack. Expecting squalid conditions, he is stunned to find himself in a luxurious parlor with Alice Lake, the head moonshiner's daughter. Roscoe picks up a nearby copy of *The Count of Monte Cristo* and reads how the hero of the book faked his death. Roscoe smears himself with catsup, fires a gun into the air, and being thought dead, is disposed of in a nearby river.

The Moth and the Flame. Two-reel drama. Pathé Frères. Released Dec. 27, 1913, by General Film Co. Based on the book by Clyde Fitch, published in New York, Apr. 11, 1898. Cast: Henry King (*Oswald*), Jeanie MacPherson (*Nellie*), Bud Harris (*Bud*), William Wolbert (*Arthur Conway*), Seymour Hastings, Dick Le Strange (*Press Clippings*, vol. 1).

Commentary: This film should not be confused with the Famous Players four-reel feature of the same title made in May 1915.

Summary: The story was about Oswald, a young farmer who becomes suspicious of the growing intimacy between his wife, Nellie, and Arthur Conway, a city visitor in the neighborhood. By playing upon Nellie's vanity, Conway persuades her that her voice and personality would make a hit upon the stage and convinces her to run away with him. Oswald returns home one night to find that he and his little son have been deserted.

Nellie goes to the city and hopes to find in wine, fine dresses, and song an antidote to the longing for her little son, but in vain. She is haunted by the vision of her deserted family and, stung by repentance, returns home. Little Bud in the meantime has run away from home to find his mother and becomes lost in the woods. He is later found unconscious by his anxious father and contracts pneumonia. The mother returns in time to find the child convalescent and is forgiven through Bud's intercession.

Review: According to the *Daily Telegram* (Jan. 24, 1914, 9:3), this film set a high-water mark in acting and production that would be hard for other companies to equal.

Mush. One-reel comedy. Joy. Made for William Fox, released by Box Office Attraction Co. (*Moving Picture World*).

Neal of the Navy. Serial. Based on a story by William Hamilton Osborne. Released Dec. 30, 1915, by Pathé Frères. Director: Harry Harvey. Cast: Edwin Brady, William Conklin, William Courtleigh, Lillian Lorraine, Henry Stanley.

The 14 Chapters: *The Survivors, The Yellow Packet, The Failure, The Tattered Parchment, A Message From the Past, The Cavern of Death, The Gun Runners, The Yellow Peril, The Sun Worshippers, The Rolling Terror, The Dreadful Pit, The Worm Turns, White Gods,* and *The Final Goal.* Chapter 1 was copyrighted Oct. 25, 1915, and Chapter 14 was copyrighted Dec. 30, 1915 (*Filmarama*, vol. 1).

Commentary: According to the *Daily Telegram* (Sept. 7, 1915, p. 12:1), this was a patriotic photoplay serial. Parts of it were filmed while the crew was in San Diego for the Panama-California Exposition. There were 2,500 marines stationed at San Diego, and the battleships in the harbor were used for the backdrop.

According to Marc Wanamaker, author and film historian, Harry Harvey was offered a bonus of $500 if he could make the serial in 12 weeks. He completed eight episodes in six weeks and finished the rest before the deadline. The rapidity of production showed, and Pathé barely accepted the hastily made episodes because of their poor quality.

Summary: *Variety* reported that Lillian Lorraine portrayed an 18-year-old orphan named Annette and William Courtleigh portrayed a former Annapolis cadet who is thrown out of the naval academy for cheating on an exam. Of course, Neal, the cadet, was framed, but he must enlist in the navy as a regular sailor. Annette has a map to Lost Island, where treasure is buried. Everyone wants to find it, and everyone is after Annette.

Poster for exhibitors.

Review: Variety (Sept. 10–Oct. 29, 1915) didn't think much of the series and reported that the audience applauded only when the American flag was portrayed.

The Neglected Wife. Serial. Copyright Dec. 18, 1916. Released by Pathé Frères. Based on Mabel Herbert Urner's famous novels: *The Journal of a Neglected Wife* and *The Woman Alone*. *Cast*: Ruth Roland, Roland Bottomley, Neil Hardin, Corrine Grant, Philo McCullough.

The 15 Chapters: *The Woman Alone, The Weakening, In the Crucible, Beyond Recall, Under Suspicion, On the Precipice, The Message on the Mirror, A Relentless Fate, Deepening Degradation, A Veiled Intrigue, A Reckless Indiscretion, Embittered Love, Revolting Pride, Desperation,* and *A Sacrifice Supreme.* Chapter 1 was copyrighted Dec. 18, 1916, and Chapter 15 was copyrighted Apr. 25, 1917 (*Filmarama*, vol. 1).

Commentary: According to the *Daily Telegram* (June 15, 1917, p. 12:5), this was a thrilling story dealing with the complex problems of married life. There were several scenes in each chapter taken in and around Long Beach. According to Tony Scott ("Southern Exposure," p. 120), Balboa Studios built a new $50,000 stage to house this serial.

Nerve. One reel. Balboa Amusement Producing Co. Made for William Fox, released by Box Office Attraction Co. *Cast*: Henry King (*Julius Booth, a miner*), Charles Dudley (*Frank Croxton, a prosperous promoter*), William Wolbert (*James, his butler*), Jeanie McPherson (*Mrs. Croxton, his wife*) (*Daily Telegram*, Nov. 14, 1914, 9: 6).

Commentary: This feature was written by H. M. Horkheimer, president of Balboa Studio. This movie depicted life in a mining town and was applauded for its accurate portrayal. It was also one of the films that showed how ore was extracted from the ground (*Press Clippings*, vol. 1, p. 117).

Summary: The *Kinematograph and Lantern Weekly* (July 16, 1914) recounts the plot:

Croxton has swindled Booth in the sale of a worthless mine. Booth comes to the city, calls on Croxton and demands reparation. Croxton will not listen to him and has him thrown out of the office. Booth, who is in desperate straits, determines to take the law into his own hands by breaking into Croxton's household and obtaining the money that Croxton had swindled him out of. Mrs. Croxton is at home alone except for the butler. She hears Booth moving about in the dining room, and comes in upon him unexpectedly. He tells her he is not a burglar, and pretending to believe him she asks him to sit at the table and tell her the story. He does so, but keeps her covered with his gun, as he is suspicious of her motives. With her foot she presses a button in the floor and summons the butler. Just before he arrives she seizes Booth's gun, which he had laid on the table for a moment while lighting a cigarette. Covering him, she commands him to remain where he is, and orders the butler to call the police. When the butler is gone Booth rises and moves towards the door, telling Mrs. Croxton that it takes nerve to kill a man daring her to shoot him. She has not the courage to do it and Booth goes out to the hall, only to be met by the police. Overcome with pity and with admiration for his courage, Mrs. Croxton tells the police that it is all a mistake; that Booth had merely called to see her husband, and before he goes she gives him the money that her husband had wrongfully taken from him [*Press Clippings*, vol. 1, p. 117].

Review: The same British article gives a favorable critique of the movie:

The succinct title of *Nerve* is a particularly well-chosen one. On the one hand we have the girl boldly facing the midnight intruder and later holding him at bay at the point of the revolver, and on the other the man contemptuously daring her to shoot — "it takes nerve to kill a man."

As a single reel this film possesses many of the virtues and few of the vices of the long exclusive. The action is quick without being clipped too short, and although it is evident that care has been taken to prevent unnecessary length in any scene, nothing relative to the theme has been eliminated.

Newsreel.

Commentary: The *Daily Telegram* (Feb. 29, 1916, 5:5) described the film:

Air race between aviators Earl Daugherty and H. P. Christofferson was filmed by Balboa and sold to the *Pathé Weekly* news pictures. The pictures are featured with a close call which the camera man, Roland Groom, had when the Christofferson machine came within a foot of striking the camera squarely as the plane left the ground. The craft was driving a beeline for the camera man, who was posted some distance away in an automobile, and managed to rise over the camera just soon enough to miss the photographer. Groom, displaying the wonderful self-control which the camera man wins in his work for the screen, steadily cranked the machine at the usual rate of speed, and caught the big bi-plane as it came rushing toward the auto. So close did the aeroplane come to hitting the camera that it becomes a big blur as it nears the camera. The pictures when developed showed perfect, and are expected to create a sensation when shown on the screen for the picture news service.

Nine-Tenths of the Law.
Six-reel northwest drama. North Woods Producing Co., Balboa Amusement Producing Co. Released May 1918, by State Rights; Atlantic Distributing Corp. *Director*: Reaves Eason. *Story*: Reaves Eason. *Cast*: Mitchell Lewis (*Jules Leneau*), Jimsy Maye (*Jane Leneau*), Reaves Eason ("*Red*" *Adair*), Breezy Reeves ("*Little Roughneck*"), Julius Frankenburg (*Pappineau*), Molly Shafer (*nurse*).

Commentary: The *American Film Institute Catalog* (p. 660) explains that the working title of this production was *The Little Roughneck*. Reaves was making the movie for the Balboa Amusement Producing Co. at the time it sold its interests to creditors in Apr. 1918. Breezy Reeves was Reaves Eason's son.

Summary: The son of a wealthy Vancouver judge is kidnapped by ruffians "Red" Adair and Pappineau. While the kidnappers are partying in their hideout, the boy makes his escape. In the woods, Jules Leneau finds the boy, who has fallen into a bear trap near

Leneau's cabin. Jules carries the boy home to his wife, Jane, who is still grieving over the loss of their only child. Red comes looking for the kidnapped child, claiming him and calling him "Little Roughneck." Jules fights Red to protect the boy, and Red dies in the struggle. Afterwards, Jules learns that the boy was kidnapped, and despite protests from his wife, he returns the boy to the judge. In doing the right thing, Jules is surprised by his reward. The judge explains that the boy was actually the child of a deceased housekeeper. Deeply touched by the bond between Jules and the boy, the judge allows Jules to claim the boy as his own adopted son. (Drawn from the *American Film Institute Catalog*, p. 660.)

No Children Wanted. Five-reel comedy. Oakdale Productions (probably Balboa Amusement Producing Co. Released Aug. 1918 by General Film Co. *Director*: Sherwood MacDonald. *Scenario*: Will M. Ritchey. *Cameraman*: Georges Rizard. *Cast*: Gloria Joy (*Dot Jarvis*), Ethel Richie (*Sylvia Jarvis*), R. Henry Grey (*Oscar Jarvis*), Edward Jobson (*Robert Chase*), Neil Hardin (*John Porter*), Daniel Gilfether (*old farmer*), Mrs. Kahler (*Mrs. Reed*), H. E. Archer (*Rankin*), Ruth Lackaye (*Mrs. Clymer*), Edward Saunders. (*American Film Institute Catalog*, p. 661.)

Commentary: According to *Henry King, Director*, the Aug. 10 1918 issue of *Moving Picture News* credits Henry King as director.

The majority of the personnel involved were associated with the Balboa Amusement Producing Co., but the film is not usually credited as being produced at Long Beach, since its production would have occurred about the very time that the Horkheimers were facing bankruptcy. However, the Horkheimers had boldly announced that Gloria Joy, the "Child Wonder," would appear in a new series, to follow the example of the "Baby Grand," Marie Osborne, who had left Balboa the previous year to make movies at her own studio in Glendale, the Diando Studios. Other features in this Balboa series with Gloria Joy include *Little Miss Grown-Up*, *The Locked Heart*, *The Midnight Burglar*, *Miss Mischief Maker*, and *Wanted — A Brother*, all of which feature Gloria Joy in the leading role.

Summary: A little girl, Dot Jarvis, lacks the love and attention of her ambitious parents who seem more interested in getting rich than in raising their own child. To be able to move into an apartment that bans children, Mr. and Mrs. Jarvis coldly decide to send Dot Jarvis to a boarding school. However, the little girl is so miserable at the school that she runs away. During her escape, Dot befriends a farmer who takes the girl to the police, and the police reunite the lost child with her parents. Pursuing a risky deal, Dot's ambitious father tries to profit from a revolution brewing in Mexico, by smuggling arms across the border. At the same time, the owner of a newspaper, Robert Chase, takes pity on the troubled family after seeing a photo of Dot and understanding her plight. Robert Chase does not reveal the smuggling operation, and, consequently, the family crisis makes Dot's parents "see the light," as they feel true remorse for neglecting their own daughter's needs. In a happy reunion, little Dot begins finally to enjoy tender loving care from her parents.

Nobody Loves a Fat Man. One-reel comedy. Joy. Made for William Fox, released by Box Office Attraction Co. (*Moving Picture World*).

Oath of Hate. Knickerbocker Star Feature. Released in 1916. *Cast*: Henry King, Marguerite Nichols, Ethel Fleming, Lewis J. Cody (*Henry King, Director*, p. 196).

Oh, You Circus Day. One-reel comedy. Joy. Made for William Fox, released by Box Office Attraction Co. (*Moving Picture World*).

The Old Monk's Tale. Edison Manufacturing Company. Based on Helen Hunt Jackson's 1884 romance *Ramona*. *Scenario*: J. Searle Dawley. *Cameraman*: J. Searle Dawley. *Cast*: Laura Sawyer (*Ramona*), James Gordon (*Allesandro*) ("Long Beach Motion Picture Industry: 1911–1923," p. 9).

On Matrimonial Seas. Comedy. California Motion Picture Manufacturing Co. Released

May 13, 1911, premiering at the Pike in Long Beach. *Cast*: Hampton Del Ruth (*Mr. Miss-Wed*), Mrs. Blakeney (*Mrs. Miss-Wed*), Roy Patchin, Miss Elora, Miss Sanchez, Miss McLean.

Commentary: This was to be the first movie shown in the new theatre built on the Pike for the California Motion Picture Manufacturing Co. It was filmed on Ocean Boulevard, the Pike, and the beach. *The Daily Telegram* (Apr. 27, 1911) stated in an article titled "Good Films Are Taken" that there had been a big crowd of spectators and "followers" on location and that many Long Beach people would see themselves in the movie. President Howland of the company encouraged the public to be at the beach scenes while the principal actors were bathing. Interestingly enough, Hampton Del Ruth, who starred in this early film, would return in the 1920s to start his own film company at the former Balboa site.

Summary: We do not have a complete description of the plot; however, the story depicts the troubles of Mr. and Mrs. Miss-Wed during an outing at the beach. Some of the scenes show their stepping down from the Pacific Electric car on Ocean Boulevard, with Mrs. Miss-Wed carrying all the parcels, their trip on the steam carousel, and their arrival on the beach, where they sit down beneath one of dozens of brightly colored beach umbrellas. Mr. Miss-Wed goes to sleep, and his wife starts off in search of other amusement. Another woman arrives on scene, joins the husband, waking him from his slumber, and they start off together, buying some candy at a Pike store. No other articles have been found explaining the rest of the plot. (Drawn from the *Daily Telegram*, Apr. 27, 1911.)

Once Upon a Time. Balboa Amusement Producing Co. Released in 1916 by Pathé Frères. Cast: Baby Marie Osborne, Henry King (*Henry King, Director*, p. 196).

The One-Eyed God see **Spellbound**

Out West. Two-reel comedy. Copyright Feb. 20, 1918; Famous Players–Lasky Corp., copyright claimant. Comique Film Corp. Paramount-Arbuckle Comedy No. A–3108. Released Jan. 20, 1918, by Paramount Pictures. *Director/Writer*: Roscoe Arbuckle. *Scene Editor*: Herbert Warren. *Scenario*: Natalie Talmadge. *Cameraman*: George Peters. *Cast*: Roscoe Arbuckle, Buster Keaton, Al St. John, Alice Lake.

Commentary: According to the *Daily Telegram* (Jan. 25, 1918), this film was staged largely at Signal Hill, where a typical Western town, "Mad Dog Gulch," was built up for the purpose. According to *Frame-up* (p. 296), this production was filmed in the San Gabriel Canyon, not Signal Hill.

Al St. John was the bad man in this picture and "Fatty" was a champion bartender from Kansas. One of the scenes has Roscoe riding into a thirst-quenching emporium on a horse. The steed itself imbibes freely of the alcoholic beverage and exhibits advanced stages of intoxication. The opening scenes of the picture were made in the desert, Fatty having been thrown off a train in the midst of a vast sandy plain (*Daily Telegram*, Jan. 23, 1918, 9:2).

Summary: The film opens in an old Western saloon. Dressed in a long black coat and stovepipe hat, Buster plays a dude gambler who casually shoots a cheating cardsharp and then rolls the body through a trapdoor in the saloon floor. The scene then shifts to Roscoe riding in the water car of a speeding train. After several high jinks on the train, Roscoe ends up stranded in the desert, where he is chased by hostile Indians. With the Indians pursuing him, Roscoe makes a spectacular entrance into town and rolls into the saloon in time to interrupt a robbery by the ruthless Wild Bill Hiccup (Al St. John). During the melee, the bartender is killed.

After Buster disposes of the body, Roscoe becomes the new bartender. Wild Bill gets fresh with Salvation Army representative Alice Lake when she asks him for a donation; Roscoe tries to subdue him by various means, succeeding at last in tickling him into submission with a feather. (Drawn from *The Complete Films of Buster Keaton*, p. 41.)

Path of Sorrow. Three-reel drama. Warner's Features, Inc. *Director*: Bertram Bracken. *Scenario*: Olga Prinzlau Clark. *Cast*: Henry

Stanley (*Philip Norton*), Fred Whitman (*Richard Harding*), Gypsy Abbott, Eugenie Forde, Victoria Ford.

Commentary: Written by Long Beach author Olga Prinzlau Clark, with the majority of scenes taken in and around Long Beach (*Daily Telegram*, Dec. 8, 1913, 7:6).

Summary: Philip Norton's life is saddened by the homecoming of his daughter Laura, a vain widow who thinks more of dress and appearance than she does of her ten-year-old son Frank. Philip's anguish is quite apparent as he observes his daughter openly making love to Richard Harding, his trusted secretary. Fortunately for the banker's peace of mind, Harding receives Laura coldly and expresses his preference for Helen, a poor seamstress. Laura finds a notebook that Harding has dropped and learns from it that he and Helen have secretly married. Taking the butler into her confidence, Laura outlines a plan for revenge that will put Harding behind prison bars.

A few mornings later Norton discovers his private safe open and the contents scattered about. Suspicion points to Harding, and when a pencil inscribed with his initials is found in the room, his doom is sealed.

A few months later Helen dies as her baby daughter comes into the world. Fifteen years later a dramatic meeting occurs between Laura and the butler who was her accomplice in the safe robbery. The shock kills Laura, who leaves a confession absolving Harding of the crime.

In the meantime, Harding's daughter has grown up as a pickpocket — the tool of some clever crooks.

The closing scenes of *The Path of Sorrow* picture the reunion of father and daughter, her welcome into the home of Laura's son, the butler's attempt to blow up the banker's home and for a climax the butler's confession that clears Harding's name. (Drawn from *Press Clippings*, vol. 1, p. 102.)

Pawnee Bill. Serial. Released in 1922. Starke-Staller. *Cast*: Pauline Starke (*Daily Telegram*, May 24, 1922, p. 19).

Commentary: According to the *Daily Telegram*, this was one of a series of 8 seven-reel pictures starring Pauline Starke.

Pay Dirt. Five-reel drama. Knickerbocker Star Features. *Distributor*: General Film Co., released June 18, 1916. *Supervisors*: H. M. Horkheimer and E. D. Horkheimer. *Director*: Henry King. *Assistant Director*: Reaves Eason. *Cast*: Henry King (*the Easterner*), Marguerite Nichols (*Kate Gardner*), Gordon Sackville (*Peter Gardner*), Mollie McConnell (*Moll*), Daniel Gilfether (*Dick Weed*), Charles Dudley (*Oby*), Philo McCullough (*Turner*), Ruth White (*Doris Wendell*), Bruce Smith (*her father*).

Commentary: The *American Film Institute Catalog* (p. 704) states that some sources credit H. M. and E. D. Horkheimer as the film's directors.

Summary: After mining all day, the Easterner gambles away his whole day's findings. Addicted herself to gambling, Moll, an old lady, urges the Easterner to end this bad habit, and he pledges to stop gambling. After successfully breaking his habit, he becomes engaged to Doris Wendell, a wealthy young woman. Kate, the daughter of Peter Gardner, loves the Easterner, but her father tries to force him out of the picture by urging the Easterner to gamble away his mining claim. The Easterner stands his ground and refuses to gamble, as he has promised himself and Moll. Later, the Easterner discovers that Moll is in reality his long-lost mother. Shocked by this discovery, Doris is not happy knowing that she will have Moll as a mother-in-law. While playing cards, Peter persuades the Easterner to stake his claim in a card game. Suddenly, after a long spell of amnesia, a man named Oby places Peter's face as that of the man who robbed him years ago. Oby draws his gun and mortally wounds Peter. Before he breathes his last, Peter confesses that Oby is Kate's father. Kate now has no reason to put on arrogant airs. With greater humility and love in their hearts, Kate and the Easterner agree to make wedding plans. (Drawn from the *American Film Institute Catalog*, p. 704.)

Pearls of Temptation. Four-reel drama. Copyright Oct. 9, 1915, Pathé Frères, LU6589. Balboa Feature Film Co. Released Oct. 11, 1915, by Pathé Exchange, Inc. *Cast*: Jackie Saunders (*Martha*).

Commentary: The American Film Institute states that this movie was also known under the title *The Perils of Temptation* and that the copyright entry incorrectly uses this latter title.

Summary: A thieving employee tries to steal some expensive earrings purchased by Mrs. Pierce. Mrs. Pierce happens to be the mother of store manager Sam Pierce, and the theft is prevented by Martha, an upright and trustworthy store clerk. In reward for her loyalty, Martha is chosen to be Mrs. Pierce's personal secretary and is invited to live at the Pierce residence. The brother of the store manager, Frank Pierce, is a thief himself and steals his mother's pearl necklace at home for his mistress, Coral. Taking advantage of Martha's presence in the house, Frank accuses Martha of the theft. However, the pearl necklace keeps making the rounds. Mrs. Pierce's husband, another dishonest family member, had pocketed the original necklace to rid himself of debts, replacing it with the false one stolen by Frank. Coral recognizes that the necklace is fake and insults Frank in front of Hamilton Cress, a conniving playwright. Cress removes Frank from Coral's flat. Looking for work, Martha seeks a secretarial post at the playwright's office. Violence and confessions mix at this point, with Frank admitting after being wounded in gunfire that he had stolen the pearl necklace. Sam, the store manager, comes to Martha's rescue in time to block Cress's advances. After being cleared of all false charges, Martha is now free to follow her heart and make wedding plans with one of the few honest and hardworking members of the Pierce family — Sam, the store manager. (Drawn from the *American Film Institute Catalog*, p. 706.)

Petticoats and Politics. Five-reel comedy-drama, Western. Plaza Pictures (probably started for Balboa Amusement Producing Co.). Released Aug. 26, 1918, by W. W. Hodkinson Corp. through General Film Co. *Director*: Howard M. Mitchell. *Scenario*: L. V. Jefferson. *Cast*: Anita King (*Ann Murdock*), R. Henry Grey (*Leonard Blair*), Gordon Sackville (*Keno Bill Maguire*), Charles Dudley (*Sheriff Joe Roberts*), Ruth Lackaye (*Mrs. Lou Winters*) (*The American Film Institute Catalog*, p. 713).

Commentary: According to the *American Film Institute Catalog*, this production is not credited to Balboa Studios; however, the release date would explain why the producer would be other than Balboa, since Balboa had gone into receivership while the production was still under way. In addition, the director, the cameraman, and the majority of the actors were Balboans. See also *Angel Child*, *The Law That Divides*, and *Whatever the Cost*, all of which seem to fall into the same category.

Summary: Ann Murdock tries to encourage women to run for office, to remove "the good-old-boy" politicians in Red Dog, Nevada, a corrupt mining town. Since the women do not have the right to vote, they persuade their husbands to vote for them to replace the incumbents. The grass-roots movement turns out to be a smashing success, with all the political seats taken over by women. With the women in power, the husbands must stay at home to manage the household and the children. The former town boss revolts against the new order by having the newly elected politicians jailed. The jailed women find a sympathizer in Leonard Blair, but he is framed for a robbery and jailed too. Ann rescues Leonard (whom she loves) and releases the women, who go back to the job of running the town.

The Phantom Shotgun. Four-reel mystery. Copyright Sept. 7, 1917, General Film Co., Inc., LP11358. Falcon Features. Released Sept. 1917, by General Film Co. *Supervisors*: H. M. Horkheimer and E. D. Horkheimer. *Director*: Harry Harvey. *Scenario*: Frances E. Guihan. *Story*: Stanley Clisby Arthur. *Cast*: Henry Grey (*Van Buren Courtland*), Kathleen Kirkham (*Elizabeth Kennedy*), Barney Furey (*Frank Marshall*), Frank Brownlee (*Hamilton Forbes*), Gloria Payton (*Betty Marshall*), T. H. Gibson Gowland (*Patton*), William Marshall (*Larkins*),

Bruce Smith (*Harding*), Capt. J. E. Nicholson (*Capt. Lloyd*).

Commentary: According to the *American Film Institute Catalog* (p. 715), some sources refer to this film as *The Phantom Shot Gun.*

Summary: Hamilton Forbes and Van Buren Courtland have become jealous partners. Forbes is steaming over the love expressed by his secretary for his business partner. To remove Courtland from the picture, Hamilton frames his business partner for forgery. During the trial, the key witness against Courtland changes his testimony, and Courtland is released from prison. While Courtland is out of town trying to clear his name, Forbes tells Elizabeth, his secretary, that Courtland has died. Elizabeth then accepts Forbes' proposal for marriage. Learning of the wedding, Courtland boards the same boat as the honeymooners. On Courtland's heels follows the reporter Larkins. On board, Forbes is attacked and killed with a shotgun. Of course, the prime suspect is Courtland. A second murder on board follows immediately. This time Patton, a deck steward, is the murder victim. Interestingly enough, Patton had a motive to kill Forbes, having been sent to prison on account of Forbes' false testimony. But if Patton shot Forbes, who shot Patton? After Patton's murder, there is another attempt to kill Courtland. To add more spice to this boiling plot, a mutiny flares up during which the shotgun used in the deaths is now used to save the captain's life. The reporter, Larkins, is hurt during the mutiny, but he is also the one to uncover the murder weapon in Frank Marshall's room. The culprit, Marshall, had killed Forbes in an act of revenge because Forbes had once seduced and dumped Marshall's sister. Marshall also killed Patton because he saw Marshall shoot Forbes. With the complicated murder case settled, Courtland and Elizabeth begin to hear wedding bells. (Drawn from the *American Film Institute Catalog*, pp. 714–15.)

A Piece of Steak. Two-reel drama. Balboa Amusement Producing Co. *Scenario:* Wallace Clifton and C. A. Manges. Based on the novel *When God Laughs* by Jack London.

Commentary: Moving Picture World (Dec. 20, 1913) announced that several Jack London stories were being prepared at Balboa, including *A Piece of Steak*, based on London's *When God Laughs* and *The Sea Wolf* and *To Kill a Man*, based on London's *The Night Born*. The announcement also stated that the following works by London were being prepared as movies at Balboa: *Martin Eden, John Barleycorn, The Call of the Wild, Smoke Bellew Series,* and *The Valley of the Moon* (*Press Clippings*, vol. 1, p. 31).

The Policewoman. Biographical drama of undetermined length. Balboa Amusement Producing Co. Release date undetermined. *Scenario*: F. M. Wiltermood. *Cast*: Alice Stebbins Wells (*herself*) (*American Film Institute Catalog*, p. 723).

Commentary: The Daily Telegram (Oct. 10, 1914, 3:3) reported:

> Mrs. Alice Stebbins Wells, the first regular policewoman in the world, a member of the Los Angeles police department for four years, is preparing to enact the leading part in a four-reel moving picture to be staged in Long Beach. Mrs. Wells, who is still a member of the Los Angeles department, believes the film will have great educational value throughout the world, in showing the erring youth.

The Port of Doom. Four-reel detective drama. Famous Players Film Co. Released, Oct. 20, 1913, by State Rights. *Director*: J. Searle Dawley. *Scenario*: J. Searle Dawley. *Cast*: Laura Sawyer (*Kate Kirby*), House Peters (*Kate's father*), Dave Wall (*Fuller*), Peter Lang (*Fornton*), Hattie Forsythe (*Vera Fornton*), Hal Clarendon (*Captain Giles*), Henrietta Goodman *(Fuller's wife)*.

Commentary: According to the *American Film Institute Catalog* (p. 727), this movie was also said to be three reels long, with H. Lyman Broening doing the cinematography. This movie was the third in the "Kate Kirby" series by Famous Players.

Summary: The *American Film Institute Catalog* (p. 727) explains the plot:

Although his daughter Vera loves Giles, the new captain of the *Morning Star*, shipowner Fornton orders her to marry his secretary Fuller. Learning that the *Morning Star* is unseaworthy, Fuller nonetheless sends it to sea, but the next day, Fornton calls detective Kate Kirby reporting that Vera has disappeared. Kate soon learns that Fuller, a drug addict, already has a wife and child, and later she convinces him to confess the truth about the *Morning Star* in exchange for some cocaine. When Kate then refuses him the drug, he attacks her, but her father appears to save her life. Kate boards a small ship and overtakes the doomed vessel, but the next day, it begins to sink during a storm. All are rescued by a passing ship, after which Vera and Giles are reunited with Fornton.

The Power of Evil. Five-reel drama. Balboa Amusement Producing Co. Made for B. S. Moss Motion Picture Corp. Released Oct. 1, 1916, by B. S. Moss Motion Picture Corp. *Directors*: H. M. Horkheimer and E. D. Horkheimer. *Scenario*: George Bronson Howard. *Cast*: Henry King (*Stuart Merwin*), Marguerite Nichols (*Laurine Manners*), Lillian West (*Jeano*), Frank Erlanger (*a valet*), Victory Bateman, Edward Peters, Gordon Sackville, Philo McCullough.

Commentary: According to the *American Film Institute Catalog* (p. 728) the Oct. 7, 1916, issue of *Moving Picture World* (p. 134) lists *The Power of Evil* at six reels. The B. S. Moss Motion Picture Corp. may have financed the production of this film.

Summary: The *American Film Institute Catalog* (p. 728) explains the plot as follows:

> Millionaire playboy Stuart Merwin reforms immediately after marriage, but his wife Laurine has no interest in a sedate life style and so leaves him for weeks at a time while she sees other men. While Laurine is away on a binge, Stuart hits Jeano with his car, and brings her back to his home to recuperate. Laurine returns, and seeing Stuart and Jeano together, she suspects the worst, and insists on a divorce. Heartbroken, Stuart reverts to his old habits, but Jeano, now healthy, convinces him to reform once again. Then, inspired by Jeano, Stuart becomes a preacher in the Salvation Army and donates all of his money to that organization, after which he and Jeano start preparing for their marriage.

Review: *Variety* (Sept. 29, 1916, p. 25) wrote that the picture showed good photography, lacked lurid sensationalism, and furnished "capital entertainment."

The Power of Print. Two-reel drama. Pathé Frères. Released Jan. 29, 1914, by General Film Co. (*Moving Picture World*). *Cast*: Charles Dudley (*J. C. Whitney*), Henry King (*Robert Whitney*), Dave Porter (*Harold Farnell*), Madeline Pardee (*Jessie, his daughter*), William Wolbert (*Cartwright*) (*Press Clippings*, vol. 1, p. 40).

Summary: The *New York Mirror* (Feb. 11, 1914) sketches the plot:

> The daughter of the political boss is wooed by the owner of the paper, the *Times*, supporting the boss. The son of the owner of the opposition paper comes home, and gets a position on the *Times*, his identity unknown to anybody in the town. He makes a record for himself, and is appointed the city editor on the opposition paper to the *Times*. So that when the owner of the *Times* tries to press his suit with the daughter of the boss, he is repulsed by the young fellow, who loves the girl and promises the boss the support of his paper in the coming election [*Press Clippings*, vol. 1, p. 40].

Review: The *New York Mirror* (p. 40) also presents a flattering critique in the same article, stating that the film had

> a forceful plot on a subject pregnant with interest. There is a slow and gradually forward movement of plot that is greatly to the credit of the play. It follows an even tenor, all the more remarkable when the divergence of interest is considered. It is an unwieldy subject at best, handled in a very able manner by the scenario writer. The intriguing between the two white-haired men is not brought out on the screen with such great clarity as might be desired. The characterization in the play is another likable feature, although the somewhat similar appearance of these two newspaper proprietors led to some of the confusion.

The acting by the above cast was fully up to the highest standard. The photography and the tinting also helped to make the film please. The end comes rather suddenly, and leaves one with a gasp that the story should be so easily finished.

A Prize in Every Package. One-reel comedy. Joy. Made for William Fox, released by Box Office Attraction Co. (*Moving Picture World*).

Professor Bugs. One-reel comedy. Joy. Made for William Fox, released by Box Office Attraction Co. (*Moving Picture World*).

Professor Oldboy's Rejuvenator. One-reel comedy. Kalem Co. Released Apr. 1, 1914, by General Film Co. *Cast*: Henry Stanley (*the professor*), Eugenie Ford (*the daughter*), Fred Whitman (*the daughter's lover*) (*Press Clippings*, vol. 1, p. 60).

Summary: The *New York Mirror* (Mar. 25, 1914) presents the plot:

> The professor has invented a machine that rejuvenates. A bulldog is changed to a puppy. An old man becomes young again before the very eyes of the audience. Then the father places himself upon the chair, and instructs his daughter to leave the current on not longer than five minutes. She forgets all about him on the chair, as she talks with her lover. The professor becomes a middle-aged man, then a young man, and lastly, a baby. The daughter comes in, and promptly takes her father in her arms, and feeds him from a bottle. After sufficient fun from this unusual situation, the daughter reverses the current and restores her father to his normal self [*Press Clippings*, vol. 1, p. 60.

Review: According to the same article in the *New York Mirror*, "this is a short comedy offering a scientific-farcical aspect that has its dramatic moments as well. It is a funny subject, well presented, and clearly staged."

The Race for a Mine. One-reel drama. Kalem Co. Released Feb. 25, 1914, by General Film Co. *Cast*: Harry Hoffman, Clifford Lee, Roy Howard, Elinor Raye.

Summary: The *Moving Picture World* (Mar. 7, 1914) presents this plot:

> The Sunset Mining Company is in sore straits, when Porter and Morton, the heads of the concern, receive a letter written by "M. B. Parker," of Hynes' Station, offering them an option on a promising borax mine. Baxter, a real estate sharp, enters the office while the partners are in the next room. The man learns of the Parker offer and resolves to take it up himself. He dashes for the railroad station. The stenographer, however, has seen Baxter read the letter. She imparts her discovery to her employers. Fearing lest Baxter will snap up the option, Morton hastens to the station. He arrives a minute too late. Undaunted, he hires a racing automobile and races away for Hynes' Station ahead of Morton [Baxter]. Hiring a rig, the man drives toward the Morton [Parker] home. Morton is compelled to stop for gasoline, and is held up for ten minutes.
>
> A Mexican holds up Margaret. After felling the girl, he robs her. Margaret recovers consciousness just as Baxter approaches. Fearing lest his rival catch up with him, the scoundrel leaves the girl lying on the road. Morton drives up a few minutes later and learns of the robbery. He goes in pursuit of the thief and surprises him in the act of examining the proceeds of the holdup. A desperate battle ensues. Morton throws the bandit from a cliff, injuring him mortally. Returning to Margaret the boy restores the valuables the Mexican had stolen. Margaret then learns that the delay has probably cost Morton a chance for a fortune. Morton tells her of Baxter's villainy. With a mysterious smile, Margaret requests him to drive her to the Parker home. The two find Baxter trying to enter the home. Margaret leaps from the machine. Taking a key from her pocket, she opens the door of the house, after which she announces that she is "M. B. Parker." Baffled, Baxter slinks away. A few minutes later Morton has the coveted option in his possession [*Press Clippings*, vol. 1, p. 57].

Review: The *New York Mirror* (Mar. 4, 1914) announced: "Well pictured especially as concerns the clear photography, the picture unreels with a great deal of suspense until the unexpected end" (*Press Clippings*, vol. 1, 57).

A Rash Revenge. One-reel comedy. Pathé Frères, released by General Film Co. (*Moving Picture World*).

Review: The *Daily Telegram* (Dec. 10, 1913, 1:7) describes this movie in the following way: "A comedy of extra fine order, containing as it does scenes familiar to every resident of the City."

The Rat. Two-reel drama. Balboa Amusement Producing Co. Made for William Fox, released by Box Office Attraction Co. *Cast:* Henry King (*The Rat, a gang leader*), Henry Otto (*Mr. Barker, the millionaire*), Belle Bennett (*Marian Barker, the daughter*), Robert Grey (*Handsome Bob, the opposing gang leader*), Charles Dudley (*Joe, a thug*).

Commentary: *Variety* (Aug. 19, 1914) remarked that when Balboa first entered the feature picture game, it turned out very long and exceedingly tiresome many-part pictures. Now, with an increasing demand for shorter features, they were hitting the mark.

Summary: This 2,200 foot film deals with Marian Barker, a slumworker who runs into a street brawl; she steps into the fight and breaks it up. One of the brawlers, the Rat, is injured, and she cares for him. In exchange, he gives her a whistle to blow three times if she is ever in any danger in the neighborhood. When Joe, a thug, kidnaps her, she remembers the whistle, and the Rat and his gang come to her rescue.

Review: *Variety* (Aug. 19, 1914) commented that Miss Bennett looked nice on screen but did very little "real" acting, while several of the other female players in the cast worked harder and carried the film.

Red Bulldogs. Seven reels. Released in 1922. *Scenario:* Willard Mack. *Cast:* Willard Mack, Sylvia Breamer.

Commentary: According to the *Daily Telegram* (Oct. 15, 1922, C6), this movie dealt with the Northwest mounted police. Mack starred and Sylvia Breamer was the leading lady. Mrs. Mack, formerly Beatrice Baynard, was also a member of the company, as were several other stage associates, including Charles Marshall, Clark Merrell, and George Sherwood.

Interestingly, the terrain about Long Beach was exactly like that in which two-thirds of the entire mounted police force of Canada performed—level rolling country with grain fields and stubble. The section between Long Beach and Westminster, to the east, was the setting for the barracks, in which much of the action took place.

The Red Circle. Serial. Balboa Amusement Producing Co. Released by Pathé Frères. *Cast:* Philo McCullough, Ruth Roland, Frank Mayo, Gordon Sackville, Corinne Grant, Mollie McConnell, Andrew Arbuckle, Bruce Smith, Bert Francis, Ruth Lackaye, Myrtle Reeves, Daniel Gilfether, Makato Inokuchi, Fred Whitman, Frank Erlanger.

The 14 Chapters (two reels each): *Nevermore, Pity the Poor, Twenty Years Ago, In Strange Attire, Weapons of War, False Colors, Third Degree or Two Captives, Peace at Any Price, Dodgin' the Law, Excess Baggage, Seeds of Suspicion, Like a Rat in a Trap, Branded as a Thief,* and *Judgment Day*. Chapter 1 was copyrighted Feb. 30, 1915, and Chapter 14 was copyrighted Sept. 3, 1916 (*Filmarama*, vol. 1).

Commentary: According to the *Daily Telegram* (Dec. 2, 1915, p. 3:6), the title is based upon the birthmark on the hand of the heroine, June Travers, played by Ruth Roland. The birthmark is noticeable only in times of stress and excitement, and a number of complications arise through this fact. There is a curse attached to this "red circle." Those who have it must steal. June is a good girl who suffers from this hereditary taint, but she uses it for good. Her first crime is to steal a moneylender's notes and return them to his victims. The story was written by the scenario editor of the Balboa Company, Will M. Ritchie, the fundamental plot being based upon an idea furnished by studio head H. M. Horkheimer.

Review: *Variety* thought highly of the series. It was a detective-crook story that took an unexpected turn early in the film and kept the viewer's interest throughout. Each chapter was complete in itself and could easily stand alone.

Roman Candles. Five-reel comedy-drama. Master Pictures. Released Sept. 13, 1920, by State Rights, M. J. Burnside, Cinart. *Director*: Jack Pratt. *Scenario*: W. S. Forsyth or Jack Pratt. *Titles*: Ralph Spence. *Story*: W. S. Forsyth. *Cameraman*: William Beckly. *Cast*: J. Frank Glendon (*John Arnold, Jr.*), Phalba Morgan (*Señorita Zorra Gamorra*), Edward M. Kimball (*John Arnold, Sr.*), Hector Sarno (*the president*), Sidney D'Albrook (*the secret service chief*), Jack Pratt (*Mendoza, the captain*), Teddy (*a dog*), Mechtilde Price, Lola Smith, William Connant, Jack Waldermeyer.

Commentary: According to the *American Film Institute Catalog* (p. 782), this movie was shown at Los Angeles' Clune Auditorium in September 1920, but it may not have had general distribution until March/April 1922, when M. J. Burnside distributed it under a different title, *Yankee Doodle, Jr.* In New York, Cinart distributed it on July 4, 1922. Press releases of 1920 announced a movie of seven reels, but its exact original length remains uncertain, because the releases for 1922 describe the movie as a five-reeler. Sources dispute whether Pratt or Forsyth was the scenarist. In 1922 the movie ended with a ten-minute fireworks display using tinted colors of the Handschlegel process. Outdoor shots were done at Exposition Park in San Diego. In 1922, reviews and trade journals listed Phalba Morgan as Zelma Morgan, Hector Sarno as Victor Sarno, and Teddy, the dog, as Teddy Whack.

Summary: John Arnold, Jr., is sent to South America by his fireworks manufacturer father. It is the son's last chance to prove himself in the business. In South America, the city of Santa Maria is preparing for a big celebration, thus providing a ready market for John's products. During his business trip, John falls in love with Zorra Gamorra, the daughter of the recently deposed president. Driven by his new passion for Zorra, John ends up making a bigger impression than ever planned. He uses the fireworks to spark a revolution, making it possible for Zorra's father to return to power. Back home, John's father is flooded with more orders than he can handle to celebrate the new regime. The son is definitely back in good standing at the home office. (Drawn from the *American Film Institute Catalog*, p. 782.)

A Romance in the Hills. Balboa Amusement Producing Co. *Scenario*: Harry Wulze. *Cast*: Jackie Saunders (*Beauty*), Bruce Smith (*Strength*), P. E. Peters (*Youth*), Mollie McConnell (*Age*).

Commentary: The *Photoplayers' Weekly* (Sept. 12, 1914) offers the following comments about this movie:

> Smith has been with the Balboa studios 8 months and has portrayed many highly artistic parts. He was for years in dramatic, operatic and vaudeville productions and gained a profound insight into the art of makeup. He is a native of Michigan, aged 35 years and is a happy Benedict, his wife being a former musical comedy star. They live in a cozy cottage beside the surf at Long Beach.
> Smith is a university graduate, and at college was the champion all-around athlete of the institution. He excels in tennis, rowing and boxing, and once gained renown as a professional baseball pitcher. Among the Balboa players he is rated a uniformly good fellow and studious actor — and his friends are legion [*Press Clippings*, vol. 1, p. 110].

Summary: The *Photoplayers' Weekly* article offered this allegorical plot: "[*A Romance in the Hills*] showed a fantasy surrounding Beauty, Youth, Age and Strength, Youth finally winning Beauty after Strength had sacrificed his own life to save Youth.

Review: According to the *Photoplayers Weekly* article, "Bruce Smith, portrayer of character parts at the Balboa studios in Long Beach, received many compliments for his highly artistic work as Strength in *A Romance of the Hills*, recently filmed at the Horkheimer Brothers' plant."

Rose Among the Briers. Copyright Dec. 30, 1915. Pathé hand-colored (*Daily Telegram*, Oct. 6, 1916, p. 2, and *Encyclopedia of the Movie Studios*, p. 234).

The Rose of the Alley. Three-reel drama. Balboa Amusement Producing Co. Made for William Fox, released Oct. 5, 1914, by Box Office Attraction Co. *Cast*: Jackie Saunders in title role (*Press Clippings*, vol. 1, p. 110).

Commentary: Not only was Jackie Saunders a successful photoplayer of renown, but she was the accredited author of at least two scenarios that became Balboa feature films: *The Rose of the Alley* and *A Mix-Up in Clothes*. In Wiltermood's article in the *Photoplayers' Weekly* (Sept. 5, 1914), Jackie expressed her concern as a screenwriter — her comments about the need for quality scenarios if filmmakers expect a successful future still apply today.

Summary: In an unidentified article in *Press Clippings*, vol. 1, p. 121, the plot is discussed:

> At an early age Rose O'Brien loses her mother, which leaves her without a relative in the world. She goes to live with some neighbors, during which time a typical Fagan discovers her plight, and through promises of pretty dresses, induces her to steal.
>
> She is arrested, found guilty, and placed in the charge of a probation officer. This officer finds a good position for her in a wealthy family. The son later falls in love with her. They are secretly married, and the following day Rose finds another woman in her husband's arms. Not knowing that he merely picked up the woman from a faint, Rose leaves her husband, and being a good dancer goes to the city, where she secures an engagement in a theatrical company.
>
> In the meantime, her husband, who loves her and who does not understand her flight, is taken abroad for his health, and rapidly declines. At the end of the year, however, he returns home, and a dinner is given in his honor.
>
> Rose, now a famous dancer, is engaged to dance at the dinner, where she and her husband are mutually surprised in their recognition. Reconciliation follows, and everything ends happily.

Review: The *Fort Worth Star-Telegram* liked the film:

> In this compelling story of a woman's soul struggle, the action leads from the slums to mansions, behind the scenes at the theater to Japan. This strong theme is backed by perfect acting and good photography. Jackie Saunders, a waif of the slums, who alone and destitute in a city, is persuaded by Raffles to attempt robbery. Her failure and arrest leads to a better life and in the end love and happiness [*Press Clippings*, vol. 1, p. 113].

Ruth of the Rockies. Serial. *Cast*: Ruth Roland ("Southern Exposure," p. 120).

Sacrificial Fires. Three-reel drama. Balboa Amusement Producing Co. Uncopyrighted. Made for William Fox, released Feb. 28, 1914, by Box Office Attraction Co. *Director*: Bertram Bracken. *Cast*: Henry King (*Dick Matthews, a young American*), Belle Bennett (*Cherry Blossom, a Japanese girl*), Madeline Pardee (*Helen Marrow, an American girl*), Frank Erlanger (*Cherry Blossom's father*).

Summary: *Motion Picture News* (Oct. 8, 1914) described the plot as being similar to that of *Madame Butterfly*, but with a different ending. Henry King plays Dick Matthews, a young American who falls in love with and marries a Japanese girl, Cherry Blossom, played by Belle Bennett. When he hears of his uncle's death, he returns to America, leaving her behind in Japan. He has been made sole heir to a vast fortune and becomes infatuated with Helen Morrow, played by Madeline Pardee. As the months pass and Dick's letters grow fewer and fewer, Cherry Blossom decides to sail for America in search of her husband. Arriving in San Francisco, she discovers him in the company of Helen, and realizing the situation, she returns to Japan without revealing her presence to Dick. Once home she takes an American flag, wraps it around her body, and kills herself with a dagger. Dick, realizing his duty to his wife, writes to tell her he will be returning. Just as he is about to mail the letter, a messenger delivers a cable which tells him that Cherry Blossom has died. Dick slowly burns the letter he had written, and clasping the picture of Helen to his breast, he buries his head in his arms.

Publicity from *Press Clippings*, vol. 1: *St. Elmo*, "the Greatest American Feature" (courtesy of Marc Wanamaker).

Cherry Blossom's family sends a young man to America to seek revenge. As Dick sits by his window one evening, the assassin kills him with a dagger. Now Dick and Cherry Blossom are ghosts together.

Review: *Motion Picture News* (Aug. 24, 1914) pointed out that the scenes, which were filmed in California and were supposed to represent Japan, were exceptionally beautiful. Reviews also appeared in *Moving Picture World* (Feb. 28, 1914) and *Kinematograph and Lantern Weekly* (Oct. 8, 1914).

St. Elmo. Six-reel drama. Balboa Amusement Producing Co. Made for William Fox, released Aug. 1914 by Box Office Attraction Co. *Cast:* William Jossey (*St. Elmo Murray*). Mollie McConnell (*Mrs. Murray*), Madeline Pardee (*Agnes*), Francis McDonald (*Murray Hammond*), Gypsy Abbot (*Edna Earle*), Henry Stanley (*Parson Hammond*), Dick Johnson (*Mr. Grady*), "Pop" Leonard (*Gabe*), Miss Jensen (*Hagar*), Fred Whitman (*Dent*), Frank Erlanger (*Clinton*).

Commentary: The *Daily Telegram* (Oct. 21, 1914, 9:5) describes this as a feature production of Mrs. Augusta Evans' celebrated Southern novel. Many local points were used as backgrounds for the scenes, notably some of the houses and grounds near Alamitos Bay. *St. Elmo* was filmed in Long Beach, California.

When *St. Elmo* was released, the novel was said to have had more readers, *Uncle Tom's Cabin* excepted, than any other fictitious narrative ever written by an American woman.

Summary: The story depicts the struggle of the powers of good and of evil to gain the mastery over the soul of the leading character, St. Elmo. St. Elmo and his cousin, Murray, love Agnes, a fickle girl who promises to marry one, although she loves the other. St. Elmo discovers this and kills Murray in a duel. From that moment on, the devil occupies his soul, and for 20 years he wanders around, a menace to all. Then he meets Edna, the daughter of a village blacksmith, whom he rescues in a wreck. Her love changes him, and the devil leaves his soul.

Review: *Motion Picture News* (July 11, 1914) said that the photography was excellent, something one expected from a Balboa production. *Moving Picture World* (July 4, 1914) also had praise for the film and the photography.

The Sand Lark. Balboa Amusement Producing Co. Released in 1916 by Pathé Frères. *Cast:* Henry King (*Henry King, Director*, p. 195).

Sands of Life. Two-reel drama. Balboa Amusement Producing Co. Made for William Fox, released by Box Office Attraction Co. *Cast:* Henry King (*Jack*), Herbert Rawlinson (*Ed Moore, a prize fighter*), Roberta Arnold (*Alice Turner, his wife*), Ivan Kahn (*Kid Connelly, a prize fighter*), William Wolbert (*Jeffries, a fight promoter*).

Commentary: According to some sources ("Southern Exposure," p. 112), this was Balboa's first film, but *Moving Picture World* (Sept. 18, 1914) and the *Daily Telegram* article (Nov. 14, 1914) lead us to conclude otherwise. The film was to be marketed by the Box Office Attraction Company, which had obtained rights for all of North and South America.

Summary: The plot revolves around a promising young man who cannot stand prosperity. When poor, he is quite happy and well-behaved, but when money and glory are his, he yields to the temptations of the carefree bachelor life (*Press Clippings*, vol. 1, p. 154). *Moving Picture World* reported that the plot was one continuous round of action, telling the story of a prizefighter, Jack (played by Henry King), who gained wealth rapidly and spent it just as quickly.

Review: According to the *Daily Telegram* (Nov. 14, 1914), "This two-reel play depicts the rise and fall of a promising young man who did not know how to deal with money and glory. Accurate portrayals of the prize ring, with enough of love and romance to develop a charming story, are features of this Balboa story with Herbert Rawlinson in the leading role." *Moving Picture World* (Sept. 18, 1914) goes on to say that the film had some excellent double exposures and the ring scenes were all true-to-life and well staged. There were also some beautiful moonlight effects. This two-reel attraction, according to *Moving Picture World*, was like other productions by this company — the photography beyond reproach, the story original and clever, and the movie further enhanced by good acting.

Saved from Himself. Balboa Amusement Producing Co. Copyright Dec. 30, 1914. Released by Pathé Frères. *Cast*: Henry King (*Henry King, Director*, p. 195).

The Sea Wolf. Three-reel drama. Balboa Amusement Producing Co. *Director*: Sidney Ayres. *Scenario*: Wallace Clifton and C. A. Manges. Based on the novel *The Sea Wolf* by Jack London. *Cast*: Henry King (*Humphrey van Weydon*), Jeanie MacPherson (*Maude Brewster*), Lawrence Peyton (*Wolf Larson*). The following company of players was expected to perform in Balboa's productions of London's works, *Martin Eden, The Call of the Wild,* and *The Sea Wolf*: Herbert Rawlinson, Jack Conway, Norman Manning, June Stone, Robert McKay, Roberta Arnold, Viola Barry, Madelene Leonard, Elsa Lorrimer, Ida Lewis. (*Daily Telegram,* Dec. 10, 1913, 11:4, and *Press Clippings,* vol. 1, pp. 5–6).

Commentary: Moving Picture World (Dec. 20, 1913) announced that several Jack London stories were being prepared at Balboa, including *A Piece of Steak*, based on London's *When God Laughs*, along with *The Sea Wolf* and *To Kill a Man* based on London's *The Night Born*. The announcement further stated that the following works by London were also being prepared as movies at Balboa: *Martin Eden, John Barleycorn, The Call of the Wild, Smoke Bellew Series,* and *The Valley of the Moon* (*Press Clippings,* vol. 1, p. 31).

The Secret of Black Mountain. Four-reel Western. Copyright Sept. 21, 1917, General Film Co., Inc., LP11442. Falcon Features. Released Sept. 29, 1917, by General Film Co. *Supervisors*: H. M. Horkheimer and E. D. Horkheimer. *Director*: Otto Hoffman. Based on the short story "The Secret of Black Mountain" by Jackson Gregory in *Western Story* (June 25, 1921). *Cast*: Vola Vale (*Miriam Vale*), Philo McCullough (*Blake Stanley*), Charles Dudley (*Ed Stanley*), George Austin (*George Cooper*), Henry Crawford (*Barton*), Mignon LeBrun (*Sarah Stanley*), James Warner (*Henry Stanley*), Lewis King (*Jake DeWitt*), Jack McLaughlin (*Jim Vale*), T. H. Gibson Gowland (*Jack Rance*), H. C. Russell (*Old Bill*).

Commentary: According to the *American Film Institute Catalog* (p. 815), the original publication date of Gregory's story is unknown.

Summary: Miriam Vale comes to California digging for clues about her deceased prospector grandfather, Jim Vale. While gathering these clues, she works as a schoolmistress to pay for her living expenses. Miriam does successfully pick up some bits of information. For example, she learns that years ago her grandfather was robbed and killed by road agents, and she learns that there is a prime suspect in the case — Henry Stanley. Since no other leads come her way and since there no way to prove Stanley's guilt, Miriam decides to go back to Vermont. Unexpectedly, Miriam is approached by an unknown man who asks her to accompany him to a seriously injured woman in his cabin. The findings in the cabin are gruesome — a woman who is breathing her last and the corpse of a stranger. The woman tells Miriam that she was beaten by her husband, Ed Stanley, and she begs Miriam to search under a stone in the chimney. Miriam learns that she has run into the Stanley clan. The unknown man who asked her to accompany him is Blake Stanley, Ed's cousin. A fight ensues, between Ed and Blake after Ed returns to the cabin. Ed is seriously injured in the fight, and Blake tells Miriam everything, explaining the death of Henry Stanley and how the secret papers of her grandfather's treasure were lost. After hearing the story, Miriam trusts Blake and decides to share with him the treasure map she has recovered under the stone in the chimney. Together Blake and Miriam go after the gold. (Drawn from the *American Film Institute Catalog,* p. 815.)

Seeds of Jealousy. Three-reel drama. Nemo. Made for William Fox, released Oct. 26, 1914, by Box Office Attraction Co. (*Moving Picture World*). *Cast*: Henry King (*Hardin, the banker*), Lucille Younge (*Louisiana, the singer*) (*Press Clippings*, vol. 1, pp. 125, and 234).

Summary: *Variety* (Nov. 28, 1914, p. 24) explains that in this story a young banker falls in love with a young gypsy woman, even though he is already engaged to an heiress. He foresakes the heiress and marries the gypsy, Anita. Seeds of jealousy creep into Anita, however, when she sees her husband speak to Miss Moore, his former fiancée. Anita faints into the arms of her music teacher. Then her husband walks into the room. He too feels the pangs of jealousy, seeing his wife in the arms of another. At a masked ball, all is cleared up, and Anita and the banker live happily ever after.

Shadows and Sunshine. Five-reel comedy-drama. Copyright Sept. 28, 1916. Pathé-Balboa. Released Nov. 12, 1916, by Pathé Exchange, Inc., Gold Rooster Plays. *Director*: Henry King. *Cast*: Baby Marie Osborne (*Little Mary*), Leon Perdue (*Shadows*), Lucy Payton (*Mary's mother*), Daniel Gilfether (*Gilbert Jackson*), Mollie McConnell (*Amelia Jackson*), R. Henry Grey.

Summary: Gilbert Jackson, who is extremely class-conscious, is so upset about his son marrying a waitress that he disowns him. After a lapse of five years, the disowned son journeys west without his wife and daughter for a few months' time in search of employment. During the young man's job search, his wife and daughter, Little Mary, move into a small dwelling next to Gilbert Jackson's residence. The old couple fall in love with the charming little girl, not knowing she is their granddaughter. Nor do the wife and child know that the old couple are blood kin. The old couple's relationship with Little Mary causes Gilbert Jackson much regret about having disowned his son and he hires a private detective to locate him. The parents send a telegram to their son, pleading that he return to see them. All identities are finally revealed, and a happy reconciliation brings young and old happily together at last. (Drawn from the *American Film Institute Catalog*, p. 823.)

Should a Wife Forgive? Five-reel drama. Copyright Oct. 29, 1915, Equitable Motion Pictures Corporation, LU6883. *Distributor*: Equitable Motion Pictures Corp., released Nov. 8, 1915, by World Film Corp. *Producer*: H. M. Horkheimer and Elwood D. Horkheimer. *Scenario*: Joseph E. Howard. *Cast*: Lillian Lorraine (*La Belle Rose*), Mabel Van Buren (*Mary Holmes*), Henry King (*Jack Holmes*), Lewis Cody (*Alfred Bedford*), William Lampe (*Dr. Charles Hoffman*), Mollie McConnell (*Mrs. Forrester*), Fred Whitman (*Reggy Stratford*), Daniel Gilfether (*Henry Wilson*), Baby Marie Osborne (*Robert Holmes*).

Commentary: The film was previously titled *The Lady of Perfume*.

Summary: La Belle Rose is a cabaret artist who attracts the attention of a young married man, Jack Holmes. Wife and son (Robert Holmes, played by Baby Marie Osborne) are forgotten as Jack uses his wife's money to back a show starring La Belle Rose. The singer also has another beau, a millionaire. The two men meet. There is a fight, and La Belle Rose is shot dead. Just before she dies she writes a note saying she is tired of the work and is going to end it all by committing suicide. Because of this note, the police believe she took her own life. The married man wishes to go back to his family, but his wife will not have him. The picture ends with the line "Should a wife forgive?" (Drawn from *Variety*, Nov. 5, 1915, p. 22.)

Review: *Variety* (Nov. 5, 1915, p. 22) thought little of the film but wrote that Lillian Lorraine wore some stunning clothes. Some of them looked familiar, however, which meant that the Horkheimer Brothers had used them in other films. Henry King, who played the married man, was a capable actor but not the sort with whom a Lillian Lorraine type of girl would fall in love. According to *Variety*, Lewis Cody did clever work and Mabel Van Buren as the wife did a good job of looking sad.

The Shrine of Happiness. Five-reel drama. Copyright Mar. 27, 1916, Pathé Exchange, Inc., LU7926. Balboa Feature Film Co. Released Feb. 18, 1916, by Pathé Exchange, Inc., Gold Rooster Plays. *Director*: Bertram Bracken.

Assistant Director: Alden Willey. *Scenario*: D. F. Whitcomb. *Cast*: Jackie Saunders (*Mary Scott*), William Conklin (*Dick Clark*), Paul Gilmore (*Ted Clark*), Gordon Sackville (*Giant*), Charles Dudley (*his partner*), Bruce Smith (*Dave Scott*).

Commentary: According to the *American Film Institute Catalog* (p. 833), although this movie was made in Balboa Studios, it was hand-colored in "Pathécolor" at Pathé's Paris laboratories.

Summary: Jackie Saunders was the star of the film, which opens with Jackie as a carefree child of the mountains, complete with bare feet, unkempt hair, and a short calico dress. Marie (Jackie Saunders) learns from her dying father the secret of a mining claim. He tells her that if anything happens to him to go to his old mining partner, Dick Clark, for protection with a string of beads which he hands to her. As the father dies, two rough men come along and fight over possession of the young girl. In the quarrel, one is killed and the other chases her through the woods. She drops a rock on his head and walks for an entire month till she reaches Clark's home.

Dick Clark tells how Marie's father saved him from an Indian attack. In gratitude, Clark told him to send the beads if he ever needed help. He will now repay his debt by raising Marie. Dick's younger brother, Ted, is infatuated with Marie, but she is in love with Dick. Dick tells her that he is too old to marry her and that she would be better off with Ted. Reluctantly she agrees to become Ted's bride. On the night before the wedding, Ted finds that Marie really loves Dick and that Dick loves Marie as well. He leaves so the couple can be happy together. (Drawn from *Variety*, Feb. 25, 1916, p. 24.)

Silver Lining. Three-reel drama. Balboa Amusement Producing Co. Made for William Fox, released by Box Office Attraction Co. *Cast*: Henry King (*Jack Alden and Paul Lamar*), other characters: *Jack's father*; *Hulda, Jack's wife*; *Lucile Preston*; *Joe Clarke*; *Marguerite, Jack's daughter* (*Press Clippings*, vol. 1, p. 247).

Summary: The movie program explains the plot:

Jack Alden has firmly decided to become an artist and tries to overcome his father's objections by assuring him of the great fame he will achieve. But no amount of persuasion moves his father to yield and Jack leaves home in anger.

He goes to a small fishing village where he hires a cottage and assumes the name of Paul Lamar. He meets Hulda, the simple and pretty daughter of a fisherman, and is much attracted by her. While painting her picture he learns to love her. Hulda consents to marry him to the great sorrow of her village sweetheart, the handsome young sea captain, Joe Clarke.

Later Jack hears of his father's serious illness and suffers remorse because of his disobedience. He decides to return at once and tells Hulda that he is going on an important business trip.

After reconciliation with his father, Jack promises to renounce his art and become a businessman.

He meets the charming Lucile Preston, a popular society girl, and their mutual admiration ends in a marriage engagement. In the meantime, Hulda searches far and wide for Paul Lamar, the name by which she knows her husband, but not finding him, she dies of a broken heart.

Captain Joe is greatly incensed against Jack because of his neglect of Hulda and discovering him at the home of Lucile Preston, denounces him as Hulda's faithless husband.

Rejected by Lucile and overcome with grief for his dishonorable behavior toward his dead wife, Jack decides to leave the scene of his humiliation and goes abroad without knowing of Marguerite, his daughter.

Soon after his return he sees the portrait of Hulda which he painted during his courtship of her and which Marguerite sold to keep from starvation. He buys the picture and hangs it at his country home.

Later Jack's auto hits Marguerite as she is walking along the road. He has her carried to his home where the greatest kindness and attention are shown to the injured girl. Something in her sweet pale face strangely stirs Jack's memory of the past and the pictures will tell you how he identified his child and began to repair the injury he did her mother [*Press Clippings*, vol. 1, p. 247].

The Smith-Jones Affair. One-reel comedy. Joy. Made for William Fox, released by Box Office Attraction Co. (*Moving Picture World*).

Sold at Auction. Five-reel drama. Balboa Amusement Producing Co. Made as a Gold Rooster Play. Released Feb. 11, 1917, by Pathé Exchange, Inc. *Producers*: H. M. Horkheimer and E. D. Horkheimer. *Director*: Sherwood MacDonald. *Scenario*: Daniel Whitcomb. *Cameraman*: Joseph Brotherton *Cast*: Lois Meredith (*Nan*), William Conklin (*Richard Stanley*), Marguerite Nichols (*Helen*), Frank Mayo (*Hal Norris*), Charles Dudley (*William Raynor*), Lucy Blake (*Raynor's sister*).

Summary: Richard Stanley, who has been jilted by his wife, sends his infant daughter Nan away to be raised by a woman named Mrs. Hopkins in order to remove all reminders of his wife's unfaithfulness. Mrs. Hopkins, the girl's new guardian, unfortunately, takes full advantage of the situation, treating poor Nan like a slave while pocketing the child's support money from her father. Stanley has no idea how badly Nan is being treated. Hal, a young reporter, offers Nan her only company and contentment. Mrs. Hopkins tells Nan that she is a mulatto, using this pretext to keep Nan under her thumb. Distraught by her many predicaments, Nan runs away from her unhappy home, although it is the only one she has known. With her prospects limited, she ends up in a "matrimonial" agency, in reality, a slave market. Nan has been treated like a slave, but now she is about to be sold as a slave. At this auction, by a strange coincidence her father outbids the other millionaires. At the end of the bidding, Hal, who has been tracking Nan down, enters to tell Stanley the true identity of the young woman he has just "bought." (Drawn from the *American Film Institute Catalog*, p. 858.)

The Solitary Sin. Six-reel social drama. New Art Film Co. Released June 1919 by Solitary Sin Corp. State Rights. *Supervisor*: George D. Watters. *Director*: Frederick Sullivan. *Scenario*: George D. Watters. *Story*: George D. Watters. *Cameraman*: King D. Gray. *Cast*: Jack Mulhall (*Bob Meredith, as an adult*), Helene Chadwick (*Mary McMillan*), Gordon Griffith (*Bob Meredith, age 14*), Pauline Curley (*Dorothy Morton*), Anne Schaefer (*Mrs. Meredith*), Irene Aldwyn (*Isabel Meredith*), Leo Pierson (*John Chamberlain*), Charles Spere (*Edward Ralston*), Edward Jobson (*Mr. Ralston*), Kate Lester (*Mrs. Ralston*), Berry Mills (*Edward Wing*), Edward Cecil (*Mr. Meredith*), Milla Davenport, Dorothea Wolbert.

Commentary: According to the *American Film Institute Catalog* (pp. 859–60), this movie was produced at the former Balboa Studios in Long Beach. The producers of the film asked state rights buyers and exhibitors to choose the title. *The Solitary Sin* received the most votes. The New Art Film Co. version is not the same as the one that starred Dorothy Gish in 1919 and 1920.

Summary: This movie served as a public announcement about safe sex. Bob Meredith, at 14 years old, is told by his father about the real hazards of sexual promiscuity. Bob's father takes his son to four hospital wards to let Bob witness in person ugly cases of venereal disease among desperately ill male patients. The sick men leave a lasting impression on Bob. On the other hand, Bob's young neighbors, John Chamberlain and Edward Ralston, remain ignorant of the dangers of sexual promiscuity because their parents stay mute about the subject. Consequently, John contracts syphilis and goes to charlatans who bleed him before his wedding, supposedly to cure him quickly, but a famous doctor intervenes to prevent the wedding. Edward, who has a history of careless companions and frequent masturbation, loses his mind. He is actually declared mad by an examining committee after he goes into a rage and engages in criminal activity. Bob, however, forewarned and prepared, avoids the excesses of his friends, and in the end, Bob is the only one to remain happy and able to wed the girl of his dreams. (Drawn from the *American Film Institute Catalog*, pp. 859-60.)

Sorefoot's Racer. One-reel comedy. Joy. Made for William Fox, released by Box Office Attraction Co. (*Moving Picture World*).

Spellbound. Five-reel drama. Balboa Amusement Producing Co. Made for Knickerbocker Star Features, released May 17, 1916, by General Film Co. *Producers*: H. M. Horkheimer and E. D. Horkheimer. *Director* Harry Harvey. *Scenario*: Bess Meredyth. *Cast*: Lois Meredith (*Elsie York*), William Conklin (*Harrington Graeme*), Bruce Smith (*Major Cavendish*), Edward J. Brady (*Katti Hab*), Frank Erlanger (*Mematu*), Edward Peters (*Azetic*), R. Henry Grey (*Graham*).

Commentary: According to the *American Film Institute Catalog* (p. 872), this film was shot at the Balboa Studios in Long Beach under the working title *The One-Eyed God*. This was the first Knickerbocker Star Feature, the name under which the General Film Co. released its five-reel films. *American Film-Index, 1916-1920* (p. xx), also explains that Knickerbocker Star Features probably began to produce films distributed by General Films as early as 1915; the offices closed in February 1917. The directors of Knickerbocker Star Feature were Henry King and Reaves Eason, and the players included Jackie Saunders, Frank Mayo, Mollie McConnell, Marguerite Nichols, Gordon Sackville, Daniel Gilfether, Margaret Landis, Lillian West, Fred Whitman, and Virginia Norden. Some sources credit H. M. and E. D. Horkheimer as the directors of *Spellbound*.

Summary: A small Hindu statue seems to place a curse on the English couple, Elsie York and Harrington Graeme. The "One-Eyed God" belonged to Elsie, and the statue started giving Elsie and Harrington problems even before their marriage. During their engagement, a yogi, Katti Hab, murdered a man during Hab's attempt to return the statue to India. Harrington was accused of the murder, but he was finally exonerated, which allowed the couple to get married. Then their marriage takes a bumpy ride because both take on bad habits. Elsie becomes a compulsive gambler, and Harrington becomes an incorrigible womanizer. All indications point to their impending separation and divorce. At this point, the yogi, Katti Hab, returns once more to make another attempt to take possession of the statue, but the "One-Eyed God" magically moves on its own, upsetting a lamp and setting fire to the house, killing the yogi. At the same time, the statue melts and the curse is lifted. Elsie and Harrington find reconciliation, and to make matters even better, dozens of precious jewels are discovered in the damaged head of the statue. (Drawn from the *American Film Institute Catalog*, p. 872.)

The Square Triangle. Three-reel drama. Balboa Amusement Producing Co. Made for William Fox, released Sept. 28, 1914, by Box Office Attraction Co. *Director*: Bertram Bracken. *Cast*: Jackie Saunders, Gypsy Abbott, Madeline Pardee, Mollie McConnell, Harriet Jansen, Joseph Singleton, Henry Stanley, Frederick Whitman, Bruce Smith, Bruce Randall, Archibald Warren, Francis McDonald.

Commentary: *The Daily Telegram* (Nov. 28, 1914) explains that this was Jackie Saunders' first film with Balboa.

Summary: According to *Variety* (Oct. 24, 1914), the story had already been told on the stage in a different way, but that didn't hinder Balboa from using the idea for a three-part feature.

Three men are acting as guardians to a young woman whose father was their close friend and lifelong companion until a skirmish with the Mexicans killed him.

Jackie Bennet, the girl, who is played by Jackie Saunders, is engaged to be wed, but her fiancé becomes enamoured with a cabaret singer. Hearing of this, her guardians take a hand. One of the guardians, Edward Trevor, played by Joe Singleton, plots to have Jackie's fiancé "see the light" about the cabaret star. But Edward himself is in love with Jackie and eventually reveals his feelings to her. She chooses Edward over the former fiancé, and they become engaged.

Review: *Variety* (Oct. 24, 1914, p. 22) thought this was one of the best films Balboa had turned out. The picture was fairly well staged, and the exterior shots were a valuable asset to the story. It did not establish any box-office records, but nine out of ten theatre-goers liked it.

The Stolen Play. Four-reel drama. Copyright Aug. 31, 1917, General Film Co., Inc., LP11345. Falcon Features. Released Sept. 1917 by General Film Co. *Supervisors*: H. M. Horkheimer and E. D. Horkheimer. *Director*: Harry Harvey. *Story*: D. F. Whitcomb. *Concept*: H. O. Stechhan. *Cast*: Ruth Roland (*Sylvia Smalley*), Edward J. Brady (*Leroux*), William Conklin (*Charles Edmay*), Lucy Blake (*Alice Mason*), Harry Southard (*Foster*), Ruth Lackaye (*Mrs. Edmay*), Makoto Inokuchi (*Togo*).

Commentary: According to the *American Film Institute Catalog* (p. 888), the alternate title of this film was *The Stolen Child*.

Summary: Charles Edmay, a blind yet distinguished playwright, and his personal secretary, Sylvia Smalley, have just completed writing a play, but the playwright hesitates to sell it to Leroux, a producer. Alice Morgan is sent by Leroux to steal the play. At the same time, Leroux kidnaps both Edmay and Sylvia, confining Edmay in the wine cellar and performing hypnosis on Sylvia. Through hypnosis, Leroux intends to have Sylvia recite the entire play, so that he can have a copy. Under hypnosis, Sylvia demonstrates enormous acting talent, so Leroux plans to cash in on this unexpected bonus. Leroux makes Sylvia the lead player of his production, but she suffers from exhaustion during her prolonged trance. When Leroux takes Sylvia out of the trance, she reprimands him so severely that he decides to set Edmay free. Not to be upstaged, Leroux plans a dramatic finish to his life by burying himself alive. Sylvia wakes up, having dreamed the whole adventure, a result of too much stress while working on the play. (Drawn from the *American Film Institute Catalog*, p. 888.)

Storms of Life. Three-reel drama. White Star. Made for William Fox, released Sept. 28, 1914, by Box Office Attraction Co. *Cast*: Henry King (*Fred Lloyd*), Dorothy Davenport (*Nan, the fisher girl*) (*Moving Picture World*, July 18, 1914).

Summary: The film involves a landowner named George Lloyd, who orders the fishermen in a coastal village to vacate the property. His son Fred Lloyd is an art student who quarrels with his father. Fred leaves home after the argument and boards a steamer, from which he falls. He loses his memory and is rescued by a fisherman known as Captain Jack. In the village he woos Nan, a fisher girl who returns his love, but another lad, Joe Porter, is also in love with Nan. Joe takes the opportunity to shoot Fred in the back when there is a battle over possession of the land. Nan nurses Fred and he recovers. They are married, but Fred is still unaware of his identity. Upset at the marriage and his failed attempt at murder, Porter leaves and joins a gang of smugglers.

Fred rediscovers his artistic talents and paints a picture of Nan. The portrait is taken to a city, where it is purchased by Blanche Dexter, Fred's former fiancée. Blanche and Fred's mother travel to the village to see the artist whose talent they admire. When Fred meets them, his memory comes back. Fred learns that his father has died and that he has inherited the estate.

Fred leaves his wife, who has just lost their baby, and goes home. He indulges himself in the luxuries that wealth can buy and forgets Nan. Porter returns, seeking Nan's love, but even though she thinks Fred is dead, Nan continues to spurn him. Instead, she rows a boat far out to sea; it capsizes and she drowns. Fred sees a vision of Nan and decides to return to her, only to find her dead, buried next to their child. (Drawn from *Press Clippings*, vol. 1, p. 105.)

The Stranger. Two reels. White Star. *Cast*: Dorothy Davenport, Henry King (*Press Clippings*, vol. 1, p. 124).

Summary: Moving Picture World (Nov. 14, 1914, p. 124), summarizes the plot as follows:

> Its hero is a detective, "the stranger," who discovers the whereabouts of a girl captive of a gang of toughs with a den hid among shanties along a wild water-front of a city. He has hair-raising adventures, but with the help of the police whom he warns by a

note thrown from a window, he brings the gangsters to justice.

Review: The same article predicted the success of the movie:

A sensational two-reel offering with the White Star brand. There is a good fighting chase in motor boats on the sea. It is a picture that will hold well and, we think, satisfy the spectators' love of adventure.

Stranglers of Paris. Four-reel drama. *Scenario*: David Belasco. Adapted by David Belasco from the French novel by Berlot. Shown in London, July 1914 (*Press Clippings*, vol. 1, p. 126).

The Sultana. Five-reel crime/drama. Copyright Oct. 14, 1916, Pathé Exchange, Inc., LU9319. Balboa Amusement Co. Released Feb. 18, 1916, by Pathé Exchange, Inc.; Gold Rooster Plays. *Director*: Sherwood MacDonald. *Scenario*: Will M. Ritchey. *Cameraman*: William Beckway. *Source:* Based on the novel *The Sultana* by Henry Cottrell Rowland (New York, 1914). *Cast*: Ruth Roland (*Virginia Lowndes*), William Conklin (*Dr. Thomas Mills*), Charles Dudley (*Peter Fulton*), Frank Erlanger (*Durand*), Daniel Gilfether (*Willoughby Kirkland*), E. T. Peters (*Gregory Kirkland*), Edwin J. Brady (*Count Strelitso*), Gordon Sackville (*Capt. Rimbert*), R. Henry Grey (*Robert Sautrelle*), Richard Johnson.

Commentary: The *American Film Institute Catalog* (p. 899) notes that according to a contemporary source, this movie was "beautified by natural [hand]coloring" at the Pathé studios in France.

Summary: Gregory Kirkland—rich and daring—proposes a wager with his friends, claiming that he can rob and put back the celebrated diamond tiara, the Sultana, without getting caught. One day the designer of the Sultana, Robert Sautrelle, pays a visit to the Kirkland residence, and Gregory takes this opportunity to swipe the tiara but loses courage before returning the tiara to its owner. To return the stolen tiara, Gregory asks a house guest to lend him a hand. The woman, Virginia Lowndes, agrees to help Gregory, but she is about to run away with her beau. When Virginia tells her suitor about her involvement in the prank, he insists that she give him the Sultana. Virginia escapes by running into the woods, while Kirkland's butler, who has been tracking Virginia, plans also on stealing the Sultana from her. Bandits disrupt the butler's scheme, however, attacking and killing him. Dr. Thomas Mills, Kirkland's friend, comes to Virginia's rescue. During all this excitement, the Sultana is finally returned to its rightful owner, and the good doctor and Virginia fall in love with each other. (Drawn from the *American Film Institute Catalog*, p. 899.)

Sunny Jane. Five-reel comedy-drama. Jackie Saunders Series. Balboa Amusement Producing Co. Released Mar. 26, 1917, by Mutual Film Corp. *President*: H. M. Horkheimer. *Cast*: Jackie Saunders (*Jane Dwight*), Edward Jobson (*Philip Dwight*), Cullen Landis (*Thomas*), Frank Mayo (*James Thornton*).

Commentary: Jackie Saunders had worked for Biograph in the East and one year for Universal before signing a contract with Balboa. E. D. Horkheimer met with Mutual Film Corp. to arrange the distribution of 6 five-part productions with Jackie Saunders. The first release was *Sunny Jane*, followed soon afterwards by *The Checkmate* and *The Wildcat*, then *A Bit of Kindling*, *Betty Be Good*, and *Bab the Fixer*.

Summary: A dreamer and adventurer, Jane Dwight spends her leisure time on her father's ranch imagining cliffhangers in which she plays the heroine. After oil is discovered on the farm, a young millionaire visits and considers buying the property, but more importantly, the visitor, James Thornton, is captivated by the charms of the tomboyish Jane. He makes, however, the mistake of proposing a finishing school for Jane. She goes to acquire the recommended polish, but when she returns all hoity-toity, he misses her tomboy spirit. Jane quickly realizes the reason for Thornton's disappointment and puts on her tougher togs, hiding herself in his car. When Thornton sits behind the wheel and sees his tomboy back again, the happy couple drive to the closest hitching post to get married. (Drawn from the *American Film Institute Catalog*, p. 901.)

Sunshine and Gold. Five-reel comedy-drama. Balboa Amusement Co. Copyright Apr. 24, 1917, Pathé Exchange, Inc.; LU10624. Released Apr. 29, 1917, by Pathé Exchange, Inc., Gold Rooster Plays. *Director*: Henry King. *Scenario*: Henry King. *Story*: Will M. Ritchey. *Cameraman*: Joseph Brotherton. *Cast*: Baby Marie Osborne (*Little Mary*), Henry King (*the chauffeur*), Daniel Gilfether (*James Andrews*), Neil Hardin (*Dr. Andrews, his son*).

Summary: During her fifth birthday party, Little Mary wanders off and is kidnapped by a band of gypsies. Hearing talk about a ransom, she runs off at night into the forest to escape her captors. The next day, Little Mary encounters an old man, James Andrews, a lonely recluse with considerable wealth stored in his cabin. The following day the family chauffeur, who has been searching for Little Mary, finds the girl still in the company of the recluse. During the chauffeur's visit, James Andrews realizes that Little Mary is actually his granddaughter. It was after a terrible quarrel between the recluse and his son that the old man went into hiding with his treasure. The recluse decides it is time to return with Little Mary, to be reconciled with his son and the entire family (Drawn from the *American Film Institute Catalog*, p. 902.)

The Test of Manhood. Three-reel drama. Balboa Amusement Producing Co. Made for William Fox, released Oct. 12, 1914, by Box Office Attraction Co. *Director*: Bertram Bracken. *Cast*: Dorothy Davenport (*Ethel Crandall*), Fred Whitman (*Ralph Crandall*), Daniel Gilfether (*John Wentworth*), Henry King (*Harry, his son*), Charles Dudley (*Jim Martin*), Joe Massey (*Jose*), Madeline Pardee (*Monte Madge*), Archie Warren (*Beanie, friend of Harry*), Bruce Randall (*Mack, friend of Harry*).

Summary: In *Press Clippings*, vol. 1, there appears a general description of the plot with a mixed review that was written by Sime for *Variety* (Oct. 31, 1914, p. 27):

This officer in the "Manhood" film knocks his men about like nine-pins, three of them escaping, including the son of a ranch owner who was sent away on his own wish to become a man, and took to the sea. In the ship scene one of the seamen climbs up the rigging and apparently makes a long jump to the ocean from a mast, as he is close pressed by pursuers. While the jump is not wholly seen, it's good enough, and there's a thrill to this. Several threads carried through the reels are nicely worked out and brought together. One of the best staged bits showed how the innocents duped the villain, and recovered money from him through gambling, to repay the amount of the mortgage the villain held on the ranch. Some of the ship's views fail to convince through the ship lying at anchor, or because they were of the studio, and others of the studio were not well produced, but *The Test of Manhood* as a melodrama in three reels is excellent for a melodrama release feature, even if the title might have happened after the picture ended.

Thou Shalt Not Steal. Two-reel drama. Released by the University Film Co. *Characters: Reverend Rupert Strathmore; Silvan; Marcia, girl thief; Doogan, outcast and crook.*

Summary: The Reverend Rupert Strathmore, rector in a Scottish village, discovers that someone has been dipping into the church treasury. He suspects Silvan, who has been caught once before appropriating church funds, but decides to let him go once more. Silvan, seeking revenge for his fancied wrong, plots to have an incriminating letter placed in the minister's house by aid of a female thief, Marcia. Strathmore discovers the girl in the act and pleads with her to give up her evil ways. Impressed with his ways, she agrees. He helps her lead a righteous life, and she returns the favor by revealing another plot Silvan has initiated against the minister.

Review: Motion Picture News (June 20, 1914) called the film delightful, saying it taught moral righteousness without being too "preachy." The review applauded the excellent double-negative work shown in several scenes, especially the one in which Strathmore appears in a vision to the converted woman, who has given way to impulse and is tempted to steal from the people who have employed and befriended her. *Motion Picture News* also thought the film was full of quaint comedy, especially in the final scene where a number of aged village women peer into the pastor's window as Rupert and Marcia reveal their love for one another.

Through Fire and Water. Two-reel drama. Nemo. Made for William Fox, released Oct. 19, 1914, by Box Office Attraction Co. (*Moving Picture World*).

Summary: The film is about Deane Maxwell, who is interested in charity work and happens to be the daughter of a wealthy banker. While working at a small orphanage, she finds a three-year-old blind child, Ruth, to whom she becomes greatly attached. In the meantime, she and Philip Osborne, her father's secretary, have fallen in love, but for some reason, he will not disclose his feelings. Philip tells her that they can never be more than friends.

One night during a severe storm, Deane is roused out of sleep, and the vision of a woman she has never seen before tells her that Ruth is in danger. Deane rushes out into the storm to go to Ruth at the orphanage. She finds the building in flames and arrives just in time to rescue the child. She takes the youngster home. Philip finds them in the library and confesses that Ruth is his daughter. He then tells her of his past, which has made him feel unworthy of Deane's love. As he is telling his story, the vision of his dead wife appears to him — the same woman that had come to Deane earlier — and tells him that all is forgiven and that he should learn to accept Deane's love. (Drawn from *Press Clippings*, vol. 1, p. 124.)

Through Night to Light. Three-reel drama. Nemo. Made for William Fox, released Oct. 5, 1914, by Box Office Attraction Co. *Cast*: Henry King (*Tom Wright, a settlement worker*), Jackie Saunders (*Dorothy Wilson*).

Summary: Tom Wright, a young man, proposes to Dorothy Wilson before leaving to take up settlement work in New York. She accepts but tells him he has to wait. While Tom is away, she falls in love with Jack Green, who becomes heir to a fortune. Both go to New York, falling victims to the life of the rich, and sink lower and lower in their wanton lives.

Dorothy finally decides to end it all, as she is not fit for decent society. She jumps in the river but is rescued by Tom Wright's co-workers in the slums. She is recognized as Tom's former sweetheart. Jack, released from the hospital after a fight, sees the error of his ways, and Tom reunites the misguided pair. (Drawn from *Press Clippings*, vol. 1, pp. 124, 246.)

The Tiger's Trail. *Cast*: Ruth Roland ("Southern Exposure," p 120).

Commentary: According to Tony Scott's article, there were live tigers in this movie that were carted in from Col. Selig's Zoo located at Eastlake Park in Los Angeles.

The Tip Off. Copyright Dec. 16, 1914. Released by Pathé Frères (*Encyclopedia of the Movie Studios*, p. 232).

To Love and to Hold. Two-reel drama. White Star. Made for William Fox, released Nov. 10, 1914, by Box Office Attraction Co. *Cast*: John Duncan, George Lane, May Granger, Rose White (*Press Clippings*, vol. 1, p. 137).

Summary: John Duncan and George Lane, traveling salesmen and pals, are on a vacation when they meet two village belles, May Granger and Rose White. John eventually marries May, and they move to the city. May does not know that her husband is fond of cards and loses heavily. He gambles everything on a horse that loses and is about to take his own life when George stops him. John goes on a drinking binge and misinterprets George's placing his hand on May's shoulder. He rushes into the room and denounces them both before they have a chance to explain. May returns to the country with her mother and her friend, Rose. John becomes a professional gambler. George, who is about to marry Rose, notices that May is making baby clothes. When the couple come across John on their honeymoon, they tell him he is about to become a father and his heart softens. He swears never to gamble again, and he goes to May and begs her forgiveness. She consents, and they happily reunite. (Drawn from *Press Clippings*, vol. 1, p. 106.)

Toilers of the Sea. Copyright Oct. 9, 1915 (*Encyclopedia of the Movie Studios*, p. 234).

Told at Twilight. Five-reel drama. Balboa Amusement Producing Co. Copyright Mar. 14, 1917, Pathé Exchange, Inc. LU10367. Released Mar. 25, 1917, by Pathé Exchange, Inc., Gold Rooster Plays. *Director*: Henry King. *Scenario*: Dan F. Whitcomb. *Cameraman*: William Beckway. *Cast*: Baby Marie Osborne (*Little Mary Sunshine*), Daniel Gilfether (*Daniel Graham*), Henry King (*the father*), Beatrice Van (*the mother*), Leon Perdue (*Piggy*).

Summary: Daniel Graham is a crusty, ill-tempered old man who lives next door to Little Mary Sunshine. One day, Mary and her playmate Piggy are out by the neighbor's fence innocently laughing. Graham crosses to the other side of the fence to see what the commotion is about and meets Little Mary Sunshine. This first encounter begins the daily routine of visits from the little girl to the old man. Little Mary Sunshine transforms the old man with her warmth and goodwill. Graham decides to throw a birthday party for Little Mary Sunshine, and when a storm brews that evening, the little girl is invited to spend the night. The very same evening the little girl's father, despondent over his investment losses, breaks into Graham's house with every intention of robbing it. When the old man and the little girl come across the intruder, Little Mary Sunshine naïvely assumes that her father has come to fetch her. Graham understands the real situation, but for love of the little girl, he decides to help her father get back on his feet, without pressing any charges. (Drawn from the *American Film Institute Catalog*, p. 939.)

Tomboy. Balboa Amusement Producing Co. Released in 1915 by Pathé Frères. *Cast*: Henry King (*Henry King, Director*, p. 195).

Too Wise Wives. Six-reel domestic drama, 5,164 ft. Copyright May 22, 1921, LP165881. Famous Players-Lasky. Released May 22, 1921, by Paramount Pictures. *Director/Scenarist*: Lois Weber. *Story*: Lois Weber, Marion Orth. *Photography*: William C. Foster. *Cast*: Louis Calhern (*David Graham*), Claire Windsor (*Marie, his wife*), Phillips Smalley (*John Daly*), Mona Lisa (*Sara, his wife*).

Commentary: See *Untitled, 2*, 1918, in this filmography for comments on the controversy at the Balboa Studios when they tried to promote Mona Lisa. Pathé refused to promote her, but the studios insisted. Balboa's publicity announced in the *Daily Telegram* (Mar. 11, 1918, 5:1), "So striking is her likeness to the famous da Vinci portrait that some of the editors have mistaken the picture of the film star for a copy of the original."

Summary: David Graham's wife, Marie, is totally dedicated to her spouse. Instead of appreciating her fidelity and care, he takes her for granted, even criticizing her for trying too much to please him. A former sweetheart, Sara, who had married another man for money, now tries to seduce Graham and take him from his wife. While on a business trip, Sara's husband asks the Grahams to keep Sara company. In a letter, Sara lets David know that she would prefer to see him alone. Marie gets hold of the letter but does not read it. Although the Grahams honor the request to keep Sara company, Marie takes the opportunity to discuss with Sara the contents of the sealed letter. In the end, David rejects Sara's overtures, denouncing the letter and the plot, finally appreciative of his wife's better qualities. (Drawn from the *American Film Institute Catalog*, p. 821.)

Tricks of Fate. *Director*: William Desmond Taylor. *Cast*: Neva Gerber, Jack Bryce, Mollie McConnell.

Commentary: The *Los Angeles Tribune* pointed out that there were many double exposures worked out to perfection by aid of a new attachment for a camera devised by William Beckway, cameraman of Balboa ("Southern Exposure," p. 118).

Twin Kiddies. Five-reel drama. Balboa Amusement Producing Co. Copyright Jan. 17, 1917, Pathé Exchange, Inc.; LU10002. Released Jan. 28, 1917, by Pathé Exchange, Inc. Gold Rooster Plays. *Director*: Henry King. *Scenario*: Calder Johnstone. *Cameraman*: William Beckway. *Cast*: Baby Marie Osborne (*Bessie Hunt/Fay Van Loan*), Henry King (*Jasper Hunt*), Ruth Lackaye (*Mrs. Flannigan*), Daniel Gilfether (*William Van Loan*), R. Henry Grey (*Baxter Van Loan*), Loretta Beecker (*Beatrice Van Loan*), Edward Jobson (*Spencer*), Mignon LeBrun (*the governess*), Lon Chaney, Leon Perdue.

Commentary: In one of the photographs of this film provided by Marie Osborne (see p. 56), the man who is wearing the hat and standing next to Marie's mother is the celebrated character actor and makeup expert, Lon Chaney. This is another interesting and little-known association between Balboa Studios and some of the film industry's greatest stars. According to clippings in Marie Osborne's scrapbooks, this movie was also called *Twin Rays of Sunshine*, a title that reflects the Spanish translation of Marie's sobriquet in her movies, "El Rayito de Sol." It is interesting to note the appearance again of the African-American child actor, Leon Perdue, who had also played "Shadows" in the film *Shadows and Sunshine*.

Summary: This is the story of a poor little rich girl by the name of Fay. Her parents, the wealthy Van Loans, shower their daughter with all that money can buy, but they deprive her of what she wants most — their affection. By sheer coincidence, there is another girl that could be Fay's twin. Bessie Hunt is the spitting image of Fay, and Bessie's father works for Fay's father as a foreman at the mine. Contrary to Fay's situation, Bessie is showered with love, but she enjoys few material comforts. In a plot recalling *The Prince and the Pauper*, the two girls meet and decide to exchange their clothes and return to the other's home to experience the difference. Fay learns what it means to receive much parental love, while her parents learn that money can't buy happiness. (Drawn from the *American Film Institute Catalog*, p. 957.)

Twin Six O'Brien aka **Smoking Trails.** Released in 1922. *Producer/Writer/Director*: Bob Horner. *Cast*: "Ranger" Bill Miller, Patricia Palmer (*Daily Telegram*, June 11, 1922, C7).

Commentary: According to the *Daily Telegram* (June 11, 1922, C7, and Aug. 3, 1922, p. 10), this film was the first of five westerns produced by Bob Horner at the Long Beach studios. It starred "Ranger" Bill Miller who was said to be the first cowboy to play leading parts in motion pictures. Patricia Palmer plays the female lead. The script was written by Bob Horner, who had become successful as a director despite the physical handicap of having lost both legs in a railroad accident when he was a child.

The Twin Triangle. Five-reel drama. Copyright May 20, 1916, Equitable Motion Pictures Corp., LU8397. Balboa Amusement Co. Released May 1, 1916, by Equitable Motion Pictures Corp.; World Film Corp. *Director*: Harry Harvey. *Scenario*: Bess Meredyth. *Cameraman*: Joseph Brotherton. *Cast*: Jackie Saunders (*Czerta/Madeline*), Mollie McConnell (*Mrs. Van Schuyler*), Ruth Lackaye (*Marco's mother*), Edward J. Brady (*Marco*), William Conklin (*MacCanley Byrnes*), Robert Grey (*Lord Fitz Henry*), Joyce Moore.

Commentary: The *American Film Institute Catalog* (p. 958) explains that this movie was the second feature made at the Long Beach studios of the Horkheimer Brothers.

Summary: A gypsy girl named Czerta learns that she was stolen as a child and adopted by a gypsy family. Marco, a member of this gypsy family, tries to seduce Czerta, and she fights back with a knife. Thinking Marco was killed in the struggle, Czerta leaves the only family she has ever known, traveling to New York with an artist that she had just met, Mac-Canley Byrnes. In the city, she elevates herself through study and training. In the meantime, while doing a portrait of Madeline Van Schuyler, Byrnes finds that his client looks a lot like an older version of Czerta. This resemblance fascinates Byrnes. Czerta becomes jealous of this new client and decides to remove herself from further disappointment, leaving Byrnes behind without saying a word. Years later, while watching a dance at the theatre, Byrnes sees Czerta as the featured dancer. Byrnes had gone to the theatre with Madeline and Madeline's mother. Madeline too recognizes Czerta and is more surprised than Byrnes. Czerta is Madeline's kidnapped daughter, stolen as a child by gypsies. The mother identifies her daughter, but Marco has chosen that very moment to take revenge on Czerta, tracking her down and stalking her at the theatre. On the other hand, Byrnes has always loved Czerta and now has a chance to prove his undying devotion to her, bravely defending her during Marco's attack, killing him in the life and death struggle. (Drawn from the *American Film Institute Catalog*, p. 958.)

The Twisted Thread. Serial. Balboa Amusement Producing Co. Released by Pathé. *Director*: Frank H. Crane. *Assistant Director*: Otto Hoffman. *Technical Director*: Thomas Swem. *Author*: H. M. Horkheimer. *Cast*: Kathleen Clifford (*leading lady*), Gordon Sackville (*leading man*), Bruce Smith (*heavy lead*), Julian Dillon (*juvenile lead*), Corinne Grant (*heavy leading woman*).

Commentary: Kathleen Clifford, a New York star, and her company were especially engaged for the production (*Daily Telegram*, Jan. 4, 1917, 2:6). The *Moving Picture World*, Mar. 3, 1917, includes an article "Visiting the Balboa Studios," in which it is explained that though the story was written by H. M Horkheimer, adaptations for the screen would be written by Will M. Ritchey.

The Understudy. Four-reel drama. Copyright Oct. 5, 1917, General Film Co., Inc., LP11603. Falcon Features. Released Oct. 5, 1917, by General Film Co. *Supervisors*: H. M. Horkheimer and E. D. Horkheimer. *Director*: William Bertram *Scenario*: Lela Leibrand. Based on the short story "The Understudy" by Leigh Gordon Giltner (publication unknown). *Cast*: Ethel Ritchie (*Georgianna Lane/Hope Van Alen*), Neil Hardin (*Gerald Fownes*), Bruce Smith (*Anthony Van Alen*), Mollie McConnell (*Evans*), Frank Erlanger (*Dr. Mache*), Albert Ellis (*Dr. Pope*).

Summary: Heading for city lights, Georgianna Lane is drawn to the excitement of performing on stage, but failing to win the spotlight, she despairs and considers killing herself. About the same time, another woman is suffering another predicament. Both meet at the hospital. Hope Van Alen, a drug addict, decides with her husband to seek rehabilitation at Dr. Pope's sanitarium. By sheer coincidence, the two troubled women look alike. Because of the striking resemblance, the Van Alens ask Georgianna to stand in for Hope during Hope's treatment at the sanitarium. This opportunity will show off Georgianna's exceptional acting skills. In fact, Mr. Van Alen's nephew Gerald falls in love with the impersonator. The poor nephew is bewildered by the circumstances, but once the story is explained after Hope's cure, Georgianna finds her happiness in Gerald, with whom she settles down to a conjugal life in the country. (Drawn from the *American Film Institute Catalog*, p. 969.)

Uneven Match. *Cast*: Hazel Tranchell, Slim Pickett (*Press-Telegram*, Aug. 8, 1963).

Commentary: Hazel Tranchell made over 150 films at Balboa Studios, receiving as much as $2,000 per month. The actress had a collection of photos covering Balboa. She lived in Long Beach and remained a resident there until her death, though she was originally from Portland, Oregon.

The Unexpected. Three-reel drama. Balboa Amusement Producing Co. Made for William Fox, released Feb. 28, 1914, by Box Office Attraction Co. *Cast*: Belle Bennett (*Dorothy Madison*), Henry King (*Dave Parks, a mountaineer*), Madeline Pardee (*Mam Parks, an old mountain woman*), Augusta Bolle (*Nell Oatsey, a mountain girl*), Fred Whitman (*Bill Oatsey, a mountaineer*), Mollie McConnell (*Mrs. Madison, a refined woman*), Baby Bennett (*Margaret Madison, a three year old*), Robert Grey (*Daniel McVey, a secret-service chief*), Charles Dudley (*James Madison*).

Summary: Dorothy Madison, a secret service operative, is sent into the West Virginia mountains to locate a still after a male operative has failed. She carries a sketching outfit and a carrier pigeon, which she hides in the woods. Walking along the road, she sees Dave Parks coming and feigns a sprained ankle. Dave takes her home to his mother, who is suspicious of the girl and barely tolerates her. Nell Oatsey, who is in love with Dave, hears of Dorothy's plight and goes to see her, saving her from a rattlesnake. Dave falls in love with Dorothy while she is trying to find evidence of his family's still. She finds the still and alerts authorities via the pigeon. When a raid takes place, Dave is hurt and Dorothy helps him escape. Nell believes Dorothy has stolen Dave from her and seeks to kill her. She traces them to Dorothy's home, only to find that Dorothy is already married and the mother of a young child. Dorothy had only helped Dave because Nell had killed the snake that menaced her. Dave and Nell are reunited. (Drawn from *Moving Picture World*, Feb. 28, 1914.)

Review: Moving Picture World (Aug. 29, 1914) described the film as a thrilling story in which a gang of moonshiners is trapped by a clever girl. The magazine reviewer loved the wild, picturesque scenery of the mountains and the unexpected ending. The review in the *Morning Telegraph* (July 26, 1914) praised the Balboa film for its use of imagery. The film began and ended with the same two figures silhouetted against sky and water, but in the beginning they were separated and in the end they were united. The review also liked the use of a real snake.

Untitled, 1. First pictures taken of firemen at Pine Avenue and Ocean Boulevard, Long Beach, California (*Daily Telegram*, Jan. 6, 1911, 1:4).

Untitled, 2. *Director:* Paul Powell. *Cast:* Mona Lisa, Wilfred Lucas, Kenneth Harlan, Ethel Ritchie, Corinne Grant, Patrick Calhoun, Haru Fugite, Percy S. Pembroke.

Commentary: According to the *Daily Telegram* (Mar. 11, 1918, 2:1), H. M. Horkheimer announced in Feb. 1918 that his search for his perfect beauty was over. He had found the new "Mona Lisa."

Years later in an article in the *Long Beach Press Telegram* (Aug. 20, 1930, A9:5), Vera Kackley reported that there was a controversy over the star. Pathé refused to take a picture featuring Mona Lisa. The Balboa management was obdurate, and two more pictures with her in the leading role were shot. Nobody bought them, and they were stacked on the shelves.

One of these films might be one at the UCLA archives: see *Too Wise Wives*, released 1921.

Vengeance of the Dead. Four-reel (drama?). Balboa Amusement Producing Co., a Fortune Photoplay. Released Mar. 1917? by General Film Co. *Cast:* Henry King, Lillian West.

Commentary: According to the *American Film Institute Catalog* (p. 985), this film also appears as *Vengeance of Death* and *Dungeons of the Dead*. Fortune Photoplays, operated by the Horkheimer Brothers, disbanded in June 1917 because of financial problems. It is even possible that this movie never made the theatre circuits. No information has been retrieved about the plot.

Vengeance of the Flames. Three-reel drama. White Star. Made for William Fox, released Nov. 17, 1914, by Box Office Attraction Co. *Scenario:* William H. Ratterman (*Press Clippings*, vol. 1, p. 55).

Commentary: The Los Angeles Tribune (Oct. 1, 1914) explained in an article entitled "Tennessee Sculptor Writing Film Plays" that William H. Ratterman had studied art in Paris, Berlin, and London. Besides being a sculptor and scenarist, he was also an authority on music. The article also stated that Balboa had purchased several other motophoto dramas that Ratterman had created (*Press Clippings*, vol. 1, p. 55).

The Vow. Three-reel drama. Nemo. Made for William Fox, released Oct. 12, 1914, by Box Office Attraction Co. *Director:* Bertram Bracken (*Daily Telegram*, Nov. 16, 1914, 10:7).

Cast: Francis MacDonald (*Bernard, a Sicilian*), Joe Singleton (*Lorenzo, his neighbor*), Fred Whitman (*Donald Hanford, an American*), Charles Dudley (*Dexter Harrison, his friend*), Lucille Younge (*Beatrice, Bernard's sister*), Henry Stanley (*Francesco, Beatrice's father*), Madeline Pardee (*Elsie, Hanford's sister*), Gypsy Abbott (*Antonetta, a happy-go-lucky Sicilian*).

Summary: Beatrice lives with her father and brother Bernard in a fishing village in Sicily. Lorenzo, a neighbor, woos Beatrice, but his attentions are not welcome, and he becomes a secret enemy of Bernard. Donald Hanford, an American author, his sister Elsie, and their friend Dexter Harrison come to the village as tourists. Bernard and Hanford quarrel over Antonetta, and the men agree to fight a duel with pistols. Bernard, not aware that Lorenzo hates him, makes him his second. Hanford, who doesn't really want to kill Bernard, takes the bullets out of his gun, but Lorenzo changes the pistols and Bernard is shot dead. Beatrice swears a vendetta against her brother's killer, even though she does not know who he is. She tells Lorenzo that she will marry him if he locates the Americans. Lorenzo remembers seeing one of the pistols marked "D. H." and mistakenly identifies Dexter Harrison as the killer. Hanford, meanwhile, goes boating, meets disaster, and is saved by Beatrice's father who takes him home. Hanford and Beatrice fall in love and Hanford proposes, but Beatrice says she is bound by a vow to Lorenzo. When Beatrice prays, a vision of her brother appears, telling her not to be bound by the vow, and she accepts Hanford's offer. In London, Lorenzo learns that Harrison is not the man who shot Bernard. He returns home to find out that the man he is to kill is betrothed to Beatrice. Lorenzo goes to a cliff to slay the lovers, but Bernard's ghost comes and accuses Lorenzo of the slaying. Lorenzo falls to his death on the rocks below. (Drawn from *New York Variety*, Mar. 14, 1914.)

Review: The *New York Telegram* (Nov. 8, 1914) said that the California scenery formed an ideal setting for the film. The rocky shores and semi-tropical gardens were "charming." The review went on to say that it was an interesting story, but it would have been more effective if the double exposures had been used in the ghost scenes instead of fade-ins.

Wanted—A Brother. Five-reel drama. Oakdale Productions (probably Balboa Amusement Producing Co.). Released Oct. 1918 by General Film Co. *Director*: Robert Ensminger. *Story*: L. Virginia Walters. *Cast*: Gloria Joy (*Bab Fanning*), Mignon LeBrun (*Mrs. Fanning*), H. E. Archer (*Mr. Fanning*), Daniel Gilfether (*Daniel Wellsley*), Julian Dillon (*Tom Wellsley*), Edward Jobson (*Officer Mulcahy*), Ruth Lackaye (*Mrs. Barton*), William Reed (*James McPherson*) (*American Film Institute Catalog*, p. 998).

Commentary: The majority of the personnel involved were associated with the Balboa Amusement Producing Co., but the film is not usually credited as being produced at Long Beach, since its production would have occurred about the very time that the Horkheimers were facing bankruptcy. However, the Horkheimers had boldly announced that Gloria Joy, the "Child Wonder," would appear in a new series, to follow the example of the "Baby Grand," Marie Osborne, who had left Balboa the previous year to make movies at her own studio in Glendale, the Diando Studios. Other features in this Balboa series with Gloria Joy include *Little Miss Grown-Up, The Locked Heart, The Midnight Burglar, Miss Mischief Maker,* and *No Children Wanted*, all of which feature Gloria Joy in the leading role.

Summary: Wanting an older brother of her own, Bab Fanning "adopts" Tom Wellsley, who ran away from his rich but strict father, Daniel Wellsley. Starting anew, the venturesome Tom sells newspapers on the streets, but the other boys resent the rich boy's ways. To put Tom in trouble, the newsies plant stolen fruit in Tom's pockets. Bab attempts without success to release Tom from the House of Correction. Tom then escapes from jail with a band of roughnecks. By coincidence, the ruffians choose Tom's father's house to rob, but Tom pulls out of the plot. Tom starts work right away on a farm, while Bab goes to the Wellsleys' home to look for Tom. There, Bab is forced to join the ruffian robbers in their break-in. Once inside, Bab manages to escape the gang and consoles Tom's depressed father. With Tom's father, Bab looks for Tom, finds him, and a family reunion follows.

The Way of the World. One-reel drama. Nemo. Made for William Fox, released by Box Office Attraction Co. (*Moving Picture World*).

Whatever the Cost. Five-reel Western. Plaza Pictures (probably started for Balboa Amusement Producing Co.). Released Oct. 7, 1918, by W. W. Hodkinson Corp. through General Film Co. *Director*: Robert Ensminger. *Story*: Captain Leslie T. Peacocke. *Cameraman*: Georges Rizard. *Cast*: Anita King (*Jess Farley*), Charles Dudley (*Uncle Dud*), Stanley Pembroke (*Steve Douglas*), Gordon Sackville ("*Black Jack*" *Fanning*), Patrick Calhoun (*Paul Otard*), Corinne Grant (*Belle*) (*The American Film Institute Catalog*, p. 1013).

Commentary: According to the *American Film Institute Catalog*, this production is not credited to Balboa Studios; however, the release date would explain why the producer would be other than Balboa, since Balboa had gone into receivership while the production was still under way. In addition, the director, the cameraman, and the majority of the actors were Balboans. See also *Angel Child*, *The Law That Divides*, and *Petticoats and Politics*, all of which seem to fall into the same category.

Summary: In the rough-and-tumble seaside town of Glen Cove, Paul Otard wants to find the secret location of John Farley's illegal whiskey shipments. To find the hiding place, Paul pretends he's in love with "Black Jack" Fanning's wife, Belle. The Fannings' daughter, Jess, is a tomboy, but she finds a dress and as she's trying it on, Paul enters and tries to kiss her. Jess defends herself by pulling out a gun. Soon afterwards, "Black Jack" is found dead. Jess wants to find her father's murderer. Jess disguises herself as a saloon dancer in the Fanning establishment. One of the customers is a detective, Steve Douglas, with whom Jess falls in love. Steve Douglas is on assignment to track down and to expose the whiskey smugglers. To Jess' dismay, it is determined that "Black Jack" was shot with Steve's gun. Jess decides to avenge her father by killing the man she loves. But in the nick of time, Jess discovers that Paul had used Steve's gun to kill her father. Relieved, Jess goes back to Steve, the man she loves.

When Fate Was Kind. Three-reel drama. Copyright Eclectic Film Co., Oct. 23, 1914. Pathé Frères, released by Eclectic Film Co. (*Encyclopedia of the Movie Studios*, p. 232).

When Might Is Right. Knickerbocker Star Features. Released in 1916.

Commentary: According to *Henry King, Director* (p. 196), this film may have been directed by Henry King.

When the Circus Comes to Town. Six reels.

Commentary: According to the *Telegram Daily* (Nov. 21, 1914, 8:2), parts of this film were photographed during a circus parade in Long Beach. This filming raised the ire of the circus owner, who had refused the movie company permission to film. He stated that all circus men were opposed to having cinematographers make free use of circus activities. Five mounted cowboys were called out of the procession and were instructed to try to lasso the camera. The crowd rallied to the defense of the movie men, while police were rushed to the scene to preserve order and to avert a near riot.

When the Troupe Closed. One-reel comedy. Joy. Made for William Fox, released by the Box Office Attraction Co. (*Moving Picture World*).

Who Is "Number One"? Serial. Nineteen Episodes. Paramount Pictures. *Producer*: H. M. Horkheimer. *Story*: Anna Katherine Green. *Cast*: Kathleen Clifford (*Aimée Villon*), Cullen Landis.

Commentary: According to the *Daily Telegram* (Nov. 1917), this was the first serial ever handled by Paramount Pictures.

Variety (Oct. 26, 1917, p. 33) wrote that

the producers had made a magnificent film, sumptuous in the extreme, and that they had spared no expense in building sets. *Variety* also remarked that the detail in the serial was wonderfully worked out and the magazine expressed the hope that the remaining 15 episodes would do equally well.

Summary: Aimée Villon, a ward of Graham Hale, comes from abroad to make her home with the Hales. Graham Hale, a financial giant and famous inventor, is for reasons unknown to him being attacked by conspirators of unlimited power and wealth. They seek his ruin and threaten his life, constantly sending him Mafia-type messages. He has a son Tommy, who is also marked by the conspirators. The mysterious Camille Arnot, who appears to be "a woman scorned," is bent on vengeance against Graham Hale, who had cast her aside. Other characters also include Thornton Rayne, a trusted friend of Hale's who is secretly in league with the conspirators, and Hugo Wald, Aimée's tutor, who is also in love with her.

In the first episode, the plotters against Hale send him a warning signed, "T-T-T," saying that after 18 years "Number One" is determined upon revenge. Hale cannot imagine who it is or why anybody would want to harm him. Aimée Villon, his ward, arrives in her new home at this time. That night the doors of the steel vault in the basement are melted away by use of a strange invention and Aimée's securities and Hale's submarine plans are stolen. In a battle with the robbers, Hale and his son Tommy rescue Aimée, who has been kidnapped. When the struggle is over, Tommy finds that he, like his father, has been marked by the "T-T-T" for a victim of "Number One."

The mystery deepens in the second episode. The thieves are escaping in a railroad engine. The Hales, accompanied by Aimée, use a "flying fortress," a sort of railway military tank to chase them. The fugitives are overtaken but escape after a hand-to-hand encounter.

The third episode opens with Hale as head of a syndicate to recover sunken treasure. The enemy seizes his submarine and goes after the treasure. Arriving at the scene, Tommy and his men don diving suits and descend to the bottom of the sea. In a desperate underwater battle, he is captured and imprisoned in the treasure ship, which the T-T-T people dynamite.

By a miracle, Tommy escapes from the blast in the fourth episode and is picked up from a floating log by his father and Aimée. The T-T-T gang goes after them and sinks their vessel. Aimée and the crew are picked up and captured, but Hale escapes. Imprisoned in an old warehouse, Aimée throws a message out of the window, and it is picked up later by a child.

Who Pays? Serial. Released by Pathé Frères. *Director*: Harry Harvey. *Scenario*: William M. Ritchey. *Cast*: Edwin J. Brady, Daniel Gilfether, Henry King, Mollie McConnell, Ruth Roland (*Filmarama*, vol. 1).

The 12 Chapters: *The Price of Fame, The Pursuit of Pleasure, Where Justice Sleeps, The Love Liar, Unto Herself Alone, House of Glass, Blue Blood and Yellow, Today and Tomorrow, For the Commonwealth, The Pomp of the Earth, The Fruit of Folly, Toil and Tyranny.* Chapter 1 was copyrighted Mar. 21, 1914, and Chapter 12 was copyrighted Oct. 13, 1915 (*Encyclopedia of the Movie Studios*, p. 234, and "Southern Exposure," p. 118).

Commentary: Recognizing the success of serialized novels in magazines, Balboa Studios decided to do the same thing in films. The *Daily Telegram* (Oct. 30, 1914, 3:3) wrote: "The first serial involves a question everybody is familiar with in one form or another. It is an old, old story—as old as love, romance or marriage, but the world has been disagreeing about it ever since the days of Adam and Eve. Now it must be settled by the motion picture patrons of the United States. It will be propounded in a strong two-reel drama. A trailer at the end of it will ask 'Who Pays?'"

Motion picture patrons of the country were to respond to the question asked at the end of each serial. In order to stimulate their active participation, the Balboa Company said that it would give one thousand dollars in gold for the best answers to the simple questions that the 12 features would pose.

Who Wins[?]. Series by Will M. Ritchey (*Daily Telegram*, Oct. 6, 1916, p. 2).

The Wildcat. Five reels. *Cast*: Jackie Saunders (*Daily Telegram*, Nov. 1917).
  Commentary: Jackie Saunders had worked for Biograph in the East and one year for Universal before signing a contract with Balboa. E. D. Horkheimer met with Mutual Film Corp. to arrange the distribution of 6 five-part productions with Jackie Saunders. The first release was *Sunny Jane*, followed soon afterwards by *The Checkmate* and *The Wildcat*, then *A Bit of Kindling, Betty Be Good,* and *Bab the Fixer*.

The Will O' the Wisp. Four-reel drama. Balboa Amusement Producing Co. Made for William Fox, released July 1914 by Box Office Attraction Co. (*American Film Institute Catalog*, p. 1042). *Cameraman*: Joseph Brotherton. *Cast*: Henry King (*Larry Thorn, novelist*), Jackie Saunders (*Hazel, Will O' the Wisp*), Madeline Pardee (*Julia Rider*), Mollie McConnell (*the widow*), Robert Grey (*Baron Von Keller*), Charles Dudley (*the miser*), Helen King (*Julia Rider*), W. Johnson (*the farmer*).
  Commentary: The *Daily Telegram* (Oct. 29, 1914, 3:4) reports that this film was produced in Feb. 1914 in the flooded lowlands near the Los Cerritos bridge north of Long Beach. This masterpiece won great praise throughout the East and England because of the many thrilling scenes shown in the 4,000 feet of film. This movie also employed novelty tinting for triple exposure scenes that was based on innovations created by Robert Brotherton of the Balboa Studios.
  The players risked their lives in crossing the storm-swollen river, tottering bridge, and flooded farm lands between Long Beach and Compton. At times the camera's vision extended several miles across the inundated area, where the actors and actresses of the Balboa Company courageously worked while filming the dramatic actions of the big photoplay. The cinematographer of the company, Joseph Brotherton, used a $1,400 camera to film the dangerous acts, and several times he had to save himself and his valuable machine from the surging currents of the flood.
  Summary: Larry Thorn is rejected by his old flame, Julia Rider, once she learns that he has been dueling with one of his rivals. Larry, a swashbuckling romantic, retreats into the wild, doffing his city clothes, dressing like a poor rustic, and living in a shack. In this very natural setting, Larry one day saves the life of a woman named Hazel, who is nicknamed "Will O' the Wisp," and he falls madly in love with her. They seem to be made for each other, and Hazel is the kind of damsel who needs Larry's gallantry and bravery. For example, Hazel's father sells her to a scoundrel who claims he wants to marry her. Larry then saves Hazel from this plight during a horrendous flood. He even tries to save the scoundrel who bought Hazel but manages only to save his sweetheart. (Drawn from the *American Film Institute Catalog*, p. 1042.)
  Review: The story stars Jackie Saunders, a ragged girl, who is the daughter of a blind miser. She runs wild in the wooded country along the banks of a small river. *Motion Picture World* (July 4, 1914) had great praise for Saunders, saying she "mixes an elfin unreality in her realistically human portrayal." The reviewer wrote that her work in the early scenes of the picture could be compared only with that of Mary Pickford. Both had an aspect of character that warmed the hearts of the viewers.

The Winner. Three-reel drama. Nemo. Made for William Fox, released Sept. 28, 1914, by Box Office Attraction Co. (*Daily Telegram*, Nov. 16, 1914, 10:7). *Director*: Bertam Bracken. *Cast:* Francis MacDonald (*Tex Reeves*), Lucille Younge (*Bess Harper*), Henry Stanley (*Al Harper*) (*Motion Picture News*, May 30, 1914).
  Summary: Two cowboys love the ranch owner's daughter; she prefers the one who has a fondness for strong drink. Her favored suitor is accused of cheating an Indian at cards, but he manages to convince the other players that the Indian was wrong. Later the Indian, seeking revenge, shoots the cowboy. The wounded cowboy loses his memory, and the rival in love is accused of the crime and sent to jail. The

Indian escapes to Canada and sends a letter which sets things straight. The suspected shooter is freed from jail and wins the hand of the girl.

Review: According to *Variety* (Oct. 10, 1914, p. 25), the film was a Western and an ordinary one at that, with the trained horse in the picture as good an actor as any of the human cast members. The magazine thought that the picture was satisfactory, however, and would do well as a feature film.

Winter Sports in Southern California. Yacht racing in San Diego and scenes of the U.S. submarine *Pike* (*Daily Telegram*, Mar. 14, 1911, 5:7).

Won by a Nose. One-reel comedy. Pathé Frères. Released Feb. 18, 1914, by General Film Co. *Cast*: Della Connor (*the girl*), Charles Dudley (*her father*), Carl Erlanger (*Count Getrich*), Harold Reese (*his rival*).

Summary: The film was described by the *Los Angeles Examiner* as "an amusing farce with plenty of action." The girl loves one man, an old and valued friend, but her father wants her to marry Count Getrich. The girl can't tolerate the Count, and when he tries to kiss her, she has a bad nose bleed. To stop it, he uses the old-fashioned remedy of putting a door key down her back. In his excitement, he locks the door before he removes the key, and when the nose bleed does not stop, he has a choice: remove the key from the girl's clothing or exit via the window. Of course, he takes the window route and is seen by a policeman who thinks he is a thief. Amid much confusion, he returns to the girl in the locked room, and they both escape through the window, and to a minister's house where, strangely, they are married. (Drawn from *Press Clippings*, vol. 1.)

The Yellow Bullet. This four-act play was adapted for the screen by William H. Lippert from a magazine story. Released by General Film Co. *Director*: Harry Harvey. *Cast*: Robyn Adair (*Fred Fowler*), Lucy Payton (*Teresa Fowler*), Bruce Smith (*Harry Holt*), Neil Hardin (*Surgeon Lloyd*), Frank Erlanger (*Pedro*), Gloria Payton (*Spanish Nell*), Ruth Lackaye (*Mrs. Black*), Charles Dudley (*Perkins*) (*Daily Telegram*, May 1, 1917, 2:1).

Review: *Variety* (Mar. 17, 1917, p. 32) thought that the picture was terrible:

> It is utterly impossible that any person of mature mind could turn out a product of this sort. Judging from this picture and *Devil's Bait*, it would seem that the name of Balboa attached to a production means that the picture is just about as impossible a product as can be expected.

You've Got to Pay. Pathé Frères. Released Dec. 10, 1913, by General Film Co. *Cast*: John Dudley, Henry King, Madeline Pardee, Bill McCoy (*Press Clippings*, vol. 1, p. 21).

Summary: *Moving Picture World* (Dec. 6, 1913) explains the plot:

> John Dudley leaves jail, where he has been serving a term for embezzlement, at the same time as Bill McCoy. Dudley, at heart a worthy man, determines to live down his past. He gets a position, but McCoy trails him and blackmails him for a portion of his earnings. Desperate at the turn of affairs, Dudley moves to another town. Here he finally secures another position, in which he makes good and is promoted. He becomes engaged to the daughter of the company's president, but his past will not [---] down. McCoy again crosses his path and threatens to tell all if he is not given $5,000. Dudley determines to give up the unequal fight and goes to his fiancée, telling her of the blot on his past, and offers to release her from the engagement. She, however, refuses to do so, in which she is supported by her father, who tells Dudley that he trusts him in spite of all [*Press Clippings*, vol. 1, p. 21].

Zollenstein. Four-reel drama. Copyright Nov. 23, 1917, General Film Co., Inc., LP11737. Falcon Features. Released Dec. 4, 1917, by General Film Co. *Supervisors*: H. M. Horkheimer and E. D. Horkheimer. *Director*: Edgar Jones. *Scenario*: Douglas Bronston. Based on the novel *Zollenstein* by William Blair Morton Ferguson (New York, 1908). *Cast*: Daniel Gilfether (*King* of Zollenstein/King of Saxonia), Monroe Salisbury (*Crown Prince, Zollenstein/John Mortimer*), Vola Vale (*Princess Fulvia/Princess Zenia*), William Edler (*Boris Von Hohenstauffen*), Frank Erlanger (*Captain Kienert*), Jane Pepperell (*Betta*), J. P. Wade (*Count Von Moltke Hertz*), Edward Jobson (*Johann Lesser*), Leah Gibbs (*Lady Maulfrey Le Fay*), Harl McInroy (*Prince Hugo*).

Commentary: According to the *American Film Institute Catalog* (p. 1081), the story was first published in *Popular Magazine*. A preproduction news item states that R. Henry Gray and Gordon Sackville were to act in this film, which was originally slated to be part of the Fortune Photoplays series.

Summary: King Zollenstein prudently arranges his son's marriage to the Princess of Saxonia, but all this careful planning is dashed by the son's impulsiveness. King Zollenstein learns that his son has secretly married Lady Maulfrey Le Fay. The furious king exiles his son to England, but the prince is called back when King Zollenstein is dying. At the same time, Lady Maulfrey Le Fay dies in childbirth. One disaster follows another. The once-exiled prince does succeed to the throne, but Boris, King Zollenstein's illegitimate brother, plots to overthrow his nephew in order to take over the kingdom. Boris pays Betta, a maid, to kill the newborn prince and rightful heir to the throne. The maid spares the royal child, however, and escapes with him while going into hiding. The unlucky monarch, already a widower and now mourning the loss of his infant son, dies in an accident, allowing his evil uncle Boris to ascend to the throne. Boris, however, has a powerful enemy in the Grand Chancellor, and the latter wants the rightful heir on the throne. The Grand Chancellor unexpectedly meets the grown-up heir who is now called John Mortimer and has an undeniable resemblance to the royal family. Unwilling to accept Boris as ruler, the Grand Chancellor proclaims John the rightful heir. Of course, Boris disputes these claims, but Betta, who raised the royal prince, is able to prove John's heritage. Once on the throne, John mends the misalliances of the past by marrying Princess Zenia, the daughter of the Saxonian princess whose intended royal match was upset years earlier by the secret marriage that caused so much grief. (Drawn from the *American Film Institute Catalog*, p. 1081.)

Bibliography

Most of the filmography contribution provided by Claudine Burnett, head of literature and photo history, Long Beach Public Library, was obtained from two Long Beach daily newspapers, the *Daily Telegram* and the *Long Beach Press*. These papers were thoroughly searched from 1910 to 1923, with all information regarding film studios in Long Beach noted and indexed in the *Long Beach Collection Newspaper Index*. Burnett also researched *Variety* thoroughly from June 11, 1910, to February 28, 1919.

The Historical Society of Long Beach provided access through its archives to the publicity scrapbook of the Balboa Studios for 1913 and 1914, identified in the filmography as *Press Clippings*, vol. 1; the second volume is presently unavailable. The following list comprises the various resources carefully culled and annotated for the book *Balboa Films*. The authors also researched the *American Film Institute Catalog*, cross-referencing as much as possible to obtain the maximum listing of films produced at Balboa Studios.

Akins, W. Appraisal of the Balboa Amusement Producing Company. Long Beach, 1919.
American Film Institute Catalog of Motion Pictures Produced in the United States. Vol. 1, Feature Films, 1911–1920. Berkeley: University of California Press, 1983.
American Film Institute Catalog of Motion Pictures Produced in the United States. Vol. 2, Feature Films, 1921–1930. Berkeley: University of California Press, 1983.
Ankerich, Michael G. *Broken Silence: Conversations with 23 Silent Film Stars*. Jefferson, N.C.: McFarland, 1993.
Barnett, Correlli. *The Great War*. London: Putnam, 1979.
Benét, William Rose. *The Reader's Encyclopedia*. New York: Thomas Y. Crowell, 1965.
Blum, Daniel. *A Pictorial History of the Silent Screen*. New York: Grosset & Dunlap, 1953.
Burnett, Claudine. "Influenza Ghosts." *Haunted Long Beach*. Long Beach: Historical Society of Long Beach, 1996.
_____. "Long Beach's Oil Strike." Unpublished manuscript. Long Beach: Long Beach Public Library, 1995–.

_____. "Timeline of Long Beach Movie Studios." Unpublished manuscript. Long Beach: Long Beach Public Library, 1995–.

Callard, Chris. "Long Beach Story: The Balboa Amusements Producing Company." *Long Beach Review* 7, no. 11 (July-August 1984).

De Atley, Richard. *Long Beach, The Golden Shore: A History of the City and the Port*. Houston: Pioneer Publications, 1988.

Doyle, Billy H. "Lost Players." *Classic Images*, no. 153 (1988).

Edmonds, Andy. *Frame-up! The Shocking Scandal that Destroyed Hollywood's Biggest Comedy Star, Roscoe "Fatty" Arbuckle*. New York: Avon, 1991.

Enclyclopedia Britannica. "Motion Picture." New Encyclopædia Britannica: Micropædia. 1988.

Enclyclopedia Britannica. "World War I." New Encyclopædia Britannica: Micropædia. 1988.

Epley, Malcolm. *Highlights & Anecdotes: Long Beach's 75 Years*. Long Beach: Long Beach Diamond Jubilee, 1963.

Esposito, Vincent J. *Concise History of World War I*. New York: Praeger, 1976.

Fernett, Gene. *American Film Studios: An Historical Encyclopedia*. Jefferson, N.C.: McFarland, 1988.

Giroux, Robert. *Deed of Death: The Story Behind the Unsolved Murder of Hollywood Director William Desmond Taylor*. New York: Alfred A. Knopf, 1990.

Griffith, Richard, and Arthur Mayer. *The Movies*. New York: Bonanza, 1957.

Grobaty, Tim. "Long Beach: One giant film set for Hollywood." *Press-Telegram*, Jan. 18, 1997, A:1ff.

_____. "Hollywood creates some traffic at Long Beach sites." *Press-Telegram* Jan. 25, 1997, A:2.

_____. "It's a bloody great time in Long Beach." *Press-Telegram*, Feb. 1, 1997, A:2.

_____. "It was a 'Mad, Mad, Mad World' on L.B. Blvd." *Press-Telegram* Feb. 22, 1997, A:2.

_____. "*Queen Mary* in for a big-time surf adventure." *Press-Telegram*, March 1, 1997, A:2.

_____. "Lights, cameras at the Pyramid, Blair Field." *Press-Telegram*, March 8, 1997, A:2.

_____. "L.B. ship *Californian* in new Spielberg film." *Press-Telegram*, April 12, 1997, A:2.

_____. "St. Mary a hot locale for TV, film." *Press-Telegram*, April 19, 1997, A:2.

_____ "Long Beach's latest onscreen role — Phoenix." *Press-Telegram*, April 28, 1997, D:1.

_____. "Comedian Tim Conway 'Speeds' and bounces all over L.B." *Press-Telegram*, May 5, 1997, D:1.

_____. "Swayze crash delays L.B. shoot." *Press-Telegram*, May 12, 1997, D:1.

Hillburg, Bill. "Back to the future." *Press-Telegram*, May 16, 1997, A:1ff.

Insurance Map of Long Beach, California. Tracts 62 and 64, pp. 48 and 50. 1914. Reprint. New York: Sanborn Map Company 1942.

James, Henry Norman. Attorney. Writ of Attachment: Thomas R. Mills, Plaintiff, vs. W. J. Conner, et al., Defendant. Los Angeles: Superior Court, 1919.

Kackley, Vera. "Story of Studio Told Here." *Long Beach Press Telegram*, Aug. 20, 1930, A9:5.

Katz, Ephraim. "Charles Pathé." In *Film Encyclopedia*. Harper Perennial, 1994.

Keaton, Buster, with Charles Samuels. *My Wonderful World of Slapstick*. New York: Doubleday, 1960.

Kline, Jim. *The Complete Films of Buster Keaton*. New York: Carol, 1993.

Knox, Richard A. "Virulent 1918 flu virus is analyzed." *Press-Telegram*, March 21, 1997, A:9.

Koegel, Kathryn I. "The Balboa Studios of Long Beach: A Rediscovery." Project of Honors Collegium II; Los Angeles Symposium. University of California at Los Angeles, 1982.

Lahue, Kalton C. *Bound and Gagged: The Story of the Silent Serials*. South Brunswick, N.J.: A. S. Barnes, 1968.

Lauritzen, Elinar, and Gunnar Lundquist. *American Film-Index, 1916–1920*. Vol. 2. Stockholm: Film-Index, 1984.

"Long Beach-Balboa Studios Fall in Path of Progress." *Los Angeles Times*, March 22, 1925, sec. II, p. 10.
Meyer, Larry L., and Patricia Larson Kalayjian. *Long Beach, Fortune's Harbor*. Tulsa: Continental Heritage Press, 1983.
Miller, Blair. *American Silent Film Comedies: An Illustrated Encyclopedia of Perons, Studios and Terminology*. Jefferson, N.C.: McFarland, 1995.
Miller, H. C. *Atlas of Long Beach*. City Engineers Office and Records of Los Angeles County, July 1915.
Minotta, Mauricio. "And the Oscar goes to ... Long Beach?" *Press-Telegram*, May 10, 1997, A:1.
Monteagudo, Luis, Jr. "Movie, TV deal signed for dome." *Press-Telegram*, Jan. 1, 1997, A:1ff.
_____. "Lights, action ... Long Beach." *Press-Telegram*, Jan. 6, 1997, B:1ff.
Moran, Cora M. Notary Public. State of California: State Archives. *Articles of Incorporation of California Motion Picture Manufacturing Company*. Long Beach: First National Bank Bldg., 1910.
Moving Picture World. From Long Beach Collection pamphlet file; no date.
Oderman, Stuart. *Roscoe "Fatty" Arbuckle: A Biography of the Silent Film Comedian, 1887–1933*. Jefferson, N.C.: McFarland, 1994.
Osborne-Yeats, Marie. Letter to author, April 9, 1997.
_____. Personal interviews, 1995–1997.
Pols, Mary F., and Bob Strauss. *Los Angeles Daily News*. "Hollywood and Oscars—to have and have not." *Press-Telegram*, May 14, 1997, A:6.
Press Clippings. Long Beach: Historical Society of Long Beach Archives, Vol. 1, 1913-1914.
Rosenthal, Harry F. Associated Press. "NASA deflects comet conspiracy theory." *Press-Telegram*, May 14, 1997, A:2.
Saunders, Jackie, Jr. Letter to the authors, April 1997.
_____. Personal interviews, 1995–1997.
Scott, Tony. "Southern Exposure." *Daily Variety*. Film Studios Anniversary Issue, 1990, 110–130.
Slide, Anthony. *The American Film Industry: A Historical Dictionary*. New York: Greenwood, 1986.
Stewart, John. *Filmarama. Vol. 1, The Formative Years, 1893–1919*. Metuchen, N.J.: Scarecrow, 1975.
_____. *Filmarama. Vol. 2, The Flaming Years, 1920–1929*. Metuchen, N.J.: Scarecrow, 1977.
Thompson, Frank, ed. *Henry King, Director: From Silents to 'Scope*. Based on interviews by David Shepard and Ted Perry. Los Angeles: Directors Guild of America, with the Giornate del Cinema Muto, 1995.
Wanamaker, Marc. "Encyclopedia of the Movie Studios." Unpublished manuscript.
Williams, Alan. *Republic of Images: A History of French Filmmaking*. Cambridge: Harvard University Press, 1992.

Index

Information, when available, has been provided in parentheses about Balboans and others associated with the Long Beach studios of the silent era.

Abbot, Gypsy (actress; first wife of Henry King; b. Atlanta GA 1897 — d. 1952) 41, 71, 103, 104, 106, 204, 210, 241, 251, 256
Abide with Me (1914) 111, 196
Academy Awards of 1997 182
Academy of Motion Picture Arts and Sciences 110, 182
The Acid Test (1915) 196–197
Acme (film company) 162, 195
The Actor 87
Actualités Gaumont (newsreel) 6
Adair, Robyn (actor) 205, 216, 269
Adams, Maude (stage actress) 26, 129
The Adventures of a Madcap (1915) 73, 118, 196
The Adventures of Martin Eden 232
The Adventures of Ruth 120, 197
Air Time 12
Alco (film company) 63, 70
Aldwyn, Irene (actress) 160, 255
The Alien Blood (1917) 189, 197
The Alien Blood (short story) 197
All on Account of Polly (1914) 197–199
Allen, Alta (actress) 170, 171, 172, 231
Allen, Elsie (actress) 71, 204
Allen, Joan (actress) 182
Allen, Richard (né Frank Barnes; actor; b. 1875 — d. 1940; interred at family plot, Crawfordville IN) 24

Alliance Films Corporation 71, 119, 194, 204, 222
Almost Crazy (1914?) 199
Alters, Easter (actor) 219
American Distributing Corporation 195
American Film Company (aka The Flying "A") 94, 108, 111, 127, 194, 229
American Releasing Corporation 172, 231
American Theatre 23, 26
American Theatrical Exchange 128
Amex (American-Mexican) Company 28
The Amistad 181
Anderson, G. M. (co-founder, Essanay Film Manufacturing Co.) 13
Angel Child (1918) 199–201, 226, 243, 266
Angels in the Outfield 182
Anger, Lou (manager for Roscoe Arbuckle) 59, 147
Animated (film company) 28
Anita King Company 75, 194
Ankerich, Michael G. (author) 137, 141, 230
Arbuckle, Andrew (actor; b. Galveston TX 1887 — d. 1932) 49, 71, 72, 104, 228, 233, 247
Arbuckle, Roscoe "Fatty" (né Roscoe Conklin Arbuckle; aka Will B. Good and William B. Goodrich; actor; b. Smith Cowter KS 1887 — d. Hollywood CA 1933) 2, 13, 30, 56, 57, 59, 75, 76, 80, 96, 101, 103, 104, 132–135, 166, 167, 197, 202, 209, 210, 217, 236, 237, 241

Archer, H. E. (full name unknown; actor) 240, 265
Arliss, George (actor; b. London, England, 1868 — d. 1946) 26
Armistice 154
Arnold, Roberta (actress) 251, 252
Arnold Stock Company 105
Arris, Henry (actor) 166, 234
Arrowhead Theatre (aka Joyland) 23
Art Film Company 62, 195
Art Theatre 186
Arthur, Bea (actress) 141
Arthur, Lee (scenarist) 202
Arthur, Stanley Clisby (writer) 243
Asai, Ichiro (pioneer motion-picture executive, Long Beach) 23
Ashton, Sylvia (actress; b. 1880 — d. 1940) 71, 204
Association of Film Commissioners International Conference 12
Astra (Film Corporation) 120, 124, 156, 194, 219
Atlantic Distributing Corporation 195, 239

Atlas Film Corporation 162, 163, 195
August, Edwin (né Edwin August Phillips Von Der Butz; actor; b. St. Louis MO 1883 — d. Hollywood CA 1964) 45, 66, 87, 88, 128, 201, 217
Austin, George (actor) 55, 165, 252
Author's League of America 37, 40, 62
The Avenging Conscience 172
The Awakening (1914) 11, 89, 201–202
Ayres, Sydney (né David Sydney Ayres; actor and director; b. New York NY 1879 — d. Oakland CA 1916) 24, 27, 39, 232, 252

B. S. Moss Motion Picture Corporation 111, 194, 204, 216, 223, 245
Bab the Fixer (1917) 114, 118, 130, 202, 203, 205, 207, 258, 268
Baby Bennett (juvenile actress) 263
(Baby) Marie Osborne Film Company (aka Marie Osborne Film Company; plaintiff against Master Pictures Corp.) 160, 162, 195
Baby Peggy (juvenile actress) 135, 228
Baby Ruth *see* Roland, Ruth
Baddeley, R. S. (full name unknown; Eastern capitalist involved in Long Beach Studio, Inc.) 173
Bailey, Dan (actor) 220
Balboa, Vasco Núñez de (b. Castile, Spain, 1475 — d. Acla, Panama, 1519; explorer, first European to sight the Pacific Ocean; H. M. Horkheimer was very interested in the life of Balboa, drawing on the name for the Horkheimers' studio) 1, 33, 70
Balboa Amusement (Producing) Company (aka Balboa Feature Film Company; aka Balboa Studios; aka Horkheimer Studios) 1, 9, 10, 11, 23, 26, 29, 30, 33, 34, 35, 36, 39, 40, 41, 42, 43, 44, 45, 46, 47, 48, 49, 51, 52, 54, 55, 56, 59, 60, 61, 62, 63, 64, 65, 66, 67, 69, 70, 71, 72, 73, 74, 76, 77, 78, 80, 81, 84, 86, 88, 90, 91, 94, 96, 103, 104, 105, 106, 107, 108, 109, 111, 112, 113, 114, 118, 119, 120, 122, 123, 124, 125, 126, 127, 128, 130, 131–132, 135, 137, 138, 139, 143, 145, 147, 148, 150, 151, 152, 153, 155, 158, 159, 160, 163, 164, 172, 175, 177, 186, 192, 193, 194, 196, 197, 199, 200, 202, 203, 204, 205, 206, 207, 209, 210, 211, 212, 213, 214, 215, 216, 218, 219, 221, 222, 223, 224, 226, 227, 228, 229, 230, 234, 235, 236, 238, 239, 240, 241, 243, 244, 245, 247, 248, 249, 251, 252, 254, 255, 256, 258, 259, 260, 261, 262, 263, 264, 265, 266, 268
Balboa Feature Film Company 114, 124, 127, 143, 228, 229, 233, 243, 253; *see also* Balboa Amusement Producing Company
Balboa Film Festival and Studio Tour (1996) 186, 187
Balboa/International Film Company (aka Hampton Del Ruth Studios) 173, 195
Balboa Studio quadrangle 79–88, 176, 187
Balboa Studios 2, 3, 5, 29, 130, 132, 159, 160, 162, 163, 164, 167, 168, 169, 170, 171, 172, 173, 174, 175, 176, 177, 183, 190, 192, 197, 232, 255, 261, 267; *see also* Balboa Amusement Producing Company
The Balboan (periodical; Balboa's newsletter, issued annually to keep employees and trade journals updated on Balboa) 73
Baldwin, Daniel (actor) 182
Ball, Lucille (actress) 141
Balshofer, Fred (producer, New York Motion Picture Co.) 12
Bank of Italy (plaintiff against Master Pictures Corp.) 160
Bankruptcy (receivership) 76
Bara, Theda (née Theodosia Goodman; actress; b. Cincinnati OH ca. 1885 — d. 1955) 30, 80
Barber, M. L. (Mr. and Mrs.; full names unknown; actors) 166, 234
Bard, Ben (theatrical producer; husband of Ruth Roland) 123
Bard, Clark (cameraman) 149
Barlett, Charles E. (director) 216
Barlow, Zada (actress) 216
A Barnyard Romance (1920) 162, 202
Barrett, Wilson (author; actor; b. ca. 1900 — d. Sussex, England, 1981) 27, 220
Barrington, Herbert (né Herbert Barrington Hollingsworth; actor; b. England, 1872 — d. Tarrytown NY 1933) 27, 220
Barrow, Robert (actor) 223
Barry, Viola (actress) 232, 252
Barrymore, Ethel (actress) 128
Barrymore, John (actor) 26
Barrymore, Lionel (actor) 26
Bartlett, Frederick Orin (author) 226
Barton Fink 181
Baruch, Bernard M. (chairman, War Industries Board, Washington, D.C.) 154
Bateman, Victory (actress; b. Los Angeles CA 1865 — d. Los Angeles CA 1926) 49, 71, 104, 245
Batman and Robin 180
Batman Forever 12, 180
Battlestar Galactica (pilot episode) 181
Baynard, Beatrice (actress) 247
Baywatch (TV) 180
Be My Wife 172
Beach, Rex (writer) 40, 62
A Bear Escape (1914?) 202
Beaubien, Julien (actress) 206, 233
Beckett, Samuel (Irish writer) 97
Beckly, William (cameraman) 248
Beckway, William (Billie) J. (chief cameraman, Balboa Studios) 41, 43, 46, 63, 70, 72, 162, 202, 203, 205, 207, 225, 233, 258, 260, 262
Beecker, Loretta (actress; Balboan from Holland) 262
Beggs, Jonathan (inventor) 157
Belasco, David (theatrical producer; playwright; b. San Francisco CA 1853 — d. New York NY 1931) 27, 119, 128, 258
The Bell Boy (1918) 135, 202–203
The Bell-Ringer's Daughter 17
Bellmore (Bellmour), Harry (actor) 163, 165, 166, 212
Ben-Hur 39
Bennett, Belle (actress; married to Fred Windemere; b. Milaca MN 1890 — d. Hollywood CA 1932) 41, 44, 63, 84, 104, 247, 249, 263
Bennett, Billie 41
Bennett, E. C. (full name unknown; general manager, Long Beach Studios, Inc.) 172
Beresford, Vincent (actor) 233
Berger, Marjorie (financial advisor for W. D. Taylor) 98
Bergman, Ingmar (Swedish filmmaker) 96
Berlot (full name unknown; French writer?) 258
Bernhardt, Sarah (French actress) 26, 90
Bernstein, I. (full name unknown; general manager of the California studios for Universal Film Manufacturing Co.) 28
Bernstein, Isidore (Mr. and Mrs.; at "Christmas Gala") 41
Bertram, William (author; director; b. Walkerton, Ontario, 1880 — d. Los Angeles CA 1933) 164, 166, 212, 263,
The Best Man (1917) 130, 203
Betty Be Good (1917) 114, 118, 202, 203, 205, 207, 258, 268
Beulah (1915) 71, 204
Beyers, Clara (actress) 41, 104
Bijou Theatre 15, 18, 22, 23, 81
Bill and Coo and Ouija Board (1920) 162, 204
Bill and the Baby (1921) 204
Bill's Sweetheart (1913) 27
Bimberg, B. K. (vice-president, National Independent Motion

Picture Board of Trade, representing Schuyler Amusement Co.) 9
Biograph (Company) 8, 12, 27, 28, 45, 113, 202, 203, 205, 207, 258, 268
Birds of Prey (1916) 204
The Birth of a Man (1915) 204
The Birth of a Nation (1915) 48, 70, 172, 204
Bisby, R. L. (full name unknown; secretary; involved in the expected move of Universal from Los Angeles to Long Beach, 1914) 28
Bishop, Pessers & Company, Ltd. (exclusive British distributor for Balboa films) 33, 44, 65, 114, 194
Bison Archives 163
Bison (Company) 22, 28
A Bit of Kindling (1917) 114, 118, 202, 203, 205, 207, 258, 268
Bitter Sweets (1914) 205
Blade 181
Blair and Company 153
Blaisdell, Charles (actor) 209, 223, 231
Blake, Eddie (Dutch; cameraman, Meteor Pictures Corp.) 165
Blake, Lucy (actress; b. Boston MA 1888 – d. ?) 49, 55, 71, 104, 213, 255, 257
Blakeney (Mrs.; full name unknown; actress) 23, 241
Bliss of Ignorance (1915) 205
Blum, Daniel (author) 26
(Bob) Horner Company 195
The Bodyguard 182
Bolle, Augusta (actress) 41, 196, 223, 263
Bolt from the Sky (1915) 205
Bonner, Joe (juvenile actor) 160
The Boob and the Bandit (1914?) 205
Booth, Julia (actress) 32
Boots and Saddles (1916) 205–206
Bopp, Thomas (amateur astronomer) 190
Bordeau, Joe (actor) 236
Borgnine, Ernest (actor) 181
Bosworth, Hobart (actor, played in more than 600 films; producer; b. Mariett OR 1867 – d. Glendale CA 1944) 39, 232
Bosworth, Inc. 232
Bottomley, Roland (actor; b. Santa Ana CA 1888 – d. Hollywood CA 1943) 52, 72, 115, 218, 238
Boucicault, Aubrey (theatrical producer) 129
Bowers, John (actor; b. Garrett IN 1899 – d. 1936) 23
Bowers, Lulu (actress) 72, 233
Bowles, Marguerite 41
Box Office Attractions (Amusements) Company 9, 42, 45, 46, 65, 66, 67, 69, 89, 94, 111, 112, 113, 114, 119, 127, 130, 131, 132, 194, 195, 199, 201, 202, 205, 206, 207, 208, 210, 211, 213, 214, 217, 218, 219, 221, 222, 223, 224, 225, 227, 229, 233, 234, 237, 238, 240, 246, 247, 249, 251, 253, 254, 255, 256, 257, 259, 260, 261, 263, 264, 266, 268
Boyle, John (cameraman) 213
The Bracelet (1914) 206
Bracken, Bertram (managing director, Balboa Studios; married to Margaret Landis 1919–1924; b. San Antonio TX 1880 – d. 1952) 41, 45, 54, 62, 66, 71, 84, 103, 104, 105, 106, 203, 204, 207, 211, 219, 223, 233, 241, 249, 253, 256, 259, 264, 268
Brady, Edwin (Edward) J. (actor; b. New York NY 1889 – d. Hollywood CA 1942) 47, 49, 55, 71, 104, 110, 213, 237, 256, 257, 258, 262, 267
Brady, William A. (theatrical producer; president, National Association of the Motion Picture Industry) 125, 154
The Brand of Man (1915) 106, 111, 206
Brando, Marlon (actor) 141
Brand's Daughter (1917) 127, 206
Breakstone, Ben (actor) 212
The Break-Up (1914?) 206
Breamer, Sylvia (actress) 247
Breese, Edmund (actor) 69
Brewer, Thurlow W. (manager, Essanay Film Manufacturing Co.; director) 173
Brewester, James W. 41
Brewster, A. H. (or A. B.) (co-director, Long Beach Studios Corp.) 169, 170
Broening, H. Lyman (cameraman) 27, 208, 244
Broken Laws (1914?) 116, 118, 206
Broncho (film company) 28
Bronston, Douglas (scenarist) 203, 205, 223, 269
Brooks, M. F. (co-director, California Motion Picture Manufacturing Co.) 13, 15, 16
Brookton, Alice (actress) 223
Brotherton, Joseph (cameraman) 41, 45, 201, 223, 226, 255, 259, 262, 268
Brotherton, Ma(r)y (in charge of Assembling Dept., Balboa Studios) 41, 43, 63
Brotherton, Robert (Bob) (chief chemist; superintendent of laboratory, Balboa Studios) 41, 43, 61, 63, 66, 67, 268
Brown, George Alisey (manager; industrial bureau, Long Beach Chamber of Commerce) 166
Brown, Linnette (among top 10, star search, 1922, Empire Theatre, Long Beach) 171
Browne, Porter Emerson (author) 70
Brownlee, Frank (actor) 203, 223, 233, 234, 243,
Bryce, Jack (actor) 210, 234, 261
Buck, Ken (tavern proprietor, Joe Jost's) 182
Buell, Kenean (director, Kalem Co., Inc.) 13
Bull's Eye (Films) 162, 195
Bumping the Bumps (1914?) 207
Burbank Public Library 118
Burnett, Claudine (head of history and literature, Long Beach Public Library) 17, 18, 24, 29, 156, 157, 181, 186, 187, 188, 194, 211, 224
Burnett, Miles 41
Burning Daylight (novel) 38
Burns, JoAnn (director of special events in Long Beach) 180
Burns, M. J. (aka Miles Burns, cameraman) 161, 163
The Butcher Boy (1917) 57, 75
Buttons, Red (actor) 181
By Impulse (1913) 111, 207
Byde a Whyle Theatre 2, 13, 132
Byrne, Jack (actor) 213

The Cable Guy 180
Cadmus, Irene (among top 10, star search, 1922, Empire Theatre, Long Beach) 171
Cain, George (writer) 203
Calhern, Louis (né Carl Vogt; actor; b. Brooklyn NY ca. 1894 – d. 1956) 261
Calhoun, Patrick (actor) 226, 264, 266
California Motion Picture Manufacturing Company 5, 10, 11, 12, 13, 15, 16, 17, 18, 19, 20, 21, 22, 23, 24, 25, 26, 27, 28, 36, 62, 79, 84, 168, 190, 194, 240, 241
The Call of the Heart (1914) 66, 207
The Call of the Wild 40, 232, 244, 252
The Call of the Wild (novel) 38
Callard, Chris (writer) 10, 13, 25
Called Back (1914) 111, 207
Cameraphone (company) 114, 227
Camp, Mr. (full name unknown; secretary, Long Beach Chamber of Commerce, at time of California Motion Picture Manufacturing Co.) 16, 17, 21
Campbell, Barley (playwright) 125
Campodonico, Emilio (gold miner) 164
Captain Kiddo (1917) 189
Carlton, Arma (actress) 209
Carlton, Lloyd B. (director) 70
Carpenter, John (filmmaker) 181

Carroll, William (actor) 227
Carruthers, Brent (actor) 223
Carruthers, Myrtle (actress) 223
Carter, Leslie (stage actress) 129
Caswell, T. (full name unknown; assistant cameraman) 161
Caught by Wireless (play) 32
Cavender, Glen (actor) 209
Cecil, Edward (actor) 160, 255
Celebrated Players Film Company 194, 204
Chadwick, Helene (actress; b. New York 1897 — d. 1940) 160, 255
Chambers, C. Haddon (author) 70
Chaney, Lon Sr. (né Alonso or Alonzo Chaney; character actor; b. Colorado Springs CO ca. 1884 – d. 1930) 56, 170, 171, 231, 262
Change of Heart 141
Chaplin, Charlie (Sir Charles Spencer Chaplin; actor; director; writer; b. London, England, 1889 — d. Switzerland, 1977) 6, 57, 59, 75, 87, 93, 96, 123, 146, 147, 156, 168
The Chase 141
Chautauqua Assembly of Long Beach 17
The Checkmate (1917) 114, 118, 127, 130, 189, 202, 203, 205, 207, 258, 268
Chelsea 7750 (1913) 27, 207–208, 221
Chesebro (Chesbro), George (actor; distributor for Clark-Cornelia agency) 166, 167, 219
The Chief's Day Off (1914?) 208
The Child (play) 32
Child Actors Bill (aka The Coogan Law) 90
Children of the Ghetto (1915) 70
Children of the Ghetto (story) 70
Christie, Nan (actress) 44, 63, 215, 223
Christmas gala (1913, Hotel Virginia) 27, 41, 62
Christy, Howard C. (artist) 112
Church, Fred (actor) 201
Cinart (distributor) 248
Circus World 141
The City (play) 172
City Center Company (plaintiff against Master Pictures Corp.) 160
City Directory Company 128
The City of San Francisco (1913) 208
Clarendon, Hal (actor) 27, 244
Clark, Marguerite (actress; b. Avondale OH 1883 — d. New York NY 1940) 26, 123
Clark, Olga Prinzlau (scenarist; Long Beach resident) 241, 242
Clark-Cornelia (agency) 166
Clarke, G(eorge) Le Roi (actor;
  general manager; supervisor, Paragon Film Co.; co-director, Meteor Pictures Corp.) 162, 163, 164, 165
Clarke, Harry Corson (promoter for film industry in Long Beach) 163
Clawson, Dal (cameraman) 231
The Clean Gun (1917) 208
The Clean Gun (short story) 208
Clear and Present Danger 180
Cleaver, Frank (actor) 214
Clements, Karen (member of Long Beach Heritage; coordinator for guided historical tour of Balboa Film Studio site, 1996) 187
Cleo and Simp (1914–1917; serial) 189; see also *Ima Simp, Detective*
Cleopatra (1963) 142
Clifford, Kathleen (actress; b. Charlottesville VA 1894 — d. Los Angeles CA 1963) 55, 75, 201, 226, 263, 266
Clifford, William (Mr. and Mrs.) 41
Clifton, Elmer (actor) 233
Clifton, Wallace (scenarist) 244, 252
The Climber (1917) 111, 208–209
Clinton, Ben F. (actor) 227
Clune, W. H. (full name unknown; Los Angeles amusement magnate) 24
Cochrane, R. H. (full name unknown; motion-picture executive) 133
Cody, Lewis J. (né Louis Joseph Côté; actor; husband of Mabel Normand; b. Berlin NH 1884 — d. 1934) 2, 44, 51, 53, 63, 71, 103, 104, 115, 137, 209, 240, 253
Coffray, Frank (actor) 166, 234
Cogley, Nick (actor) 171, 231
Cohan, Mary Ann (née Mary Anne Jane Cohen; aka Mary Ann Gibson; actress; daughter of Jackie Saunders) 117
Cohen, Joseph Ward (second husband of Jackie Saunders) 117, 118
Cohl, Émile (French pioneer animator) 6
Coleman, Ronald (actor; b. Richmond, England, 1891 — d. 1958) 110
College Life (play) 103
The College Widow (play) 32
Collier, William Sr. (stage actor) 128
Colonel Selig's Zoo 120, 260
Columbia Film Company 162, 195
Comique Film Corporation 56, 57, 75, 76, 132, 135, 194, 202, 209, 210, 217, 236, 241
The Common Law (play) 106
Commonwealth (Pictures) Company 169, 170, 195
Comrade John (1915) 120, 124, 209
Congo 180
  Conklin, Chester (actor; b. Oskaloosa IA circa 1886 — d. 1971) 163
Conklin, William (actor; b. Brooklyn NY 1872 — d. Hollywood CA 1935) 49, 55, 71, 104, 204, 212–213, 237, 254, 255, 256, 257, 258, 262
Connant, William (actor) 248
Conner, W. J. (full name unknown; co-partner, Master Pictures Corp.) 160
Connor, Della (Delia) (actress) 198, 269
Connor, H. R. (full name unknown; publicity director, Empire Theatre, Long Beach) 170
Conway, Jack (actor) 252
Coogan, Jackie (juvenile actor; b. Los Angeles CA 1914 — d. 1984) 135, 228
The Coogan Law see Child Actors Bill
The Cook (1918) 135, 209–210
Cook, Frederick A. (explorer; d. New Rochelle NY 1940) 215
Cooke, Caroline Frances (actress) 227
Costner, Kevin (actor) 180, 182
Counsel for the Defense (1915) 210
The Count of Monte Cristo (novel) 168
The Counterfeit (1913 or 1914) 46, 210
A Country Hero (1917) 57, 75, 132, 135, 210
Courtleigh, William Jr. (actor; b. Buffalo NY 1892 — d. Philadelphia PA 1918) 49, 71, 104, 237
Coveted Heritage (1914) 48, 210
Coxen, Ed (actor) 120
Crane, Erle (actor) 213
Crane, Frank H. (director) 263
Crane, George 41
Crawford, Henry (actor) 55, 252
Creation Can't Be Bought see *Martin Eden*
The Criminal Code (1914) 127, 130, 210–211
The Crooked Road (1917) 111, 130, 211
Crown City Trust and Savings Bank (plaintiff against Master Pictures Corp.) 160
The Cruise of the Hell Ship (1914) 66, 211
Crystal (film company) 28
Crystal, Billy (actor) 181
Cunningham, Jack (scenarist) 219
Curley, Pauline (actress) 160, 255
Currier, R. C. (full name unknown; editor) 161
Cush, Joe (switchboard operator, Milburn Morante Comedy Co.) 163
Cyclone Racer 183, 184, 185; see also The Pike
Cyclonic Western Serials 219

Index

Dad Voute (full name unknown; actor) 203
D'Albrook, Sidney (actor) 248
Dale Violet (actress) 32
The Dancer (1913) 211, 212
The Dances of the Ages (1913) 26, 211–212
Daniels, Jeff (actor) 182
Dark Skies 180
Darkest Russia (play) 125
Darnall, J. L. (full name unknown; co-director, Meteor Pictures Corp.) 165
Daro, Mr. (full name unknown; wrestling promoter) 174, 175
The Dashing Ranger (1921) 166, 212
The Daughter of the Hills (1913) 27, 212
Davenport, Dorothy (actress; wife of Wallace Reid; b. Boston MA 1895 – d. 1977) 103, 116, 171, 206, 213, 233, 257, 259
Davenport, Milla (actress) 255
David Trattner Production Company 162, 195, 224
Davies, David (actor) 27, 212
Davies, Howard (actor) 227
Davis, H. R. (full name unknown; co-director, California Motion Picture Manufacturing Co.) 13, 15, 16
Davis, L. (full name unknown; co-partner, Long Beach Studios) 170
Davy Crockett (play) 88, 124
Dawley, J. (Jim) Searle (director; scenarist; studio manager for Edison in Long Beach; b. De Norte CO 1877 – d. 1940s) 10, 20, 24, 26, 27, 35, 36, 208, 212, 221, 240, 244
Dawson's Dancing Dolls 112
Deal, Nina (actress) 41, 104
Deane-Tanner, Denis (brother of William Desmond Taylor) 96, 101
De Carlton, George 70; *see also* Fox Features
Deely, (J.) Ben(ard) Deeley (vaudeville comic; actor; b. California 1878 – d. Hollywood CA 1924) 44, 63, 88, 223
Defending Your Life 180
Defying Destiny 116, 118, 212
De Gaston, Percy (cameraman) 44, 66, 67, 223
De Gonzales, Carmen (actress) 27, 212
Delano, F. C. (full name unknown; representative for New Art Film Co.) 160
Dell, Ethel M. (novelist) 99
Delmont, Mandy 134
Del Ruth, Hampton (actor; managing director, Long Beach Studios, Inc.; b. 1879 – d. Woodland Hills CA 1958) 23, 168, 169, 170, 171, 172, 173, 174, 231, 241
DeMille, Cecil B(lount) (motion-picture executive; director; b. Ashfield MA 1881 – d. Hollywood CA 1959) 10, 25
DeMille (Mrs.) 42
Demolition Man 181
De MoLouis, R. (full name unknown; plaintiff against Master Pictures Corp.) 160
Dempsey, Frank J. (Marie Osborne's first husband) 142
De Niro, Robert (actor) 181
Detective Dale and Mudflats Gang (1914) 212; *see also The End of the Bridge*
Devereaux, A. F. (full name unknown; co-director, R. D. Films) 163
The Devil (play) 106
The Devil's Bait (1917) (aka *Devil's Pet*) 124, 189, 212–213, 269
The Devil's Needle 172
Devil's Pet see *The Devil's Bait*
Dewees, Scott 12
Dewey, Percy 41
Dey, Jane (actress) 221
The Diamond from the Sky 94, 95
Diando Film Company (Glendale CA) (aka Diando Studios) 139
Diando Studios 57, 138, 230; *see also* Diando Film Company
Dickson, William (Edison's assistant; inventor of motion picture camera) 6
Dillon, Julian (actor) 263, 265
Directors Guild of America 110
Disney, Walt (film producer) 16
Disney Productions 145
Dividing Walls (1914?) 213
Dixey, Henry E. (actor; b. Boston MA 1859 – d. Atlantic City NJ 1943) 27, 208
Dixon, Denver (actor for Vitagraph westerns; manager, R. D. Films) 163
Dodge, Anna (actress; b. River Falls WI 1867 – d. 1947) 24
Donnelly and Girard Company 128
Doran, William C. (deputy to district attorney during W. D. Taylor's murder trial) 101
Dorothy Chandler Pavilion 182
Dos Passos, John (writer) 99
Douglas, Kirk (actor) 141
Douglas, W. A. S. (full name unknown; co-founder, Diando Film Co.) 139
Doyle, Billy H. (writer) 103
Drag Harlan (1920, rereleased 1925) 115, 116, 118, 189, 213
Drake, Charles Rivers (Colonel) (railroad magnate, responsible for the Pike amusement zone, Long Beach, 1902) 18, 184
Drake, Gene (son of Col. Drake) 184
Dream of Loco Juan (1914) 213–214
Dressler, Marie (actress) 26, 168
Drew, John (actor; b. Philadelphia PA 1854 – d. Dante Sanitarium 1927) 26, 128
Drum, S. B. (full name unknown; co-director, R. D. Films) 163
Drummer Manufacturing Company 167
Dudley, Charles (né Charles Dudley Heaslip; actor; b. Ft. Grant AZ 1883 – d. Woodland Hills CA 1952) 44, 49, 55, 63, 71, 103, 104, 196, 197, 202, 204, 205, 206, 211, 213, 218, 223, 228, 235, 236, 238, 242, 243, 245, 252, 254, 255, 258, 259, 263, 266, 268, 269
Dudley, John (actor) 269
Duhem, V. L. (full name unknown; motion-picture expert; general manager, California Motion Picture Manufacturing Co.) 16, 17
Duke of York's Theatre 130
Dumas, Alexandre (French author) 168
Duncan, John (actor) 260
Dungeons of the Dead see *Vengeance of the Dead*
Du Pont (company) 76
Dupree, Minnie (stage actress) 129–130
Durbin, Deanna (actress) 141
Du Ree, Squire F. (manager, Bijou Theatre, Long Beach) 18
Durfee, Minta (actress; wife of Roscoe Arbuckle; b. Los Angeles CA 1889 – d. Woodland Hills CA 1975) 13, 103, 132
Dwan, Allan (testified to Taylor's crusade against drug traffickers) 94
Dyer, Elmer G. (cameraman) 170, 171

Eagon (company) 28
The Earth Is Mine (1959) 141
Eason, Reeves (director, Knickerbocker Star Features; b. Friars Point MS 1886 – d. Sherman Oaks CA 1956) 53, 74, 239, 242
Eclair (company) 28
Eclectic Film Company 47, 48, 194, 266
Edgewood Folks (play) 125
Edison, Thomas Alva (inventor; motion-picture pioneer; b. Milan OH 1847 – d. Orange NJ 1931) 6, 7, 8, 10
Edison Manufacturing Company (aka Edison Motion Picture Company) 194, 208, 211, 212, 224, 227, 240

Edison (Motion Picture Company) 10, 17, 24, 25, 27, 28, 34, 35, 36, 44, 55, 57, 74, 78, 79, 84, 114, 145; *see also* Edison Manufacturing Company
Edith Sterling Productions 162, 195
Edler (Elder), Charles (actor) 208, 215
Edler, William (actor) 270
Edwards, J. Gordon (studio chief; managing producer, Academy of Music, New York) 69, 70, 213
Eggs and Water (1914?) 214
Ehfe, William (actor) 203, 223
Electric Theatre Supply Company 9
Elliott, William (actor) 209
Ellis, Albert B. (actor) 203, 263
Elora (Miss; full name unknown; actress) 23, 241
Empire Stock Company 128
Empire Theatre 170, 171
Empress, Marie (actress) 216
The End of the Bridge 130, 212, 214; see also *Detective Dale and Mudflats Gang*
Ensminger, Robert (Bert) (actor; director; assistant director to Henry King) 209, 216, 231, 235, 265, 266
Equitable Motion Pictures Corporation 127, 131, 143, 194, 253, 262
Erlanger, Carl (actor) 198
Erlanger, Frank A. (actor) 41, 49, 71, 104, 209, 214, 215, 216, 235, 245, 247, 249, 251, 256, 258, 263, 269, 270
Erwin, Mr. (manager, La Petite Theatre, 1907) 17
Escape from L.A. 180, 181
Essanay (Film Manufacturing Company) 8, 13, 28, 52, 57, 63, 70, 145, 173, 204
Evans, Augusta (author) 204, 251
Everett, Charles (Shorty) (master of properties) 161, 163
The Execution of Private Slovick 181
Executive Decision 180
The Explorer (1914) 215
The Explorer (novel) 215
An Eye for an Eye (1914) 48, 67, 215

Fairbanks, Douglas Sr. (actor) 26
Fairbanks (studio) 166
The Fairy of the Spring 17
Fairyland Theatre 24
Faith's Reward (1916) 111, 215
Falcon Features (brand name for Balboa Films, Aug. 1917–Feb. 1918) 54, 75, 111, 124, 128, 130, 131, 194, 206, 208, 215, 219, 225, 231, 232, 243, 252, 257, 263, 269
Famous Players (Film) Company (aka Famous Players–Lasky) 17, 26, 27, 28, 36, 160, 194, 195, 207, 210, 212, 221, 244

Famous Players–Lasky (Corporation) 169, 171, 202, 209, 210, 217, 236, 241, 261; *see also* Famous Players (Film) Company
Fantasmagorie 6
Fantômas 6
Farnum, William (actor; b. Boston MA 1876 – d. Hollywood CA 1953) 115, 116, 213, 220
The Fatal Ring 120
The Fatal Thirty (1919) 161, 215
Feet of Clay (1917) 215–216
Feet of Clay (story) 215
Feldman, Adam (property manager, Gumbiner Properties) 187
Fellini, Federico (innovative filmmaker) 177
Fellows, Howard (W. D. Taylor's chauffeur) 97, 101
Ferguson, Elsie (actress; b. New York NY 1883 – d. 1961) 26
Ferguson, William Blair Morton (author) 269
Fielding, Howard (aka Charles Whitherle Hooke; author) 223, 234
Film exchanges 8
Film Supply Company 28
Film Welfare League 117
Finch, Peter (British actor) 141
Fisher, Harrison (artist) 112
Fitch, Clyde (playwright) 32, 128, 237
Fitzmaurice, George (director) 120, 219
Flatau, Lawrence 41
Fleming, Ethel (actress) 49, 71, 104, 240
The Flexible Man 17
The Flying "A" *see* American Film Company
Fonda, Jane (actress) 141
A Fool There Was (1915) 70
A Fool There Was (story) 70
Ford, Eugenie (actress) 242, 246
Ford, Glenn (actor) 232
Ford, Victoria (actress) 242
Forget Paris 181
Forrest, Edwin (actor) 126
Forsyth, W(illiam) S. (co-partner, Master Pictures Corp.) 160, 248
Forsythe, Hattie (actress) 27, 244
Fortune Photoplay 130, 194, 197, 211, 212, 223, 231, 264
Foster, William C. (cameraman) 261
Fowler, F. D. (full name unknown; general manager, Morante Producing Co.) 166
Fox, William (né Wilhelm Fried; pioneer distributor and motion-picture executive; president and co-director, National Independent Motion Picture Board of Trade,

representing the William Fox Amusement Co.; b. Tulchva, Hungary, 1879 – d. New York NY 1952) 8, 9, 24, 44, 46, 47, 65, 66, 69, 70, 89, 94, 111, 112, 114, 115, 119, 127, 130, 131, 132, 133, 153, 156, 171, 199, 201, 202, 205, 206, 207, 208, 210, 211, 213, 214, 217, 218, 219, 221, 222, 223, 224, 225, 227, 229, 233, 234, 236, 237, 238, 240, 246, 247, 249, 251, 252, 254, 255, 256, 257, 259, 260, 261, 263, 264, 266, 268
Fox Features (aka Fox Film Corporation) 3, 69, 118, 195, 213, 220
Fox (Film Corporation) *see* Fox Features
Foxhall, George (author) 208, 209
Francis, Bert (actor) 49, 71, 104, 247
Frankenburg, Julius (actor) 239
Franklyn, Sidney (actor) 213
Frantzen, Nell (actor) 223
Frechette, LeRoy J. (scenic artist, Balboa Studios) 41, 69, 70
Frederick, Pauline (née Pauline Beatrice or Beatrice Pauline Libbey; actress; b. Boston MA circa 1883 – d. 1938) 26
Freeman, Max (stage actor) 130
Fremont, Al (actor) 213
Freshwater, C. E. (full name unknown; assistant manager, Empire Theatre, Long Beach) 170
Friends I Have Known and Liked (book) 105
Frist, Helen and A. C. (full name unknown; proprietors of the American Theatre, Long Beach) 24
Frohman, Charles (theatrical manager; founder of Theatrical Syndicate; established Empire Stock Company; younger brother of Daniel and Gustave Frohman; b. Sandusky OH 1860 – d. at sea 1915) 128, 129
Frohman, Daniel (theatrical manager; b. Sandusky OH 1851 – d. New York NY 1940) 26, 125
From Manger to Cross 24
Frontier (company) 28, 114, 227
Fugite, Haru (actor) 264
Furey, Charles M. (co-partner, Master Pictures Corp.) 160
Fury, Barney (actor) 215, 226, 243

Gaden, Alexander (actor; b. 1880 – d. ?) 27, 212
Gallagher, Ray(mond) (actor; b. 1895 – d. 1975) 41, 105, 218, 222, 224
Garbutt, Frank A. (Jack London's associate and fellow plaintiff in

copyright lawsuit against Balboa Studios) 39, 62
Garnett (full name unknown) 197
Gasnier, Louis J. (filmmaker) 120, 231
Gaumont Palace 6, 20
Gaumont (Pictures) 6, 7, 65, 114, 227
The Gay Divorcee 141
Gayton, Betty (among top 10, star search, 1922, Empire Theatre, Long Beach) 171
Geiger, Caroline (among top 10, star search, 1922, Empire Theatre, Long Beach) 171
General Film Company, (Inc.) 8, 47, 53, 54, 73, 74, 75, 111, 112, 119, 124, 127, 130, 131, 194, 195, 196, 197, 200, 203, 206, 207, 208, 212, 215, 219, 223, 224, 225, 229, 231, 233, 234, 235, 236, 237, 242, 243, 245, 246, 247, 252, 256, 257, 263, 264, 265, 266, 269
Gentlemen's Agreement (1915) 216
Geographical Feature Film Corporation 51
George, Burton (director) 197
Gerber, Neva Delorez (actress; lover of W. D. Taylor while at Balboa) 44, 46, 63, 70, 89, 90, 201, 210, 213, 215, 217, 225, 261
Gerrard, Douglas (actor) 227
Gerstad, Harry W. (cameraman) 228
Gervais, Aimie (donator, Historical Society of Long Beach) 78
Gheller, Ed (cameraman) 162, 224
Gibbs, Leah (actress) 209, 234, 270
Giblyn, Charles (director; scenarist) 227
Gibson, Mary Ann *see* Cohan, Mary Ann
Gibson, Tom (scenarist; director) 163, 166, 167, 170, 171, 234
Gibson-Gowland, T. H. (aka Gibson Gowland; actor; b. Spennymoor, England, ca. 1875 — d. 1951) 209, 243, 252
Gilbert, Florence (actress) 160
Gilfether, Daniel (actor; b. 1840s — d. Long Beach CA 1919) 47, 49, 53, 54, 71, 72, 74, 88, 103, 104, 110, 115, 124–127, 128, 137, 201, 205, 206, 207, 210, 216, 219, 225, 228, 229, 233, 235, 240, 242, 247, 253, 256, 258, 259, 261, 262, 265, 267, 269
Gillette, William (stage actor) 128, 129
Gilmore, Paul (actor; b. Rochester NY) 49, 71, 104, 254
Gilson (Gillson), Amelia P. (actress; co-director, Meteor Pictures Corp.) 165
Gilson, Richard (continuities) 166

Giltner, Leigh Gordon (author) 263
The Girl of the Golden West (play) 32
The Girl That Didn't Matter (1916) 216
The Girl Who Doesn't Know (1916) 216–217
The Girl Who Won (1916) 217
The Girl's Angle (1917) 127, 130, 216
Giroux, Robert (author) 87, 89, 90, 93, 94, 95, 96, 97, 101, 133, 134, 201, 225
Gish, Dorothy (actress) 255
Glasgow, Ellen (writer) 40, 62
Glendon, J. Frank (actor) 248
Glenn, Byron P. (president, Long Beach Studios Corp.) 169, 170, 172
Glenn, Claire (actress) 206
The Godfather, Part II (aka *The Godfather II*) 142, 181
The Gold Diggers of 1937 116
Gold Rooster Play *see* Pathé Exchange, Inc.
Gold Seal (film company) 28
Goldberg, Jesse L. (secretary, National Independent Motion Picture Board of Trade, representing Life Photo Film Corp.) 9
Golden, Susan (head of public relations, Museum of Latin American Art) 187
Goldfish, Samuel (né Schmuel Gelbfisz; aka Samuel Goldwyn; motion-picture executive; b. Warsaw, Poland, 1870s — d. Beverly Hills CA 1974) 10, 76, 133
Goldwyn, Samuel *see* Goldfish, Samuel
Goldwyn Pictures Corporation 76
Good, Will B. *see* Arbuckle, Roscoe "Fatty"
Good Night, Nurse (1918) 135, 189, 217
Goodman, Henrietta (actress) 27, 244
Goodrich, William B. *see* Roscoe "Fatty" Arbuckle
Gordon, Grace (actress) 160
Gordon, Huntley (actor) 231
Gordon, James (actor; b. Pittsburgh PA 1871 — d. 1941) 24, 27, 220, 240
Gould, Norma (actress) 211
Gowland, Gibson (actor) 55; *see also* Gibson-Gowland, T. H.
Graham, Martha (dancer) 211
Grandin, Francis 41
Granger, May (actress) 260
Grant, Corinne (also spelled Corenne, Corene; actress; b. New Orleans LA 1888 — d. ?) 49, 53, 71, 104, 196, 204, 226, 238, 247, 263, 264, 266

Grant, L. A. (full name unknown; service station helper) 97, 98; *see also* Taylor, W. D.
Grant, Paul 41
Grapevine Video 189
Graustark (play) 106
Gray, Clifford (B.) (actor) 53, 71, 197, 203, 204, 223
Gray, King D. (cameraman) 255
Gray, Phyllis (actress; b. 1880s — d. Los Angeles CA 1922) 51, 71, 104
Gray, R. Henry *see* Grey, R. Henry
Gray (Grey), Robert (actor; born in Houlton, ME) 49, 71, 104
Great Divide (play) 32
A Great Secret (1914) 217–218
The Great War *see* World War I
Green, Anna Katherine (writer) 55, 75, 266
Green, Dorothy (actress) 227
Green Temptation 99
Greenwood, Win(n)ifred (actress; b. Geneseo NY 1885 — d. Woodland Hills CA 1961) 53, 197, 223
Gregory, Jackson (author) 252
Grey, Henry *see* Grey, R. Henry
Grey, Jane (actress) 172
Grey, R. Henry (aka R. Henry Gray, Henry Grey, Robert H. Grey; actor) 41, 71, 72, 104, 105, 202, 205, 206, 207, 215, 216, 218, 221, 223, 224, 234, 240, 243, 247, 256, 258, 262, 263, 268, 270
Grey, Robert (H.) *see* Grey, R. Henry
Greybeal, O. A. (full name unknown; greatest shareholder of Hampton Del Ruth Studios; Wyoming oil man; backer of *The Marriage Chance*) 174, 175, 176
Griffith, D(avid) W(ark) (pioneer filmmaker) 42, 48, 70, 96, 112, 156, 162, 172, 204
Griffith, Gordon (actor) 160, 255
Griffith and Mayer (authors of *The Movies*) 8
The Grip of Evil (1916 serial) 52, 72, 115, 118, 218
Grobaty, Tim (journalist, *Press-Telegram*) 180, 181, 182
Guazzoni, Enrico (pioneer filmmaker; b. Rome, Italy, 1876 — d. Rome, Italy, 1949) 6
Guihan, Frances E. (scenarist) 231, 243
Guinan, Texas (née Mary Louise Cecelie Guinan; actress; b. Waco TX 1885 — d. Vancouver BC 1933) 161
Guns and Garlic (1914?) 218
Gunshy 181
Guys and Dolls 141
Gypsy Love (1914) 66, 119, 218–219
Gyton, George (actor) 163

Haines, Rhea (actress) 232
Hal Roach's Our Gang 63
Hale, Alan (amateur astronomer) 190
Hamilton, James Shelley (early film critic) 93
Hampton, Ray (character actress) 160, 163
Hampton Del Ruth Productions 231
Hampton Del Ruth Studios *see* Balboa/International Film Company
Hands Up! (serial) 120, 124, 189, 219
Hansen, Florence 51, 71, 104
Hansen, Juanita (actress; b. Des Moines IA ca. 1885 — d. 1961) 94
Hansen, Louis P. 41
Hardin, Neil (actor) 201, 228, 235, 238, 240, 259, 263, 269
Harding, Tiny (actor) 165
Harlan, Kenneth (actor; b. Boston MA ca. 1895 — d. 1967) 226, 264
Harlan, Rita (actress) 201
Harlow, Charles W. (oil man; financier) 175, 176, 177
Harris, Bud (full name unknown; actor) 237
Harris, Henry B. (theatrical manager) 106
Hart, William S. (actor) 123
Hart Studio 156
Harte, Betty (née Daisy Mae Light; actress; b. 1880s — d. 1965) 24, 27, 220
Hartley, Grant Floyd (service station owner) 97, 98; *see also* Taylor, W. D.
Harvey, Harry (director) 47, 48, 55, 71, 114, 206, 208, 212, 215, 227, 237, 243, 256, 257, 262, 267, 269
Hastings, Seymour (actor) 237
Hay Market Theatre 103
Hayden, Charles E. (director) 49, 71
Hayes, Johnny (actor) 215
Hays, Will (head of Motion Picture Producers and Distributors Association) 133
Hays Office 133
Hayworth, Rita (actress) 141
Heart of the Brute (1914) 219
Hearts of the Range (1921) 164, 219
Heat 180, 181
Henderson, Hazel (actress) 71, 204
Herman, Jay (actor) 204
Hewston, Alfred (actor) 166, 234
Hewston, H. (full name unknown; character actor) 160
Heyes, Herbert (actor; b. Vader WA ca. 1889 — d. 1958) 227
Hiers, Walter (actor) 227
Hillburg, Bill (journalist; special reports for *Press-Telegram*) 184
His Conquered Self (1915) 219
His Old-Fashioned Dad (1917) 127, 130, 219–220
Historical Films Company 169, 195

Historical Society of Long Beach 62, 82, 143, 183
Hodkinson, W. W. (full name unknown; distributor) 226, 233, 243
Hoffman, Harry (actor) 55, 246
Hoffman, Otto (director; b. New York NY 1879 — d. Woodland Hills CA 1944) 55, 252, 263
Holden, Ed (stage manager) 119
Holly Comedy Company 161, 195
Hollywood Heritage Museum 10
Holmes, Stuart (né Joseph Liebschen; actor; b. Chicago IL or Schweidnitz, Germany, 1882 — d. 1971) 70
Homer, Audrey (among top 10, star search, 1922, Empire Theatre, Long Beach) 171
Hoodman Blind (1913) 27, 220
Hoodman Blind (play) 27, 220
Hopkins, Anthony (actor) 12
Horkheimer, Cecelia (née Hirsch; mother of H. M., Elwood, and Florence Horkheimer) 31, 32
Horkheimer, Elwood D. (electrical engineer; pioneer filmmaker; treasurer and secretary, Balboa Studios; b. Wheeling WV 1881 — d. Los Angeles CA 1966) 29, 30, 32, 33, 34, 35, 36, 38, 39, 40, 41, 42, 43, 44, 45, 46, 47, 48, 51, 53, 54, 55, 57, 59, 60, 61, 63, 65, 66, 67, 70, 71, 73, 74, 75, 76, 77, 81, 87, 103, 106, 107, 109, 114, 115, 116, 117, 118, 119, 127, 128, 130, 132, 145, 147, 148, 151, 152, 153, 154, 155, 157, 159, 162, 167, 170, 171, 172, 174, 176, 177, 182, 192, 194, 200, 202, 203, 204, 205, 206, 207, 208, 210, 215, 216, 219, 223, 226, 231, 233, 242, 243, 245, 252, 253, 255, 256, 257, 258, 263, 268, 269
Horkheimer, Florence (sister of H. M. and Elwood Horkheimer and silent partner of the Horkheimer Studios) 36, 77, 167
Horkheimer, H. M. (theatrical manager; pioneer filmmaker; founder, president and general manager, Balboa Studios; vice-president and co-director, National Independent Motion Picture Board of Trade, representing Balboa Feature Films; b. Wheeling WV 1882 — d. Hollywood CA 1962) 9, 12, 17, 29, 30, 31, 32, 33, 34, 35, 36, 37, 38, 39, 40, 41, 42, 43, 44, 45, 48, 51, 53, 54, 55, 56, 57, 59, 60, 61, 62, 63, 65, 66, 67, 70, 71, 73, 74, 75, 76, 77, 81, 87, 90, 91, 94, 96, 106, 107, 108, 109, 112, 114, 119, 120, 121, 122, 127, 128, 130, 132, 139, 145, 146, 147, 148, 151, 152, 153, 154, 155, 157, 159, 162,

167, 170, 171, 172, 174, 175, 176, 177, 180, 182, 192, 194, 199, 200, 203, 205, 206, 207, 208, 210, 215, 219, 223, 225–226, 231, 233, 238, 242, 243, 245, 247, 252, 253, 255, 256, 257, 258, 263, 264, 266, 269
Horkheimer, Jacqueline Junior Saunders *see* Saunders, Jackie Jr.
Horkheimer, Morris (father of H. M., Elwood D., and Florence Horkheimer) 31, 32, 167
Horkheimer, Mrs. H. M. (full name unknown; first wife of H. M.) 85
Horkheimer, Vivian (second wife of Elwood D. Horkheimer) 118
Horkheimer Studios *see* Balboa Amusement Producing Company
Horne, James W. (director) 219
Horner, Bob (film producer, specializing in western movies) 169, 262
Horner (Company) 169
Hotel McAlpin 8, 66
Hotel Virginia 2, 10, 13, 14, 15, 27, 41, 42, 62, 163, 167, 168, 170, 172
An Hour Before Dawn (1913) 27, 208, 221
House, Pat (museum director, Museum of Latin American Art, site of former Balboa Studios) 187
The House Divided (1913?) 221
The House of a Thousand Candles (play) 106
The House of Hate 120
Houston, Whitney (singer; actress) 182
How to Make an American Quilt (TV) 180
Howard, Clifford (actor) 41, 105
Howard, George Bronson (scenarist) 245
Howard, Joseph E. (scenarist) 253
Howard, Roy (actor) 246
Howland, T. L. (full name unknown; president, California Motion Picture Manufacturing Co.) 13, 15, 16, 17, 22, 23, 241
Howling, G. H. (full name unknown; filmmaker) 51
Hoyt Theatre 134
Hudson, Rock (actor) 141
Hueston, Alfred (Tex) (actor; makeup artist) 163
Huff, Horace (pitcher for University City's baseball team) 86
Hughes, Gareth (actor) 171
The Human Soul (1914) 66, 221–222
Humphrey, Doris (dancer) 211
The Hunchback of Cedar Lodge (1914) 66, 113, 119, 131, 222
Hunt, George J. (co-partner, The International Film Co.) 161, 162
Hunt, Helen (actress) 162
Hunt, Irene (actress) 162
Huntsman, C. P. (full name unknown; scenarist) 174

Hurst, William O. H. (author) 223
Huston, Anjelica (actress) 182
Huston, John (director) 96
Hutton, Betty (actress) 141
Hyde, Mabel (actress) 226

I.A.T.S.E. (aka International Alliance of Theatrical Stage Employees) 156
The Idler 70
The Idler (story) 70
Ill-Starred Babbie (1914) 119, 222
Ill-Starred Babbie (novel) 222
Ima Simp, Detective (1914 serial) 44, 222–223
The Imprint (1913) 111, 223
In the Bishop's Carriage (1920) 224
In the Bishop's Carriage (book) 162, 224
In the Hands of the Law (1917) 223
In the Hands of the Law (novel) 223
In the Stretch 37
Ince, Thomas Harper (film director) 156
Independent Motion-Picture Company (IMP) 8, 22, 28
The Infamous Miss Ravell 116, 119, 223
Influenza epidemic (1918) 156, 157
Ingersoll, William (actor) 32
Inokuchi, Makato (actor) 49, 55, 247, 257
The Inspirations of Harry Larrabee (1917) 223–224
The Inspirations of Harry Larrabee (short story) 223
International Alliance of Theatrical Stage Employees *see* I.A.T.S.E.
International Film Company 161–162
International Moving Picture Company 23
Intolerance 172
The Intrigue (1914) 46, 119, 131, 224
Iowa Cedar Rapids Swine Show *see* Influenza epidemic of 1918
Irene (full name unknown; costume designer) 118
Ironsides (TV) 181
Irwin, May (stage actress) 128
It Happened One Night (1914?) 224
It Will All Come Out in the Wash (1914?) 224
Ivers, Ann (actress) 232
Ivers, Julia Crawford (suspect in W. D. Taylor's murder) 101

Jaccard, Jacques (director) 94
Jack (full name unknown; assistant director) 149
Jack London Motion Picture Company 39, 232
Jackie Saunders Series 258
Jackrabbit Racer *see* The Pike (amusement zone)
Jackson, Helen Hunt (writer) 240
Jacobsen, Arma (actress) 231
JAG (TV) 180
James, Darren (Cyclone Racer exhibit coordinator and volunteer, Historical Society of Long Beach) 183
Jansen, Harlett *see* Jansen, Harriet
Jansen, Harriet (aka Harlett Jansen, Harriet Janson, Miss Jensen; actress) 41, 105, 218, 225, 251, 256,
Janson, Harriet *see* Jansen, Harriet
Jarrel, Dixie (actress) 51, 71, 104
Jasset, Victorin (French director; pioneer of crime films) 6
Jefferson, Fred A. (head of Paragon Pictures Corp. of America; director, Long Beach Comedy Co. and Meteor Pictures Corp.) 162, 164, 165
Jefferson, L. V. (full name unknown; scenarist) 216, 243
Jefferson, Mrs. (full name unknown; wife of Fred A. Jefferson) 165
Jenner, William H. (Pacific coast manager, American Releasing Corp.) 172
Jensen (Miss) *see* Jansen, Harriet
The Jewels of the Madonna (1913) 24, 224
Jewett, Christine (W. D. Taylor's neighbor's maid) 97, 99
Jibenosay (play) 125
Jillison, Ken (promoter of amusement zone revival in Long Beach) 183, 184
Jobson, Edward (actor) 160, 205, 207, 208, 215, 236, 240, 255, 258, 262, 265, 270
Jobst, Lou (Long Beach columnist) 122
Joe's Restaurant 80
John Barleycorn 40, 232, 244, 252
Johnson, Constance (actress) 227
Johnson, Ligon (Balboa's lawyer during lawsuit with London) 39
Johnson, Olive (juvenile actress) 63
Johnson, Richard (Dick) (actor; b. Denver CO 1867 – d. ?) 41, 49, 71, 81, 104, 204, 219, 251
Johnson, W. (full name unknown; actor) 268
Johnston, Lorimer (producer) 227
Johnstone, Calder (scenarist) 262
Joker (company) 28
Joly, Henri Joseph (early partner of Charles Pathé) 7
Jones, Edgar (director) 216, 226, 234, 269
Jones, Grover (writer; director) 161, 215
Jones, Henry Arthur (author) 27, 220
Jones, Tommy Lee (actor) 180
Jordan, Michael (basketball celebrity) 12
Jossey, William (author; actor; b. Macon GA 1867 – d. Macon GA 1937) 85, 251
The Journal of a Neglected Wife (novel) 238
Joy, Gloria (juvenile actress) 200, 228, 229, 235, 236, 240, 265
Joy (company) 194, 199, 202, 205, 207, 208, 214, 218, 224, 237, 240, 246, 255, 256, 266
Joy and the Dragon (1916) 52, 55, 71, 107, 111, 131, 138, 143, 224–225, 228, 230
Joyland *see* Arrowhead Theatre
Joyce, James (Irish writer) 97
The Judge's Wife (1914) 94, 127, 225

Kackley, Vera (journalist, Long Beach *Press-Telegram*) 264
Kahler, Clara (aka Mrs. Kahler; actress) 202, 240
Kahler, Mrs. *see* Kahler, Clara
Kahn, Ivan (actor) 251
Kalem (Company, Inc.) 8, 13, 28, 39, 46, 119, 120, 122, 131, 139, 194, 224, 246
Kane, J. Inman (scenarist) 166, 234
Kathleen Clifford Company 76, 194
Katz, Ephraim (author) 153
Kay-Bee (company) 28, 114, 227
Keaton, Buster (né Joseph Francis Keaton; actor; b. Piqua KS 1895 – d. Woodland Hills CA 1966) 30, 56, 59, 75, 76, 80, 132, 133, 147, 202, 209, 210, 217, 236, 237, 241
Keaton, Joseph (actor) 202, 210
Keeler, H. P. (full name unknown; scenarist) 213
Keith and Orpheum Circuit 13
Kelly, Helen (among top 10, star search, 1922, Empire Theatre, Long Beach) 171
Kelsey, Fred A. (director) 162, 224
Kelsey Company 162, 195
Kerigan Studio 156
Kerr, James (actor) 209
Kerrigan, Warren 41
Kessel, Adam, Jr. (founder, New York Motion Picture Co.) 12
Keystone Kops 6, 132
Keystone Studios 26, 28, 63, 70, 104, 168
KFI's "Hollywood Extra Program" (radio) 141
Kid Komedy Kompany 63
Kiefer, Jack (production manager, Columbia Film Co.) 162
Kimball, Edward M. (actor) 248
Kinemacolor (company) 28

King, Anita (actress; b. 1899 — d. Hollywood CA 1963) 148, 200, 216, 243, 266
King, Helen (actress) 268
King, Henry (actor; director; b. Christianberg VA 1886 — d. Teluca Lake CA 1982) 2, 29, 41, 45, 47, 51, 52, 53, 56, 66, 67, 71, 74, 80, 81, 90, 91, 103, 104, 105–112, 115, 120, 135, 138, 141, 142, 150, 196, 206, 207, 208, 209, 211, 213, 215, 223, 225, 227, 228, 229, 231, 233, 237, 238, 240, 241, 242, 245, 247, 249, 251, 252, 253, 254, 257, 259, 260, 261, 262, 263, 264, 266, 267, 268, 269
King, Lewis (actor) 53, 55, 252
Kirk, Mr. (full name unknown; actor) 149
Kirkman (Kirkham), Kathleen (actress; b. Menominee MI 1895 — d. Santa Barbara CA 1961) 53, 206, 208, 243
Kirkwood, James (actor; b. Grand Rapids MI 1883 — d. 1963) 170
The Kitty (farce) 128
Kleine, George (co-founder, Kalem Co., Inc.) 13
Kleine (company) 8
Kline, Jim (author) 132, 202, 209, 210, 217, 236
Knickerbocker Star Features 53, 54, 73, 74, 75, 111, 112, 127, 131, 194, 240, 242, 256, 266
Knight, F. A. (full name unknown; attorney representing Balboa Studio creditors) 76
Koehring, David (musician) 187
Kuan, Moru (actor) 226
Kurosawa, Akira (Japanese film director) 96

Labor Commission 151
Lackaye, Ruth (actress; b. Oregon City OR 1869 — d. ?) 49, 55, 71, 104, 202, 209, 216, 226, 235, 236, 240, 243, 247, 257, 262, 265, 269
Lackaye, Wilton (actor) 70
The Lady in the Library (1917) 225–226
The Lady in the Library (story) 226
The Lady of Perfume (1915) see *Should a Wife Forgive?*
Laemmle, Carl (pioneer distributor and motion-picture executive) 8, 24, 28, 133
Lagard, Garald (writer) 80
Lahue, Kalton C. (author) 47
Lake, Alice (actress; b. Brooklyn NY circa 1896 — d. 1967) 116, 202, 209, 210, 217, 223, 236, 241
La Marr, Barbara (née Reatha Watson; actress; b. Richmond VA 1896 — d. 1926) 94

Lamont (La Monte), Dixie (actress) 164, 166, 212
Lamothe, Julian (scenarist) 216
Lampe, William (actor) 51, 71, 104, 253
Landis, Cullen (actor; b. Nashville TN 1895 — d. 1975) 53, 55, 75, 137, 207, 225, 231, 258, 266
Landis, Margaret (née Margaret Cullen; actress; b. Nashville TN 1891 — d. Oakland CA 1982) 53, 74, 203, 207, 215, 223, 233, 256
Lane, George (actor) 260
Lang, Fritz (director) 142
Lang, Peter (actor; b. 1859 — d. New York NY 1932) 27, 244
Langley, Edward M. (studio superintendent, Balboa Studios) 41, 65
La Petite Theatre 17
La Reno, Richard (Dick) (actor; b. New York NY 1863 — d. Hollywood CA 1945) 24
Lascelle, Ward (head of Special Pictures Corp.) 162
Lasky, Jesse L. (pioneer motion-picture executive; b. San Francisco CA 1880 — d. Beverly Hills CA 1958) 10, 42, 95, 190
Lasky, Ronnie (actor; grandson of Jesse Lasky) 190
La Varnie, Laura (actress) 171, 231
The Law That Divides (1918) 201, 226, 243, 266
Lawson, Shields (business manager, David Trattner Production Co.) 162
Learn, Bessie (actress) 212
LeBrun, Mignon (actress; b. New York NY 1888 — d. Los Angeles CA 1941) 53, 55, 203, 252, 262, 265
Lee, Clifford (actor) 246
Lee, Stan (producer) 181
The Legend of Lylah Clare 141
Leibrand, Lela (scenarist) 208, 209, 226, 263
Lenard, Madeline (actress) 41, 105
Lenore, Alta (among top 10, star search, 1922, Empire Theatre, Long Beach) 171
Leonard, "Pop" (full name unknown; actor) 44, 64, 83, 137, 214, 251
Leonard, Madelene (actress) 252
The Lesson (1918) 227
Lester, Kate (actress) 160, 255
Le Strange, Dick (actor) 237
Letters Entangled (1915) 111, 227
Lewis, Edgar (director) 70
Lewis, Ida (actress) 252
Lewis, Mitchell (actor; b. Syracuse NY 1880 — d. 1956) 231, 239
Liberty Theatre 81
Library of Congress 189
Liepold, George (actor) 222

Life Photo Film Corporation 9
Life's Shop Window (1915) 70
The Light in a Woman's Eye (1914) 227
Linder, Max (né Gabriel [Max] Leuvielle; actor; b. St. Loubès, France, 1883 — d. Paris, France, 1925) 6, 172
Linn, Harold (proprietor, Art Theatre, Long Beach) 186
The Lion and the Mouse (play) 69, 106
Liotta, Ray (actor) 182
Lippert, William H. (writer) 269
Lisa, Mona (actress) 151, 261, 264
Little Jack (1914) 45, 112, 113, 119, 227–228
Little Mary Sunshine (1916) 11, 52, 71, 91, 106, 111, 131, 135, 137, 138, 142, 143, 189, 228, 230
Little Miss Grown-Up (1918) 228–229, 235, 236, 240, 265
A Little Ray of Sunshine (1916?) 71, 111, 138, 140, 143, 228, 229, 230
The Little Roughneck (1918) (aka *Nine-Tenths of the Law*) 239
Little Sunbeam (1914) 45, 113, 119, 229
The Littlest Rebel (play) 70
Livingstone, Jack (actor) 49, 71, 104
L-KO Studio 156
Lloyd, Beatrix Demarest (author) 54, 232
Lloyd, Harold (actor; b. Burchard NB 1893 — d. Beverly Hills CA 1971) 24, 99, 224
The Locked Heart (1918) 111, 127, 229–230, 235, 236, 240, 265
Loew, Marcus (motion-picture executive) 133
Logan, J. E. (full name unknown; director, Long Beach Studios, Inc.; Logan and E. F. Thorine purchased Balboa Studios and surrounding grounds in 1921) 167, 169, 172
London, Jack (né John Griffith Chaney; writer; adventurer; motion-picture producer; b. San Francisco CA 1876 — d. Glen Ellen CA 1916) 35, 37, 38, 39, 40, 42, 53, 62, 96, 232, 244, 252
The Lonely Guy 181
Long, Samuel (co-founder, Kalem Co., Inc.) 13
Long Beach Comedy Company see Long Beach Motion Picture Company
Long Beach Community Producers 166
Long Beach Convention and Entertainment Center 182
Long Beach Heritage 187
Long Beach Motion Picture Company (aka Long Beach Comedy

Company, Long Beach Studios, Long Beach Studios Corporation) 162, 164, 165–166, 168, 169, 170, 171, 172, 173, 195, 212
Long Beach Public Library 17, 18, 19, 77, 79, 143, 157, 186, 187, 194
Long Beach Public Library Centennial Book Fund (1996) 187
Long Beach Studios Corporation *see* Long Beach Motion Picture Company
Long Beach Studios, Inc. *see* Long Beach Motion Picture Company
Looff, Arthur (son of Charles I. D. Looff) 184
Looff, Charles I. D. (teamed with Col. Drake in 1902 to build the Pike amusement zone in Long Beach; Looff was a park developer and ride designer who also built the first carousel at New York's Coney Island) 184
Lopez, John E. (scenarist) 216
Loraine, Robert (stage actor) 129
Lorimer, Wright (actor) 125
Lorimore, Alec (sales manager, Gaumont; publicity manager, Méliès and Box Office Attraction Co.) 65, 66, 67
Lorraine, Leota (actress) 215, 233
Lorraine, Lillian (née Mary Ann Brennan; actress; b. 1892 – d. New York NY 1955) 49, 71, 104, 237, 253
Lorrimer, Elsa (actress) 252
Los Angeles Wholesalers Board of Trade 60, 75, 77, 151, 163
Lost at Sea 231
Lotto, Arthur A. (assistant general manager, Balboa Studios) 36, 41
Lovell, C. H. (full name unknown; co-director, California Motion Picture Manufacturing Co.) 13, 15, 16
Lovell, M. C. (co-director, California Motion Picture Manufacturing Co.) 13, 15, 16
"Love's Old Sweet Song" (song) 130
Lubin (aka Western Lubin Company) 8, 70, 104, 106, 169
Lucas, Wilfred (né James Bruce; actor; b. Ontario, Canada, 1871– d. 1940) 264
Luke, Norman W. (actor) 206
Lumière, Louis (inventor; pioneer manufacturer of photographic equipment; b. Besançon, France, 1864 – d. Bandol, France, 1943) 6
Lumière Brothers (French inventors; film making pioneers) 6, 7
The Lure of Youth 171

M. J. Burnside (distributor) 248
McAllister, Jessie (actor) 24
McCardell, Roy (scenarist) 70
McCarthy, A. S. (full name unknown; director) 174
McCauley, John William (co-partner, The International Film Co.) 161, 162
McClary, Clyde (assistant manager, R. D. Films) 163
McConnell, Mollie (aka Mollie Sherwood; actress; b. Chicago IL 1865 – d. Los Angeles CA 1920) 41, 47, 49, 53, 71, 74, 81, 103, 104, 128–132, 137, 202, 203, 204, 207, 209, 210, 211, 214, 216, 219, 222, 224, 225, 228, 233, 242, 247, 248, 251, 253, 256, 261, 262, 263, 267, 268
McConnell, Will A. (writer; editor, *New York Morning Telegraph*; theatrical magnate; husband of Mollie McConnell) 128, 130
McCoy, Bill (actor) 269
McCoy, Clyde (director; actor) 162
McCullough, Philo (actor; b. San Bernardino CA 1894 – d. Burbank CA 1981) 48, 49, 55, 71, 72, 104, 115, 196, 218, 233, 238, 242, 245, 247, 252
M(a)cDonald, Francis (actor; aka McDonald, J. Francis; b. Bowling Green KY 1891– d. 1968) 84, 214, 221, 251, 256, 268
McDonald, (J.) Francis *see* M(a)cDonald, Francis
MacDonald (McDonald), Sherwood (director) 49, 55, 71, 72, 202, 203, 205, 207, 222, 228, 233, 235, 240, 255, 258
Mace, Fred (producer; executive; 1872–1917) 26, 35, 71, 77
McGee, James L. (manager, Selig Polyscope Co.) 12
McInroy, Carl (aka Hal McInroy, Harl McInroy; actor; scenarist) 201, 208, 215, 226, 233, 270
McInroy, Hal *see* McInroy, Carl
McInroy, Harl *see* McInroy, Carl
McIntosh, Burr (actor) 209
Mack, Willard (scenarist) 247
McKay, Robert (actor) 252
McKenzie, Alec (explorer) 215
McLaughlin, Jack (director) 55, 209, 252
MacLean, Douglas (actor; b. Philadelphia PA ca. 1892 – d. 1967) 109
MacLean, Faith (W. D. Taylor's neighbor) 97, 100, 101
McLean, Miss (full name unknown; actress) 23, 241
MacManigal, E. L. (full name unknown; actor) 166, 234
MacMillan Company 39
McP(h)erson, Harry F(arnsworth) (actor; assistant director to Harry Harvey) 215
M(a)cPherson, Jeanie (actress at Balboa Studios; scenarist for DeMille's silent version of *The Ten Commandments*) 237, 238, 252
Macy, William H. (actor) 182
Maid of the Wild (1915) 137, 138, 143, 189, 230–231
The Mainspring (1917) 54, 111, 231
The Mainspring (story) 54, 231
Majestic (company) 28, 44, 162, 204
Majestic Pavilion 86
Malitz, Felix (vice-president and general manager, Pathé Frères and Pathé Exchange; executive, Piedmont Corp.) 148, 149, 151
Maloney, Leo (actor) 164, 166, 212
Mame 141
A Man of Sorrow 220
The Man Who Came to Dinner (play) 116
The Man with Green Eyes (1914?) 119, 231
Manges, C. A. (full name unknown; scenarist) 244, 252
Mannering, Mary (stage actress) 26
Manning, Norman (business and studio manager, Balboa Studios) 36, 71, 74, 80, 82, 86, 252
Mansfield, Richard (stage actor) 130
Mantell, Robert (Shakespearean actor) 125
Marie Osborne Film Company *see* (Baby) Marie Osborne Film Company
Marion, Frank (co-founder, Kalem Co., Inc.) 13
Marlo, Zada (actress) 213
Marlowe, Julia (stage actress) 26
The Marriage Chance (1922) 171, 172, 173, 231–232
Marsh, Mrs. (full name unknown; actress) 203
Marshall, Charles (actor) 247
Marshall, Edward (artist; correspondent or *Variety*) 170
Marshall, Tully (actor) 170, 171, 172, 231
Marshall, William (actor) 208, 215, 243
Martin Eden 40, 232, 244, 252
Martin Eden (novel) 38, 232
The Martinache Marriage (1917) 54, 131, 233
The Martinache Marriage (story) 54, 233
Marvin, Henry Norton (founder, Biograph Co.) 13
The Mask (1914) 111, 233
Massey, Joe (actor) 259
Master Pictures (Corporation) 78, 160, 161, 195, 248

Matilda 180
The Matrimonial Martyr (1916) (aka *A Matrimonial Martyr*) 52, 72, 73, 120, 124, 127, 233–234
Maugham, Somerset (British writer) 215
Maupassant, Guy de (French author) 217
Maxwell, E. W. (full name unknown; the Deelys' friend) 88
Mayakovsky, Vladimir (Russian actor) 232
Mayall, Herschel (actor) 213
Maye, Jimsy (actor) 239
Mayer, Louis B. (né Eliezer [Lazar] Mayer) (motion-picture executive; b. Minsk, Russia, 1885 – d. Hollywood CA 1957) 1, 3
Mayo, Frank (actor; b. New York NY 1886 – d. Laguna Beach CA 1963) 48, 49, 53, 71, 74, 88, 104, 122, 124, 196, 207, 247, 255, 256, 258
Mayo, Melvin (actor) 53, 206, 234
Medan, Leopold (actor) 71, 204
Méliès, Gaston 104
Méliès, Georges (pioneer motion-picture executive, innovator, actor; b. Paris, France, 1861 – d. Paris, France, 1938) 1, 6, 7, 8, 65, 96
Melville, Wilbur (friend of Henry King) 106
Menacing Past (1922) 167, 234
Mentioned in Confidence (1917) 189, 234
Mentioned in Confidence (short story) 234
Mercury Comedy Company 160, 195
Meredith, Lois (actress) 255, 256
Meredyth, Bess (scenarist) 256, 262
Merrell, Clark (actor) 247
Merrill, Lynch & Company 153
Mesh of the Net (1915) 234
A Message from Reno (play) 32, 233
Message of the Mind (1914) 234–235
A Messenger from Jarvis Section (play) 125
Mestayer, W. A. (full name unknown; stage actor) 128
Meteor Pictures Corporation 165, 166, 195
Metro (studio) 156
Metro-Goldwyn-Mayer (MGM) 1, 2, 3, 39, 109, 118
Metropolitan Motion Picture and Producing Company 51
Metropolitan Theatre 124
MGM-Pathé 153
MGM/UA 153, 180
Michelson, Miriam (author) 162, 224
Mickey 168
The Midnight Burglar (1918) 229, 235, 236, 240, 265
A Midnight Call (1913) 235–236

Milburn Morante Comedy Company *see* Morante (Motion Picture) Company 163
Miller, Ashley (director) 212
Miller, Henry (stage actor) 26
Miller, "Ranger" Bill (actor) 169, 262
Miller, Victor (cameraman) 223
Millett, Arthur (actor) 213
Mills, Berry (actor) 255
Mills, Milton (actor) 170
Mills, Thomas R. (plaintiff against Master Pictures Corp.) 160
Minter, Mary Miles (née Juliet Reilly; actress; b. Shreveport LA 1902 – d. Santa Monica CA 1984) 95, 101, 160, 171
Miss Mischief Maker (1918) 229, 235, 236, 240, 265
Mr. X (Taylor's supposed murderer) 97, 98, 99, 100, 101
Mitchell, Howard M. (director) 226, 243
A Mixup in Clothes (1914) 114, 119, 236, 249
Mona Lisa Company 76, 194
Monopol Feature Film Company 28, 104
Monteagudo, Luis, Jr. (journalist, *Press-Telegram*) 180
Montgomery, A. B. (full name unknown; general manager, co-director, Meteor Pictures Corp.) 165
The Moods of Medora (1916) 236
Moonshine (1918) 135, 236–237
Moore, Anna Boyle (stage actress) 106
Moore, Joyce (actress) 49, 71, 104, 204
Moore, Tom (actor; County Meath, Ireland ca. 1884 – d. 1955) 171, 225, 226
Moore, Victor (actor) 26
Moran, Dan (actor) 227
Morante, Al (assistant director; head of the Morante Motion Picture Co.) 161, 162, 163
Morante, "Dad" 163
Morante, Joseph (technical director) 161, 163
Morante, Milburn (motion-picture producer; b. San Francisco CA 1887 – d. Pacoima CA 1964) 160, 163, 164, 204, 219
Morante (Motion Picture) Company (aka Milburn Morante Comedy Company, Morante Producing Company) 161, 162, 163, 164, 166, 167, 169, 170, 195, 204, 219, 234
Morante Producing Company *see* Morante (Motion Picture) Company
Moreno, Antonio (actor; friend of W. D. Taylor) 98

Morgan, "Kewpie" (full name unknown; actor) 213
Morgan, Phalba (actress; aka Zelma Morgan) 248
Morgan, Tom (actor) 215, 223
Morgan, Zelma *see* Morgan, Phalba
Morris, Lewis O. 41
Morton, Luther (scenarist) 215
Morton, William (writer) 215
Moses, Barr (author) 208
The Moth and the Flame (1913) 111, 237
Motion Picture Directors Association 95
Motion Picture Guild 117
Motion Picture Patents Company (Edison trust) 8, 15, 20, 24, 28, 47, 67
Motion Picture Producers and Distributors Association 133
Moulton, Dorothy (juvenile actress) 63
Mt. Olympus Distribution 195
Ms. X (Taylor's supposed murderess) 101
Mulhall, Jack (actor; b. Wappingers Falls NY ca. 1888 – d. 1977) 160, 255
Multiplicity 180, 181
Mulvane, Margaret (actress) 71, 204
The Muses (Mnemosyne) 97
Museum of Latin American Art 187, 188
Museum of Modern Art 189
Mush (1914?) 237
Mutoscope 114, 227
Mutual (Film Company/Corporation) 28, 57, 114, 118, 119, 127, 130, 145, 194, 200, 202, 203, 205, 207, 258, 268
Mutual Star Productions 118, 127, 130, 203, 205, 207
My Partner (play) 125
Myers, Ray (actor) 232

Nance, Frank A. (coroner, Taylor's murder) 101
Nares, P. W. (full name unknown; actor) 27, 212
Nash, Carrie Browning 41
Nash, Mr. and Mrs. (full names unknown; at "Christmas Gala") 41
National Archives of Canada 189
National Association of the Motion Picture Industry 154
National Association of Theatrical Producing Managers 33
National Bank of Pasadena (plaintiff against Master Pictures Corp.) 160
National Independent Motion Picture Board of Trade 8, 9, 66, 67
The Natural 181

Natural Gas (play) 128
Nazimova (actress) 26
Neal of the Navy (1915 serial) 47, 48, 67, 71, 81, 89, 120, 237–238
The Neglected Wife (1916–17 serial) 47, 48, 50, 67, 120, 124, 130, 189, 238
Neilan, Marshall (actor) 120
Nelson, Evelyn (actress) 164, 204, 219
Nelson, Fred (motorcycle officer) 86
Nemo (company) 69, 195, 205, 206, 252, 260, 264, 266, 268
Nerve (1914) 111, 238–239
Nestor (company) 28
New Art Film Company (aka New Art Film Corporation) 160, 195, 255
New Art Film Corporation 77; *see also* New Art Film Company
"The New Bellboy" (sketch) 223
New York Motion Picture Company 12
Newsreel (1916) 239
Nichols, Marguerite (Margaret) (aka Marguerite Roach; actress; b. 1900 – d. Los Angeles CA 1941) 49, 53, 71, 72, 74, 104, 204, 228, 230, 233, 240, 242, 245, 255, 256
Nicholson, J. E. (Capt.) (full name unknown; actor) 203
Nick Carter 6
Nielsen, Leslie (actor) 12
Nielsson, Anna Q(uerentia) (actress; b. Ystad, Sweden, ca. 1888 – d. 1974) 170
The Night Born (story) 232, 244, 252
Nimmo, Winifred (among top 10, star search, 1922, Empire Theatre, Long Beach) 171
Nine-Tenths of the Law (1918) see *The Little Roughneck*
Nixon 12, 180
No Children Wanted (1918) 111, 127, 229, 235, 236, 240, 265
Nobody Loves a Fat Man (1914?) 240
Norden, Virginia (actress) 53, 74, 256
Norma Talmadge Film Corporation 57, 75
Normand, Mabel (actress; close friend of W. D. Taylor; wife of Lewis Cody; b. Staten Island NY 1892 – d. Monrovia CA 1930) 76, 87, 94, 95, 97–101, 103, 123, 168
North Woods Producing Company 195, 239
Northmore, Mary (actress) 228
Nostalgia Family Video 189
Novak, Jane (actress; b. St. Louis MO 1896 – d. 1990) 231
Novak, Kim (actress) 141
Nye, G. Raymond (actor) 213

Oakdale Productions 111, 127, 228, 229, 235, 236, 240, 265
Oakley, Laura 41
Oakley (company) 162
Oath of Hate (1916) 111, 240
O'Brien, Eugene (actor; b. Boulder CO 1882 – d. 1966) 171
Oh, You Circus Day (1914?) 240
Olcott, Chauncey (theatrical manager) 125
Old Heidelberg (play) 129, 130
The Old Monk's Tale (1913) 24, 240
Olivier, Laurence (English actor) 141
Olympian Production Company of New York 166
Omnia (theatre) 6
On Matrimonial Seas (1911) 20, 23, 168, 240–241
Once Upon a Time (1916) 241
The One-Eyed God (aka *Spellbound*) 189, 241, 256
Oppenheim, James 212
Orpheum Stock Company 112
Orth, Marion (writer) 261
Osborn[e], Edyth (actress; mother of Baby Marie) 139
Osborn[e], Leon (theatre manager; actor; co-founder, Diando Film Co.; father of Baby Marie) 139
Osborne, Baby Marie (née Helen Alice Myres; aka Marie Osborne-Yeats, Helen Marie Osborne; nicknames: "Little Majesty Marie," "Baby Grand," "Little Mary Sunshine," "Merry Sunshine," "Baby Bernhardt"; child star; costumer; b. Denver CO 1911) 2, 29, 49, 50, 52, 54, 55, 56, 62, 64, 71, 74, 80, 82, 89, 90, 91, 92, 103, 104, 107, 108, 110, 120, 121, 125, 126, 129, 131, 135–143, 164, 187, 188, 189, 198, 225, 228, 229, 230, 241, 253, 259, 261, 262
Osborne, Gloria (sister of Baby Marie) 164
Osborne, Helen Marie *see* Osborne, Baby Marie
Osborne, William Hamilton (scenarist) 48, 237
Osborne-Yeats, Marie *see* Osborne, Baby Marie
Oscar (trophy, Academy of Motion Picture Arts and Sciences) 182
Othello (play) 125
Otto, Henry W. (actor; producer; b. St. Louis MO 1877 – d. Los Angeles CA 1952) 87, 88, 104, 199–201, 207, 218, 247
Out West (1918) 135, 189, 241
Owen, Seena (actress; b. Spokane WA ca. 1895 – d. 1966) 172

Pacino, Al (actor) 181
Paid in Full (play) 32, 172

Palestine 174
Palmer, Cy 24
Palmer, Patricia (actress) 169, 171, 262
Panama-California Exposition (aka Panama-Pacific International Exposition) 237
Panama-Pacific International Exposition (aka Panama-California Exposition) 33, 34, 70
Paragon Pictures Corporation of America 162, 165, 195, 204
Paramount (Pictures) 19, 20, 55, 57, 75, 95, 109, 135, 141, 194, 195, 200, 202, 209, 210, 217, 236, 241, 261, 266
Paramount-Arbuckle Comedy 202, 209, 210, 217, 236, 241
Pardee, Joan (actress) 210
Pardee, Madel(e)ine (actress) 49, 71, 72, 104, 196, 207, 213, 214, 221, 233, 245, 249, 251, 256, 259, 263, 268, 269
Parker, Edwin B. (judge; head of Priorities Committee of the Board, War Industries Board) 154
The Pasadena Peach 120
Patchin, Roy (actor) 23, 241
The Path of Sorrow (1913) 46, 241
Pathé, Charles (pioneer motion-picture executive; b. Paris, France, 1863 – d. Monte Carlo, Monaco, 1957) 7, 8, 47
Pathé, Émile (French producer; associate and brother of Charles Pathé) 7, 8, 47
Pathé/Balboa 127, 131, 143, 253
Pathé Communications Corporation 153
Pathé Exchange, Inc. (Gold Rooster Play) 47, 68, 72, 111, 112, 118, 119, 124, 127, 131, 135, 137, 143, 148, 151, 152, 153, 154, 155, 194, 196, 200, 219, 224–225, 228, 229, 233, 243, 253, 255, 258, 259, 261, 262, 264
Pathé Film Committee 47, 48
Pathé (Frères) 1, 3, 6, 7, 8, 17, 28, 33, 47, 48, 49, 50, 52, 54, 55, 57, 59, 63, 67, 70, 71, 73, 77, 91, 104, 106, 111, 112, 114, 118, 120, 124, 127, 131, 132, 138, 140, 143, 145, 148, 177, 194, 195, 196, 197, 206, 207, 209, 210, 215, 227, 230, 235, 237, 238, 241, 243, 245, 247, 248, 251, 252, 260, 261, 263, 266, 267, 268
Pathé Journal (newsreel) 6
Pathé of New York 218
Pawnee Bill (1922) 170, 242
Pay Dirt (1916) 111, 127, 131, 242
Payton, Gloria (actress) 206, 243, 269
Payton, Lucy (actress) 219, 253, 269
Peaceful Valley (play) 125
Peacocke (Peacock), Leslie T. (Capt.)

(scenarist) 197, 201, 202, 203, 206, 207, 208, 234, 266
Pear Productions 182
Pearl of the Army 120
Pearls of Temptation (1915) (aka *The Perils of Temptation*) 243
Pearson, Leo (actor) 160, 255
Peavey, Henry (valet and cook of W. D. Taylor) 95, 97, 98, 99, 101
Peck, Charles Mortimer (vice-president and assistant manager, Balboa Studios) 9, 10, 35, 43, 70, 71
Pembroke, Percy S. (actor) 264
Pembroke, Stanley (actor) 226, 266
Pepperell (Pepprell), Ethel (actress) 228, 231, 235, 236
Pepprell, Jane (actress) 226, 270
Perce, L. A. (full name unknown; medical doctor) 85
Perdue, Leon (juvenile actor) 54, 229, 253, 261, 262
The Perils of Temptation (1915) see *Pearls of Temptation*
Perlus, William (orchestra leader; at "Christmas Gala") 63
Pete (the Bear) 142, 228; see also *Little Mary Sunshine*
Peters, E. T. (full name unknown; perhaps the same person as Edward Peters; actor) 258
Peters, Edward (actor) 245, 256
Peters, George (cameraman) 202, 210, 217, 236, 241
Peters, House (né Robert House Peters; actor; b. Bristol, England, 1880 — d. 1967) 25, 27, 208, 212, 221, 244
Peters, P. E. (full name unknown; actor) 248
Petroleum strike (Long Beach, 1921) 147, 152
Petticoats and Politics (1918) 201, 226, 243, 266
Peyton, Lawrence (actor) 232, 252
Phantasm 181
The Phantom Shotgun (1917) 54–55, 243–244
Pheilen, George (actor) 206
The Philadelphia Story (play) 116
Philippi, Charles E. (co-director, Meteor Pictures Corp.) 165
Phoenix 182
Photoplayers Club 66, 84
Pickett, "Slim" (actor) 81, 263
Pickford, Jack (né Jack Smith; actor; brother of Mary Pickford; b. Toronto, Canada, 1896 — d. 1933) 95
Pickford, Mary (née Gladys Smith; actress; b. Toronto, Canada, 1893 — d. 1979) 27, 34, 41, 63, 87, 95, 122
Pickford, Mrs. (full name unknown) 41

A Piece of Steak (1913) 39, 40, 232, 244, 252
Piedmont Corporation 148
Pietz, Lucille (actress) 209
The Pike (amusement zone) 2, 13, 17, 18, 19, 20, 22, 23, 24, 26, 54, 70, 80, 132, 162, 166, 183, 184, 185, 186, 190, 241
Pilot Films Corporation (aka Pilot Films Company) 17, 27, 194, 220
Pitou, Augustus (theatrical producer) 125
Pitts, Ella (actress) 226
Pixley, Annie (stage actress) 125
Playter, Wellington A. (actor; b. Rawcliffe, England, 1879 — d. Oakland CA 1937) 27, 212
Plaza Pictures 199, 226, 243, 266
Pleasantville 182
The Policewoman (1914; played by Alice Stebbins Wells) 244
A Poor Relation (play) 125
The Port of Doom (1913) 27, 244–245
Porter, David 41, 223, 245
The Poseidon Adventure 181
Powell, Paul (director) 264
The Power of Evil (1916) 111, 245
The Power of Print (1914) 111, 245–246
Powers (company) 28
Pratt, Jack (director) 248
Prestell(e), Mae (actress; b. Iowa 1878 — d. Los Angeles CA 1952) 71, 204
Preston, Stanley J. (actor) 208
Prevratil, Joseph (operator, Queen Mary, Long Beach) 184
Price, Kate (actress) 217
Price, Mechtilde (actor) 248
Prickly Pear Productions 182
A Prize in Every Package (1913 or 1914) 246
Proctor, George D. (writer) 37
Proctor, Joseph (theatrical producer) 124, 125
Professor Bugs (1913 or 1914) 246
Professor Oldboy's Rejuvenator (1914) 246
Prohibition 99
Proust, Marcel (French author) 97
Purviance, Edna (actress; neighbor of W. D. Taylor) 97, 101

Queen Mary (Long Beach) 180, 181, 184
Quo Vadis 6

R. D. Films, Inc. 163
The Race for a Mine (1914) 246
Radcliffe, Violet (child actress; b. 1908 — d. 1926) 63
Rae, W. C. (full name unknown; co-director, R. D. Films) 163

Rambeau, Lillian (actress) 227
Randall, Bruce (actor) 41, 214, 223, 256, 259
Rappe, Virginia (actress) 133, 134
A Rash Revenge (1913) 247
The Rat (1914) 66, 111, 247
Ratterman, William H. (artist) 264
The Raven 172
Rawlinson, Herbert (actor; b. Brighton, England, circa 1885 — d. 1953) 232, 251, 252
Raye, Elinor (actress) 246
Red Bulldogs (1922) 247
The Red Circle (1915–16 serial) 47, 48, 49, 67, 120, 121, 124, 127, 130, 131, 247
The Red Cross 42, 75
Redford, Robert (actor) 141
Reed, Charlie (stage actor) 128
Reed, William (actor; b. circa 1893 — d. W. Los Angeles CA 1944) 51, 71, 104, 203, 204, 216, 226, 265
Reelcraft Corporation 165, 195
Reese, Harold (actor) 269
Reeves, Alf (Chaplin's studio manager) 147
Reeves, Breezy (actor) 239
Reeves, Edith (actress) 51, 71, 104
Reeves, Myrtle (actress; wife of Oliver Hardy of "Laurel and Hardy" fame) 49, 199, 213, 247
Reid, Wallace (né William W. Reid; actor; husband of Dorothy Davenport; b. St. Louis MO circa 1890 — d. 1923) 95, 103, 116, 133, 167, 170
Reid, Wallace (Mrs.) 171; see also Davenport, Dorothy
La Reine Elizabeth (1912) 26
Reliance (company) 114, 162, 227
Republic (company) 141
Retail Merchants Credit Association of Los Angeles 160
Revett, John (actor) 225
Revier, Harry 35
Revier Studio 26, 62
Rex (company) 28
Rhea, Henry (publicity director, Empire Theatre, Long Beach) 170
Riccardi, Constantine V. (attorney) 83, 84
Rice, Louise (author) 197
Rich, Irene (née Irene Luther; actress; b. Buffalo NY 1891 — d. Hope Ranch CA 1988) 116, 170, 171, 212, 231
Rich, Vivian (actress) 166, 169, 234
Rich Man, Poor Man (TV) 180
Richelieu (play) 125
The Rise of the Sunset 105
Ritchey or Ritchie (Richie), Ethel (actress) 205, 235, 240, 263, 264
Ritchey or Ritchie, Will(iam) B. (M.) (scenario editor, Balboa Studios; b. circa 1882 — d. Los Angeles CA

1937) 51, 71, 122, 203, 204, 212, 222, 225, 240, 247, 258, 259, 263, 267, 268
Rizard, Georges (cameraman) 107, 225, 229, 240, 266
RKO 153
Roberson, Jessylee (actor) 226
Roberts, Theodore (stage actor) 129
Robinson, John 180; *see also* Burns, JoAnn
Robson, Eleanor (stage actress) 26
Rockett, Albert (actor) 236
Roe, Emil (actor) 220
Rogers, Ginger (actress; dancer) 141
Rogers, Gustavus A. (legal counsel for the National Independent Motion Picture Board of Trade) 9
Rogers, Suzanne (actress) 223
Roland, Ruth (aka Baby Ruth; child performer; actress; b. San Francisco 1892 — d. Hollywood CA 1937) 2, 30, 41, 44, 47, 48, 49, 50, 55, 63, 68, 71, 72, 80, 103, 104, 106, 110, 119–124, 137, 197, 209, 212, 233, 238, 247, 249, 257, 258, 260, 267
"Roll of Loyalty" 41
Roman Candles (1920) 248
A Romance in the Hills (1914) 119, 131, 248
Rose Among the Briers (1915) 73, 248
The Rose of the Alley (1914) 113, 114, 119, 236, 248
Rosenbluh, Louis (co-director, National Independent Motion Picture Board of Trade) 9
Rosenthal, E. M. (full name unknown; vice-president, David Trattner Production Co.) 162
Rossier, Ben (actor) 203
Roth, Marion (actress) 217
The Rough House 209
Rowland, Henry Cottrell (author) 258
Rubens, Alma (née Alma Smith; actress; b. San Francisco CA 1897–1931) 95
Rush, Bertha 41
Russell, H. C. (full name unknown; actor) 55, 205, 252
Russell, Kurt (actor) 180
Russell, Sol Smith (theatrical producer) 125
Russell, William (né William Leach or Lerche; actor; W. D. Taylor's friend; b. Bronx NY ca. 1885 — d. 1929) 95
Russo, Rene (actress) 180
Ruth of the Rockies 120, 124, 189, 249
Ruth Roland, Detective 120
Rutledge, Gladys 41
Ryan, Joseph (actor) 216

Saalman, Nell (actress) 236
Sable Torch 172
Sackville, Gordon (actor; b. Ontario, Canada, 1880 — d. Los Angeles CA 1926) 24, 49, 53, 71, 74, 104, 201, 203, 204, 206, 213, 216, 226, 230, 234, 242, 243, 245, 247, 254, 256, 258, 263, 266, 270
Sacrificial Fires (1914) 45, 66, 111, 249–251
St. Denis, Ruth (choreographer; wife of Ted Shawn, who together would form the Denishawn Dancers) 211
St. Elmo 11, 46, 66, 70, 104, 130, 131, 204, 250, 251
St. John, Al ("Fuzzy") (actor; nephew of Roscoe Arbuckle; b. Santa Ana CA 1892 — d. Viatalia GA 1963) 80, 132, 133, 202, 209, 210, 217, 236, 241
Sais, Marin (née Mae Smith?; actress; b. San Rafael CA ca. 1888 — d. 1971) 120
Salisbury, Monroe (actor) 270
Salkow, Sidney (director) 232
Salvini (full name unknown; theatrical manager?) 125
Sammis, Walter (executive secretary, National Independent Motion Picture Board of Trade) 9
Sanchez (Miss; full name unknown; actress) 23, 241
The Sand Lark (1916) 111, 251
Sandborn maps 77, 78, 160
Sands, Edward F. (cook and secretary of W. D. Taylor) 95, 98, 101
Sands of Life (1914) 66, 111, 251–252
Sarno, Hector (actor; aka Victor Sarno) 248
Sarno, Victor *see* Sarno Hector
Saunders, Eddie [Edward] (assistant cameraman; brother of Jackie Saunders) 149, 208, 228, 236, 240
Saunders, Jackie (née Anna Jackal; actress; b. Philadelphia PA 1892 — d. Palm Springs CA 1954) 2, 29, 34, 35, 41, 44, 45, 49–51, 52, 53, 63, 71, 72, 74, 80, 82, 86, 103, 104, 112–119, 120, 121, 196, 202, 203, 205, 206, 207, 212, 213, 218, 222, 223, 224, 227, 229, 231, 236, 243, 248, 249, 254, 256, 258, 260, 262, 268
Saunders, Jackie, Jr. (née Jacqueline Junior Saunders Horkheimer) 32, 33, 35, 36, 37, 52, 115, 116, 117, 118, 188, 189, 190
Saved From Himself (1914) 48, 111, 252
Sawyer, A. H. (director, National Independent Motion Picture Board of Trade) 9
Sawyer, H. J. (full name unknown; vice-president and co-director, National Independent Motion Picture Board of Trade, representing Sawyer, Inc.) 9
Sawyer, Laura (Laura S. Wolff; actress; b. Long Beach CA 1885 — d. Matawan NJ 1970) 24, 27, 208, 212, 221, 240, 244
Sawyer, Inc. 9
Schaefer, Ann (actress) 160, 255
Schenck, Joseph M. (studio executive) 56, 75
Schuyler Amusement Company 9
Schwalbe, S. (full name unknown; vice-president, National Independent Motion Picture Board of Trade, representing Electric Theatre Supply Co.) 9
Scott, Tony (writer for *Variety*) 114, 119, 120, 121, 122, 128, 138, 227, 230, 260
The Scout 182
Scoville, Gus (actor) 164, 166, 212
Scripture Film Company 167–168
The Sea Wolf (1913) 39, 40, 111, 232, 252
The Sea Wolf (novel) 35, 244, 252
The Secret of Black Mountain (1917) 55, 252
The Secret of Black Mountain (short story) 252
Seeds of Jealousy (1914) 111, 252–253
Select Pictures Corporation 195, 227
Selig, William N. (founder, Selig Polyscope Co.) 12
Selig (Polyscope Company) 8, 12, 28, 57, 67, 104, 145, 162, 168
Selten, Morton (stage actor) 130
Seltzer, Charles Alden (writer) 213
Selznick, Lewis J. (motion-picture executive; co-director, National Independent Motion Picture Board of Trade) 9, 57, 133, 145
Sennett, Mack (motion-picture pioneer; suspect in W. D. Taylor's murder) 101
Sennett Studio 156, 168
Serwill, Lucille (actress) 213
Seven Years Bad Luck 172
Shadows and Sunshine (1916) 52, 54, 71, 107, 112, 127, 131, 138, 143, 228, 230, 253, 262
Shafer, Molly (actress) 239
Shawn, Ted (choreographer; husband of Ruth St. Denis, who together would form the Denishawn Dancers) 211
Shear, J. M. (full name unknown; vice-president, National Independent Motion Picture Board of Trade, representing Solax Co.) 9
Sheehan, Winfield R. (motion-picture executive; treasurer, National Independent Motion Picture Board of Trade, representing Box Office Amusements Co.) 9, 133

Sheer, William (actor) 204
Shelby, Charlotte (suspect in W. D. Taylor's murder) 101
The Shepherd King (play) 125
Sherman, Lowell (actor) 231
Sherwood, George (actor) 247
Sherwood, Mollie (stage name of Mollie McConnell; actress) 130
Sherwood, W. F. (Mollie McConnell's father) 130
The Shielding Shadow 120
Shirley, Arthur (actor; b. London, England, 1853 — d. London, England, 1925) 53, 202, 203, 205
Should a Wife Forgive? (1915) (aka *The Lady of Perfume*) 112, 120, 121, 127, 131, 138, 143, 230, 253
Shrine Auditorium 182
The Shrine of Happiness (1916) 52, 73, 119, 253–254
Shriver, H. L. (full name unknown; man who claimed to be Baby Marie's natural father) 140
Shuberts (brothers: Jacob J., Lee, Sam S.; theatrical managers) 130
Shupe, Irene (among top 10, star search, 1922, Empire Theatre, Long Beach) 171
Sills, Milton (actor) 171, 172, 231
Silver Lining (1914?) 112, 254–255
Simmons, Jean (actress) 141
Singleton, Joseph E. (chief chemist, Balboa Studios) 84, 256
Skinner, Otis (stage actor) 128
Skirts 168, 171
Skretvedt, Randy 199
Slide, Anthony (author) 12, 13, 193
Sloan, Tod (jockey) 168
Smalley, Phillips (actor) 261
Smiley, Joseph (actor) 227
Smith, Alice (actress) 220
Smith, Bruce (actor; 1880–1942) 49, 51, 71, 104, 209, 215, 221, 234, 242, 247, 248, 254, 256, 263, 269
Smith, Courtland (motion-picture executive) 133
Smith, Lola (actress) 248
Smith, Mr. (full name unknown; cameraman) 149
Smith, Syd (actor) 161
Smith, Vola *see* Vale, Vola
The Smith-Jones Affair (1914?) 255
Smoke Bellew Series 40, 232, 244, 252
Smoking Trails (1922) see *Twin Six O'Brien*
Snipes, Wesley (actor) 181
Solax Company (film company) 9, 114, 227
Sold at Auction (1917) 55, 255
Soldiers of Fortune (play) 32
The Solitary Sin (1919) 255
Solitary Sin. (Corp.) (company) 195, 255
The Son of the Wolf (novel) 38

Sorefoot's Racer (1913 or 1914) 256
La Sortie des usines lumière (1895) 6
Sothern, Louise (actress) 53, 208
Southard, Harry (né Harry D. Weill; actor; b. Buffalo NY 1881— d. 1939) 55, 257
Southern California Motion Picture Baseball League 86
Space Jam 180, 182
Spartacus 141
Spear, Charlie (actor) 149
Special Pictures Corporation 162, 195
Speed 12, 181
Spellbound see *The One-Eyed God*
Spence, Ralph (titles) 248
Spere, Charles (actor) 160, 255
Spielberg, Steven (filmmaker) 181
Spinx Serial Company 161, 195, 215
Spoor, George K. (co-founder, Essanay Film Manufacturing Co.) 13
Spy Hard 12
The Square Triangle (1914) 45, 113, 119, 131, 256–257
Stabler, Harry S. (writer) 206
Stahl, Rose (stage actress) 26
Standing, Guy (actor) 220
Stanley, Henry (actor; b. New York NY 1864 — d. ?) 41, 49, 71, 103, 104, 204, 213, 214, 216, 218, 221, 222, 223, 224, 237, 241–242, 246, 251, 256, 268
Star Films 1, 6, 7, 104
Stargate 12, 180
Starke, Pauline (actress) 170, 242
Starke-Statter (Corporation) 170, 195, 242
Starship Troopers 182
State Rights (Distributor) 65, 194, 195, 204, 208, 212, 216, 220, 221, 233, 239, 244, 248, 255
Stechhan, H. O. (full name unknown; scenarist; assistant general manager, Balboa Studios) 33, 55, 257
Stedman, Myrtle (actress) 232
Sterling, Mae (actress) 51, 71, 104
Sterling (company) 63
Stevens, Bert 41
Stewart, Violet (actress) 220
Stockwell, Dean (actor) 110
The Stolen Child (1917) see *The Stolen Play*
The Stolen Play (1917) (aka *The Stolen Child*) 55, 124, 257
Stollar, Dora 41
Stone, Georgie (juvenile actor) 63
Stone, June (actress) 252
Stone, Oliver (filmmaker) 12
Storms of Life (1914) 257
Strand Theatre 46, 163
The Stranger (1914?) 112, 257–258
Stranglers of Paris (1914) 258
The Streets of Paris 172

Streisand, Barbra (actress; singer) 141
The Strugglers (play) 32
Sullivan, Fred(erick) (associate, New Art Film Co.; general director with Thanhouser Film Co.) 160, 255
Sully, Janet M. (actress) 149
The Sultana (1916) 52, 73, 124, 127, 258
The Sultana (novel) 258
Sunny Jane (1917) 114, 119, 202, 203, 205, 207, 258–259, 268
Sunshine and Gold (1917) 55, 71, 74, 107, 112, 126, 127, 138, 143, 189, 228, 230, 259
Super-Feature (Film) Corporation 173, 174
Sutro, Alfred (playwright) 69
Sutton, Charles (actor; b. circa 1856 — d. Englewood NJ 1935) 24
Sutton, Ralph 41
Swem, Thomas (technical director) 263

The Tabernacle (auditorium) 17
The Talker (play) 172
Talmadge, Constance (actress; b. Brooklyn NY ca. 1899 — d. 1973) 227
Talmadge, Natalie (scenarist) 241
Talmadge, Norma (actress; b. Jersey City NJ ca. 1895–d. 1957) 172
Tarkington, Booth (writer) 40, 62
Tarzan of the Apes 160
Taubenberger, Jeffrey K. (medical researcher) 156
Taylor, Elizabeth (actress) 142
Taylor, W(illiam) D(esmond) (né William Cunningham Deane-Tanner; actor; director; b. Ireland 1877 — d. Hollywood CA 1922) 2, 30, 45, 46, 61, 66, 70, 80, 82, 89, 90, 93, 94–101, 166, 167, 201, 210, 213, 215, 217, 225, 231, 261
Teddy (dog; aka Teddy Whack) 248
Temple, Shirley (child actress) 52, 135, 228
Terrace Theatre 182
Terry, R. A. (full name unknown; medical doctor) 83
The Test of Manhood (1914) 112, 127, 259
Texas Guinan Company 161, 195
Thanhouser Film Company 28, 160
Thanhouser/Imp lot 27, 35
Théâtre du Gymnase 6
Theatrical Syndicate 128
Theilan, George (actor) 216
The Thief (1915) 70
Thomas, Augustus (playwright) 128
Thomas, Olive (actress) 95
Thomas Ince Company 109
Thompson, Edith (Ruth Roland's aunt) 123

Thorine, E. F. (full name unknown) 167, 169; *see also* J. E. Logan
Thorne, L. C. (full name unknown; co-director, Long Beach Studios) 170
Thou Shalt Not Steal (1914) 259–260
Through Fire and Water (1914) 260
Through Night to Light (1914) 112, 119, 260
Thurman, G. P. (full name unknown; actor?) 86
Thurman, Robert G. 41
Thurwald, Frank (actor) 213
Tiffany Productions 231
The Tiger's Trail 120, 124, 260
Tillie's Punctured Romance 168
Tin Cup 180
The Tip Off (1914) 48, 260
Title Insurance and Trust Company (plaintiff against Master Pictures Corp.) 160
To Kill a Man 40, 232, 244, 252
To Live and Die in L.A. 181
To Love and to Hold (1914) 260
Toilers of the Sea (1915) 261
Told at Twilight (1917) 55, 71, 74, 112, 125, 127, 138, 143, 189, 228, 230, 261
Tomboy (1915) 112, 261
Too Wise Wives (1921) 189, 261
Tranchell, Hazel (actress; made more than 150 movies at Balboa) 80, 81, 165, 263
Tranchell, Hugh E. (husband of Hazel Tranchell) 80
Tranchell, Katherine (daughter of Hugh and Hazel Tanchell, residents of Long Beach) 80
Trattner, David (president, David Trattner Production Co.) 162
Trattner, Erwin (secretary and treasurer, David Trattner Production Co.) 162
Triangle Film Company 57
Tricks of Fate (1914?) 46, 70, 131, 261
Tucker 181
Turkin, Nikandr (Russian director) 232
Turnley, Ned (founder of an American reform colony) 94
20th Century–Fox 108-109
23½ Hours Leave 109
Twin Kiddies (1917) 55, 56, 71, 74, 112, 127, 138, 143, 228, 230, 262
Twin Rays of Sunshine (1917) 55, 74, 138, 143, 230, 262
Twin Six O'Brien (1922) (aka *Smoking Trails*) 169, 262
The Twin Triangle (1916) 52, 131, 262–263
The Twisted Thread (1917) 75, 263

UCLA Film and Television Archive 189

Uncle Dan'l (play) 125
The Understudy (1917) 55, 131, 263
The Understudy (short story) 263
Underwood, Clarence (artist) 112
Uneven Match 81, 263
The Unexpected (1914) 66, 112, 131, 263–264
Unique Theatre 20
United Artists 108
Universal (aka Universal City, Universal Company, Universal West Coast studio, Universal Studios) 19, 28, 29, 45, 86, 94, 113, 114, 156, 166, 227
Universal City *see* Universal
Universal Company *see* Universal
Universal Ike 28
Universal Studios *see* Universal
Universal West Coast studio *see* Universal
University Film Company 46, 76, 104, 128, 195, 210, 259
Unknown Video 189
Untitled, No. 1 (1911) 264
Untitled, No. 2 (1918) 264
Urner, Mabel Herbert (author) 238
Usonia (film company) 44

Vale, Vola (aka Vola Smith; actress) 53, 55, 226, 229, 234, 252, 270
The Valley of the Moon 40, 232, 244, 252
Les Vampires 6
Van, Beatrice (actress) 261
Van Buren, Frank (actor) 27, 212
Van Buren, Mabel (actress) 253
Van De Water, Virginia Terhune (writer) 227
Vance, Louis Joseph (writer) 54, 231
Vanderpool, "Spike" (full name unknown; assistant cameraman) 163
The Vanishing 182
Vaughn, Theresa (stage actress) 128
Vengeance of Death see Vengeance of the Dead
Vengeance of the Dead (aka *Dungeons of the Dead*, *Vengeance of Death*) 112, 189, 264
Vengeance of the Flames (1914?) 264
Verhoeven, Paul (director) 182
Verne, Jules (French writer) 7
Victor (company) 28
Vidor, King (Wallis) (motion-picture director) 94
Virginius (play) 125
Vitagraph 8, 28, 52, 57, 145, 154, 163
Von Der Esch, Leigh (president, Association of Film Commissioners International Conference, Long Beach, 1995) 12
Von Harleman, G. P. (full name unknown) 74
Vosburgh, Jack (actor) 226

The Vow (1914) 264–265
Le Voyage dans la lune 7

W. C. and Me 181
W. Hodkinson Corporation 199, 266
Wade, J. P. (full name unknown; actor) 205, 215, 270
Wager, Duane (actor) 24
Waldermeyer, Jack (actor) 248
Walker, Christy (actress) 227
Wall, David (Dave) (actor; b. Coburg, Canada, ca. 1870 — d. New York NY 1938) 27, 244
Wallace, Lew (playwright) 39
The Walls of Jericho (1915) 69, 70
The Walls of Jericho (play) 69
Walter, Eugene (playwright) 32, 205, 206
Walters, (L.) Virginia (writer) 265
Walthall, Henry B. (actor; b. Shelby City AL 1878 — d. Monrovia CA 1936) 48, 70, 71, 170, 171, 172, 204, 231
Wanamaker, Marc (archivist, Bison Archives; film historian; author) 11, 13, 26, 57, 59, 62, 75, 89, 122, 146, 148, 149, 150, 162, 163, 177, 237, 250
Wanted — A Brother (1918) 229, 235, 236, 240, 265–266
Wanted, an Heir 120
Warfield, David (stage actor) 26
Warner, James (actor; b. Nebraska 1895 — d. Los Angeles CA 1924) 53, 55, 226, 252
Warner Bros. 116, 118, 179, 180, 183
Warner's Features, Inc. 46, 195, 241
The Warning 160
Warren, Archibald (Archie) (actor) 44, 63, 213, 223, 256, 259
Warren, Herbert (scene editor) 202, 210, 217, 236, 241
Watters, George D. (vice-president and general manager, New Art Film Co.) 160, 255
The Way of the World (1914?) 266
The Way We Were 141
Wayne, John (actor) 141
Wayne, Marie (actress) 44, 63, 223
Webber, Gladys (actress) 51, 71, 104
Weber, Lois (director; scenarist) 261
Weber Studio 156
Webster, Noah (lexicographer) 105
Weidman, Charles (dancer) 211
Welch (Welsh), Eddie W. (aka W. Welch; manager, The International Film Co.; business manager and co-director, Meteor Pictures Corp.) 162, 165
Welch, W. *see* Welch (Welsh), Eddie W.
Weller, William L. (pedestrian; extra) 85
Welles, Orson (actor; director) 96

Wells, Alice Stebbins (the first regular policewoman, Los Angeles Police; featured in *The Policewoman*) 244
Wells, H. G. (British writer) 7
West, Lillian (Mildred) (actress; 1890; from New York, NY) 49, 53, 71, 74, 104, 205, 245, 256, 264
West, William (actor) 212
Western Costume Company 141
Western Lubin Company *see* Lubin
Weycross, Robert (actor) 206, 208, 226
Whalen, William Wilfrid (author) 222
Whatever the Cost (1918) 201, 226, 243, 266
When Fate Was Kind (1914) 48, 266
When God Laughs (novel) 40, 232, 244, 252
When Might Is Right (1916) 112, 266
When the Circus Comes to Town (1914) 266
When the Troupe Closed (1914?) 266
Whitcomb, Dan F. (scenarist) 91, 107, 138, 228, 229, 254, 255, 257, 261
White, Pearl (Fay) (actress; b. Greenridge IL 1889 — d. Paris, France, 1938) 30, 80, 121
White, Rose (actress) 260
White, Ruth (actress) 216, 242
White Fang (novel) 38
White Star (film company) 69, 89, 94, 111, 112, 127, 195, 201, 206, 217, 223, 225, 233, 257, 261, 264
Whitman, Fred(erick) G. (J.) (actor; b. Findlay OH 1887 — d. South Pasadena CA 1945) 37, 41, 49, 52, 53, 71, 72, 74, 103, 104, 213, 214, 222, 233, 242, 246, 247, 251, 253, 256, 259, 263
Whitman, Velma 41
Whitney, Claire (actress) 70
Whittlesey, William 41
Who Is Guilty? 71
Who Is "Number One"? (1917 serial) 55, 75, 266–267
Who Pays? (1914–15 serial) 11, 47, 67, 71, 106, 110, 112, 120, 124, 127, 130, 132, 186, 189, 267
Who Wins? (1916 serial) 268
Wickersham, Billie (dancer; Hollywood socialite) 117
Wickersham, Ella (dancer; Hollywood socialite) 117
The Wildcat (1917) 114, 119, 202, 203, 205, 207, 258, 268
Wilhelm, Harry (author; scenarist) 22
The Will o' the Wisp (1914) 45, 66, 86, 113, 114, 119, 130, 132, 268
Willets, Gilson (scenarist) 219
Willey, Alden (assistant director) 71, 204, 228, 254
William Fox Amusement Company 9
William Fox Sunshine Comedies 169
William Thompson Company 169, 170, 195
Williams, Alan (writer) 7
Williams, Frank D. (director of Kid Komedy Kompany) 63
Wilson, Ben(jamin) (F.) (actor; b. Corning IA 1876 — d. Glendale CA 1930) 24, 25
Wilson, William (photographer) 96
Wiltermood, Frank M. (scenario editor, Balboa Studios) 43, 66, 113, 114, 215, 221, 227, 244
Windsor, Claire (née Clara Cronk; actress; b. Cawker City KS ca. 1897 — d. 1972) 261
The Winner (1914) 268–269
Winter Sports in Southern California (1911) 23, 269
Winters, Shirley (actress) 181
Wise, Thomas (stage actor) 128
Wither, Eugene (dramatic editor, *Daily Telegram*) 170
Wolbert, Dorothea (actress) 255
Wolbert, William (director; b. Petersberg VA 1883 — d. Los Angeles CA 1918) 44, 45, 66, 196, 198, 207, 215, 223, 237, 238, 245, 251
The Woman Alone (novel) 238
Won by a Nose (1914) 269
Wonderful Plays and Players 69
Wood, Alice Jean (among top 10, star search, 1922, Empire Theatre, Long Beach) 171
Wood, Dorothy (actress) 149
Woodman, Josephine (extra; *Bill's Sweetheart*) 27
World Film Company (aka World Film Corporation) 57, 112, 127, 130, 131, 143, 145, 216, 253, 262
World Film Corporation *see* World Film Company
World War I (aka Great War, First World War) 1, 5, 7, 11, 30, 41, 46, 47, 59, 77, 93, 94, 145, 147, 148, 151, 152–153, 154, 155, 156, 159, 194
Wright, William (director, Kalem Co., Inc.) 13
Wulze, Harry (director) 44, 64, 248
Wyse, John (stage manager, Balboa Studios) 41, 43, 63

Yankee (company) 114, 227
Yeats, Murray F. (Marie Osborne's second husband) 142
The Yellow Bullet (1917) 269
Yohe, May (stage actress) 128
Yorke Studio 156
Young, Joan (née Joan Dempsey, daughter of Marie Osborne and Frank J. Dempsey) 142
Young(e), Lucille (actress; b. ca. 1892 — d. Hollywood CA 1934) 44, 64, 207, 234, 253, 268
You've Got to Pay (1913) 112, 269

Zangwill, Israel (author) 70
Zecca, Ferdinand (French motion-picture pioneer) 6
Zimlick, Celeste (actress) 165
Zollenstein (1917) 55, 128, 269–270
Zollenstein (novel) 269
Zukor, Adolph (motion-picture executive; b. Ricse, Hungary, 1873 — d. Century City CA 1976) 26, 133